Bohdan Peter Rebshynskyj
9/18/2018 NYC
75
Memoria tene !

Assembler Language Programming:
the IBM System/360 and 370

Second Edition

Assembler Language Programming: the IBM System/360 and 370

Second Edition

GEORGE W. STRUBLE / University of Oregon

ADDISON-WESLEY PUBLISHING COMPANY

Reading, Massachusetts / Menlo Park, California
London / Amsterdam / Don Mills, Ontario / Sydney

ISBN 0-201-7322-6
KLMNOPQR-DO-898765432

PREFACE

The fact that the use of computers is becoming ever more widespread needs no repetition here. Almost as obvious is that the tasks to which computers are put are becoming ever more varied. New computers, new programming languages, new theory and technique, and new applications continue to make the computing field exciting and very rewarding to those who approach it with a zest for new knowledge and adventure.

Assembler languages occupy a unique place in the computing world. Since most assembler-language statements are symbolic of individual machine-language instructions, the assembler-language programmer has the full power of the computer at his disposal in a way that users of other languages do not. Because of the direct relationship between assembler language and machine language, assembler language is used when high efficiency of programs is needed, and especially in areas of application that are so new and amorphous that existing problem-orientep languages are ill-suited for describing the procedures to be followed.

This volume couples the study of assembler-language programming and programming techniques to the study of a particular series of computer, the IBM System/360 and 370. Study of assembler language *must*, by the nature of the language, be relative to *some* machine, and some particular machine, at that. The IBM System/360 and 370 series is a good choice for two principal reasons: (1) IBM System/360 and 370 computers are in use by the thousands, so thousands of computer users will find a study of the specifics of this computer immediately applicable; (2) the IBM System/360 or 370 exemplifies features of many other current computers, so concepts and techniques learned with respect to this computer will be applicable to other computer systems as well.

The aim of this text is therefore to introduce the detailed structure of the IBM System/360 and 370 and their instruction repertoire, programming in assembler language for this computer, and techniques useful in the applications of computers, especially those more easily programmed in assembler language than in higher-level languages.

It is assumed that the reader of this book is already familiar to some extent with programming, probably in Fortran. The particular language of the student's previous exposure is unimportant; what matters is experience in analyzing a problem, and developing an algorithm in flowchart form for a computer solution. Many basic concepts are reviewed or presented in a framework that supports my development of further material, so a reader with a basic background should find this book suitable for individual study.

The book is intended primarily for use as a class text, in a "second" course in computing (though a teacher who wishes to use the book as an introductory text should be able to do so, with a reasonable amount of supplementary explanation). It may be used in a course similar to "Course B2, Computers and Programming" in the curriculum recommended by the ACM Curriculum Committee on Computer Science, in *Communications of the ACM*, March, 1968, pp. 151–197. It may also be used in conjunction with a more general or theoretical text on computer organization or information structures or as a stand-alone text. There is more than enough material for a semester, and sufficient opportunity for an instructor to omit or substitute other material. The text is also flexible in that the order of presentation of material after Chapter 12 can be rearranged at will, and parts of Chapter 12 can be introduced earlier without any difficulties.

Chapter 1 introduces the reader to the structure of a computer, especially the structures of the IBM System/360 or 370 and the ways information is represented in them.

Chapter 2 is an introduction to the machine language of the IBM System/360 and 370, and Chapter 3 follows immediately with the introduction of assembler language. Throughout the remainder of the book assembler language is used, though the student understands the machine language he is writing symbolically.

Chapter 4 begins the study of the characteristics and uses of individual IBM System/360 and 370 instructions, with the binary integer arithmetic and information move instructions. Chapter 5 introduces the very important concept of a subroutine and the conventions employed in defining and using subroutines in the IBM System/360 and 370.

Chapter 6 contains a variety of miscellaneous information, which is included at this point to prepare the reader to write and run his own example programs and subroutines. Practice is an extremely important part of the learning of programming, and the student should test his understanding by actual trial during the remainder of the book.

The most frustrating problem for teachers of assembler language for IBM System/360 or 370 systems is that a student must learn a fairly large amount of information before he can submit his first laboratory exercise to the computer. It is a problem inherent in teaching powerful and flexible systems. Use of input/output subroutines such as the READATA and PRINT subroutines illustrated can cut down some immediate requirements (READATA and PRINT are available on request from me). Another approach attractive to some instructors is a coalition with a higher-level language such as Fortran; either a Fortran main program may call the student's assembler language subroutine for some data manipulation, or an assembler language program may call Fortran subroutines to do its input and output. Either way, some burdens are lifted from the student in the early period of his study. Appendix A is devoted to exposition of the necessary linkages, and an instructor may introduce this material with or after, say, Chapter 5. Of course some higher-level language other than Fortran could be substituted; Fortran is included here because it most likely coincides with the previous background of the students.

Chapter 7 brings in the branch instructions, and Chapter 8 continues with the concepts and patterns of looping and address modification.

Chapter 9 endeavors to help the reader in his problems of debugging programs. Techniques and debugging aids are described, and some advice is given which—I hope—will help the user minimize the need for debugging.

Chapters 10 and 11 deal with byte (character) and bit manipulation. In assembler language these functions are simple, direct, and efficient; this is one of the areas in which the power of assembler language, as compared to most other languages, is realized.

Chapter 12 introduces manipulation of data sets, both within a program by means of the input and output macros, and external to the program by means of job control statements. Basics of the OS/360 and OS/VS operating systems are illustrated and explained; instructors whose installations use a different operating system should have little difficulty in substituting details of their own systems.

Chapters 13 and 14 introduce two other modes of arithmetic available in the IBM System/360 and 370: floating-point and decimal.

Chapter 15 describes five sophisticated and powerful instructions: Translate, Translate and Test, Edit, Edit and Mark, and Execute; these instructions are typical of efforts by computer manufacturers to extend the standard instruction repertoire.

Chapter 16 introduces the facility for defining macros in assembler language.

Chapter 17 introduces virtual storage concepts, program status word formats and manipulation, input and output instructions and channel programming, interrupt handling and the storage protection system—the pieces of computer structure that are used by operating systems programmers, not applications programmers. The chapter is intended as an introductory survey to give the reader some understanding of a part of the computer structure he will not directly use; even a little understanding can relieve anxiety and promote more efficient use of the facilities of the operating system.

An important feature of the book is that it discusses a number of common information processing problems, introduces significant computing techniques, and illustrates implementation of these techniques in assembler language. Thus, while the student is learning to handle certain features of the IBM System/360 and 370, he is also learning valuable techniques which he can use in many situations. Among the techniques discussed are generation of pseudo-random numbers, manipulation of linked lists, binary search, scatter storage and hashing methods, and a sort-merge algorithm.

This book, then, describes fairly thoroughly the instruction repertoire usable by applications programmers of the IBM System/360 and 370. Functions reserved to the operating system are introduced, because an applications programmer needs some understanding of what lies behind supervisor functions he calls upon, and because budding systems programmers must start somewhere too. However, the functions used only in supervisor state are treated in much less detail than the others, and some of the more specialized, especially those of System/370, are not even mentioned. Assembler language is introduced and used extensively, but several advanced features of the assembler language are not mentioned. Instructions for use of facilities of the operating system are even less complete; a user must learn more details from appropriate IBM manuals and must get information on the configuration in use at his own computing center. I have tried to follow the terminology of IBM manuals to facilitate transition from this book to the manuals. It will be helpful if a good set of manuals is available to the student for reference while he is studying this text.

I would like to express my deep appreciation to the many people who contributed to the development of both the original and this revised edition. Most of the material, of course, is derived from various IBM manuals; the IBM Corporation has been generous in allowing me to use excerpts from the manuals listed in the bibliographies at the end of each chapter, and individuals within IBM have been encouraging and helpful in their explanations of further points. Robert Heilman, John MacDonald, Thom Lane, Michael Harrison, Tim Hagen, Norman Beck, Sally Browning, Gordon Ashby, Kevin McCoy, and Ed Rittenhouse made valuable suggestions and criticisms. Sharon Burrowes, Jenny Brown, and Barbara Demezas did a masterful job of typing the manuscript.

Finally, I wish to acknowledge the contributions of users of the book who have helped to debug and strengthen the ideas and presentation as they endeavored to learn about assembler language and the IBM System/360 from preliminary versions and the first edition of this book.

Eugene, Oregon   G.S.
February 1975

CONTENTS

Chapter 1

Introduction to Computer Structure: The IBM System / 360 and 370

This chapter introduces the structure of a stored-program digital computer. Since this book is about programming, the structure is described as it appears to a programmer, not to an electronic engineer or a space layout designer. The first section introduces number systems, especially the binary system, used internally in many computers, and the hexadecimal system, used for description of contents of the IBM System/360 and 370. Section 2 contains a short analysis of the functional subsystems of a computer. Sections 1 and 2 will be review for many readers. They may be skimmed; their value is mainly in the introduction of terms and an orientation to the approach taken in this text. The reader unfamiliar with number systems other than decimal may also skim Section 1 if he wishes, and refer to it when the need arises.

Section 3 is a survey of the structure of the IBM System/360 and 370; it attempts to show the overall pattern into which details will be fitted in the remainder of the book. Section 4 begins the actual detailed presentation of the IBM System/360 and 370 by discussing the representations of various types of information; this section should be read for content.

1. DECIMAL, BINARY, AND HEXADECIMAL NUMBERS

The student of the IBM System/360 and 370 must understand three number systems: the decimal, binary, and hexadecimal systems. He must know the nature and advantages of each, how to convert quantities from one representation to another, and how to do arithmetic in each. Skill comes only slowly, and is developed through practice. But first must come understanding of the nature and processes of the systems. Fortunately, the three systems can be presented as three instances of a central idea, the idea of positional representation.

Positional representations

A *positional representation* of a number is a representation by which the position of each digit gives its value, or more precisely, gives the power of some *radix* by which it is multiplied. Our usual representation of numbers, which we call decimal, is a positional representation with radix 10. In the number 379, for example, the position of the three digits in the representation determines their value:

$$379 = 3 \times 10^2 + 7 \times 10^1 + 9 \times 10^0$$
$$= 300 + 70 + 9$$

The same digits arranged differently represent a different number; we recognize the digit pattern 793 to represent a number different from 379.

By contrast, the Roman system of number representation is *not* a positional representation. The numeral X means ten regardless of its position in the representation, though whether the ten is to be subtracted or added depends on whether or not the X precedes C or L.

The binary representation of numbers is a positional representation using 2 as a radix. We call numbers expressed in this form *binary numbers*. For example, the binary number 101011 has the meaning

$$101011 = 1 \times 2^5 + 0 \times 2^4 + 1 \times 2^3 + 0 \times 2^2 + 1 \times 2^1 + 1 \times 2^0$$
$$= 32 + 8 + 2 + 1 = 43$$

In any positional representation system, the set of digits required runs from zero up to a digit representing the number that is one less than the radix. Therefore in the decimal system we need ten different digits 0–9. In the binary system only two different digits are required: 0 and 1. It is natural for computers to use binary representations, since most of its components are two-state devices whose two states are easily associated with the digits 0 and 1.

Arithmetic

Addition of two numbers is performed according to the same rules, regardless of the radix of the representation. A pair of digits in corresponding positions of two numbers, and possibly a carry from the previous pair, are added, with the following results.

1. If the sum is less than the radix, it is expressed as a single digit, and there is a 0 carry.
2. If the sum is equal to or greater than the radix, it is reduced by the radix to yield a digit of the result, but a 1 is carried to be added with the next digit.

Put into this context, addition of the decimal numbers 273 and 465 is carried out as follows:

```
  3           7                        2
  5 ,    then 6              then      4
 ___         ___                     ___
  8           3 with 1 carry,       + 1 carry,
                                     ___
                                      7
```

which we normally write

$$273$$
$$465$$
$$\overline{738}$$

With binary numbers, the addition table is especially simple:

$$\begin{array}{cccc} 0 & 0 & 1 & 1 \\ +0 & +1 & +0 & +1 \\ \hline 0 & 1 & 1 & 0 \text{ with 1 carry} \end{array}$$

A carry, of course, adds another 1 to the sum. Addition of the binary numbers 10110 and 10011 is carried out, according to our rules, as follows:

$$\begin{array}{ccccc} 0 \quad 1 & 1 & 0 & 1 & (0) \\ +1 +1 & +0 & +0 & +1 & (0) \\ \hline 1 \quad 0 \text{ with 1 carry} & +1 \text{ carry} & +1 \text{ carry} & 0 \text{ with 1 carry} & +1 \text{ carry} \\ & & 0 \text{ with 1 carry} & 1 \text{ no carry} & & 1 \end{array}$$

Collecting and writing in the usual way,

$$10110$$
$$10011$$
$$\overline{101001}$$

Subtraction is the obvious converse process; if borrowing is necessary, a 1 borrowed from the next position has the value of the radix when used in the current position. For example, the difference of two binary numbers 101001 (decimal 41) and 1100 (decimal 12) is

$$\begin{array}{r} 101001 \\ -\ 1100 \\ \hline 11101 \end{array} = \text{decimal 29}$$

Multiplication of binary numbers is performed in essentially the same manner as multiplication of decimal numbers, but is much easier since the product of a digit by the multiplicand is either the multiplicand itself (1 × the multiplicand) or zero (0 × the multiplicand). For example, the product of 1101 (decimal 13) and 101 (decimal 5) is

$$\begin{array}{r} 1101 \\ 101 \\ \hline 1101 \\ 0000 \\ 1101 \\ \hline 1000001 \end{array} = \text{decimal 65}$$

Division of binary numbers is also easier than division of decimal numbers, since each digit of the quotient is either 1 or 0 and it is easy to tell which, by mere comparison. The quotient of 10011001 (decimal 153) divided by 1011 (decimal 11) is found to be

$$
\begin{array}{r}
1101 \;=\; \text{decimal } 13 \\
1011 \overline{)10011001} \\
1011 \\
\hline
10000 \\
1011 \\
\hline
10101 \\
1011 \\
\hline
1010 \;=\; \text{decimal } 10
\end{array}
$$

These examples of binary arithmetic are provided for two reasons. The first is to show that arithmetic in any positional representation system is carried out according to the same rules which govern decimal arithmetic. Only the addition and multiplication tables are different, and these only in the digit symbols used and the carries generated. The second reason is that the student of a binary computer such as the IBM System/360 or 370 may need to do some binary arithmetic on occasion; since binary arithmetic is actually *easier* than decimal arithmetic, the student should not panic at the prospect.

Conversions between decimal and binary

Our example above showed how the definition of the positional representation of binary numbers can be used to help us find the decimal representation of a binary number. Each binary digit corresponds to a certain power of 2, depending on its position; these powers of 2, or rather, those corresponding to 1's in the binary number, are added to find the decimal equivalent. There are easier and more efficient conversion techniques, however. One can regard a number expressed in a positional representation as a polynomial in the radix, where the digits of the number are the coefficients of the polynomial. Then one can use the process called *nesting* for evaluation of a polynomial in evaluating, that is converting, the number. The technique of nesting consists of the following steps:

1. Start with the highest-order (leftmost) digit.

2. Multiply by the radix (2).

3. Add the next digit to the right.

4. If there are more digits, return to step 2 and continue; that is, multiply the result of each step by the radix 2, etc.

We illustrate with the binary number 101011,

$$
\begin{array}{ccccc}
\textcircled{1} & 2 & 5 & 10 & 21 \\
\times\,2 & \times\,2 & \times\,2 & \times\,2 & \times\,2 \\
\hline
2 & 4 & 10 & 20 & 42 \\
+\,\textcircled{0} & +\,\textcircled{1} & +\,\textcircled{0} & +\,\textcircled{1} & +\,\textcircled{1} \\
\hline
2 & 5 & 10 & 21 & 43
\end{array}
$$

where the binary digits are circled and the decimal equivalent derived is 43, as shown earlier. This technique is a simple one to apply, and has the advantage that if there are n digits in the binary number, only $n - 1$ multiplications are required, each a multiplication by 2, and $n - 1$ additions. The technique assumes that the arithmetic is done in the number system *to which* the number is being converted—decimal arithmetic in this case.

The same technique is used by computers in converting numbers from decimal to binary. If, for example, each of the digits of the decimal number 347 is coded in binary (0011, 0100, 0111), the conversion of the number 347 to binary follows the scheme above but with 2's replaced by (decimal) 10's and all arithmetic done in binary:

$$
\begin{array}{rl}
\ \ \textcircled{0011} & (3) \\
\times\ 1010 & (10) \\
\hline
00110 & \\
0011 & \\
\hline
11110 & \\
+\ \textcircled{0100} & (4) \\
\hline
100010 & \\
\times\ 1010 & \\
\hline
1000100 & \\
100010 & \\
\hline
101010100 & \\
+\ \textcircled{0111} & (7) \\
\hline
101011011 & (347)
\end{array}
$$

In decimal arithmetic, conversion from decimal representation to binary is done by a division process. The decimal number is divided by 2, and the remainder is the units' digit of the number's binary representation. The quotient is divided by 2, and the new remainder is another digit of the binary representation. The process of dividing each new quotient by 2 continues; each remainder is another digit of the binary representation. The process terminates when the quotient is reduced to zero. We illustrate with the conversion of the decimal number 347 to binary:

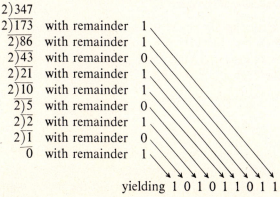

$$
\begin{array}{rll}
2\,)\,347 & & \\
2\,)\,\overline{173} & \text{with remainder} & 1 \\
2\,)\,\overline{86} & \text{with remainder} & 1 \\
2\,)\,\overline{43} & \text{with remainder} & 0 \\
2\,)\,\overline{21} & \text{with remainder} & 1 \\
2\,)\,\overline{10} & \text{with remainder} & 1 \\
2\,)\,\overline{5} & \text{with remainder} & 0 \\
2\,)\,\overline{2} & \text{with remainder} & 1 \\
2\,)\,\overline{1} & \text{with remainder} & 0 \\
\overline{0} & \text{with remainder} & 1
\end{array}
$$

yielding 1 0 1 0 1 1 0 1 1

The same process, done in binary arithmetic and substituting 1010 (decimal 10) for 2, converts binary numbers to decimal. As an illustration, conversion of 110100111 proceeds as follows:

$$
\begin{array}{r}
\underline{101010} \\
1010\overline{)110100111} \\
1010 \\
\hline
1100 \\
1010 \\
\hline
1011 \\
1010 \\
\end{array}
\qquad
\begin{array}{r}
\underline{100} \\
1010\overline{)101010} \\
1010 \\
\hline
\end{array}
\qquad
\begin{array}{r}
0 \\
1010\overline{)100} \\
0 \\
\hline
\end{array}
$$

Remainder: 010 = decimal 2   Remainder: 100 = decimal 4

Remainder: 11 = decimal 3

Since the digits are generated in low-to-high-order sequence, the decimal-number equivalent to 110100111 is 423.

Hexadecimal representation

It is natural for a computer to deal with numbers expressed in a binary representation, since the electronic elements used are two-state devices. One of the states of each device can be identified with the digit 0, and the other with the digit 1. Only these digits are needed for binary representations. A computer can easily deal with fairly long strings of binary digits, with each digit in the string represented by one electronic element.

It is not natural for us, however, to write, recognize, work with, or remember long strings of digits. We prefer strings of fewer digits, and our minds more easily accept a variety of digits than do computer elements. We sometimes need to show, examine, and work with numbers *as the computer does*, and a shorter representation closely related to binary is helpful. For dealing with System/360 and 370 we choose a positional representation with radix 16, calling the *hexadecimal representation*. The hexadecimal representation is chosen because 16 is 2^4, and therefore equivalent to combining binary digits in groups of four. There are 16 four-digit binary numbers; the characters we choose to represent them in a hexadecimal representation are 0, 1, . . . , 9, A, B, C, D, E, F, as shown in Fig. 1–1.

Conversions with hexadecimal numbers

Conversions between hexadecimal and binary are very easy; hexadecimal representations were chosen with this in mind. To convert a binary integer to hexadecimal one merely groups its digits into groups of four, starting from the right, and then converts each group to a hexadecimal digit according to Fig. 1–1. For example,

$$
\underbrace{101}_{5}\underbrace{1001}_{9}\underbrace{0001}_{1}\underbrace{1101}_{D}
$$

shows that the hexadecimal equivalent of 101100100011101 is 591D. Conversion from hexadecimal to binary is even easier: one merely converts each hexadecimal digit to binary according to Fig. 1–1 and strings the binary digits together. The

Fig. 1-1 Hexadecimal digits

Hexadecimal digit	Binary equivalent	Decimal equivalent
0	0000	0
1	0001	1
2	0010	2
3	0011	3
4	0100	4
5	0101	5
6	0110	6
7	0111	7
8	1000	8
9	1001	9
A	1010	10
B	1011	11
C	1100	12
D	1101	13
E	1110	14
F	1111	15

conversion of the hexadecimal number 6C08 illustrates the process:

$$6 \quad C \quad 0 \quad 8$$
$$0110110000001000$$

These conversion processes can be expressed in terms of the techniques shown above for binary-decimal conversions, and are equivalent to them.

Conversions between decimal and hexadecimal can be done by the techniques developed above for conversions with binary numbers. The number 16 replaces the number 2 where it appears in the descriptions of those techniques. For example, conversion of the hexadecimal number 6C08 to decimal is as follows:

$$
\begin{array}{cccc}
⑥ & 108 & 1728 \\
\times\ 16 & \times\ 16 & \times\ 16 \\
\hline
96 & 1728 & 27648 \\
+⑫\ (C) & +⓪ & +⑧ \\
\hline
108 & 1728 & 27656 = \text{decimal equivalent}
\end{array}
$$

Conversion of the decimal number 17307 to hexadecimal proceeds as shown below:

$$
\begin{array}{cccc}
1081 & 67 & 4 & 0 \\
16)\overline{17307} & 16)\overline{1081} & 16)\overline{67} & 16)\overline{4} \\
16 & 96 & 64 & 0 \\
\hline
130 & 121 & ③ & ④ \\
128 & 112 \\
\hline
27 & ⑨ \\
16 \\
\hline
11 = ⑧
\end{array}
$$

The hexadecimal equivalent is 439B.

Arithmetic in hexadecimal is a strain on our decimal-oriented minds. We will have occasion to do addition and subtraction of hexadecimal numbers, but very rarely multiplication or division. One adds and subtracts by thinking of the decimal equivalents of each hexadecimal digit, adding or subtracting the decimal equivalents, then reconverting the results. Doing this, digit by digit, involves much less work than a full conversion of the numbers to decimal. The best way to multiply or divide hexadecimal numbers is to convert them to binary first and do the multiplication or division in binary.

Using hexadecimal arithmetic, hexadecimal-to-decimal conversion is done by division (by A = 10), and decimal-to-hexadecimal conversion by multiplication. However, these are recommended only as rather severe mental exercise.

2. SUBSYSTEMS OF A STORED-PROGRAM DIGITAL COMPUTER

A programmer deals with five major aspects of the modern stored-program digital computer which, for clarity, we will treat as discrete subsystems. They are: the *main storage*, an *input subsystem*, an *output subsystem*, an *arithmetic and logic subsystem*, and a *control subsystem*. We can consider these subsystems to be connected as shown in Fig. 1–2. Although this description is a drastic oversimplification (for the actual connections are quite complex), it helps us to understand the function of each subsystem in the computer's structure.

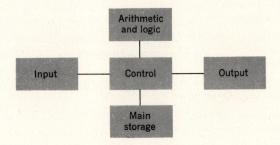

Fig. 1–2   Subsystems of a digital computer.

Main storage

The *main storage* of a computer, sometimes called its memory, holds information for the job (or jobs) being done by the computer at the moment. The information kept in storage may be of several kinds: programs in machine language that give directions to the computer, input data, constants used in the program, and intermediate and final results.

The main storage of modern computers is composed of elements that accept and hold a magnetic charge. Each element (ferrite core, spot on a film, etc.) may accept a charge in either of two orientations. These two orientations or states can be interpreted as *on* and *off*, *yes* or *no*, *0* and *1*. The information stored in one element as the choice between the two states is called a *bit*, which is a contraction

Fig. 1-3   Binary representation of decimal digits

Decimal digit	Binary representation
0	0000
1	0001
2	0010
3	0011
4	0100
5	0101
6	0110
7	0111
8	1000
9	1001

of *binary digit*. The interpretation as 0 and 1 suggests naturally the representation of quantities as binary numbers, since in a binary representation every digit is 0 or 1. Practically all computers take advantage of this natural binary nature of the storage medium, although some superimpose a decimal structure.

We seldom have use for only one bit of storage, or for a number whose length is one bit. Instead we may wish to use a number equivalent to seven decimal digits, or four alphabetic characters, or an instruction to the computer. Therefore, the cores making up the computer's storage are grouped. In some computers, such as the IBM System/360 and 370, the groups are called *bytes*. A byte is a fairly small group, eight bits in the IBM System/360 and 370, so bytes are further grouped into larger units called *words*.

By a *binary computer* we mean a computer in which each number is represented in binary form. In using a binary computer we input quantities in decimal form since we are accustomed to dealing with decimal numbers. The computer converts the input numbers into their binary representations. Similarly, before output the computer can convert binary quantities into decimal equivalents and output the results in decimal form.

In binary computers the words are usually of fixed size. In a *decimal computer*, by contrast, main storage elements are first grouped in some fashion—in the IBM System/360 and 370 the grouping is by fours; each group of four represents a decimal digit. Each decimal digit is itself represented in binary, as shown in Fig. 1-3. Some decimal computers further group these decimal-digit groups into larger groups, again called *words*, of fixed length, for example, ten decimal digits plus sign. Other computers have the ability to handle groups of digits of varying length.

In any computer, units of storage must be identified, so that a program can store information in a particular storage location and retrieve it later from the same location. The locations are given *addresses;* a program retrieves a piece of information in storage by giving the address of the location of the information. The basic groups are numbered, ordinarily from an address of zero; hence the largest address would of course be one less than the number of storage groups in the computer. In a computer with a byte structure, each byte in storage has its individual address; in other computers, with fixed word length, each word has an address.

Input

The input subsystem of the computer enables the computer to accept information from the outside world. The information, comprising data and instructions, is read from punched cards, magnetic tape, or other similar media, and stored in the computer's main storage.

The most widespread vehicle for the initial introduction of programs and data into a computer is the *punched card*, though preparation of the initial input on magnetic tape or paper tape is gaining increasing acceptance. The cards are most commonly punched by a person operating a typewriter-like device called a *card punch*. The card punch puts the typed information into cards in the form of punched holes. Computers have card readers which sense the holes in the cards and emit electrical impulses corresponding to these holes. The electrical impulses are sent to the computer's main storage, where they magnetize some of the magnetic storage elements, thus storing in the computer's main storage the information punched in the cards. Punched cards are used widely because they are standardized, inexpensive even for small-volume operations, durable, and easily manipulated. Cards can be punched in a relatively simple operation; they can be perused visually, rearranged and replaced by hand or by machine.

Magnetic tape is an efficient storage medium. The capacity of a reel of tape may be several million characters, and the tape can be written and read rapidly. The speed of tape drive units varies from 30,000 or less to 340,000 characters per second during actual information transfer. This speed is partly achieved by the high recording density: a density of 800 characters per inch of tape is standard, though densities of 200, 556, and 1600 characters per inch are also common. The high density, of course, is another factor contributing to the large capacity of a reel of tape.

Fig. 1–4 Information recorded on a magnetic tape.

Physically, information is recorded on magnetic tape, as shown in Fig. 1–4. The tape unit has sets of *writing heads* which record information by magnetizing spots on the ferrite coating of the tape. *Reading heads* sense the magnetic spots and construct electrical impulses representing the information from the magnetized spots; the impulses can be sent to the main storage subsystem of the computer, where they magnetize some cores in main storage, thus completing the transfer of information from magnetic tape to main storage. The information on a magnetic tape is written in discrete *records*, each consisting of several characters, with an *interrecord gap* between the records. Figure 1–5 shows a magnetic tape unit used by the IBM System/360.

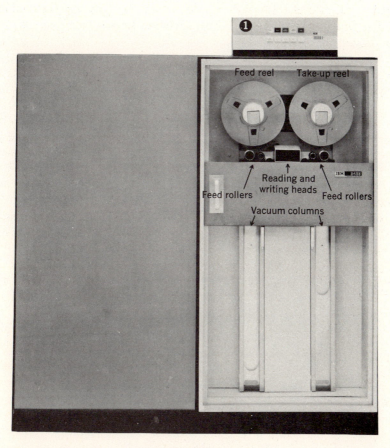

Fig. 1–5 An IBM Model 2403 magnetic tape unit. (Courtesy of International Business Machines Corporation.)

Magnetic ink character readers and *optical mark or character readers* are very useful where source documents can be prepared by their originators for direct computer entry, bypassing keypunching or equivalent steps. The savings in elimination of data preparation lags and costs are substantial.

The majority of the data processed by computers are organized sequentially. That is, the program starts at the beginning of the data and proceeds, item by item, to the end. Some computer data, however, possess a more elaborate organization. If the nature of each record is known, as perhaps in an ordered table, the program may well need information from, say, the 27th record, then the 83rd record, then the 51st. An input device that will permit retrieval of these records without retrieving all records in between is called a *direct access* device.

Fig. 1–6 An IBM 3330 Disk Storage System. (Courtesy of International Business Machines Corporation.)

A *magnetic disk pack* is one kind of direct access device. It has a series of revolving plates, looking much like phonograph records but coated with a magnetic oxide; these plates revolve at high speed, and magnetic heads suspended close to the disk surface read or write information as they would on a magnetic tape. An IBM 3330 Disk Storage System used with IBM System/370 computers is shown in Fig. 1–6. The advantage of a disk pack over a tape is that the heads can move to any given track and be prepared to read or write information there in a fraction of a second, while it may take as much as three *minutes* to read selected information from a tape. Therefore, if the order of the sequence of accesses to the data is not the same as the order in which the data are placed on the disk, a disk pack is of advantage since the access time to the data on disk is low, whereas if the information were on tape, a large amount of winding, rewinding, and back-spacing would be necessary and the access time required would be large. On the other hand, magnetic tape has the advantage of lower cost, greater compactness for storage, and interchangeability among a wider variety of computers. When access is desired to the data in the sequence in which the data are stored on the tape or disk, speeds are comparable for both storage alternatives but will depend on such things as the length of the block of data to be read or written at a time.

A distinction should be made between devices for *primary input*—the input of data and programs on the first presentation to the computer from the outside world—and devices for what is called *backing store*. Backing store is storage, external to the main storage immediately addressable by the central processing unit of a computer, but yet accessible to and readable only by a computer. A computer writes into the backing store information for later reuse and stores this information (programs, data, intermediate and even final results) for relatively quick retrieval. Backing store is usually composed of direct access devices, since retrieval may well be needed in a sequence different from that in which the information was originally written.

Magnetic disk units are good examples of backing store. They are used mostly for temporary storage or for programs or data to which frequent access is required. Magnetic tapes are often used as backing store, but where several kinds of backing store are available, they are used chiefly for storage of information to which frequent access is not necessary. Punched cards and punched paper tape are not considered backing store but primary input, though they can be punched by a computer and later read back.

Besides magnetic disk packs, several other devices are used as backing store. There are *magnetic drums*, cylinders which rotate under sets of magnetic reading and writing heads. In general, drums have smaller capacities than disk units, usually in the range of one million characters. Their advantage is that they permit faster access than disk units. *Data cells*, on the other hand, contain magazines of strips of magnetic material; the drive unit can select one of the strips for reading or writing, but the access is still slower than that of disk units. The capacity, however, is much greater, being in the neighborhood of 400 million characters.

Direct data entry to computers through video terminals, teletypes, banking terminals, point-of-sale terminals, etc. is becoming more widespread. Its advantages, especially for major applications, lie primarily in the possibility of immediate response, either for immediate correction of errors, return of information required for completion of a transaction, or information for time-critical management decisions. General-purpose typewriter or video-screen terminals are used in many situations where interaction between a person and the computer is desired. In such situations, if the programs in the computer are well designed, the person directs the computer in its processing, and the computer in turn supplies information— *feedback*—to the person, enabling him to make progress toward the solution of his problem or to direct the computer in a new round of processing. The human and the computer can thus be partners in problem-solving or information retrieval. The use of direct data entry devices is practical only when the computer is able to service several of them simultaneously. Such simultaneous use is called *time sharing*.

Output

The output subsystem enables the computer to give information to the outside world. The information coming from the computer's main storage is written onto output media such as punched cards, paper, magnetic or punched paper tape, or magnetic disk packs. We can distinguish logically the functions of input and output, but the devices are often not separate. The same magnetic tape drives

Pen moves horizontally along tracks   Pen unit   Paper is wound and unwound from roller

Fig. 1-7   A Calcomp Model 563 digital incremental plotter.   (Courtesy of California Computer Products, Inc.)

read from and write onto the magnetic tapes, and the same disk drives read from or write onto the magnetic disk packs.

For the magnetic media of tape, disk, drum, and data cell, the output data rates are the same as the input rates.   Cards and paper tapes are punched by devices separate from card and paper tape readers, and the output rates are much slower.

Printers attached to computers typically print a line at a time, and can print 1200 or more lines of 132 characters each per minute.   Printers provide most of the output that is accessible to human understanding.   Therefore printer output constitutes the bulk of computer output and is the end result of most computational procedures.   Other forms of computer output serve primarily to prepare input for some later process in the computer.

Pen-and-ink plotters can be attached to computers to draw graphs and diagrams.   It usually takes longer for a plotter to prepare a diagram than it takes a computer printer to print a thousand words; however, a complicated diagram may be well worth many thousand words (and especially numbers).

Special-purpose output devices convert computer output to analog form to drive machines.   Other devices display the information at consoles, either on a cathode-ray tube as characters, points, or lines, or printed by a console typewriter.

Arithmetic and logic

The arithmetic and logic subsystem of the computer contains the circuitry that performs all arithmetic operations, comparisons, and other transformations of data.

The operations available are addition, subtraction, multiplication, and division; multiplication is performed by repeated addition, and division by repeated subtraction. Operands can be compared and an indicator set to record the result of the comparison. More sophisticated computers are capable of more than one kind of number representation, for example integer and *floating-point* (a floating-point number consists of some significant digits and an indicator of the placement of the decimal point), and can deal with various lengths of numbers of each type. The circuitry must be able to perform the arithmetic and comparison operations on numbers expressed in each representation.

Other manipulations which transform data are also performed by the arithmetic and logic section. Many computers have instructions that convert numbers from one representation to another. The circuitry to perform these instructions, as well as shifts and other logical operations described in Chapter 11, is located in the arithmetic and logic section.

Operands for all these operations are taken from the main storage of the computer, and results of the operations are stored again in the main storage.

Control

In the center of Fig. 1-2 is the control sybsystem, which controls the activities of each of the other sections. The sequence in which operations are performed is supervised by the control subsystem; this subsystem retrieves instructions from main storage and decodes them for execution. It also takes charge of getting operands needed by the arithmetic and logic or output subsystems from the appropriate locations in main storage, and storing arithmetic results or information from the input subsystem into main storage.

The unit of control in a computer is the *instruction;* a *program* is a set of instructions. An instruction is coded numerically and kept in the computer's main storage. The sequence of operations in retrieving, decoding, and executing instructions can be described as follows.

A computer has an *instruction address register* which always holds in main storage the address of the next instruction to be executed. Execution of an instruction can be divided into two parts, an *instruction cycle* and an *execution cycle*. During the instruction cycle, the control subsystem retrieves the instruction from the location addressed by the instruction address register, and decodes the instruction preparatory to executing it. During the decoding process, the control subsystem identifies from the *operation code* in the instruction the type of operation to be performed. It decodes the rest of the instruction accordingly and sets up data paths for the execution of the instruction.

During the execution cycle, the operation specified by the instruction is actually performed—arithmetic, information move, the start of an input operation, etc. The instruction address register is also updated during the execution cycle. Usually it is changed to refer to the instruction immediately following (in main storage) the instruction being executed; some instructions are *branch* instructions in which part of the execution of the instruction itself is to replace the contents of the instruction address register by one of the operands of the instruction.

Instruction and execution cycles alternate in the execution of a program. The instruction and execution cycles for one instruction are followed by instruction and execution cycles for the next instruction, and so on, until the whole program has been executed.

The control, arithmetic and logic, and main storage subsystems are usually housed in the same computer unit; the distinctions made here between the functions are defined for pedagogical reasons, and do not represent a clear separation of circuitry elements.

3. STRUCTURE OF THE IBM SYSTEM / 360 AND 370

There are several models of IBM System/360 computers and an even greater variety of input and output device configurations. In addition to the differences in the number and variety of peripheral devices attached to the basic units, models differ in main storage capacity and speed. The larger models are faster, of course. Here we will describe several of the functional characteristics that are common to all IBM System/360 computers.

The IBM System/370 is newer, and it also comes in a wide range of models. Besides generally greater speed and storage capacity, there are features in System/370 in addition to those available on System/360. The newer features are introduced mainly to enable implementation of more sophisticated operating system services; the most noteworthy of these features is dynamic address translation, which enables development of virtual storage systems. Since the additional System/370 features are mostly invisible to the user (partly by design, to aid compatibility between System/360 and System/370 programs), nearly all the presentation in this text will be equally applicable to System/360 and System/370 users. Toward the end of the book, especially when presenting the architectural features used primarily by the supervisor, we will draw distinctions between the systems.

Main storage and arithmetic

The main storage of the IBM System/360 and 370 is organized into *bytes*, each of which consists of eight bits. We will refer to either an eight-bit quantity or the storage required to hold it as a byte—the meaning in each case should be clear from the context. Each byte of storage has an address, and the capacity of main storage ranges from 8192 bytes in the smaller models to 2,097,152 bytes or even more in some larger ones. For arithmetic and logical operations, the bytes in turn are grouped into *words* of four bytes each, *half-words* of two bytes each, and *double words* of eight bytes each. This grouping will be discussed in more detail in later sections.

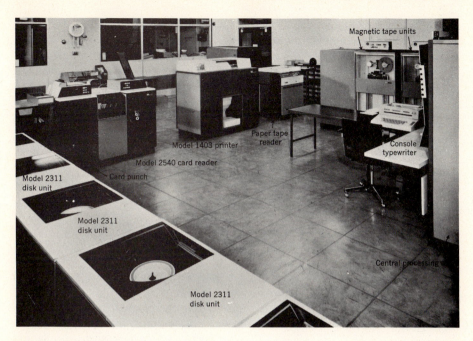

Fig. 1–8 An IBM System/360 computer. (Courtesy of D. H. Rooks, A.I.I.P., University College, London, Physics Department.)

   In addition to the main storage, there is a set of 16 general-purpose *registers*, each one word (4 bytes or 32 bits) long. These registers are used in specifying addresses of operands and in performing binary integer arithmetic and most logical operations. Their addresses are 0 to 15. Still another set of four registers is used in floating-point arithmetic. These four registers, of 64 bits each, have addresses 0, 2, 4, and 6. The context of an address in an instruction determines whether the address refers to a floating-point register, a general register, or a location in main storage. Implicit in the operation code for each instruction are the addressing characteristics of each of its operands.

   In the IBM System/360 and 370, arithmetic can be performed on numbers in three different representations. A set of instructions is provided for each of the three types, and the number representation assumed by each instruction is implicit in the operation code of the instruction. The first representation is *binary integer*. Numbers are represented in binary form, with lengths of 16 and 32 bits. Specific details of representation and the arithmetic instructions that operate on the numbers will be discussed in Section 4 of this chapter and in Chapter 4. A second representation is called *floating point*. Exponents and fractions are both represented in binary, sharing 32-bit, 64-bit, or 128-bit storage areas. The use of floating-point numbers is familiar to FORTRAN, PL/1, or ALGOL programmers; more details about floating-point number representation and System/360 and 370 instructions for manipulating floating-point numbers are given in Chapter 13. The third number representation is *decimal*. Each decimal digit can be represented in four bits, so two decimal digits can be packed into one byte. Decimal arithmetic can be performed on numbers varying in length from 1 to 16 bytes, with one half-byte always reserved for the representation of the sign. This mode of arithmetic is discussed in greater detail in Chapter 14.

In addition to the three representations of data for which arithmetic instructions are furnished, there are other representations which permit nonarithmetic manipulations. Data in character form are represented one character to a byte; the characters can be tested, moved, and changed in main storage. Certain data are best represented by single bits, which can efficiently record yes or no, 1 or 0, present or absent, etc. Logical and shift instructions (discussed in Chapter 11) operate on information in bit form.

Input-output

Each IBM System/360 or 370 computer has one or more input and output *channels*, and several devices may be attached to each channel. There are two types of channels, *selector* and *multiplexor* channels. A given computer may have one or more selector channels. One of the devices on each selector channel may be active for transmission at any one time. Usually high-speed devices, such as magnetic tape units, magnetic disk drives, and magnetic drums, are attached to the System/ 360 through selector channels. Slower-speed devices are attached through a *byte-multiplexor* channel, which is capable of simultaneously transmitting to and receiving from several slow-speed devices. Thus one multiplexor channel can maintain active transmission with a card reader, card punch, printer (even the 1403-N1 printer, at 1100 lines per minute, is slow enough to be serviced by the multiplexor channel), pen-and-ink plotter, typewriter console—in fact, with several of each. A System/370 computer may also have a *block-multiplexor* channel, which

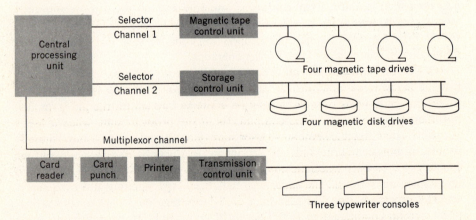

Fig. 1–9 An input-output configuration.

can control several active high-speed devices concurrently, though only one can be transmitting data at a time. A typical input-output configuration is diagrammed in Fig. 1–9.

A channel of System/360 or 370 is not only a means of communicating information between the main storage and input or output devices on command, but it is a small special-purpose computer in its own right. It has its own program, made of *commands* (the word "command" is used to distinguish the instruction executed by the channel from the instruction executed by the central processor). Of course, the channel is subordinate to, and executes its programs as requested by, the central processor.

Operating system

The *operating system* of System/360 or 370 is a series of programs designed to aid and supervise both the internal activities of the computer and its input and output. Such an operating system has the twofold purpose of helping users utilize the complex and sophisticated features of the hardware and making such use efficient by means of careful planning and overlapping of activities. To ensure efficient computer use, the operating system provides for a high degree of concurrency: several input and output operations can be performed at the same time that instructions are being executed in the central processing unit. For this concurrency to be possible, the computer must have some fairly sophisticated features, and the operating system makes use of these features in ways that individual programs would find terribly burdensome. Thus, by means of the operating system, services can be provided in a comprehensive and consistent manner, relieving the individual programmer of many laborious chores.

Concurrency of operations means that often the output for one job, internal processing for a second job, and input for a third job are performed simultaneously. Immediately after the processing for one job is finished, processing for another job begins. Still more sophisticated operating systems allow *time-sharing*, under which programs and data for several jobs are in the computer at the same time, taking turns at execution. In such environments as these, which are necessary to the efficient use of computers, the data of one job must be protected from destruction by the data of another job; the operating system provides this protection.

One of the hardware features that helps the *supervisor* (part of the operating system) perform its functions is the *privileged* nature of certain instructions. When the computer is running, it may be in one of two states: the problem state and the supervisor state. The computer is in the problem state when a user's program is running; it is in the supervisor state only when the supervisor is running. Input and output instructions, among others, are *privileged*, which means they can be executed only when the computer is in the supervisor state. Therefore, a user's program *must ask* the supervisor to do any input and output required.

The supervisor can also make use of the *interrupt* feature of System/360 or 370. Certain conditions, such as errors, requests from the user's program, and input or output terminations, can cause interruptions of the user's program and transfer of control to the supervisor. The supervisor may start new input or output transmission, honor requests for service by the user's program, analyze and correct errors—any or all of these—before returning control to the user's program. The interrupt feature thus allows the supervisor to operate input and output devices in a sophisticated and efficient manner and to retain firm control over the activities of the user's program.

An important part of the IBM System/360 or 370 computer is the *program status word*, PSW for short. The program status word is 64 bits long. It contains much important information about the status of the program currently being run, including the instruction address register. Also included are indicators for problem or supervisor state, bits specifying whether certain conditions should cause interrupt, a key designating which areas of main storage are available to the program, and other items of information. The supervisor can store a program status word and load a new one when the computer is in the supervisor state.

As we see, the supervisor is a ubiquitous part of the IBM System/360 or 370 computing system. We will be learning about various aspects of it throughout this book.

4. REPRESENTATION OF INFORMATION

Storage structure

The IBM System/360 and 370 are basically binary computers, in which numbers, including addresses, are represented in binary form. The *bit* is the smallest unit of information and represents a simple choice: 0 or 1. Bits are grouped into bytes of eight bits each; in the IBM System/360 and 370 the byte is the smallest *addressable* unit of information—the smallest unit which has a distinct address. Since a byte is eight bits long, it can hold 2^8 or 256 different patterns of information or numbers—the binary forms run from 00000000 to 11111111. Since a byte is eight bits long, it holds exactly two hexadecimal digits. This is the reason for preferring the hexadecimal system for description of IBM System/360 and 370 contents.

Addresses in System/360 and 370 are 24-bit numbers. The addresses of bytes start at 0 and increase to the capacity of the storage available in any particular computer. Smaller models may have 8192 bytes of storage, so addresses go from 0 to 8191 or, in binary, from

$$000000000000000000000000$$

to

$$000000000001111111111111.$$

Larger models may have more storage: 2^{16}, 2^{17}, 2^{18} or 2^{19} bytes; the capacity is usually a power of 2.

The bytes are also grouped to form words, each of which is four bytes in length. A word in storage is addressed by its *highest-order* byte, i.e., the byte holding the most significant part of a number, or the leftmost segment, as one would ordinarily picture the arrangement of storage. A word (sometimes called a *full word* to ensure clarity or to distinguish it from a half-word or a double word) must begin on a word *boundary;* that is, its address must be divisible by 4. (To state the rule differently, the *lowest-order* two bits of its address expressed in binary must be 0's.) Figure 1–10 shows a full word in storage, four bytes long, beginning with the byte addressed (decimal) 19424. Note that 19424, divisible by 4, is a word boundary.

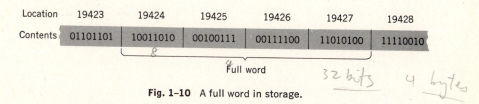

Fig. 1–10 A full word in storage.

Similarly, a *half-word* is a group of two bytes or 16 bits. In storage it must be located at a half-word boundary; that is, its address must be divisible by 2. A *double word* is a group of eight bytes. In main storage it must be located at a double-word boundary; that is, its address must be divisible by 8.

In addition to the main storage, there are two sets of registers in the IBM System/360 or 370. There are 16 general registers, each a full word in length, with addresses 0 to 15, or 0000 to 1111 in binary. Registers are *not* part of the main core storage, but independent units with much faster access. There is no ambiguity as to whether a given address refers to a register or to a location in main storage because only certain portions of computer instructions contain register addresses, whereas other portions are used to define main storage locations of operands. The 16 general registers are used to hold operands and results of all binary integer arithmetic operations, to specify addresses in main storage, and for many other purposes.

The second set consists of four *floating-point registers*. Each is 64 bits long, since floating-point numbers may be 32 or 64 bits long. The addresses of the registers are 0, 2, 4, and 6. Some instructions address floating-point registers, and others address general registers; the context of a register address determines whether a general or floating-point register will be used, and there can be no ambiguity. All floating-point computations are performed in the floating-point registers.

Representation of binary integers

A binary integer is usually represented in a full word of 32 bits. For purposes of specifying bits within a word, we number the bit positions from 0 through 31, left to right, as shown in Fig. 1–11. In binary integers, bit position 0 holds the sign of the number. If the sign bit is a 0, the number is positive; if it is a 1, the

Bits   [0|0|0|0|0|0|0|0|0|0|0|0|0|0|0|0|0|0|0|0|0|0|0|0|0|0|0|0|1|1|0|1|0]
Bit positions   0 1 2 3 4 5 6 7 8 9 . . .   30 31

Fig. 1–11 The binary integer equivalent to 26 (decimal).

number is negative. For example, Fig. 1–11 shows the binary integer representation of the decimal number $+26$. (For the rest of this section we will show the 32-bit numbers just as strings of 1's and 0's, omitting the boxes representing bit positions.)

A negative number is represented in what is called *2's-complement notation*. This means that if x is positive, $-x$ is represented by the 32-bit number $2^{32} - x$. The arithmetic is not difficult in binary. For example, to represent -26, we subtract 26 from 2^{32} in their binary forms as follows:

$$2^{32} = \quad 100000000000000000000000000000000$$
$$- \ 26 = - \ 00000000000000000000000000011010$$
$$\overline{11111111111111111111111111100110} = \text{representation of } -26$$

The 32-bit number shown as the difference is the binary representation of -26. Note that the sign bit is 1, denoting a negative number.

Another equivalent procedure for finding the 2's-complement of a number is to form its *bit complement* (also called the *1's complement*); that is, we change every 1 to a 0 and every 0 to a 1, and then add the number 1. The representation of -26 by this procedure is as follows:

$$26 = 00000000000000000000000000011010$$
$$\text{Bit complement:} \quad 11111111111111111111111111100101$$
$$\text{Add 1:} \qquad\qquad\qquad\qquad\qquad\qquad\qquad\qquad 1$$
$$\overline{11111111111111111111111111100110}$$

The two procedures are equivalent because the bit complement of a 32-bit number is in fact the result of subtracting the number from $2^{32} - 1$, which is a string of 32 1's.

Binary integers which are small enough are sometimes represented in half-words of 16 bits each. The representation is essentially the same: bit position 0 holds the sign and negative numbers are in 2's-complement form. To find the 16-bit 2's-complement of a number, one must of course subtract the number from 2^{16}, not 2^{32}. The 2's-complement of 1111001101100111, for example, is found by subtracting as follows:

$$2^{16} = \quad 10000000000000000$$
$$- \ 1111001101100111$$
$$\overline{0000110010011001} \ .$$

Any number from $-32{,}768$ to $32{,}767$ can be represented by a half-word.

Representation of characters

A *character* is represented in one byte of eight bits; instructions allow processing of character strings up to 256 characters long. There are 256 different eight-bit numbers, and any of these could be used to represent characters. Of these, 62 numbers are actually assigned to characters for standard IBM use, including 26 for the upper-case alphabet, 10 for the digits 0–9, and the remainder for 25 special characters,

$$¢ \quad . \quad < \quad (\quad + \quad | \quad \& \quad ! \quad \$ \quad * \quad) \quad ; \quad \neg \quad - \quad /$$
$$, \quad \% \quad > \quad ? \quad : \quad \# \quad @ \quad ' \quad = \quad "$$

and a blank. Codes have also been assigned to the lower-case alphabet, but these are reserved for special purposes. The character representations generally used are called the EBCDIC (Extended Binary Coded Decimal Interchange Code); they are listed in a table in Appendix D.

The character representation of decimal digits is also called *zoned decimal*. The first half of the byte, i.e., the first hexadecimal digit, represents a *zone punch* (+, − or blank); the second half of the byte contains the representation of one of the digits from 0 through 9. The word "zones" as used here derives from punched card descriptions, in which the +, −, and 0 punches are called zone punches, especially in the representation of letters and special characters. The zone punches are converted to four-bit codes in the EBCDIC representation as follows:*

Zone	Code
+	1100 or hexadecimal C
−	1101 or hexadecimal D
Blank	1111 or hexadecimal F

An example of a zoned decimal number is shown in Fig. 1–12. The three bytes represent the number +387, with the zones for blank in the first two bytes and the zone for + in the last byte.

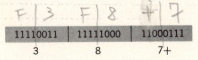

11110011	11111000	11000111
3	8	7+

Fig. 1–12 A zoned decimal number.

---

* These are the codes *produced* by the computer. It will recognize any digit A, B, C, D, E, or F as a sign.

Decimal numbers: packed decimal representation

A decimal digit can be represented in four bits; therefore, two decimal digits can be packed into one byte. The IBM System/360 and 370 can do arithmetic on numbers expressed in this form, which is called *packed decimal.* The sign of the number is represented in the *low-order* four bits of the low-order byte: usually 1100 for plus, 1101 for minus. The low-order byte also holds the least significant digit of the number; other bytes hold two decimal digits each. Arithmetic may be performed on numbers whose lengths may vary from 1 to 16 bytes; numbers can therefore include from 1 to 31 decimal digits. Figure 1–13 shows a packed decimal field, two bytes long, holding the number −196.

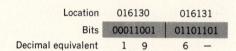

Fig. 1–13 A packed decimal number.

The number is always *addressed* by its highest-order byte—location 016130 in Fig. 1–13, for example. Instructions which deal with packed decimal numbers include the lengths of the operands as arguments. Such instructions are described in Chapter 14.

Floating-point numbers

Floating-point numbers are used for calculations with numbers of mixed and variable magnitudes when we wish that the computer retain as many significant digits as possible while keeping track of the magnitudes of the numbers. In a binary computer, this is accomplished by making one part of each number a *characteristic,* indicating a power (positive or negative) of two, and the other part a *fraction,* a binary number considered to be less than one. The number represented is the product of the power of two and the fraction.

In the IBM System/360, floating-point numbers can be of two sizes: 32 bits and 64 bits, called *short* and *long* (or *single-* and *double-precision*). In both, bit position 0 contains the sign, and bit positions 1–7 contain the characteristic. In the IBM System/360 this characteristic indicates a power of 16; that is, adding 1 to the characteristic multiplies the number represented by 16. Values coded by the characteristic may range from −64 to +63, so the range of representable numbers is roughly from 16^{-64} to 16^{63}, or 10^{-78} to 10^{+75}. Thus the IBM System/360 can be fairly called a hexadecimal computer with respect to floating-point.

In System/370 and in a few System/360 models, a third size of floating-point numbers, called *extended precision,* is recognized. Extended-precision numbers are each 128 bits long.

The fraction occupies bit positions 8–31 in short floating-point numbers, or 8–63 in long floating-point numbers. This capacity allows the equivalent in

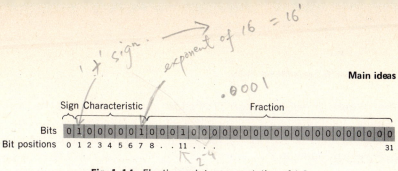

Fig. 1–14 Floating-point representation of 1.0.

binary of about seven decimal digits of precision in short floating-point numbers, and about 16 decimal digits in long floating-point numbers. Negative numbers are represented in true form; the sign bit is set to 1, but both the exponent and the fraction are shown as if the number were positive.

Figure 1–14 shows a short floating-point number representing the number 1.0. The fraction (binary) is .0001; the 1 in the fraction is in the position representing 2^{-4}. The characteristic has a 1 in bit position 1; this represents a positive power of 16 and is sometimes called a *bias quantity*. The 1 in bit position 7 represents an exponent of 1, so the true number represented is 16^1 times the fraction: $16^1 \times 2^{-4} = 1.0$.

Floating-point arithmetic and instructions are treated in Chapter 13.

5. MAIN IDEAS

a. Binary numbers consist of 1's and 0's in a positional representation with radix 2. Hexadecimal numbers consist of digits 0–9 and A–F in a positional representation with radix 16. Conversion from binary to hexadecimal or from hexadecimal to binary is a matter only of compression of four-digit binary groups or expansion of single hexadecimal digits.

b. The major logical subsystems of a computer are input, output, storage, arithmetic, and control.

c. Storage is comprised of groups of bits; each group has an address.

d. Input and output subsystems allow communication between the computer and the outside world, through such media as magnetic tapes and disks, punched cards, printers, pen-and-ink plotters, and typewriter terminals.

e. The control subsystem directs activities of the other subsystems by interpreting and executing instructions.

f. Arithmetic in the IBM System/360 and 370 is performed on binary integers, floating-point numbers, and decimal numbers.

g. Input and output in the IBM System/360 and 370 take place through channels: selector channels handle high-speed devices; a multiplexor channel can handle several devices simultaneously.

h. The supervisor in the IBM System/360 or 370 maintains control of processing, especially input and output, with the help of interrupt facilities and privileged instructions.

i. Main storage in the IBM System/360 or 370 is organized in eight-bit bytes, each of which is addressable. An address is 24 bits long. Bytes are grouped to form four-byte words, two-byte half-words, and eight-byte double words.

j. The 16 general registers, each 32 bits long, have addresses 0–15. The four floating-point registers, each 64 bits long, have addresses 0, 2, 4, 6.

k. Binary integers in the IBM System/360 and 370 are expressed in 2's-complement notation.

l. A character has a representation (EBCDIC) in eight bits or one byte.

m. Decimal numbers can be represented in the packed-decimal form, two digits per byte, with the sign represented in the lowest-order half-byte.

n. Floating-point representation, including an exponent of 16 and a fraction, is used for numbers that vary greatly in magnitude.

QUESTIONS FOR REVIEW AND IMAGINATION

1. Learn the core storage size and input/output configuration of the computer you will be working with.

2. Make a list of other computers you know or can read about and their storage organizations and capacities.

3. Each byte of storage in the IBM System/360 contains eight bits of information and one parity bit. The parity bit is redundant; it is used only to guarantee that information bits are not lost. The parity bit is set to 1 or 0 so as to make the sum of 1's represented in the nine bits an odd number. For example, the character / is represented in eight bits (in EBCDIC) by 01100001. The parity bit to go with this character will be 0, because there are three 1's among the information-carrying bits. The character Q is represented by 11011000, and the parity bit is set to 1, so there will be five 1-bits among the nine. These representations with parity bit (we call this *odd parity*) are also used in magnetic tape and disk storage associated with the IBM System/360. Using the character representation table of Appendix A, code your name and telephone number in eight-bit EBCDIC representations, and add the correct parity bit to each character.

4. Computers used to be decimal or binary, but no one computer was both. Either kind was used for business data processing and scientific work. Only since the early 1960's have computers had *both* decimal and binary arithmetic capabilities. Given a computer with both, in what problems would you use decimal arithmetic? floating-point? binary integers? Ignore considerations of storage and timing efficiency, and base your answers on such things as accuracy and naturalness.

5. By using the positional representation definition of binary numbers, convert the binary numbers 10101 and 1110111 to decimal.

6. By using the positional representation definition of hexadecimal numbers, convert the hexadecimal numbers A8 and 24D to decimal.

7. Write the hexadecimal number 24D in binary; the binary number 11011001110001 in hexadecimal.

8. Show the full-word 2's complement binary integer representation of the decimal number -18.

9. Express the number 7 as a full-word binary integer, and show how it would be added to the representation of -18.

10. There is a number expressible as a full-word binary integer in the IBM System/ 360 or 370, whose complement (negative) cannot be expressed in a full word. What is this number, and why can't it be expressed in a full word? Sometimes this number is used as the representation for "missing data" or "undefined quantity." Think of reasons for or against this convention.

11. Some computers represent negative numbers in what is called 1's complement notation, in which a complement is formed by changing every 1 to 0 and every 0 to 1. In this notation, are there numbers whose complement cannot be taken? What is the complement of the number 0, and how can it be interpreted? Addition and subtraction in a 1's complement machine require that a carry out of the high-order (sign) position be added to the units' position. Illustrate. Then think of advantages of 1's-complement notation over 2's-complement notation, and vice versa.

12. If a maximum of 64 different characters are to be represented in storage, six bits are enough to provide unique codes for the characters. Before the advent of the IBM System/360, most binary computers used six bits for storage of each character. The fact that words were multiples of six bits facilitated the handling of six-bit characters. The IBM System/360, with its eight-bit representations of characters, introduces an inefficiency of two bits per character. This is partly offset by the efficiency of storage of decimal numbers in the packed-decimal format: two digits into eight bits. Calculate the ratio of characters to decimal digits in storage for which the eight-bit character and two-digit byte are just as efficient as a six-bit system. With fewer characters than this break-even ratio, the eight-bit system is more efficient.

REFERENCES

Amdahl, G. M., "The Structure of SYSTEM/360: Part III—Unit Design Consideration," *IBM Systems Journal* 3 (1964), pp. 144–64. An explanation of the rationale of the IBM System/360 structure.

IBM System/360 System Summary, GA22-6810, IBM Corporation. An introductory description of the System/360, especially the input and output units.

IBM System/370 System Summary, GA22-7001, IBM Corporation. A similar description of the System/370.

Stone, Harold S., *Introduction to Computer Organization and Data Structures* (New York: McGraw-Hill, 1972). Thorough discussions of number representations based on a binary radix, and other computer organization considerations.

Wegner, Peter, *Programming Languages, Information Structures, and Machine Organization* (New York: McGraw-Hill, 1968). A theoretical and general description of computer structure. Portions of this book bear on the next few chapters too.

Chapter 2

Introduction to IBM System / 360 and 370 Machine Language

In this chapter we introduce in some detail the basic features of machine language of the IBM System/360 and 370, including the addressing of operands and the formats of the six types of instructions.

1. THE NATURE OF MACHINE LANGUAGE

It was stated in Chapter 1 that the unit of control of a computer is an *instruction.* Instructions are coded numerically and kept in main storage during execution of the program. A set of instructions which are executed in sequence is a *program,* and the activity of programming is, strictly speaking, writing sequences of instructions. Each instruction contains an operation code, which designates the operation to be performed by the computer. Instructions also contain operand addresses, to instruct the computer which storage locations or registers to use in the operation. Some instructions also carry other information that helps to define the operation to be performed.

Instructions can be put into classes according to the computer subsystems they use. There are arithmetic instructions, which instruct, through the control subsystem of course, the arithmetic and logic subsystem to perform arithmetic or logical operations. Some instructions are classed as input/output instructions; they instruct the input and output subsystems to take action. Other instructions are information move instructions; they move information from one location to another in the storage subsystem, sometimes making simple transformations in the information as it is moved. Still other instructions are classed as control instructions. Control instructions do not cause arithmetic to be performed, information to be moved in main storage, or input or output to be accomplished; they affect the flow of control by changing the program status word in some way. The most common and important control instruction is the conditional branch, which makes a test, then depending on the result, either allows the computer to go on to the next instruction in main storage or, by replacing the contents of the instruction address register with the operand of the conditional branch instruction, starts execution of a different sequence of instructions. This kind of instruction is extremely important; it permits repetition of instructions and complexity of programs, as we will see in Chapters 7 and 8.

We will see examples of instructions in later sections of this chapter, and spend the rest of the book learning how to use them effectively. In the next section we examine the addressing structure of the IBM System/360 and 370; the ways in which instructions in System/360 and 370 address their operands are rather complex, so the reader is urged to pay special attention.

2. OPERAND ADDRESSING IN MACHINE LANGUAGE

Rules for operand address representation

An operand in a register is addressed by the register number. This register address is a number from 0 to 15, and is expressed in four bits. We will show this number in examples as one hexadecimal digit, 0 to F, corresponding to the binary representations 0000 to 1111.

The address of an operand in main storage can be expressed in instructions in either of two ways. First is the sum of

contents of a register

$C(B) + D$
base register

and

a 12-bit number called a *displacement*.

3 nibbles = 4 bit @

The register used is called a *base register*, or more simply, a *base*. Second, and similar is the sum of

contents of a base register

$C(B) + C(X) + D$

and

contents of another (or the same) register, called an *index*,

and

a 12-bit displacement.

Figure 2–1 illustrates the forming of an operand address from base and displacement and from base, index, and displacement. Figure 2–1(a) shows how a pointer to a register used as a base and a displacement define the address of an operand. Figure 2–1(b) includes an index as well.

Some instructions use operands addressed by base and displacement; others use operands addressed by base, index, and displacement. In order to use the instructions correctly, we must know the addressing characteristics of each. The instructions in the IBM System/360 and 370 are organized and named, as we shall see, to help us keep this information clearly in mind.

After the sum of base and displacement—or base, index, and displacement—has been formed, only the low-order 24 bits are used as an address. For compact-

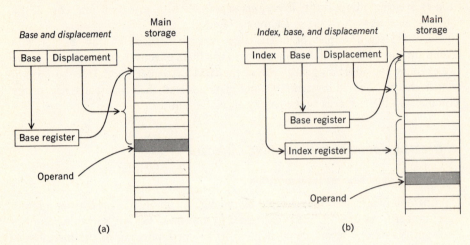

Fig. 2–1 Forming an operand address (a) from base and displacement, and (b) from index, base, and displacement.

ness we will show register contents, displacements, and actual addresses in hexadecimal in our examples. Program listings and debugging information printed by the IBM System/360 and 370 also show addresses in hexadecimal, so familiarization with hexadecimal representations is necessary.

In storage address specifications, a base or index of 0 is a special case. By convention, it is taken to mean the *number* 0, *not* the contents of register 0. This allows for situations in which we want to specify an address by only base and displacement in instructions where addressing by base, index, and displacement is standard, and also for cases in which addresses are to be specified by displacement only.

In System/370 virtual storage systems, the addresses generated by base, index, and displacement as explained above are taken to be addresses in a virtual (almost imaginary!) storage. The virtual address is automatically translated by the *dynamic address translation* feature into physical main storage addresses for access of actual operands and instructions. The system does the translation so consistently and thoroughly that the user operates entirely within his virtual storage, and need not be aware of the translation system until he is doing quite advanced and complex manipulations. So far as he knows, virtual storage is identical to main storage. Therefore we will ignore the address translation until Chapter 17.

Storage addressing examples

a. Suppose that in an instruction addressing its operand in storage by base and displacement, the specification is a base of 9 and a displacement of 00E (hexadecimal). Suppose further that register 9 contains (hexadecimal, as all numbers in this section) 00006844. The actual operand address—which we call

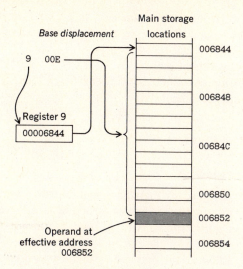

Fig. 2–2 The addressing of an operand.

the *effective address*—is formed as $\quad c(R_i) + D$

$$
\begin{array}{ll}
\text{contents of register 9} & \text{00006844} \\
+ \text{ displacement} & \underline{\hspace{1.2em} \text{00E}} \\
& \text{006852}
\end{array}
$$

The effective address is the low-order 24 bits of the sum, 006852. The contents of register 9 are not altered; the addition is performed in a special nonaddressable register in the central processing unit. The addressing of the operand can be represented in diagram form such as that shown in Fig. 2–2.

b. Suppose register B (decimal 11) contains 50011C48. An instruction specifying base B and displacement 46A will address

$$
\begin{array}{ll}
\text{contents of register B} & \text{50011C48} \quad c(B) + D \\
+ \text{ displacement} & \underline{\hspace{2.0em} \text{46A}} \\
& \text{0120B2}
\end{array}
$$

The effective address is 0120B2.

c. An instruction using base, index, and displacement may call for base **B**, index 4, and displacement 46A. If register 4 contains 00001240, the effective address computation is

$$
\begin{array}{ll}
\text{contents of register B} & \text{50011C48} \quad c(B) + c(x) + D \\
+ \text{ contents of register 4} & \text{00001240} \\
+ \text{ displacement} & \underline{\hspace{2.0em} \text{46A}} \\
& \text{0132F2}
\end{array}
$$

The effective address is 0132F2.

d. An instruction which normally uses base, index, and displacement may call for base B, index 0, and displacement 074. The effective address computation is

contents of register B	50011C48
+ (*not* the contents of register 0)	0
+ displacement	074
	011CBC

The effective address is 011CBC.

Rationale of addressing structure

Most computers are designed so that the actual address of an operand is in the instruction itself. This simple addressing structure is often enhanced by index registers and indirect addressing. With *indirect addressing*, the address in the instruction is not the address of the operand itself but that of a place in storage which contains the address of the operand. An addressing structure with indirect addressing and index registers is straightforward and reasonably powerful.

The addressing structure of System/360 and 370 is quite different from that of other computers, and compared to other addressing schemes it has both notable advantages and disadvantages. One disadvantage is that addressing in the IBM System/360 and 370 is difficult to learn. One principal advantage is economy of storage required for instructions. An IBM System/360 or 370 instruction requires only 16 bits for base and displacement specification; a full address, if placed in the instruction, would take 24 bits.

When a program is loaded into main storage for execution, the operating system must assign available space and load the program into this space. Since the storage locations may not be the same on different occasions, the program must be able to run properly no matter where it is loaded in main storage. This means that operand addresses in instructions must be adjusted to refer to the actual locations used. The process of loading the program and adjusting the address is called *relocation*, and the ability of a program to be relocated is called *relocatability*. In some computers, every operand address is modified as the program is loaded to make the address consistent with the address assigned currently to the program and its data areas. In System/360 and 370, relocatability is mostly accomplished by adjustment of the contents of base registers, and, as we shall see in Chapter 5, this is largely automatic. Thus another advantage of the System/360 and 370 addressing structure is the easy relocatability of programs and data blocks.

Often a loop in a program must address successive pieces of data in successive passes through the loop. The addresses in the instructions referring to these data must be modified so that successive executions of the instructions will in fact treat successive pieces of data. A programmer using an algebraic language like FORTRAN can refer to successive pieces of data by means of subscripted variables, but the programs translated into machine language must modify effective addresses of operands during execution. Another advantage of the addressing scheme of System/360 and 370 is the manner in which it facilitates address computation and modification. Doing arithmetic on the quantity in the index register is a most convenient way of modifying an effective address. Modification of a base register can also be a convenient and efficient means of address modification.

3. MACHINE LANGUAGE INSTRUCTION FORMATS

Machine language instructions follow six different formats. The formats differ in the addressing characteristics—whether operands are in registers, in the instruction itself, or in main storage addressed by base and displacement or by base, index, and displacement. Because of the variation in space required for specification of storage operand addresses, register addresses, and data in the instruction, some instructions occupy two bytes of storage, others are four bytes long, and still others are six bytes long.

In all instructions the first one or two bytes are the *operation code*, which indicates the length of the instruction and the type of operation to be performed.

RR instructions

The simplest of the five instruction forms is the *RR type*. Both operands of each of these instructions are in registers, giving the type the name RR, standing for register to register. Four bits hold each register address, so the address of the first operand is in bits 8–11 of the instruction, and the address of the second operand in bits 12–15. The instruction is therefore two bytes long, as shown in Fig. 2–3.

RR type   Op code | R1 | R2   = 4 hex. digit.

Bits 0   3 4   7 8   11 12   15

Fig. 2–3 Format of an *RR* instruction.

As an example, the instruction coded in hexadecimal as 1837 is an RR-type instruction. The operation code, 18, means load from a register. The operand addresses are 3 and 7; execution of the instruction causes the contents of register 7 to be loaded into register 3, replacing the previous contents of register 3. The contents of register 7 remain unchanged.

RX instructions

An instruction of *RX type* has the form shown in Fig. 2–4.

The first operand is a register operand, with address *R1* given in bits 8–11 of the instruction. The second operand is located in main storage; its address is specified by a base *B2* (register whose address is given in bits 16–19), index *X2* (a register whose address is given in bits 12–15) and a displacement given in bits 20–31 of the instruction.

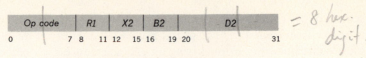

Fig. 2-4 Format of an *RX* instruction.

As an example, the instruction coded in hexadecimal as 5B35C024 is an RX-type instruction. The operation code is 5B meaning subtract (binary integer). The first operand is in register 3. The field *X2* is 5, the field *B2* is C, the displacement is 024; together they define the address of the second operand. Suppose register 5 contains 00000050 and register C (or 12) contains 00007404. Then the second operand address is generated as shown below:

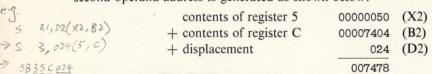

	contents of register 5	00000050	(X2)
+	contents of register C	00007404	(B2)
+	displacement	024	(D2)
		007478	

The effective address is 007478.

This instruction will be executed as follows: The contents of location 007478 (actually the full word in locations 007478 to 00747B) will be subtracted from the contents of register 3. The result will be left in register 3; the contents of all storage locations are unchanged.

This is a good time to explain the notation and type fonts we will be using through the remainder of the text. Italics are used for three purposes. One, of course, is emphasis of particularly notable words. Second, the first and defining use of a term is italicized. In that context, *RX type* was italicized in its first mention at the beginning of this subsection, but is not in the text following. Third, italics are used to denote symbols that represent a possible range of actual values. In this context, *R1*, *X2*, *B2*, and *D2* are italicized because each represents a variety of possible values. Typewriter type, such as GSQ and 00747B, is used to denote actual values, codes, instructions and statements as they might be submitted to the computer or be reported by the computer. These conventions are not followed to ultimate extremes; when no ambiguity should result, we stick to the regular text-type font to avoid the visual confusion of constantly changing fonts.

RS instructions

An instruction of *RS type* has the form shown in Fig. 2–5. The first operand is a register operand, with address *R1* given in bits 8–11 of the instruction. The second operand is located in main storage, with address specified by a base *B2* (register whose address is given in bits 16–19 of the instruction) and a displacement *D2* given in bits 20–31 of the instruction. The RS-type instructions are the only ones which have three operands; the third operand is a register operand, whose address *R3* is given in bits 12–15 of the instruction.*

---

* There are some RS instructions, however, which do not have a third operand. In these, the *R3* portion of the instruction is ignored.

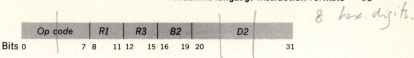

8 hex. digits.

Bits 0   7 8   11 12   15 16   19 20   31

Fig. 2–5 Format of an *RS* instruction.

For example, the instruction coded in hexadecimal as 9868C024 is an RS-type instruction. The operation code is 98, meaning *load multiple*. The first operand is register 6, the third operand is register 8. The second operand is defined by the base C and displacement 024. If register C contains 00007404, the second operand address is defined:

LM   R1,R3,D2(B2)

contents of register C	00007404
+ displacement	024
	007428

→ LM   6,8,024(C)

→ 98 68 C024

The effective address is 007428.

The execution of this instruction will be as follows. Registers from 6 (first operand) to 8 (third operand) will be loaded from consecutive locations of main storage, starting with location 007428. Register 6 will be loaded therefore from locations 007428 to 00742B, register 7 will be loaded from locations 00742C to 00742F, and register 8 will be loaded from locations 007430 to 007433. Previous contents of registers 6, 7, and 8 are lost; contents of all storage locations are unchanged.

SI instructions

An instruction of *SI type* is of the form shown in Fig. 2–6. The first operand is in main storage, with address specified by base *B1* and displacement *D1*. The second operand is the eight-bit quantity in bits 8–15 of the instruction itself. It is called *I2*, or the *immediate* operand.

For example, the instruction coded in hexadecimal as 92F3C231 is an SI-type instruction. The operation code is 92, meaning *move immediate*. The first operand is in main storage in a location defined by base register C and displacement 231. If register C contains 00007404, the operand address is determined by:

MVI   D1(B1),I2

contents of register C	00007404
+ displacement	231
	007635

→ MVI   231(C),F3

Thus the effective address is 007635. The second operand is the eight bits coded in hexadecimal as F3, from the second byte of the instruction.

In the execution of this instruction, the byte of immediate data, the second operand F3, is stored at location 00007635 of the main storage.

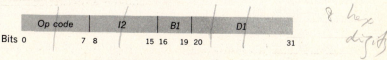

Bits 0   7 8   15 16   19 20   31

8 hex digits

Fig. 2–6 Format of an *SI* instruction.

SS instructions

An instruction of *SS type* is of the form shown in Fig. 2–7. It is the only type of instruction which is six bytes long. Both operands are in main storage: the address of the first is given by base *B1* and displacement *D1* from bits 20–31; the address of the second operand is given by a base *B2* (whose address is given in bits 32–35 of the instruction) and displacement *D2* from bits 36–47. Instructions of SS type are flexible in that the operands may be of various lengths, the actual lengths coded in bits 8–15 of the instructions. Numbers from 0 to 255 can be expressed in the length field of the instruction; they represent lengths of 1 to 256 bytes: $L=0$ implies an operand length of 1 byte, $L=1$ implies an operand length of 2 bytes, etc.

Op code	L	B1	D1	B2	D2

Bits 0   7 8   15 16   19 20   31 32   35 36   47

Fig. 2–7 Format of an *SS* instruction.

12 lex digits.

MVC   D1(L,B1),D2(B2)

For example, the instruction coded in hexadecimal as D202C106C735 is an SS-type instruction. The operation code of D2 means *move character*. The first operand address is defined by base register C and displacement 106. Given that register C contains 00007404, the address computation is

contents of register C   00007404
+ displacement   106
─────────
00750A

The effective address is 00750A.

Similarly, the second operand address is

contents of register C   00007404
+ displacement   735
─────────
007B39

The length field contains 02, so each operand is three bytes long.

In the execution of this instruction, the three bytes beginning at location 007B39 (the second operand) are moved to three storage locations beginning at 00750A (the first operand). That is, the byte from location 007B39 is moved to location 00750A, the byte from 007B3A is moved to 00750B, and the byte from 007B3B is moved to 00750C.

In some SS instructions the two operands may be of different lengths. In these instructions the length field is broken into *L1*, a four-bit field in bit positions 8–11 giving the length of the first operand, and *L2*, a four-bit field in bit positions 12–15 giving the length of the second operand. The numbers in these four-bit fields may be 0 to 15, representing, by a transformation as above, actual operand lengths 1 to 16.

The instruction F224C248CA82 is this kind of SS instruction. The operation code of F2 means *pack*. The length field of the first operand contains a 2, so the first operand is three bytes long. The address of the first operand is

$$
\begin{array}{lr}
\text{contents of register C} & 00007404 \\
+ \text{ displacement} & \underline{\hspace{1.5em} 248} \\
& 00764C
\end{array}
$$

The length field of the second operand contains 4, so the second operand is five bytes long. The address of the second operand is

$$
\begin{array}{lr}
\text{contents of register C} & 00007404 \\
+ \text{ displacement} & \underline{\hspace{1.5em} A82} \\
& 007E86
\end{array}
$$

The execution of this instruction takes the five bytes from locations 007E86–007E8A (second operand) assumed to be in the zoned decimal format and converts the characters to packed decimal form. The resulting packed decimal number is stored in the three-byte area 00764C–00764E (the first operand).

One distinction made between single-length and two-length SS instructions is that those with only a single length process their operands from left (high-order byte) to right. Those that define a length for each operand process their operands from right (low-order) byte to left.

S instructions

An instruction of *S type* is of the form shown in Fig. 2–8. This is the only type in which the operation code is two bytes long. The single operand (called the second operand in reference material!) is determined by base *B2* and displacement *D2* in the usual way. All S instructions are connected with advanced functions which we will not introduce until Chapter 17; almost all of them are reserved for use in supervisor state.

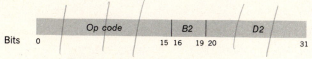

Bits   0   15 16   19 20   31

Fig. 2–8   Format of an S instruction.

Summary

The variety of instruction types is designed to give flexibility in length and location of operands. Figure 2–9 shows the operand configurations of the six instruction types. We shall see, however, that a few instructions are exceptions.

In all instructions, the operation code occupies the first byte. A main storage reference is always given by base and displacement, except in RX-type instructions,

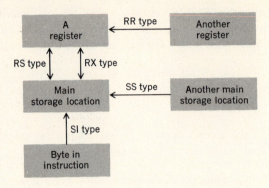

Fig. 2–9 Operand configurations of instructions.

where a register can also be used as index. A register address is given in four bits. Instructions of SS type involve variable-length fields in main storage, so a length (or two lengths) must be specified in the instruction. But when only one byte of data is to be processed, the SI instructions provide extra efficiency by eliminating a storage reference. The individual instructions and their use will be studied in the next several chapters.

4. AN EXAMPLE OF A PROGRAM SEGMENT

We can examine the structure of machine language more thoroughly and convey the flavor of System/360 and 370 processing by following even a trivial example. The following program segment illustrates program sequencing and the use of a few instructions.

Location	Instruction
008114	9824C304
008118	1A42
00811A	5040C310
00811E	9200C310
008122	D207C438C30C
008128	. . .

Instructions, as we have seen, are stored in two, four, or six bytes of main storage. They are executed sequentially, with the next instruction in storage being the next executed, except when a branch instruction causes a jump to an instruction sequence elsewhere, or an interrupt suspends execution of the current program and gives control to the supervisor. Each instruction must begin on a half-word boundary, that is, an even-numbered storage location.

Let us assume that before execution of the segment the contents of various registers and storage locations, expressed in hexadecimal, are as follows:

Registers	Contents	Storage locations	Contents
2	00003404	00830C	00000848
3	00127CD8	008310	03362103
4	FFF30E56	008314	1DCBA987
12 (C)	00008008	008318	23FE5631

Execution begins with the instruction at 008114. The operation is *load multiple*. The effective storage address is

$$\begin{array}{lr} \text{contents of register C} & 00008008 \\ + \text{ displacement} & 304 \\ \hline & 00830C \end{array}$$

The register operands are 2 and 4. This instruction causes register 2 to be loaded with 00000848, the contents from location 00830C; register 3 to be loaded with 03362103, from the next location, 008310; and register 4 to be loaded with 1DCBA987, from location 008314. The load multiple instruction is a four-byte instruction, so the next instruction is taken from location 008118. The operation code is 1A; it stands for *add to register* and is recognized as a two-byte RR-type instruction. The contents of register 2 (second operand) are added to register 4 (first operand):

$$\begin{array}{r} 1DCBA987 \\ + 00000848 \\ \hline 1DCBB1CF \end{array}$$

The result is left in register 4.

The next instruction is taken from location 00811A, since the add-to-register instruction was two bytes long. The instruction 5040C310 is a *store* instruction, of RX type. The effective main storage address is

$$\begin{array}{lr} \text{contents of register C} & 00008008 \\ + 0 & 0 \\ + \text{ displacement} & 310 \\ \hline & 008318 \end{array}$$

The contents of register 4 (first operand), 1DCBB1CF, is stored at location 008318 (meaning, as usual, the four bytes beginning at 008318), replacing the previous contents. The fourth instruction, 9200C310, is the SI-type instruction *move immediate*. It has the same effective address as the last instruction; the "immediate" byte, 00, is stored at location 008318. The four bytes beginning at 008318 are now 00CBB1CF.

The last instruction, D207C438C30C, is an SS-type instruction *move character*. The length field contains 07, so eight bytes are moved. The second operand

address is

	contents of register C	00008008
+	displacement	30C
		008314

The first operand address is

	contents of register C	00008008
+	displacement	438
		008440

Eight bytes are moved from locations 008314–00831B to locations 008440–008447. The eight bytes moved are 1DCBA98700CBB1CF; they replace previous contents of locations 008440 to 008447. This instruction is recognized as a six-byte instruction, so the next instruction is taken from location 008128.

5. MAIN IDEAS

a. A *program* in machine language is a sequence of instructions.

b. The most important components of instructions are the *operation code* and *specification of operands*.

c. Instructions can be classed by function as *arithmetic*, *input-output*, *information move*, and *control*.

d. In the IBM System/360 and 370 the address of an operand in main storage is specified by a *base*, sometimes an *index*, and a *displacement*. The contents of the register(s) and the displacement are added to form the effective address.

e. Six different instruction formats provide for different operand locations: register, main storage, immediate data. The types are RR, RX, RS, SI, SS, and S.

QUESTIONS FOR IMAGINATION AND REVIEW

1. The IBM System/360 and 370 calculate addresses in a 24-bit register, adding together a displacement, the low-order 24 bits of a base register and, if applicable, the low-order 24 bits of an index register. Overflows are ignored. Convince yourself that the resulting address is the same as if the entire base and index registers and the displacement were added together in a 32-bit register, and the low-order 24 bits taken as the effective address.

2. Given contents of registers (in hexadecimal):

Register	Contents
0	00012345
1	00006213
2	000024A2
3	00005310

What effective address will result from each of the following?

Base	Index	Displacement
2	–	104
3	–	000
0	–	OCE
1	3	101
2	0	233
0	2	233
0	0	FFF
3	1	101

(handwritten annotations:) 104 + 24A2 = 25A6; 000 5310; OCE 0CE; 101 + 12345 + 5310 = 17756; 233 + 6213 = 6446; 233 + 24A2 = 26D3; 101 + 6213 5310 11523 = 11624

(left margin handwritten:) 101 / 12345 / 5310 / 17766 / FFFFF / 7766

3. Given that register 10 contains the hexadecimal number 00009336, compute the displacement *d* such that *d* and base register 10 address the location 00958A.

4. A displacement is three hexadecimal digits. With fixed contents of a base register and varying displacements, how many main storage locations can be addressed? This number is often insufficient to hold all the program that needs to be addressed, let alone data areas. Several approaches to addressing more locations than can be addressed with fixed contents of one base register are possible in System/360 and 370, and some will be developed later in this volume. You are invited to think ahead and imagine what solutions to the problem you would set up in the hardware, in the operating system, or in the user's program.

5. An attempt was made in the design of the instruction set to let source operands of instructions be second operands, and destination operands, first operands. Thus MVC moves characters from the second operand address (and bytes following) to the first operand address. This is not possible with all instruction types; we need a STore instruction, which will store the contents of a register into main storage, and this is best defined as an RX instruction with second operand as destination. With what instruction types is it possible for the second operand always to be source and the first operand, destination?

REFERENCES

IBM System/360 Principles of Operation, GA22-6821, IBM Corporation. For a reference description of instruction formats.

IBM System/370 Principles of Operation, GA22-7000, IBM Corporation. Similar descriptions.

(handwritten calculations at bottom:) 958A / 9336 / 254; 6213 / 5310 / 101 / 8624; 24A2 / 233 / 26D5; 6213 / 5310 / 101 / 8624

Introduction to Assembler Language

An assembler language is a symbolic form of machine language. While machine language is numeric, assembler language allows alphabetic names for operation codes and storage locations. A program called an *assembler* translates a program written in assembler language into machine language which can be executed by the computer.

This chapter is an introduction to assembler language. We shall study the format of statements and forms for addressing operands in OS Assembler Language and OS/VS Assembler Language.

There are several assemblers for the IBM System/360; they accept languages which are compatible in most ways. There are minor differences, which are summarized in Appendix I of the Manual *OS Assembler Language*, GC28-6514. One's choice of assembler is dictated almost entirely by the level of operating system used at his installation. In order of increasing complexity, the IBM System/360 Basic Assembler is used in small-machine environments *without* an operating system. The IBM System/360 BOS Assembler is used under the Basic Operating System (BOS/360), the IBM System/360 DOS/TOS Assembler is used under the Disk Operating System (DOS/360) or Tape Operating System (TOS/360), and the IBM OS/360 Assembler is used under the Operating System (OS/360). The OS/VS Assembler is used under OS/VS systems in System/370.

After this chapter we will start describing the individual instructions available in the IBM System/360 and 370; we will not show their use in the context of a machine-language program, but in the context of assembler language, since programs are no longer written directly in machine language but in assembler language. The student must bear in mind the formats of the machine-language instruction types, and should have a clear picture of the machine-language instruction which would be produced by the assembler from the assembler-language statement.

1. A FIRST LOOK AT ASSEMBLER LANGUAGE

If we write programs directly in machine language, we must perform several clerical activities. We must keep track of exactly what locations are used for which instructions, data areas, and constants, so that we may refer to these locations correctly later in the program and also so that our program does not erase data, instructions, or constants by inadvertently using the same space for another purpose. We must refer to tables, so we can write the numerical operation codes required by the computer. We must express constants in binary, making conversions ourselves with the help of tables.

Until the early 1950's all programming was done directly in machine language. It was tedious, and the performance of clerical jobs by programmers resulted in many clerical errors. Assembler languages evolved as symbolic ways of writing machine language. The clerical tasks are, as far as possible, delegated to the *assembler*, which is a program that translates programs written in assembler language into machine language. The assembler keeps track of the storage locations used; the programmer refers to them symbolically, using names suggestive of the actual meaning in the problem the program is being written for. The assembler language programmer is also allowed to write operation codes in symbolic form; STM, for instance, may be written for "STore Multiple" and the assembler will translate STM to the numerical operation code 90.

An assembler also allows the programmer to specify constants and data areas symbolically. The constant may be given in the form in which the programmer thinks of it, such as 1.0 for a floating-point constant, or SUM = for a representation of the characters SUM =. The length of the storage area to be assigned to the constant may be specified, as well as a symbolic name by which the programmer will refer to the constant. The assembler will do the necessary conversions of the constants to binary representations, allocate storage, and keep a table of names and corresponding addresses. The same storage allocation and symbol table procedures are used for data areas.

The assembler language programmer can conveniently write calls on subroutines that are written by himself, written by others and kept in a standard library, or included in the supervisor of the computer. The assembler generates the necessary linkages and prepares for the communication of parameters. The assembler also prepares a table of subroutine references with the assembled program. When the program is prepared for loading and execution, the operating system will retrieve the appropriate subroutines from a library if necessary. When all the programs and subroutines are loaded into main storage for execution, the table of subroutine references makes it possible for the actual addresses of entry points of subroutines to be filled in the subroutines where they are needed. These complex tasks of finding subroutines and filling in the proper linkages between calling and called subroutines are performed well in a standard fashion from the information generated by the assembler.

Modification of programs written in assembler language is much easier than modification of programs written directly in machine language. Insertion of instructions, for example, changes the allocation of all storage addresses after the point of insertion. In a program written directly in machine language, the programmer would have to change the addresses of all affected instructions and constants, *and all references to them,* with the strong likelihood of error. Changing the size of a data area has similar hazards. To change an assembler language program, however, it is usually necessary only to change or insert the directly affected assembler language; the assembler will reassign all addresses and references to instructions, constants, and data areas according to the current structure of the program. Thus the assembler helps us avoid many potential mistakes in the changing of a program.

The assembler produces a printed listing of the program, showing the assembler language, the corresponding machine language generated, and diagnostic error messages. Many programming errors are caught in the assembly process, and do not have to be found, one by one, through debugging execution runs. The listing of the program, plus other tables printed, such as a cross-reference table listing all references to each symbol, help in the analysis and correction of logical errors uncovered during the debugging process.

Still another service performed by an assembler for the IBM System/360 or 370 is the automatic calculation of displacements and specification of base register for operands which are addressed symbolically. As we shall see in more detail later, one or more registers are designated as *implied base registers*, and their contents made known to the assembler. A location addressed symbolically is then expressed by the assembler as the sum of the contents of one of the implied base registers and a displacement calculated by the assembler; the assembler fills in the base register address and displacement in the machine language instruction.

2. FORMAT OF AN ASSEMBLER-LANGUAGE PROGRAM

In general, one *statement* of the assembler-language program corresponds to and is translated into one machine-language instruction. A statement is usually punched into one card for input to the assembler, though several cards can be used for longer statements. A statement has four fields which contain different aspects of the instruction to be coded. These fields are *name*, *operation*, *operands*, and *remarks*, each variable in length; the fields are separated by one or more blanks. Unless a statement is continued onto more than one card, it is not necessary for any field except the name field to begin in any particular card column. Some consistency, however, on the part of the programmer or keypuncher improves readability and is heartily recommended. A reasonable convention is that an operation code should begin in column 10 and the operands field in column 16. Greater leeway is given for remarks, but to begin most remarks in, say, column 30, helps.

When a statement is continued beyond one card, column 72 of each card except the last must contain a nonblank character, and the continued part of the statement must begin in exactly column 16 of the next card. At most two continuation cards for a statement are allowed (making three cards in all).

The first field of the assembler-language statement is reserved for the *name* or *location* symbol of the instruction, constant, data area, or other definition. The name field *must* begin in column 1 of the card. A symbol (to be defined later) may be entered in this field, or the field may be left blank. Use of the name is analogous to the use of a statement number in FORTRAN: the name is optional, and used only when the instruction, etc., is referred to elsewhere in the program.

After the name and at least one blank, or beginning in column 2 or later if no name is given, is the *operation* field. The operation is always given symbolically. Several kinds of operations can be specified:

a) machine-language instructions,

b) constant or symbol definition,

c) instructions to the assembler,

d) macro-instructions.

Generally, machine-language instructions will predominate. After all, the program is meant to be a collection of machine-language instructions; the other types of operations mentioned are merely given in support of the assembler in its job of generating machine-language instructions. Symbols defining data areas or constants are specified in the name field of a statement; the operation field of such a statement specifies the type of definition. Some operations are used to give directions to the assembler about how to behave in assembling future statements. Some of these operations control options available in the listing or *object* (machine-language) *program;* others give information to the assembler, such as which register to use in addressing symbolically specified operands. Finally, a *macro-instruction* is a statement that will be translated into possibly several lines of assembler language according to some given macro pattern. Macros are used for commonly used sequences of instructions (and constants), such as subroutine calls and requests for supervisor services. A one-line macro-instruction written by the assembler-language programmer is expanded by the assembler into the full sequence, saving the programmer work.

The third field contains *operands* for the operation. The operands field is separated from the operation field by at least one blank. The operands within the operands field are separated by commas, but no blanks. Different operations have different numbers of operands, and of course the nature of the operands varies with different operations. To show what operands are appropriate to each operation and how to use them to advantage is one of the major concerns of this book.

The fourth field is the *remarks* field, separated from the operands field by one or more blanks. The remarks do not affect assembly; they are reproduced into the program listing where they help document and explain the program.

We see that blanks are important. The name, operation, operands, and remarks fields are each separated by one or more blanks. Blanks are not allowed *inside* the name, operation, or operands fields, except in some operands inside quotation marks, where blanks are valid characters. Blanks are permitted in the remarks field.

A *symbol* used as a name may be from one to eight characters in length. The first character of the symbol must be a letter A–Z or $, #, or @, which are called "national characters" in the IBM OS or OS/VS assembler language. Characters, if any, after the first character in a name may be letters, national characters, or digits 0–9, intermixed in any fashion. No special characters or blanks are permitted in symbols. Thus F, P81B, $3, #0ZG38Q, and @ are valid names but for one reason or another 3$, Z*3, and ABCDE3456 are not valid symbols. Programmers should be warned, however, that some systems have adopted special conventions using $, @, and # as the first characters of symbols; to ensure compatibility with these systems, the student is urged to avoid beginning a symbol with $, @, or #.

A symbol is *defined* when it is used in the name field of an assembler language statement. Each symbol used in a program must be defined, and may be defined only once. In general, a symbol may be used in an operand before or after it is defined. There are uses of symbols, especially uses that affect the quantity of storage allocated, which require that the symbol be *previously defined*, that is, defined in an earlier statement; these uses will be noted specifically when they arise.

3. AN EXAMPLE

Let us now examine a segment of a program written in assembler language. We will follow this example through assembler language into machine language, loading into main storage, and execution.

Let us pay some attention to the general sequence of operations. First is the assembly process. The assembler is the program currently in execution in main storage. Input is the *source deck*, cards containing assembler-language statements. The program in assembler language is called the *source program*. The assembler reads the source program and produces an equivalent machine-language program, called the *object program* or *object module*. The object program is either punched into cards, which are then called an *object deck*, written onto a direct access device, or both. The program may have to be combined with subroutines required to support its functions; combining the routines, completion of references between them as required, and general molding into a consistent set of routines are often done by a *linkage editor*, though if the required tasks are appropriately restricted, they can be performed by the *loader*. Most of our examples will show bypassing the linkage editor and using a loader, which is more efficient of computer time. The loader combines modules as necessary, resolves references from each to others, and places the combined module into main storage ready for execution. The student should note that *all* instructions are loaded before they are executed; the complete program is loaded all at once (we ignore in this volume the concept of overlay). *Constants* are loaded as an integral part of the program.

After all the program and constants have been loaded into main storage, execution of the program begins. Instructions are executed in sequence except when a sequence is broken by a branch or an interrupt. Input data are read on command, and output produced. If new information is stored in areas in which constants were loaded, the constants are replaced, and can only be restored by execution of subsequent machine-language instructions.

The segment as written in assembler language follows. When punched into cards, the E of the name EXPL in the first statement is punched in column 1. Operation codes must follow at least one blank after the name field, so usually begin in column 10. The operands must follow at least one blank after the operation field, so usually begin in column 16.

```
EXPL    L     3,24(8,9)
        A     3,=F'29'
        LR    4,3
        S     4,B
        STM   3,4,B+4
        MVC   L(12),B
        MVI   L,X'0E'
```

The example may look brutally incomprehensible to the student at this point. Sorry about that. Explanations of the example follow, but what is important as the student follows the example is not the computations performed by the individual instruction or by the segment but the flavor of the assembly process and its relationship to actual execution of the instructions.

The intentions of the programmer in writing the segment are as follows. The first instruction will load register 3 from a location addressed by the sum of (decimal) 24 and the contents of registers 8 and 9. The (decimal) number 29 is added to the new contents of register 3. Register 4 is loaded with the contents of register 3, the result of the addition. The number at location B is subtracted from the contents of register 4. Contents of registers 3 and 4 are stored starting at a location four bytes beyond B. The next-to-last instruction moves 12 (decimal) characters starting at location B (up to and including B+11) to an area starting at location L. Finally, the byte whose hexadecimal contents are 0E is moved to location L.

Assembly

To show what the assembler does with this segment we must make some assumptions about affairs in the rest of the program. Let us suppose first that EXPL has been assigned to (relocatable) location 000086. Also, that B and L have been assigned to 000218 and 000344 respectively. Since storage is assigned sequentially, these assignments depend on statements not shown here. Lastly, we assume that register 12 has been declared the implied base register, with (relocatable) contents 000006.

The assembler listing of our segment is then as shown in Fig. 3–1. Machine-language equivalents are shown opposite each assembler language statement. Locations are given in hexadecimal at the extreme left. Then follows the hexadecimal representation of the machine-language instructions, arranged in two-byte groups. ADDR1 and ADDR2 fields show the relocatable locations addressed symbolically, or the displacement in cases like the first instruction, where contents of registers 8 and 9 are not known to the assembler. Statements are numbered consecutively by the assembler; in our example we see that (supposedly) the

```
 LOC   OBJECT CODE     ADDR1 ADDR2   STMT    SOURCE STATEMENT

000086  5838 9018            00018   57 EXPL      L      3,24(8,9)
00008A  5A30 C512            00518   58           A      3,=F'29'
00008E  1843                         59           LR     4,3
000090  5B40 C212            00218   60           S      4,B
000094  9034 C216            0021C   61           STM    3,4,B+4
000098  D20B C33E C212 00344 00218   62           MVC    L(12),B
00009E  920E C33E      00344         63           MVI    L,X'0E'
```

Fig. 3-1 Assembly listing of program segment.

statement named EXPL is number 57 in the assembly. The numbers are followed by a reproduction of the statements themselves.

The first instruction begins, as we assumed, at location 000086. The operation code of 58 corresponds to L for *Load*. The first operand of 3 is followed by 8, the index register designated; 9, the base register designated; and the displacement 018, which is the hexadecimal equivalent of 24.

Since the first instruction is four bytes long, the second begins at location 000086 + 4 = 00008A. The noteworthy aspect of this instruction is the treatment of the second operand. A *self-defining term* can be a value, in single quotation marks, preceded by a single letter prefix giving the type of self-defining term. For example, F'29' specifies a full-word binary integer whose value is (decimal) 29. The operand =F'29' is called a *literal;* it causes a full word to be set aside at the end of the program—in the *literal pool*—which will contain the constant 29. The *address* of this constant is coded in this instruction. We will assume that the literal is assigned to location 000518; its address is specified in the instruction by index 0, the implied base register C (with its assumed contents 000006), and displacement 000518 − 000006 = 000512, of which the last 12 bits are used.

Since the second instruction is also four bytes long, the third begins at location 00008A + 4 = 00008E. It is an RR-type instruction, so the only operand addresses are the register addresses 4 and 3.

The next instruction, subtract, begins at 00008E + 2 = 000090. After the operation code, 5B, the register operand address 4 is followed by the specification of the second operand. The index register was unspecified, so it is 0; the base register is the implied C; and since B is at location 000218, the displacement is 000218 − 000006 = 212.

The fifth instruction is of RS type, so the second byte contains the register addresses 3 and 4 of the operands R1 and R3. Location B+4 is 000218 + 4 = 00021C, as shown in the ADDR2 column; this is the address of the next full word beyond B. Base and displacement are as in the previous instruction, but as might be expected, the displacement used in addressing B+4 is 4 greater than the displacement used in addressing B.

The sixth instruction, MVC (or MoVe Character), is of SS type. The second byte is a length specification; the actual length in decimal is 12, so the coded length is (decimal) 11 or hexadecimal 0B. The locations B and L are both in main storage, addressed by base and displacement. As before, the implied base register

C is used, and the displacements are 000344 – 000006 = 33E and 000218 – 000006 = 212.

Since the MVC instruction is six bytes long, the last instruction, MVI, begins in location 000098 + 6 = 00009E. The second operand X'0E' is a self-defining term standing for hexadecimal (X) value 0E. The MVI instruction includes the second operand in the second byte of the instruction, just after the operation code 92. The address L is specified as in the MVC instruction above.

Loading and execution

Now let us suppose that the program, including this segment, is loaded into main storage preparatory to execution. Since the first section (low addresses) of main storage contains the supervisor portion of the operating system, the program is loaded into storage somewhere beyond the first section. Suppose the storage available for the program starts at location 009020. Then the piece of the object program shown in the listing as beginning at location 000000 is actually loaded into locations starting at 009020. All addresses are similarly relocated, or shifted, by 009020, so the actual locations of our segment are as follows:

Relocatable location	Actual location	Contents		
000086	0090A6	5838	9018	
00008A	0090AA	5A30	C512	
00008E	0090AE	1843		
000090	0090B0	5B40	C212	
000094	0090B4	9034	C216	
000098	0090B8	D20B	C33E	C212
00009E	0090BE	920E	C33E	

Suppose B, which was assigned to relocatable location 000218 and now actual location 009238, contains (hexadecimal) 000004F9. Also suppose that the byte at L, actual location 000344 + 009020 = 009364, is a hexadecimal 80.

Here, as in Chapter 2, we note that the user of a Virtual Storage system should consider "actual locations," as used in explanations here, to be locations in virtual storage. The translations to real storage are performed consistently so the user need not be aware of them. In Chapter 17 we explore the manner in which this is done.

Let us now simulate execution of the program segment. First, we must make some more assumptions, mostly about register contents. Register 12 was declared the implied base register, with relocatable contents 000006. Therefore we must assume that register 12 actually contains 00009026. Let us also assume that register 8 contains 00009834, and register 9 contains 00000014. All these register contents are presumably the results of previous segments of the program.

The first instruction in our segment loads register 3. The operand address is

contents of register 8	00009834
+ contents of register 9	00000014
+ displacement	018
	009860

If we assume that the word at location 009860 is 000043E4, this number is loaded into register 3, replacing previous contents of register 3. The second instruction adds to register 3 the number from location 009026 + 512 = 009538. The contents of the word at location 009538 is a hexadecimal 0000001D, equivalent to the decimal number 29 specified in the literal in the assembler language instruction. This makes the contents of register 3

$$000043E4$$
$$+\ 0000001D$$
$$00004401$$

The third instruction, executed from location 0090AE, loads register 4 from register 3. After this instruction, both registers 3 and 4 contain 00004401. The fourth instruction subtracts from register 4 the number from location

contents of register 12	00009026
+ displacement	212
	009238

This is the location named B, so register 4 will contain

$$00004401$$
$$-\ 000004F9$$
$$00003F08$$

Note, however, that register 3 still contains 00004401. Also note how the addressing of relocatable operands is accomplished in the IBM System/360 and 370 by the proper setting of the base register, not by modification of the addresses in each actual instruction. The assembler-language listing showed the address of the operand in this instruction as 00218, which would be relocated to 009020 + 00218 = 009238. The instruction was not changed during loading; proper setting of register 12 to 009020 + 000006 takes care of the addressing of all operands in the segment which are addressed symbolically.

The fifth instruction has a main storage operand address of 009026 + 216 = 00923C. The instruction stores registers 3 and 4 starting at this location, so locations 00923C through 009243 will contain 0000440100003F08. The MVC instruction moves twelve bytes, from locations starting at 009026 + 212 = 009238 to locations beginning at 009026 + 33E = 009364. Therefore locations 009364 through

00936F will contain

000004F90000440100003F08

Finally, the MVI instruction puts the byte 0E in location 009364, thus changing the word in locations 009364–009367 to 0E0004F9.

4. ADDRESSING OF OPERANDS IN ASSEMBLER LANGUAGE

This section will specify in some detail the components used in operands and operand addresses in assembler language. The reader should try to assimilate the main points and get a good idea of what can be done before going on to the next chapter. After that he will do best to refer to this section for details of how to do what he finds he wants to do, and every now and then to refresh his memory of the options available.

Let us define the words which give structure to this section. First, an *operand* of an instruction is a piece of information which is operated with or upon by the instruction. Operands are defined by *expressions* or appropriately restricted *combinations of expressions;* an *expression* is a *term* or an *arithmetic combination of terms;* a *term* can be a *symbol*, a *self-defining term*, a *location counter reference*, a *literal*, or a *symbol length attribute reference*. The symbol length attribute reference is mentioned only for completeness, and will henceforth be ignored until Chapter 16. The other types will be taken up in turn.

Symbols

According to Section 2 of this chapter, a symbol is 1 to 8 characters long, is composed of letters, $, #, @, and digits, and begins with $, #, @, or a letter. A symbol is defined, that is, given a value during assembly, when it appears in the name field of an assembler language statement.

Self-defining terms

A value can be defined directly in what are called self-defining terms. The value may be expressed in several ways—decimal, hexadecimal, binary, and character— but in all cases the assembler converts the value to its binary equivalent for use by the assembler or for inclusion in the object program.

Decimal values should be and are the most natural to write; they are written in assembler language simply as unsigned decimal numbers, like 15 or 3729.

Values expressed in hexadecimal, binary, or character forms are enclosed in single quotes, and a prefix denotes the form used. Hexadecimal values are written with the prefix X, as in X'0E' or X'F863'. Binary values are written with the prefix B, as in B'101' or B'00001110' (note that the latter defines exactly the same value as X'0E'). Character self-defining terms are written with the prefix C, as in C'AB9' or C'$'. Because the assembler uses the characters ' and & in a special way, if a single quote (apostrophe) or ampersand is wanted in a character self-defining term, *two* must be written. The string of characters &A' would be written C'&&A'''.

Self-defining terms are used throughout the assembler language, for specification of register addresses, storage addresses or displacements in instructions, immediate portions of SI-type instructions, and, as we shall see later, in the definition of constants. We choose the form (decimal, hexadecimal, binary, or character) that seems most direct and natural at the moment. For example, if we wish to move the character / to an output area, the simplest way of expressing the term is C'/', though X'61', B'01100001', and 97 would all be equivalent. On the other hand, if we wish to construct a byte whose bit pattern is 01010101, the simplest and most direct form is B'01010101', with perhaps X'55' as a close second.

Literals and Constants

A literal is a constant preceded by an equals sign (=). The constant may be one of several types, such as decimal, binary, character, hexadecimal, floating-point, packed-decimal, and some special types of addresses. The value of the constant is usually enclosed in single quotes (apostrophes), with a prefix designating the type of constant, as in a self-defining term.

Definition of constants is treated in detail in Chapter 6. However, an introduction to some types is valuable at this point, so that they can be used from now until Chapter 6. Some types are

X	Hexadecimal
B	Binary
F	Full-word fixed-point number
H	Half-word fixed-point number
C	Character

If a constant is specified as hexadecimal (X), the value given in apostrophes must be a string of hexadecimal characters whose binary equivalent will be the actual constant assembled. If a constant is specified as binary (B), the value given in assembler language must be a string of 0's and 1's. If the constant is of F or H type, the value written in assembler language must be a decimal integer, with sign optional. The binary equivalent of the value of an F-type constant is assembled into four bytes, and will be located on a full-word boundary. The binary equivalent of the value of an H-type constant is assembled into two bytes, and will be located on a half-word boundary. The value of a character constant (C) is given as a string of characters whose EBCDIC representations are assembled into the object program, one character to a byte.

The definition of constants, therefore, is much like the definition of self-defining terms. However, as we will see in Chapter 6, there are many more options in the definition of constants than there are in the definition of self-defining terms.

When a literal appears in an assembler language program, the assembler takes the following action. The constant described is assigned space in an area called the *literal pool*, usually in storage following the rest of the program. The constant is assembled into this space, and its address is the term used in assembling the instruction in which the literal was encountered.

We saw an example of a literal in the last section, in the instruction

$$A \qquad 3,=F'29'$$

The prefix F designated the literal as a constant to be assembled as a full-word binary integer, whose value is expressed in the literal as a decimal number. The value itself was 29, so the assembled constant is the binary equivalent of 29, or

$$00000000 \ 00000000 \ 00000000 \ 00011101.$$

The address of this constant was the term used in assembling the instruction; the address was coded into base and displacement using the implied base register. This is the normal use of a literal; as the need for a constant in our program arises, we can insert the definition and reference to the constant into the instruction that needs it. The logic of the program is clear, and it is not necessary to make up a symbol which must be later defined and associated with a constant.

Location-counter reference

The assembler keeps many pointers, among them one called the *location counter*, which always contains the address of the next available location in storage for the instructions, data areas, and constants in the program. The location counter is increased during the assembly of each statement that requires allocation of storage, which includes the overwhelming majority of the statements written.

A programmer may refer to the current contents of the location counter by using an asterisk (∗). The asterisk can be used as a term in a statement; the associated value is the location of the first byte of currently available storage. We will see some examples shortly.

During assembly of an instruction, the location counter refers to the address of the instruction, whether or not a name is given to the instruction. Therefore, if a name *is* given to an instruction, the location counter has the same value as the name (but only during processing of that instruction).

Absolute and relocatable terms

When a program is assembled, all addresses are assigned relative to some initial value of the location counter, usually 000000. When a program is loaded prior to execution, it is loaded into main storage relative to some actual origin (which is *not* 000000, because the lower portion of main storage must be reserved for the supervisor). The difference between the actual origin and the initial value of the location counter is called the *relocation factor*. For example, if the initial value of the location counter is 000000 but the program is actually loaded in main storage starting at location 009020, the relocation factor is 9020.

An *absolute term* is a term whose value is independent of the relocation factor. Register addresses, most constants (but not *addresses* of constants), and values of some other symbols are absolute terms. A *relocatable term* is a term whose value must be adjusted by adding the relocation factor. Addresses of instructions, constants, and data areas in main storage are relocatable terms.

Let us be more specific about which terms are absolute and which are relocatable. A self-defining term is an absolute term; the value defined in a self-defining term does not change with relocation. The value of a literal is the address of a constant, so it is a relocatable term. The location-counter reference is clearly a relocatable term, since it represents an address of a statement in the program. A symbol may be either relocatable or absolute. If a symbol appears in the name field of a statement which defines a machine-language instruction, data area, or constant (in all but supervisor programming), the symbol is relocatable. A symbol may be defined by an EQU (EQUivalence) statement, which equates the symbol to the value of some expression. If the defining expression is relocatable, the symbol is relocatable, but if the expression is absolute, the symbol is also absolute.

Expressions

An operand entry in an assembler-language statement may be an expression. Valid expressions include terms and, subject to some restrictions, arithmetic combinations of terms. Terms and expressions may be added, subtracted, multiplied, and divided to form new expressions. Addition, subtraction, multiplication, and division are represented by

$$+ \quad - \quad * \quad /$$

respectively; parentheses may be used to enclose subexpressions.

The important rules are:

1. An expression may not start with an arithmetic operator or contain two consecutive operators or two consecutive terms.

2. An expression may not consist of more than 16 terms or have more than five levels of parentheses. There may be more than five pairs of parentheses, but any point inside the expression may not be enclosed by more than five.

3. An expression consisting of more than one term may not contain a literal.

4. No relocatable term or expression may enter a multiply or divide operation.

5. Expressions must be either relocatable or absolute. Relocatable terms may enter an absolute expression, but must be *paired*, meaning that for each relocatable term (or subexpression) added into the expression, one must be subtracted. Relocatable terms and subexpressions must also be paired in the definition of relocatable expressions: all but one of the relocatable terms and

subexpressions must be paired, and the unpaired one must be added to the expression; it cannot be subtracted.

Suppose *rel* stands for any relocatable term or expression, and *abs* for any absolute term or expression. Then the pairing rule means that allowable operations are restricted to the following, with meanings as shown:

$$rel \pm abs: \text{ relocatable expression}$$
$$rel - rel: \text{ absolute expression}$$
$$abs \pm abs: \text{ absolute expression}$$
$$abs * abs: \text{ absolute expression}$$
$$abs / abs: \text{ absolute expression}$$

6. Except when parenthesis specify otherwise, operations are performed from left to right, with addition and subtraction after multiplication and division.

7. Division always yields an integer result, with no rounding. For example, $2/3*10=0$. Division *by zero* is allowed, and yields a result of zero!

Suppose A, B, and C are relocatable symbols, and G and H are absolute symbols. The following are valid absolute expressions:

```
G
B-A+X'1C'
H+24
*-B+2*G
B'10111'
37
```

The following are valid relocatable expressions:

```
A
*-4
*+B'101'
=F'4095'
G*H+A-B+C
```

The following are invalid for the reasons indicated:

=F'4095'+4	Literal in a multiterm expression
2*A-B	Multiplication involving a relocatable term
A+B-G	Pairing rule violated

The programmer must keep in mind that the operations

$$+ \quad - \quad * \quad /$$

discussed here are performed by the *assembler* on values which are addresses and constants. They result in values which are included in the object program. These operations *are not* performed during execution of the object program.

Specifying operands in instructions

A register address in an instruction may be specified by any absolute expression whose value is in the range 0 to 15. Such an absolute expression can be used for *R1*, *R3*, *B1*, *B2*, and *X2*, as we name the register operands or portions of operands in the various instruction formats.

Programmers sometimes find it worth while to use a symbol to refer to a register. If a programmer who is beginning to write a program is unsure how many registers he will need and how they can most conveniently be arranged, he can put off his decision until later by referring to all registers symbolically; however, before *assembling* his program, he must equate all such symbols to specific registers. A common convention is to name registers REG1, REG4, etc. Among other things, this helps distinguish register operands from other uses of small numbers and makes programs more readable.

Main-storage operand addresses in assembler-language instructions are given by expressions combined with punctuation as shown in Fig. 3–2. Base registers are either explicit or implied, but if explicit, they are absolute expressions with values 0 to F. Note the three sets of forms for RX instructions: if no *X2* is specified, as in the second set of forms, *X2*=0 is assumed, which will mean no indexing in that instruction. Similarly, if *B2* is left out, *B2* = 0 is assumed. Since base and index registers enter the address computations in the same way, we need not distinguish (until Chapter 15) between *D2(,B2)* and *D2(X2)*. For example, 4(1) and 4(,1) will indicate the same address. Therefore in most cases we use the third form *D2(X2)*, saving the trouble of punching the comma.

An *I2* operand, the second operand in an SI-type instruction, must be given as an absolute expression with value less than or equal to 255 (decimal), which is sufficiently small to fit in one byte. Self-defining terms of one character or two hexadecimal digits are the usual self-defining terms given.

A value of *L1* or *L2* (in SS-type instructions with two lengths) must be in the range 0 through 16 (inclusive); a value of *L* (in SS-type instructions with a single length) must be in the range 0 to 256. The usual definition is a decimal integer.

Fig. 3–2 Main storage address specification forms

Instruction type	Explicit address form	Implied address form
RX	*D2(X2,B2)*	*S2(X2)*
	D2(,B2)	*S2*
	D2(X2)	*S2*
RS	*D2(B2)*	*S2*
SI	*D1(B1)*	*S1*
SS (single length)	*D1(L,B1)*	*S1(L)* or *S1*
	D2(B2)	*S2*
SS (two-length)	*D1(L1,B1)*	*S1(L1)* or *S1*
	D2(L2,B2)	*S2(L2)* or *S2*

D1, D2, X2, B1, B2, L, L1, L2 are absolute expressions;
S1, S2 are relocatable expressions.

Some examples of entire assembler-language instructions with operands follow. The L (Load) instruction is of RX type, LM (Load Multiple) of RS type, MVI (MoVe Immediate) of SI type, and MVC (MoVe Character) of SS type.

```
L     0,4(1)
L     1,A+4(8)
L     2,A+4*N        N IS AN ABSØLUTE SYMBØL
L     3,=F'4095'
L     14,*+X'10'
LM    14,REG2,SAV+12 REG2 IS AN ABSØLUTE SYMBØL
LM    14,REG2,12(13)
MVI   12(13),X'FF'
MVI   LNG,G3         G3 IS AN ABSØLUTE SYMBØL
MVC   ØUT(10),CØNV   10 IS THE LENGTH
MVC   *+8(12),4(1)   12 IS THE LENGTH, 1 IS THE BASE B2
MVC   30(LTH,7),156(7)   LTH IS AN ABSØLUTE SYMBØL USED AS LENGTH
MVC   0(17,8),=C'STRING ØF */+$&&&&-'
```

Note that the letter O (oh) is written Ø to distinguish it clearly from the digit 0 (zero). We follow this convention in the description of any statement or card that is fed to the computer.

Summary

An address in main storage is specified by a relocatable expression or by absolute expressions for displacement and base. In addition, some instructions allow for specification of an index or a length, either of which is also an absolute expression.

Expressions are terms or arithmetic combinations of terms; they are relocatable if their values change with relocation of the program, absolute otherwise. The writing of expressions is subject to restrictive rules, but most things we would like to do are allowed. Terms studied here are symbols (relocatable and absolute), self-defining terms (absolute), literals (relocatable), and location-counter reference (relocatable).

5. MAIN IDEAS

a. Assembler language permits the symbolic writing of machine-language instructions, thus contributing to speed and accuracy of the programming and debugging processes.

b. An assembler-language statement consists of a name (optional), an operation code, operands, and remarks. Blanks are used as delimiters between these fields.

c. Register operands in assembler language are specified by absolute expressions; main-storage operands are specified by relocatable expressions or by absolute expressions for base and displacement.

d. An expression is a literal or an arithmetic combination of terms which may be symbols, self-defining terms, and location-counter references.

QUESTIONS FOR REVIEW

1. Point out which of the following are valid assembler language symbols.

A3	(B9)	GIH2J3K4	#@$&
$3	7X	GIH2J3K4L5	#34$Q

2. Which of the following are valid assembler language expressions? Of the valid ones, which are absolute, which relocatable? Assume that G, H and K are absolute symbols, P, Q, R, and W are relocatable symbols.

G	*
P	*−7
X'123F'	*+X'123F'
=X'123F'	*+G
X'123F'+G	R+G+H
X'123F'+P	Q−(P−K)+B'10100'
=X'123F'+G	G−(P−K)
*−P	C'4578'−G−X'F4F23E4A'
P+4*X'CE'	P+Q+R−W−(*+4)

3. Which of the following are valid assembler-language statements? Assume that G, H and K are absolute symbols, P, Q, R and W relocatable symbols.

L	4,5(G)	L IS AN RX INSTRUCTIØN
L	19,19(H)	
L	G,W(H)	
L	G,5(H,K)	
L	7,W(H,K)	
L	B'101',*+8	
L	10,P+Q−R−X'CE'(G−5+R−Q)	
L	W,4(4)	
L	4(4),W	
LR	4,P	LR IS AN RR INSTRUCTIØN
LR	5,K	
LR	K,X'E'	

```
LM     K,W            LM IS AN RS INSTRUCTIØN
LM     3,4,W+4
LM     3,G,W-Q+K
LM     3(4),Q
LM     3,4,Q(5)
MVI    4,5            MVI IS AN SI INSTRUCTIØN
MVI    R,5
MVI    Q,X'CE'
MVI    R,Q
MVI    G(4),C'/'
MVC    R(2),W         MVC IS AN SS INSTRUCTIØN
MVC    X'24'(2,11),W
MVC    G(8),W
MVC    W(8),P(8)
MVC    W(8,9),*+8
```

4. The machine-language instruction generated from the following assembler-language instruction is assigned to relocatable location 009A40. What is the second operand address?

$$L \quad 15,*+8$$

5. During an assembly in which the implied base register is register 10, with assumed relocatable contents 00000C, suppose the next available space in the literal pool is at relocatable location 0003CC. How is the statement

$$L \quad 6,=F'24'$$

assembled, and what actions must the assembler take with respect to the literal pool?

6. Simulate the assembler in assembling the operands of the following instructions in a program segment. Assume that the implied base register is declared to be register 9 and to contain relocatable 000006. Assume that the symbol G is equated to absolute 10, and T and V are assigned relocatable addresses 000458 and 00082C, respectively.

```
L      4,T
LM     5,6,V-4
AR     4,5
A      6,T(G)
MVI    V+4,X'FF'
ST     4,T+4(G)
MVC    12(8,9),V+5
```

7. An absolute term is one whose value is independent of relocation of the program; a relocatable term is one whose value must be adjusted upon relocation by addition of the relocation quantity. Absolute and relocatable expressions are defined similarly. Using arithmetic operations on relocatable terms, it is possible to write expressions which are, by our definitions, neither relocatable nor absolute. Illustrate. How are the rules for formation of valid expressions, especially the rules on pairing of relocatable symbols, related to the definitions of absolute and relocatable expressions?

REFERENCES

OS Assembler Language, GC28-6514, IBM Corporation. For reference and more advanced features, this is *the* manual.

OS/VS and DOS/VS Assembler Language, GC33-4010, IBM Corporation. A parallel description for Virtual Storage systems.

Wirth, Niklaus, "PL360, a Programming Language for the 360 Computers," *Journal of the Association for Computing Machinery* **15** (1968), pp. 37–74. Another approach to realizing the power and directness of machine language, yet also some of the advantages of higher-level languages.

Chapter 4

Information Move
and Binary Integer Arithmetic

In any digital computer, the instruction repertoire must include instructions that move information from one place to another within the computer. These instructions are simple to describe, are used often, and for the IBM System/360 and 370 illustrate well the use of the various instruction types. Therefore we begin our detailed discussions of the instruction repertoire with the information-move instructions.

Any digital computer also needs instructions that do integer arithmetic. In this chapter we describe the binary integer arithmetic instructions of the IBM System/360 and 370, leaving the more complicated decimal arithmetic to Chapter 14. With information move and binary integer arithmetic instructions we can illustrate and discuss real and significant program segments, and the reader can begin to comprehend and write meaningful program segments.

1. GENERAL STRUCTURE

Instructions must be provided for moving information to and from all parts of the IBM System/360 or 370 computer accessible to the programmer. In particular, we must be able to move information from a register to another register, from a location in main storage to another location in main storage, and between a register and a location in main storage. Movement to and from floating-point registers must also be provided for, but this aspect will be discussed in Chapter 13. We can diagram the requirements as shown in Fig. 4–1.

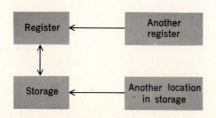

Fig. 4–1 Information Move requirements.

In contrast, binary integer arithmetic need only be provided for operands in registers. If it is possible to do arithmetic operations with all operands in registers, and to move numbers to and from registers, it is then possible to do arithmetic on numbers located anywhere and to place the result anywhere. All that is necessary is to move all operands to registers if they are not there already, do the arithmetic, then move the results wherever we please.

System/360 and 370 provide more than the minimum set of instructions. In every binary integer arithmetic operation the first operand is expected to be in a register, and the result will generally be left in the same register. Parallel sets of instructions permit the second operand to be either in a register or in main storage. Thus, if all operands and results are to reside eventually in main storage, a sequence of instructions like

1. place one operand in a register,
2. perform arithmetic with one register and one operand in main storage,
3. store result from a register into main storage

will be satisfactory.

Symbolic notation

We introduce some symbolic notation to help us describe the working of instructions.* We denote the address of a register by $R1$, $R2$, or $R3$, depending on whether it is used as first, second, or third operand in an instruction. The *contents* of a register used as first, second, or third operand will be denoted by $c(R1)$, $c(R2)$, or $c(R3)$. A location in main storage specified by base and displacement or by base, index, and displacement will be denoted by $S1$ or $S2$, indicating first or second operand in the instruction. The contents of main-storage location $S1$ or $S2$ will be denoted by $c(S1)$ or $c(S2)$. Such contents will be understood to be full words at locations beginning with $S1$ or $S2$, unless there is indication to the contrary.

When necessary, we will use subscripts to $R1$, $R2$, $R3$, $S1$, and $S2$ to indicate particular bit positions. Bits in a register are numbered 0 to 31, so the last 24 bits in register $R2$ will be denoted, for example, by $c(R2)_{8-31}$. Similarly, contents of a one-byte area in main storage can be denoted by $c(S1)_{0-7}$, which specifies bits numbered 0 to 7, starting from the leftmost bit of the main-storage byte addressed by $S1$. We may also denote fields of destination operands as, for example, $R1_{8-31}$ and $S1_{0-7}$.

In the manuals *IBM System/360 Principles of Operation*, GA22-6821 and *IBM System/370 Principles of Operation*, GA22-7000, which are the basic sources of information on the structure of the computer and details of its instruction repertoire, fields in instructions are sometimes abbreviated R_1, R_2, B_2, X_2, D_2, I_2, etc. We avoid this notation in order to use subscripts to show bit positions.

---

* The notation we introduce is derived from that advanced in Kenneth Iverson, *A Programming Language* (New York: Wiley, 1962). The complete description of the IBM System/360 in Iverson notation is included in A. D. Falkoff, K. E. Iverson, and E. H. Sussenguth, "A formal description of SYSTEM/360," *IBM Systems Journal* **3**, 3 (1964).

We use an arrow pointing to the left to indicate the act of placement. Thus, $R1 \leftarrow c(R2)$ means that the contents of the register whose address is $R2$ are placed in the register whose address is $R1$.

The "immediate" byte of an SI-type instruction will be denoted by $I2$.

This notation and a few additions to it will be used in the remainder of this book in the definition of instructions. It is summarized in Appendix B.

2. INFORMATION MOVE INSTRUCTIONS

Register to register

First, we will examine the information move instructions both of whose operands are in registers. These are RR-type instructions; each operand address is of course a register address. We will identify the instructions by the names or abbreviations used for them in assembler language, not by their numeric operation codes. A move instruction into a register is called a load, so the RR-type move instructions will all be called load instructions, and their names begin with the letter L. Every RR-type instruction name (with a few minor exceptions) ends with the letter R; this convention helps one to remember and recognize instructions. Four RR-type move instructions are:

LR   Load from Register
LCR   Load Complement from Register
LPR   Load Positive from Register (absolute value)
LNR   Load Negative from Register (negative of absolute value)

In each of these, as in all RR-type instructions, the first operand address is the address of the register which is the destination of the move; the second operand address is the address of the register whose contents are to be moved to the destination.

Therefore the

LR   R1,R2

instruction loads the $R1$ register with contents of the $R2$ register. The instruction

LR   5,8

for example, loads register 5 from register 8; the previous contents of register 5 are lost, and register 8 remains unchanged.

The

LCR   R1,R2

instruction loads the $R1$ register with the complement of the contents of the $R2$ register. The

LPR   R1,R2

instruction loads the $R1$ register with the absolute value of the contents of the $R2$ register. That is, if the contents of register $R2$ is a positive number, it is loaded into register $R1$; if the contents of register $R2$ is a negative number, its complement (a positive number) is loaded into register $R1$. The

$$\text{LNR} \quad R1,R2$$

instruction does the opposite in loading the negative (or complement) of the absolute value of the contents of register $R2$ into register $R1$. That is, if the contents of register $R2$ is a negative number, this number is loaded into register $R1$; if the contents of register $R2$ is a positive number, the complement of this number is loaded into register $R1$.

Suppose registers 3 and 4 have as initial contents the binary numbers

Register 3:   00001111 00000000 00001111 11110000
Register 4:   11111111 11110000 00000000 00001111

Then the following instructions will have the indicated results.

Instruction		Register changed	New contents
LR	5,3	5	00001111 00000000 00001111 11110000
LCR	5,3	5	11110000 11111111 11110000 00010000
LCR	5,4	5	00000000 00001111 11111111 11110001
LPR	6,3	6	00001111 00000000 00001111 11110000
LPR	6,4	6	00000000 00001111 11111111 11110001
LNR	7,3	7	11110000 11111111 11110000 00010000
LNR	7,4	7	11111111 11110000 00000000 00001111

In the notation of the last section, the general action performed by the RR-type move instructions is

$$
\begin{aligned}
\text{LR:} &\quad R1 \leftarrow c(R2) \\
\text{LCR:} &\quad R1 \leftarrow -c(R2) \\
\text{LPR:} &\quad R1 \leftarrow |c(R2)| \\
\text{LNR:} &\quad R1 \leftarrow -|c(R2)|
\end{aligned}
$$

Between registers and main storage

The second group of information move instructions includes those that load registers from locations in main storage, or store contents of registers into main storage. These instructions are of RX type; the first operand address is always the register, whether source of the information to be moved (as in a store instruction) or destination (as in a load instruction). Similarly, the second operand address is a main storage address given by base, index, and displacement, as described in Chapter 3. The four instructions in this group are given below.

L	Load (from main storage):	$R1 \leftarrow c(S2)$
ST	STore (into main storage):	$S2 \leftarrow c(R1)$
LH	Load Half-word:	$R1_{16-31} \leftarrow c(S2)_{0-15},\ R1_{0-15} \leftarrow c(S2)_0$
STH	STore Half-word:	$S2_{0-15} \leftarrow c(R1)_{16-31}$

In the

L   *R1,D2(X2,B2)*

instruction the register *R1* is loaded from the four bytes of main storage addressed by *B2, X2,* and *D2.* The second operand is a full word, and therefore its address (address of its first byte) must be on a full-word boundary, that is, divisible by 4. The contents of main storage are unchanged by this instruction; the previous contents of register *R1* are lost.

The instruction

ST   *R1,D2(X2,B2)*

is exactly the converse of the load instruction. The contents of register *R1* are stored in the word addressed by *B2, X2,* and *D2.* The main storage address must be divisible by 4. In computer systems which include the *byte-oriented operand* feature, it is not necessary to align operands on nonprivileged instructions to full-word, half-word, or double-word boundaries. There is a penalty in execution time, however, if the boundary alignment rules shown here are not followed. Therefore it is advisable for programmers on all systems to follow the alignment rules.

The instruction

LH   *R1,D2(X2,B2)*

loads register *R1* with the number found in the half-word in main storage addressed by *B2, X2,* and *D2.* The address of the half-word must be on a half-word boundary, that is, be divisible by 2. The high-order bit of the 16 bits in the half-word to be loaded is taken to be a sign bit. The half-word is loaded into the low-order (rightmost) half of the register *R1,* and 16 copies of the sign bit from the half-word are placed in the high-order 16 bits of *R1.* This preserves in the full word the value of the number expressed in the half-word as a sign and 15 bits. For example,

01111111 11111111

is the largest positive number expressible in a half-word. If it is loaded into register 8 by the LH instruction, register 8 will contain

00000000 00000000 01111111 11111111.

Similarly, the negative number in the half-word

11111110 00000000

will be loaded into a register by the LH instruction as

11111111 11111111 11111110 00000000.

The

STH   *R1,D2(X2,B2)*

instruction stores the low-order 16 bits of register *R1* in the half-word addressed by *B2, X2,* and *D2.* The second operand must be on a half-word boundary. No check for sign or size of the number in register *R1* is made; the low-order 16 bits of the register are stored, regardless of the other bits in the register.

For example, suppose that the initial contents are as follows:

Register 2: 00000000 11110000 11111111 00001111
Register 9: 00000000 00000000 10010000 10000000
(hexadecimal 00009080)

Locations 009094–7: 00001111 11001100 11111111 01010101

Then the following instructions will have the indicated results.

Instruction	Register or locations changed	New contents
L 4,20(0,9)	Register 4	00001111 11001100 11111111 01010101
ST 2,0(0,9)	Locations 009080–3	00000000 11110000 11111111 00001111
LH 5,20(0,9)	Register 5	00000000 00000000 00001111 11001100
LH 6,22(0,9)	Register 6	11111111 11111111 11111111 01010101
STH 2,4(0,9)	Locations 009084–5	11111111 00001111

Note that in the first instruction, the effective address is computed as shown below.

base: register 9: hexadecimal 00009080
index: 0: 0
displacement: decimal 20 = hexadecimal 014
009094

In the execution of the instruction

LH 5,20(0,9)

the two bytes loaded into the low-order half of register 5 have a high-order bit of 0, so the high-order 16 bits of the register are set to 0's. In the execution of the instruction

LH 6,22(0,9)

the half-word loaded into the low-order half of register 6 has a high-order bit of 1, so the high-order bits of the register are set to 1's. Both 009094 and 009096 are addresses located on half-word boundaries; 009094 is also on a full-word boundary, as was required in the

L 4,20(0,9)

instruction.

Storage to storage

One instruction for moving information from one place to another in main storage is sufficient. The MVC (MoVe Character) instruction discussed briefly in the previous chapter has the flexibility of moving character or byte strings of length from 1 to 256 bytes, with no restrictions as to full-word boundaries and the like. Instructions that have both operands in main storage are all of SS-type and all have the destination or result as first operand and the source as second operand. Source and destination operands of the MVC instruction are naturally of the same length, so only one length is specified in the instruction. The MVC instruction is usually written with both operands expressed as symbols:

$$\text{MVC} \qquad \text{STØRE(8),PLACE}$$

will cause eight bytes to be moved from PLACE to STØRE. The length is coded in the second byte of the machine-language instruction; in assembler language it is the first quantity enclosed in parentheses in the definition of the first operand. While looking at program listings, the programmer should bear in mind that in assembler language the actual length of the string to be moved is specified as the length, but in the assembled machine-language instruction this number is decreased by one.* Thus

$$\text{MVC} \qquad \text{8(4,9),24(9)}$$

assembles into D20390089018. The actual length of the string to be moved is four bytes; the length coded in the machine language instruction is 03.

Another instruction which moves information to a location in main storage is the MVI (MoVe Immediate) instruction, which was also used as an example in the last chapter. As an SI-type instruction, MVI has a first operand which is a location in main storage and a second operand which is a one-byte datum in the second byte of the instruction itself. The first operand is the destination, the second operand the source of the information to be moved. The MVI instruction is used when a one-byte constant is to be moved to a location in main storage.

Suppose that registers and main storage locations have the following initial contents.

Register 9:	00000000 00000000 10010000 10000000
	(hexadecimal 00009080)
Locations 009280–83:	11110000 00001100 10011001 11111111
Locations 009398–9B:	00000000 00110011 11000011 01110111

Then the following instructions have the indicated results.

Instruction		Locations changed	New contents
MVC	513(2,9),792(9)	009281–2	00000000 00110011
MVC	64(1,9),512(9)	0090C0	11110000
MVI	20(9),20	009094	00010100
MVI	21(9),C'E'	009095	11000101
MVI	22(9),X'0E'	009096	00001110
MVI	23(9),B'00001111'	009097	00001111

---

* Exception: the length of a one-byte field may be given in assembler language as either 0 or 1.

Let us consider another set of examples, including use of symbolic addresses and showing in hexadecimal the contents of main storage and registers. Suppose that the following are initial contents:

$$
\begin{array}{ll}
\text{Register 0:} & \text{FCA02705} \\
\text{Register 1:} & \text{0000347C} \\
\text{Register 2:} & \text{D00342A3} \\
\text{Register 9:} & \text{00000004} \\
\text{Register 10:} & \text{00009080} \\
\text{Location Q} & \\
\text{(full word):} & \text{FFF432AD} \\
\text{Location Y} & \\
\text{(two words):} & \text{003881E4 00000014}
\end{array}
$$

Then the following instructions will have the indicated results.

Instruction		Action	
L	3,Q	Register 3:	FFF432AD
L	3,Y(9)	Register 3:	00000014
LH	3,Y+2	Register 3:	FFFF81E4
ST	2,Y+8	Location Y + 8:	D00342A3
MVC	Q+3(7),Y+1	Location Q + 3:	3881E400000014
		(first byte:	38 replaces AD at Q+3)
MVI	Q+2,X'EE'	Location Q + 2:	EE

Let L indicate the length of an operand used in an SS instruction, in particular the coded length (0–255) as formed in the machine-language instruction itself. Then, if we denote by BL the value $8L + 7$, the action of the MVC and MVI instructions can be summarized as

$$
\begin{array}{ll}
\text{MVC:} & S1_{0-BL} \leftarrow c(S2)_{0-BL} \\
\text{MVI:} & S1_{0-7} \leftarrow I2
\end{array}
$$

3. BINARY INTEGER ADD AND SUBTRACT INSTRUCTIONS

Since binary integer addition and subtraction are performed in registers, the instructions performing the arithmetic are of RR and RX types. The register in which the arithmetic is performed is always the first operand of the instruction; one of the numbers taking part in the operation must already be in that register, and the result is left there. The second operand may be either in a register or in main storage.

The six instructions can be described symbolically as follows:

$$
\begin{array}{lll}
\text{AR:} & \text{Add Register} & R1 \leftarrow c(R1) + c(R2) \\
\text{SR:} & \text{Subtract Register} & R1 \leftarrow c(R1) - c(R2) \\
\text{A:} & \text{Add} & R1 \leftarrow c(R1) + c(S2)
\end{array}
$$

S:	Subtract	$R1 \leftarrow c(R1) - c(S2)$
AH:	Add Half-word	$R1 \leftarrow c(R1) + c(S2)_{0-15}$
SH:	Subtract Half-word	$R1 \leftarrow c(R1) - c(S2)_{0-15}$

AR (Add Register) and A (Add) are simple: the two operands are added and the result left in $R1$. The SR (Subtract Register) and S (Subtract) are nearly as simple, but the programmer must remember that the instructions subtract the second operand from the first. Rules of signs prevail; for example, if we subtract a negative number, the number in $R1$ is increased.

In a half-word addition or subtraction, the half-word operand is aligned with the low-order portion of the register operand. The whole word in the register (first operand) participates. We may think of the half-word as expanded into a full word before addition or subtraction, with the sign bit of the half-word copied into the upper half of the full word, as in the LH instruction.

Suppose the following are initial contents of registers and storage locations.

Register 0:   0000123A
Register 1:   00000051
Register 2:   FFFFFFFE
Location Q: 01CEBDEC
Location Y: 0001FFC2

Then the following instructions will have the indicated results. In each instruction, we assume that we deal with the initial conditions listed above—not, as in a program, with the results of the immediately preceding instruction.

Instruction		Register changed	New contents
AR	0,1	0	0000128B
SR	0,1	0	000011E9
SR	1,2	1	00000053
A	1,Q	1	01CEBE3D
S	2,Q	2	FE314212
AH	1,Y	1	00000052
SH	0,Q	0	0000106C
SH	2,Q+2	2	00004212

Let us now examine some instruction sequences to see how the arithmetic and information move instructions can be used together on actual problems. Suppose that quantities named k, m, and j are stored at full-word storage locations named K, M, and J, and a quantity called jr is stored in register 4. Then the following instruction sequences perform the indicated computations.

Compute n as $k - m$:	L	5,K
	S	5,M
	ST	5,N

Compute n as $k - jr$:	L	5,K
	SR	5,4
	ST	5,N
Compute n as $k - jr$:	LCR	5,4
(a second way)	A	5,K
	ST	5,N
Compute n as $m + k - 5000$:	L	5,M
	A	5,K
	S	5,=F'5000'
	ST	5,N

4. BINARY INTEGER MULTIPLICATION

Specifications of instructions

Binary integer multiplication is performed in registers, and as in the binary integer add and subtract instructions, one operand is in a register at the beginning of the operation. Instructions of both RR and RX types are provided so that the second operand may be in either a register or main storage.

When two 32-bit numbers are multiplied, the product is 64 bits long. Therefore two registers are used in the operation. In System/360 and 370, whenever two registers are used as a connected pair, the first, holding the most significant part of the number, is a register with an even address; the second register is the one immediately following. Therefore instructions using register pairs must use registers 0 and 1, 2 and 3, 4 and 5, 6 and 7, 8 and 9, 10 and 11, 12 and 13, or 14 and 15. Conventions establish special uses for registers 0 and 1, 13, 14, and 15, so normally only 2–12 are available.

The full word multiply instructions are

MR	Multiply Register:	$[R1, R1 + 1] \leftarrow c(R1 + 1)*c(R2)$
M	Multiply:	$[R1, R1 + 1] \leftarrow c(R1 + 1)*c(S2)$

The *first operand address*, $R1$, must be an *even* register address, the address of the first register of the register pair to be used. However, the *multiplier* is the contents of the following register, the one with *odd* address, $R1 + 1$. The product is left in the register pair $R1$ and $R1 + 1$; the brackets [ ] in our symbolic definition of the operation indicate the concatenation of the two registers.

For example, the instruction

$$\text{MR} \quad 2,8$$

multiplies the numbers in registers 3 and 8, leaving the product in registers 2 and 3.

Detailed logic of the process

It is instructive to describe in some detail the multiplication process as implemented in the IBM System/360 or 370 computer; the description should remove

Fig. 4-2   Multiplication in four-bit registers

	Reg. 2	Reg. 3

1. 0110 enters the special multiplicand register.

2. Register 2 is cleared to 0000. For the remaining steps, we show registers 2 and 3.

   | 0000 | 0101 |

3. Examine the low-order bit of register 3. It is 1, so add the multiplicand.

   +0110

   | 0110 | 0101 |

4. Shift both registers right one bit.

   | 0011 | 0010 |

5. Examine the low-order bit of register 3. It is 0, so the multiplicand is *not* added.

   | 0011 | 0010 |

6. Shift.

   | 0001 | 1001 |

7. Examine the low-order bit. It is 1, so add the multiplicand.

   +0110

   | 0111 | 1001 |

8. Shift.

   | 0011 | 1100 |

9. Examine the low-order bit. It is 0, so no addition.

   | 0011 | 1100 |

10. Shift.

   | 0001 | 1110 |

some of the bewilderment caused by the instruction specifications. We will consider a multiplication in which both operands are positive, though the instructions handle perfectly well negative operands. Complementation of operands and recomplementation of results if necessary take care of cases in which one or both operands are negative.

The first actions in multiplication are:

1. The multiplicand (second operand) is put in a special nonaddressable register.

2. Register $R1$ is cleared to 0.

Then come 32 repetitions of the following sequence:

3. The low-order bit of register $R1 + 1$ is examined. If this bit is 1, the multiplicand is added into register $R1$.

4. Registers $R1$ and $R1 + 1$ are shifted right one bit. That is, the bit from bit position 63 (in the register pair) is lost, the bit from position 62 is moved into position 63, the bit from position 61 is moved to position 62, . . . , the bit from position 0 is moved to position 1, and a 0 is filled in position 0.

Thus the multiplier is gradually shifted away and lost, and the product is gradually shifted down until it fills the entire register pair.

For purposes of illustration, let us consider fictitious registers four bits long instead of 32. The process is the same, but an illustration using 32-bit registers would be more tedious. Consider four-bit register 3 containing 0101, equivalent to the decimal number 5. Let us suppose that four-bit register 8 contains 0110, or decimal 6. The steps shown in Fig. 4-2 perform MR   2,8.

The series of examine, add, and shift is carried out only four times, since we are dealing with fictitious four-bit registers. The result is the binary number 00011110, or decimal 30.

Note that this process is exactly equivalent and quite similar to our normal method of doing long multiplication. Compare the foregoing with a pencil-and-paper multiplication of 0101 and 0110:

$$
\begin{array}{r}
110 \\
101 \\
\hline
110 \\
110 \\
\hline
11110
\end{array}
$$

Use in a program

When the result of a multiplication is left in a register pair, it is a 64-bit integer. The only arithmetic operation that can be performed by the IBM System/360 in a straightforward manner on 64-bit integers is division, as we shall see in the next section. Therefore, some 32-bit segment of the 64 bits must usually be stored. In most cases, the low-order 32 bits, the contents of register $R1 + 1$, will contain all the significant (that is, non-sign) bits of the result, and we can store the product merely by storing register $R1 + 1$. When this is not sufficient, some scaling analysis must be made, and a 32-bit segment of the product shifted into a register for storage. (Shift instructions will be considered in Chapter 11.) However, if quantities are expected to be generated which are larger than 2^{31} (about 2×10^9), floating-point arithmetic will usually be used.

Let us now show the results of binary integer multiply instructions in the actual 32-bit registers of the IBM System/360. Suppose the following are the initial contents expressed as hexadecimal numbers:

Register 2:	00EA539F
Register 3:	00000200
Register 4:	5F349ABD
Register 5:	FFFFD000
Register 9:	00240C32
Storage location U:	FFFFEEEF

Assuming that these are the initial conditions before *each* of the following instructions, the instructions have the indicated results.

Instruction		Register pair	New contents
MR	2,9	2, 3	00000000 48186400
MR	2,5	2, 3	FFFFFFFF FFA00000
M	4,U	4, 5	00000000 03333000
M	8,U	8, 9	FFFFFFFD 998BDEAE

The following computations can be performed by program segments as shown.

1. Multiply contents of registers 7 and 8, storing the low-order bits of the result in BTF:

```
MR    6,8
ST    7,BTF
```

2. Square the number in register 7, leave the contents of register 7 itself unchanged:

```
LR    9,7
MR    8,9
```

The result will then be in registers 8 and 9.

3. Perform (A+B)*Q, where A, B, and Q are all full-word integers in main storage, and store the low-order 32 bits of the result in Y:

```
L     5,A
A     5,B
M     4,Q
ST    5,Y
```

Our terminology becomes looser here. We say "Perform (A+B)*Q," meaning add and multiply certain quantities, full words A, B, and Q, in main storage. But A, B, and Q are really, for purposes of writing programs, *addresses* of locations containing the quantities to be added and multiplied. It is convenient to talk about the contents of the location named A as also being A, and we will often do so, when the meaning is clear. However, when we start doing much address arithmetic we must be clear whether B + 4, for example, means address B plus the number 4 or the number at location B plus the number 4.

The half-word multiply instruction

There is one other multiplication instruction of RX type which makes use of a full-word first operand in *any* register, multiplies it by a *half-word* in main storage, and leaves the low-order 32 bits of the product in the first operand register:

MH   Multiply Half-word: $R1 \leftarrow (c(R1)*c(S2)_{0-15})_{16-47}$

A 16-bit quantity times a 32-bit quantity will give a 48-bit product. The usual rule of signs will prevail. But of bits 0–47 of this product, only the last 32 are kept as a result by the computer. If the absolute value of the actual product is greater than 2^{31}, the sign bit of the result as left in the register does not necessarily agree with the actual sign of the product.

An example of the use of the MH instruction will conclude this section. Suppose that a half-word integer is stored at location G, and another half-word at K. Their product is to be stored at Z, as a full word.

```
LH    2,G
MH    2,K
ST    2,Z
```

5. BINARY INTEGER DIVISION

Specifications of the instructions

The dividend in a binary integer divide instruction in System/360 or 370 is in a register pair. As in any instruction using a register pair, the most significant part of the number must be in the register with even address, and the last 32 bits in the next register. The register pair is addressed by its first register, the one with even address. The address of the register pair containing the dividend is the first operand, $R1$, in the divide instructions.

Instructions are provided to allow for the divisor to be in a register or in a full word in main storage. The DR (Divide Register) instruction is of RR type; the D (Divide) instruction is of RX type. Both quotient and remainder are left as results of the division. The *quotient* is left in the *odd*-addressed register, and the *remainder* in the *even*-addressed register. The instructions are as follows:

DR   Divide Register: $R1 \leftarrow$ Remainder of $[c(R1), c(R1 + 1)]/c(R2)$
$R1 + 1 \leftarrow$ Quotient of $[c(R1), c(R1 + 1)]/c(R2)$
D   Divide: $R1 \leftarrow$ Remainder of $[c(R1), c(R1 + 1)]/c(S2)$
$R1 + 1 \leftarrow$ Quotient of $[c(R1), c(R1 + 1)]/c(S2)$

The sign of a nonzero remainder is always the same as the sign of the dividend. The sign of a nonzero quotient is determined by the rule of signs; i.e., the quotient is positive if both dividend and divisor have the same sign; if dividend and divisor are of opposite sign, the quotient is negative.

Detailed logic of division

As with the multiply instructions, a detailed explanation of the computer's process should help the student understand how to use the divide instructions. Here too, we will assume that both dividend and divisor are positive. The division process repeats 32 times the sequence of steps listed below.

1. The register pair $R1$ and $R1 + 1$ is shifted *left* one bit: the bit in position 0 is lost, the bit in position 1 is moved to position 0, the bit in position 2 is moved to position 1, ..., the bit in position 63 is moved to position 62, and position 63 is filled with 0.

2. The divisor is subtracted from the contents of register $R1$, which must now be considered as a 32-bit unsigned number.

3. *If* the subtraction causes an overdraft, that is, if the divisor is greater than the quantity in register $R1$, the divisor is added back to restore the previous contents of register $R1$.

4. If there is no overdraft, the bit in position 63 is changed to a 1.

Each time this sequence is performed, another bit of the quotient is formed in bit 63. These bits, through shifting, ultimately fill the entire register $R1 + 1$ with

Fig. 4–3   Division in four-bit registers

1. Register pair 4–5 is shifted left one bit.	0101 | 0110
2. The divisor 0111 is subtracted from register 4.	0111
	1110 | 0110
3. The overdraft requires adding back.	0111
	0101 | 0110
4. Register pair 4–5 is shifted.	1010 | 1100
5. The divisor is subtracted.	0111
	0011 | 1100
6. No overdraft, so change last bit to 1.	0011 | 1101
7. Shift.	0111 | 1010
8. Subtract.	0111
	0000 | 1010
9. No overdraft, so set quotient bit to 1.	0000 | 1011
10. Shift.	0001 | 0110
11. Subtract.	0111
	1010 | 0110
12. Overdraft, so add back.	0111
	0001 | 0110

the quotient. The remainder, literally the number remaining after the division by repeated subtraction, is left in register $R1$.

Let us illustrate the process, again with four-bit registers to avoid tiresome repetition of the steps. Let us consider division of the eight-bit quantity 00101011 (decimal 43) in four-bit registers 4 and 5 by 0111 (decimal 7) in register 9. The steps outlined in Fig. 4–3 perform

$$\text{DR} \quad 4,9$$

The quotient is 0110, or 6; the remainder is 0001, or 1. Compare the sequence with the layout for pencil-and-paper long division of the same problem:

$$
\begin{array}{r}
0110 \\
111\overline{)101011} \\
111 \\
\overline{111} \\
111 \\
\overline{0001}
\end{array}
$$

If the relative sizes of dividend and divisor are such that the quotient cannot be expressed as a 32-bit word including sign, no division is performed, and a program interruption occurs. Program interruptions are described more fully in Chapter 9.

Examples

To illustrate further the action of the divide instructions, we will show the results of several instructions on System/360 or 370 full 32-bit registers. The following are the initial contents:

Register pair 4–5:	0000000000001D6	(decimal 470)
Register pair 6–7:	FFFFFFFFFFFFF12	(decimal −238)
Register 9:	00000028	(decimal 40)
Storage location P:	FFFFFFB6	(decimal −74)

Each of the following instructions, starting from these initial contents, will have the indicated results.

DR	4,9	Register 5	(quotient):	0000000B	(decimal 11)
		Register 4	(remainder):	0000001E	(decimal 30)
DR	6,9	Register 7	(quotient):	FFFFFFFB	(decimal −5)
		Register 6	(remainder):	FFFFFFDA	(decimal −38)
D	4,P	Register 5	(quotient):	FFFFFFFA	(decimal −6)
		Register 4	(remainder):	0000001A	(decimal 26)
D	6,P	Register 7	(quotient):	00000003	(decimal 3)
		Register 6	(remainder):	FFFFFFF0	(decimal −16)

Use of division in program segments

When a programmer uses a divide instruction, he must fill both registers of the register pair being used for the dividend. If the dividend is generated by a multiply instruction, it is automatically in the right form for division. If the dividend comes from a full word in storage, it should be loaded into the register with odd address. The register with even address, the first register of the pair, must then be filled with sign bits of the dividend: 0's if the dividend is positive, 1's if the dividend is negative. We will learn in later chapters how this can be done easily when the sign of the dividend is not known to the programmer in advance.

The following instruction sequences perform the arithmetic indicated:

1. Compute E as P*Q/Y.

```
L    5,P
M    4,Q
D    4,Y
ST   5,E
```

2. Compute E as P/3 assuming P positive.

```
L    5,P
L    4,=F'0'
D    4,=F'3'
ST   5,E
```

3. Compute E as Y/(Q+3) assuming Y negative.

L	9,Q
A	9,=F'3'
L	5,Y
L	4,=F'−1'
DR	4,9
ST	5,E

4. Compute G as the remainder of P/3, assuming P positive.

L	5,P
L	4,=F'0'
D	4,=F'3'
ST	4,G

5. Compute G as P/(Q+3)+Y/5,
    assuming P positive, Y negative.

L	9,Q
A	9,=F'3'
L	5,P
L	4,=F'0'
DR	4,9
L	7,Y
L	6,=F'−1'
D	6,=F'5'
AR	5,7
ST	5,G

6. THE LM AND STM INSTRUCTIONS

The LM (Load Multiple) and STM (STore Multiple) instructions are information move instructions of RS type. They cause the movement of several words at a time between consecutive registers and consecutive main storage locations. The first and third operands (written first and second in the assembler-language statement) are register addresses, defining a block of registers which take part in the move. If $R1$ is less than $R3$, all registers $R1$, $R1+1$, $R1+2$, ..., $R3$ are loaded or stored. But if $R1$ is greater than $R3$, the registers $R1$, $R1+1$, ..., 15, 0, ..., $R3$ are loaded or stored. In other words, the registers are considered as forming a loop, with register 0 following register 15, so that every register has a successor. The registers loaded or stored are in every case $R1$ and all succeeding registers in the loop up to and including $R3$. In main storage, a consecutive block of full words is used, starting at the address given by the second operand.

We illustrate with some examples.

The instruction

$$\text{LM} \quad 3,4,Q$$

loads register 3 from the full word at location Q, and register 4 from the next word, at location Q+4.

The instruction

$$\text{LM} \quad 4,3,Q$$

loads register 4 from the full word at location Q, register 5 from the word at

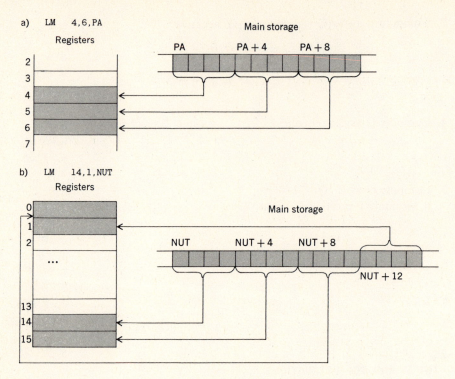

Fig. 4–4 Examples of LM instructions.

Q+4, register 6 from Q+8, . . . , register 15 from Q+44, register 0 from Q+48, . . . , register 3 from Q+60.

The instruction

$$\text{LM} \quad 4,4,Q$$

loads register 4 from the word at Q, and therefore produces the same result as

$$\text{L} \quad 4,Q$$

Further examples are illustrated in Fig. 4–4.

The STM instruction operates with exactly the same pattern of registers, with the flow of information reversed: the contents of registers are stored in main storage. The instruction

$$\text{STM} \quad 14,0,Y$$

would cause the contents of register 14 to be stored at the full word Y, contents of register 15 at Y+4, and contents of register 0 at Y+8.

The LM and STM instructions are used primarily in linkage to subroutines, as we will see in the next chapter. They are also useful for loading and storing blocks of data.

For example, suppose that we wish to compute E as

$$3*Q/P + 3*Q/R + 3*Q/S.$$

A program segment to accomplish this is given below.

```
L      5,=F'3'
M      4,Q
STM    4,5,DIVD       DIVD MUST BE DEFINED AS A TWØ-WØRD AREA
D      4,P            CØMPUTES 3*Q/P
LM     6,7,DIVD
D      6,R            CØMPUTES 3*Q/R
AR     5,7            SUM ØF QUØTIENTS IN REGISTER 5
LM     6,7,DIVD
D      6,S            CØMPUTES 3*Q/S
AR     5,7            SUM ØF THREE QUØTIENTS
ST     5,E
```

7. THE LA INSTRUCTION

The LA (Load Address) instruction is an important information move instruction of RX type, but is peculiar in that it does not access main storage. We can describe the instruction symbolically as

$$LA \quad \text{Load Address: } R1_{8-31} \leftarrow S2$$
$$R1_{0-7} \leftarrow 0$$

The address $S2$ is generated from base, index, and displacement as in any RX-type instruction. Since the normal address calculation circuitry is used, only the low-order 24 bits are kept. These 24 bits themselves are loaded into the low-order 24 bits of register $R1$, and the first 8 bits are cleared to 0's.

The instruction was designed to allow us to load actual addresses into registers; we will learn the usefulness of this possibility when we consider problems of address modification. The instruction is also useful for performing loads and additions with small numbers. Suppose, for example, that we wish to load the number 3 into register 5. Instead of requiring that a constant 3 be kept in storage for loading into register 5, we can issue an instruction

$$LA \quad REG5,3$$

The second operand 3 is a self-defining term. The assembler will assemble the instruction with

$$R1 = 5 \text{ (EQUivalenced to REG5)}$$
$$X2 = 0$$
$$B2 = 0$$
$$D2 = 003$$

In execution of this instruction, the second operand address will be

$$
\begin{array}{ll}
B2: & 000000 \\
X2: & +\ 000000 \\
D2: & +\ \underline{\qquad 003} \\
& 000003
\end{array}
$$

Therefore, 00000003 will be loaded into register 5.

Furthermore, the LA instruction can be used as an efficient add instruction for small numbers whose sum is small and positive. One or two numbers in registers can be added to a positive constant up to (decimal) 4095. Consider the instruction

LA   REG3,69(6,7)

The contents of register 6, the contents of register 7, and the (decimal) number 69 are added, and if the sum is positive and less than 24 bits in length, it is loaded correctly into register 3. While this example is slightly exotic, a very common use of the instruction is to add 1 to a register whose contents are known to be positive. For example,

LA   4,1(4)

The following instruction sequences perform the arithmetic indicated:

1. Compute E as $(P+3)/Q$ assuming P small and positive.

```
L    REG5,P
LA   REG5,3(REG5)
LA   REG4,0
D    REG4,Q
ST   REG5,E
```

2. Put the address of HPK plus the (small) number N found in register 4 into HPKN.

```
LA   5,HPK
AR   5,4
ST   5,HPKN
```

or

```
LA   5,HPK(4)
ST   5,HPKN
```

3. The address of the word in the first column and first row of an array of full words in main storage is ARBASE. The words in a column are stored sequentially, and the next column begins immediately after the 20th word of the preceding column. Given M as the row index of a particular word (that is, this word is in the Mth row) and N as the column index, load the word into register 6.

```
L    5,N
S    5,=F'1'      c(N)−1 is the number of columns to be skipped.
M    4,=F'20'     20 words to a column.
A    5,M          c(M)−1 is the number of words to be skipped
S    5,=F'1'         in a column to get to the Mth row.
```

```
M    4,=F'4'          Four bytes to a word.
LA   5,ARBASE(5)      Add base address.
L    6,0(5)           Load word from computed address.
```

8. GENERATION OF PSEUDO-RANDOM NUMBERS

One of the significant uses of computers is simulation of environments and activities in the real world, such as traffic flow patterns, drawing from and replacing inventory, flow of jobs through a digital computer, inheritance of genetic traits, interaction of people in a group, etc. In many of these simulations, actions occur at chance or random intervals or involve attributes whose values inside the computer must be assigned somewhat by chance. For example, in an inventory simulation the time at which the next customer makes a demand for an item should be considered to be determined at least partly by chance. Furthermore, the *number* of items he wishes to buy is a variable whose value should be determined by chance (under restrictions, of course). If a computer is performing the simulation, it must assign values to variables like "length of wait until next customer" and "size of transaction." A table of values carefully produced at random could be fed into the computer, but if the computer can produce its own random values easily, the program can be simpler and more efficient.

Pseudo-random numbers

If a computer starts producing truly random numbers, i.e., numbers which cannot be adequately explained from knowledge of the machine's contents and input, we call for repair. If we attempted to build particular elements into a computer which would yield random values, we would have an extremely difficult time controlling the distribution of values produced. As it turns out, it is far better to produce *pseudo-random numbers*. Pseudo-random numbers are not random, but sequences of them have many of the properties that we desire sequences of random numbers to have. Some of these properties are:

1. *Controlled distribution.* We want to be able to designate the fraction of numbers in the sequence that attain a certain value or fall into a certain interval, but if the number sequence merely has some *known* distribution, we can transform its values to any desired distribution by programming.

2. *Independence of successive values.* The value of one number of the sequence should not affect the next value. We usually generate pseudo-random numbers *from their predecessors*, so this condition is clearly not met. But it can be met approximately, in the following sense: knowing only that a number in a pseudo-random sequence lies in some fairly small interval does not help one to predict the next number of the sequence; in other words, the distribution of numbers following numbers which may lie in the given interval is the same as the distribution of numbers following numbers in any other interval of similar size.

Multiplicative congruence method

One widely used method for generating pseudo-random numbers is called the *multiplicative congruence method.** This method is as follows:

1. A beginning value X is chosen, the first number of the pseudo-random sequence.
2. X is multiplied by some constant multiplier.
3. The product is divided by some constant (called the *modulus*) and the *remainder* taken as a new X, the next pseudo-random number.
4. Steps 2 and 3 are repeated for every successive pseudo-random number desired.

For binary computers, some theory has been developed about proper beginning values, multipliers, and moduli. First, if the modulus is chosen as a power of 2, no division need be performed at all; all that is necessary is to clear some of the *most significant* bits of the product. In System/360 and 370, for example, a word is 32 bits long; hence a convenient choice of modulus is 2^{32}, and instead of performing a division we need only *ignore* the first word of a product. Second, it can be shown that the last three bits of the multiplier should be 011 or 101, for if they are, the sequence of pseudo-random numbers can be made not to repeat until 2^{30} numbers have been generated (assuming the 2^{32} modulus). The only additional requirement for achieving a period of 2^{30} before repetition is that the last bit of the starting number X be 1. More conditions should be set on the multiplier, however. It should be close to the square root of the modulus in order to have maximum apparent independence of successive values, and to minimize the time required for the multiplication (on some computers) the number of 1-bits in the multiplier should be as small as possible! Therefore a good value for the multiplier in System/360 or 370 is $2^{16} + 5$ or 65,541.

The multiplicative congruence method yields a quite uniform distribution of numbers over the possible range of generation. For example, considering that there are 2^{32} possible 32-bit numbers, if the full sequence of 2^{30} different numbers were generated, it would include 2 out of every 8 consecutive numbers of the 2^{32}. The distribution of less than the full sequence of 2^{30} numbers would not be as even.

Programming

Suppose that the current pseudo-random number, an integer in the range -2^{31} to $2^{31}-1$, is always stored at RN. A program segment sufficient to generate the next pseudo-random number is

```
L    7,RN
M    6,=F'65541'
ST   7,RN
```

---

* For a more formal description and further references, see Shan S. Kuo, *Computer Applications of Numerical Methods* (Reading, Mass.: Addison-Wesley, 1972).

Suppose that in our *use* of pseudo-random numbers, what we really want is a digit randomly selected from 0 to 9, with each digit to be selected with equal likelihood. After the above instruction sequence, we can perform

```
M    6,=F'10'
LA   6,5(6)
ST   6,RDIGIT
```

A number RN in register 7 is between -2^{31} to 2^{31} (noninclusive, since it must end in 1). The

```
M    6,=F'10'
```

instruction produces a number between -10×2^{31} and 10×2^{31} or -5×2^{32} and 5×2^{32}. Adding 5 to register 6 is equivalent to adding 5×2^{32} to the product; so after the

```
LA   6,5(6)
```

instruction the number in register pair 6–7 is between 0 and 10×2^{32}. If we take only the portion in register 6, we are in effect taking the *quotient* upon division by 2^{32}. Since 10×2^{32} is approached but not attained as a value, 10 is never generated in register 6; the values of RDIGIT will be uniformly distributed among the numbers 0 to 9.

9. MAIN IDEAS

a. We describe the action of instructions symbolically, with notation as summarized in Fig. 4–5.

Fig. 4–5 Notation for symbolic description of instructions

R1, R2, R3	Register addresses given as operands.
S1, S2	Main storage addresses given as operands.
I2	"Immediate" byte of an *SI* instruction.
c(R1)	Contents of register *R1*.
c(S2)	Contents of full word at location *S2*.
Quantity$_{a-b}$	Bits numbered *a* to *b* of the *Quantity*.
[Quantity 1, Quantity 2]	Concatenation of *Quantity 1* and *Quantity 2*.
A ← Quantity	The *Quantity* is placed at location *A*.

b. Information move instructions permit the moving of information from a register to another register, from register to main storage, from main storage to a register, and from main storage to other main storage locations.

c. Binary integer arithmetic is always performed in registers. One operand is in a register; the second operand may be either in a register or in main storage, but the result is always put in a register.

d. Most binary integer arithmetic operations use full words, but some RX load, store, and arithmetic instructions allow for half-word operands from main storage.

e. The action of the instructions in this chapter is summarized in Fig. 4–6.

f. The usual instruction sequence for performing arithmetic is:
Load an operand into a register from main storage.
Perform the arithmetic, possibly more than one operation.
Store the result.

Fig. 4–6 Information move and binary integer arithmetic instructions

Mnemonic name	Type	Full name	Action
LR	RR	Load from Register	$R1 \leftarrow c(R2)$
LCR	RR	Load Complement from Register	$R1 \leftarrow -c(R2)$
LPR	RR	Load Positive from Register	$R1 \leftarrow |c(R2)|$
LNR	RR	Load Negative from Register	$R1 \leftarrow -|c(R2)|$
L	RX	Load	$R1 \leftarrow c(S2)$
ST	RX	STore	$S2 \leftarrow c(R1)$
LH	RX	Load Half-word	$R1_{16-31} \leftarrow c(S2)_{0-15}$, $R1_{0-15} \leftarrow c(S2)_0$
STH	RX	STore Half-word	$S2_{0-15} \leftarrow c(R1)_{16-31}$
MVC	SS	MoVe Character[1]	$S1_{0-BL} \leftarrow c(S2)_{0-BL}$
MVI	SI	MoVe Immediate	$S1_{0-7} \leftarrow I2$
LM	RS	Load Multiple	$[R1, \ldots, R3] \leftarrow c(S2)$[2]
STM	RS	STore Multiple	$S2$[2] $\leftarrow [c(R1), \ldots, c(R3)]$
LA	RX	Load Address	$R1_{8-31} \leftarrow S2$, $R1_{0-7} \leftarrow 0$
AR	RR	Add Register	$R1 \leftarrow c(R1)+c(R2)$
SR	RR	Subtract Register	$R1 \leftarrow c(R1)-c(R2)$
A	RX	Add	$R1 \leftarrow c(R1)+c(S2)$
S	RX	Subtract	$R1 \leftarrow c(R1)-c(S2)$
AH	RX	Add Half-word	$R1 \leftarrow c(R1)+c(S2)_{0-15}$
SH	RX	Subtract Half-word	$R1 \leftarrow c(R1)-c(S2)_{0-15}$
MR	RR	Multiply Register[3]	$[R1, R1+1] \leftarrow c(R1+1)*c(R2)$
M	RX	Multiply[3]	$[R1, R1+1] \leftarrow c(R1+1)*c(S2)$
MH	RX	Multiply Half-word	$R1 \leftarrow (c(R1)*c(S2)_{0-15})_{16-47}$
DR	RR	Divide Register[3]	$R1 \leftarrow$ remainder of $[c(R1), c(R1+1)]/c(R2)$ $R1+1 \leftarrow$ quotient of $[c(R1), c(R1+1)]/c(R2)$
D	RX	Divide[3]	$R1 \leftarrow$ remainder of $[c(R1), c(R1+1)]/c(S2)$ $R1+1 \leftarrow$ quotient of $[c(R1), c(R1+1)]/c(S2)$

Notes
1. $BL = 8L + 7$, where L is the length coded in the machine-language instruction
2. If $R1 \leq R3$, $4*(R3-R1) + 4$ bytes of the main storage operand $S2$ participate
   If $R1 > R3$, $4*(R3+16-R1) + 4$ bytes of the main storage operand $S2$ participate
3. $R1$ must be an even address; $R1+1$ is of course the address of the following register

g. Multiply (except half-word) and divide instructions use register pairs, beginning at a register with even address, for their processes of successive add and shift or subtract and shift.

h. Pseudo-random numbers are helpful in simulation programs; they are easily generated by the multiplicative congruence method.

QUESTIONS FOR REVIEW AND IMAGINATION

1. What sequence of two instructions, not including LPR, will have the same effect as

LPR   2,7

2. A quick way to set a register, say register 5, to zero is to perform

SR   5,5

List two other ways of setting a register to zero.

3. The LA instruction can be used to add a small positive constant to the contents of a register without requiring definition of the number as a constant in main storage. Why can it not subtract a small positive constant just as well?

4. Suppose that the initial (hexadecimal) contents of registers and storage locations are as given below.

Register 1:	0000002E	Location G (full word):	000001D6
Register 2:	FFFFFFC0	Location K (full word):	FFFFFFF6
Register 3:	456789AB	Location Q (full word):	BA987654
Register 4:	CDEF0123	Location Q+4:	3210FEDC

Assuming that these are the contents before *each* of the following instructions, show the result of each instruction.

```
LPR   7,2      A    1,K        STM   2,4,Q
LNR   8,4      S    1,K        LM    5,6,Q
AR    1,2      SH   1,K        LH    7,Q+6
AR    2,1      AH   3,Q+2      STH   3,K
SR    1,2      MVI  Q+5,17     LA    8,2(3,4)
SR    2,1      MVC  K+1(5),Q+2 S     2,Q
```

5. Distinguish among the effects of the instructions

```
LR    5,4
LA    5,4
L     5,4
L     5,0(4)
LA    5,0(4)
```

6. Suppose that the initial contents in registers and main storage locations of the binary integer representations of the following decimal values are:

Register 2:	0	Location U:	16
Register 3:	49	Location Y:	−5
Register 4:	−1		
Register 5:	−84		
Register 7:	12		
Register 9:	−30		

Assuming that these are the contents before *each* of the following instructions, show the results of each instruction.

```
MR    8,9       DR    2,7
MR    6,9       DR    4,7
M     8,U       DR    4,9
MH    7,U+2     D     2,Y
```

7. If a number is loaded into a register to become the dividend in a divide instruction, its sign must be extended into all bit positions of the even-numbered register of the register pair. If the sign of the number is unknown, one way to extend it is to multiply the number by 1. Illustrate this in a sequence which will divide the number at location K by the number in location Q, storing the result at location Z, even though signs of the numbers at K and Q are unknown.

8. The scheme for multiplication in System/360 and 370 involves starting with the multiplier in the lower half of the product area, adding the multiplicand at appropriate times into the upper half, and shifting right. Illustrate a valid scheme (at least for positive numbers), starting with the multiplier in the top half of the product area, adding the multiplicand to the lower half, and shifting left.

9. Can an equivalent scheme for division be devised which involves shifting right instead of left, similar to the alternative scheme just mentioned for multiplication? Illustrate such a scheme or explain why one cannot be constructed.

10. In general, if the dividend in a divide instruction fits completely in the odd-numbered register and the divisor is nonzero, there is no possibility of overflow in the divide instruction. There is one exceptional pair consisting of a dividend which is wholly in the odd-numbered register and a divisor which does produce an overflow (that is, the quotient cannot be expressed in 32 bits). What is this dividend and divisor pair?

11. Write program segments to perform the following:

Compute E as $K+3$.
Compute E as $(K+3)/Q$, K positive.
Compute E as $(K+U)*R$, where U is in register 6.
Compute E as $(K-T+R*P)/(Y-5)$, where T is a half-word.

REFERENCES

Falkoff, A. D., K. E. Iverson, and E. H. Sussenguth, "A Formal Description of SYSTEM/360," *IBM Systems Journal* **3** (1964), pp. 198–261. A comprehensive description of the structure and instruction repertoire of the IBM System/360, in the Iverson notation.

IBM System/360 Principles of Operation, GA22-6821, IBM Corporation. Descriptions of the instructions introduced in this chapter.

IBM System/370 Principles of Operation, GA22-7000, IBM Corporation. A parallel description for System/370 users.

Iverson, Kenneth, *A Programming Language* (New York: Wiley, 1962). Develops a symbolic language for description of computer processes, and discusses several data processing techniques expressed in the language. This study led to implementation of *APL* as a computer language.

Kuo, Shan S., *Computer Application of Numerical Methods* (Reading, Mass.: Addison-Wesley, 1972). A good discussion of generation of pseudo-random numbers.

Knuth, Donald E., *The Art of Computer Programming, Vol. 2: Seminumerical Algorithms* (Reading, Mass.: Addison-Wesley, 1969). Chapter 3 deals comprehensively with generation of pseudo-random numbers.

Chapter 5

Subroutine Linkage;
Declaring a Base Register

A sequence of instructions that is to be executed at several different points in a computer program need not be included in its entirety at each such point. It can be enclosed and called a subroutine. Then at each point where execution of the sequence is desired, the right kind of branch to the subroutine is sufficient. Enough information must be given to the subroutine so that it knows what information to work with and where to return control when it is finished. The idea is to replace the storage and control structure of Fig. 5–1(a) with the structure shown in Fig. 5–1(b). The structure shown in Fig. 5–1(b), using the subroutine, requires less storage space than the other, since sequence A is loaded in main storage only once.

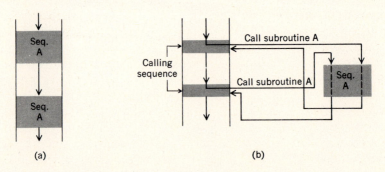

Fig. 5–1 Storage and control: (a) without a subroutine; (b) with sequence A as a subroutine.

A subroutine structure has many advantages: It allows easy use of previously programmed solutions to subtasks of the programming problem. It facilitates debugging by allowing each small subroutine to be debugged separately when called by a minimal master program designed purely to test the given subroutine. It makes programming easier by breaking down the problem into pieces, each of which has only a minimal and explicit number of relationships with the others.

We introduce in this chapter the conventions governing the linkage between subroutines in the IBM System/360 and 370, showing the responsibilities of both calling and called subroutines.

In Section 4 of this chapter we explain the mechanism for declaring and setting the implied base register. With this done, we are able to exhibit complete subroutines, which we do in examples at the end of this chapter.

1. REGISTER CONVENTIONS AND REGISTER SAVE AREAS

Register conventions

A *subroutine* is a closed sequence of instructions (and perhaps data areas and constants) which is called by another program or subroutine. It usually returns control to the calling program. This is in distinction to a main program, which conceptually is in direct control, not subsidiary to or called by any other program. Actually, in the IBM System/360 and 370, a main program is regarded as a subroutine by the supervisor; however, the concept of a main program as one not called by any other program or subroutine belonging to the user is still a useful one. A main program may or may not call subroutines, and subroutines may or may not call other subroutines. If we restrict our attention to a section that calls a subroutine, we see that it does not matter to the calling structure whether the section is a main program or a subroutine, so we use the blanket term *routine*, which applies to either.

Every program or subroutine in the IBM System/360 uses the general registers; practically nothing can be done without them. A routine (main program or subroutine) *A* which calls a subroutine *B* would be difficult indeed to write if the subroutine changed contents of all the registers. The subroutine *B* must use the registers, but writing the calling routine *A* will be much easier if its register contents are undisturbed, except for the registers explicitly used in communication with subroutine *B*. Fortunately, it is possible to set up procedures and conventions so that a few designated registers have special uses in the subroutine communication. All registers can be used by the subroutine but almost all are restored to the calling routine's contents before the subroutine returns control to the calling routine. This amounts to having our cake and eating it too: both calling routine *A* and subroutine *B* have the use of registers; the cost of following certain register conventions is quite low. We will learn the uses set by convention for registers 0, 1, 13, 14, and 15; other registers may be used in any way the programmer desires in any routine.

Register 0 contains the single-word output of a subroutine. For example, the value of an integer function written in FORTRAN is left by the function in register 0, and from there retrieved by the calling routine. Contents of register 0 upon entry to the subroutine are lost.

Register 1 contains the address of an area of main storage which contains addresses of parameters, both input parameters to and output parameters from, the subroutine.

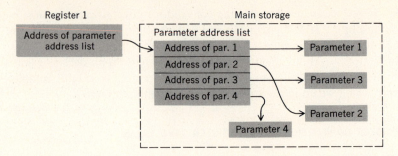

Fig. 5-2 The parameter address list.

For example, suppose subroutine B has four parameters, two of which are input parameters and two are output parameters. The routine A which calls on subroutine B may wish to supply parameters T and U as input to subroutine B and have the results of subroutine B placed at V and W. Routine A will therefore put the *addresses* of T, U, V, and W in consecutive words, and place the address of the first word of this area (the word containing the address of T) in register 1, as shown in Fig. 5–2. This may be done by defining a block of address constants

```
ADDS        DC      A(T)
            DC      A(U)
            DC      A(V)
            DC      A(W)
```

among other constants and storage definitions, and loading the address of the block

```
            LA      1,ADDS
```

before entry to subroutine B. The A-type constant is for defining addresses, as we shall see in more detail in the next chapter.

Subroutine B may get the second parameter by

```
            L       3,4(1)
            L       8,0(3)
```

The first of these instructions loads register 3 with the word four bytes beyond the location whose address is in register 1; this word is the address of U as placed there by routine A. The second instruction, assuming that U is a full word, loads U into register 8. Addresses of all four parameters can be loaded into consecutive registers by, say

```
            LM      3,6,0(1)
```

Let us examine several possible ways of passing parameters to subroutines. First, if there are only one or two parameters, and they are full-word quantities, we could place the quantities themselves in register 1 or registers 0 and 1. Second, we could put the *addresses* of the parameters in registers 0 and 1. Leaving an address in register 0 is not the most helpful thing we can think of; remember that 0 in a *Bl*,

B2, or *X2* field is taken to mean no register participation for that element in the address computation. The third alternative, that of the *block* of parameter addresses, is the standard that will enable greatest compatibility between routines, especially if some are written in languages other than assembler language. Especially when there is only one parameter, it seems silly to have put the address *of an address* (the "block" of parameter address is one address long) of the parameter in register 1. It is also not easy to understand. Let us explore several alternative specifications.

a. Suppose the fields named PSAT and NAME are to be passed to a subroutine. With other definitions of constants we can define the parameter address block:

```
ADBLØCK     DC      A(PSAT)
            DC      A(NAME)
```

Just before entry to the subroutine, we load register 1 with the address of the block:

```
            LA      1,ADBLØCK
```

b. Suppose we wish to call the same subroutine. The value of the first parameter is in register 3, and the address of the 108-byte area containing characters of the second parameter is in register 6. We must construct an address block as before. The parameter block may be defined

```
ADBK1       DC      A(FPARAM)
            DS      1F
```

DS is a pseudo-operation standing for Define Storage; the operand specifies definition of one full word. We will present the DS statement in more detail in the next chapter. The first parameter must be stored in main storage, perhaps by

```
            ST      3,FPARAM
```

The second parameter is already in main storage, but its address must be stored:

```
            ST      6,ADBK1+4
```

which places the address in the full word for which we defined the storage space with the DS 1F statement. Finally, the address of the parameter address-block is loaded:

```
            LA      1,ADBK1
```

c. Suppose we are preparing to enter another subroutine, whose single parameter is a binary integer. The subroutine could be written to accept the number itself in register 1, but we presume it follows the standard conventions. If the number is in, say, register 5, we store it:

```
            ST      5,NUM
```

We need a parameter address block, even though it contains only one address; it could be defined

```
ADNUM       DC      A(NUM)
```

Finally, before entry to the subroutine, we load the address of the parameter address block:

```
LA      1,ADNUM
```

Register 14 contains the return address, the address in the calling routine to which the subroutine should return control when finished. Register 15 sometimes contains the address of the entry point in the subroutine, the address to which the calling routine branches when calling the subroutine. There are ways of branching to the subroutine, however, which do not involve register 15. The instructions used to enter the proper addresses into registers 14 and 15 and to transfer control to the subroutines and back will be discussed in Section 2.

Register 13 contains the address of an area in which register contents can be stored by the subroutine. The layout and use of this area are the next topic to be discussed.

The register save area

It is a great convenience for a calling program to be able to set up registers 1, 13, 14, and 15 for a subroutine call, transfer control to the subroutine, and then expect all registers except register 0 to be unchanged when control is returned. Both calling and called routines need to use and change registers; a system for preserving the register contents left by the calling routine and restoring them just before return of control to the calling routine will allow both routines full use of registers.

The area used for storage of registers is 18 words long; it has the format shown in Fig. 5–3. The first and third words are not used in the more elementary linkage patterns. The called subroutine stores the contents of registers 14, 15, 0, 1, . . . , 12 in words 4 to 18 of the save area. Preservation of these register contents can be accomplished by the instruction

```
STM     14,12,12(13)
```

at the beginning of the called subroutine, since register 13 contains the address of the save area. Similarly, the registers can be restored by the single instruction

```
LM      14,12,12(13)
```

just before exit from the subroutine.

The calling program supplies the area (that is, puts the address of an area in register 13) in which the called subroutine stores the register contents as left by the calling program (read that again—carefully!). However, the called subroutine must make special arrangements for storing register 13. The called subroutine,

Fig. 5-3 A register save area

Word	Address	Contents
Word 1	SAV	
Word 2	SAV+4	Address of calling program's save area
Word 3	SAV+8	
Word 4	SAV+12	Contents of register 14
Word 5	SAV+16	Contents of register 15
Word 6	SAV+20	Contents of register 0
Word 7	SAV+24	Contents of register 1
⋮	⋮	⋮
Word 18	SAV+68	Contents of register 12

subroutine *B*, usually stores the contents of register 13 in word 2 of the save area which *it* provides. The remainder of this area would be used by a subroutine *C*, called by subroutine *B*, to store the contents of registers as left by subroutine *B*. Alternatively, the called subroutine may store register 13 in an entirely separate location, or guarantee not to call any subroutines or change register 13.

To justify special treatment for register 13, we draw an analogy. If we bury a treasure, we make a treasure map. It does no good to bury the map with the treasure; we must store the map elsewhere, so we can use it in finding the treasure again. So it is with register contents. We can bury the contents of registers 14, 15, and 0–12 at a location recorded in our treasure map, register 13, but we must keep the contents of register 13, namely the treasure map, elsewhere.

In Section 3, we will explore further the actions taken by calling and called subroutines.

2. THE BR AND BALR INSTRUCTIONS

A number of different branch instructions, conditional and unconditional, are needed in any digital computer. The instructions and their use are discussed at length in Chapter 7; here we only describe two unconditional branch instructions used in subroutine linkage.

The BR and BALR instructions are both RR-type instructions. In both, the second operand is the address to which control is transferred, called the *branch address*. That is, the register specified as *R2* contains the address of a main storage location from which the next instruction is to be taken. Instructions are then taken from locations subsequent to the branch address until another branch is performed.

The BR operation code is a simplification of BCR 15, where 15 is the first operand. It will become clear in Chapter 7 why 15 is a first operand which makes a BCR (Branch Conditional to Register) instruction into an unconditional branch. The unconditional branch is important enough to warrant a separate alphabetic abbreviation and a simplification. Thus we write BR with only one operand, which in the normal RR-type pattern is the second operand. The instruction causes a branch to the location whose address is in register 14. If, for example, location 009426 contains the BR   14 instruction and register 14 contains 00009630, the instruction executed after the BR   14 will be the instruction located (that is, beginning) at location 009630.

A special convention attaches to a 0 as second operand in the BR and BALR instructions. The specification of 0 means that no branch takes place; the next instruction is taken from main storage directly following the BR or BALR instruction. Therefore BR   0 is a dummy instruction, the one used when a "no-operation" instruction is desired. The BALR instruction whose second operand is 0 does not reduce to a no-operation instruction; the action taken with respect to the first operand is explained below.

The BALR instruction performs a branch in exactly the same way as the BR instruction, but first loads the address of the instruction immediately after the BALR into the register whose address is given in the first operand. Suppose, for example, that location 009472 (really 009472 and 009473) contains the instruction BALR   14,15, and that register 15 contains 0000BC76. The BALR instruction causes two actions. The first is that 00009474, the address of the instruction immediately following the BALR instruction, is loaded into register 14, the first operand. The second action is the branch to location 00BC76.

Actually, the BALR instruction loads some bits of the program status word into positions 0–7 of register $R1$, in addition to loading the address of the next instruction (actually bits 40–63 of the program status word) in positions 8–31 of register $R1$. Therefore the first two hexadecimal digits of register 14 in the above example may not be 00. The contents of register 14 usually serve only as a branch address, however, and so the eight high-order bits are irrelevant.

The next sections will show the usefulness of these instructions.

3. AN IMPLIED BASE REGISTER; THE USING PSEUDO-OPERATION

The USING pseudo-operation

In Chapter 3 we discussed the action of the IBM 0S/360 or 370 assembler in converting the address of a symbol to base-and-displacement form. The assembler puts in the assembled machine-language instruction the base register address which was declared previously to be used as an implied base register. The declaration of the implied base register also includes information about what relocatable address is assumed to be in that register, so the correct displacement can also be generated by the assembler. Now we show how the implied base register is declared.

An assembler-language statement that is not translated into instructions or constants which become part of the machine-language program is called a *pseudo-operation*. The pseudo-operation gives information or commands to the assembler, influencing the output of the assembler, either by specifying the form of the listing or object program or by instructing the assembler how to assemble subsequent instructions. The USING pseudo-operation instructs the assembler by giving it the information it needs in order to convert relocatable expressions to base-and-displacement form.

For this purpose, the most elementary form of the USING pseudo-operation is

$$USING \quad *,r$$

The second operand is a decimal integer designating the register to be used as the implied base register; the asterisk used as first operand is the location-counter reference symbol. The statement informs the assembler that the register named in the second operand contains the relocatable address currently in the location-reference counter. This address is usually the address of the next instruction. For example, consider the following sequence of instructions with addresses assigned as indicated.

```
                        USING    *,9
        000014          L        8,G
                        ⋮
        000156   G      DC       F'-1'
```

The implied base register is declared to be register 9, and it is declared to contain the relocatable address 000014. Therefore in assembly of the L   8,G instruction, the base designation *B2* inserted by the assembler is 9. The displacement *D2* is 000156 − 000014 = 142. The entire assembled instruction is 58809142.

The BALR, USING pair

The USING pseudo-operation makes a promise to the assembler about the contents of a named register. The BALR instruction enables us to keep that promise. As discussed in the previous section, it loads the register named as first operand with the address of the next instruction. When a BALR instruction immediately precedes the USING statement, the USING becomes not a promise but a notice of action previously taken. The BALR instruction is used to load the register, but there is usually no need to branch at the same time, so the second operand of the BALR instruction is 0.

For instance, we may have

```
                BALR     9,0
                USING    *,9
                L        8,G
                ⋮
        G       DC       F'-1'
```

The BALR   9,0 instruction loads register 9 with the address of the next instruction, but does not branch, since its second operand is 0. Therefore the next instruction to be executed is the next one in main storage, that is, L   8,G. The USING pseudo-operation has told the assembler how to construct base and displacement, so G will be loaded correctly into register 8.

Relocatability

The BALR instruction, used as we have just shown, permits a program to work properly independently of its placement in main storage. As long as the *differences* between addresses of various parts of the program are maintained and double-word boundaries are where they were planned to be during assembly, displacements from the address placed by the BALR instruction in the implied base register will be correct.

Let us examine once more our example, showing assembler-assigned locations and actual core locations. Suppose that the program is relocated by (hexadecimal) 009020, so that every relocatable address is added to 009020. Then the program in main storage can be shown as

Actual location	Assembled location	Assembled instruction		Assembler language	
⋮	⋮	⋮		⋮	
009032	000012	0590		BALR	9,0
				USING	*,9
009034	000014	58809142		L	8,G
⋮	⋮	⋮		⋮	
009176	000156	FFFFFFFF	G	DC	F'-1'

The execution of the BALR instruction loads 00009034 into register 9. During the execution of the load instruction, the displacement 142 is added to the contents of register 9, 00009034, to yield an effective address of 00009176, which is the actual address of G: 009020 + 000156.

More on USING

Several registers may be declared available for use as implied base registers by one USING pseudo-operation. The first operand of USING is any relocatable expression not involving a literal. This first operand is followed by from 1 to 16 absolute expressions whose values are register addresses. We can express the syntax of USING as

Name	Operation	Operands
Blank	USING	*V,r1[,r2, . . . ,r16]*

where the brackets around *r2, . . . ,r16* indicate that these are optional operands. Register *r1* is assumed to contain *V*, the value of the relocatable expression. If a third operand *r2* appears, register *r2* is assumed to contain the value *V* + 4096. Similarly, if *r3, r4, . . .* are specified, registers *r3, r4, . . .* are assumed to contain

values $V + 2*4096$, $V + 3*4096$, ... More than one implied base register must
be declared if the length of program and data areas is so great that some addresses
exceed the address in the first base register by more than 4095 (the largest possible
displacement).

A location, or an expression specifying it, is said to be *addressable* if its address
is greater than the address declared to be in some implied base register and less
than 4096 greater than the address declared to be in that register. This is a practical requirement which makes sure that the assembler will find one of the declared
implied base registers and construct a displacement to go with it to address the
desired location. No expression referring to a main storage location and involving
a symbol or literal may be used as an operand in an instruction before the USING
statement which makes it addressable. Register 0 can be declared in a USING
pseudo-operation, but special rules which we shall not consider govern its use.

A base register may be redefined to have a different value in a subsequent
USING pseudo-operation. A register may be made unavailable for further use as
an implied base register by a DRØP pseudo-operation. The form of this operation
is shown below.

Name	Operation	Operands
Blank	DRØP	From 1 to 16 absolute expressions referring to registers, of the form *r1*[,*r2,r3*, . . . ,*r16*]

We show an example of a more advanced usage of USING.

Name	Operation	Operands
	BALR	9,0
	USING	BASE,9,10,11
BASE	LM	10,11,BADDR
⋮		
BADDR	DC	A(BASE+4096,BASE+8192)

The BALR instruction and USING make 4095 bytes starting at BASE addressable.
After seeing USING   BASE,9,10,11 the assembler believes that all addresses up
to BASE+12287 are addressable; we can see that locations BASE+4096 to BASE+12287
cannot in fact be correctly addressed until the LM   10,11,BADDR instruction is
executed, loading the proper values into registers 10 and 11. Note that for this
procedure to work properly, BADDR must be located not more than 4094 bytes
beyond BASE.

4. SUBROUTINE LINKAGE

Expected status at the time of call: responsibility of calling routine

The calling routine must make the arrangements for linking to the subroutine which it calls; the responsibilities of the subroutine called are merely to recognize the arrangements the calling routine has made and to do its work without upsetting anything. Before transferring control to the subroutine, the calling routine must do all of the following.

1. prepare the input parameters to the subroutine,
2. put the addresses of all parameters in a main storage area,
3. load the address of that area into register 1,
4. load the address of an 18-word register save area into register 13,
5. load into register 14 the address of the instruction to be executed immediately upon return from the subroutine,
6. branch to the subroutine.

Instructions normally used by the calling routine to fulfill its responsibilities for subroutine linkage are as follows. First, near the beginning of the routine, register 13 is loaded with the address of a register save area by the instruction

LA   13,SAV

The symbol SAV (any symbol may be used, of course) must refer to an 18-word area. The definition of this area and other constants and symbols is usually placed at the end of the program. SAV can be defined by

SAV DS   18F

The operand specifies definition of 18 full words; the symbol SAV is equated to the address of the first of the 18 words.

The register save area used during a call on a subroutine contains, except for the second word, no pertinent information after return from that subroutine. Therefore the same area can be used to save register contents during subsequent subroutine calls from the same routine. For this reason, loading the address of the register save area into register 13 is done just once, usually near the beginning of the calling routine; it need not be done just before every subroutine call.

After the input parameters to the subroutine are prepared, their addresses can be put in a main storage area and the address of the area loaded into register 1, as explained in Section 1.

The location of the first instruction of a subroutine is called its *entry point*. The address of the entry point of a subroutine to be called is loaded into register 15 before the branch to the subroutine. If the subroutine is in the same control section (roughly, a control section is an independent assembly) as the calling routine, the entry point address can be loaded with, say, an instruction such as

LA   15,SUBR

If the subroutine is in a different control section from the calling routine, as is usually the case, the entry point must be defined as an external symbol. The calling routine may define an external address constant as

SUBRAD   DC   V(SUBR)

where SUBR is the symbol used in the subroutine to designate the entry point. The assembler notes this address as an external symbol in the external symbol dictionary prepared with the machine-language program. When the program is prepared for execution by the linkage editor or loader, the actual address of the subroutine entry point is inserted in the location SUBRAD of the calling routine. During execution of the calling routine, this address is available to be loaded into register 15 by the instruction

L   15,SUBRAD

After the entry point address has been loaded, steps 5 and 6, loading the return address and branching, can be accomplished by the single instruction

BALR   14,15

As explained in Section 2, the BALR instruction first loads the first operand, register 14, with the address of the next instruction, then branches to the address given in the second operand, register 15. Since register 15 contains the entry point address of the subroutine, control is passed to the subroutine. Register 14 contains the address of the next instruction in the calling routine; that instruction will be the one first executed after the subroutine returns control to the calling routine.

Responsibilities of the called subroutine

Immediately after gaining control, the subroutine should store the register contents as left by the calling routine. At the entry point of the subroutine, the instruction to accomplish this task is

STM   14,12,12(13)

This instruction stores all registers except register 13 in the area provided by the calling program.

Usually the subroutine follows the STM instruction with

BALR   12,0
USING   *,12

to define an implied base register. Some register other than 12 could, of course, be used. After these instructions have established the addressability of relocatable expressions in the subroutine, the subroutine may save the contents of register 13 by

```
ST    13,SAVØWN+4
```

The sequence of these instructions is important; a programmer varies them only at everyone's peril. Before register 13 can be stored, addressability of the subroutine's register save area must be established. Since establishing that addressability changes the contents of a register, at least that register must be stored in the calling routine's register save area. But all registers 14, 15 and 0–12 may be stored as easily as one with the STM instruction.

If the calling routine loaded the entry point address into register 15, which is not always done, then it might be possible to leave out the BALR and declare register 15 to be the implied base register:

```
SUBR    STM     14,12,12(13)
        USING   SUBR,15
        ST      13,SAVØWN+4
```

While this arrangement is satisfactory for lowest-level subroutines which neither call other subroutines nor call for supervisor services such as input or output, it cannot be safely used in others. Some subroutines and some supervisor services that might be called by SUBR place a "return code" in register 15 indicating success or exceptional conditions in the subroutine; if register 15 is thus not restored, the addressability of relocatable expressions is destroyed.

Return from the subroutine

When the subroutine has done its work and placed all of its results either in locations given in the parameter list by the main program or in register 0, it must return control to the main program. First, however, it must restore the register contents as left by the calling routine. Register 13 is reloaded first, since it is used in the restoring of the other registers. The instruction may be

```
L    13,SAVØWN+4
```

the converse of the instruction that stored register 13. If register 0 does not contain an output from the subroutine, registers 14, 15 and 0–12 may be restored by

```
LM    14,12,12(13)
```

the converse of the STM instruction which preserved the register contents. If register 0 contains an output from the subroutine, it must *not* be restored, but 14, 15, and 1–12 must be restored. This is accomplished by

```
LM    14,15,12(13)
LM    1,12,24(13)
```

Finally, the return instruction itself is

$$\text{BR} \quad 14$$

The unconditional branch transfers control to the return address placed in register 14 by the calling routine.

Of course, only registers which are changed during execution of the subroutine need be restored. If, say, registers 7–12 are unused and unchanged by the subroutine, the register save instruction may be

$$\text{STM} \quad 14,6,12(13)$$

and the corresponding restore instruction would be

$$\text{LM} \quad 14,6,12(13)$$

Although the same number of instructions are executed, execution time is reduced.

5. SUMMARY OF A CALLED PROGRAM'S ACTIONS

In this section we summarize the statements described earlier in this chapter for subroutine linkage. There are two cases: a lowest-level subroutine which does not call on any other subroutines or on any supervisor services, and higher-level subroutines which do call on other subroutines, supervisor service, or both.

Lowest-level subroutine

There are two possibilities in the case of a lowest-level subroutine. If register 15 contains the entry-point address, the statements at the beginning of the subroutine may be

```
subr-name      STM      14,12,12(13)
               USING    subr-name,15
```

If register 15 cannot be counted on to contain the entry-point address, the beginning statements will be

```
subr-name      STM      14,12,12(13)
               BALR     12,0
               USING    *,12
```

After doing its work, the return sequence is either

```
               LM       14,12,12(13)
               BR       14
```

if register 0 does not contain output of the subroutine, or

```
               LM       14,15,12(13)
               LM       1,12,24(13)
               BR       14
```

if register 0 contains a result to be used by the calling routine. The actions are shown below.

```
SUBR    STM    14,12,12(13)          SUBR    STM    14,12,12(13)
        USING  SUBR,15          or           BALR   12,0
                                              USING  *,12
```

Body of subroutine

```
        LM   14,12,12(13)                     LM   14,15,12(13)
        BR   14                   or          LM   1,12,24(13)
                                              BR   14
```

Higher-level subroutine or main program

A higher-level routine should not use register 15 as its implied base register. The linkage statements needed, including those for branching to a subroutine, are given below.

```
A         STM    14,12,12(13)
          BALR   12,0               Any register 2–12 may be used.
          USING  *,12
          ST     13,SAV+4
          LA     13,SAV
          ⋮
          L      15,SUBRAD
          BALR   14,15              Branch to subroutine.
          ⋮                         Continue after return from subroutine.
          L      13,SAV+4
          LM     14,12,12(13)       Or two LM instructions if register 0
          BR     14                    contains output.
SAV       DS     18F
SUBRAD    DC     V(subr)            subr is name of subroutine called by A.
          ⋮
```

Note especially the sequence of the three instructions dealing with register 13. The first stores the contents of register 13 in word 2 of the SAV block. The second (LA) loads the *address* of the SAV block. The third, just before return, reloads the original contents of register 13.

6. EXAMPLES OF COMPLETE SUBROUTINES; PSEUDO-RANDOM NUMBER GENERATION

In the last chapter we discussed the generation of pseudo-random numbers, and showed how the multiplicative congruence method could be incorporated into a program. Here we will show these same statements in a complete subroutine. Then we construct a higher-level subroutine which uses this one, and follow the execution step by step.

RANDØM: a lowest-level subroutine

The subroutine RANDØM shown in Fig. 5–4 computes a pseudo-random number, an integer between -2^{31} and 2^{31}, and leaves the number in register 0. Every successive call on the subroutine yields a new number (at least, for the first 2^{30} calls). There are no input parameters, which is rare among subroutines. Note that registers 14 and 15 are in no way changed inside the subroutine, so they need not be restored.

Fig. 5–4   The subroutine RANDØM

```
RANDØM      STM      14,12,12(13)
            BALR     12,0
            USING    *,12
            L        7,RN
            M        6,=F'65541'
            ST       7,RN
            LR       0,7
            LM       1,12,24(13)
            BR       14
RN          DC       F'8193'
```

RDIGIT: a subroutine using RANDØM

The RDIGIT subroutine shown in Fig. 5–5 yields a random number in a more restricted range. Given a number N as an input parameter, RDIGIT returns a pseudo-random number in the range 0 to $N - 1$, with all these numbers more or less equally likely. The parameter N is to be a binary integer less than 2^{30}. The parameter N is in a main storage location whose address is stored at a location we may call *param-addr*. The address of the location *param-addr* is in register 1, in accord with the normal subroutine linkage, when the subroutine begins execution. The subroutine RDIGIT must use two Load instructions in retrieving the value of N; the first Load instruction loads *param-addr*.

Fig. 5–5   The subroutine RDIGIT

```
RDIGIT      STM      14,12,12(13)
            BALR     12,0
            USING    *,12
            ST       13,SAV+4
            LA       13,SAV
            L        4,0(1)        ADDRESS OF PARAMETER
            L        5,0(4)        DIGIT LIMIT
            L        15,RANDAD
            BALR     14,15
            LPR      7,0           ABSOLUTE VALUE OF RN
            M        4,=F'2'
            MR       4,7
            LR       0,4
            L        13,SAV+4
            LM       14,15,12(13)
            LM       1,12,24(13)
            BR       14
SAV         DS       18F
RANDAD      DC       A(RANDØM)
```

The two instructions

$$
\begin{array}{ll}
\text{L} & \text{15,RANDAD} \\
\text{BALR} & \text{14,15}
\end{array}
$$

are sufficient to call the subroutine RANDØM. When we define RANDAD as an A-type address we are assuming that RANDØM is in the same assembly as RDIGIT. If RANDØM and RDIGIT are assembled separately for later linking, RANDAD must be defined as a V-type address.

When the statement after BALR   14,15 is executed, control has been returned from the subroutine RANDØM, and the output of RANDØM is available in register 0. The scheme used to develop random numbers between 0 and 9 which we described in Chapter 4 is not applicable here, because N might be an odd number. Here we take the absolute value of the random number, yielding a number between 0 and 2^{31}, and then multiply that number by $2*N$. The product is a number between 0 and $2^{32}*N$; the even register of the pair contains an integer between 0 and $N - 1$ inclusive.

Now let us trace the execution of these subroutines. Before execution, we must simulate assembly and loading to the extent of assigning addresses. We assume that RANDØM and RDIGIT are being assembled as part of a larger assembly including perhaps a main program. Let us suppose that RANDØM comes first, and starts at relocatable location 000602 (most likely after some other subroutines),

Fig. 5–6   Subroutines RANDØM **and** RDIGIT **with addresses assigned**

Actual address	Assembled address		Instruction	
00EE22	000602	RANDØM	STM	14,12,12(13)
00EE26	000606		BALR	12,0
			USING	*,12
00EE28	000608		L	7,RN
00EE2C	00060C		M	6,=F'65541'
00EE30	000610		ST	7,RN
00EE34	000614		LR	0,7
00EE36	000616		LM	1,12,24(13)
00EE3A	00061A		BR	14
00EE3C	00061C	RN	DC	F'8193'
00EE40	000620	RDIGIT	STM	14,12,12(13)
00EE44	000624		BALR	12,0
			USING	*,12
00EE46	000626		ST	13,SAV+4
00EE4A	00062A		LA	13,SAV
00EE4E	00062E		L	4,0(1)
00EE52	000632		L	5,0(4)
00EE56	000636		L	15,RANDAD
00EE5A	00063A		BALR	14,15
00EE5C	00063C		LPR	7,0
00EE5E	00063E		M	4,=F'2'
00EE62	000642		MR	4,7
00EE64	000644		LR	0,4
00EE66	000646		L	13,SAV+4
00EE6A	00064A		LM	14,15,12(13)
00EE6E	00064E		LM	1,12,24(13)
00EE72	000652		BR	14
00EE74	000654	SAV	DS	18F
00EEBC	00069C	RANDAD	DC	A(RANDØM)

and that RDIGIT follows immediately. Let us further suppose that in the loading process the entire program is relocated by 00E820. Figure 5–6 shows the assembled and actual loading addresses of each instruction, constant and data area in this segment.

Now let us suppose that the subroutine RDIGIT is being called. At the moment of the call, the contents of relevant information are:

Register 1:   0000E890
Register 13:   0000E848
Register 14:   0000E838
Location 00E890:   0000E844
Location 00E844:   0000000B

The parameter address area is at location 00E890; the parameter itself, at location 00E844 is 0000000B. This is the decimal number 11, so we infer that a random number between 0 and 10 (inclusive) is called for. The computer proceeds as follows.

Instruction	Location changed: new contents	Explanation
STM 14,12,12(13)	Locations 00E854–00E88F: Contents of registers 14–12. For example, 00E854 : 0000E838	Store register contents as left by calling routine, in locations provided by calling
BALR 12,0	Register 12 : 0000EE46	routine.
ST 13,SAV+4	00EE78 : 0000E848	Store register 13 in
LA 13,SAV	Register 13 : 0000EE74	RDIGIT's area.
L 4,0(1)	Register 4 : 0000E844	Address of parameter.
L 5,0(4)	Register 5 : 0000000B	Parameter.
L 15,RANDAD	Register 15 : 0000EE22	Address of RANDØM.
BALR 14,15	Register 14 : 0000EE5C	Return address in RDIGIT. Transfer control to location 00EE22.

Note that at this point the routine which called RDIGIT is suspended, waiting for return. Its register contents are all stored. Subroutine RDIGIT is now also suspended, while RANDØM begins to do its work.

STM 14,12,12(13)	00EE80–00EEBB: Contents of registers 14–12 as left by RDIGIT	
BALR 12,0	Register 12 : 0000EE28	
L 7,RN	Register 7 : 00002001	Decimal 8193 = hexadecimal 00002001

M	6,=F'65541'	Register 6	:	00000000	Decimal 65541
					= hexadecimal
					00010005
		Register 7	:	2001A005	= decimal
					536977413
ST	7,RN	00EE3C	:	2001A005	Replaces 00002001
LR	0,7	Register 0	:	2001A005	
LM	1,12,24(13)	Registers 1–12	:	Restored to	
				contents as	
				they were	
				when RANDØM	
				was entered.	
BR	14				Transfer control to
					location 00EE5C, in
					subroutine RDIGIT.

Note that subroutine RDIGIT is in control again. The net result of subroutine RANDØM was that register 0 now contains 2001A005, as does location 00EE3C (RN).

LPR	7,0	Register 7	:	2001A005	2001A005 is positive.
M	4,=F'2'	Register 4	:	00000000	
		Register 5	:	00000016	
MR	4,7	Register 4	:	00000002	Product in hexadecimal
		Register 5	:	C023C06E	is 2C023C06E.
LR	0,4	Register 0	:	00000002	Output of RDIGIT.
L	13,SAV+4	Register 13	:	0000E848	
LM	14,15,12(13)	Register 14	:	0000E838	
		Register 15	:	Contents	
				left by	
				routine	
				calling	
				RDIGIT.	
LM	1,12,24(13)	Registers 1–12	:	Restored to	
				condition	
				as of	
				entry to	
				RDIGIT.	
BR	14				Transfer to location
					00E838, in calling
					routine.

Both subroutines have done their work. The registers of the calling routine are intact, except that register 0 contains the pseudo-random number 2, the output of RDIGIT.

7. MAIN IDEAS

a.   When a subroutine is called, the registers of the calling routine are stored; they are restored just before return from the subroutine. This gives both calling and called routines freedom to use registers without interference.

b.   By convention, registers 0, 1, 13, 14, and 15 have special use:

Register 0:   output from subroutine
Register 1:   address of area containing parameter addresses
Register 13: address of register save area
Register 14: return address
Register 15: entry point address

The actions of subroutine linkage are primarily those of properly preparing these registers.

c.   When registers are stored at the beginning of a subroutine, contents of registers 14, 15, 0–12 are stored in the area supplied by the calling routine; register 13 is stored in the area supplied by the called routine.

d.   The BR instruction is an unconditional branch to a location whose address is in the register operand. It is used to return control from a subroutine.

e.   The BALR instruction stores the address of the next instruction before branching; if the second operand is 0, no branch takes place. It is used in branching to a subroutine.

f.   The combination of a USING pseudo-operation preceded by a BALR instruction establishes one or more implied base registers.

QUESTIONS FOR REVIEW AND IMAGINATION

1.   Word 3 of subroutine A's register save area is designated to hold the address of the save area provided by the subroutine called by A. The action is not mandatory, but it permits the supervisor to provide in some situations diagnostic information not otherwise available. The address can be stored by expanding the instruction

```
LA      13,SAV
```

of the beginning sequence in a subroutine to the three-instruction sequence

```
LR      2,13
LA      13,SAV
ST      13,8(2)
```

First, simulate the instructions to see precisely what is stored where. Second, modify examples of this chapter to include this convention. Third, analyze where and when the address of the save area provided by subroutine B is stored, if A calls B, and B, in turn, calls C.

2. How would you expect the actions of the instructions

$$\text{BALR} \quad 12,0 \quad \text{and} \quad \text{BALR} \quad 12,12$$

to differ, if at all?

3. There is a BAL (Branch and Link) instruction which has the same action as BALR except that the branch address is given in base + index + displacement form according to the RX instruction format. The BAL instruction can be used to branch to a subroutine when it is convenient to express the entry point to the subroutine in base + index + displacement form, especially in symbolic form. When and why would you branch to a subroutine by a BAL instruction?

4. Routine A may call three different subroutines, but may transmit via register 13 the same register save area for all three subroutines. How does this work?

5. Give reasons why it would be awkward for routine A to save all of its own register contents before branching to subroutine B and then restore the registers after return from B. Is it even possible? If so, how? If not, why not?

6. Would it be feasible for subroutine B, called by routine A, to store all of A's register contents in an area provided by subroutine B?

7. Normally, subroutine B stores the contents of register 13 of the calling routine in word 2 of B's register save area. What difficulties would be encountered if register 13 were saved at a location SAV13 defined by B apart from its register save area?

8. When the supervisor interrupts a program being executed, it must store the program's register contents. Is it safe for the supervisor to store them in the area addressed by the current contents of register 13? What must the supervisor do?

9. Suppose register 11 contains a base address. Show several ways of loading register 12 with an address 4096 greater than the address in register 11. Can it be done with an LA instruction?

10. In the example subroutine RANDØM, what are the base register, index register, and displacement assembled in the instruction below?

$$\text{L} \quad 7,\text{RN}$$

11. In the traced execution of RANDØM shown in Section 6, just after the LR   0,7 instruction, what are the contents of register 4?

12. After the execution of RDIGIT shown in Section 6, the number RN is changed to 2001A005. If RDIGIT is called a second time, what number will RANDØM return? What number will RDIGIT return?

13. Rewrite RANDØM, taking advantage of the fact (or assumption) that register 15 contains the entry point address of RANDØM.

14. In the subroutine RDIGIT, the address of RANDØM is defined as an A-type address, which can only be done if RANDØM and RDIGIT are assembled during the

same execution of the assembler. Could the address of RANDØM be loaded into register 15 in RDIGIT by the instruction given below?

```
        LA    15,RANDØM
```

Does the order of assembly make any difference?

15. If the instruction

```
        L    13,SAV+4
```

near the end of subroutine RDIGIT were accidentally left out, what would be the consequences? To what address would the subroutine return? Then what?

16. If, in RDIGIT,

```
    USING   *,12    and    BALR   12,0
```

appeared in this order instead of in the conventional order, how would you expect the error to show up?

17. Write a lowest-level subroutine which will return the cube of its binary integer argument. Assume that the result will not overflow one register.

18. Write a higher-level subroutine that will, given parameters A and B, return $A^3 + B^3$. Use the cube subroutine described in Problem 17.

19. Any register from 2 to 12 is available for use as a base register. It does not matter much which is used. One principle is that a number of instructions, such as Multiply and Divide, use register pairs; so by using register 12 as base register, we preserve as many register pairs for use by the program as possible. Think of other considerations that might influence the choice of a base register.

20. What is the difference in effect among the instructions

```
        LA      4,=A(TENNIS)
        LA      4,TENNIS
        L       4,=A(TENNIS)
        L       4,TENNIS
```

REFERENCES

IBM System/360 and System/370 Bibliography, GA22-6822, IBM Corporation. Listing of IBM manuals by subject, system and number, with abstracts. The source for finding your way to the right manual.

IBM OS/360 Operating System Supervisor Services and Macro Instructions, GC28-6646, IBM Corporation. The detailed reference manual.

IBM System/360 Operating System Introduction, GC28-6534, IBM Corporation. Overview of the operating system, with some discussion of subroutine management and linkage techniques.

OS Assembler Language, GC28-6514, or *OS/VS and DOS/VS Assembler Language*, GC33-4010, IBM Corporation. Reference on the USING and DRØP statements.

OS/VS Supervisor Services and Macro Instructions, GC27-6979, IBM Corporation. Similarly for OS/VS Systems.

Stone, Harold S., *Introduction to Computer Organization and Data Structures* (New York: McGraw-Hill, 1972). An overview of subroutines, coroutines, and parameter passing.

Appendix A, on linking assembler language routines with Fortran routines.

Chapter 6

Conversions; Constants and Housekeeping in Assembler Language

In this chapter we discuss a number of matters. After studying this chapter and learning some details about local configuration and procedures, the reader should be able to assemble and run complete programs with the help of subroutines to perform input and output. The programs the reader could write will be of a fairly trivial nature, but to see his way completely through even a minor problem should contribute to his understanding of the processes.

The material on constant and storage definition includes a great amount of detail. The reader should not expect to remember all of it before he has used the material extensively. While studying this chapter, he should try to remember the most important features of constant and storage definition, and prepare to retrieve additional details as he needs them.

1. CONVERSIONS

When numeric data are read by the IBM System/360 or 370 from a card, they are coded in the EBCDIC or zoned decimal code. We cannot perform meaningful arithmetic on data in this form; instead, we must convert the data to packed decimal or binary form and perform our arithmetic on these representations. Then, if we wish to print or punch the results in readable form, we must convert them to EBCDIC form.

In the IBM System/360 or 370, the conversions can be done by single instructions. We shall consider four instructions which convert as follows:

PACK:	EBCDIC to packed decimal
CVB:	packed decimal to binary
CVD:	binary to packed decimal
UNPK:	packed decimal to EBCDIC

The strategy of the use of the instructions is shown in Fig. 6–1.

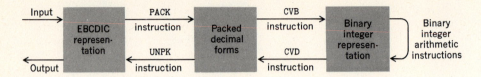

Fig. 6-1 The strategy of use of conversion instructions.

The PACK instruction

The PACK instruction converts a string of bytes, 1 to 16 bytes long, from the EBCDIC or zoned decimal format to a string, also 1 to 16 bytes long, in the packed decimal format. Both operands are in main storage, so the instruction is of SS type. The second operand specifies the source string, the bytes to be converted; the first operand specifies the destination, the location of the packed decimal representation. Each operand is of variable length, and the lengths need not be the same. Therefore the length suboperand portion of the instruction is divided into two parts: a four-bit $L1$, the length of the first operand string, and a four-bit $L2$, the length of the second operand string. As explained in Chapter 3, the number entered in each length field is one less than the actual length of the string. If the instruction contains an $L1$ of 2 and an $L2$ of 5, a six-byte EBCDIC string will be converted into a three-byte packed decimal string. In assembler language, however, we give the actual lengths. For example,

$$\text{PACK} \quad \text{A}(8),\text{INP}(6)$$

will cause a six-byte string starting at INP to be converted to packed decimal form; the packed decimal form will be stored in eight bytes, starting at A.

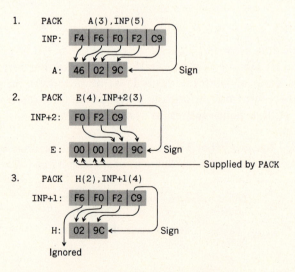

Fig. 6-2 Execution of PACK instructions.

The PACK itself acts as follows. The operands are processed from right to left. The upper four bits of the rightmost byte of the second operand are assumed to contain a representation of the sign of the number, and are moved to the low-order bit positions of the rightmost byte of the first operand. After that, the low-order four bits of each byte in the second operand string are packed into consecutive four-bit groups, made up of both lower and upper portions of bytes, in the first operand string. Zeros are filled or padded into the leftmost bytes of the first operand string if the second operand is too short to supply data to fill the first operand string. On the other hand, if the length of the first operand string is too small to accommodate all the digits from the second operand, the remaining digits are ignored. Figure 6–2 gives several examples illustrating how the PACK instruction is executed.

The UNPK (**UNPacK**) instruction

We next consider the UNPK instruction. The instruction UNPK (or UNPacK) is the converse of the PACK instruction. Also of SS type, it changes a string of packed decimal data specified in the *second* operand into a string of zoned decimal bytes, and stores them, starting at the location given in the first operand. Lengths of each operand are specified in the instruction.

During execution of the UNPK instruction, the strings are processed from right to left. Digits, that is, four-bit groups from the second operand, are expanded into full bytes. The upper four bits of each byte are filled with 1111 except for the rightmost byte, whose upper four bits are filled by the sign of the packed decimal string. If necessary, the packed decimal string is expanded (for purposes of conversion, but not altered in main storage) by adding zeros on the left before con-

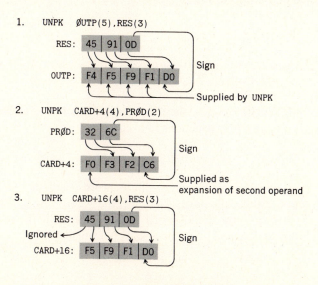

Fig. 6–3 Execution of UNPK instructions.

version. On the other hand, if the length of the first operand string is too small to accommodate all the digits from the packed decimal string, the high-order digits are ignored. Figure 6–3 illustrates the execution of the UNPK instruction.

The CVB (ConVert to Binary) instruction

The CVB (ConVert to Binary) instruction converts a number from the packed decimal to binary integer form. Since binary integer arithmetic is performed in registers, the binary integer result is left in a register. The packed decimal source operand is located in main storage, so the instruction is of RX type. The second operand is the packed decimal source, the first operand is the register to contain the result. The packed decimal source operand is assumed to be exactly eight bytes long and to begin on a double word boundary. The low-order four bits of the packed decimal string are interpreted as a sign: 1010, 1100, 1110, and 1111 (A, C, E and F in hexadecimal) are recognized as plus, and 1011 and 1101 (B and D) as minus. If a minus sign is found, the result is, of course, in 2's complement form.

Some examples follow.

	Source	Result
CVB 3,G	00000000 0000025C	00000019

Both source and result are representations of the decimal number 25.

CVB 4,H	00000000 0000025D	FFFFFFE7

Both are representations of the decimal number −25.

The CVD (ConVert to Decimal) instruction

The CVD (ConVert to Decimal) instruction is the converse of the CVB instruction. Also of RX type, it converts a binary integer addressed by *R1* into a packed decimal number in a double word addressed by *B2*, *X2*, and *D2*.

With operands of 3,G and 4,H, the CVD instruction would exactly reverse the action performed by the CVB instructions above.

Programming

Since the CVB and CVD instructions assume double-word operands in main storage, the PACK instruction will usually have a first operand whose length is 8 and whose address is defined to be on a double-word boundary, even if the number to be converted is known to be small. A typical sequence might be

```
        PACK    DBLE(8),INP(6)
        CVB     4,DBLE
```

Conversely, when converting results to the EBCDIC form for output, a typical sequence might be

```
CVD     7,DB
UNPK    ØUTP+16(4),DB(8)
```

One further attribute of the UNPK instruction should be noted. The rightmost byte of the converted string *will* have a sign. When the characters are printed, all digits except the rightmost one will print as ordinary digits. If the rightmost digit is 1–9, with a plus sign, one of the letters A–I will be printed. If the rightmost digit is 1–9 with a minus sign, one of the letters J–R will be printed. If the rightmost digit is 0 with either sign, a blank will be printed. There are several ways of avoiding this; we shall mention some in Chapters 11 and 14.

2. DEFINITION OF CONSTANTS IN ASSEMBLER LANGUAGE

The statement that defines a constant in IBM OS or OS/VS assembler language is of the form

Name	Operation	Operands
Optional constant name	DC	One or more operands separated by commas

Each statement may define one or more constants, occupying consecutive locations in main storage. Each operand may have the following operand subfields, *not* separated by commas or blanks:

a. duplication factor, optional

b. type of constant, required

c. modifiers, optional

d. value of the constant or constants, required

Each operand subfield will be described below.

The duplication factor

If a duplication factor is present in an operand defining a constant, the constant defined will be duplicated in successive locations as many times as this factor specifies. In a DC statement the duplication factor may be an unsigned decimal integer or, when the factor is enclosed in parentheses, another kind of absolute expression. Any symbol used in the expression must have been previously defined. Thus, the operands

```
2F'19'
(X'E')F'19'
(G)F'19'
```

where G is a previously defined absolute symbol, are valid operands including duplication factors. A duplication factor of zero is permitted: *no* constant is assembled, but boundary alignment is performed according to the type of constant, as will be explained below. The absence of a duplication factor is equivalent to the presence of a duplication factor of 1.

Modifiers

The definition of constants may be modified by length modifiers, scale modifiers, and exponent modifiers. The modifiers are optional. We shall ignore the scale and exponent modifiers, and discuss only the length modifiers. The length modifier defines the length in bytes of the constant; it is written Ln, where n is given as either an unsigned decimal integer or an absolute expression in parentheses. Any symbol used in an expression defining length must have been previously defined. Thus in an operand of a DC statement, length modifiers L9 and L(G+4) where G is a previously defined symbol, are valid; in a literal, L(G+4) is not valid.

The *length attribute* of a named constant is kept by the assembler in a table. The length is either set by the length modifier in the constant definition or is set to a default value. Permitted length and default lengths for each type of constant are shown in Fig. 6–4. In SS-type instructions, the length of each symbolic operand may be left unspecified; in this case, the assembler inserts the length attribute associated with the symbol. For example, the statement

```
BSQ     DC      CL9'123456789'
```

defines BSQ to have a length attribute of 9. Therefore the assembler-language statement

```
PACK    GQ(5),BSQ
```

is equivalent to

```
PACK    GQ(5),BSQ(9)
```

Similarly,

```
MVC     BSQ,XH
```

is equivalent to

```
MVC     BSQ(9),XH
```

but in the instruction

```
MVC     GQC,BSQ
```

the length will be supplied according to the length attribute of GQC.

Lengths can also be stated in bits instead of in bytes, but we will not explore this possibility in this book.

Type and value of constant

The type of each constant or set of constants is given as a single alphabetic character. We will discuss the following types:

C	character	E	floating-point, single precision
X	hexadecimal	D	floating-point, double precision
B	binary	P	packed decimal
F	fixed-point (normally full word)	A	address
H	half-word	V	external symbol address

How values are given in assembler-language operands and the representation of the constant as placed in main storage must be discussed for each type separately.

Alignment

Some types of constants are expected to be used by certain classes of instructions, and therefore the constants are aligned by the assembler on an appropriate boundary. The conventions are summarized in Fig. 6–4. H-type constants are expected to be used in half-word instructions such as LH, AH, SH, MH, and therefore each H-type constant is aligned to a half-word boundary. F-type constants are expected to be used in instructions like L, A, M, D, LM, so each F-type constant is aligned to a full-word boundary. E-type and D-type constants are expected to be used by single- and double-precision floating-point instructions, respectively, so they are aligned on full- and double-word boundaries. Address constants of A- and V-types are aligned on full-word boundaries, but constants of other types (X, B, C, and P) are begun at the first available byte of storage. However, *if a length modifier is specified* in the definition of *any* constant, boundary alignment is suppressed, and the constant begun at the first available byte of storage. Ways of forcing alignment are explained in Section 3.

Fig. 6–4   Summary of attributes of constants

Type	Alignment	Length range	Implied length	Specified by	Constants per operand	Truncation or padding
C	Byte	1–256	As in value	Characters	One	Right
X	Byte	1–256	As in value	Hexadecimal digits	One	Left
B	Byte	1–256	As in value	Binary digits	One	Left
F	Word	1–8	4	Decimal digits	Multiple	Left
H	Half-word	1–8	2	Decimal digits	Multiple	Left
E	Word	1–8	4	Decimal digits	Multiple	Right
D	Double-word	1–8	8	Decimal digits	Multiple	Right
P	Byte	1–16	As in value	Decimal digits	Multiple	Left
A	Word	3–4	4	Relocatable expression	Multiple	Left
A	Word	1–8	4	Absolute expression	Multiple	Left
V	Word	3–4	4	Relocatable symbol	Multiple	Left

Padding and truncation

In some constant definitions, such as character (C) and hexadecimal (X), if length is not specified, it is determined by the length of the constant value given. For example,

C'12345'   will define a constant whose length is 5,
X'123456'   will define a constant whose length is 3, and
X'0000123456'   will define a constant whose length is 5.

For other types a specific length is assumed if none is stated. For example, F'19' defines a constant whose length is 4.

If a specific length is assumed or if a length modifier for any constant is given, this length takes precedence over the length that may be implied by the length of the string of characters determining the constant. If, for example, we define CL5'123', we are defining a constant of length 5, whose first three characters are 123. Padding of two character blanks (hexadecimal 4040) is supplied by the assembler to fill the last two bytes of the five-byte constant. On the other hand, CL5'123456' also defines a five-byte constant. Not all the characters given can be stored, so the 6 is lost. The constant will contain the characters 12345. Padding or truncation, whichever is necessary, will take place at the same end of the constant. Character constants are padded or truncated on the right, almost all others on the left. However, special explanations are necessary for the floating-point constants.

We now discuss the types of constants one at a time.

Character constants (C)

Any of the 256 eight-bit patterns may be entered into a character constant. Special arrangements must be made for apostrophes and ampersands desired within character constants: two apostrophes or two ampersands are written in the assembler-language statement wherever one is desired in the character constant. For example, C'''&&' defines a character constant of length 2; the characters in the two bytes will be '&. As mentioned above, the length of the constant is determined by the number of characters specifying its value unless a length modifier is given; in either case, 256 is the upper limit on the length of the constant. Each character is entered into one byte of main storage, exactly as written in the value portion of the constant definition. Padding with blanks or truncation is done at the right.

Only one character constant per operand may be defined, though a duplication factor may be used. For example,

        REPEAT   DC   3CL5'NØWIS'

will generate the constant NØWISNØWISNØWIS.

Hexadecimal constants (X)

A hexadecimal constant is specified as a sequence of hexadecimal digits which are entered into main storage two digits per byte. If no length modifier is specified, the length of the constant is what is required to accommodate the digits. If, say, n digits are given, n even, the length of the constant is $n/2$ bytes. If n is odd, the length of the constant is $(n+1)/2$ bytes, with 0's occupying the four high-order bit positions of the leftmost byte. If a length modifier is specified, padding with zeros or truncation takes place on the left. The length of a hexadecimal constant may be from 1 to 256 bytes. Only one constant may be specified per operand, but a duplication factor may be used.

It is often convenient to use a hexadecimal constant to set a pattern of particular bits in a word. Care must be taken, however, to ensure proper boundary alignment if the constant is to be used as an operand in instructions that require full-word, half-word or double-word operands. Forcing alignment will be discussed in Section 3.

For example,

```
CPX   DC   X'A1245'
```

defines a three-byte constant whose hexadecimal digits are 0A1245.

```
PQR   DC   XL2'A1245'
```

defines a two-byte constant 1245.

```
STUV  DC   XL5'A1245'
```

defines a five-byte constant 00000A1245.

Binary constants (B)

A binary constant is written as a string of 1's and 0's. The 1's and 0's are entered into main storage, eight to a byte, so that each 1 or 0 defines a bit in a binary number. If no length modifier is specified, the length of the constant is just sufficient to hold the bits written. Padding with zero bits is done on the left. If a length modifier is specified, padding with zeros or truncation takes place on the left. The maximum length is 256 bytes. Only one constant can be defined per operand, but a duplication factor may be used.

For example,

```
BITTE  DC   B'10110'
```

defines BITTE as a one-byte constant whose bit pattern is 00010110.

```
BIT2   DC   BL2'10110'
```

defines BIT2 as a two-byte constant whose bit pattern is 0000000000010110.

Fixed-point constants (F and H)

A fixed-point constant is written as a decimal number, which may be signed and may include a decimal point. It may also be followed by a decimal exponent of the form E*n* where *n* is a decimal integer with or without sign. The number is adjusted by the power of 10 specified by the exponent, then converted to binary. The integer portion of the resulting binary number is the constant stored in main storage. The implied length is 4 for an F-type constant and 2 for an H-type constant; boundary alignment is made so that an F-type constant begins on a full-word boundary, an H-type constant on a half-word boundary. Either type may be declared by a length modifier to have a length of from one to eight bytes; if the

Fig. 6–5   Examples of F- and H-type constants

Assembler language statement	Constants generated
NINETN DC F'19'	Full-word binary integer, representing 19 (00000000 00000000 00000000 00010011).
BIØ DC FL1'513'	One-byte constant 00000001, formed by truncating the binary equivalent of 513 to eight bits.
G34 DC 2F'0'	Two full-word constants containing zeros.
PARAMS DC F'20,−17,371'	Three full-word binary integers: binary equivalents of 20, −17(2's complement), 371.
MAG DC FL3'1.234E2'	A three-byte binary integer: binary equivalent of $1.23 \times 10^2 = 123$ (00000000 00000000 01111011).

length modifier is given, no boundary alignment is performed. Truncation and padding are made on the left. Multiple constants, separated by commas, can be defined with one operand; a duplication factor may also be used. Figure 6–5 shows some examples of F- and H-type constants.

Floating-point constants (E and D)

The value of a floating-point constant is written precisely the same as the value of a fixed-point (F or H) constant. The value is converted to binary and expressed in the standard floating-point form described briefly in Chapter 3 and in more detail in Chapter 13. If an E-type constant has no length modifier, it has an implied length of four bytes and is aligned on a full-word boundary. If a D-type constant has no length modifier, it has an implied length of eight bytes and is aligned on a double-word boundary. If either has a length modifier, the length must be from one to eight bytes; no boundary alignment is made.

Since the numbers in floating-point form are normalized, any extra zeros of padding are added on the right; similarly, any digits that must be lost because of lack of space are the less significant digits that are lost from the right. Multiple constants in one operand and duplication factors may be used. Examples are:

```
FLØNE      DC   E'1'
PI         DC   D'3.14159265'
FLLIST     DC   E'2.6E−4,7.94136,−1000.27E+5'
LISTØNES   DC   6D'1.0'
```

Packed decimal constants (P)

The value specified in a packed decimal constant is a decimal number; sign and decimal point are optional. No exponent is allowed. The decimal point does not affect the constant in any way, and is permitted only as a possible help to reading and understanding the program. The number is put into the packed decimal form for placement in main storage.

If no length modifier is given, the length is determined as the minimum required to hold the digits given. If n digits are given, n odd, the constant will be

$(n + 1)/2$ bytes long. If n is even, the constant will be $(n + 2)/2$ bytes long; the high-order four bits will be padded with zeros. If a length modifier is given, truncation or padding is on the left. In any case, the length must be from 1 to 16 bytes. Multiple constants may be defined in one operand, and duplication factors may also be used. The following are valid packed decimal constant definitions, which cause definition and loading into storage of the corresponding constants, shown in hexadecimal:

```
PDQ        DC    P'-357'                 357D
TAXRATE    DC    PL3'.26'                00026C
PERCENTS   DC    PL2'78.3,22,-.3'        783C022C003D
PHØNE      DC    2PL3'0'                 00000C00000C
DEPØSIT    DC    P'999999.99'            099999999C
```

Address constants (A and V)

An address constant is a main storage address contained in a constant. Unlike other constants, whose values are enclosed in apostrophes, address constants are enclosed in parentheses. Several addresses may be specified in one operand; they are separated by commas and the whole list is enclosed in parentheses.

An A-type constant may be specified as an absolute expression or as a relocatable expression (see definitions, Chapter 3). A V-type constant is the value of an *external symbol*—a relocatable symbol which is external to the current control section. The V-type address constants are used for branching to locations in other control sections, not for addressing data.

The assembler constructs the address of an absolute expression in an A-type constant in a straightforward manner. For a relocatable expression, the assembler defers actual filling in of the address until the program is loaded, since the actual value of the constant is dependent on the relocation factor. The address of an external symbol is partially filled in by the linkage editor or loader, which must find the symbol in another control section. Both the control section which *uses* the external symbol and the control section which defines it are entered into the *load module,* the module of programs and subroutines ready to be loaded together. Filling in relative addresses of external symbols is merely part of the linkage process; as with A-type constants, the final filling in of the V-type constant will occur with the loading of the program.

Implied length of an address constant is four bytes; the constant is aligned on a full-word boundary. A length modifier of 3 or 4 for a relocatable expression or 1 to 8 for an absolute expression may be given, in which case no boundary alignment takes place.

The following are valid address constants.

```
GSUBAD     DC    V(READATA)
AREAD      DC    A(AREA+40)
BASEREG    DC    A(BEGIN+4096,BEGIN+2*4096)
```

Literals

Literals were mentioned briefly in Chapter 3; they provide us the facility to define constants in assembler-language statements that translate into machine-language instructions. The duplication factor, type, modifiers, and value are written as in definition of other constants, but they are preceded by an equals sign. They can be used where we would use a main-storage operand *but not* as a destination field of an instruction. The assembler understandably objects if we try to define a constant and store something else there at the same time! There are other minor restrictions on the use of literals:

1. A literal may have only one operand, unlike a DC statement which may have several. The literal can define several constants, as in the instructions

    ```
    MVC     B(20),=5CL4'1234'
    LM      REG4,REG5,=F'-1,-879'
    ```

    but cannot define the equivalent of

    ```
    G       DC      F'25',XL4'AC8'
    ```

2. Duplication factors and length modifiers in literals may be only positive decimal integers; other self-defining terms and symbols, even if previously defined, are not allowed. A duplication factor of zero is not allowed.

All constants defined by literals are put by the assembler in a *literal pool*, usually at the very end of the program. The *address* of each literal is coded in base-and-displacement form in the machine-language instruction which refers to it.

Literals are arranged within the literal pool so as to respect as many boundary alignments as necessary. All 8-byte (and multiples thereof) literals are located first in the literal pool and aligned on a double-word boundary. Then come all 4-byte (and odd multiples thereof) literals, which are aligned on word boundaries. Then all 2-byte (and odd multiples thereof) literals, each aligned on a half-word boundary. Finally come all literals of an odd number of bytes, which presumably used no particular alignment. Therefore, we can safely use an instruction like

```
L       REG3,=X'FFFF0000'
```

since the literal will be aligned on a word boundary as required.

One example of the use of a literal is the definition of a parameter address block. We saw in Section 5.1 the definition of a block

```
ADDS    DC      A(T)
        DC      A(U)
        DC      A(V)
        DC      A(W)
```

We may note now that exactly the same definition could be made in the single statement

```
ADDS    DC      A(T,U,V,W)
```

However, the combination of this statement *and* the instruction which loads its address

    LA   1,ADDS

can be replaced by

    LA   1,=A(T,U,V,W)

3. THE DS (DEFINE STORAGE) AND EQU (EQUATE SYMBOL) STATEMENTS

The DS statement

The DS or Define Storage statement directs the assembler to allocate storage but not to put a constant in the space. By using DS statements, we can name and reserve work areas.

The format of the DS statement is identical to the format of the DC statement; the same operands and suboperands are used, with the same meanings. However, two differences must be noted. The maximum lengths for character (C) and hexadecimal (X) data types are 65,535 bytes in DS statements, rather than the 256-byte maximum in DC statements.

The second difference between the two statements is the central one. In the DC statement, the value of the constant or constants is a required suboperand; in the DS statement the value is optional, and usually omitted. If the value is omitted, the length of the storage space to be reserved is determined by the implied length or by a length modifier. The implied length of a C, X, B, or P field is one byte. However, if a constant-value suboperand is used, the length of the field is determined in exactly the same way as in a DC statement. No constant is assembled, but the constant specified governs the length assigned.

Forcing alignment

Unless a length modifier is used, a DC or DS operand of types F, H, E, D, A, or V forces alignment of the constant or storage area to the beginning of the next half-word, full word, or double word. Storage space skipped over to align boundaries is not counted as part of the length of the constant or storage area, and this space is not set to anything in particular.

The programmer defines his constant or storage with desired boundaries in mind. Often he can choose the type of constant or storage area that will best meet his needs. Sometimes, however, he may wish to express a certain kind of constant but need a boundary alignment other than that provided automatically with his choice of constant type. The programmer can then make effective use of the DS statement with a duplication factor of 0. Such a statement performs boundary alignment and may attach a name to a location, but does not reserve storage. For example, a programmer who wishes to use a full-word constant

Fig. 6–6 Constant and storage area definition

Assembler language statement		Location	Length attribute
	DS 0H	000130	
MULT	DS X'4005'	000130	2
SAV	DS 18F	000134	4
ENDCHAR	DC C'END'	00017C	3
ASTER	DS CL2'**'	00017F	2
ZERØAR	DC 20F'0'	000184	4
ØUT	DC 132C''	0001D4	1
ØUT2	DC CL133''	000258	133
DBL	DS D	0002E0	8
GSUBAD	DC V(READATA)	0002E8	4
PARAMAD	DC A(G,W,K−4)	0002EC	4

whose hexadecimal digits are FFFF0000 may write

$$\text{DS}\quad 0F$$
$$\text{CØNFØ}\quad \text{DC}\quad \text{X'FFFF0000'}$$

The symbol CØNFØ will be aligned on a full-word boundary.

Figure 6–6 shows the storage allocation of a series of constants and storage areas. Note that the length attribute of a constant or storage area is independent of the duplication factor. Storage is allocated, of course, for all duplicates made according to the duplication factor, but the length attribute as listed in the symbol table refers to just one copy. For example, the instruction using implied length

$$\text{MVC}\quad \text{ØUT,ASTER}$$

is equivalent to

$$\text{MVC}\quad \text{ØUT(1),ASTER}$$

Storage space is skipped for boundary alignment before SAV, ZERØAR, and DBL.

The EQU statement

The EQU statement is used to define a symbol by equating it to an expression. The general form is

Name	Operation	Operand
A symbol	EQU	An expression

The expression may be either relocatable or absolute; the symbol equated will be relocatable or absolute accordingly. All symbols in the expression must be previously defined. The symbol has the same length attribute and value as the expression; the length attribute of an expression is the length of its first term, with the convention that the location-counter symbol * and the self-defining terms each have a length attribute of 1.

For example,

$$\text{REG4}\quad \text{EQU}\quad 8$$

equates the symbol REG4 to 8; REG4 can be used as a register address in any instruction. Also

                    DRBACK   EQU   ØUT+25

defines DRBACK as equivalent to the address ØUT+25. The length attribute of DRBACK
is the same as the length attribute of ØUT. ØUT must have been defined, i.e., have
appeared as the name in a statement, before the definition of DRBACK.

4. ASSEMBLER CONTROL STATEMENTS

The statements described in this section are all pseudo-operations: they control
the assembler but do not correspond to instructions or constants which are assembled into the object program.

   The first one we discuss is the START statement. It is optional; it attaches a
name to the control section and supplies an initial value to the location counter.
The general form is

Name	Operation	Operand
A symbol or blank	START	A self-defining term or blank

If a symbol is given in the name field, that symbol is the name given to the control
section. If an operand is given, it is used as the initial setting of the location counter. If the operand is blank, the location counter is initially set to zero.

A word should be said here about control sections. A control section is a block of coding that can be relocated independently of other blocks. An assembly, one execution
of the assembler, is composed of one or more control sections. We will not describe
here the complications of assembling more than one control section in the same assembly;
the reader who wishes to define more than one control section per assembly should consult one of the assembler language manuals for details. Sometimes, for example, in
speaking of V-type constants, we mention symbols, etc., in other control sections; the
reader may think of these as symbols in control sections created in different assemblies.

   We next mention the listing control statement, TITLE. The general form is

Name	Operation	Operand
Name or blank	TITLE	A string of up to 100 characters enclosed in apostrophes

The name, if entered, may be of from one to four alphabetic and numeric characters in any combination. These characters will be punched in columns 73–76
of all cards of the object deck (if any) produced by the assembly. The string
specified in the operand field is printed at the top of every page of the listing of
the program. At any time in a program a new TITLE statement may give a new
title for the pages that follow, but only the first TITLE statement may have an
entry in the name field.

An ØRG statement may reset the location counter at any time. The ØRG statement must
not have a name; its operand is a relocatable expression or blank. If a relocatable expres-

sion is given, the location counter is set to the value of the expression; all symbols in the expression must have been previously defined. The value in the location counter may be reduced by the ØRG statement, but it must not be reduced to less than the initial value in the control section. If it has been reduced, say for the purpose of redefining an area, it can be restored to its highest previous value by an ØRG without operand.

The LTØRG statement causes all the literals used since the last LTØRG to be assembled in a new literal pool. The LTØRG statement has no operands; it may have a name, which is associated with the first byte of the literal pool. The beginning of the literal pool is aligned on a double-word boundary.

When two completely identical literals are used in the range of a LTØRG, only one is assembled. For example, =X'FC' and =X'FC' used in two different statements are identical, and only the first is stored; however, ='FC' and =B'11111100' are not considered identical although they define the same constant; hence both are stored. The literals =A(*-4) and =A(*-4) used in two different statements are not identical, since the value of * will be different in each statement. Therefore both literals must be stored.

The LTØRG statement is not usually necessary in a program. If it is omitted, the literals are assembled automatically at the end of the program. However, if the length of the program and the definition of implied base registers are such that literals assembled at the end of the program cannot be addressed in the instructions in which they are used, a LTØRG statement can force assembly of the literals at a location at which they can be addressed.

The END statement is required as the last statement in an assembly; it signifies the end to the assembler. The END statement has no name, but may have an operand. The operand is a relocatable expression, identifying the location at which execution of the edited and loaded program should begin. The operand therefore should be specified only in main programs, never in subroutines.

One further kind of card should be mentioned. A card with an asterisk (*) in column 1 is a *remarks card;* a remarks card can be inserted in an assembler-language program and not affect assembly. It is reproduced in the output listing for the edification of those reading the program. Remarks, either on remarks cards or in remarks fields of assembler-language statement cards, should be sprinkled liberally throughout a program to help in its documentation.

5. SAVE AND RETURN MACROS

There are standard sequences of instructions that are used often. General patterns of some of these sequences are defined in what is called the *macro library*. A pattern, or *macro*, can be incorporated into a user's program at an appropriate place, with parameters particular to the user's program inserted into the pattern if necessary. The user writes a *macro-instruction*, which has an optional name, an operation code which is the macro name, and operands which are parameters to the macro. The assembler inserts the instructions (and perhaps constants and other assembler-language statements) of the macro pattern, incorporating the parameters given, into the program in place of the macro-instruction. A sequence like this is sometimes called an *open subroutine*—to distinguish it from a *closed* subroutine (the customary kind), which is self-contained, and is entered by a branch from the current sequence of instructions.

We describe here two macros which simplify linkage at the beginning and end of a subroutine. The first is the SAVE macro. The general form of the SAVE macro-instruction (we ignore some optional parameters) is

Name	Operation	Operand
A symbol or blank	SAVE	(*r1,r2*)

The suboperands *r1* and *r2* are absolute expressions used as register addresses. Note the parentheses enclosing the suboperands. The assembler-language coding which replaces the macro-instruction in the assembled program is called the *expansion of the macro*, or *macro-expansion*. The expansion of the SAVE macro-instruction is a single STM (STore Multiple) instruction which stores registers *r1* to *r2* in the appropriate words of the register save area. The advantage of the SAVE macro-instruction is that the programmer need not compute the correct displacement in the STM instruction; the assembler does the job. For example,

```
SUBR  SAVE  (14,12)
```

has the expansion

```
SUBR  STM   14,12,12(13)
```

The macro-instruction

```
      SAVE  (2,5)
```

has the expansion

```
      STM   2,5,28(13)
```

The second macro we discuss here is named RETURN. The form of the RETURN macro-instruction is (again ignoring some optional parameters)

Name	Operation	Operand
Symbol or blank	RETURN	(*r1,r2*)

where the subparameters enclosed in parentheses are, as in a SAVE macro-instruction, absolute expressions interpreted as register addresses. The expansion of the RETURN macro-instruction is an LM (Load Multiple) instruction restoring registers *r1* to *r2* from the register save area, and the instruction BR   14 which returns control to the calling routine. For example

```
      RETURN (14,12)
```

has the expansion

```
      LM    14,12,12(13)
      BR    14
```

The macro-instruction

$$\text{RETURN} \quad (2,4)$$

has the expansion

```
LM      2,4,28(13)
BR      14
```

6. JOB CONTROL

When a user of the IBM System/360 wants the computer to do work for him he submits a *job*. A job is a series of interdependent steps; it is sealed off by the operating system from interaction with other jobs. The operating system is a set of programs and subroutines that controls the computer and the data and programs submitted to the computer. Some parts of the operating system remain in the computer's main storage at all times, controlling all input and output (among other tasks).

The operating system deals with programs and data sets. A *data set* is a set of data treated as an entity by the operating system. The data set is composed of records. The individual records are read or written on command, but the data set is the unit made available to the user for processing of his program.

A user submits in his job the program or programs he wants run, the data set he wants used by his programs, and some *job control statements* that direct the operating system in the organization of processing. Of course, some of the programs and data sets may be already available to the operating system, often on direct-access devices; the user has only to request these programs and data sets by name in his job control statements.

The job control statements give the operating system directions about how to process a job: which programs to run, which data sets to make available to each program, and whom to charge for the run. The job control statements for a series of jobs are submitted in what is called the *main job stream;* some data sets may also be submitted in the main job stream.

The job control statements are punched into cards which naturally are called *job control cards*. The job control statements are prepared in a special language called *job control language*. There are only a few different kinds of statements in the job control language; we describe them briefly. Every job begins with a JØB *statement* which names the job and identifies the user. An EXEC *statement* calls for execution of a program, or of a catalogued procedure, which we will soon describe in greater detail. Definition and assignment of a data set are accomplished by a DD (Data Definition) *statement:* the DD statement names and defines one data set. There is one further type of card: a *delimiter* card is used to mark the end of a data set in the main job stream.

In general, the format of job control cards is as follows: Columns 1 and 2 of a JØB, EXEC, or DD card contain slashes (//); columns 1 and 2 of a delimiter card contain /*. The format of the rest of each job control card is much like the format of an assembler-language statement. A name is usually required, and must begin in column 3. At least one blank must follow the name; the next field is called the *verb* field and contains one of the verbs JØB, EXEC, or DD. (The delimiter card has /* in columns 1 and 2, but nothing else in the card.) The verb is followed by at least one more blank and then come the operands. As in assembler language, the operands are separated by commas but not by blanks.

Certain sequences of job control statements are standard. For example, execution of the assembler always requires the same data sets for temporary storage, a macro library, an output listing, and an object deck if desired. Each of these data sets requires definition in a job control statement. To save duplication of effort in the preparation of standard job control sequences for each user, the operating system keeps a library of *catalogued procedures*. A catalogued procedure can be called by an EXEC statement; the sequence of job control statements in the catalogued procedure will essentially be substituted for the EXEC statement which calls it. Thus the catalogued procedure is used like a macro. The job control statements in the catalogued procedure will in turn call for execution of programs and define data sets.

One of the standard catalogued procedures available in almost every installation using the operating system OS/360 or OS/VS is ASMFCG, which calls for assembly and execution of a program written in assembler language. The ASMFCG procedure has two steps, that is, it calls for execution of two distinct programs. The first is the assembler. The assembler translates the assembler-language program into machine language, creating what is called an *object module* which contains the program assembled in machine language. The second step is execution of the *loader* program. The loader links together the object modules presented to it both from the previous assembly step and from an object deck or a module on disk. It then loads the completed program into core and begins execution of the program. When more complex linking tasks must be done, we must invoke a similar procedure, ASMFCLG, which invokes the *linkage editor* as a second step, with execution of the completed program as a third step. Our examples will show ASMFCG.

Now we describe the job control necessary to submit a job using the ASMFCG procedure. The first two cards are

```
//TYPICAL      JØB  (267576),STRUBLE
//             EXEC ASMFCG
```

A job always needs a name; "TYPICAL" is used in our example. Operands in the JØB card include account number and programmer name, but each installation has its own requirements about JØB card operands, so the student must learn those appropriate to his installation. The second card calls for the execution of the ASMFCG procedure.

The remaining EXEC statements and most of the data set definitions are in the catalogued procedure ASMFCG. The user need provide only data set definitions that must be modified from or added to those defined in ASMFCG.

For the first step of ASMFCG, only the program to be assembled need be provided. The program is presented to the assembler as an input data set, most likely in the main job stream. Just after the statement calling for execution of ASMFCG, we include

```
//ASM.SYSIN    DD    *
```
Assembler–language program (source program)
```
        /*
```

The DD card declares that the SYSIN data set for the ASM step in the procedure follows immediately in the main job stream (this is the meaning of *). The program itself is followed by a delimiter card signaling the end of assembly.

The loader will load and execute the program just assembled. If an object deck (a machine-language program or subroutine punched into cards by a previous assembly) or a subroutine in a library are needed, job control statements must provide them to the loader too. The statements could be

```
//GØ.ØBJECT    DD    *
```
Object Deck
```
             /*
```

or, in case of a subroutine in a direct access data set,

```
//GØ.ØBJECT    DD    operands specifying definition and
                     location of subroutines
```

Finally, in the GØ step, which executes the assembled and link-edited program, no data set definitions are supplied by the catalogued procedure; all data set definitions must be supplied by the user. The simplest, defining card input and printed output, would be

```
//GØ.SYSPRINT  DD    SYSØUT=A
//GØ.SYSIN     DD    *
```
Data cards
```
        /*
```

The operand SYSØUT=A directs the data set to the printer. The names SYSPRINT and SYSIN are standard names for printed and card input data sets, but other names could be used, as specified in the input and output sections of the program to be executed.

In summary, the simplest assemble, link-edit, and execute job would be submitted in cards as shown in Fig. 6–7.

Fig. 6–7 Job deck for simple assemble, link-edit, and execute

```
//TYPICAL       JØB   (267576),  STRUBLE
//              EXEC  ASMFCG
//ASM.SYSIN     DD    *
Source program
/*
//GØ.SYSPRINT   DD    SYSØUT=A
//GØ.SYSIN      DD    *
Input data
/*
```

7. A FULL EXAMPLE

Let us examine a complete job to see the sequence and structure of the card deck submitted. The problem we take for our example is a trivial one: read a data card which has a number in columns 1–6 and another in columns 9–12, find their sum and product, and print on a line the original numbers, the sum, and the product. We assume we may call on a subroutine named READATA to read a card and make its contents available to us, and on a subroutine named PRINT to print a line for us.

First let us examine the program, shown in Fig. 6–8. The logic is simple. After the initial steps, we call on READATA to read a card. The call is simple: the

Fig. 6–8   A complete program in assembler language

```
EXAMPLE1    START     0
*           STANDARD LINKAGE AND BEGINNING CØNVENTIØNS
            SAVE      (14,12)
            BALR      12,0
            USING     *,12
            ST        13,SAV+4
            LA        13,SAV
*           READ A CARD. THE SUBRØUTINE READATA HAS ØNE
*           INPUT PARAMETER - THE ADDRESS ØF THE AREA
*           INTØ WHICH THE CARD CØNTENTS SHØULD BE PUT
            L         15,READADDR
            LA        1,CARDADDR
            BALR      14,15
*           CØNVERT NUMBERS TØ BINARY FØRM
            PACK      DBL(8),CARD(6)
            CVB       5,DBL
            PACK      DBL(8),CARD+8(4)
            CVB       7,DBL
*           FØRM SUM AND PRØDUCT
            LR        6,7
            AR        6,5
            MR        4,7
*           STØRE ØRIGINAL NUMBERS, SUM, PRØDUCT IN ØUTAREA
            MVC       ØUTAREA(6),CARD
            MVC       ØUTAREA+8(4),CARD+8
            CVD       6,DBL                        SUM
            UNPK      ØUTAREA+14(7),DBL(8)
            CVD       5,DBL                        PRØDUCT
            UNPK      ØUTAREA+23(10),DBL(8)
*           PRINT A LINE FRØM ØUTAREA
*           THE SUBRØUTINE PRINT HAS ØNLY ØNE PARAMETER -
*           THE ADDRESS ØF A 120-BYTE AREA TØ BE PRINTED
            L         15,PRINTADD
            LA        1,ØUTAREAD
            BALR      14,15
*           END ØF PRØCESSING - RETURN
            L         13,SAV+4
            RETURN    (14,12)
*           CØNSTANT AND STØRAGE DEFINITIØNS
SAV         DS        18F
CARD        DS        CL80
ØUTAREA     DC        CL120'        '
DBL         DS        D
READADDR    DC        V(READATA)
PRINTADD    DC        V(PRINT)
CARDADDR    DC        A(CARD)
ØUTAREAD    DC        A(ØUTAREA)
            END
```

address of the entry point of READATA is loaded into register 15, and the address of the parameter address area into register 1. The BALR instruction transfers control to the subroutine.

After the subroutine has returned control, our program can go to work on the contents of the card read. The numbers are converted to binary integer form, added, and multiplied, and all numbers are stored in the output area. The PRINT subroutine is called in the same way as the READATA subroutine, and the program is finished. It returns control to the operating system just as if it were a subroutine to the operating system. Constant and storage definitions conclude the program.

The complete card deck that might be submitted as a job to do our little problem is shown in Fig. 6–9. The JØB and EXEC cards are followed by subdecks supplementary to the ASMFCG job control statements for each of the steps ASM and GØ. The subdecks are arranged as explained in the previous section. The object deck contains the already assembled subroutines READATA and PRINT. If they were to be used a lot, we should keep them on a disk pack instead; one JCL statement would call for them to be found on the disk pack and loaded with the assembled program. Note the single data card in the GØ step, preceded by a DD statement and followed by a delimiter card.

Figure 6–10 shows the output of the job, which consists of seven sheets of computer output. If no trouble develops, we need pay attention only to page 3,

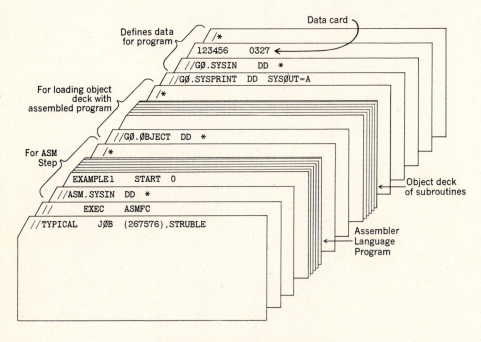

Defines data for program

Data card

/*

123456   0327

//GØ.SYSIN   DD   *

//GØ.SYSPRINT   DD   SYSØUT=A

For loading object deck with assembled program

/*

//GØ.ØBJECT   DD   *

For ASM Step

/*

EXAMPLE1   START   0

//ASM.SYSIN   DD   *

//   EXEC   ASMFC

//TYPICAL   JØB   (267576),STRUBLE

Object deck of subroutines

Assembler Language Program

Fig. 6–9 Card deck submitted as a job.

Fig. 6–10 Printed output of a job. ▶

H A S P   S Y S T E M   L O G

```
$ 17.38.08 JOB 164 -- TYPICAL  -- BEGINNING EXEC - PART 1 - CLASS A
N 17.39.18 JOB 164 END EXECUTION.


//TYPICAL  JOB  (267576),STRUBLE                         JOB 164
//         EXEC ASMFCG
XXASM      EXEC PGM=IEUASM,PARM='LOAD,NODECK'                 00000010
XXSYSGO    DD   DSNAME=SYS1.SCRATCH4,DISP=OLD,               X00000020
XX              DCB=(RECFM=FB,BLKSIZE=800,LRECL=80)           00000030
XXSYSLIB   DD   DSNAME=SYS1.MACLIB,DISP=SHR                   00000040
XXSYSPRINT DD   SYSOUT=A                                      00000050
XXSYSPUNCH DD   SYSOUT=B                                      00000060
XXSYSUT1   DD   DSNAME=SYS1.SCRATCH1,DISP=OLD                 00000070
XXSYSUT2   DD   DSNAME=SYS1.SCRATCH2,DISP=OLD                 00000080
XXSYSUT3   DD   DSNAME=SYS1.SCRATCH3,DISP=OLD                 00000090
//ASM.SYSIN DD   *
IEF236I ALLOC. FOR TYPICAL ASM
IEF237I 133 ALLOCATED TO SYSGO
IEF237I 131 ALLOCATED TO SYSLIB
IEF237I 030 ALLOCATED TO SYSPRINT
IEF237I 040 ALLOCATED TO SYSPUNCH
IEF237I 130 ALLOCATED TO SYSUT1
IEF237I 131 ALLOCATED TO SYSUT2
IEF237I 132 ALLOCATED TO SYSUT3
IEF237I 020 ALLOCATED TO SYSIN
IEF142I - STEP WAS EXECUTED - COND CODE 0000
IEF285I    SYS1.SCRATCH4                          KEPT
IEF285I    VOL SER NOS= WORK22.
IEF285I    SYS1.MACLIB                            KEPT
IEF285I    VOL SER NOS= RES212.
IEF285I    SYS1.SCRATCH1                          KEPT
IEF285I    VOL SER NOS= RES211.
IEF285I    SYS1.SCRATCH2                          KEPT
IEF285I    VOL SER NOS= RES212.
IEF285I    SYS1.SCRATCH3                          KEPT
IEF285I    VOL SER NOS= WORK03.
XXGO       EXEC PGM=LOADER,PARM='MAP,PRINT,NOCALL,LET'        00000100
XXSYSLOUT  DD   SYSOUT=A                                      00000110
XXSYSLIN   DD   DSNAME=SYS1.SCRATCH4,DISP=OLD,               X00000120
XX              DCB=(RECFM=FB,BLKSIZE=800,LRECL=80)           00000130
XX         DD   DDNAME=OBJECT                                 00000140
```

Handwritten annotations:

Reproduction of messages to operator's console.

JOB and EXEC statements from card deck.

Job control for ASM step of the procedure.

Device allocations for ASM step, assigned according to job control statements.

Status of ASM step

Dispositions of data sets at end of step.

Job control for GO step, from cataloged procedure.

```
//GO.OBJECT DD  *          ⎫ Job control for GØ step,
//GO.SYSPRINT DD SYSOUT=A  ⎬ added from card deck.
//GO.SYSIN    DD  *        ⎭
//
IEF236I ALLOC. FOR TYPICAL  GO
IEF237I 030  ALLOCATED TO SYSLOUT    ⎫ Device allocations
IEF237I 133  ALLOCATED TO SYSLIN     ⎬ for GØ step.
IEF237I 021  ALLOCATED TO            ⎭
IEF237I 031  ALLOCATED TO SYSPRINT
IEF237I 022  ALLOCATED TO SYSIN
IEF142I - STEP WAS EXECUTED - COND CODE 4000 ← Status of GØ step
IEF285I SYS1.SCRATCH4              KEPT ⎫ Disposition at end
IEF285I VOL SER NOS= WORK22.           ⎬ of step.
```

                                                    PAGE
                                              17.38 8/26/

EXTERNAL SYMBOL DICTIONARY
← Lists symbols which have relationships
  outside this program.

```
SYMBOL    TYPE ID  ADDR   LENGTH LD ID

EXAMPLE1  SD 01 000000 000190 ← Length of EXAMPLE1 is
READATA   ER 02                 (hexadecimal) 190
PRINT     ER 03
                 ↑ Beginning address
                   of EXAMPLE1 is
                   (relocatable) 000000.
```

↳ Name of assembled section

Names from other sections. The addresses
corresponding to these symbols must be
entered in this section.

```
LOC    OBJECT CODE  ADDR1 ADDR2  STMT  SOURCE STATEMENT            F01FEB73  8/26

000000                              1 EXAMPLE1 START 0
                                    2 *  STANDARD LINKAGE AND BEGINNING CONVENTIONS
                                    3     SAVE  (14,12)
000000                              4+    DS   0H
000000 90EC D00C            0000C   5+    STM  14,12,12(13)  SAVE REGISTERS
000004 05C0                         6     BALR 12,0
000006                              7     USING *,12
000006 50D0 C066            0006C   8     ST   13,SAV+4
00000A 41D0 C062            00068   9     LA   13,SAV
                                   10 *  READ A CARD.  THE SUBROUTINE READATA HAS ONE
                                   11 *  INPUT PARAMETER - THE ADDRESS OF THE AREA
                                   12 *  INTO WHICH THE CARD CONTENTS SHOULD BE PUT
00000E 58F0 C17A            00180  13     L    15,READADDR
000012 4110 C182            00188  14     LA   1,CARDADDR
000016 05EF                        15     BALR 14,15
                                   16 *  CONVERT NUMBERS TO BINARY FORM
```

```
000018 F275 C172 C0AA 00178 000B0   17        PACK  DBL(8),CARD(6)
00001E 4F50 C172       00178         18        CVB   5,DBL
000022 F273 C172 C0B2 00178 000B8   19        PACK  DBL(8),CARD+8(4)
000028 4F70 C172       00178         20        CVB   7,DBL
                                     21  *     FORM SUM AND PRODUCT
00002C 1867                          22        LR    6,7
00002E 1A65                          23        AR    6,5
000030 1C47                          24        MR    4,7
                                     25  *     STORE ORIGINAL NUMBERS, SUM, PRODUCT IN OUTAREA
000032 D205 C0FA C0AA 00100 000B0   26        MVC   OUTAREA(6),CARD
000038 D203 C102 C0B2 00108 000B8   27        MVC   OUTAREA+8(4),CARD+8
00003E 4E60 C172       00178         28        CVD   6,DBL
000042 F367 C108 C172 0010E 00178   29        UNPK  OUTAREA+14(7),DBL(8)
000048 4E50 C172       00178         30        CVD   5,DBL
00004C F397 C111 C172 00117 00178   31        UNPK  OUTAREA+23(10),DBL(8)
                                     32  *     PRINT A LINE FROM OUTAREA
                                     33  *     THE SUBROUTINE PRINT HAS ONLY ONE PARAMETER -
                                     34  *     THE ADDRESS OF A 120-BYTE AREA TO BE PRINTED
000052 58F0 C17E       00184         35        L     15,PRINTADD
000056 4110 C186       0018C         36        LA    1,OUTAREAD
00005A 05EF                          37        BALR  14,15
                                     38  *     END OF PROCESSING - RETURN
00005C 58D0 C066       0006C         39        L     13,SAV+4
                                     40        RETURN (14,12)
000060 98EC D00C       0000C         41+       LM    14,12,12(13)  RESTORE THE REGISTERS
000064 07FE                          42+       BR    14 RETURN
                                     43  *     CONSTANT AND STORAGE DEFINITIONS
000068                               44  SAV      DS   18F
0000B0                               45  CARD     DS   CL80
000100 40404C4040404040             46  OUTAREA  DC   CL120' '
000178                               47  DBL      DS   D
000180 00000000                      48  READADDR DC   V(READATA)
000184 00000000                      49  PRINTADD DC   V(PRINT)
000188 000000B0                      50  CARDADDR DC   A(CARD)
00018C 00000100                      51  OUTAREAD DC   A(OUTAREA)
000000                               52           END  EXAMPLE1
```

RELOCATION DICTIONARY

Lists addresses whose contents
must be relocated during loading.

POS.ID	REL.ID	FLAGS	ADDRESS
01	01	0C	000188 (CARD)
01	01	0C	00018C (OUTAREA)
01	02	1C	000180 (READATA)
01	03	1C	000184 (PRINT)

PAGE   8/26/7

PAGE   8/26

CROSS-REFERENCE helps in reading, debugging, and maintaining programs.

Length → / Value, usually the address / Statement no. of defining statement

REFERENCES—to each symbol in other statements

SYMBOL	LEN	VALUE	DEFN	REFERENCES							
CARD	00080	000080	00045	0017	0019	0026	0027	0050			
CARDADDR	00004	000188	00050	0014							
DBL	00008	000178	00047	0017	0018	0019	0020	0028	0029	0030	0031
EXAMPLE1	00001	000000	00001	0052							
OUTAREA	00120	000100	00046	0026	0027	0029	0031	0051			
OUTAREAD	00004	00018C	00051	0036							
PRINTADD	00004	000184	00049	0035							
READALDR	00004	000180	00048	0013							
SAV	00004	000068	00044	0008	0009	0039					

means no errors found

NO STATEMENTS FLAGGED IN THIS ASSEMBLY
STATISTICS   SOURCE RECORDS (SYSIN) =   48   SOURCE RECORDS (SYSLIB) =   608
OPTIONS IN EFFECT   LIST, NODECK, LOAD, NORENT, XREF, NOTEST, ALGN, OS, NOTERM, LINECNT = 55
81 PRINTED LINES

} Report from the assembler.

Shows how the LOADER assigns addresses.   OS/360 LOADER

OPTIONS USED - PRINT,MAP,LET,NOCALL,NORES,NOTERM,SIZE=140640,NAME=**GO

NAME	TYPE	ADDR	NAME	TYPE	ADDR	NAME	TYPE	ADDR	NAME	TYPE	ADDR	NAME	TYPE	ADDR
EXAMPLE1	SD	D2F0	READATA	SD	D480	PRINT	LR	D4C0						

TOTAL LENGTH   3F8
ENTRY ADDRESS   D2F0

123456   0327   012378C   004037011B   The single line of output from the program.

assembler listing, and page 7, *output of the program*. The relocation dictionary and cross-reference tables produced by the assembler and loader contain information that can be helpful when we need to debug or modify a program. The reports of allocation and disposition of data sets are useful only in much more sophisticated jobs or when processing of the data sets causes trouble.

8. MAIN IDEAS

a. Conversions from EBCDIC to packed decimal to binary integer and back are performed by the instructions PACK, CVB, CVD, and UNPK. With these instructions, data can be read and printed in character form, while binary integer forms of the data are used in arithmetic operations.

b. DC and DS statements define constants and storage in assembler language. Literals are in general defined according to the same rules that govern the definition of constants. The subfields of a DC or DS instruction or literal definition are duplication factor, type, modifiers, and values.

c. Constant types C, X, B, F, H, E, D, P, A, and V allow for a variety of data representations, boundary alignment rules, and padding and truncation.

d. Assembler language statements START, TITLE, ∅RG, LT∅RG, and END control the assembly of programs, but are not translated directly to machine language.

e. Macro-instructions are expanded by the assembler into one or more assembler language statements. SAVE and RETURN macros relieve the programmer of some slight burdens and enable him to write his program in a more straightforward manner.

f. A user submits a job to the IBM System/360 or 370, with job control statements containing directions as to programs and data sets to be used.

g. Job control statements include J∅B, EXEC, and DD statements; catalogued procedures provide job control for standard tasks.

QUESTIONS FOR REVIEW AND IMAGINATION

1. Under what conditions will the PACK instruction overflow? That is, under what conditions will the destination field be too small to hold properly the PACKed result? Under what conditions will UNPK, CVB, and CVD overflow?

2. If a field is PACKed and the result is UNPacKed, in what ways may the UNPacKed result be different from the original field?

3. Suppose a field N holds a packed decimal number. The field is three bytes long, and not aligned on any particular boundary. Write a sequence of instructions that will convert the contents of this field to a binary integer.

4. Trace execution of the instruction pair

```
PACK    D(8),Q(1)
CVB     4,D
```

assuming that D is a double-word and the byte at Q is 11000111 (C7 in hexadecimal).

5. Trace execution of the instruction pair

```
CVD     7,D
UNPK    U(3),D(8)
```

assuming that register 7 contains the (hexadecimal) number 0000006B. What would be different if the UNPK instruction were changed to the following?

```
UNPK    U(3),D+5(3)
```

6. Write a sequence of instructions that will take a field G of length five bytes containing a number in the EBCDIC form and construct a new field K of length seven containing the product 37*G in EBCDIC form.

7. Show the bit patterns generated from the constant definitions

```
DC    C'0'          DC    PL4'0'
DC    CL4'0'        DC    C'A'
DC    X'0'          DC    X'A'
DC    XL4'0'        DC    F'19'
DC    F'0'          DC    XL4'19'
DC    E'0'          DC    HL4'19'
DC    P'0'
```

8. A CVB instruction requires a double-word source operand. Suppose we know that a number to be converted is small (for example, if it is being PACKed from only three bytes). We could save some time in the PACK instruction if its first operand (destination) were only two or three bytes instead of eight. We must then see that the two or three bytes are in the low-order portion of a double-word whose upper portion is filled with zeros, before the CVB instruction is executed. Write DC or DS statements and a PACK instruction that will follow this suggestion.

9. Write DC statements for

a) a list of three full words containing binary integer equivalents of (decimal) −11, +373, 0;

b) a list of ten full words containing zeros;

c) a half-word whose binary bits are 1100100100100100;

d) a double-word whose EBCDIC contents is EGC123*$;

e) a three-byte field, each byte containing hexadecimal E4;

f) four 120-byte areas, each containing the EBCDIC characters RESULT= followed by blanks.

10. State the difference between

a)   C1   DC   FL2'19'   and   C2   DC   H'19'

and that between

b)   C3   DC   F'367'   and   C4   DC   HL4'367'

11. Change the program of Fig. 6–8 so that

   a) the input numbers are taken from columns 17–22 and 30–33 of the input card;

   b) the number 1 is subtracted from each of the two numbers before their sum and product are taken;

   c) the output line includes identifications such as

          A=   B=   SUM=   PRØDUCT=

12. Write an appropriate TITLE statement to be included in the program of Fig. 6–8.

13. Rewrite the program of Fig. 6–8 so that literals are used instead of the constant definitions READADDR, PRINTADD, CARDADDR, and ØUTAREAD.

14. Look up the macros SAVE and RETURN in a *Supervisor Services and Macro-Instructions* manual; there are optional parameters which may be helpful.

15. Analyze the following, each of which purports to set up parameters to send to a subroutine, and determine which are correct, which are incorrect, and why.

   a) There is one parameter, located at BBB:

```
              L      1,BADDR
              ⋮
BADDR    DC    A(BBB)
```

   b) There is one parameter, located at BBB:

```
              L      1,=A(BBB)
```

   c) There is one parameter, located at BBB:

```
              LA     1,=A(BADDR)
              ⋮
BADDR    DC    A(BBB)
```

   d) There is one parameter, located at BBB:

```
              L      1,=A(BADDR)
              ⋮
BADDR    DC    A(BBB)
```

   e) There are three parameters, located at FF, GG, and HH:

```
              L      1,=A(FF,GG,HH)
```

   f) There are three parameters, located at FF, GG, and in register 4:

```
              ST     4,TP
              LA     1,=A(FF,GG,TP)
```

g) There are three parameters, located at FF, GG, and a main storage location whose address is in register 7:

```
            ST    7,TP
            LA    1,BADDR
            ⋮
BADDR       DC    A(FF,GG,TP)
```

h) There are three parameters, located at FF, GG, and a main storage location whose address is in register 7:

```
            ST    7,BADDR+8
            LA    1,BADDR
            ⋮
BADDR       DC    A(FF,GG)
            DS    1F
```

i) There are three parameters, located at FF, GG, and HH:

```
            BAL   1,*+16
            DC    A(FF,GG,HH)
```

16. Some subroutines should accept a variable number of parameters, and the subroutine must therefore be able to recognize the length of a parameter list. The convention adopted in OS and OS/VS is that the first byte of each 4-byte parameter address is 0 except the last, whose high-order bit is set to 1. For example, the parameter address block could be set up

```
PLIST       DC    A(T,U,V)
            DC    X'80'
            DC    AL3(W)
```

This convention need not be followed where the number of parameters is fixed and well understood. Write a program segment which will test a parameter address block and determine its length. Also, think of subroutines which should accept a variable-length parameter list.

17. Decide on a suitable convention for naming all available registers, and write the appropriate EQUate statements.

18. Write statements which perform the following:
    a) Reset the location counter to 100 hexadecimal.
    b) Equate the symbol PØRG with the value 256 decimal.
    c) Move the location counter to a full-word boundary if necessary and assign a full word to have the value 300 decimal. The location should be named DEC300.
    d) Create a symbol ØUTBUF which represents a location whose contents are the address of ØUTSTR.
    e) Create a 132-character storage area called ØUTSTR.
    f) Stop the assembler from processing further statements.

19. One common way to set an entire field in main storage to zero, or blanks, or something, is to move one copy into the first byte, and then "cascade" its

movement through the rest of the field with a MVC instruction. For example, we can store blanks in the 133-byte field PRTLINE by

```
MVI    PRTLINE,C' '
MVC    PRTLINE+1(132),PRTLINE
```

Trace how the blank is propagated through the entire field, and find examples previously given where this technique can be used to advantage. Overlap of fields in any manner is permitted the MVC instruction; explore other effects achieved by overlapping of fields.

REFERENCES

IBM System/360 Operating System: Job Control Language Reference, GC28-6704, or *OS/VS JCL Reference*, GC28-0618, IBM Corporation. Details of Job Control Language.

IBM System/360 Operating System: Job Control Language, Users Guide, GC28-6703, or *OS/VS JCL Services*, GC28-0617, IBM Corporation. A survey of facilities and options provided through job control language.

IBM System/360 Principles of Operation, GA22-6821, or *IBM System/370 Principles of Operation*, GA22-7000, IBM Corporation. Details on conversion instructions.

Presser, Leon, and John R. White, "Linkers and Loaders," *Computing Surveys*, **4**, 3 (Sept. 1972), pp. 149–167. A tutorial presentation on linking and loading programs in System/360.

OS Assembler (F) Programmer's Guide, GC26-3756, or *OS/VS Assembler Programmer's Guide*, GC33-4021, IBM Corporation. References on data sets, parameters, and job control needed by the assembler.

OS Assembler Language, GC28-6514, or *OS/VS and DOS/VS Assembler Language*, GC33-4010, IBM Corporation. Complete reference descriptions of DC, DS, EQU and assembler control statements.

See also introductory references listed in Chapter 5.

Chapter 7

Transfer of Control

A computer program must be able to make tests and follow alternative paths (that is, execute alternative sequences of instructions) as a result of those tests. The instruction that enables the computer to choose and follow one of two paths is the *conditional branch*. Depending on the result of such tests, the conditional branch instruction will decide that the next instruction to be executed is *either* the instruction from the physically next location in main storage *or* the instruction whose address is an operand of the branch instruction.

With the conditional branch, a programmer can write programs of logical complexity; furthermore, he can program loops, i.e., sequences of instructions which can be executed repeatedly, then left when sufficient repetitions have been taken. The ability to loop provides much of the power of the modern digital computer: instructions written once, entered into the computer's storage once, but executed many times greatly expand the productive capacity of the man-computer partnership.

1. THE PROGRAM STATUS WORD AND THE CONDITION CODE

The program status word (abbreviated *PSW*) has been mentioned earlier. It is a special 64–bit register containing information on the status of the computer and the program being run. Bits 40–63 of the PSW contain the instruction address, the address of the next instruction to be executed. During the instruction cycle for every instruction, the computer retrieves the instruction to be executed from main storage locations addressed by bits 40–63 of the PSW. Then the instruction address is increased by 2, 4, or 6, depending on the length of the current instruction; this enables the next instruction cycle to retrieve the next instruction from storage. The execution of a branch consists of storing a new value in the instruction address portion of the PSW; the value is specified by an operand of the branch instruction, and the effect of storing an address in the PSW is to force execution of the instructions starting at that new address.

Another important part of the program status word is the *condition code* (often abbreviated CC). The condition code is kept in bits 34 and 35 (or, as we shall see later, bits 18 and 19) of the PSW and therefore can take on the binary values 00, 01, 10, 11, or the decimal values 0, 1, 2, and 3. The condition code is set by each of a number of instructions, including many arithmetic instructions. The value to which the condition code is set depends on the result of the instruction; for example, the condition code may be set to reflect whether the result of an arithmetic operation is negative, zero, or positive.

The condition code can be tested by a conditional branch instruction; the value of the condition code determines whether or not the branch will be taken. Thus the condition code is an extremely important intermediary between arithmetic instructions and conditional branch instructions. It is set by the arithmetic instructions and tested by the conditional branch instructions, and therefore allows a branch to be conditional on the result of an arithmetic instruction. We shall explore the use of condition codes and conditional branch instructions in the remainder of this chapter.

2. SETTING THE CONDITION CODE

Figure 7–1 shows the values to which the condition code is set as a result of each of the instructions we have so far encountered. Of all the instructions we have discussed, only some loads and the binary integer add and subtract instructions set condition codes. If the result of such an instruction is zero, the condition code is set to 0. If the result is negative, the condition code is set to 1; this outcome is possible for all except the LPR instruction. If the result is positive and greater than zero (an outcome possible for all but the LNR instruction), the condition code is set to 2.

Fig. 7–1 Condition codes set by binary integer arithmetic instructions

Instruction		Condition code set			
		0	1	2	3
LPR	Load Positive Register	Zero	–	>Zero	Overflow
LNR	Load Negative Register	Zero	<Zero	–	–
LCR	Load Complement Register	Zero	<Zero	>Zero	Overflow
LTR	Load and Test Register	Zero	<Zero	>Zero	–
AR	Add Register	Zero	<Zero	>Zero	Overflow
SR	Subtract Register	Zero	<Zero	>Zero	Overflow
A	Add	Zero	<Zero	>Zero	Overflow
S	Subtract	Zero	<Zero	>Zero	Overflow
AH	Add Half-word	Zero	<Zero	>Zero	Overflow
SH	Subtract Half-word	Zero	<Zero	>Zero	Overflow

If the result is too large—positive or negative—to be expressed properly, that is, if the result is less than -2^{31} or greater than $2^{31} - 1$, we consider the result to have *overflowed* the register. When this happens as a result of a binary integer addition or subtraction, the overflow bit is lost, and the remaining contents of the result register are incorrect by exactly 2^{32}. In all overflow cases, the condition code is set to 3, regardless of whether the actual result left in the result register is

Fig. 7-2   Instructions not affecting condition code

LR	Load Register	MVC	MoVe Character
L	Load	MVI	MoVe Immediate
ST	STore	LM	Load Multiple
LH	Load Half-word	STM	STore Multiple
STH	STore Half-word	LA	Load Address
MR	Multiply Register	BR	Branch to Register
M	Multiply	BALR	Branch And Link to Register
MH	Multiply Half-word	PACK	PACK
DR	Divide Register	UNPK	UNPacK
D	Divide	CVB	ConVert to Binary
		CVD	ConVert to Decimal

positive, negative, or zero. An overflow cannot occur as a result of an LNR instruction; it can occur as a result of an LCR or LPR instruction only if the second operand is -2^{31} (hexadecimal 80000000).

We introduce another load instruction at this point. The instruction Load and Test Register (LTR) is exactly the same as the LR instruction, except that it sets the condition code. The condition code is set to 0 if the result (in register $R1$) is zero, to 1 if the result is negative, and to 2 if the result is greater than zero.

When a condition code is set by execution of one of the instructions listed in Fig. 7–1, the previous value of the condition code is lost. The condition code remains unchanged by instructions that do not set a condition code, even the instructions that *test* the condition code. The instructions we have discussed so far that do *not* affect the condition code are listed in Fig. 7–2.

As an example, consider the program segment

```
LCR    4,7
M      6,4
ST     7,MINUSASQ
A      7,=F'4000'
```

Suppose that when the machine-language translation of the assembler-language segment has been executed, register 7 contains the binary equivalent of the decimal number 35. As a result of the LCR instruction, register 4 contains −35, so the condition code is set to 1. During the multiply instruction (yielding a result of −1225) and store instructions the condition code remains 1. As a result of the add instruction, however, the condition code is set to 2, since the addition yields 2775.

3. THE COMPARE INSTRUCTIONS

We introduce here three instructions whose sole result is the setting of the condition code. The instructions compare two operands, and the only differences between the three instructions are the assumed locations and lengths of the operands. The CR (Compare Register) instruction is of RR type, and compares the contents of two registers. The C (Compare) instruction is of RX type and compares the contents of a register (first operand) with a full word in main storage (second operand). The CH (Compare Half-word) instruction is of RX type; it compares the contents of a register with the contents of a half-word in main storage. We may think of the half-word as expanded to a full word by propagation of the sign bit into the upper 16 bits of a full word (as in the LH instruction) before comparison.

The condition-code settings resulting from the compare instructions are:

First operand = second operand: CC = 0
First operand < second operand: CC = 1
First operand > second operand: CC = 2

Since these instructions do not yield an arithmetic result, there is no possibility of overflow. Therefore the condition code is never set to 3 as a result of a compare instruction. In other respects, the condition code is set exactly as if a subtract instruction with the same two operands were executed.

Suppose that the initial contents of registers and main storage locations are as follows:

Register 3:   000046E9
Register 4:   FFBD2380
Location Q: 234689AC
Location W: FE3046E9

The following compare instructions will set the condition code as indicated, but will not change the contents of registers or main storage locations:

Instruction		Condition code set
CR	3,4	2
CR	4,3	1
C	3,Q	1
C	4,W	2
C	3,W	2
CH	4,W	1
CH	4,W+2	1
CH	3,W+2	0
CH	3,Q+2	2

4. THE BC AND BCR INSTRUCTIONS

The instructions which do or do not branch, depending on the value of the condition code, are BC (Branch on Condition) and BCR (Branch on Condition to Register); BC is of RX type, BCR of RR type.

The second operand designates the branch address. In execution of the BC instruction, the second operand, defined by $B2$, $X2$, and $D2$ in the usual way, is the address which is stored in bit positions 40–63 of the PSW and is therefore the

Fig. 7-3   Values of *M1* and branching control

Mask	Value of mask	Condition codes causing branch	Comparison results causing branch	Arithmetic results causing branch
1000	8	0	$Op_1 = Op_2$	=0, no overflow
0100	4	1	$Op_1 < Op_2$	<0, no overflow
0010	2	2	$Op_1 > Op_2$	>0, no overflow
1100	12	0,1	$Op_1 \leq Op_2$	≤0, no overflow
1010	10	0,2	$Op_1 \geq Op_2$	≥0, no overflow
0110	6	1,2	$Op_1 \neq Op_2$	≠0, no overflow
1110	14	0,1,2	All	No overflow
0000	0	None	None	None
0001	1	3	None	Overflow
1111	15	All	All	All
1001	9	0,3	$Op_1 = Op_2$	0 or overflow
0101	5	1,3	$Op_1 < Op_2$	<0 or overflow
0011	3	2,3	$Op_1 > Op_2$	>0 or overflow
1101	13	0,1,3	$Op_1 \leq Op_2$	≤0 or overflow
1011	11	0,2,3	$Op_1 \geq Op_2$	≥0 or overflow
0111	7	1,2,3	$Op_1 \neq Op_2$	≠0 or overflow

branch address. In the execution of the BCR instruction, the second operand *R2* designates a register *whose contents* (last 24 bits of the contents) is stored in bit positions 40–63 of the PSW. For example, if register 11 contains 0000A244, a BC instruction with *B2*, *X2*, and *D2* of 11,0,0 and a BCR instruction with *R2* = 11 both cause a branch to location 00A244.

The first operand of either the BC or the BCR instruction is called a *mask* and designated as *M1*. The four-bit pattern *M1* and the condition code jointly determine whether the branch is taken or not, that is, whether the second operand is stored in bits 40–63 of the PSW. Each of the four bits of *M1* determines whether or not one of the four possible values of the condition code (CC) will cause a branch; *a branch is taken if $M1_{cc} = 1$, and not if $M1_{cc} = 0$.* For example, if the condition code is 2 and *M1* bit 2 (bit 10 of the instruction) is 1, a branch will take place; if CC = 2 and $M1_2 = 0$, no branch takes place and the next instruction in the normal sequence is executed.

Following the implications of this rule, the instruction

> BC   B'1001',BRPTA

will cause a branch to the instruction named BRPTA if at the time the instruction is executed the condition code is 0 or 3; if the condition code is 1 or 2 the branch will not be taken. As a second example, the instruction

> BCR   B'0100',9

will cause a branch to the address held in register 9 if the condition code is 1, but no branch if the condition code is 0, 2, or 3.

In our assembler-language instructions we usually do not state *M1* as a binary value, but as its decimal equivalent. All 16 combinations of 1's and 0's in *M1* can be used to make branches occur under certain condition codes and not under others. We summarize the masks in Fig. 7-3. All possible values of *M1* are shown, both in binary and in their decimal equivalents, as well as the condition codes which would cause a branch with each value of *M1*. In the last two columns, we show which results of a compare instruction or of one of the binary integer arithmetic instructions listed in Fig. 7–1 will cause branching under each mask.

Several features of Fig. 7–3 are worthy of note.

1. Since a condition code of 3 cannot occur as the result of a compare instruction, bit 3 of the mask is irrelevant. This shows up in duplicate entries in the fourth column of the table; for example, after a compare instruction, a branch instruction with *M1* of 1001 or 1000 will cause branching under exactly the same conditions, namely, equality of the two operands.

2. The arithmetic results listed in the fifth column are the actual bit patterns left in the result register *R1*. It *is* possible to have a result of 0 *and* an overflow: consider addition of the hexadecimal numbers 80000000 and 80000000. The condition code will, of course, be set to 3.

3. If *M1* has the value 0, no branch will result, regardless of the condition code. The instruction

BCR   0,0

is therefore a no-operation instruction. It has its uses.

4. If *M1* has the value 15, a branch will always occur, regardless of the condition code. The instruction

BCR   15,14

therefore is an *unconditional* branch to the address held in register 14.

The following instruction sequences will perform the branches indicated.

a. C   6,BSQ   Branch to BEQ if the contents of register 6 equals the
   BC   8,BEQ   word at BSQ.

b. CR   6,9   Branch to PBA if the contents of register 6 is *not greater*
   BC   12,PBA   *than* (is less than or equal) the contents of register 9.

c. S   5,=F'1'   Subtract 1 from the contents of register 5. Then branch
   BC   7,LØØPB to LØØPB if the new contents of register 5 is not zero.

5. USE OF THE BRANCH INSTRUCTIONS: AN EXAMPLE

We construct in this section a program segment using the compare and branch instructions in a situation which has some degree of logical complexity. Suppose we have full words A and B, each containing either 1, 2, or 3. Values 1 and 3 represent positive and negative attributes, 2 is a neutral value. If the attributes of A and B are both positive or both negative, we are directed to add 1 to a counter of *affinities*, named AFF. If one is positive and the other negative, we are directed to add 1 to a counter of *incompatibilities*, named INCØMPAT. If either is neutral, we are to add nothing. We can represent the logic by the flowchart shown in

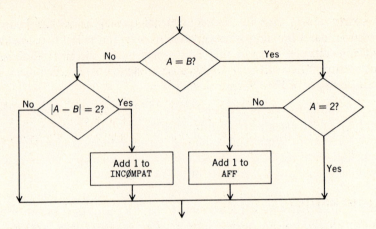

Fig. 7–4 Flowchart for a simple branching problem.

Fig. 7–4. The flowchart and the program segment we construct from it assume that A and B indeed contain 1, 2, or 3. The assumption that data are correct and valid as represented is always a dangerous one. In a real problem, data must be checked at every possible opportunity, but for simplicity we assume clean data here. A program segment following the logic of our flowchart follows.

```
          L     4,A
          C     4,B          IS A = B
          BC    8,PØSSAFF     IF SØ, GØ TØ PØSSAFF
          S     4,B          IF NOT, CHECK FØR INCØMPATIBILITY
          LPR   4,4
          C     4,=F'2'
          BC    7,NEXT
          L     5,INCØMPAT    UPDATE INCØMPAT
          LA    5,1(5)
          ST    5,INCØMPAT
          BC    15,NEXT
PØSSAFF   C     4,=F'2'       CØMPARE A WITH 2
          BC    8,NEXT
          L     5,AFF         A=B, BUT A IS NØT 2,
          LA    5,1(5)          SØ ADD 1 TØ AFF
          ST    5,AFF
NEXT      ...
```

The first branch (to PØSSAFF) is taken if A and B are found to be equal. If they are not equal, the subtract instruction is executed next. If the difference between A and B is not exactly 2, the computer branches to NEXT without adding to either AFF or INCØMPAT. If the difference is exactly 2, the value of INCØMPAT (assumed to be nonnegative and less than 2^{24}) is increased by 1 before an unconditional branch to NEXT. If we follow the branch to PØSSAFF, recognizing that the sequence of five instructions beginning at PØSSAFF is executed only if A = B, we see that 1 is added to AFF only if A = B = 1 or A = B = 3; otherwise the computer branches to NEXT. In any case, the instruction at NEXT is executed after the appropriate instructions of our program segment.

The student should take several pairs of values of A and B in turn and trace the execution of the program segment. He can also with profit try to rearrange the flowchart to provide the same result and write a program segment from his own flowchart.

6. EXTENDED MNEMONICS

OS and OS/VS assembler language provides for the use of alphabetic operation codes that will be translated by the assembler into both the numeric operation code and the *M1* part of a branch instruction. For example,

$$\text{BE} \qquad \text{ADDPR}$$

will be assembled into the same machine-language instruction as

$$\text{BC} \qquad \text{8,ADDPR}$$

The code BE stands for "Branch on Equal," and is called an *extended mnemonic*. It includes the definition of not only the operation code 47 (for BC) but also the *M1* portion of the instruction, which is 8 in a test for equality. Since the first operand of the instruction becomes in effect part of the operation code, only the second operand remains, and is written as a single operand. Use of the extended mnemonics simplifies the writing of programs in that the programmer need not think of or write the *M1* portion of a branch instruction.

Figure 7–5 lists extended mnemonics recognized by the OS/360 assembler. The BR instruction introduced in Chapter 5 is merely an extended mnemonic for BCR 15. Extended mnemonics are provided for BCR instructions with *M1* codes other than 0 and 15; we do not list them here, since in practice almost all conditional branches are BC instructions.

Extended mnemonics are provided which are natural for use after a compare operation and others which are natural after an arithmetic operation. The codes are interchangeable, however; for example, BZ can be used after a compare instruction and BL after an arithmetic instruction.

Extended mnemonics could be used in the segment given in the previous section. The branch instructions used there and their extended mnemonic equivalents are:

BC	8,PØSSAFF	BE	PØSSAFF
BC	7,NEXT	BNE	NEXT
BC	15,NEXT	B	NEXT
BC	8,NEXT	BE	NEXT

Fig. 7-5 Extended mnemonics

Meaning	Extended code		Equivalent	
Unconditional Branch	B	*S2*	BC	15,*S2*
Unconditional Branch to Register	BR	*R2*	BCR	15,*R2*
No OPeration	NØP	*S2*	BC	0,*S2*
No OPeration (Register)	NØPR	*R2*	BCR	0,*R2*
For use after a compare instruction:				
Branch on Equal	BE	*S2*	BC	8,*S2*
Branch on Low	BL	*S2*	BC	4,*S2*
Branch on High	BH	*S2*	BC	2,*S2*
Branch on Not Equal	BNE	*S2*	BC	7,*S2*
Branch on Not Low	BNL	*S2*	BC	11,*S2*
Branch on Not High	BNH	*S2*	BC	13,*S2*
For use after an arithmetic instruction:				
Branch on Zero	BZ	*S2*	BC	8,*S2*
Branch on Minus	BM	*S2*	BC	4,*S2*
Branch on Plus	BP	*S2*	BC	2,*S2*
Branch on Not Zero	BNZ	*S2*	BC	7,*S2*
Branch on Not Minus	BNM	*S2*	BC	11,*S2*
Branch on Not Plus	BNP	*S2*	BC	13,*S2*
Branch on Overflow	BØ	*S2*	BC	1,*S2*
Branch on Not Overflow	BNØ	*S2*	BNØ	14,*S2*

Note: S2 refers to an implied or explicit address appropriate as second operand in an RX-type instruction. *R2* refers to an expression appropriate to a register address.

7. EXAMPLE: INSERTION IN A LINKED LIST

In a computer data items are often conveniently stored in list form. When the items in the list are to remain fixed or when insertions and deletions are to be made only at the bottom of the list, the data items can be efficiently stored in consecutive main storage locations. However, when insertions and deletions may be required anywhere in the list, storage in consecutive locations is not efficient. Room for an insertion would have to be made by moving all data items which are beyond the point at which the insertion is to be made. Deletions require either collapsing the list or substituting for the deleted item a value representing "vacant" space.

In situations requiring many insertions and deletions a *linked list* has advantages. In a linked list each data item is kept in what is called a *cell*. If we assume that a data item is one word long, a cell must be two words long. The first word of each cell contains the address of the next cell in the list; the second word of the cell contains the data item itself. Thus a segment of a list could be stored as follows.

First cell:

Location 00A248: 0000A360 (Link to second cell)
        00A24C: C3D4F640 (First data item)

Second cell:

Location 00A360: 0000A290 (Link to third cell)
        00A364: E7E4C9E2 (Second data item)

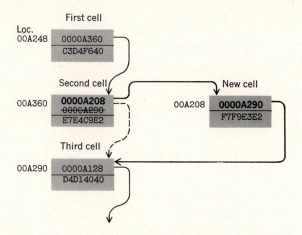

Fig. 7–6 Insertion in a linked list.

Third cell:

Location 00A290:   0000A128   (Link to fourth cell)
          00A294:   D4D14040   (Third data item)

        etc.

We may adopt as a convention that the *last cell* in the list has zero in its first word.

An insertion may easily be made at any point of a linked list. Suppose that given the list segment shown above, we wish to insert an item after the second cell. Suppose that the item F7F9E3E2 is in a cell whose address is, say, 00A208. We need only change two link addresses to make the insertion:

Second cell:

Location 00A360:   0000A208   (Link to new cell)
          00A364:   E7E4C9E2   (Second data item)

New cell:

Location 00A208:   0000A290   (Link to former third cell)
          00A20C: F7F9E3E2   (Inserted data item)

Figure 7–6 shows the change in the list structure; the broken line represents the connection replaced in the insertion process, and the changes are shown in boldface. Given the address of cell 2 in register 5 and the address of the new cell in register 6, the change of link addresses accomplishing the insertion can be done by

```
L    7,0(5)      ADDRESS ØF NEXT CELL
ST   7,0(6)      STØRE IN NEW CELL
ST   6,0(5)      STØRE ADDRESS ØF NEW CELL
```

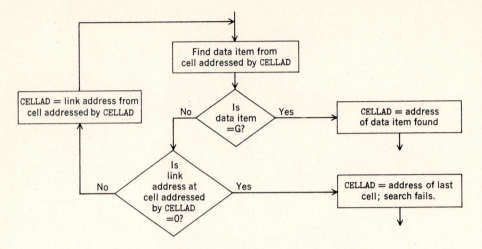

Fig. 7–7   Flowchart for a search for an item in a linked list.

Search for a given item on a linked list is also reasonably easy. The search steps can be represented in the flowchart shown in Fig. 7–7, if the word at CELLAD first contains the address of the first cell of the list and G contains the given data item we are searching for.

We exhibit in Fig. 7–8 a subroutine which has the following input parameters.

1. The address of the first cell of a list.

2. The address of a data item. A new item is to be inserted in the list after the cell whose data item matches the data item addressed by parameter 2.

3. The address of a cell containing the new item.

The subroutine searches the list for a cell containing a data item equal to that given by parameter 2; if it finds such a cell, it inserts the cell whose address is the third parameter after the cell found. Otherwise, the new cell is inserted at the bottom of the given list. There is no formal output from the subroutine.

The subroutine is a lowest-level subroutine, and it therefore need not provide a register save area of its own. The input parameters are loaded into registers 2, 3, and 4 by a single LM instruction. A loop of seven instructions, completed by the unconditional branch to SEARCH, performs a search for the given data item. Two BE instructions provide exits from the loop when either the given data item is found or the end of the list is reached. Upon branch to LINK from the loop, register 2 contains either the address of the cell containing the matching data item or the address of the last cell in the list. In either case, the new cell is to be inserted after the cell addressed by register 2. If the cell is inserted at the end of the list, the zero indicating the end of the list is moved to the new cell just as a normal cell address would be.

Fig. 7–8 Subroutine for insertion in a linked list

```
INSERTLK SAVE     (14,12)
         BALR     12,0
         USING    *,12
         LA       6,0         ZERØ FØR CØMPARISØNS
         LM       2,4,0(1)    GET PARAMETERS
*    REGISTER 2 WILL BE 'CELLAD'
*    REGISTER 3 CØNTAINS ADDRESS ØF DATA ITEM G TØ SEARCH FØR
*    REGISTER 4 CØNTAINS ADDRESS ØF CELL TØ BE INSERTED
*    SEARCH LØØP FØLLØWS
SEARCH   L        5,4(2)      LØAD DATA ITEM
         C        5,0(3)      CØMPARE WITH GIVEN ITEM
         BE       LINK        IF EQUAL, GØ INSERT
         C        6,0(2)      CØMPARE LINK ADDRESS WITH ZERØ
         BE       LINK        IF END ØF LIST, INSERT AT END
         L        2,0(2)      PREPARE TØ EXAMINE NEXT CELL
         B        SEARCH
*    INSERT NEW CELL AFTER CELL ADDRESSED IN REGISTER 2
LINK     L        7,0(2)      GET ADDRESS ØF NEXT CELL (ØR ZERØ)
         ST       7,0(4)      STØRE IN NEW CELL
         ST       4,0(2)      STØRE ADDRESS ØF NEW CELL
*    END ØF NECESSARY WØRK.  RETURN.
         RETURN   (2,12)
         END
```

8. MAIN IDEAS

a. Conditional branch instructions are essential to the use of the computer; they permit loops and logical complexity of programs.

b. The program status word contains the instruction address register and the two-bit condition code. The condition code is set by compare, add, and subtract instructions, and serves as an indicator of the instructions' results.

Fig. 7–9 Compare and branch instructions

Mnemonic name	Type	Full name	Action
CR	RR	Compare Register	$CC \leftarrow \begin{cases} 0 \text{ if } c(R1) = c(R2) \\ 1 \text{ if } c(R1) < c(R2) \\ 2 \text{ if } c(R1) > c(R2) \end{cases}$
C	RX	Compare	$CC \leftarrow \begin{cases} 0 \text{ if } c(R1) = c(S2) \\ 1 \text{ if } c(R1) < c(S2) \\ 2 \text{ if } c(R1) > c(S2) \end{cases}$
CH	RX	Compare Half-word[1]	$CC \leftarrow \begin{cases} 0 \text{ if } c(R1) = c(S2)_{0\text{-}15} \\ 1 \text{ if } c(R1) < c(S2)_{0\text{-}15} \\ 2 \text{ if } c(R1) > c(S2)_{0\text{-}15} \end{cases}$
BCR	RR	Branch on Condition to Register[2,3]	$\rightarrow c(R2)$ if $(M1)_{CC} = 1$
BC	RX	Branch on Condition[2,3]	$\rightarrow S2$ if $(M1)_{CC} = 1$

Notes
1. For purposes of comparison, the $S2$ operand is considered as expanded to a full word by propagation of the sign bit, bit 0 of the half-word, into the upper 16 bits of a full word.
2. We extend the notation introduced in Chapter 4. An arrow pointing to the right indicates a branch: $\rightarrow c(R2)$ specifies a branch to the address contained in $R2$. The arrow meaning branch is distinguished from that meaning store by its direction; storage of a quantity is always indicated by an arrow pointing to the left.
3. $M1$ represents the mask, bits 8–11 of the instruction. Whether a branch is taken depends on whether or not a particular bit of $M1$ is a 1.

c. The conditional branch instructions are BC and BCR. The first operand, *M1*, indicates which condition codes would cause branching to occur; the second operand designates the branch address. These and the compare instructions are summarized in Fig. 7–9. Extended mnemonics in assembler language combine the operation code with *M1*, making the writing of branch instructions easier.

d. When data items are kept in a list and many insertions and deletions are required, a linked list is a time-saving device; searching, insertion, and deletion are fast.

PROBLEMS FOR IMAGINATION AND REVIEW

1. Write as many different instructions as you can, each setting the condition code to 0 if and only if the contents of register 4 is zero.

2. Why is an overflow possible with the LPR and LCR instructions, but not with LNR?

3. Given the following contents of registers and storage locations,

$$
\begin{array}{ll}
\text{Register 2:} & \text{0000697A} \\
\text{Register 3:} & \text{49564EDB} \\
\text{Register 4:} & \text{80039FF0} \\
\text{Location Q:} & \text{FFFFFCD4} \\
\text{Location Y:} & \text{00000000} \\
\text{Location W:} & \text{FFFF9686} \\
\end{array}
$$

before *each* of the instructions listed below, determine the condition code set by each instruction.

SR	3,4		CR	4,3
S	2,W		CR	3,4
SH	2,W+2		C	3,Y
A	4,Q		LTR	3,3
C	4,Q			

4. What relationship must hold between contents of register 9 and storage location T for each of the following sequences to result in a branch to PRØGPT2?

a) C   9,T
    BC   12,PRØGPT2

b) C   9,T
    BC   5,PRØGPT2

c) A   9,T
    BC   5,PRØGPT2

d) S   9,T
    LPR 9,9
    S   9,=F'30'
    BC   6,PRØGPT2

5. Write a program segment not using the LPR or LNR instructions which will perform the equivalent of

$$LPR \quad 5,5$$

Then go to the instruction named CØNTIN.

6. Revise the flowchart and program segment of Section 5 to test A and B for validity. In particular, add 1 to AFF if A = B = 1 or A = B = 3 or add 1 to INCØMPAT if A and B are 1 and 3 or 3 and 1, but add nothing to either if A or B is 2 *or any number other than 1, 2, or 3.*

7. A certain neophyte programmer wished to provide a branch to statement S1 if A < −B, to S2 if A = −B, and to S3 if A > −B. He programmed the segment

$$
\begin{array}{ll}
L & 4,A \\
A & 4,B \\
BM & S1 \\
BP & S3 \\
\end{array}
$$

which he followed immediately with the segment beginning at *S2*. The program worked well most of the time, but on a few occasions the segment beginning at S2 was executed when A and −B were decidedly not equal. Why? How could you correct the segment?

8. Deletion of a data item from a linked list is slightly more complicated than insertion of a data item if we know only the address of the cell containing the item to be deleted and not the address of its predecessor. Considering only the case in which the item to be deleted is *not* in the last cell in the list, we proceed as follows: The data item *and link address* from the subsequent cell are put into the cell whose original data item is to be deleted; the subsequent cell is then considered to be empty and is deleted from the list. Diagram and program this process. What difficulties arise if the item to be deleted is in the last cell of a list? How might you avoid the difficulties?

9. During a process of insertions and deletions, the cells not in use will become scattered throughout the storage region used for list cells. The usual stratagem for keeping track of cells not in use is to string them onto a list of their own, called the available space list. So the complete process of adding a data item to a list is to delete a cell from the available space list, put the data item in the cell, then insert that cell into the desired list. To delete a data item from a list, we follow first the steps described in the previous problem, then add the deleted cell to the available space list. From where on the available space list is it most efficient to take a cell? Where should one be put back? Program the entire process of deleting a given data item from a list, including return of the deleted cell to the available space list.

10. There is a macro, CNØP, which inserts no-operation instructions into the object program in order to align the subsequent instruction at a particular boundary. There are two operands. The second operand should be 4 if alignment with respect to a full-word boundary is desired, 8 if double-word boundary alignment. The first operand specifies where within the full or double word the subsequent instruction should start. For example,

```
            CNØP    0,4
    BP      L       3,A
```

will cause assembly of one half-word no-operation instruction, or nothing, so that BP will be located on a full-word boundary. If the CNØP operands had been 2,8, BP would be two bytes after the beginning of a double word. CNØP is used within instruction sequences so that execution of instructions can be unbroken, up to an instruction for which boundary alignment is desired.

Another use is in assuring that relative addressing is carried out properly. In the segment

```
            B       *+8
    A       DS      1F
            L       3,A
```

the Branch instruction may or may not go to the Load instruction, depending on whether the branch instruction is on a full-word boundary or not. Show how a CNØP instruction solves this problem. Then think of other uses for CNØP.

11. Write a program segment which will skip the next instruction if the contents of register 1 is zero.

12. Without flagging it as such, we introduced an example of a linked list in Chapter 5. The chain of register save areas is a linked list; if we regard the area provided by the currently active subroutine as the cell at the head of the list, word 2 is the link that points to the next cell. Go back to problem 1 at the end of Chapter 5 and see how the register save areas also form a linked list when viewed in the opposite direction. Such a list is called a *doubly linked list*; try to think of cases where it is useful to have links pointing both directions.

REFERENCES

IBM System/360 Principles of Operation, GA22-6821, or *IBM System/370 Principles of Operation*, GA22-7000, IBM Corporation. For reference on the program status word, compare and branch instructions.

Knuth, Donald E., *The Art of Computer Programming, Vol. 1: Fundamental Algorithms*, *2nd ed.* (Reading, Mass.: Addison-Wesley, 1974). Chapter 2 includes a comprehensive presentation of the theory and principles of list processing.

Chapter 8

Looping and Address Modification

In Chapter 7 we discussed briefly the importance of looping, introduced the conditional branch statements that make a loop and its exit possible, and presented an example of a loop. Now we shall discuss the structure of a loop in more detail. We shall further illustrate the use of the conditional branch instruction, and introduce some other instructions that are logically equivalent to sequences of instructions we already know but which help in the writing of program loops. We shall also introduce address modification and discuss the techniques used in constructing loops in which the addresses of data items used in repetitions of the loop vary.

The subject of looping and address modification is an extremely vital one. The structure of the IBM System/360 and 370 helps us perform the functions of looping and address modification in several different ways, each of which has advantages in some situations. The reader should pay special attention to following and learning the techniques discussed in this chapter; he will have opportunity to see them used in subsequent chapters as well.

1. THE STRUCTURE OF A LOOP

In analyzing the structure of a loop we find four steps that can be clearly identified: initialization, the body of the loop, an adjustment step, and a test for exit. They are, of course, related to one another, and sometimes two of these steps are included in the same instruction. On some occasions no instructions are required to perform the functions of one of the steps. In any event, we find the division into these four steps to be profitable to our discussion. We take up the steps one by one.

The body

The *body* of the loop is the segment containing the instructions which are the principal business of the loop—the real work we want the computer to do. The body includes input, output, arithmetic computations, information move, tests, and branches within the loop—whatever we want done repetitively. The other three steps have only one purpose—to ensure that the body will be performed the right number of times on the right data.

The adjustment step

The *adjustment step* of the loop is often a set of instructions that adds to a counter of the number of repetitions of the loop that have already been performed, or subtracts from a counter of the number of times the loop has yet to be performed. Such a counter is, of course, a register or storage location which we treat as a counter with ordinary arithmetic instructions. As we shall see in more detail later, the adjustment step may also include adding to or subtracting from a register which specifies the address of the data items to be used in the next repetition of the loop. The adjustment step may also include moving some information around so that it will be in the correct place for the next repetition of the loop. Thus the adjustment step has the functions of updating a quantity to be used in the test for exit and of ensuring that the right data are available to the next repetition of the loop.

Exit from the loop

Obviously, in all but the most trivial problems the computer needs an *exit* from the loop as well as an entry to it. The exit must be some sort of conditional branch that is not always taken; otherwise there would be no loop at all! So a test for exit is a branch point involving a test: if certain conditions occur, control leaves the loop; if other conditions occur, the loop is continued. The structure of the loop may be complicated by several possible exits, so that any of several possible conditions will cause exit from the loop. For example, in a loop whose main business is the search for a certain piece of data, there may be one possible exit which is taken if and when the piece of data is found, and another possible exit which is taken when the data to be searched are exhausted and the search has therefore failed. Often a test for exit is a test of whether the body has been repeated a given number of times, specifically, a comparison of the counter of repetitions of the loop with some predetermined limit, and a branch on the condition code resulting from the comparison. Other conditions which may be tested for possible exit will be illustrated in examples in this chapter and in later chapters. The student will realize that any possible test that can be made by a computer may be a possible test for exit from some loop.

Initialization

The body, adjustment step, and test for exit are repeated over and over again inside the loop. The *initialization step* takes place outside the loop, preferably before execution of the loop begins. In the initialization step, all counters, addresses of first data items, and other conditions necessary to the proper functioning of the loop itself are set. A location to be used as a counter of the number of times the body of the loop has been executed will be filled with zero; a location used to address the data items in a list as the body of the loop is executed will be set to address the first item on the list, etc.

It is important that the initialization be performed by instructions executed before entry to the loop. To understand this point, let us examine two inferior alternatives. The first alternative is initialization of the counters, etc. by constant definitions. Definitions can be made so that at first entry, the loop proceeds properly. However, if after exit from the loop we wish to enter the loop from the beginning a second time, the counters and other items that have changed during execution of the loop will not be properly set. The second alternative is an improvement on the first: reset the counters, etc. after exit from the loop. The difficulties with this approach are more subtle. In the first place, there may be several possible exits, with perhaps different actions needed to reset the appropriate quantities after each exit. So the coding of the reinitialization becomes longer and more complex than if initialization were done before entry in the first place. Secondly, reinitialization after exit from the loop complicates the logic of the program and confuses the programmer, thereby creating a greater danger of programming errors. Third, the programmer may see from the total logic of his program that shortcuts can indeed be taken in reinitialization, or that certain loops can be left without reinitialization because they will not be entered again. However, if it is necessary to modify the program at a later date—and any worthwhile program is often modified to fit slightly different circumstances—then the shortcuts taken will likely increase the work of making and debugging the modifications way out of proportion to the time saved by the shortcuts in the first place.

Therefore the initialization comes before execution of the loop itself. The body, adjustment step, and test for exit may appear in any order, and, indeed, they may be mixed together. The most common structures are those shown in Fig. 8-1. The first of these, structure (a), is often used, and is quite straightfor-

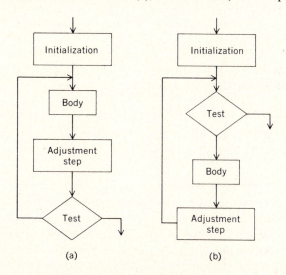

(a)   (b)

Fig. 8-1   Two common loop structures.

ward. The machine language corresponding to a FORTRAN DØ statement follows this pattern. Structure (b) has the advantage that special cases in which the body of the loop should be executed *no* times can be handled by the regular test for exit, thus avoiding the necessity of a separate test prior to entry to the loop.

Examples of loop structure

Now let us illustrate loop structure with some simple examples. Our first example is the addition of 20 numbers, which we will call A_0, A_1, . . . , A_{19}. Figure 8–2 is a flowchart for the addition. Each of the four steps in our loop structure is represented by one box in the flowchart. The body is the addition of A_i to the sum; the other steps serve to make the body be executed exactly 20 times, adding the proper numbers to a location which has the appropriate initial contents. The quantity i is used both as an indicator of which A is to be added next and as a counter of how many times the loop has been executed; incrementing of i is the only adjustment needed in the adjustment step. The test for exit is a comparison of i with a limit of 20; when i has reached 20, the loop is left. The only quantities changed during the loop are *Sum* and i, so they are the only quantities that need to be initialized.

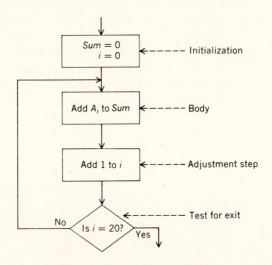

Fig. 8–2 Addition of 20 numbers.

As a second example, suppose that we wish to search 20 numbers A_0, A_1, . . . , A_{19} in consecutive main storage locations for the first (if any) equal to a given X. Figure 8–3 is a flowchart for this search. Again i is used both as a pointer to the proper A to consider next and as a counter of times through the loop. The quantity i is also the only output of the loop; the result is either the pointer, indicating the correct entry in the table of A's, or the number 20, indicating failure of the search. The test for $A_i = X$ is the body of the loop, the principal

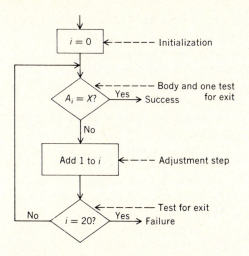

Fig. 8–3 Search of 20 numbers for one equal to X.

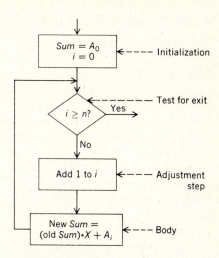

Fig. 8–4 Evaluation of a polynomial by Horner's method.

business of the loop, but since it includes a branch out of the loop, it must also be considered a test for exit.

As a third, and more complex, example, let us consider polynomial evaluation. Suppose we have quantities $A_0, A_1, \ldots, A_n$ which are coefficients of a polynomial of degree n: $A_0x^n + A_1x^{n-1} + \cdots + A_{n-1}x + A_n$. The polynomial can be rewritten for efficiency of computation as

$$((\cdots((A_0x + A_1)x + A_2)x + \cdots)x + A_{n-1})x + A_n,$$

which can be evaluated as

$$A_0x + A_1,$$
$$(A_0x + A_1)x + A_2,$$
$$((A_0x + A_1)x + A_2)x + A_3,$$
$$\vdots$$
$$(\cdots((A_0x + A_1)x + A_2)x + A_3)\cdots)x + A_{n-1},$$
$$((\cdots((A_0x + A_1)x + A_2)x + A_3)\cdots)x + A_{n-1})x + A_n.$$

This technique, called *Horner's method* and also sometimes called *nesting*, was introduced in the discussion of number conversions in Chapter 1. It requires only n multiplications and n additions, and can easily be programmed in a loop as shown in Fig. 8–4. We assume that X, the value at which the polynomial is to be evaluated, is available. *Sum* and i are the only quantities changed during execution of the loop, so they are the only ones that need to be initialized. By making the test for exit first, we have made our loop able to evaluate polynomials of 0 degree, namely constants. The body and adjustment step are straightforward.

2. PROGRAMMING A SIMPLE LOOP

Let us illustrate the concepts of the various steps of a loop with a program segment. Suppose that we have a deck of 20 cards, each containing a number A_i in columns 8–12, in the EBCDIC representation. Our problem is to read each of the cards in turn and add all 20 A's together. The flowchart may be like that shown in Fig. 8–5.

Assuming that a subroutine READATA is available to read a card, we can code the program segment in assembler language as follows:

```
*           INITIALIZATION
        L       15,=V(READATA)
        LA      1,=A(CARD)
        LA      8,0             SUM = 0
        LA      9,0             I = 0
*           BEGINNING ØF LØØP ITSELF
*           BØDY ØF LØØP
LØØP    BALR    14,15           BRANCH TØ READATA SUBRØUTINE
        PACK    DB(8),CARD+7(5) CØNVERT A TØ BINARY
        CVB     6,DB
        AR      8,6             ADD TØ SUM
*           ADJUSTMENT STEP
        LA      9,1(9)          INCREASE I BY 1
*           TEST FØR EXIT
        C       9,=F'20'
        BNE     LØØP
*           SEGMENT AFTER END ØF LØØP
        ⋮
DB      DC      1D
CARD    DS      CL80
        ⋮
```

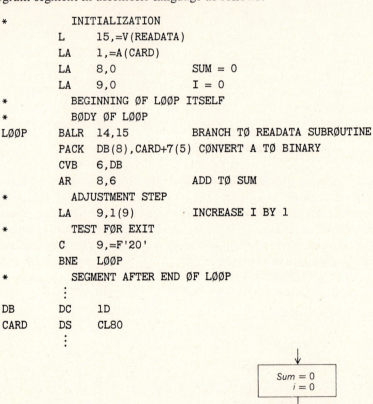

Fig. 8–5 Flowchart for adding numbers from 20 cards.

The instructions loading registers 1 and 15 preparatory to entering the READATA subroutine could logically be considered as belonging to the body of the loop. However, these instructions need be executed only once; the addresses will remain in registers 1 and 15 during the repetitions of the body, adjustment step, and test for exit, so it is most efficient to include the instructions loading registers 1 and 15 with the initialization.

In the body of the loop, the subroutine READATA is actually entered. When it returns control, the number in columns 8–12 of the card, now in locations CARD+7 to CARD+11, is converted to binary and added to the sum which is being kept in register 8. The adjustment step is performed by the single instruction

$$\text{LA} \qquad 9,1(9)$$

The test for exit involves a comparison of the counter i, register 9, with the number 20. The extended mnemonic BNE (Branch Not Equal) is used to return control to LØØP for another repetition if i has not yet reached 20. When i reaches 20, no branch will take place, and control will leave the loop by proceeding to the next instruction.

3. ADDRESS MODIFICATION: CHANGING AND TESTING CONTENTS OF A BASE REGISTER

In many loops the data items to be treated in repetitions of the body of the loop are found in main storage. Often the data items will be stored in consecutive locations. On other occasions the items, while not in consecutive locations, will at least be in evenly spaced locations. In such a situation, we can derive the address of each data item after the first by adding a constant to the address of its predecessor. This addition can be done naturally as part of the adjustment step of a loop.

For example, in the problem of Fig. 8–2, the numbers A_i to be added together may be in consecutive full words in main storage, starting at location AA. If the address of the A_i just added to the sum is kept in a register, the number 4 can be added to the contents of that register; the result is the address of the next number to be added. Figure 8–6 shows a program which follows the flowchart of Fig. 8–2, with the added assumption that the A_i are stored in consecutive full words. Register 7 is initialized to AA, the address of A_0. Each time the adjustment step is executed, the quantity in register 7 is increased by 4. Thus the second time the instruction

$$\text{A} \qquad 8,0(7)$$

is executed, the address in register 7 is 4 greater than the address of A_0; therefore it is the address of A_1. The third time the body of the loop is executed, the address in register 7 has been increased again, so A_2 is added to the growing *Sum*. The process of adding an A_i and adjusting the address continues until execution of the loop is terminated.

Note that for addressing the A's we use the implied base register specified (earlier) in the USING statement only for loading the address AA into register 7.

Fig. 8-6   A program to add 20 numbers from main storage

```
*       A SEGMENT TO ADD 20 NUMBERS FRØM
*       CØNSECUTIVE FULL WØRDS IN MAIN STØRAGE
*       INITIALIZATION
            LA    8,0               SUM = 0
            LR    9,8               I = 0
            LA    7,AA              ADDRESS ØF FIRST A
*           BODY:  ADD A(SUB I)     TØ SUM
LØØP        A     8,0(7)
*       ADJUSTMENT STEP
            LA    9,1(9)            INCREASE I
            LA    7,4(7)            GET ADDRESS ØF NEXT A
*       TEST FØR EXIT
            C     9,=F'20'
            BNE   LØØP              BRANCH BACK IF I NØT YET 20
*                                   GØ ØN ØUT ØF LØØP WHEN I = 20
```

Then register 7 holds the address of the *A* to be used next. If we had tried to use the implied base register for addressing all the *A*'s, incrementing it by 4 each time through the loop, the *A*'s could have been correctly addressed, but everything else, like the address LØØP and the address of the literal =F'20', would be incorrect.

The counter *i*, which is kept in register 9, is incremented in a regular pattern, attaining the values 0, 1, 2, . . . , 20. The contents of register 7 are also incremented in a regular pattern, attaining the values

$$AA, \qquad AA+4, \qquad AA+8, \qquad \ldots, \qquad AA+80$$

We exit from the loop when the contents of register 9 is 20, and when the contents of register 7 is AA+80. *We could test for exit from the loop with a test of register 7 just as well as by a test of register 9;* the compare instruction would be changed to

$$C \qquad 7,=A(AA+80)$$

and the branch instruction is unchanged. The program is equivalent to the original: it will produce exactly the same results. But with the change, it is no longer necessary to use register 9 at all; we can eliminate it from the program. The resulting, more efficient program is shown in Fig. 8–7.

Fig. 8-7   A shorter program to add 20 numbers from main storage

```
*       A SEGMENT TØ ADD 20 NUMBERS FRØM
*       CØNSECUTIVE FULL WØRDS IN MAIN STØRAGE
*       INITIALIZATIØN
            LA    8,0               SUM = 0
            LA    7,AA              ADDRESS ØF FIRST A
*       BØDY: ADD A(SUB I) TØ SUM
LØØP        A     8,0(7)
*       ADJUSTMENT STEP
            LA    7,4(7)            GET ADDRESS ØF NEXT A
*       TEST FØR EXIT
            C     7,=A(AA+80)
            BNE   LOOP              BRANCH BACK IF ADDRESS NØT YET AA+80
*                                   GØ ØN, ØUT ØF LØØP, WHEN = AA+80
```

Some points illustrated by this problem are the following:

1. A sequence of data items arranged in a regular pattern in main storage can be addressed easily in successive repetitions of the body of a loop.

2. The adjustment step of a loop obtains the address of the next data item by incrementing the address of the last one.

3. Since these addresses are advanced in a regular pattern, they can be tested and used to cause exit from the loop at the appropriate time. The register containing the addresses is thus essentially a counter of times through the loop.

These points will be illustrated by further examples.

Program segment for a polynomial evaluation loop

Next, let us consider polynomial evaluation, following the procedure shown in the flowchart of Fig. 8–4. Again we assume that the coefficients are in consecutive full words in main storage, but that they start at location CØEF. Let us further assume that N, the degree of the polynomial, is in register 2, and that X is a binary integer in register 3. A program segment following the flowchart in Fig. 8–4 is shown in Fig. 8–8. We assume that the sums and products will not overflow one register.

Note that the branch out of the loop is taken on the condition that I is equal to *or greater than N*. We expect N to be nonnegative, and if N *is* nonnegative, I will reach N by coming up from underneath. However, if by some mischance N is negative, I will never be equal to N; our test, which costs no more in time or space than the plain test for equality, will cause a quick exit from the loop anyway. It is always good practice to make programs secure against mischances in the data. Any time we can do it with no extra effort, we certainly should; however, the security may sometimes cost more than it is worth to us.

   In this example we could have the program calculate the limiting address, CØEF+4*N, that register 7 should attain before exit from the loop, and then have it test register 7 for exit. If we did, we could abolish all references to I and register 9, as we did in Fig. 8–7.

Fig. 8–8 Evaluation of a polynomial by Horner's method

```
*           EVALUATION ØF A PØLYNØMIAL BY HØRNER'S METHØD
*           CØEFFICIENTS AO, A1, ..., AN ARE STØRED IN CØNSECUTIVE
*              FULL WØRDS STARTING AT CØEF, CØEFFICIENT ØF X**N FIRST.
*           N IS IN REG. 2, X IN REG. 3.
*           **INITIALIZATIØN**
            LA    7,CØEF         ADDRESS ØF CØEF. TØ REG. 7.
            L     5,0(7)         SUM = AO
            LA    9,0            I = 0
*           **TEST FØR EXIT**
LØØP        CR    9,2            CØMPARE I WITH N
            BNL   ØUT            IF I NØT LESS THAN N, EXIT
*           **ADJUSTMENT STEP**
            LA    9,1(9)         ADD 1 TØ I
            LA    7,4(7)         PREPARE TØ ADDRESS NEXT CØEFFICIENT
*           **BØDY ØF LØØP**
            MR    4,3            SUM*X
            A     5,0(7)         NEW SUM = SUM*X + AI
            B     LØØP
ØUT                             CØNTINUE PRØGRAM AFTER LØØP
```

Fig. 8-9   Search of 20 numbers for one equal to X

```
*        PRØGRAM SEGMENT TØ SEARCH 20 NUMBERS AT
*           ARG, ARG+80, ARG+160, ..., FØR EQUALITY WITH X.
*        X IS IN REGISTER 3.
*        **INITIALIZATIØN**
         LA      7,ARG
*        **BØDY**
LØØP     C       3,0(7)
         BE      ØUT                BRANCH ØUT IF EQUALITY
*        **ADJUSTMENT STEP**
         LA      7,80(7)
*        **TEST FØR EXIT**
         C       7,=A(ARG+20*80)
         BNE     LØØP
*        REACH ØUT EITHER BY NØT BRANCHING BACK TØ LØØP,
*           WHICH INDICATES FAILURE ØF SEARCH BY LEAVING
*           ARG+20*80 IN REG. 7,
*        ØR BY BRANCH WHEN SUCCESSFULLY CØMPLETING SEARCH
ØUT      ~†
```

We leave this conversion of the segment as an exercise for the student. The student will find that

a) his segment is expanded by one instruction,

b) his loop is one instruction shorter, so will run faster, and

c) the logic of the segment is somewhat more obscure.

Either segment may be preferable, under different circumstances. Real programming problems are usually accompanied by considerations that help the programmer make his choice between segments such as these.

As a final example in this section, let us consider the searching procedure shown in Fig. 8-3. Let us assume that the numbers A_i to be searched are full words located 80 bytes apart (perhaps read each one from a card), beginning at location ARG. That is, the A's to be searched are at locations

$$ARG, \qquad ARG+80, \qquad ARG+2*80, \qquad ..., \qquad ARG+19*80$$

We also assume that before entry to our search segment, the quantity X we are searching for is in register 3.

The program segment for the search is shown in Fig. 8-9. The logic follows that in the flowchart in Fig. 8-3. However, the quantity i is used only implicitly as reflected in the address of the next A to be compared. If, for instance, the third A were found equal to X, the address of the third A, ARG+160, would be left in register 7. This address would be the only result of the loop.

4. ADDRESS MODIFICATION: USE OF INDEX REGISTERS

An effective address in the IBM System/360 or 370 is generated either as the sum of a displacement and contents of a base register or as the sum of displacement and

---

† The sign $\sim$ indicates that program control continues in the next segment of the program.

Fig. 8-10   Search of 20 numbers, using an index register

```
        LA     7,ARG
        LA     10,0            SET INDEX REG.
LØØP    C      3,0(10,7)       ADDRESS NUMBER BY BASE + INDEX
        BE     ØUT
        LA     10,80(10)       INCREASE INDEX
        C      10,=F'1600'     TEST INDEX
        BNE    LØØP
ØUT     ~
```

contents of base and index registers. The effective address specified in a particular repeated instruction can therefore be modified by changing the displacement, changing the contents of a register used as a base, or changing the contents of a register used as an index. In Section 3 we illustrated techniques associated with change in the base register. Address modification by change in the displacement in an actual instruction is possible but awkward; we will not illustrate it here, but leave it as a challenging exercise to the student. Comparable techniques are necessary in the use of some computers.

In this section we introduce the use of an index register in modification of an effective address. Of course, this technique can be used only when the instructions addressing the items with varying addresses are RX-type instructions. The index register specification was included in RX-type instructions especially to make address modification easy, and since many instructions are of RX type, index register techniques can be widely used.

We shall first illustrate the use of an index register by twice changing the program segment shown in Fig. 8-9, which searches 20 numbers for one equal to X. The first changed segment is shown in Fig. 8-10. The logic of the segment has not been changed at all; the remarks in Fig. 8-9 have been stripped away to allow us to show more easily the changes made. One extra instruction sets the initial contents of the index register. The instruction at LØØP addresses by base and index registers one of the numbers to be searched; the contents of the base register is left fixed, and the index register (10) is incremented and tested for exit. We have not improved the program segment with our use of an index register; we have in fact made it longer!

If all the modification of effective addresses is done by changing the value in an index register, it becomes possible to use the implied base register. Our second change to the same program segment, shown in Fig. 8-11, makes use of the

Fig. 8-11   Search of 20 numbers, using an index register and an implied base register

```
        LA     10,0
LØØP    C      3,ARG(10)
        BE     ØUT
        LA     10,80(10)
        C      10,=F'1600'
        BNE    LØØP
ØUT     ~
```

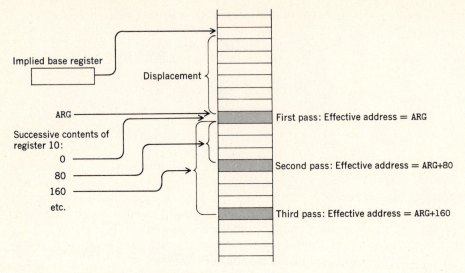

Fig. 8-12 Addressing successive operands by ARG(10).

implied base register and again shortens the segment. The specification ARG(10) is the only change in the program segment from the segment of Fig. 8–10. Register 7 is no longer used, so the segment is shortened by deletion of the instruction that loaded it. In constructing a machine-language instruction corresponding to

$$\text{C}\qquad 3, \text{ARG}(10)$$

the assembler inserts the address of an implied base register as the base register *B2* for the second operand. The assembler also calculates and inserts the proper displacement *D2* so that *D2* and *B2* together address ARG. The assembler includes *X2* = 10, but without knowledge or thought of the contents of register 10. During repeated execution of the instruction, the base and displacement together always address ARG, and the contents of register 10 is also added, yielding effective addresses

$$\text{ARG},\qquad \text{ARG+80},\qquad \text{ARG+160},\qquad \ldots$$

In diagram form, the addressing of successive operands by ARG(10) can be represented as shown in Fig. 8–12. The change in the contents of register 10 changes the effective address.

Now that we have illustrated how an index register can be used in a simple situation, let us show another in which the use of the index register is clearly advantageous. Consider a problem in which there are 20 numbers, $A_0, A_1, \ldots, A_{19}$, stored in consecutive words in main storage starting at AA, and 20 numbers, $B_0, B_1, \ldots, B_{19}$, stored in consecutive words in main storage starting at BB. We wish to calculate 20 numbers: $C_0 = A_0 + B_0$, $C_1 = A_1 + B_1$, $\ldots$, $C_{19} = A_{19} + B_{19}$, and store the 20 C's in consecutive words beginning at location CC. In a loop, effective addresses of an A, a B, and a C must be used and modi-

Fig. 8-13   Computation of $C_i = A_i + B_i$, $(i = 0, \ldots, 19)$ by modifying the base register

```
            LA    7,AA          INITIALIZATIØN
            LA    8,BB
            LA    9,CC
LØØP        L     4,0(7)        BØDY.   GET A
            A     4,0(8)                ADD B
            ST    4,0(9)                STØRE C
            LA    7,4(7)        ADJUSTMENT STEP.    ADDRESS ØF A
            LA    8,4(8)                            ADDRESS ØF B
            LA    9,4(9)                            ADDRESS ØF C
            C     7,=A(AA+80)   TEST FØR EXIT
            BNE   LØØP
```

fied. Using the base-register modification techniques of Section 3, we would need
a program segment like that shown in Fig. 8-13. There are eleven instructions,
including eight which are executed each repetition of the loop. However, using
index register techniques, we can have a shorter and faster segment, as shown in
Fig. 8-14. Only one register needs to be initialized and modified; the same register
serves to vary the effective addresses in three instructions, giving a clear reduction
in storage space and time required and making a more readable program segment.

We will see more examples of the modification of contents of base registers
and index registers in later sections and chapters.

Fig. 8-14   Computation of $C_i = A_i + B_i$ $(i = 0, \ldots, 19)$ by modifying the index register

```
            LA    10,0          INITIALIZATIØN
LØØP        L     4,AA(10)      BØDY
            A     4,BB(10)
            ST    4,CC(10)
            LA    10,4(10)      ADJUSTMENT STEP
            C     10,=F'80'     TEST FØR EXIT
            BNE   LØØP
```

5. THE BXH AND BXLE INSTRUCTIONS

In many of the examples of loops we have seen in this chapter, the adjustment
step and test for exit have followed the pattern

```
            LA    REG1,INCR(REG1)
            C     REG1,LIMIT
            BNE   LØØP
```

This three-instruction loop control sequence and slight variants of it are indeed
standard in many computers. In the design of the IBM System/360 and 370, thought
was given to facilitation of the looping process, and the instructions BXLE and BXH
were provided. Either of these instructions, in different situations, can be substituted for the three-instruction loop control sequence. To prepare for BXLE or
BXH usually requires additional initialization instructions, but the reduction in
instructions repeated in the loop gives a net saving of time.

The BXH and BXLE instructions are of RS type; there are two register operands, *R1* and *R3*, and a main storage operand. The operands for the two instructions are the same; only the branching criterion is different. The first operand *R1* is the register that will be incremented and then tested. The second operand *D2(B2)* is the address to which control will branch if the branch criterion is met.

Examining the three-instruction loop control sequence, we see that the increment and the limit to be compared against must still be specified. Since it is impossible to specify four operands in any IBM System/360 instruction, we are driven to the use of an even-odd pair of registers, so that one operand address can specify two operands, one in the even register, the other in the odd register. The operand address *R3* can therefore be the address of a register pair. Register *R3* contains the increment which is added to register *R1*. The addition performed is ordinary binary integer addition; note that either or both registers could contain negative numbers. The odd register, register *R3* + 1, contains the limit which is compared with register *R1* after *R1* has been incremented. Branching depends on the result of the comparison. The BXH instruction (BXH stands for Branch on indeX High) will cause a branch to operand 2 if the contents of *R1*, as incremented, is greater than the contents of register *R3* + 1. The BXLE instruction (BXLE stands for Branch on indeX Less than or Equal) will cause a branch if the contents of register *R1*, as incremented, is less than or equal to the contents of register *R3* + 1. There is one further wrinkle to the BXH and BXLE instructions: register *R3* can be specified as an odd register. If it is, the contents of register *R3* is used as *both* increment and limit.

The BXLE and BXH instructions can therefore be summarized as follows:

$$\text{BXLE} \quad R1,R3,S2: \qquad R1 \leftarrow c(R1) + c(R3);$$

If *R3* even:
$$\rightarrow S2 \text{ if } c(R1) \leq c(R3 + 1)$$

If *R3* odd:
$$\rightarrow S2 \text{ if } c(R1) \leq c(R3)$$

$$\text{BXH} \quad R1,R3,S2: \qquad R1 \leftarrow c(R1) + c(R3);$$

If *R3* even:
$$\rightarrow S2 \text{ if } c(R1) > c(R3 + 1)$$

If *R3* odd:
$$\rightarrow S2 \text{ if } c(R1) > c(R3).$$

Neither instruction affects the setting of the condition code.

Let us illustrate the action of these instructions before we use them in program segments. Suppose that the initial contents of the registers are

Register 2:	00000001	Register 6:	00000026
Register 3:	0000004A	Register 7:	0000006E
Register 4:	FFFFFFFF	Register 9:	FFFFFFFC
Register 5:	00000000	Register 12:	00009434

The following instructions, each starting from these initial contents, will have the results indicated:

BXLE 6,2,0(12) Contents of register 6 is incremented by the contents of register 2, to 00000027. The number 00000027 *is* less than 0000004A, so branch to location 009434.

BXH 6,2,0(12) Similarly, contents of register 6 is increased to 00000027. The number 00000027 is *not* higher than 0000004A, so no branch.

BXLE 7,2,0(12) Contents of register 7 is increased to 0000006F, which is *not* less than or equal to 0000004A, so no branch.

BXH 6,4,0(12) Contents of register 6 is incremented (but decreased) to 00000025, which *is* higher than 00000000, so branch to 009434.

BXH 3,9,0(12) Contents of register 3 is incremented (by −4) to 00000046, which *is* higher than FFFFFFFC, so branch to 009434.

Examples of use of BXLE and BXH instructions

Now that we have explained the instructions, let us illustrate their use. Our first example will be the last problem presented in Section 4: computation of $C_i = A_i + B_i$ $(i = 0, 1, \ldots, 19)$. Modifying the program segment shown in Fig. 8–14, we are able to replace the last three instructions by a BXLE instruction, as shown in Fig. 8–15. In the execution of the BXLE instruction, register 10 is first incremented by the 4 contained in register 8, then compared with the 76 in register 9. The first 19 times the instruction is executed (when register 10 contains 4, 8, 12, . . . , 72, 76 after incrementing) control branches back to LØØP. The twentieth time the BXLE instruction is executed, the contents of register 10 is raised to 80, which is *not* less than or equal to 76, so no branch takes place, and control passes from the loop. Note that the limit in register 9 is the number 76, the last contents of register 10 with which the body of the loop should be executed. Two extra instructions had to be added to the loop initialization, so the total segment shown in Fig. 8–15 is the same length as the segment shown in Fig. 8–14. The advantage of the segment in Fig. 8–15 is in the smaller number of instructions to be executed repeatedly.

Fig. 8–15 Computation of $C_i = A_i + B_i$ $(i = 0, \ldots, 19)$, using the BXLE instruction

```
        LA    10,0        INITIALIZATIØN
        LA    8,4           INCREMENT
        LA    9,76          LIMIT
LØØP    L     4,AA(10)    BØDY
        A     4,BB(10)
        ST    4,CC(10)
        BXLE  10,8,LØØP   ADJUSTMENT AND TEST FØR EXIT.
```

Fig. 8-16   Evaluation of a polynomial, which illustrates the BXH instruction

```
        LA    7,CØEF        INITIALIZATIØN
        L     5,0(7)        SUM = A SUB 0
        LA    9,0           I = 0
        LA    10,1            INCREMENT = 1
        LR    11,2            LIMIT = N, FRØM REG. 2
LØØP    BXH   9,10,ØUT      ADJUSTMENT AND TEST FØR EXIT
        LA    7,4(7)        ADJUST ADDRESS
        MR    4,3           BØDY
        A     5,0(7)
        B     LØØP
ØUT     ~
```

For a second example, we return to the problem of polynomial evaluation. We retain the logic of Fig. 8-4 except that in the single instruction BXH the adjustment step comes before the test for exit. Figure 8-16 is a modification of Fig. 8-8, using the BXH instruction to exit from the loop at the appropriate time. Again we see that the number of instructions repeated in the loop is reduced by two, but two instructions must be added to the initialization step. However, we point out that if N were made available in register 11 in the first place instead of in register 2, the instruction

$$\text{LR} \qquad 11,2$$

would be unnecessary. The student is invited to simulate execution of the segment, to convince himself that the change of the branch test from Branch if Not Low to Branch on High, coupled with the incrementing of register 9 before the test instead of afterwards, makes the segment execute properly.

Note that although the names of the instructions BXH and BXLE suggest that a register *used as an index* is incremented and tested, there is no requirement that the incremented and tested register be used for anything in particular. In Fig. 8-15, register 10, incremented and tested by the BXLE instruction, was in fact used as an index. In Fig. 8-16, however, register 9, incremented and tested by the BXH instruction, was used as a base register, not as an index. In still another example, the incremented and tested register might be used only as a counter, and not at all in the forming of an address. Each instruction operates by itself, without knowledge in the computer of what else its operands may be used for.

We consider a third example. The contents of 20 cards are to be read into the computer and stored backwards in a block from locations TABLE to TABLE+1599. That is, the first card is to be stored at locations TABLE+1520 to TABLE+1599, with the characters from the card columns stored in normal order: column 1 at TABLE+1520, column 2 at TABLE+1521, . . . , column 80 at TABLE+1599. The second card read is to be stored at locations TABLE+1440 to TABLE+1519, etc. The last card is to be stored at locations TABLE to TABLE+79. We use a register as an index in a load address instruction that generates the address into which the READATA subroutine is directed to read the contents of a card. The contents of the register used as index must decrease in steps of 80; and the last time used, it must contain 0.

Fig. 8–17 A program to read 20 cards and store them at decreasing locations

```
*READ 20 CARDS.  STØRE FIRST AT TABLE+1520,
*SECØND AT TABLE+1440, ..., TWENTIETH AT TABLE
*USE READATA SUBRØUTINE.
*          **INITIALIZATIØN**
           L    15,=V(READATA)
           LA   1,VARAD          ADDRESS ØF ADDRESS TØ READ INTØ
           L    9,=F'-80'        INCREMENT AND LIMIT
           LA   8,1520           BEGINNING INDEX
*          **BØDY ØF LØØP**
LØØP       LA   7,TABLE(8)       SET ADDRESS TØ READ INTØ
           ST   7,VARAD
           BALR 14,15            READ CARD
*          **LØØPING CØNTRØL**
           BXH  8,9,LØØP
```

The BXH instruction, with suitable register contents, can handle looping control by testing the contents of the register used as index.

The program segment to perform this task is shown in Fig. 8–17. Conforming to standard subroutine linkage, register 15 is set to contain the entry address of the subroutine READATA, and register 1 contains the address of the parameter list. The single parameter in the parameter list is the address into which the card is to be read (actually, column 1 of the card: the other columns of the card are read into successive locations). In our problem the address is variable, but we can store it in a constant location whose name is VARAD. Looping control is prepared by initialization of register 8 to 1520 and register 9 to a number that turns out to be usable as *both* increment and limit: −80. In the body of the loop, the address into which the card is to be read is generated by the load address instruction as the sum of the address TABLE and the contents of register 8. In successive repetitions of this instruction, the effective addresses generated (and then stored at VARAD for use in the READATA subroutine) are

$$\text{TABLE+1520,} \qquad \text{TABLE+1440,} \qquad \text{TABLE+1360,} \qquad \text{etc.}$$

After execution of the subroutine, the single looping control instruction

$$\text{BXH} \qquad \text{8,9,LØØP}$$

completes the loop. On first execution, the contents of register 8 is reduced to 1440, and since it is higher than −80, the branch back to LØØP closes the instruction loop. Similarly, the second execution reduces the contents of register 8 to 1360 and branches back. Finally, after executing the subroutine READATA with VARAD holding the address TABLE, the contents of register 8 is reduced to −80, which is *not* higher than −80 so the branch does not take place and the loop concludes.

The programming process

Let us examine the sequence of steps in programming, as compared to the sequence of steps in the program itself. First, programming of an entire job should be broken into sections, and the logical design of the sections refines defined tasks into smaller blocks. The blocks can be organized into combinations of elements, such as simple loops and choices of alternate computations. The information structures required for each of the elements and blocks should be analyzed, and tentative decisions made about storage area and register use, so that the pieces of program fit together smoothly.

When it comes time to code individual elements, some different processes take over. A program listing shows the program roughly in order of execution. In particular, the initialization of a loop precedes the body of the loop, although *the code is not designed in that order*. Loops are written from the inside first. We design the body of the loop, including the way in which addresses, counters, or indexes will vary. Second, we usually design the adjustment step, including all incrementing and adjusting needed to prepare for the next execution of the body. Third, we design the test for exit, which may include a loop-control instruction such as BXLE. *Last, we design the initialization;* we can do that only when we know what is being changed inside the loop, how the variable items (and others) must begin, and in short, the complete requirements of the activities in the repeated portions of the loop.

6. THE BCT AND BCTR INSTRUCTIONS

The BCT and BCTR instructions, Branch on CounT and Branch on CounT to Register, are special looping control instructions that are easier to use than BXLE and BXH but are less flexible and less generally applicable.

The BCT and BCTR instructions are of RX and RR type, respectively. The second operand of each instruction defines a branch address: the second operand of the BCT instruction is the sum of *D2* and contents of registers *X2* and *B2*. If the second operand (*R2*) of the BCTR instruction is zero, no branching will occur, regardless; otherwise, a branch if taken will be to the address given in register *R2*.

The first event in the execution of BCT or BCTR is that the contents of register *R1* is decreased by 1. Then the branch occurs if the result in register *R1* is not zero. A result either greater or less than zero will cause a branch; only in case the result is exactly zero will there not be a branch. The condition code is not affected by either the BCT or BCTR instruction.

The action of the BCT and BCTR instructions can be described formally as:

$$\text{BCT} \quad R1,S2: \quad R1 \leftarrow c(R1) - 1;$$
$$\rightarrow S2 \text{ if } c(R1) \neq 0$$

$$\text{BCTR} \quad R1,R2: \quad R1 \leftarrow c(R1) - 1;$$
$$\rightarrow c(R2) \quad \text{if} \quad \begin{cases} c(R1) \neq 0 \text{ and} \\ R2 \neq 0. \end{cases}$$

Thus the BCT instruction is similar to the BXH and BXLE instructions. Register *R1* is incremented, but by a constant -1 instead of the contents of an operand register; it is compared to a limit, but a constant limit 0 instead of the contents of an operand register. Branching takes place or not as a result of the comparison, but on a criterion of not equal.

As examples, let us detail the effects of the following instructions.

1. Suppose that register 6 contains 000000F4. The instruction

                    BCT   6,BRCHAA

will reduce the contents of register 6 to 000000F3, and since this result is not zero, control will branch to BRCHAA.

2. Suppose that register 7 contains FFFFFFEA and register 10 contains 0000A344. The instruction

                    BCTR   7,10

will reduce the contents of register 7 to FFFFFFE9, and since the result is not zero, control will branch to 00A344.

3. Suppose register 3 contains 00000001. The instruction

                    BCT   3,LØØP

causes the contents of register 3 to be reduced to 00000000; since the result is zero, no branch takes place.

The BCT instruction is most often used when the branching control needed is a simple count of the number of times the loop should still be executed. The structure is

```
                L    REG1,LIMIT
        LØØP                  BØDY ØF LØØP
                  ⋮
                BCT    REG1,LØØP
```

The number of repetitions desired is entered into a register as part of the initialization step. The BCT instruction at the end of the loop decreases the contents of that register by one every time it is executed, in effect making the register keep the number of times the loop is yet to be executed. Until the number reaches zero, there are still more repetitions desired; the BCT instruction causes a branch back to LØØP. The register is reduced to zero immediately after the last desired repetition of the loop body; the BCT instruction does *not* cause a branch, and control exits from the loop.

As an example program segment, let us return to the problem given in Section 2: reading 20 cards and adding the numbers from columns 8–12. No address modification is required; we need only a looping control that repeats the body of the loop 20 times. The program segment for the problem, which uses the BCT instruction, is shown in Fig. 8–18. The program segment is exactly like the segment given in Section 2 except for the use of the BCT instruction, which shortens the segment by two instructions.

Fig. 8-18   Read 20 cards and form the sum of their values

```
        L     15,=V(READATA)
        LA    1,=A(CARD)
        LA    8,0          SUM = 0
        LA    9,20         REPEAT CØUNT
LØØP    BALR  14,15
        PACK  DB(8),CARD+7(5)
        CVB   6,DB
        AR    8,6
        BCT   9,LØØP
```

7. ORDERED LISTS AND BINARY SEARCH

We illustrated earlier in this chapter some serial search procedures. In this section we shall consider more deeply the subject of list organization and, finally, present a procedure called binary search, which is quite efficient in some search situations.

A list is made up of data items which we may call records. Records may all be of some fixed size or of different sizes. Usually, if records have varying lengths, a list of pointers is created, each record of which is of fixed size and serves mostly to point to the locations of the variable-length records. So we will restrict our attention in the following discussion to lists of fixed-length records.

Each record in the list is identified with a *key;* the key is a data item in the record. When we want information from a record, we have a data item called a *search key*, which bears some relation to the key of a record in the list; the search problem is that of finding the record with the right key. We say that the data item we have "bears some relation" to the key in the right record; the relationship could be any simple or complex relationship that can be tested for by program. We shall restrict our attention to matching the data item with the key, since no conceptual problems of the search attend other relationships.

Assuming that consecutive keys are stored in locations which differ by some constant amount, we can search for the key associated with the record we desire. We also assume that the record is located in constant relation to the key, so that once the key is found, we can easily calculate the address of the information in the desired record from the address of the key.

Fig. 8-19   Atomic numbers and weights of chemical elements

Atomic number	Atomic weight
1	1.008
2	4.003
3	6.940
4	9.013
5	10.820
6	12.011
7	14.008
8	16.000
9	19.000
10	20.183
18	39.944
36	83.8
54	131.3
86	222.

Let us describe two lists for illustrative purposes. First is the functional table of chemical elements shown in Fig. 8–19. The atomic numbers, which we would normally call the arguments in the table, are the keys in the list. The arrangement in the computer might be that all the keys are stored in consecutive words beginning at ATØMNØ and all the atomic weights are stored (in packed decimal or floating-point form) in consecutive words starting at ATØMWT. If the address of a particular atomic number (key) is generated in, say, register 6, the address of the corresponding atomic weight can be derived simply by

$$A \qquad 6,=A(ATØMWT-ATØMNØ)$$

Our second example of a list is a payroll information file, in which the information on each employee is held in an 80-byte record. Each employee may have an employee number, which can act as key to the list. The employee number may be stored in the 80-character record, as perhaps the first word. The records may be stored in consecutive 80-byte blocks of storage. A search for the employee with some particular employee number could be as shown in Figs. 8–3, 8–9, and 8–11. For example, suppose that the employee number is in the first four bytes of the record and the year's earnings to date is stored in the ninth through twelfth bytes. Once the address of the employee number of the desired employee is found through a search, the address of his year's earnings to date can be derived by adding 8 to the address of the employee number.

List density

We shall suppose that consecutive blocks are set aside in the computer's main storage for the items (keys and records) of a list. There may not be a list item in each block. If there are gaps in the storage of list items, the storage not used will usually have to contain some indicator which, by convention, is taken to mean absence of a list item. If there are gaps, we call the list *loose*. If there are no gaps, we call the list *dense*. For efficient storage, and often for efficient retrieval, a dense list is best.

We can also talk about a *key-dense* list, in which there is a common fixed increment between consecutive keys. The first 10 keys in the list of chemical elements given in Fig. 8–19 are consecutive integers; therefore this portion of the list is key-dense. The entire list as given is not key-dense, because the eleventh to fourteenth keys do not follow the same pattern of consecutive integers.

For retrieval of information from a key-dense list it is not necessary to search for a key. The address of the desired key can be *calculated* from the key itself. Therefore in the following discussions about searches, we shall assume a list which is dense (sometimes called *item-dense* for extra clarity) but not key-dense.

Ordered lists

If the keys of consecutive records are in some order, either ascending or descending, the list is said to be *ordered*. A key-dense list is a special case of an ordered list. If the list is not ordered, there is, in general, no search strategy that is more efficient than the *serial search* (search of consecutive records) illustrated earlier in the chapter. On the average, we would expect to search half the list before finding the desired record. If the list is ordered, we can still use a serial search, with the same expectation of a search of half the list before finding the desired item. With an ordered list, however, a different strategy called *binary search* is more efficient.

Binary search

In a binary search of an ordered list, the principal idea is that each comparison of a data item against a key is made on the key in the middle of the segment of the list to which the desired record might belong. The result of a comparison is either that the desired record is found or that one of the two pieces is rejected as not containing the desired record. Thus with each comparison the segment remaining to be searched is cut in half.

To describe the binary-search procedure in detail, let us adopt some notation. Let L be the ordered list to be searched for a data item x. Let the length of the list L be N items, and the keys be denoted by $L_1, L_2, \ldots, L_N$. By enclosing a quantity in square brackets [ ], we denote the largest integer not greater than the quantity: $[16.7] = 16$, $[15.0] = 15$, etc. Figure 8–20 describes in flowchart form

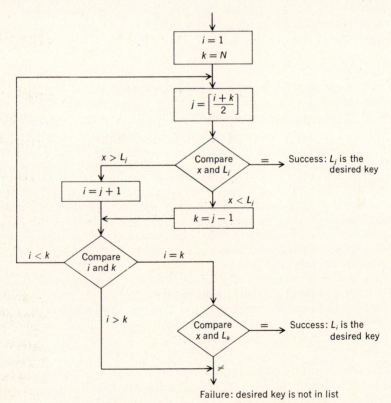

Fig. 8–20 Flowchart for a binary search.

the binary search procedure. The variables i and k always define the limits of the list segment in which the desired record must lie (if in fact it is in the list at all). The variable j defines the midpoint of the segment; after the comparison of L_j and x, the segment remaining to be searched is cut in half by a revision of one of its limits. So long as there remains a segment to search, the loop continues. If i and k are found to be equal, only one item remains to be tried. If i becomes greater than k, no segment remains to be searched; the search has failed.

Program segment for a binary search

Figure 8–21 shows a program segment which follows the flowchart in Fig. 8–20 for binary search. The segment is different from others in this chapter in the nature of its adjustment step and the address calculations. Variables I and K (in registers 4 and 5, respectively) are the only pointers that change in successive repetitions of the loop. These control the ultimate exit from the loop and also the

Fig. 8–21   Program segment for binary search

```
*           ASSUME AN ØRDERED LIST, WHØSE KEYS START AT ARG
*               AND ARE M LØCATIONS APART.  M IS IN MAIN STØRAGE.
*           THE LIST IS N ITEMS LØNG.  N IS IN MAIN STØRAGE.
*           THE SEARCH IS FØR A KEY MATCHING THE ITEM IN REG. 2
*           RESULT IS EITHER
*               THE ADDRESS ØF THE DESIRED KEY, IN REG. 3
*           ØR IN CASE ØF FAILURE, ZERØ IN REG. 3
*           **INITIALIZATIØN**
            LA    4,1            LØAD I
            L     5,N            LØAD K
            LA    11,ARG
            S     11,M           ADDRESS ØF ZERØ'TH KEY
*           **BØDY ØF LØØP**
LØØP        SR    6,6
            LA    7,0(4,5)       I+K
            D     6,=F'2'        J IN REG. 7
            LR    3,7            SAVE J
            M     6,M            DISPLACEMENT FRØM ZERØ'TH KEY
            C     2,0(7,11)      SUM ØF REGS. 7,11 IS ADDR. ØF J'TH KEY
            BE    SUCC
            BH    ADJI
*           **ADJUSTMENT STEP**
            LR    5,3
            S     5,=F'1'        K = J - 1
            B     CØMPIK
ADJI        LA    4,1(3)         I = J + 1
*           **TEST FØR EXIT**
CØMPIK      CR    4,5            CØMPARE I,K
            BL    LØØP
*           **LEAVE LØØP**
            BH    FAIL
            LR    7,5            DØ LAST CØMPARE
            M     6,M
            C     2,0(7,11)
            BE    SUCC
FAIL        SR    3,3            ZERØ IN REG. 3
            B     NEXT
SUCC        LA    3,0(7,11)      ADDRESS ØF CØRRECT RECØRD
*           **END ØF SEARCH SEGMENT**
NEXT        ~
```

address calculations within the loop. The address of the Jth key is J*M greater than the address of the zeroth key (which of course does not exist); the two portions of the address are used together in C and LA instructions as base and index, thus avoiding actual addition in a register.

Let us illustrate execution of a binary search with the table of atomic weights and numbers. Suppose the keys are stored in consecutive words (M = 4) beginning at location 009840 (ARG). There are N = 14 keys in the table, and the search key happens to be 10. In the initialization phase, I = 1, K = 14, and the address of the zeroth key is computed as 00983C. In the first execution of the loop, J = 7, and J*M = (hexadecimal) 0000001C. The search key, 10, is compared with the seventh key (at location 00983C+00001C = 009858). The search key is larger, so a branch is taken to ADJI, where I is recomputed as 8. The segment containing (possibly) the search key is now known to comprise items 8 through 14 of the list. The second time through the loop J = 11, J*M = 0000002C, and the comparison of the search key with the key at location 009868 shows the search key smaller. This time K is recomputed to be 10, and we loop again. After the third execution of the body of the loop, key number 9 is found to be too small, so the segment containing the search key now begins and ends with the 10th key. This is examined after exit from the loop and found to be the correct key.

Since the segment remaining to be searched is approximately halved during each execution of the loop, the loop must be executed approximately $\log_2 N$ times. This number is close to the *expected and maximum* numbers of iterations required. For example, if the list contains 256 items, eight executions of the loop will suffice. This compares to an expected number of 128 executions of a serial-search loop and shows the binary-search technique to be more efficient. Each execution of the body in a binary-search loop takes longer than an execution of the serial-search loop, so the binary search is more efficient only for lists of perhaps 16 items or more. The student is invited to try to calculate a more precise estimate of the break-even point.

8. MAIN IDEAS

a. The general loop structure includes initialization before the loop, and a body, adjustment step, and test for exit inside the loop.

b. When a list of data items is used in a loop, the effective addresses of the items can be conveniently modified in the adjustment step of the loop by incrementing a register used as base or index in addressing the data items. A register used as index can serve as modifier for several lists at once.

c. The test for exit may be made on the register used in modifying effective addresses. The BXH, BXLE, and BCT instructions are specially designed for looping control; they can perform adjustment and test for exit in one instruction.

d. When a list of records is searched for the record with a certain key, and the list is ordered (by key), a binary search can be much more efficient than a serial search.

PROBLEMS FOR REVIEW AND IMAGINATION

1. After initialization,

$$\boxed{i = N} \, ,$$

arrange the body, adjustment step, and test for exit,

$$\boxed{\text{Body}} \qquad \boxed{\text{Decrease } i \text{ by } 1} \qquad \langle \text{Is } i{=}0? \rangle \xrightarrow{\text{Yes}} \text{Exit,}$$

in all possible permutations to form loops. Then analyze each according to the following questions:

a) Assuming $N>0$, how many times is the body executed?
b) If $N=0$, how many times is the body executed?
c) What is the value of i during the first execution of the body?
d) What is the value of i during the last execution of the body?

Each of these permutations may be most efficient in some situations.

2. Making suitable assumptions, write program segments following each of the flowcharts constructed in problem 1, both using the special looping control instructions and not using them.

3. Suppose that we have a list of numbers, $A_0, A_1, \ldots, A_{19}$, in consecutive full words of main storage starting at AA. We wish to compute $B_0, B_1, \ldots, B_{18}$, as $B_i = A_i - A_{i+1}$ $(i = 0, 1, \ldots, 18)$ and to store the results in consecutive full words starting at location BB. The body of the loop is the sequence

```
L      5,AA(3)
S      5,AA+4(3)
ST     5,BB(3)
```

Design the adjustment step and the test for exit to follow the body, and determine the initialization necessary to complete a segment to do the problem. Try to do the problem twice, once using, and once not using, the BXLE instruction.

4. Suppose that in the evaluation of a polynomial by Horner's method we try to keep the intermediate sums. Figure 8–4 would be modified by replacing the initialization by

$$\boxed{\begin{array}{c} B_0 = A_0 \\ i = 0 \end{array}}$$

and the body by

$$\boxed{B_i = B_{i-1} * X + A_i}$$

The procedure, as modified, is known as *synthetic division*, and it is used in a change of variable, computation of the derivative, and other mathematical operations. Design the program segment so that the coefficients B_i are stored at consecutive full-word locations beginning at BB. You will find an index register useful.

5. Examine and simulate the following program segment which is designed to store 80-byte blank areas in a block of main storage. From where to where in main storage are blanks actually stored by execution of this segment?

```
              LA    7,PRTAREA
              LA    8,80
              LA    9,PRTAREA+1920
      LØØP    MVC   0(80,7),BLANKS
              BXLE  7,8,LØØP
              ⋮

      BLANKS  DC    CL80' '
```

Note that a register cannot be used as an index in this problem since MVC is not an RX-type instruction.

6. The following segment is designed to store copies of the contents of register 4 in a block of consecutive words in main storage. Assume that C is located on a full-word boundary. Will the store instruction always have a second operand address which is a full-word boundary? If so, how many times will the store instruction be executed? In exactly what block of main storage is the contents of register 4 stored?

```
              LA    7,48
      LØØP    ST    4,C(7)
              S     7,=F'3'
              BCT   7,LØØP
```

7. The following segment is intended to add the 10 full-word numbers starting at location BB, and to store the sum at SUM. The effective address of the second operand of the add instruction is modified by the process of modification of the displacement in the instruction. Make suitable assumptions, then simulate execution of the segment. Beware: the half-word at location LP+2 is used as part of an instruction, but it is also composed of numbers in main storage so it can be, and is, changed by execution of the program. What are the contents of the half-word at LP+2 when the program segment is completed? Is the initialization complete; that is, if the segment were entered a second time, would it form the sum of the numbers in the same 10 locations? If not, how can you complete the initialization?

```
              SR    6,6
              LA    8,10
      LP      A     6,BB      (cont. on next page)
```

```
*              ADDRESS MØDIFICATIØN
        LH     5,LP+2
        LA     5,4(5)
        STH    5,LP+2
*              LØØPING CØNTRØL
        BCT    8,LP
        ST     6,SUM
```

8. Suppose that we have a list of 29 numbers stored in consecutive full words starting at FF, and that we wish to store the list *in reverse order* in consecutive full words starting at BB. Each of the following segments can perform correctly the body, adjustment step, and test for exit of this problem. Supply the proper initialization for each segment to make each segment work.

(1)
```
        LØØP    L      3,0(6)
                ST     3,0(7)
                S      6,=F'4'
                BXLE   7,8,LØØP
```

(2)
```
        LØØP    L      3,FF(8)
                ST     3,BB(9)
                LA     8,4(8)
                BXH    9,7,LØØP
```

9. There is a list of 17 consecutive full words in main storage, starting at location GG. Every word in the list whose contents is 4 should be replaced by a zero. Write first a flowchart for a loop that performs this task, and identify on your flowchart the initialization, body, adjustment step, and test for exit. Then write a program segment to accomplish the task, following the logic of your flowchart.

10. There is a list of 17 consecutive full words in main storage, starting at location GG. Write a flowchart and program segment for the task of finding the address of the largest number in the list. If there are ties, take the first of the equal numbers.

11. Adapt one of the program segments for evaluation of a polynomial by Horner's method into a subroutine. Have as parameters the address of the beginning of the coefficient list, the order N of the polynomial, and the value X at which the polynomial is to be evaluated. The output, the value of the polynomial, should be left in register 0.

12. Adapt one of the program segments in Figs. 8–13, 8–14, or 8–15 to form $C_i = A_i + B_i$ for a list of indefinite length, the length (in words) being stored at location N.

13. Try to make some general statements concerning the exact proper situation under which to use a BXLE instruction, a BXH instruction, or a BCT instruction, and cite the exact initialization steps (instructions and operands) that must be written in preparation.

14. In the flowchart for binary search shown in Fig. 8–20, the comparison of i and k can be replaced by

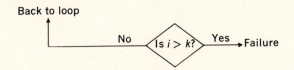

Back to loop

No — Is $i > k$? — Yes → Failure

Why is this change possible? What effect does it have on efficiency of the procedure?

15. Make the program segment shown in Fig. 8–21 into a subroutine. Have as parameters the address of the first key in the list, the difference between locations of successive keys, the number of items in the list, and the search key. Output should be the address of the key found, or 0 if the search ends in failure; the output should be left in register 0.

16. Using the subroutine constructed in problem 15 above, write a program segment for the following problem.

A student information record is 80 bytes long, and there are NN records in the list at the moment. The list is stored as consecutive 80-byte records starting at STUDINF. In the record the first word contains a student number, and the fifth word contains the total number of credits the student has earned. The list is ordered, and the student number is the key.

A particular student, whose student number is stored at CURRNØ, has earned additional credits in transfer work; the number of additional credits is stored in CREDUP. Update the student's record by adding the additional credits to his total. Remember that the output from the subroutine is an address in register 0, but register 0 cannot be used directly in addressing main storage.

17. One way to store and access a table in main storage is to define a vector (list) of addresses which point to rows of the table. (Assume that the table is stored "row-wise"—that is, all entries of the first row, then all of the second row, etc.) Declare storage for a table of ten rows, each row containing ten full words. Also create a vector of addresses, starting at a location called RØW, which point to the rows of the table. Show how the vector addresses help in accessing

a) all entries in a given row in succession,

b) all entries in a given column in succession,

c) a single entry, given row and column indexes.

REFERENCES

IBM System/360 Principles of Operation, GA22-6821, or *IBM System/370 Principles of Operation*, GA22–7000, IBM Corporation. Reference on the looping control instructions.

Knuth, Donald E., *The Art of Computer Programming, Vol. 3: Sorting and Searching* (Reading, Mass.: Addison-Wesley, 1973). Chapter 6 is a detailed discussion of search techniques over various data structures, including lists.

Price, C. D., "Table Lookup Techniques," *Computing Surveys* **3**, 2 (June 1971), pp. 49–65. A tutorial article on search techniques.

Chapter 9

Debugging

We place our emphasis on writing correct programs. Yet even with our best efforts, our programs will contain errors. What happens in case of error, how we can diagnose errors, and how we can try to prevent errors in the first place are the subjects of this chapter. First we explore what happens when we break the rules for use of individual instructions—the interrupts, error messages, and dumps we get. We discuss how to read the messages and dumps and pinpoint the actual errors. Then we explore the advance preparation we can make for debugging, and the partial dumps and the execution traces we can call for. Finally, we pay attention to the qualities and considerations of a programmer which can reduce the number of errors made in the first place.

1. EXCEPTIONS AND INTERRUPTS

When we described each IBM System/360 instruction we introduced, we gave restrictions on the operands—restrictions like proper boundaries, coding of signs in a CVB instruction, etc. The inquiring student probably felt a nagging question of what would happen if the restrictions were not met. Breaking one of the rules is what is called an *exception*, and the usual effect is an interruption of the program. The program can be designed to control whether or not some exception conditions cause interrupts, but most of the interrupts are automatic.

As was mentioned in Chapter 1, the effect of an interrupt is that execution of the current program is suspended. The entire program status word is stored at a special main storage location. A new program status word is loaded from a fixed location in the portion of storage controlled by the supervisor, and this starts execution of the appropriate interrupt-handling routine. It is possible for the user's program, working through the supervisor, to send control to a user-written interrupt routine for any particular kind of interrupt. For program exceptions, however, the usual action is the supervisor's default option of terminating the program and the job step, outputting diagnostic information as directed. We will study later in this chapter the various kinds of diagnostic information that can be obtained, and when and how to call for and get information from it.

Let us now describe some of the exceptions that might be encountered.

Interruption code 1: Operation

The operation code in the instruction currently being executed is illegal. That is, there does not exist any such operation, at least not on that particular model of the System/360 or 370. The operation is suppressed before interrupt.

Interruption code 2: Privileged operation

The operation code is of an existing operation, but one that can be executed only in the supervisor mode. Such an operation is called *privileged;* if execution of a privileged operation is attempted while in the problem (opposite of supervisor) state, this kind of interrupt occurs. The operation is suppressed. Privileged operations are mainly those that change the more sensitive parts of the program status word or directly affect input or output operations. None of the operations we have introduced thus far is privileged.

Interruption code 4: Protection

There is a four-bit storage key associated with each 2048-byte block of main storage. Many blocks may have the same key; the keys are stored in a special area which is inaccessible to a program operating in the problem state. The keys designate which areas of main storage are to be available to a program. Bits 8–11 of the program status word contain a protection code which is matched with the storage key for a main storage location that the program is attempting to access. When the protection code and storage key match or when the protection code is zero (used by the supervisor) the access is allowed. A mismatch is a protection exception.

In some IBM System/360 models, there is no storage protection; any part of main storage may be used in any way without generating a protection exception. In some, protection is furnished for store operands only: the storage and protection key comparisons are invoked only on instructions that store results into main storage. Of the instructions we have studied, the following could generate protection exceptions:

CVD	ConVert to Decimal (first operand)
MVI	MoVe Immediate
MVC	MoVe Character (first operand)
PACK	PACK (first operand)
ST	STore
STH	STore Half-word
STM	STore Multiple
UNPK	UNPacK (first operand)

In still other models of System/360 and 370, protection is furnished on the store operations noted above and also on *fetches*, instructions which use information from main storage. In no models is a *branch* monitored for protection violations; one is always permitted to branch to any location in main storage.

If a protection exception is generated by the first reference to main storage used by the instruction, the operation is suppressed. But sometimes some of the operation is carried out—for example, movement of several characters by an MVC instruction—before an address is generated which causes a protection key mismatch. In such cases, the operation is terminated as soon as the violation is sensed.

For example, if a program is running with a protection code in the program status word of (binary) 0001, it has access to all blocks of storage whose storage key is 0001. When the program attempts to store information in a block whose storage key is 0010, an interrupt occurs. The storage keys are set by the supervisor before the program begins execution.

Interruption code 5: Addressing

If an address of a specified instruction or data (to store or fetch) is outside the limits of available storage on the particular computer, an addressing exception is generated. The operation is terminated before interrupt. Any instruction that accesses main storage in any way can generate an addressing exception.

In a virtual storage System/370, the protection and addressing exceptions result from faults discovered in the *real* main storage addresses, not the virtual addresses. The virtual address and dynamic address translation system will be studied in more detail in Chapter 17.

Interruption code 6: Specification

A specification exception occurs when there is something wrong with the way in which an operand is specified in an instruction. (When something is wrong with an operand itself, other exceptions result.)

There are some instructions that require a register operand address to be even. Those we have encountered are

D	Divide
DR	Divide Register (first operand)
M	Multiply
MR	Multiply Register (first operand)

If a first operand address is odd in any of these instructions, a specification exception results.

Floating-point register addresses are 0, 2, 4, 6; floating-point register operand addresses 1, 3, 5, or 7 through 15 will cause specification exceptions.

Most specification exceptions are generated by main storage operand addresses that do not conform to required boundary alignment. Some instructions require half-word alignment, some full-word alignment and some double-word alignment.

All of these instructions are of RX or RS type; the ones we have seen are

A	Add	full word
AH	Add Half-word	half-word
C	Compare	full word
CH	Compare Half-word	half-word
CVB	ConVert to Binary	double word
CVD	ConVert to Decimal	double word
D	Divide	full word
L	Load	full word
LH	Load Half-word	half-word
LM	Load Multiple	full word
M	Multiply	full word
MH	Multiply Half-word	half-word
ST	STore	full word
STH	STore Half-word	half-word
STM	STore Multiple	full word
S	Subtract	full word
SH	Subtract Half-word	half-word

For example, if a program attempts to execute an LH instruction whose second operand address (as defined by base, index, and displacement) is 009340, the operand specification is legal (009340 is a half-word, full-word, and double-word boundary), but an operand address of 009341 is illegal and will cause a specification exception.

If the *byte-oriented-operand* feature is installed, the system allows main storage operands of nonprivileged instructions to begin at any address, not necessarily at half-word, full-word, or double-word boundaries. This cuts down the conditions that cause specification exceptions. We continue to emphasize alignment, however, not only for systems that require it but because instruction execution using non-aligned operands is slowed by use of the byte-oriented-operand feature.

A branch instruction may also generate a specification exception by attempting to branch to an odd address. All instructions must begin on even half-words, even where the byte-oriented-operand feature is installed.

Interruption code 7: Data

The ConVert to Binary (CVB) instruction assumes that the operand is in the packed decimal format. If the codes in the operand are not the expected valid digit and sign codes, a data exception results. The instruction is terminated after an invalid code is discovered. The data exception can also result from other instructions having to do with packed decimal data, as we shall learn in Chapter 14.

Interruption code 8: Fixed-point overflow

A fixed-point overflow results from the binary integer load, add, and subtract instructions when they yield results too large to be expressed in 32 bits in the 2's complement form. These instructions are

A	Add
AH	Add Half-word
AR	Add Register
LCR	Load Complement Register
LPR	Load Positive Register
S	Subtract
SH	Subtract Half-word
SR	Subtract Register.

A fixed-point overflow by these instructions sets the condition code to 3, as we learned in Chapter 7. The overflow is also recognized as a fixed-point overflow exception. A fixed-point overflow exception may cause an interrupt. The option can be controlled by the program itself; if the first bit of the *program mask* in the program status word is 1, a fixed-point overflow exception causes an interrupt, but if that bit of the PSW is 0, a fixed-point overflow exception does not cause an interrupt.

One of the fields of the program status word is called the *program mask*. The bits of the program mask enable *masking* (controlling) of the interrupts resulting from four of the 15 different causes. We shall learn in Chapter 17 how the program may change the program mask; it is one of the few pieces of the program status word that can be accessed and changed by a program in the problem state.

In the case of a fixed-point overflow interruption, the operation is completed, and the result left in the register is too large or too small by 2^{32}.

Interruption code 9: Fixed-point divide

A fixed-point divide exception can result from either of two conditions. First is binary integer division by zero or the development of a quotient too large to be expressed in 32 bits in the 2's complement form. Either D (Divide) or DR (Divide Register) can produce these results. The second condition leading to a fixed-point divide instruction is that the result of a CVB (ConVert to Binary) instruction is too large to be expressed in 32 bits in the 2's complement form.

Division is suppressed if a fixed-point divide exception arises; a CVB instruction is completed, but the portion of the result which would fall outside the register is ignored. Interruption of the program is automatic in either case.

Other interruption codes

There are other conditions which cause interrupts. Interrupts that result directly from attempts at invalid program execution are called program or program-check interrupts; they are identified by codes, eight of which have been described above. Seven more result from execution of instructions which we have not yet studied; briefly, they are as shown in Fig. 9–1. Each of these will be explained when the

Fig. 9-1   Additional interruption codes

Code number	Code name	Causes
3	Execute	Invalid use of the EXECUTE instruction.
10	Decimal overflow	Overflow in addition or subtraction of packed decimal numbers.
11	Decimal divide	Quotient in a packed decimal division is too large.
12	Exponent overflow	The result of a floating-point operation is 16^{64} or greater.
13	Exponent underflow	The result of a floating-point operation is smaller than 16^{-64}.
14	Significance	The result of a floating-point operation is an all-zero fraction.
15	Floating-point divide	Floating-point division by zero.

instructions producing it are discussed. Decimal overflow, exponent underflow, and significance are the three conditions besides fixed-point overflow which can be (independently) masked on or off by the program mask.

Besides program-check interrupts, there are four other classes of interrupts. *Input and output* conditions can cause interrupts, as will be described in Chapter 17. There are *external* interrupts, resulting from signals from external lines or the console interrupt key or from overflow of the interval timer. *Supervisor call* interrupts take place when a program executes the SVC (SuperVisor Call) instruction to request some action by the supervisor. *Machine check* interrupts occur when the computer discovers that some part of its circuitry has failed. The interrupt system as a whole will be discussed more thoroughly in Chapter 17.

2. INDICATIVE DUMPS

The programmer may furnish his own routine to handle various kinds of interrupts; the supervisor gives control to this routine if and when the appropriate kind of interrupt occurs. Usually, however, the programmer does not supply any interrupt-handling routines, and in case of a program check interrupt the supervisor terminates the job step. As the job step is terminated, an *indicative dump* is printed, with information about the program and the cause of the interrupt.

The indicative dump is of variable length, but is usually about 13 printed lines long. The programmer must learn to read indicative dumps and deduce most of his errors from them. The second and third lines should be read first. The completion code, on the second line, is a code furnished by the operating system to designate the reason for termination of the step. Completion codes and their meanings are listed in the IBM manuals *IBM System/360 Operating System Messages and Codes*, GC28-6631; *IBM System/360 Operating System Programmer's Guide to Debugging*, GC28-6670; *OS/VS1 Debugging Guide*, GC24-5093, *OS/VS2 Debugging Guide*, GC28-0632, and various other OS/VS system manuals. In case of program-check interruption, the first two digits of the completion code are 0C, and the third is (in hexadecimal) the interrupt code number: 1 for operation, 6 for specification, etc. The third line gives in words a short description of the cause of the interrupt.

In the lines following the third are one or two sets of register contents. Instead of explaining the conditions under which there are one or two sets, we advise that if there are two sets given, examine the second. The contents of registers as they were when the interrupt occurred are given in hexadecimal; these contents should be very valuable in showing exactly what the program was doing and what it had done. Contents of the implied base register should be checked, as well as other registers being used to define addresses. Operands and results in registers may also help to point to the bug in the program.

The 12-byte region of main storage including and just preceding the instruction that was being executed before interrupt is displayed in hexadecimal. Often when something illegal is being executed as an instruction, a glance at the contents of the main storage area where the instruction should be will tell the programmer what was put there by mistake, and he can then figure out why.

Floating-point register (abbreviated as FPR) contents are also given in hexadecimal, if the floating-point feature is installed in the computer.

The part of the indicative dump that needs the most explanation is the ACTIVE RB LIST. This section includes program status information from all of the currently active *request blocks*. In general, every request for a service from the supervisor generates a request block, and the active request blocks are associated with requests that have not yet been fulfilled. When an indicative dump is being printed, the first request block in the list represents the request for an indicative dump. There may be one or two other request blocks active; the one of most interest to the programmer will be the one identified by PRØGRAM ID=LØADER (or whatever his own job step is named.)   On the same line as the identification PRØGRAM ID=LØADER is the ENTRY PØINT. This is the main storage location at which execution of the program began.

If the LØADER is used, as in our examples, the entry point shown on the dump will be the point at which the *loader* was entered. The loader reserves some space for itself, so the entry point to *our* program is not the same. The page of output from the loader identifies the entry point to our main program and other external symbols, such as entry points to subroutines.

The *relocation quantity* can be computed as the entry point to our program minus the relocatable entry-point location as shown in the program listing produced by the assembler. For example, if the ENTRY ADDRESS reported by the loader is 00D2F0 and the relocatable entry point is 000000, which is common, the relocation quantity is

$$00D2F0 - 000000 = 00D2F0$$

The relocation quantity is added to each relocatable address in the program listing to give the corresponding actual address.

The second line of the request block information gives information from the program status word. Some of the codes are

SM=   Gives the system mask, showing what input/output and external
           interruptions are masked on.
K=   Gives the protection key assigned to the program.
IL+CC=   Gives the instruction length (times 2, so 4 means two bytes, 8 means
           four bytes, and 12 means six bytes) of the current instruction, and
           the condition code.
           For example, IL+CC=6 means a two-byte instruction was being exe-
           cuted, and the condition code was 2.
PM=   Gives the program mask, showing whether interrupts on fixed-point
           overflow, decimal overflow, exponent underflow, and significance
           are masked on or off.
IA=   Gives the instruction address, usually of the instruction just after the
           instruction causing interrupt.

By subtracting the relocation quantity from IA, the programmer can pinpoint exactly where to look in his program listing for the instruction which caused the interrupt.

To recapitulate, the programmer first finds out what kind of condition caused the interrupt (or other termination). Second, he usually looks at the entry point and instruction address, then finds the place in his listing of the offending instruction. The listing reminds him not only of what instruction should be executed there but also why, and it gives him an indication of what in general the computer should have been doing just before interrupt. A look at the instruction image as reported in the indicative dump confirms that the expected instruction is there, or tells what is. Often by this time the programmer has realized his error. If he has not, further sleuthing, aided by register contents and anything else relevant, is necessary.

Figure 9–2 is an example of a program and the indicative dump produced by execution of the program. The program was designed to be entered at relocatable location 000000, so the entry point reported by the loader, 00D2F0, is the relocation quantity. The error noted is an operation exception, the kind we often get if we are executing instructions where there are no instructions. By subtracting the relocation quantity from the reported interruption address of 00D2FE, we find the offending instruction is at relocatable address 00000E. We see from the program listing that this instruction is just before and in our SAV area, where we do not intend to be executing instructions at all. What is there is not a valid instruction, so program execution is terminated. The error in the program is placing the SAV area directly after the instruction

                          LA   13,SAV

The definition of the SAV area must either be moved or else a branch instruction

Fig. 9-2 A program and indicative dump.

```
LOC    OBJECT CODE        ADDR1  ADDR2  STMT  SOURCE STATEMENT                          F01FEB73

000000                                    1 EXAMPLE2 START 0
000000                                    2          SAVE  (14,12)
000000                                    3+         DS    0H
000000 90EC D00C                  0000C   4+         STM   14,12,12(13)  SAVE REGISTERS
000004 05C0                               5          BALR  12,0
000006                                    6          USING *,12
000006 50D0 C00E          00014           7          ST    13,SAV+4
00000A 41D0 C00A          00010           8          LA    13,SAV
000010                                    9  SAV     DS    18F
000058 58F0 C162          00168          10          L     15,=V(READATA)
00005C 4110 C166          C016C          11          LA    1,=A(CARD)
000060 4180 0000          00000          12          LA    8,0           SUM = 0
000064 4190 0014          C0014          13          LA    9,20          REPEAT COUNT
000068 05EF                              14  LOOP    BALR  14,15
00006A F274 C15A C099     00160  0009F   15          PACK  DBL(8),CARD+7(5)
000070 4F60 C15A          00160          16          CVB   6,DBL
000074 1A86                              17          AR    8,6
000076 4690 C062          00068          18          BCT   9,LOOP
00007A 4E80 C15A          00160          19          CVD   8,DBL
00007E F367 C0E8 C15A 000EE 00160        20          UNPK  OUTAREA+6(7),DBL(8)
000084 58F0 C16A          00170          21          L     15,=V(PRINT)
000088 4110 C16F          00174          22          LA    1,=A(OUTAREA)
00008C 05EF                              23          BALR  14,15
00008E 58D0 C00E          00014          24          L     13,SAV+4
                                         25          RETURN (14,12)
000092 98EC D00C                  0000C  26+         LM    14,12,12(13)  RESTORE THE REGISTERS
000096 07FE                              27+         BR    14  RETURN
                                         28 *  CONSTANT AND STORAGE DEFINITIONS
000098                                   29  CARD    DS    CL80
0000E8 E2E4D4407E404040               30  OUTAREA DC    CL120'SUM = '
000160                                   31  DBL     DS    D
000000                                   32          END   EXAMPLE2
000168 00000000                          33          =V(READATA)
00016C 00000098                          34          =A(CARD)
000170 C0000000                          35          =V(PRINT)
000174 000000E8                          36          =A(OUTAREA)
```

```
                                          OS/360 LOADER

OPTIONS USED - PRINT,MAP,LET,NOCALL,NORES,NOTERM,SIZE=140640,NAME=**GO


  NAME TYPE ADDR     NAME TYPE ADDR     NAME TYPE ADDR     NAME TYPE ADDR     NAME TYPE

EXAMPLE2  SD  D2F0   REACATA  SD  D468   PRINT  LR  D4A8

TOTAL LENGTH    3E0
ENTRY ADDRESS   D2F0  <- Use this entry point in calculations

                Shows the program halted because of an illegal operation code.

CONTROL BYTE=C0  TCB FLAGS=A1  NO. ACTIVE RB=2  NO. LOAD RB=0
COMPLETION CODE - SYSTEM=0C1  USER=0000
PROGRAM INTERRUPTION (OPERATION) AT LOCATION 00D2FE  <- Shows where.
REGISTER SET 1
GPR 0-7   00003558   000346F0   800346F4   00D346F0   00D347FA   FFFFFFFF   00034798   000300FF
GPR8-15   0C0067F0   00034648   000347E0   000D02F6   4C0D0300   000D0142   000D2F0
INSTRUCTION IMAGE  C0DE41D0C00AE6D3D6C1C4D9
FPR 0-4   44813400   413CC651   C0496590   EC339AF0   4168D06A   00000000   45186A00   00000000
ACTIVE RB LIST
PROGRAM ID= ;   801C   RB TYPE=D0   ENTRY POINT=004188
RESUME PSW  SM=00  K=0  AMWP=4   IC=0007  ILtCC=5  PM=0  IA=004188
PROGRAM ID=LOADER   RB TYPE=00   ENTRY POINT=00D020
RESUME PSW  SM=FF  K=2  AMWP=5   IC=00D0  ILtCC=C  PM=0  IA=00D304
IEF285I   SYS1.SCRATCH4                       KEPT
IEF285I   VOL SER NOS= WORK22.
```

should be supplied to branch around the area and prevent use of the garbage left in the area as instructions.

3. ERROR MESSAGES

Often the computer, through whatever system is in control, will discover an error before affairs degenerate to the point of invalid instruction and interrupt. The FORTRAN compiler, the assembler, COBOL and PL/1 translators, etc., all catch syntax errors and print messages pointing out the errors. Warning messages are given for conditions that are not necessarily errors but which are often symptomatic of an error somewhere. During execution, error messages are given on discovery of errors in input data validity, data set format, and other things that can be caught by the operating system. Each error message is short, but a longer explanation of the error and often of how to correct it is given in the manual *IBM System/360 Operating System Error Messages and Codes*, Form C28-6631.

The programmer must remember that the error messages and their explanations reflect the error as seen by the system. The *cause* of the error may be something quite different from the cause suggested by the message; the programmer must try to find not necessarily what error the message said he made, but instead what error he made that would *look* to the system like the error the system said he made. All the ingenuity the programmer can muster may be needed to ascertain the real cause.

4. FULLER DUMPS

Sometimes the information given in an indicative dump is not sufficient to enable the programmer to find his error. The clues needed may be in main storage instead of in registers, so he needs a dump of at least a portion of main storage.

A programmer can get a dump of the relevant portions of main storage when his program is terminated. An ABDUMP (standing for ABnormal DUMP) is one kind of storage dump; it also includes information on the system parameters associated with the program. The ABDUMP can be called by an ABEND macro-instruction executed in the normal course of the program. The form of the macro-instruction is

Name	Operation	Operands
Symbol optional	ABEND	Completion code,DUMP

The completion code is an unsigned decimal integer less than or equal to 4095; it can help identify the location of initiation of the dump. A job control card must also be provided; it is usually of the form

```
//GØ.SYSABEND   DD   SYSØUT=A
```

if the program being run is in the GØ step of a catalogued procedure; if the program is being executed without a catalogued procedure, the job control statement is

//SYSABEND   DD   SYSØUT=A

The ABDUMP will be provided automatically instead of an indicative dump in case of abnormal termination of the program, if the job control statement defining the SYSABEND data set is present.

We shall outline briefly the information provided in an ABDUMP; full details must be found in one of the manuals on debugging mentioned in Section 3, perhaps supplemented by information on options taken in the student's local installation.

The ABDUMP is identified by job, step, time, and date. The completion code is given, as is a message about the cause of initiation of the dump. The program status word is given as it was at time of initiation of the ABDUMP. Task control blocks and request blocks are given; the first line under ACTIVE   RBS includes a vital piece of information: the *entry point*, identified by USE/EP. Otherwise, the TCBs and ACTIVE   RBS are intelligible only to a systems programmer familiar with the design and use of these blocks. If a programmer's debugging problem requires analysis of these blocks (then he's *really* in trouble), the programmer should seek help from a systems-programming consultant at his computing center.

An important feature of an ABDUMP is the Save-Area Trace. The routine which provides the ABDUMP can find in register 13 the address of the register save area in current use. The contents of this area are printed. In the second word of the save area, however, is the address of the register save area of the routine which called the current one. The ABDUMP routine prints the contents of this area too. By continuing this chain, the ABDUMP traces the status of registers (at the time of subroutine call) of all routines from the current routine back up the chain of subroutines called, to the main program.

There is other miscellaneous information on data sets and a trace table of supervisor calls and interrupts, mostly unintelligible except to systems programmers.

Finally, the contents of main-storage locations are printed. The "nucleus" or operating system space is printed first, and the user's space last. Both are printed both in hexadecimal and, where possible, in character form. Not every byte in storage represents a printable character; letters and digits are printed according to their representations, and periods designate other bytes. The main-storage addresses of each line of dump are well identified.

In virtual storage systems, it is the user's virtual storage area, not fragments of real storage, which appear in the dump. This is as it should be; the virtual storage addresses are the ones meaningful to the programmer, and the operating system takes complete care of the correspondence with real storage.

The ABDUMP presents a programmer with many pages of output, which contain more information than he usually wants or needs. A smaller dump is provided which has the same form as the ABDUMP but leaves out the trace table of supervisor calls and interrupts and the dump of nucleus storage. The smaller dump is provided if the job control statement in effect specifies a ddname of SYSUDUMP instead of SYSABEND. The job control statement would be

$$//GØ.SYSUDUMP \quad DD \quad SYSØUT=A$$

if the program is executed by the GØ step of a catalogued procedure.

The use of a full ABDUMP or SYSUDUMP might be as follows. The programmer first examines the completion code to discover the immediate cause of program termination. With a puzzled look, he asks "How did that happen?" He next examines register contents, the program status word, and the listed entry point of his program, to find what portion of his program was being executed when the termination occurred. Still puzzled, he asks what data were being used. To determine which data were being used, he must look at his main storage dump, calculating addresses of data areas by adding the relocation quantity to the data area addresses in his listing and independently calculating them from register contents and displacements which he can see from the dump. By looking carefully at the input data and intermediate results in main storage, the programmer can deduce a great deal about what his program did. The save-area trace helps him to follow the path his program took in arriving in the current subroutine. However, the save-area trace follows only the direct chain and does not contain information about subroutines whose executions have been completed.

Let us follow an example of the use of a SYSUDUMP. Suppose that we need a program which will read 20 cards into a block of main storage and then go on to manipulation of the data from the cards. A difficulty in this particular application is that the cards are not to be stored in the order they are read in; each of the 20 cards contains a number between -10 to 9 (inclusive) in columns 79–80, and its place in the block of storage is to be computed from this number. The card containing -10 is to be placed first in the block, the card containing -9 is to be placed second, and so on, regardless of the order in which the cards are presented to the program.

Following good programming practice, we check out our program section by section, and the first section we write and check out merely reads in the 20 cards, places them in their block in the proper order, then prints the contents of the block. Figure 9–3 shows this program. After each card is read into CARD, the address in the block WØRK for storing the contents of the card is computed, and the contents of the card are moved to the proper place. After all 20 cards are read, another section of the program prints the block.

When the program is executed, it does not work. The first time we get an indicative dump showing something preposterous as instruction image. We cannot find the cause of the trouble from the indicative dump (maybe we should be able

Fig. 9–3   A program to be debugged. ▶

```
LOC    OBJECT CODE     ADDR1 ADDR2  STMT  SOURCE STATEMENT

000000                             1 WSORT  SAVE  (14,12)
                                   2+WSORT  DS    0H
000000 90EC D00C        000C       3+       STM   14,12,12(13)  SAVE REGISTERS
000004 05C0                        4         BALR  12,0
000006                             5         USING *,12
000006 50D0 C06A        0070       6         ST    13,SAV+4
00000A 182D                        7         LR    2,13
00000C 4100 C06C        003C       8         LA    13,SAV
000010 50D2 0008        0008       9         ST    13,8(2)
                                  10 *  READ 20 CARDS, PUTTING THEM IN ORDER IN WORK
000014 58F0 C752        0758      11         L     15,=V(READATA)
000018 4190 0014        0014      12         LA    9,20
00001C 4110 C750        075C      13 LR      LA    1,=A(CARD)
000020 05EF                       14 LR      BALR  14,15
000022 F271 C082 C108   0088 00038 15        PACK  D(8),CARD+78(2)
000028 4F50 C032        0088      16         CVB   5,D
00002C 5C40 C75A        0760      17         M     4,=F'80'
000030 4155 000A        000A      18         LA    5,10(5)
000034 4155 C10A        0110      19         LA    5,WORK(5)
000038 D24F 5000 C08A   0000 00000 20        MVC   0(80,5),CARD
00003E 4690 C01A        0020      21         BCT   9,LR
                                  22 *  NOW PRINT THE CARDS IN ORDER
000042 4170 C10A        0110      23         LA    7,WORK
000046 4180 0050        0050      24         LA    8,80
00004A 4190 C6FA        0700      25         LA    9,WORK+19*80
00004E 4110 C74A        0750      26         LA    1,CARDAD
000052 58F0 C75E        0764      27         L     15,=V(PRINT)
000056 5070 C74A        0750      28 LPR     ST    7,CARDAD
00005A 05EF                       29         BALR  14,15
00005C 8778 C050        0056      30         BXLE  7,8,LPR
                                  31 *  END OF PRINT SECTION
000060 5800 C06A        0070      32         L     13,SAV+4
                                  33         RETURN (14,12)
000064 98EC D00C        000C      34+        LM    14,12,12(13)  RESTORE THE REGISTERS
000068 07FE                       35+        BR    14            RETURN
00006C                            36 SAV     DS    18F
000088                            37 D       DS    1D
0000C0                            38 CARD    DS    CL80
000110 4040 C040 4040 4040        39 WORK    DC    20CL80' '
000750                            40 CARDAD  DS    1F
000758                            41         LTORG
000758 00000000                   42                =V(READATA)
00075C 000000C0                   43                =A(CARD)
000760 00000050                   44                =F'80'
000764 C0000000                   45                =V(PRINT)
```

Fig. 9-4 Example of a SYSUDUMP.

```
* ABDUMP REQUESTED *

JOB CH9SYSUD        STEP GO        TIME 162017    DATE 74242                                         PAGE 0001

COMPLETION CODE      SYSTEM = 0C1

PROGRAM INTERRUPTION (OPERATION) AT LOCATION 00D32E ← Address of invalid instruction

INTERRUPT AT 00D334

PSW AT ENTRY TO ABEND  FF25000D D00D0334

TCB 002FB8  RB   00033928   PIE    00000000   DEB  00033BA4   TIOT 0003A6F8   CMP  800C1000   TRN  00000000
            MSS  00003088   PK/FLG 20A10008   FLG  000006F0   LLS  00000000   JLB  00000000   JST  00002FB8
            FSA  0503479B   TCB    00000000   TME  000030A0   PIB  E0009E88   NTC  00000000   DTC  00000000
            LTC  00000000   IQE    00000000   ECB  00000000   XTCB 00000000   LP/FL F0050000  RESV 00000000
            STAE 00000000   TCT    00000000   USER 00000000   DAR  00000000   RESV 00000000   JSCB 8700CEC0
            RESV 00000000   IOB    00000000


ACTIVE RBS

PRB  00D000   NM LOADER    SZ/STAB 005C01D0   USE/EP 000D0020    PSW FF25000D D00D0334   Q 000000   WT/LNK 00002FB8

SVRB 0345A0   NM SVC-601C  SZ/STAB 0012D062   USE/EP 0004188     PSW FF040033 40004338   Q 980398   WT/LNK 00000000
     RG 0-7   0000355B   0000DA4C   0000D2F0   FFFFFFFF   0000D31A   00034798   000000FF
     RG 8-15  000067F0   0000000F   0000D2E0   40000D2F6  0000D35C   5000D312   0000DA58

SVRB 033928   NM SVC-A05A  SZ/STAB 000CD062   USE/EP 0004188     PSW FF040290 80004350   Q E003E0   WT/LNK 00035A0
     RG 0-7   00034148   00034600   4000418A   00002FB8   000345A0   0003DCC8   00002FB8
     RG 8-15  00034148   0000DE3A   0003086    00009DC    00002FB8   0000DCC8   80004262   1000D32E


SAVE AREA TRACE

LOADER    WAS ENTERED         AT EP IEWLCTRL
                                                        ┌ Entry point to our program
                                                        │ as also reported by the loader.
SA 03478B  WD1 00000000  HSA 00000000  LSA 00034630  RET 00006840  EPA 5000D020  R0  FD00009C
           R1  000347E0  R2  00034800  R3  0000EE44  R4  0003478C  R5  0000009C  R6  00002FB8
           R7  0003478C  R8  00000000  R9  00000000  R10 00034798  R11 00034508  R12 6000D74A

SA 034630  WD1 00000203  HSA 00034798  LSA 0000D35C  RET 4000D142  EPA 00000D2F0  R0  00003558
           R1  000346D8  K2  00034680  K3  0000D2F2  R4  000347FA  R5  FFFFFFFF   R6  00034798
           R7  000000FF  R8  000067F0  R9  00034630  R10 000347E0  R11 0000D2E0  F12 5000D034
```

```
REGS AT ENTRY TO ABEND

FL.PT.REGS 0-5    43.258000 00000000   00.000000 00000000   46.800000 CEC32000   40.507507 00000000

REGS 0-7     00003558  0000DA4C  00000000  0000D020     FFFFFFFF  0000D2F6  0000D31A  00000000FF
REGS 8-15    000067F0  0000000F  00000000  0000D2E0     00034630  0000D35C  5000D312  0000DA58
```

[hw: 0003+798 / 5000D312]   [hw: boxed 0000D31A / 0000D35C — "Address for storing CARD not good!"]

```
P/P STORAGE

00D000  D3D6C1C4 C5D94040 00EC01D0 0000D020   FF25000D D000D334 00000000 00002F88  *LOADER..........*
00D020  47F0F00E 08C9C5E6 D3C3E3D9 D3009DEC   D00C05C0 18A1186D 58410000 +8740000  *.00.IEWLCTRL....*
00D040  417700AE 13C74510 C01B0A0A 00105888   90A09200 80744710 C04A92D9 90B84100  *....JK..B.....J.*
00D060  00C818D1 D2079084 C2644180 00105888   00C09110 80744710 C04A92D9 90B84100  *...........B....*
00D080  90841611 0A0B1B1A 58410000 4874C000   18574070 90BE1277 4780C08A 95614C02  *.............B..*
00D0A0  4780C07C 41440000 4650C068 47F0C080   9601908C 58210000 18754072 00018F00  *...........B....*
00D0C0  05EF18B1 1830187F 41009084 0A091B77   49F0C25A 47D0C0B0 95D99D08 4770C21E  *.........0.....B*
00D0E0  47F0C124 18144320 90AC5620 C2545020   90A80650 405090AC 41700DFF 1255472D  *.....R..0B.....R*
00D100  C0D8D701 20C02000 47F0C0FE 4950C25C   47D0C0E4 18750670 4740C25E 4850C25C  *...........0A...*
00D120  1255472D C0FE4A20 C25C4A40 C25C47F0   C0D895D9 90B84770 C13618F3 4I109DA8  *.Q..........B..B*
00D140  05EF187F 58180008 12114780 C124580B   0000A08A 5810000 58B0B0004 40            *.O...B..0.B.Q.R.*
00D160  41110000 0A0A47F0 C21ED233 9048C26C   5080D004 1B885080 907C4110 90A841F0  *.....B...A......*
00D180  90484150 907CD7D2 F009F009 56EF0008   50EF0048 41E00004 0A2A5010 90A841F0  *....P....B...P.O*
00D1A0  90C04110 907C4100 0C010A01 943F907C   58709D80 9180101D 478DC218            *.O.K..B.........*
00D1C0  45106C1C 003A3000 0C3566F1 5F09C940   D9406040 E4E2C5D9 40C7D9D6 40C7D906  *.A...IEW191I ERROR - USER PRO*
00D1E0  C7D9C1D4 40C8C1E2 40C1C2D5 D6D9D4C1   D3D3E840 E3C5D9D4 C9D5C1E3 C5C4000  *GRAM HAS ABNORMALLY TERMINATED...*
00D200  4020A023 41800010 5880D000 4B80C258   795F2800 D2D9D090 C2A04180 00000000  *B.2..B.K..B.....*
00D220  90BC5811 00104111 0C000A00 41109D80   C28E4780 C20A9180 8000471D C2185810  *.........B......*
00D240  00000201 1009D908 18195800 90A04111   906C4780 C224947F A0005B1A            *.........B..7.0.*
00D260  92FFD00C 07FE47F0 80000000 00030004   40100200 20024003 C9C5E6D3 D6C1C440  *...........K...IEWLOAD*
00D280  00000000 00000000 00000000 00000000   00000000 02000000 40404040 40404040  *................*
00D2A0  40404040 00000000 00009E8 00000000    000000D4 00000000 00000000 40100C66  *................*
00D2C0  00000000 00000000 00000000 00000000   05C050D0 C061060 40400C066            *................*
00D2E0  50D20008 58F0C752 41900014 411DC726   05EFF271 C0B2C108 4F50C2E4 E340C6D7  *.K.Y.............K.*
00D300  D6D4440E3 C8C540E2 E3C1D5C4 D7D6C9D5   E340D6C6 40E3C8C5 40D5C5E6 40E3C8C5  *.K..OG.......G.2..A..BUT FR*
00D320  D6D9E868 40C9E340 C9E240C1 D3D3C040   C5D3C1E3 C9E5C5C6 40404040 40404040  *OM THE STANDPOINT OF THE NEW THE*
00D340  40404040 40404040 40D03312 0000D458   00003558 00013630 0000D2F0 0000D2F6  *GRY. IT IS ALL RELATIVE...... KO*
00D360  00000000 0000D4FA 00003478 00000003D   C2E4E340 C6D9D6D4 40E3C8C5 40E2E3C1  *OLL.................K.*
00D380  D5C4D7D6 C9D5E340 D6C640E3 C8C540D5   C5E640E3 C8C5D6D9 E840E3C8 C9E25B20  *.K6.K.......M....BJT FROM THE STA*
00D3A0  40C1D3D3 40D9C5D3 C1E3C9E5 C540404D   40C1E240 C9D54240 C5D9C5E3 C5C44400  *NDPOINT OF THE NEW THEORY. IT IS *
00D3E0  C8C9D7D7 C9C5E240 C1D9D4C1 C3C8C9D5   C5E240C1 D9C540D5 C5C9E3C8 C5D94000  *ALL RELATIVE.................OL*
00D400  E240C9D5 E3C5D9C5 E2E3C9D5 C740D6D9   40C1E240 C9D5E3C5 D9C5E2E3 C5C44000  *HIPPIES ARMACHINES ARE NEITHER A*
00D420  E340D7C5 D6D7D3C5 40404040 40404040   40404040 F0F04040 40404040 40404040  *S INTERESTING OR AS INTERESTED A*
00D440  40404040 40404040 40404040 40404040   40404040 40404040 40404040 40404040  *S PEOPLE.................OO*
00D460  40404040 40404040 40404040 40404040   40404040 40404040 40404040 40404040  *................*

LINES 00D480-00D4C0  SAME AS ABOVE

00D4E0  40C4C040 40404040 40404040 40404040   40404040 40404040 C5D3C5C7 C5C7C1D5  *.........................ELEGAN*
00D500  E36B40C2 E4E34040 40C3D6D4 D7D3C5E3   C540E2D3 D6C240C9 C640E8D6 E440D2C4  *T. BUT A COMPLETE SLOB. IF YOU K*
00D520  D5D6E640 E6C8C1E3 40C9C040 D4C5C1D5   40404040 C9C2C640 D6C264D4 40404040  *NOW WHAT I MEAN.................*
00D540  40404040 40404040 40404040 40404040   40404040 40404040 40404040 F0F34040  *.............................O3*
00D560  40404040 40404040 40404040 40404040   40404040 40404040 40404040 40404040  *................*

LINES 00D580-00D600  SAME AS ABOVE
```

[hw notes: "Our page extends down to here" (arrow near 00D000); "The BCT instruction should" (near 00D2E0 / 411DC726); "Area 2 card"; arrow pointing to "BJT FROM THE STA"] to, but that would spoil the example), so on the next run we call for a SYSUDUMP by inserting a card

//GØ.SYSUDUMP   DD   SYSØUT=A

Portions of the first three pages of dump are shown in Fig. 9–4. The entry point is 00D2F0, which we find as EPA (Entry Point Address) in the second block of the Save Area Trace. The first block of the Save Area Trace shows affairs as they are stored by the loader; the second is the block stored by our program upon entry, and thus shows the entry point address of our program. The relocation quantity is therefore 00D2F0; the interruption occurred at 00D32E, so the instruction causing the interruption was at relocatable location 00D32E − 00D2F0 = 00003E. From our listing, we see that the instruction at that location is supposed to be

BCT   9,LR

We find in the listing also that the machine-language instruction is 4690   C01A, and that is what we should find on the dump at location 00D32E. Instead, we find C9D5E340. A hint to the origin of this garbage is provided by the character part on the right of the dump, where this general area seems to contain STANDPØINT ØF THE NEW.   More investigation, including a peek at the area CARD (locations 00D2F0 + 0000C0 = 00D3B0 on) and our data deck, shows that these characters come from a data card.

　　We have made progress; the problem now is to find how the contents of our data card strayed into the instruction area. The instruction presumably executed just before the interruption was

MVC   0(80,5),CARD

which was supposed to move the contents of the card to an appropriate place. A glance at register 5 shows 0000D31A, the address of a most inappropriate place. We now examine the instructions that computed such an address, and the light dawns: after multiplying the number from the card by 80, we must correct for the lowest card number −10 by adding 800, not 10. With this correction made, the program segment runs properly.

5. ADVANCE PREPARATION

While programming, one should bear in mind the necessity for debugging his program later, and plan ahead for the debugging. Not that we should plan to make errors that will need debugging, but we should maintain a healthy humility and realize that every step we write *may* contain an error.

　　It is difficult to read a program and to understand its intent. Even very good programmers find it almost impossible to follow the logic of a program of more than average complexity. Often a programmer has trouble following or remembering the logic of his *own* program. Therefore, the program must be documented, and the most opportune time is the time of writing.

Comments and notes should be sprinkled liberally through the program; they are always available in the program and therefore are the most enduring form of documentation. There are programs in which comment statements are more than twice as numerous as executable statements. Specifications for input and output, explanation of program options, labeling of sections, descriptions of symbols, notes on particular logical procedures—all are welcome as comments. They make the debugging process much easier, since they facilitate understanding of the program. Also, they simplify enormously the task of anyone else who may have to understand or modify the program; any program which is useful, well written, and well documented, *will* be modified to fit the slightly different needs of someone else.

A flowchart is another useful tool. Many programmers write flowcharts before their programs, especially on large problems. This helps in breaking the problem into smaller, manageable pieces, and thus simplifies the programming task. Also, with fewer ramifications to consider while programming any given step, the programmer is better able to avoid making errors. The program evolved will probably deviate from the preliminary flowchart, so that in any case a new flowchart should be written after the program, describing *the actual program*. This is the one to be used in the debugging process.

The programmer should write his program so that it will maintain stability in the face of unexpected data patterns. He may know what the data *should* be like, but he usually does not have enough control to guarantee that it *will always* conform to his ideas. Where there is a possibility of data that would derange the program, he should build into the program error checks that will guard against the possibility. For example, if an address is computed from the data read in, a few tests of the data will ensure that the address actually computed falls within the allowable bounds. If a computed quantity is supposed to be positive, a check is in order before the computer attempts to find its square root. Note that this kind of check is not represented as a check on *program* correctness, but on data validity. Therefore, unlike techniques mentioned in Sections 6 and 7, it should be retained in the program after completion of the debugging phase. This kind of error check may help catch bugs in the program, however, since some program bugs produce invalid data patterns from entirely innocent input data. Such a test should be inserted in the program of Fig. 9–3, for example.

An initial test of any program must be carried out with carefully prepared data. This data should be the simplest possible which still affords a significant test of the program's features. The programmer should be able to check the computer's output for correctness on this set of data—he should not be satisfied that it "looks reasonable." The programmer may make the correctness check by carrying out himself the calculations to be done by the computer. Or the problem may be such that a test of the results in another fashion, after they are calculated, is more efficient. For example, if a program is to take the square root of a number T, it is easier to square the output and compare with T than to follow the procedure of finding the square root. For some large problems neither may be possible for the whole process; in this case the program should be checked out section by section, with a computational check on each section.

6. PARTIAL DUMPS

The ABDUMP, SYSUDUMP, and indicative dumps are taken only at the point of termination of the program. Among the three types the completeness of the information provided varies. There are many debugging situations in which a dump at the time of termination is not the best information to have. At times it is much more helpful to have dumps, not necessarily of everything, at intervals throughout execution of the program. With such a dump we can analyze the program's actions by sections: Up to this point in the program such-and-such should have been done; was it? If not, the problems are localized to the particular section of program; if so, we look at the dump after another section to see the results of its actions. Since some errors compound themselves and their effects sometimes even wipe out the evidence of their causes, periodic dumps can be very valuable indeed.

Partial dumps can be implemented in several ways. First, of course, is to call in the regular fashion (subroutine call or macro-instruction) for the output of a line of intermediate results, with format, conversions, and identification all handled in the program itself. This is the most flexible but also the most difficult method of obtaining intermediate dumps. Any desired output can be accomplished by programming, but at the risk of introducing additional errors! Not only is there the possibility of creating errors through the writing of the instructions that provide intermediate output, but also there is the possibility that the removal of the instructions after the debugging process is "completed" will introduce further errors.

Another way to get a partial dump during execution of a program is to call on the SNAPSHØT feature of the operating system. The SNAP macro-instruction permits the programmer to obtain a dump in the ABDUMP or SYSUDUMP format, then continue execution of his program. Of course, this provides a very comprehensive dump, almost always containing much more information than the programmer needs. There are requirements for preparation of the SNAPSHØT data set that we will not discuss here; one of the manuals on debugging listed in Section 3 contains full details, but information on the input and output macro-instructions (which we shall study in Chapter 12) is prerequisite.

Still another way to get partial dumps is to use special dump subroutines that are available at most installations. The subroutine PDUMP, written for use in FORTRAN but also usable with assembler language, is an example. Parameters to PDUMP come in groups of three: the first two parameters of each group are addresses of locations between which storage contents are to be printed. The third parameter of each group defines the representation in which the storage contents are to be printed: hexadecimal, decimal equivalent of a binary integer, or decimal floating-point equivalent of the IBM System/360 floating-point format, either single or double precision. Several areas can be dumped with one call on PDUMP. Since PDUMP is written for use with FORTRAN, it assumes an output on a data set with ddname FT03F001, so a job control statement

$$//G\emptyset.FT03F001 \quad DD \quad SYS\emptyset UT=A$$

must be provided even though another data set may already be assigned to the printer.

If the printing is being done directly onto the printer and two or more data sets are assigned to the printer, then each request for an output line from any of the data sets will cause a line to be printed immediately after the line last requested. This means that if requests for output to the data sets are mixed, the output will similarly be mixed. If, on the other hand, the data sets are saved for later printing, each data set will be printed intact, and therefore we lose all information as to whether a particular line of one data set was requested before or after a particular line of another data set. This can be a debugging inconvenience; each programmer must learn of the data-set-handling practices at his installation if he wishes to assign two or more data sets to the same device.

Besides the PDUMP subroutine, each installation has dump subroutines built for various purposes: display of register contents, dumping information in character form, etc.

7. TRACE FEATURES

A trace of a program can be regarded as a special case of a partial dump. A full trace reports each instruction executed and its results; a flow trace reports each branch instruction and the direction of branch. Either one gives information about the flow of execution of instructions. A trace is useful especially in situations where the programmer cannot follow the flow of control from partial dumps and his program listing.

A trace involves a full interpretive execution of at least the portion of the program being traced; that is, a program examines and interprets each instruction, retrieves operands, and stores results; in short, it simulates the operation of the computer. This obviously takes time and storage space for the trace program as well as the user's program, and it can produce a whale of a lot of paper. Therefore any trace feature allows the trace to be turned on and off at various times according to various criteria.

IBM System/370 installations have access to the *General Trace Facility* (GTF); users may consult the *Services Aids* manual, GC28-6719, for details. System/370 also contains *program event recording* and *monitoring* features, which can assist greatly in the implementation of debugging systems that provide some flexible trace features without impinging very much on the program being debugged. As time goes on, we can expect significant developments in this area.

Some computer installations may have other trace features of their own. Other computing centers discourage tracing, feeling that with dumps and careful thought the alert programmer can find his errors, and therefore traces, with their invitation to over-dependence, are unnecessary. In any case, the object of this section, like others in the chapter, is to introduce the reader to facilities about which he may wish to learn to help him cope with future debugging situations. Tracing is helpful when the programmer cannot follow and understand the flow of control through his program; partial dumps are helpful when intermediate results in main storage which lead to erroneous output must be examined. Dumps obtained upon termination are usually sufficient to help the programmer find the error in an invalid instruction. The programmer is urged to remember the basic debugging tools, and develop sophistication and skill at using these tools to the degree of sophistication required by his programs (and errors).

8. MATURITY AND GOOD CITIZENSHIP

Maturity in programming shows, like maturity in automobile driving. Maturity is not synonymous with skill or experience, though it is related; maturity is the use of good judgment on problems and consideration for others. Let us discuss some of its aspects; first we shall give some hints about the way in which a mature programmer debugs his programs.

A good programmer always has a completely up-to-date listing of his program as it was actually submitted for the last run. He debugs from this listing, not from an older one on which he has indicated corrections or changes he has since made. How many novice programmers have trouble finding errors because they are debugging from listings of what they intended to submit and therefore do not see the "corrections" which they made incorrectly! Most systems produce listings of the programs they are translating; the wise programmer does not turn off production of these listings except when he has made *absolutely no change whatever*.

A programmer learns not to be hasty in correcting an apparent error and rushing his program back to the computer. He examines his output carefully, and tries to ensure that he knows exactly what caused his erroneous results. Only then can he truly correct the error. The best programmers are not satisfied to find and correct one error after a run; they examine their results to try to find and correct all errors possible. The effort spent in this kind of examination is amply repaid in fewer debug runs and shorter total debugging time.

In order to be an effective programmer, one must learn the detailed specifications of at least the features and instructions he is trying to use. One of the requirements of almost-error-free programming is that the programmer knows what he *knows* and what he does not. What he does not know or is unsure of he must look up and then use correctly, because what he doesn't know could cause errors. One loses much time if he must look up everything, but it is the mark of a professional to know where to look for information and to refer to it when necessary.

Before being certified as debugged, a program should be tried under all combinations of circumstances that could possibly lead to different treatments by the program. This is difficult to define precisely, and difficult to achieve if taken literally. Therefore programs are often found, after years of presumably error-free use, to contain subtle bugs which show up only under certain combinations of circumstances. We must do the best we can, and this takes a good deal of work.

Not only does the mature programmer test his program with a variety of data; he collects and maintains carefully a comprehensive set of test data. Whenever the program needs to be changed by the addition of some new feature, for example, a run with the set of test data can verify that the program still works properly under the circumstances originally planned for. The addition of a new feature will usually necessitate the generation of more test data to test the new feature, perhaps in connection with a variety of other features.

A program should have stability in its actions on unexpected data. During the life of a good program, data will be submitted in just about every wrong way imaginable. A really good program tests for and recognizes bad data, and treats them as such without becoming paralyzed; it issues a message identifying the particular data record which is invalid and why, then takes some default action like ignoring the record or assuming that the offending data item is zero. After that it continues as usual, providing a reasonable output. Thus the program points out not only the first data invalidity but all of them, and in a way that is helpful to the user who of course wishes to correct his data.

In recent years there has been significant study of the nature of the programming process, and there have been developments that enable us to write programs with fewer bugs in the first place and later to *prove* that the programs work properly. Weinberg and Dijkstra (see the references at the end of the chapter) are perhaps foremost on this area. A primary thrust is that simplification of the control structures used in programming aids in more error-free program development. Restrictions, especially on the placement of branch instructions, clean up the thinking, debugging, and correctness proof considerably. These ideas of structured programming are being applied to the design of higher-level languages with good results. Attempts are being made to apply the principles to assembler language programming as well, with more or less success. One problem is that this thrust is contradictory to the principle that one uses assembler language to get the full power and flexibility permitted by his computer. We have a lot of work ahead of us before we find the proper balance—preserving power, yet utilizing good structured programming principles in a system that is straightforward and easy to write error-free programs in!

Meanwhile, we should strive for honesty and straightforwardness in programming. There is enough room for ingenuity and efficiency in the intended capabilities of almost any system that a programmer should avoid usage contrary to advertised features. He should also avoid involved and complex structures when possible. This aspect of good citizenship has two benefits. First, the debugging process is much simplified, not only because the program to debug is simpler, but also because there are likely to be fewer errors. Besides, a correction is less likely to cause new errors. Second, good programs have a life in which they grow, change, and are transplanted. New features are added, old ones are modified, the program is transcribed to run on a different computer. These changes are facilitated by straightforward programming and prevented by the tricky use of nonstandard subtleties. It is the mark of a novice that his programs, even if they work, cannot be understood, and the mark of a responsible professional that his programs can be understood and adapted readily to new demands.

9. MAIN IDEAS

a. Each instruction in the IBM System/360 and 370 has its requirements of operand validity. When these requirements are not met, the condition is called a program check *exception*. Most exceptions will always cause an interrupt and termination of the program. The most important types of exceptions are operation, privileged operation, protection, addressing, specification, data, fixed-point overflow, and fixed-point divide.

b. In the absence of other requests, an exception and interrupt will cause an *indicative dump*, which prints for the programmer some information on register contents, program status word fields, and the instruction currently attempted.

c. Error messages are printed by the operating system when it detects requests that cannot be satisfied by the operating system components or by assemblers, etc.

d. Debugging aids available besides the indicative dump and error messages are fuller dumps at termination of the program, partial dumps taken during execution, and various sorts of traces. Their use can be planned before the debugging process begins, or additional aids can be called when an error arises whose cause cannot be found from the information at hand.

PROBLEMS FOR REVIEW AND IMAGINATION

1. The subroutine shown in Fig. 9–5 is designed to search a list in which full word data items follow immediately their full word keys. The data item corresponding to the largest full word key is returned as the result. Write a flowchart which *describes* the workings of the subroutine.

2. Write remarks in the subroutine of Fig. 9–5 to help document the program.

3. Design a set of test data to use in testing the subroutine of Fig. 9–5.

4. Rewrite the subroutine of Fig. 9–5 to include tests for input errors; for example, a nonpositive number of items to search or a beginning address of the table which is not on a full-word boundary. Assign return codes in register 15 of 0 for successful completion, 4 for invalid number of data items, etc.

5. Outline a procedure you might follow in debugging the subroutine of Fig. 9–5 (or subroutines like it which contain a variety of errors). In relation to debugging aids in particular, in what situations, and why, would an indicative dump be sufficient? In what situations, and why, would a dump of segments of main storage be helpful? What segments? At what times should these

Fig. 9–5   A subroutine

```
SRCHLARG SAVE    (14,12)
         BALR    12,0
         USING   *,12
         LM      2,3,0(1)
         L       6,0(2)
         LR      4,3
         L       5,0(4)
LP       C       5,0(3)
         BNL     ARØUND
         LR      4,3
         L       5,0(4)
ARØUND   LA      3,8(3)
         BCT     6,LP
         L       0,4(4)
         RETURN  (2,12)
         END
```

dumps best be taken?   Would monitoring the segments for changes be an acceptable substitute?   What kinds of trace would be helpful; when, how much, and why?

6. Add to the program of Fig. 9–3 a test on the number read from the card to make sure it *is* between −10 and 9, or what should amount to the same thing, a test on the address computed to make sure that it falls within the area WØRK.

REFERENCES

Dahl, O. J., E. W. Dijkstra, and C. A. R. Hoare, *Structured Programming* (New York: Academic Press, 1972).

IBM System/360 Operating System: Messages and Codes, GC28-6631, IBM Corporation. Error messages and completion codes: their meanings and suggested corrective measures.

IBM System/360 Operating System: Programmer's Guide to Debugging, GC28-6670, *OS/VS1 Debugging Guide*, GC24-5093, or *OS/VS2 Debugging Guide*, GC28-0632, IBM Corporation.   How to call for various dumps, and formats of the dumps.

Stevens, W. P., G. J. Myers, and L. L. Constantine, "Structured Design," *IBM Systems Journal*, **13**, 2 (1974), pp. 115–139.

Weinberg, Gerald M., *The Psychology of Computer Programming* (New York: Van Nostrand Reinhold, 1971).

Chapter 10

Character or Byte Manipulation

The byte is a basic unit of information in the IBM System/360, chiefly because it holds the coding of one character. Many of today's problems and more of tomorrow's will be problems of processing text, i.e., characters. The IBM System/360 has a good set of instructions that facilitate byte manipulation. Those instructions that are exclusively byte processors are discussed in this chapter. In the next chapter we shall discuss manipulation of bits and groups of bits; the bit manipulation facilities also help us to process bytes, which are, after all, just groups of eight bits.

1. BYTE TRANSFER OR MOVE INSTRUCTIONS

In the IBM System/360 and 370 single bytes can be moved from one main storage location to another or to a register, from a register to a main storage location, and directly from an instruction to a main storage location, as can be seen pictorially in Fig. 10–1. In addition, a string of several bytes can be moved from one main storage location to another.

The MVC and MVI instructions were discussed in Chapter 4; we will further illustrate their use here.

The IC (Insert Character) instruction is of RX type. It inserts a character from the byte addressed as the second operand to the low-order bit positions, 24–31, of the register $R1$. Bit positions 0–23 of register $R1$ are unchanged by the instruction. Thus the IC instruction is different from the LH (Load Half-word) instruction which loads a half-word from main storage into a register but changes the contents of the whole register.

The STC (STore Character) instruction is the converse of IC. Also of RX type, it stores the low-order eight bits of the register $R1$ into a main storage location addressed as the second operand.

The two instructions can be described as

$$IC: \quad \text{Insert Character:} \quad R1_{24-31} \leftarrow c(S2)_{0-7}$$
$$STC: \quad \text{STore Character:} \quad S2_{0-7} \leftarrow c(R1)_{24-31}$$

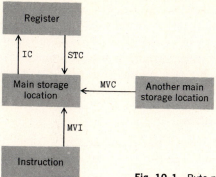

Fig. 10–1 Byte move instructions.

The main storage operands are only one byte long, so do not have to begin on any word or half-word boundary. Thus a specification exception cannot occur in the execution of these instructions; the only exceptions possible are access exceptions. The condition code is not affected by either instruction.

Consider the following examples. The instruction

                    IC   6,INAREA

inserts the byte from location INAREA into the low-order eight bits of register 6. So if INAREA contains (hexadecimal) F7 and register 6 contains F3C2D540 before the instruction, execution of the instruction will change contents of register 6 to F3C2D5F7. Similarly, the instruction

                    STC   5,ØUT+14

will store the low-order eight bits of register 5 into the main storage byte at location ØUT+14.

2. CHARACTER COMPARE OPERATIONS

The meaning of "logical" in IBM System/360 and 370

Certain instructions work with data in a "logical" fashion. Some of these correspond to logic functions of *or* and *and*, and are discussed in the next chapter. Others deal with data as numeric quantities, but without sign. This latter is the use of the word "logical" that concerns us in this section; it has nothing to do with logic or reasonableness, and is really only a synonym for *unsigned*. All bits in the quantity, including the highest-order, are considered as numeric bits, so all logical quantities are nonnegative. If we have quantities

          A: 11111111 00000000 11110000 00001111

and

          B: 00000000 11111111 11111111 00001111,

the relationship depends on whether they are considered as arithmetic or logical. As an arithmetic quantity, A is negative and therefore less than B. However, as a logical quantity, A is positive and greater than B. A System/360 or 370 computer allows comparisons in either arithmetic or logical mode. We shall discuss logical instructions further in the next chapter, but since the character compare instructions are logical instructions we discuss them next.

The CLC and CLI instructions

The CLC (Compare Logical Character) and CLI (Compare Logical Immediate) instructions are designed to permit comparison of characters and strings of characters. Both perform logical, that is, unsigned, comparisons, setting the condition code to

       0   if the two operands are equal,
       1   if the first operand is less than the second operand,
       2   if the first operand is greater than the second operand.

The CLC instruction is of SS type; it permits comparison of strings of characters from 1 to 256 bytes long in main storage. Only one length, which describes both operands, is specified. The CLI instruction is of SI type; it performs a comparison of a first operand, which is one byte in main storage, with a second operand, which is a byte in the instruction itself.

Neither instruction requires any particular boundary alignment of its operands; only protection and addressing exceptions can occur. For example,

                    CLI   INAREA+4,C'%'

compares the character in main storage at INAREA+4 with the character %, setting the condition code accordingly. The instruction

                    CLC   NAME(24),INAREA+10

compares the 24-byte string starting at NAME with the 24-byte string starting at INAREA+10.

The instructions can be described symbolically as

$$\text{CLI} \quad \text{Compare Logical Immediate} \quad CC \leftarrow \begin{cases} 0 \text{ if } c(S1) = I2 \\ 1 \text{ if } c(S1) < I2 \\ 2 \text{ if } c(S1) > I2 \end{cases}$$

$$\text{CLC} \quad \text{Compare Logical Character} \quad CC \leftarrow \begin{cases} 0 \text{ if } c(S1)_{0-BL} = c(S2)_{0-BL} \\ 1 \text{ if } c(S1)_{0-BL} < c(S2)_{0-BL} \\ 2 \text{ if } c(S1)_{0-BL} > c(S2)_{0-BL} \end{cases}$$

where if L is the length operand coded in the machine-language instruction, $BL = 8L + 7$ so $L + 1$ bytes of each operand are tested. It must be understood that the quantities are compared as unsigned integers.

In the remainder of the chapter we shall explore character manipulation techniques and give examples of the use of these instructions.

3. AN EXAMPLE: SEARCHING FOR A NAME

Consider the following problem: A file consists of records, each 120 bytes long. Considering the first byte of each as byte 0, each record contains a person's name in bytes 10–33 and his street address in bytes 34–93. The file is in main storage, starting at location PEØPLE. The name of one of the people in the file is at location NAME; the problem is to find from the file his address and place it at ADDR. Let us suppose that the records are ordered on some key other than name, so the names are not ordered. We must therefore make a sequential search. Suppose the number of records in the file is in register 7.

A program segment to accomplish this task is shown in Fig. 10–2. Register 9 holds the address of the record currently being considered. It is therefore incremented by 120 in each execution of the body of the loop. The specification 10(9) addresses the first byte of the name in the current record, and 34(9) specifies the corresponding street address. The CLC instruction is used to compare the names; all 24 bytes are compared by the single instruction. Note that an index register method of address modification cannot be used in this problem, since CLC and MVC are of SS type and therefore do not include index specification in their operand addressing.

Some remarks on the reality of this example are in order. In the first place, searching for an (exact) name is a perilous business. Everyone knows that names are written in many ways, with full middle name, middle initial, no middle name, wife's first name or Mrs. and her husband's name, etc., not to mention the neverending misspellings. If the name to be found comes from, say a credit card charge plate, consistency with the name in the file can be assumed. In other cases, failure to find an exact match in the file should cause a much more sophisticated search for a name which is most likely to be the correct one. The more sophisticated search would perhaps include first a search for all records with the last name correct (the last name is all the characters up to the first blank, and we can find *that*), then a survey of first and middle names and initials. The program would still suffer from both errors of omission and commission.

In the second place, a reasonable file to be searched would not likely be kept in main storage. A reel of magnetic tape or something else of large capacity would hold the file, and only small portions of it would be brought into main storage. The program segment

Fig. 10–2 Program segment to search for a name

```
*    SEARCH FILE ØF 120-BYTE RECØRDS FØR ADDRESS
*    CØRRESPØNDING TØ NAME, STØRE IN ADDR.
*    NAME IN EACH RECØRD IS IN BYTES 10 - 33, ADDRESS
*    IN BYTES 34 - 93.
*    REG. 7 CØNTAINS LENGTH (IN RECØRDS) ØF FILE.
          LA      9,PEØPLE        USE REG. 9 TØ ADDRESS NAMES IN FILE.
LØØP      CLC     NAME(24),10(9)  CØMPARE NAMES
          BE      ØUT
          LA      9,120(9)        MØVE TØ NEXT RECØRD
          BCT     7,LØØP
          B       FAIL            BRANCH TØ FAIL IF NAME NØT IN FILE
ØUT       MVC     ADDR(60),34(9)  RETRIEVE ADDRESS
          :
```

given could be a search through a portion of the file, with FAIL introducing the program segment which brings a new portion of the file into main storage. Furthermore, if possible in the application, names whose street addresses are needed would be grouped, so that one pass through the file would search for, say fifteen names.

4. AN EXAMPLE: CHARACTER REPLACEMENT

An IBM Model 026 card punch produces different punch configurations for the characters =+() from those produced by the IBM Model 029 card punch. In fact, the characters =+() as punched by an IBM Model 026 card punch are interpreted as #&%< in the EBCDIC representation used by the IBM System/360 and the IBM Model 029 card punch. Let us consider a subroutine which is to examine a string of characters and replace all occurrences of the characters #&%< with EBCDIC representations of =+(), correspondingly. That is, each # is to be replaced by =, each & replaced by +, each % replaced by (, and each < replaced by). With this subroutine available, an IBM System/360 user can use the IBM Model 026 card punch to prepare input to the IBM System/360.

Figure 10–3 shows a subroutine that will do the task. First, the looping strategy is to keep in register 4 the address of the byte in the string currently being tested. Register 7 is set to the address of the last byte in the string, for looping control. In the loop itself, the byte currently addressed by register 4 is compared

Fig. 10–3   Subroutine to change #&%< to =+( )

```
*       SUBRØUTINE TØ REPLACE #&%<
*          WITH CØRRESPØNDING =+() IN A CHARACTER STRING.
*       INPUT PARAMETERS ARE ADDRESS ØF STRING AND LENGTH.
*       THE STRING IS CHANGED IN PLACE.
CHNGSTR  SAVE    (14,12)
         BALR    12,0
         USING   *,12
         LM      4,5,0(1)        ADDRESS ØF STRING IN REG. 4
         L       5,0(5)          LENGTH IN REG. 5
         LA      6,1
         LA      7,0(4,5)
         S       7,=F'1'         ADDRESS ØF LAST BYTE IN STRING
LØØP     CLI     0(4),C'#'       TEST FØR #
         BE      REPL1
         CLI     0(4),C'&&'      TEST FØR &
         BE      REPL2
         CLI     0(4),C'%'       TEST FØR %
         BE      REPL3
         CLI     0(4),C'<'       TEST FØR <
         BNE     LØØPCØNT
         MVI     0(4),C')'       IF <, REPLACE BY )
         B       LØØPCØNT
REPL1    MVI     0(4),C'='       IF #, REPLACE BY =
         B       LØØPCØNT
REPL2    MVI     0(4),C'+'       IF &, REPLACE BY +
         B       LØØPCØNT
REPL3    MVI     0(4),C'('       IF %, REPLACE BY (
LØØPCØNT BXLE    4,6,LØØP        LØØP CØNTRØL
         RETURN  (4,12)
```

with each of the characters #&%<, in turn, and if one of these four is found, it is replaced by =+(or), respectively. Remember that the self-defining term containing & must be defined by && in assembler language.

The CLI and MVI instructions are good instructions to use in this problem. Each can work on one byte without disturbing or being affected by any adjacent bytes. The CLC and MVC instructions with lengths of 1 could be used, but the instructions would be longer, take longer to execute, and require definition of constants holding the eight character representations.

In Chapter 15 we shall learn of a translate instruction which does the problem described here even better in the IBM System/360. The approach taken in Fig. 10–3, however, can be used in other computers with character manipulation facilities.

5. AN EXAMPLE: COUNTING DIGITS

A common use of a computer is tabulation of various sorts of things. Let us take an example in which we construct a table of the frequencies of digits occurring in a particular position of a record and the frequencies counted over a group of records, and show how the character manipulation instructions facilitate the task.

Suppose that a record is read or somehow generated in main storage starting at REC. The position within the record is in register 9; for example, if we are to tabulate positon (byte) 23 of the record (assuming the first byte to be position 0), the number 23—hexadecimal 00000017—is in register 9. Any of the digits 0–9 are expected to be in that positon of the record, represented as EBCDIC characters, and we wish to count, over a group of records, just how many 0's, how many 1's, . . . , how many 9's, occur. It is likely that we may be asked to generate several tables from a group of records, so storage space may be at a premium. Let us suppose, then, that no count will exceed 255, so we can keep each counter in one

Fig. 10–4 Counting digits

```
*       PRØGRAM SEGMENT TØ UPDATE CØUNTERS ØF DIGITS
*       BY CØUNTING DIGIT IN CURRENT RECØRD.
*       REGISTER 9 CØNTAINS THE INDICATØR ØF WHICH PØSITION
*          IN THE RECORD NAMED REC CØNTAINS THE DIGIT
*       ADDRESS ØF 10–BYTE CØUNTER AREA IN REG. 10
UPCNT   LA      6,0
        LA      5,0
        IC      5,REC(9)        CHARACTER TØ BE CØUNTED
        S       5,=F'240'       CØDE FØR DIGIT 0
        BM      TILT
        C       5,=F'10'        MAKE SURE CHAR. IS DIGIT
        BNL     TILT
        IC      6,0(10,5)       GET APPRØPRIATE CØUNT
        LA      6,1(6)             ADD 1
        C       6,=F'255'
        BH      TILT1
        STC     6,0(10,5)       STØRE IT
*       CØNTINUE
*       BRANCH TØ TILT IF ATTEMPT TØ CØUNT ILLEGAL CHAR.
*       BRANCH TØ TILT1 IF CØUNT BECØMES TØØ LARGE.
```

byte. To keep ten counters, one for counting each of the digits 0–9, we need 10 bytes of main storage; we assume that the address of the first byte of this area is in register 10.

Figure 10–4 shows a program segment which adds 1 to the appropriate counter, depending on the digit found in the current record. The IC instruction is used in two ways. First, it brings into register 6 the digit to be counted. The IC instruction is of RX type, so indexing is possible and used to advantage here. The character is brought into a register so arithmetic can be done on it. The EBCDIC codes for the digits 0–9 are hexadecimal F0–F9, or decimal 240–249. Therefore if 240 is subtracted from the EBCDIC representation, a number 0–9 results, and the second IC instruction uses the digit as an index to grab the right counter to update!

If each of the counters had been two bytes long, the number 0–9 remaining after the subtraction of 240 would have been multiplied by 2, and the result would have been used to obtain a counter in the same way; however, the instruction to bring a counter into a register would then have been

```
LH    6,0(10,5)
```

If it is suspected that the counters might sometimes but rarely exceed 255, it may be worth while to maintain the counters at one byte each but provide a small overflow area to hold counts that have exceeded 255. The program segment at TILT1 could start overflow counts.

The segment of Fig. 10–4 would likely be the body of a loop entered for each record of a group of records. Perhaps there would be an intermediate loop, counting several positions (into several counter areas) in each record. The two instructions

```
LA    6,0
LA    5,0
```

could be placed outside the loop if the high-order 24 bits of registers 5 and 6 were not changed during the loop. The instructions are necessary *somewhere* since the IC instruction changes only the low-order eight bits of a register.

When the counters are finally to be printed, the IC instruction can again be used to bring the counter into a register for conversion to decimal and unpacking.

6. ADDITIONAL CHARACTER INSTRUCTIONS FOR SYSTEM/370

Users of IBM System/370 systems have five additional character-manipulation instructions at their disposal. We present them in this section.

Move Character Long

A programmer often wishes to move a block of information from one place in main storage to another. The MVC instruction does that, but we find it annoying that MVC can move at most 256 characters; sometimes we want to move much longer strings. The instruction MVCL (MoVe Character Long) moves arbitrarily long strings. MVCL is an RR-type instruction; each register address is the address of an even-odd pair of registers. The first pair defines the address and length of the destination field: $c(R1)$ designates the beginning (leftmost) address of the destination field, and $c(R1 + 1)$ designates the length of the field to be filled. The second pair similarly defines the address and length of the source field. However, bits 0–7 of register $R2 + 1$ are a *padding character*; if the destination field is longer than the source field, the padding character is copied into the remainder of the destination field after the source field is exhausted. (If the source field is longer, only enough of it is moved to fill the destination field.)

Unlike MVC, the number of characters moved is not one more than is specified by the length codes. One result is that if a length of 0 is coded in register $R1 + 1$, *no* characters are moved.

Some examples will illustrate the action.

a. Suppose the address P has been loaded into register 2, the address Q into register 4. The hexadecimal contents of register 3 is 000004E0, and contents of register 5 is 400001B4. The instruction

$$\text{MVCL} \qquad 2,4$$

will move
  i) 1B4 characters starting at location Q to a field starting at location P;
 ii) 32C (4E0–1B4) copies of the padding character 40 into locations starting at P+1B4, which is immediately after the last character from Q.

b. With the same original contents, the instruction

$$\text{MVCL} \qquad 4,2$$

will move 1B4 characters from location P to location Q.

The registers $R1$ and $R2$ are incremented by 1 each time a character is moved, and $R1+1$ and $R2+1$ are each decremented by 1. Therefore the final results in the registers will be

Register $R1$ is incremented by the original contents of $R1+1$.
Register $R1+1$ is set to 0.
Register $R2$ is incremented by the smaller of the original contents of $R1+1$ and $R2+1$ (ignoring the padding character).
Register $R2+1$ is decremented by the same amount that $R2$ was incremented.

The condition code is set by MVCL to

  0 if the field counts are equal,
  1 if the first operand count is lower,
  2 if the second operand count is lower,
  3 if no movement is performed because of destructive overlap.

The destructive overlap condition is recognized if a byte is used as a source after it is used as a destination.

Use of the fill character makes MVCL a useful instruction for clearing a section of storage to zeros, or storing blanks in it, or filling it with copies of any single character. For example,

```
L      2,Y
LA     3,800
L      4,*
L      5,=F'0'
MVCL   2,4
```

will set the 800 bytes beginning at Y to zeros. The address in register 4 can be any valid address not causing destructive overlap, since no characters are moved from the second operand field; all are copied from the padding character.

Compare Logical Character Long

The instruction CLCL (Compare Logical Character Long) is very similar to MVCL. CLCL is an RR-type instruction, and the registers define fields and a padding character in exactly the same way as MVCL. The difference, of course, is that instead of moving contents of one field to another, the two fields are compared. The result of the comparison is expressed in the condition code, which is set

0 if the operands are equal or if both fields have zero length,
1 if the first operand is low,
2 if the first operand is high.

The comparison treats the fields as unsigned binary integers, and it continues until either a mismatch is found or the *longer* field is exhausted. If either field is shorter than the other, the shorter field (note: *either* field if shorter) is considered to be extended by the padding character.

If the operation ends because of a mismatch, the contents of the registers identify the byte of mismatch. The contents of registers $R1+1$ and $R2+1$ are decremented by the number of bytes that match, except that they stop at 0 when the comparison is continued by use of the padding character. Registers $R1$ and $R2$ are incremented by the same quantities that the count fields are decremented.

The instructions MVCL and CLCL are *interruptible*; that is, execution can be interrupted before completion. Since the instructions can take a long time (at least in comparison with other instructions), the interruptibility is essential in preserving the system's timely response to interrupts, such as some input/output and clock-generated interrupts which impose a time pressure for prompt action. No other instructions are interruptible (except, of course, for interrupts generated by conditions arising in execution of the instructions themselves); interruptions are held until after execution of an instruction is completed. One reason so much information used by MVCL and CLCL is kept in registers is that the information will therefore be available for restart of the instruction after interruption. The interruptibility of the instructions is of concern to the programmer in that he should avoid letting the destination (first) operand area of MVCL contain the MVCL instruction itself; it might be gone when needed for resumption!

The instructions ICM, STCM, CLM

The three instructions ICM (Insert Characters under Mask), STCM (STore Characters under Mask), and CLM (Compare Logical under Mask) form a family. All are RS-type instructions. In each, *R1* designates a register operand, *S2* an operand in main storage. In each, the third operand, *M3*, is not another register operand but a mask that designates which bytes of the register *R1* participate in the instruction. Each of the four bits of the mask determines whether a corresponding byte of the register is used in the instruction. The assignments are as follows:

Mask bit	Mask value	Register byte	Register bit positions
1	8	1	0–7
2	4	2	8–15
3	2	3	16–23
4	1	4	24–31

For example, a mask of 4 selects the second byte of the register; a mask value of 6 ($= 4 + 2$) selects the middle two bytes of the register. In each case, the same number of bytes in main storage, starting at the location *S2*, participate.

The actions of the three instructions can be guessed: ICM inserts characters from main storage into the selected byte positions in the register, leaving the non-selected bytes unchanged. STCM stores selected bytes from the register into main storage. CLM compares the number formed by the selected bytes in the register with an equal number of bytes in main storage; the operands are considered as unsigned binary integers.

These instructions are more flexible extensions of other insert, load, compare, and store instructions. For example,

                 ICM   REG7,1,Y

is equivalent in action to

                 IC   REG7,Y

Similarly,

                 STCM   REG7,3,HLF

is equivalent to

                 STH   REG7,HLF

except that STCM does not require HLF to be on a half-word boundary. The point is that any subset of bytes in a register can be compared with a character string in main storage, or stored in a contiguous main storage field, or can be replaced by the contents of a main storage field. The selected bytes in a register operand need not be contiguous, but the corresponding main storage field will always be con-tiguous bytes. For example,

                 STCM   REG7,10,Y

stores the first byte of REG7 (bits 0–7) at Y and the third (bits 16–23) at Y+1.

Both CLM and ICM set the condition code:

	CLM	ICM
0	selected bytes equal, or mask = 0	all inserted bits are 0, or mask = 0
1	selected field of 1st operand is low	first bit of inserted field is 1
2	selected field of 1st operand is high	first bit of inserted field is 0, but not all inserted bits are 0

7. AN EXAMPLE: GENERATING A SYMBOL TABLE

One of the tasks for any computer-language translator—assembler, compiler or whatever—is the generation and use of a symbol table. All the names of storage areas, etc. must be kept in a table, along with information about the nature of the symbol and addresses and lengths assigned by the translator. The problem is not unique to language translators; many diverse applications require generation of tables of similar sorts of information. We use the symbol table for the IBM System/360 or 370 assembler as an example, because, since the reader is already familiar with the language, definition of the problem is not difficult.

In the IBM System/360 or 370 assembler systems, a symbol or name is from one to eight characters long. The table must store all characters of each symbol. It is most convenient to allow space for eight characters for each symbol in the table, filling in blanks on the right if necessary. Several other pieces of information are necessary:

the length attribute of the symbol, a half-word;
the address assigned to the symbol, three bytes;
an indicator whether relocatable or absolute, one bit;
an indicator whether or not yet defined, one bit;

and a few other small pieces of information. To hold all of this, let us allocate four words, or 16 bytes, to each symbol entry. We may call each four-word space a cell in the table.

Several different operations must be performed on the symbol table. First is insertion of a symbol in the table, which must be performed once for each symbol. Second is search and retrieval of information, which may be required several times for each symbol, but this "several" is more likely to be four times than 400.

Depending on the organization of the assembler, a third operation of search, followed by insertion or further definition, may be required. For example, if a symbol is entered into the symbol table when first encountered, either as name or operand, each subsequent encounter will require a search, but a subsequent encounter in the name field will at last cause definition of the symbol.

The symbol table as a list; derived keys

The symbol table is a list, according to the definition of list given in Chapter 8; the key in the list is the symbol itself. Since the IBM System/360 or 370 assembler language allows over 10^{10} different symbols, a key-dense list is out of the question.

The list could be ordered, which would minimize search time in the list. However, the cost in time spent in sorting the list could be great. Insertion time can be minimized if we put the entries in the list in consecutive cells as they are encountered, but a significant amount of time would thereafter be spent in searching. So both the completely ordered list and the unordered, easy-to-generate list have their disadvantages.

Other alternatives are available. From our eight-byte key, the symbol itself, we can derive a new key by division or other manipulation of the symbol. The *derived key* can then be a pointer to a particular cell in the list. Search and insertion can be a matter of deriving a key from the symbol and then looking in the space pointed to by the derived key. The process is not this simple, however, since many original keys can correspond to one derived key. This raises a *collision* problem. For example, a first symbol may generate the derived key 8, and it can be inserted into cell 8 in the list. A second symbol may also generate derived key 8, so it must be put elsewhere. The collision problem can be minimized if we can derive keys to be as uniformly distributed as possible, so we attempt to do that.

Collision management

There are several ways of handling collisions. One is to put the new entry into the next available cell. The organization of the list is simple; to retrieve any particular entry one starts a sequential search at the cell corresponding to the derived key. The search ends upon either finding the right entry or finding a blank cell. The efficiency of this solution decreases as the list gets full and overflow entries have to be stored farther away from the cell corresponding to their derived keys. Main storage is used efficiently, however.

This treatment can be improved. Given that there is a collision of an element whose derived key is $k_0^{(0)}$ with another element already at cell $k_0^{(0)}$, let us denote the cells searched by $k_0^{(1)}$, $k_0^{(2)}$, $k_0^{(3)}$, ... Let us understand that each index is reduced by an appropriate multiple of N, the table size, so that the residue used to address a cell is in the range 0 to $N - 1$, inclusive. If cells are taken in sequence, so that $k_0^{(1)} = k_0^{(0)} + 1$, $k_0^{(2)} = k_0^{(0)} + 2$, etc., clusters tend to develop, because a search starting from $k_1^{(0)} = k_0^{(0)} + 1$ covers the same cells $k_0^{(2)}$, $k_0^{(3)}$, ... in the same order. If we can derive a scheme by which a search starting at $k_1^{(0)} = k_0^{(1)}$ does *not* cover cells $k_0^{(2)}$, $k_0^{(3)}$, ..., in this order, searches will be shortened. One such scheme is called *quadratic probing**; according to this scheme, the sequence of cells searched is k_0, $k_0 + a + b$, $k_0 + 2a + 2^2b$, $k_0 + 3a + 3^2b$, ... with appropriate choices of a and b. For example, we can generate a sequence by

$$k_0^{(i)} = k_0^{(i-1)} + i, \qquad i = 1, 2, \ldots,$$

or by

$$k_0^{(i)} = k_0^{(i-1)} + (N + 1)/2 - i, \qquad i = 1, 2, \ldots$$

---

* W. D. Maurer, "An Improved Hash Code for Scatter Storage," *Commun. Assoc. Comput. Mach.* **11**, No. 1 (January, 1968), pp. 35-38.

The table size N is required to be a prime number, and a search sequence will cover $(N + 1)/2$ cells before repeating. The result that the table is declared full if a cell is not available among the $(N + 1)/2$ cells searched is usually acceptable, especially since the $(N + 1)/2$ cells searched for one derived key are not precisely the same as those for another derived key.

Another collision management technique is the provision of a separate overflow area, where only overflow entries are stored. The overflow area can be filled sequentially; if the derived keys are well assigned, only a small fraction of the entries will be in the overflow area.

Links can be appended to each cell, so that in case of collision a particular next cell to search is indicated. Thus if entries have been made for derived keys 8 and 9, and a new entry is encountered with derived key 8, it could be stored in cell 10, and the link in cell 8 would point to cell 10. Thus cell 9 would not be searched for an entry with derived key 8. If an entry with derived key 10 were encountered next, it could be stored in cell 11, and that fact recorded in cell 10. Still other entries encountered with derived keys 8 or 10 would be mixed in what is essentially the same linked list. The link technique can also be used in connection with an overflow area, to minimize still further the burdens of search.

Another technique is called *bucketing*. Keys are derived in such a way that there are fewer different derived keys, and each derived key points to, say, a group of 10 cells, which is called a bucket. Entries associated with the same derived key are placed in the bucket in the order they are encountered. Insertion and searching are reasonably fast since only one bucket of 10 cells will usually have to be searched. Most of the overflows are averaged out, so there will be many fewer overflows from the buckets than from individual cells associated with individual keys. Overflow areas will not usually be buckets associated with other keys, but more likely separate areas. The programming required for bucketing is more complicated than for other techniques, but not prohibitive.

A search using any of these techniques is in most cases actually much faster than a binary search of a completely sorted list, since only a very few tests are required even in a large table until the table is 80 or 90 percent full.

Implementation: an example

Let us now examine one of the simpler techniques as it might be implemented in the IBM System/360 or 370. Our procedure will derive keys which will be associated with individual cells, perhaps allowing for 509 cells in our table. The first task is to derive the keys in such a way as to minimize the chance of collision. There is no known solution to the problem, but there are considerations that will at least enable us to get a distribution that is more uniform than a completely random distribution would be.

Programmers use symbols which are similar; that is, many of the symbols used in a program will differ in only one character out of eight. Our procedure then should assign different derived keys to symbols that differ in only one character. We should also derive keys in such a manner that if two symbols are different merely by the interpose of two characters, we obtain different keys. Many different procedures will conform to these requirements. One can think of more require-

Fig. 10–5　**Deriving a key from a symbol**

S2	L	5,SYMBØL+4	
	LA	4,0	
	D	4,=F'253'	DIVIDE SECØND HALF
	L	5,SYMBØL	FØRM NEW DIVIDEND FRØM REM. AND FIRST HALF
	D	4,=F'509'	DERIVED KEY IS REMAINDER ·IN REG. 4

ments, but for the purposes of this volume we will be satisfied with these. Our procedure is first to divide the last half of the symbol by 253. A new dividend is formed as the remainder from the first division (say in register 4), followed by the first half of the symbol (in register 5), and the derived key is the remainder after this dividend is divided by 509. We thus derive keys that may take on 509 different values; each will point to a cell. If the symbol is stored in a double word called SYMBØL, the program segment shown in Fig. 10–5 would derive a key from it.

Finding a symbol

Let us examine more phases of our problem. The first thing to be done, of course, is to find a symbol. For our example, we shall restrict ourselves to looking for a symbol in the name field, which vastly simplifies the job we undertake. We remember that a name is optional, but if one is present, it begins in column 1 of the card and is terminated by the first blank encountered. Supposing that a card containing a new assembler-language statement has just been read, and that it is stored at STATMENT, our procedure might be as shown in Fig. 10–6.

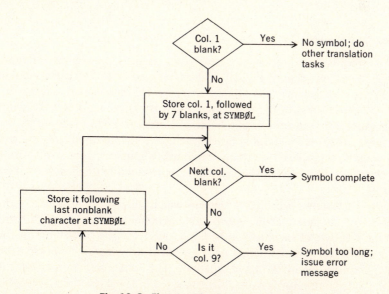

Fig. **10–6**　Flowchart for finding a symbol.

Fig. 10–7   Find a symbol

```
*       STATEMENT CARD READ INTØ STØRAGE AT STATMENT
*       FIND NAME, IF IT EXISTS, STØRE AT SYMBØL
*          THEN GØ TØ S2
*       IF NØ SYMBØL, GØ TØ S5
*       IF SYMBØL LØNGER THAN 8 CHARS., GØ TØ ER1
S1      CLI     STATMENT,C' '
        BE      S5
        MVC     SYMBØL(1),STATMENT        FIRST CHAR. TØ SYMBØL
        MVC     SYMBØL+1(7),BLANK          FILL WITH BLANKS
        LA      4,0                       INITIALIZE FØR LØØP
        LA      8,1
        LA      9,7
        LA      5,0
S1LP    IC      5,STATMENT+1(4)           GET NEXT CHAR.
        C       5,=F'64'                  64 IS DEC. EQUIV. ØF BLANK
        BE      S2                        IF EQUAL, SYMBØL CØMPLETE
        BXH     4,8,ER1                   INCREASE INDEX. IF 8, GØ TØ ER1
        STC     5,SYMBØL(4)               STØRE CHARACTER
        B       S1LP
BLANK   DC      CL7' '
SYMBØL  DS      1D
```

A program segment for the phase of the problem covered in the flowchart in Fig. 10–6 is given in Fig. 10–7. The first character of the name is moved by an MVC instruction. We could use this instruction to move subsequent characters also, but two addresses would have to be adjusted in the loop, one in the STATMENT area and one in the SYMBØL area. Instead, the segment shown uses the IC and STC instructions, which can be indexed. The BXH instruction is used for looping control: if a ninth nonblank character is encountered, the BXH instruction increases the index in register 4 to 8, causing a branch to ER1. Usually, the loop is left by the discovery of a blank.

Searching for a symbol

After a symbol is found, a key can be derived from it; the segment of Fig. 10–5 thus logically follows that of Fig. 10–7. Next we can try to find the symbol in our table. A program segment may have three possible outcomes: (1) the symbol is found, and the address of the cell containing it is presented, or (2) the symbol is not in the table, but the address of a blank cell appropriate for entering the symbol is presented, or (3) the symbol is not in the table, but no blank cell is available. Such a segment is usable either when one wants to enter or to retrieve information about a symbol. The logic of the segment is represented in the flowchart shown in Fig. 10–8.

Figure 10–9 shows a program segment which follows the flowchart shown in Fig. 10–8. We assume that the empty table is initialized by storage of blanks in at least the first byte of every cell of the table; thus a CLI instruction testing for one blank is a sufficient test of whether or not a cell is still empty. To compare entire symbols, however, we use a CLC instruction. The BXLE instruction at once increments the index and returns control to S3A if the index is less than 16*509, but if

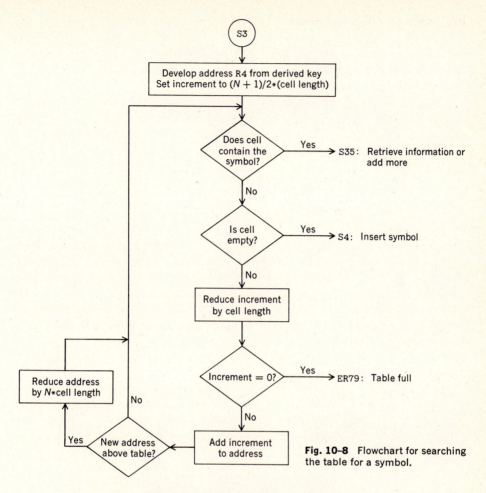

Fig. 10–8 Flowchart for searching the table for a symbol.

Fig. 10–9 Search a table for a symbol

```
*       FIND ADDRESS ØF CELL CØNTAINING SYMBØL
*          ØR IF THE SYMBØL IS NØT IN THE TABLE,
*          THE ADDRESS ØF AN APPRØPRIATE BLANK CELL
*       TABLE SIZE 509, INCREMENTS FØR INDEX 254*16, 253*16, ..., 16
*          CØNSTITUTING QUADRATIC PRØBING
S3      LM      6,9,=F'-16,8144,4080,8128'
        LR      5,4
        M       4,=F'16'
*       REG. 5 CØNTAINS INDEX ØF CURRENT CELL TØ BE TESTED
*       REG. 4 USED FØR ADDRESS ØF CURRENT CELL
*       REG. 8 CØNTAINS CURRENT INCREMENT
S3A     LA      4,TABLE(5)
        CLC     SYMBØL(8),0(4)      IF SYMBØL FØUND,
        BE      S35                     GØ TØ S35
        CLI     0(4),C' '           IF CELL EMPTY,
        BE      S4                      GØ TØ S4 TØ INSERT SYMBØL
        AR      8,6                 REDUCE INCREMENT,
        BNP     ER79                    GØ TØ ER79 IF TABLE FULL
        BXLE    5,8,S3A             INCREMENT INDEX,
        SR      5,7                     REDUCE BY 509*16 IF NECESSARY
        B       S3A
```

the index is 16∗509 or greater, control first passes to the next instruction, where 16∗509 is subtracted, thus ensuring that the index plus the base address of the table yields an address *inside* the table.

As an illustration, suppose that the symbols START, STARSTAR, GMTC, A, NLEC, SASØT, and ENUF are encountered in this order and placed in a table of size 509 according to the procedures we have described. The first four symbols generate no collisions, and so are placed in the table in cells

START	cell	84
STARSTAR	cell	243
GMTC	cell	309
A	cell	471

The symbol NLEC generates a derived key 309, which creates a collision; NLEC must be stored at cell $309+254-509=54$. The symbol SASØT generates a derived key of 54; although 54 is not the derived key of another symbol encountered, it generates a collision nevertheless, with NLEC, which was just stored at cell 54. Cell $54+254=308$ is used for SASØT. Finally, ENUF has a derived key of 309, so must be stored at $54+253=307$. In summary, the symbols are associated with keys and cells as follows:

Symbol	Derived key	Cell
START	84	84
STARSTAR	243	243
GMTC	309	309
A	471	471
NLEC	309	54
SASØT	54	308
ENUF	309	307

8. MAIN IDEAS

a. Instructions are available for moving one or more characters between main storage locations, and for moving single characters between main storage and a register or from an immediate byte in an instruction to a main storage location.

b. Character compare operations CLI and CLC permit comparison of one or more characters without bringing the characters into registers. The comparisons are made on byte strings considered as unsigned integers.

c. When a list is to be generated, but relatively few retrievals are to be made from the list later, the labor of ordering the list is uneconomical. Derived keys can be used to minimize total search and insertion time.

PROBLEMS FOR REVIEW AND IMAGINATION

1. Write a sequence of instructions which do not include IC that will have the same result as

    IC   4,AB

    Do the same for

    STC   6,G

2. Write a program segment that will move the eight characters stored starting at SØURCE to a field at RESULT, reversing the order of the characters.

3. The program segment of Fig. 10–3 can be written in other forms. Illustrate by rewriting it so that the bytes in the record are scanned from right to left, using the IC and STC instructions, indexing their operand addresses, and using BCT for looping control.

4. Rewrite the program segment shown in Fig. 10–4 to keep count regions of a half-word per count.

5. Rewrite the program segment shown in Fig. 10–4 to keep count regions of a byte each, but provide a small region for overflow counts so that one or two totals could become larger and still be counted. Then write a segment that would follow the counting and put each count, including overflows if any, in a full word (perhaps preparatory to output).

6. Making suitable assumptions, write loops around the segment shown in Fig. 10–4 that will read (using READATA subroutine) a number of records (find the number at location NREC), and count all positions 0 through 39 of the record.

7. Write a program segment that will start examining characters at an address given in register 4. The first character should be the apostrophe ('). Characters following should be moved to location CHARCØN, with the following conditions:

    a) if two consecutive ampersands (&) are encountered, only one is placed in the new string;

    b) if two consecutive apostrophes are encountered, only one is placed in the new string; and

    c) transfer ends with an apostrophe which is not a member of a consecutive pair, or (with transfer to ER63) when the next character to be examined would be at location CARD+70.

    Count the number of characters put in the string at CHARCØN; leave the number in register 5.

8. What additional character-handling instructions would you like to see in computers? Explain advantages with respect to particular problems.

9. The arguments made in Section 6 about the time spent in insertion and search of items in a list are rather sketchy. Outline how you would evaluate each proposed organization and choose one for a class of uses.

10. Devise and program a procedure for deriving keys to be used given that each of 50 derived keys is to be associated with a bucket of, say, 10 cells.

11. Program the insertion of an item in a list using one of the organizations mentioned but not illustrated in Section 6—an overflow area used sequentially, links to overflow cells, or bucketing techniques.

12. Rewrite the segment of Fig. 10–7 to use MVC instead of IC and STC instructions to move the characters into the SYMBØL area.

13. Why can we not divide both halves of our symbol by 509 in the segment at the right (replacing Fig. 10–5) in order to derive a key?

```
L     5,SYMBØL
LA    4,0
D     4,=F'509'
L     5,SYMBØL+4
D     4,=F'509'
```

14. Write a program segment for System/360 that will have the same effect as a given CLCL instruction.

15. Use the System/370 instructions to spread the 400 characters from HEAD into every second byte of the area DHEAD, namely DHEAD, DHEAD+2, DHEAD+4, etc. Have blanks put in the intervening bytes of DHEAD.

16. Most examples in the text use only the IBM System/360 instruction set, so that the examples and techniques illustrated will be useful in both System/360 and 370 computers. Find examples and exercises in which some special System/370 instructions would be helpful, and rewrite the program segments accordingly.

REFERENCES

IBM System/360 Principles of Operation, GA22-6821, IBM Corporation. Reference for byte manipulation instructions in System/360.

IBM System/370 Principles of Operation, GA22-7000, IBM Corporation. As above, but including System/370 instructions.

Knuth, Donald E., *The Art of Computer Programming*, *Vol. 3: Sorting and Searching* (Reading, Mass.: Addison-Wesley, 1973). A presentation and analysis of hashing and collision resolution.

Maurer, W. D., "An Improved Hash Code for Scatter Storage," *Commun. Assoc. Comput. Mach.* **11**, No. 1 (January 1968), pp. 35–38. Introduction to quadratic probing.

Wegner, Peter, *Programming Languages, Information Structures, and Machine Organization* (New York: McGraw-Hill, 1968). Discussion of organization of symbol tables.

Chapter 11

Bit Manipulation

In previous chapters we have learned to do manipulations of an arithmetic nature and movement of character data. Not all data is numerical or character in form, so some must be manipulated in still different ways. In this chapter we shall study logical operations and operations that can set or change any preselected pattern of bits in a word or character string. We shall also study the shift instructions that move bits from right to left or left to right in a register. All these instructions are useful and necessary for performing a number of processes, as we shall see in examples.

1. LOGICAL INSTRUCTIONS: ARITHMETIC ON UNSIGNED NUMBERS

In Chapter 10 the nature of logical instructions in the IBM System/360 and 370 was introduced; these instructions treat data as unsigned integers. In Chapter 10 only the logical instructions CLC and CLI were discussed, since that chapter was concerned with character manipulation. There are also logical instructions that deal specifically with full words; we introduce them now. There are six, including the RR and RX forms, which perform the functions of add, subtract, and compare.

The add and subtract operations leave the same results in the first operand register as do the normal add and subtract operations. The difference is in the setting of the condition code and the exceptions that can possibly cause interrupts. The add and subtract instructions can be described as:

Instruction	Type	Full name	Action
AL	RX	Add Logical	$R1 \leftarrow c(R1) + c(S2)$
ALR	RR	Add Logical Register	$R1 \leftarrow c(R1) + c(R2)$
SL	RX	Subtract Logical	$R1 \leftarrow c(R1) - c(S2)$
SLR	RR	Subtract Logical Register	$R1 \leftarrow c(R1) - c(R2)$

The condition code records whether the result is zero or nonzero and also whether or not there is a carry out of the high-order (sign) position. The carry represents overflow of the addition of the two unsigned numbers, which is not at all the same as overflow of the addition of the same words considered as signed numbers. Subtraction is performed by adding the 2's complement of the second operand to the first operand, so a carry must be interpreted in that light. For example, if both operands of an SL instruction are hexadecimal 33333333, the result in the first operand register will be zero, but a carry is generated since the operation is really addition of 33333333 and CCCCCCCD. The first bit of the condition code is set to 0 if the operation (AL, ALR, SL, SLR) results in no carry and 1 if a carry is generated. The second bit of the condition code is set to zero if the result of the instruction is zero and to 1 if the result is not zero. We can summarize condition code settings of the four instructions as

$$CC \leftarrow \begin{cases} 0, \text{ if result is zero, no carry;} \\ 1, \text{ if result is not zero, no carry;} \\ 2, \text{ if result is zero, carry;} \\ 3, \text{ if result is not zero, carry.} \end{cases}$$

The logical compare instructions that apply to registers are equivalent to the character-oriented compare logical instructions studied in Chapter 10. The comparisons are made assuming that both operands are unsigned 32-bit integers; the results are

CL   Compare Logical $$CC \leftarrow \begin{cases} 0, \text{ if } c(R1) = c(S2); \\ 1, \text{ if } c(R1) < c(S2); \\ 2, \text{ if } c(R1) > c(S2). \end{cases}$$

CLR   Compare Logical Register $$CC \leftarrow \begin{cases} 0, \text{ if } c(R1) = c(R2); \\ 1, \text{ if } c(R1) < c(R2); \\ 2, \text{ if } c(R1) > c(R2). \end{cases}$$

Since none of the six instructions recognizes such a thing as an overflow, there is no possibility of a fixed-point overflow exception. The only exceptions possible as a result of AL, SL, or CL are access and specification. No exception can result from an ALR, SLR, or CLR instruction.

An efficient means of setting the contents of a register to zero is to subtract the contents from itself with an SLR instruction. The instruction

SLR   5,5

sets register 5 to zero, just as does

SR   5,5

As an example of the use of these instructions, let us consider the problem of multiple-precision integer arithmetic, in which a number is represented in several words. As the most trivial case, let us add two integers A and B, each occupying double words in main storage, leaving the result in a double word at location C. Each integer has a sign in the high-order bit in the first of the two words; the numbers are in 2's complement form, but the high-order bit in the second word

Fig. 11-1   Addition of 64-bit integers

```
*        A AND B ARE DØUBLE WØRDS HØLDING INTEGERS
*        IN 2'S-CØMPLEMENT FØRM.  THIS SEGMENT PUTS THEIR
*        SUM AT LØCATION C.
         LM    4,5,A
         AL    5,B+4      ADD LØWER HALVES
         BC    12,NØCAR
         AL    4,=F'1'    ADD CARRY FRØM LØWER HALVES
NØCAR    AL    4,B        ADD UPPER HALVES
         STM   4,5,C      STØRE RESULT
```

is an ordinary information-carrying bit. The sum of A and B can be derived and put in C by the segment shown in Fig. 11-1.

The segment shown in Fig. 11-1 ignores the possibility of overflow in the total process. The condition for overflow is that the sign bits of A and B be alike but different from the sign bit of the result. After studying the logical instructions introduced in Section 4, the student can test the sign bits and set an overflow indicator of his own; this is suggested as problem 2 at the end of the chapter.

2. SHIFT INSTRUCTIONS

Shift instructions move data "sideways" within registers. The movement from right to left is in one sense equivalent to a multiplication by a power of 2, and movement from left to right is equivalent to a division by a power of 2. A shift of any distance is possible; the second operand of each instruction specifies the distance desired.

General description of the instructions

There are eight shift instructions; they differ in three ways. First, there are left shifts (bits move right to left) and right shifts (left to right). Second, there are single and double shifts. In single shifts, contents of one register are shifted, but in a double shift, contents of a register pair are shifted, with contents of one register flowing into the other just as though they formed a single register 64 bits long. Third, there are arithmetic shifts and logical shifts. In a logical shift all 32 or 64 bits are shifted uniformly, and no considerations of sign are made. In an arithmetic shift the high-order bit of the 32 or 64 is considered to be a sign and is not moved. Each of these characteristics of the shift instruction will be described in more detail below. The eight instructions are

SLA	Shift Left single Arithmetic,
SRA	Shift Right single Arithmetic,
SLDA	Shift Left Double Arithmetic,
SRDA	Shift Right Double Arithmetic,
SLL	Shift Left single Logical,
SRL	Shift Right single Logical,
SLDL	Shift Left Double Logical,
SRDL	Shift Right Double Logical.

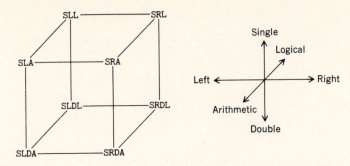

Fig. 11-2 The shift instructions.

The three dimensions of difference can be seen in the three-dimensional diagram shown in Fig. 11–2.

All shift instructions are of RS type, but the *R3* field of the instruction is ignored. The first operand specification *R1* designates the register or register pair to be shifted; in shift double instructions this must be an even register address, specifying an even register and the odd register following. The second operand, specified by *B2* and *D2* as usual, gives the number of bit positions by which the contents of register *R1* are to be shifted. However, only the low-order six bits of the sum of *B2* and *D2* are used, so the maximum shift that can be specified is 63. Since the maximum length of a field to be shifted is 64, a shift of 64 or more bit positions is unnecessary.

Logical shifts

Let us now examine the logical shift instructions, which are simpler in operation than the arithmetic shifts. The SLL (Shift Left Logical) instruction shifts the contents of one register to the left. Bits are lost from the left end of the register (we say they fall into the "bit-bucket"), and zeros are filled on the right in the bit positions vacated in the shift. Figure 11–3 shows the movement of bits through the register. For example, if register 4 contains

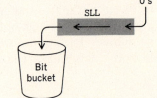

10011001111111111100110010000001,

an instruction

          SLL   4,6

will change the contents of register 4 to

Fig. 11-3 Action of the SLL instruction.

01111111111100110010000001000000.

The six leftmost bits of the original contents, 100110, are lost; the remaining 26 bits are moved to the left six bit positions, and 000000 is filled in the rightmost positions.

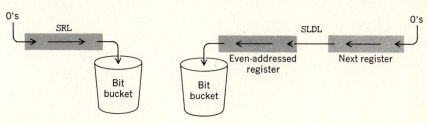

Fig. 11–4 Action of the SRL instruction.   **Fig. 11–5** Action of the SLDL instruction.

Similarly, SRL (Shift Right Logical) shifts a single register's contents to the right, losing bits from the right end and filling in with zeros on the left end. Figure 11–4 shows movement of bits performed by SRL.

The double-register logical shifts are performed similarly on what is essentially a 64-bit register. In a SLDL (Shift Left Double Logical) instruction the leftmost bits of the even-addressed register are lost, and other bits are moved left. The leftmost bits of the odd-addressed register are moved to the rightmost portion of the even-addressed register; other bits are moved left in the odd-addressed register, and zeros are filled in the rightmost bit positions of the odd-addressed register. Figure 11–5 shows the movement of bits in the two registers. For example, suppose registers 4 and 5 contain

        Register 4   Register 5

10011001111111111100110010000001   00001110000000001111111101010101.

Execution of the instruction

SLDL   4,6

will change the contents of registers 4 and 5 to

        Register 4   Register 5

01111111111100110010000001000011   11000000001111111101010101000000.

The six bits 100110 are lost from register 4; the remaining 26 bits are moved left. The low-order six bit positions of register 4 are filled with 000011, the high-order bits from register 5. The low-order 26 bits of register 5 are moved left six positions, and six zeros are filled in the rightmost end of register 5.

Similarly, a SRDL (Shift Right Double Logical) instruction shifts the contents of an even-addressed register into the following odd-addressed register. The entire register pair acts as a 64-bit register with bits moving to the right, some bits being lost from the right end, and zeros being filled in at the left end, as shown in Fig. 11–6.

None of the four logical shift instructions, SLL, SRL, SLDL, or SRDL, affects the condition code.

The only possible program check exception to occur on a logical shift instruction is a specification exception; this occurs if *R1* is given as an odd register address in a double-register shift instruction, SLDL or SRDL.

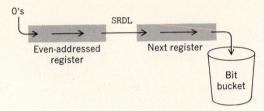

Fig. 11–6   Action of the SRDL instruction.

The logical shift instructions are often used to pack data. For example, suppose that there is a two-bit quantity IND in register 4 in the low-order bit positions, a 15-bit quantity P in the low-order positions of register 5, and a 15-bit quantity Q in the low-order positions of register 6 that are to be stored in one word W in the order IND, P, Q. Multiplications and additions could be performed, but shifts are simpler and faster, and do not require assumptions about the contents of the high-order bit positions in the registers containing IND, P, and Q. The packing can be done by

```
SLL    5,17    P TØ UPPER PART ØF REG. 5
SLDL   4,15    IND,P IN REG. 4
LR     5,6     Q TØ REG. 5
SLL    5,17    Q TØ UPPER PART ØF REG. 5
SLDL   4,15    IND,P,Q IN REG. 4
ST     4,W     STØRE AT W.
```

The reader is urged to diagram the exact placement of IND, P, and Q after each instruction, and to convince himself that contents of upper-order bit positions of registers 4, 5, and 6 are irrelevant to this sequence.

Similar shift instructions can be used to break a word down again into its component parts. Such packing and unpacking are often quite necessary to reduce the space required for data and intermediate results and to permit them to be kept in main storage, where the alternative is to store some of the data on external devices such as magnetic disk, drum, or tape, and to recall the data when it is needed. The savings in time spent writing and retrieving the data far outweigh the cost in time of packing and unpacking data kept in main storage.

In Section 4 of this chapter we shall see how any one particular field may be retrieved more efficiently by logic and shift instructions than by shift instructions alone.

Arithmetic shifts

The four arithmetic shift instructions, SRA, SLA, SRDA, and SLDA, follow the same patterns as the logical shift instructions. There are right shifts (SRA, SRDA) which move bits to the right in registers, and left shifts (SLA, SLDA) which move bits to the left. There are single-register shifts (SRA, SLA) and double-register shifts (SRDA, SLDA), which couple a register pair just as is done for the logical double shifts. The arithmetic shift instructions differ from the logical shifts only in their treatment of signs and fill bits and in the setting of condition code.

The bit in position 0, the sign bit, does not participate in an arithmetic shift; only the low-order 31 bits (or 63 bits in a double-register shift) are shifted. Thus the sign of the original number is always preserved. During a left shift, bits filled at the right of the register or register pair are zeros. This is consistent with treating the arithmetic shift as a multiplication by 2, regardless of the sign of the original number. A shift of a bit *unlike the sign bit* out of the high-order portion during a left arithmetic shift constitutes an overflow. The overflow is recorded in the condition code, which is discussed below.

In a right arithmetic shift, bits filled on the left of the register or register pair are *copies of the sign bit*. This is necessary if the result of the shift is to be considered as a division of the original number by 2. Actually, the right shift is equivalent to a division by 2 or a power of 2 *with rounding down*. For example, the result of shifting a number 7 right one position is the number 3, but the result of shifting −7 right is the number −4. This is in distinction to the action of the divide instructions; a division of −7 by 2 would give a quotient of −3 and a remainder of −1. Among other things, the rounding down implies that if all "significant" bits of a negative number are shifted right and lost, as, for example, in a SRA   5,34 instruction, the result will be a string of 32 1's in the register,

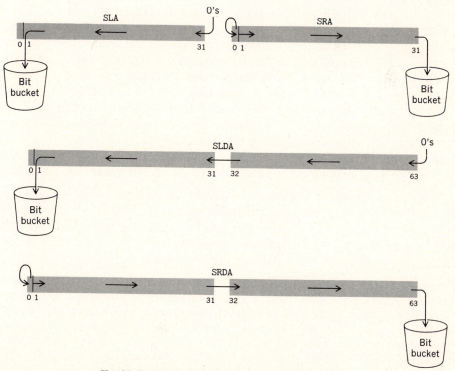

Fig. 11-7   Action of the arithmetic shift instructions.

which is equivalent to the number -1. Similarly, if all significant bits of a negative number are shifted out and lost in a left shift, the sign bit of 1 will remain and the result will be -2^{31}.

The arithmetic shifts can be represented pictorially as shown in Fig. 11–7.

An arithmetic shift instruction sets the condition code. The condition code is set to

> 0, if the result $= 0$;
> 1, if the result < 0;
> 2, if the result > 0;
> 3, if there is an overflow on a left shift.

Let us consider some examples of arithmetic shifts. Assume the contents of register 4 to be

$$10011001111111111100110010000001$$

and the contents of register 5 to be

$$00001110000000011111111101010101.$$

With these contents before *each* of the following instructions, results will be as follows:

SRA	4,1	Register 4:	11001100111111111110011001000000	CC:1
SLA	4,1	Register 4:	10110011111111111001100100000010	CC:3
SRA	4,31	Register 4:	11111111111111111111111111111111	CC:1
SLA	4,31	Register 4:	10000000000000000000000000000000	CC:3
SRA	5,1	Register 5:	00000111000000001111111110101010	CC:2
SRA	5,28	Register 5:	00000000000000000000000000000000	CC:0
SLA	5,3	Register 5:	01111000000001111111101010101000	CC:2
SLA	5,4	Register 5:	01110000000011111110101010100000	CC:3
SLA	5,31	Register 5:	00000000000000000000000000000000	CC:3
SLDA	4,8	Register 4:	11111111110011001000000100001111	
		Register 5:	00000000111111110101010100000000	CC:3
SRDA	4,8	Register 4:	11111111100110011111111111001100	
		Register 5:	10000001000011100000000011111111	CC:1

Two program-check exceptions may occur on arithmetic shift instructions. On the double-register instructions SLDA and SRDA a specification exception occurs if *R1* specifies an odd address for a register pair. In case of overflow, the left shifts generate a fixed-point overflow exception, which causes interrupt if the fixed-point-overflow bit in the program mask is set to 1.

Because of their treatment of signs and possibilities of overflow, the arithmetic shift instructions are less well suited to packing of fields than are the logical shift instructions. The arithmetic shift instructions, however, are better suited to performing what should amount to multiplication and division by powers of 2. The reader can find in program segments and problems of earlier chapters several instances in which an arithmetic shift is more convenient than the multiply or divide instruction actually shown. Other ex-

Fig. 11-8 Counting the 1-bits in a word

```
*       CØUNTS THE 1'S IN A WØRD AT AFFW.
*       STØRES THE CØUNT IN AFF
        L       3,AFFW
        SLR     5,5         CLEAR REG. 5
*       REG. 5 WILL CØNTAIN THE RUNNING CØUNT
        LA      6,32
LP      SLR     2,2         CLEAR REG. 2
        SLDL    2,1         MØVE A BIT INTØ REG. 2
        AR      5,2         ADD BIT TØ CØUNT
        BCT     6,LP
        ST      5,AFF       STØRE CØUNT
```

amples cannot be improved by the use of shift instructions, given the statement of the problem, but if some length or other parameter is given as a power of 2, a shift instruction can replace a multiply and simplify the segment.

Counting bits in a word

Let us examine another short example of the use of a shift instruction. Figure 11-8 shows a program segment which counts the 1-bits in the word AFFW. Each bit is moved into the low-order bit position of register 2, from where it is added to register 5. Thus each 1-bit is added, forming the count. The 0-bits are added too, but of course they do not affect the sum, and it is easier to add them than to decide not to. Note that the instruction SLR   2,2 must be inside the loop so that 1-bits once found do not have a chance to be shifted over and add 2, 4, 8, etc. to register 5.

3. AN EXAMPLE: HEXADECIMAL CONVERSION

At times we want the hexadecimal contents of a register printed. Each of the hexadecimal digits must be converted to printable characters; the shift instructions can help us in the conversion.

Fig. 11-9 Conversion from hexadecimal to character

```
*       SEGMENT TØ CØNVERT 8 HEXADECIMAL DIGITS
*       IN REG. 0 TØ CHARACTER FØRM.
*       ADDRESS ØF RESULT IS TAKEN FRØM REG. 1
        LR      3,0         HEX DIGITS TØ REG. 3
        SLR     4,4         INITIALIZE REG. 4
*       REG. 4 TØ BE USED FØR LØØP CØNTRØL AND TØ INDEX STØRE INSTR.
        LA      6,1         LØØP INCREMENT
        LA      7,7           LIMIT
LP      SLR     2,2         CLEAR REG. 2
        SLDL    2,4         MØVE ØNE HEX. DIGIT TØ REG. 2
        LA      2,240(2)    ADD HEX. FO, FØR CHARS. 0-9.
        C       2,=F'250'   STORE IT IF LESS THAN HEX. A
        BL      STØRE
        S       2,=F'57'    IF HEX. DIGIT IS A OR LARGER, REDUCE
                            CHAR. REPRESENTATIØN TØ RANGE C1 TØ C6.
STØRE   STC     2,0(4,1)    STØRE IN REGIØN ADDRESSE⅃ BY REG. 1
*                           INDEXED BY REG. 4
        BXLE    4,6,LP
```

The procedure we illustrate in the program segment of Fig. 11–9 is to move the hexadecimal digits one at a time into a register, add a factor to each to generate the appropriate printable character, and store it in a character string. The segment uses a double-length shift instruction to move a hexadecimal digit into register 2; the result of a logical or arithmetic instruction would be the same, since the entire register 2 contains zeros before the shift.

The segment uses knowledge of the structure of the EBCDIC representations, which are as follows:

Digit	Character representation	Decimal equivalent
0	F0	240
1	F1	241
2	F2	242
⋮	⋮	⋮
8	F8	248
9	F9	249
A	C1	193
B	C2	194
C	C3	195
D	C4	196
E	C5	197
F	C6	198

The reader can see that the character equivalents of hexadecimal digits form two sequential segments: the digits 0–9 have character representations F0–F9, and the digits A–F have character representations C1–C6. Therefore a hexadecimal digit can be converted to its printable character representation by adding F0 (decimal 240) to each of the digits 0–9, and B7 (decimal 183) to each of the digits A–F (decimal 10–15). For example, $5 + 240 = 245$; $11 + 183 = 194$. The segment makes the assumption first that the digit is in the range 0–9, and therefore adds 240. The segment then tests the result, and if the result is 250 or greater, it adjusts by subtracting 57 ($240 - 183$).

The character is then stored; the address is the sum of the beginning address of the string (in register 1) and an index in register 4 which increases from 0 to 7.

4. LOGICAL INSTRUCTIONS: AND **AND** ØR

This section introduces a class of logical instructions that are quite different from those discussed in Chapter 10 and in Section 1 of this chapter. The logical instructions now to be defined perform manipulations on individual bits, manipulations related to the functions used in logic, instead of arithmetic on unsigned numbers.

Definition of the functions

We shall define four logical functions before we discuss their implementation in a computer. Suppose that we have two operands, each with a value 0 or 1. We can define the AND function as a function of two operands; the value of the function is 1 if *both operands* have the value 1, and 0 otherwise. We can illustrate or define the function as

AND:

| | Second operand | |
	0	1
First operand 0	0	0
1	0	1

where the numbers in the boxes show the value of the function in each of the four possible cases.

There are two varieties of OR functions; they differ in their treatment of the case in which both operands are 1. First, the EXCLUSIVE OR function has a value 1 if either of the two operands, *but not both*, has the value 1; the value is 0 if both operands are 0 or if both are 1. In tabular form, the function can be described as

EXCLUSIVE OR:

| | Second operand | |
	0	1
First operand 0	0	1
1	1	0

The third function is OR, or for emphasis, INCLUSIVE OR. The value of the OR function is 1 if *either or both* of the operands is 1, and 0 only if both operands are 0. In tabular form we have

INCLUSIVE OR:

| | Second operand | |
	0	1
First operand 0	0	1
1	1	1

The fourth function is the NOT function, which is a function of one operand. Its value is what the operand is not; that is, the value is the opposite of the operand.

The value is 1 if the operand is 0, and 0 if the operand is 1. In tabular form we have

NOT: Operand: 0   1

Value: | 1 | 0 |

Use of the logical functions in symbolic logic

The logical functions get their names from their original use in the representation of symbolic logic. Let the value 1 represent the truth of a proposition (a proposition, roughly speaking, is a statement), and 0 that the proposition is false. Then we can talk about truth or falsity of various new propositions made from other propositions with the aid of connectives AND, OR, and NOT.

A compound proposition, (proposition 1) AND (proposition 2), is true if both proposition 1 and proposition 2 are true, false if either or both are false. If t_1 is a value 1 or 0 representing the truth or falsity of proposition 1, and t_2 acts similarly for proposition 2, then t_1 AND t_2, where AND is the logical function defined above, yields a value 1 or 0 correctly representing the truth or falsity of (proposition 1) AND (proposition 2). The OR, EXCLUSIVE OR, and NOT functions similarly help in assigning values to represent truth or falsity of compound propositions or statements formed using OR and NOT connectives. Mathematicians and logicians always use OR to mean the *inclusive* OR (either or both), and the definition of logical functions here follows this usage. The EXCLUSIVE OR is a useful function, however.

As an example, suppose that proposition 1 is "This book is lousy," and proposition 2 is "so is the IBM System/360." We can form a compound proposition "This book is lousy AND NOT so is the IBM System/360," which in better English is "This book is lousy but the IBM System/360 is not." Suppose that proposition 1 is true; the variable t_1 has the value 1. Suppose also that proposition 2 is false, so $t_2 = 0$. The truth of the compound proposition is represented by t_1 AND NOT t_2, which has the value

$$1 \text{ AND } (\text{NOT } 0) = 1 \text{ AND } (1) = 1$$

so the compound proposition is true.

Use of the logical functions in Boolean algebra

In the 19th century, George Boole developed the algebra which bears his name. In Boolean algebra all quantities have values 0 or 1, and arithmetic is defined by

$$
\begin{aligned}
0 + 0 &= 0, & 0 \times 0 &= 0, \\
0 + 1 &= 1 + 0 = 1, & 0 \times 1 &= 1 \times 0 = 0, \\
1 + 1 &= 1, & 1 \times 1 &= 1,
\end{aligned}
$$

The only abnormal relationship is that $1 + 1 = 1$. Subtraction and division are not usually used. Boolean algebra is used in circuit design and analysis and in many other instances of manipulation of binary-choice data.

The AND logical function is equivalent to Boolean multiplication; if X and Y are Boolean variables (having values 0 or 1), the Boolean product $X \times Y$ is the same as the logical function X AND Y. Either has the value 1 if and only if both X and Y are 1.

The INCLUSIVE OR function is equivalent to Boolean addition. The Boolean sum $X + Y$ has the same value as the logical function X OR Y: either is 1 if at least one of the variables X and Y has the value 1, and 0 only if both X and Y are zero.

Implementation in the IBM System/360 and 370

There are twelve instructions in the IBM System/360 and 370 which perform the logical functions AND, OR, and EXCLUSIVE OR on a number of bits in parallel. For each of the three logical functions there are four instructions of different types, allowing for operands in various places and of various lengths. The mnemonic operation codes of the 12 instructions can be shown in a table as follows:

Type	AND	OR	EXCL. OR
RR:	NR	ØR	XR
RX:	N	Ø	X
SI:	NI	ØI	XI
SS:	NC	ØC	XC

In the RR instructions, for example, two full-word operands are in registers. Each logical function is performed on 32 bit pairs in parallel: on the bit in position 0 in the first operand and on the bit in position 0 of the second operand to yield a result in bit position 0 of the first operand, and so on for each of the other 31 bit positions. These logical instructions are distinguished by the fact that the function, AND, OR, or EXCLUSIVE OR, is performed on each of the 32 pairs of bits in corresponding positions independently of the action on other bit positions; there are no carries or other interactions.

The RR-type instructions NR, ØR, and XR perform the corresponding logical instructions on contents of two registers. The RX-type instructions N, Ø, and X perform the logical functions on contents of two full words, one in a register and one in main storage; the result is placed in the register named as first operand. The SI-type instructions NI, ØI, and XI perform logical functions on the contents of one byte in main storage and a byte $I2$ in the instruction. The SS-type instructions NC, ØC, and XC perform the logical functions on two strings of bytes in main storage. The lengths of the two strings are equal, so only one length is specified; strings from 1 to 256 bytes long can be accommodated.

The condition code is set by each of the 12 logical instructions. It is set to 0 if the result of the instruction is 0, that is, if every bit is 0; and to 1 if at least one bit of the result is 1. Condition codes 2 and 3 are not used by these instructions.

Fig. 11–10   Results of logical instructions

Instruction		Result		Cond. code
NR	5,6	00000011000000110000001100000011	in Reg. 5	1
ØR	5,6	00111111001111110011111100111111	in Reg. 5	1
XR	6,5	00111100001111000011110000111100	in Reg. 6	1
N	5,Q	00000101000001010000010100000101	in Reg. 5	1
Ø	6,Q	01110111011101110111011101110111	in Reg. 6	1
XI	Q,B'11000011'	10010110	at Q	1
NI	P+2,X'F0'	00110000	at P+2	1
ØC	Q(3),P	010101011111111101111101	at Q	1
XC	P+1(2),Q+2	1010101001101001	at P+1	1
NC	Q(1),P	00000000	at Q	0
XI	Q+1,B'01010101'	00000000	at Q+1	0

Let us examine some examples of the instructions. Suppose that the initial contents of registers and main storage are

Register 5:	00001111000011110000111100001111
Register 6:	00110011001100110011001100110011
Word at main storage location Q:	01010101010101010101010101010101
Three bytes at main storage location P:	000000001111111100111100

If these contents are assumed before *each* of the following instructions, the results will be as indicated in Fig. 11–10.

Program-check exceptions are possible in most of the logical instructions. Access exceptions are possible in all but the RR-type instructions, since these instructions can make reference to nonexistent main storage or to storage protected for other use. Specification exceptions can be generated by the N, Ø, and X instructions since they require full words in main storage. No other program checks are possible.

There is no instruction specifically for the NOT logical function, but it can be performed by any of several instructions. An EXCLUSIVE OR operation, with 1 as its second operand, has the same result as a NOT operation on its first operand; that is: (*a* EXCLUSIVE OR 1) is the same as (NOT *a*). We can use this fact in implementing NOT in the IBM System/360 or 370:

$$XI \quad G,X'FF'$$

performs a NOT function on each of the bits of G. The four types of EXCLUSIVE OR instructions make it easy enough to perform a NOT function on any number of bytes in main storage or on the contents of a register. Besides the EXCLUSIVE

OR, there are other ways to perform the NOT function. For example,

```
L     4,=F'-1'
S     4,WRØNG
```

places NOT WRØNG in register 4. The reader can verify this, and also the claim that there is no possibility of overflow on the subtraction!

Use of the logical instructions in bit manipulation

We may interpret the logical instructions as selectively changing bits in an operand. The bits to be changed are in the first operand; which bits are eligible for change are determined by the bits in the second operand, which thus acts as a mask, covering and protecting some bits while leaving other bits exposed and eligible for change.

The AND instructions NR, N, NI, and NC selectively set bits in the first operand to 0, in bit positions where the second operand has 0's. Thus in the mask a 1 bit protects the bit in the corresponding position of the first operand from change; a 0 bit in the mask directs that the bit in the corresponding position of the first operand be set to 0 regardless of its previous value. For example,

```
NI     G,B'00001111'
```

directs that the first four bits of the byte at location G be set to 0's while the last four bits remain unchanged.

The condition code can be thought of as recording whether there are any 1's left in the first operand (CC=1) or whether all bits are now 0's (CC=0).

The INCLUSIVE OR instructions ØR, Ø, ØI and ØC selectively set bits in the first operand to 1, in positions where the corresponding bits of the second operand are 1's. In positions where the bits of the second operand are 0, the bits in corresponding positions of the first operand are left unchanged. As an example,

```
ØC     R(2),=B'1111000011110000'
```

directs that the four high-order bits of each of the two bytes at R and R+1 are to be set to 1's; the four lower-order bits of each byte are to remain unchanged. There is thus a kind of symmetry to the masks used by AND and OR functions in selectively setting bits: if bits are selectively to be set at 0's, 0's appear in corresponding positions in the mask used by an AND instruction; if bits are to be set to 1's, then 1's appear in corresponding positions of the mask used by an OR instruction.

The EXCLUSIVE OR instructions XR, X, XI, and XC selectively change or complement bits in the first operand in positions where the bits in the second operand are 1's, but leave unchanged bits in positions where the corresponding bits in the second operand are 0's. For example,

```
XI     SWITCH,X'01'
```

will change the last bit of the byte SWITCH from 1 to 0 or from 0 to 1, whichever it finds, and leave the other seven bits unchanged. Note that execution of this instruction a second time will change the contents of SWITCH back to what it was before the first XI instruction. Thus location SWITCH can act as a switch, causing certain actions on alternate passes through a segment. For example,

```
                    MVI    SWITCH,X'00'
                    . . .
        LØØP        XI     SWITCH,X'01'
                    BZ     ØN
        ØFF         . . .
```

will cause a branch to ØN on the second, fourth, sixth, . . . time control is passed to LØØP; the segment beginning at ØFF will be executed the first, third, fifth, . . . time control is passed to LØØP.

An example: Resolving the sign of an unpacked number

When a number is unpacked, perhaps by the instruction

```
            UNPK   CHAR(8),PAKD(8)
```

its sign is placed in the upper four bits of the last (units) digit. For printing, it is preferable to have the upper four bits all 1's so that the digit will be printed like other digits. First, assuming the number to be positive, we can set the bits to 1's by

```
            ØI     CHAR+7,X'F0'
```

which, as noted above, sets the four upper-order bits to 1's while leaving the lower-order bits intact.

Second, if the sign is unknown, we may wish to store the sign as a printable character at CHAR-1, as well as changing the coding of the units digit as before. We must use the information that a plus sign is coded as 1100 (hexadecimal C) over the units digit and a minus sign is coded as 1101 (hexadecimal D) over the units digit. Figure 11–11 shows a segment which performs the entire task.

Fig. 11–11   Separation of sign from units digit

```
*       SEGMENT TØ PLACE THE SIGN ØF AN UNPACKED NUMBER
*       BEFØRE THE DIGITS AS A PRINTABLE CHARACTER AND CHANGE
*       UNITS DIGIT TØ PLAIN PRINTABLE DIGIT
            CLI    CHAR+7,X'D0'
            BL     PØS               CHAR. CØDED BEGINNING WITH C IS PLUS
            MVI    CHAR-1,C'-'       STØRE MINUS
            B      CHDIG
PØS         MVI    CHAR-1,C'+'       STØRE PLUS
CHDIG       ØI     CHAR+7,X'F0'      FIX UNITS DIGIT
```

An example: Retrieving a field from a word

In Section 2 we considered the task of packing several fields into a word, and indicated that the fields could be separated again by the converse of the same process.

This technique is quite satisfactory if we wish to separate all the fields, but if we wish to retrieve or change just one field, we can use the logical instructions to advantage.

For example, suppose a word W is composed of three fields: a two-bit field IND, a 15-bit field P, and a 15-bit field Q, in that order. Suppose also that we wish to retrieve field P, that is, put it in a register by itself. This can be done with the sequence

```
L    3,MASKP
N    3,W        FIELD P ØNLY LØADED INTØ REG. 3
SRL  3,15       RIGHT-JUSTIFY
```

where the constant MASKP is defined by

```
MASKP   DS   0F
        DC   BL4'00111111111111111000000000000000'
```

The AND function performed by the instruction N   3,W sets to 0 in register 3 all bits outside the P field, and loads P in register 3 in its corresponding positions. The shift instruction moves the field to the right of the register. Note that in the definition of MASKP a DS 0F pseudo-operation is given to force the following constant onto a full-word boundary. This is necessary since B-type constants do not force any alignment, yet a full word is required in the L   3,MASKP instruction.

Again, suppose that a new 15-bit quantity has been generated which is to replace the P field in the word W, but IND and Q are to remain unchanged. This can be accomplished by the segment (assuming that the upper-order 17 bits of register 3 containing the new P are 0's):

```
L    4,W
N    4,MASKNØTP     ERASE P
SLL  3,15           MØVE NEW P INTØ PØSITIØN
ØR   4,3            INSERT NEW P
ST   4,W
```

where MASKNØTP is defined by

```
MASKNØTP DS   0F
         DC   BL4'11000000000000000111111111111111'
```

An example: Matching and opposing configurations

Suppose that we wish to describe a set of objects and have a list of 32 aspects; each object may be represented by whether it is a positive example, a negative example, or a neutral example of each aspect. We may describe an object then in two full words in main storage of a System/360 or 370 computer; each bit position

Fig. 11–12   Find matches and oppositions

```
*       ØBJECTS ARE DESCRIBED IN 32 ASPECTS BY A WØRD
*         SHØWING PØSITIVE INSTANCES FØLLØWED BY A WØRD
*         SHØWING NEGATIVE INSTANCES.
*       THE ADDRESS ØF THE FIRST (PØSITIVE) WØRD ØF ØNE
*         ØBJECT IS IN REG. 8, THE ADDRESS ØF A SECØND ØBJECT
*         IN REG. 9
*       THIS SEGMENT CØNSTRUCTS WØRDS MATCH AND ØPPØSE
*         SHØWING INCIDENCE ØF MATCHES AND ØF ØPPØSITIØNS.
        L       3,0(8)          PØS. WØRD, ØBJ. 1
        N       3,0(9)            BØTH PØS.
        L       4,4(8)          NEG. WØRD, ØBJ. 1
        N       4,4(9)            BØTH NEG.
        ØR      3,4             CØMBINE MATCHES
        ST      3,MATCH
        L       3,0(8)          PØS. WØRD, ØBJ. 1
        N       3,4(9)            AND NEG. WØRD, ØBJ. 2
        L       4,4(8)          NEG. WØRD, ØBJ. 1
        N       4,0(9)            AND PØS. WØRD, ØBJ. 2
        ØR      3,4             CØMBINE ØPPØSITIØNS
        ST      3,ØPPØSE
```

of a word holds information about one of the aspects. In the first of the two words a 1-bit represents a positive instance of the aspect, a 0 represents a neutral or negative instance. In the second word, a 1 represents a negative instance and a 0 represents a neutral or positive instance. Thus a positive instance would be recorded as 1 in the first word and 0 in the corresponding position of the second word, a neutral instance would be recorded as 0's in both words, and a negative instance would be recorded as 0 in the first word and 1 in the second word.

Now suppose that two objects so described are to be compared as to the aspects in which they match (either both positive or both negative) and the aspects in which they are opposed (one positive and the other negative.) The objects might be boys and girls being paired for dates, and the aspects such important things as "like Chinese food?," "squeeze toothpaste from the top of the tube?," and "root for the New York Yankees?." Or the objects may be subgoals and initial positions in a problem-solving situation, and the aspects be properties that allow one to decide which of several subgoals is closest to the initial conditions and therefore the one with most promise for further work. In any case, we are to construct a word MATCH in which a 1 represents a match of an aspect and 0 represents either opposition or at least one object neutral, and another word ØPPØSE in which a 1 represents opposition of the two objects with respect to the aspect and 0 represents either match or at least one object being neutral.

Figure 11–12 shows a program segment that constructs the words MATCH and ØPPØSE. AND instructions are used to generate coincidences of 1's in all four relevant pairs of words. The both-positive coincidences and the both-negative coincidences are combined by means of an OR instruction (XR should yield the same result) to form the word to be stored in MATCH, and the positive-negative coincidences are combined similarly to form the word to be stored in ØPPØSE.

5. GENERATING MOVES IN CHECKERS

As an example in which bits in a word have no arithmetic or character significance but only meanings as individual bits to be manipulated, we show a small part of a checker-playing program. This example shows the use of the bit manipulation facilities provided by logical and shift instructions.

Describing the board

The squares on a checkerboard are usually numbered from 1 to 32, which would seem to be nicely suited to use of the 32-bit word of the IBM System/360. How-ever, we shall see that a much more convenient numbering for our purposes is that given in Fig. 11–13. The advantage to this numbering is that a move from a square x forward and to the right is always a move to square $x + 5$, and a move from square x forward and to the left is always a move to square $x + 4$. This numbering was first used by Arthur Samuel in his computer checker-playing experiments in the mid 1950's;* the numbering was especially happy for him since the computer he was working with, the IBM 704, had a 36-bit word length. In the IBM System/360 or 370 we can commit the first 36 bits of a double word to a board picture, and still realize significant execution-time efficiencies. The contents of square 1 will be recorded in bit position 0, square 2 in bit position 1, etc.

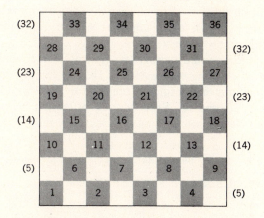

Fig. 11–13 Numbering squares on a checkerboard.

Still following Samuel's scheme, we allocate four 36-bit sequences (in the IBM System/360 or 370, four double words) to the complete description of a board position. We assume that the bottom row (squares 1–4) is the home position for black; that is, black moves up the board, while red moves down. We will record

* A. L. Samuel, "Some Studies in Machine Learning Using the Game of Checkers," *IBM J. Res. Develop.* **3**, pp. 210–229 (1959).

in the first of the four double words describing a board position a 1 in the bit position corresponding to each square on which there is any black *forward-active* piece, that is, a man or king. In the second of the four double words we record a 1 corresponding to black *backward-active* pieces, that is, kings. Thus at the beginning of a game, bits 1–4, 6–9, and 10–13 of the first double word would contain 1's, with all other bits in that double word set to 0's. All the bits in the second double word would be 0, since there are no black kings. The third word contains the configuration of red forward-active pieces, forward-active meaning up the board from black's viewpoint, actually backward for red. Thus the third word records the positions of red kings. The fourth word records the positions of red backward-active pieces, that is, men and kings. In none of these double words will there be a 1 in positions corresponding to "squares" 5, 14, 23, and 32, and we must see to it that we never try to move a man into one of these "squares."

We shall assume that the four double words describing a board position are consecutive, and that the address of the first is given in register 1.

Generating moves

The small parts of the checker-playing problem which we shall illustrate are the generation of possible moves and the manipulations required to make a move or jump. First we illustrate how all possible right forward moves (not jumps) can be generated *at once* by use of logical and shift instructions. This is the advantage of the square numbering we have adopted.

Figure 11–14 shows a short program segment that accomplishes this task. A word is generated showing which squares are not eligible for moving into by performing OR functions on the squares occupied by black and by red and on the fictitious squares 14, 23, and 32. Everything is shifted left 5, first so that a single word can hold the relevant information (black cannot move *forward* into squares

---

Fig. 11–14   Generating black's forward right moves

```
*           SEGMENT TØ GENERATE PØSSIBLE FØRWARD
*             MØVES TØ THE RIGHT FØR BLACK
      LM    4,5,0(1)       LØAD BLACK FØRWARD-ACTIVE (BFA)
      SLDL  4,5            MØVE BACK 5 SQUARES
      LM    6,7,24(1)      LØAD RED MEN AND KINGS (RBA)
      SLDL  6,5            MØVE BACK 5 SQUARES
      ØR    4,6            CØMBINE
      Ø     4,MM5          COMBINE WITH BITS FØR PØS. 14, 23, 32
*       REGISTER 4 NØW CØNTAINS 1 IN EVERY SQUARE THAT IS
*       NØT ELIGIBLE FØR MØVING INTØ, EITHER BECAUSE ØCCUPIED
*       ØR BECAUSE NØNEXISTENT.
      X     4,=F'-1'       CHANGE SØ 1 REPRESENTS ELIGIBLE SQUARE
      N     4,0(1)         BLACK FØRWARD-ACTIVE AND ELIGIBLE SQUARE
      ST    4,FØRDRGHT
      :
MM5   DS    0F
      DC    BL4'00000000100000000100000000100000'
```

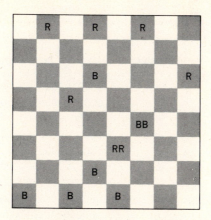

Fig. 11-15 A sample board position.

1-4) and second so that the bits will correspond with squares from which black men or kings might move. After the word of ineligible squares is generated, the configuration of eligible squares is generated by a NOT, actually an EXCLUSIVE OR with an operand full of 1's. The AND instruction N   4,0(1) is almost anticlimatic; it matches black pieces with positions that are free to be moved into, leaving a word in which each 1 indicates the position of a black piece that can move forward to the right.

To illustrate the processes shown in this segment, let us follow its execution with respect to the board configuration shown in Fig. 11-15. A red man is shown by the letter R, a red king by RR; similarly, black men and kings are shown by B and BB. The first 36 bits of each of the double words representing this board position are as follows.

Black forward active (BFA):

$$111000100000000010000000100000000000$$

Black backward active (BBA):

$$000000000000000010000000000000000000$$

Red forward active (RFA):

$$000000000001000000000000000000000000$$

Red backward active (RBA):

$$000000000001000000010000001000001110$$

Black men are shown in squares 1, 2, 3, 7 and 25, and a black king in square 17. Red men are shown in squares 20, 27, 33, 34 and 35, and a red king in square 12.

Execution of the segment shown in Fig. 11–14 will have the following result:

Instruction	Register	New contents
LM 4,5,0(1)	4	11100010000000001000000010000000
	5	00000000000000000000000000000000
SLDL 4,5	4	01000000000100000001000000000000
LM 6,7,24(1)	6	00000000000100000001000000100000
	7	11100000000000000000000000000000
SLDL 6,5	6	00000010000000100000010000011100
	7	00000000000000000000000000000000
ØR 4,6	4	01000010000100100001010000011100
Ø 4,MM5	4	01000010100100100101010000111100
X 4,=F'-1'	4	10111101011011011010101111000011
N 4,0(1)	4	10100000000000001000000010000000
ST 4,FØRDRGHT		

The result records that the men (or kings) in squares 1, 3, 17 and 25 can move
forward and to the right.

Separating the possibilities

For an analysis of the moves, it is necessary to separate them so that they can be
considered one at a time. Figure 11–16 shows a program segment that will separate
the 1-bits of a word like FØRDRGHT. First, the word is loaded into register 5. If
there are no 1-bits, an immediate branch is taken to NØNE. Otherwise, the bits are
moved one at a time into register 4. When a 1-bit is found, it is moved to register 8,

Fig. 11–16   Separating possible moves

```
*           SEGMENT TØ GENERATE A WØRD FØR EACH PØSSIBLE MØVE.
*           WHEN ØNE IS FØUND, IT IS LEFT IN REG. 9, WITH JUMP TØ ANAL.
*           AFTER A MØVE IS ANALYZED, JUMP BACK TØ REIN FØR ANØTHER.
*           WHEN NØ MØRE REMAIN, JUMP TØ NØNE.
            L     5,FØRDRGHT
            LA    6,0           INITIALIZE SHIFT CØUNT TØ ZERØ
REIN        LTR   5,5           REENTER HERE.
            BZ    NØNE          ANY PØSSIBLE MØVES?
LP          LA    4,0
            SLDL  4,1           MØVE A BIT INTØ REG. 4
            LA    6,1(6)        UPDATE SHIFT CØUNT
            LTR   4,4
            BZ    LP            IF NØT 1, GØ SHIFT AGAIN
            LR    8,4
            LA    9,0
            SRDL  8,0(6)        MØVE 1-BIT FØUND BACK TØ ITS
            B     ANAL              ØRIGINAL PØSITION
```

and shifted back to its original position, but by itself in register 9. Note the use, which is fairly rare, of a register holding the count by which another register is shifted. After a position is analyzed, a branch back to REIN will cause search for the next possible move, if any. With the board position given as shown in Fig. 11–15, our segment will generate, in turn, the words

```
1000000000000000000000000000000000
0010000000000000000000000000000000
0000000000000000100000000000000000
0000000000000000000000010000000000
```

and after generating each one, control will branch to ANAL; on a last return to REIN control will branch to NØNE.

Making a move

One of the first steps in the analysis of any move is to generate the board position that would result from it. We ignore for now the assumption that contents of registers 5 and 6 must be saved for use on the branch back to REIN, and we show how the logical instructions may be used to generate a new board position. We assume that register 1 still contains the address of the eight-word description of the current board position, and that register 2 contains the address of an eight-word block into which we are to put the description of the new board position.

Figure 11–17 shows a program segment that generates a new board position. The entire old board position is moved to the new area; the red configuration remains unchanged, and the black configuration can most easily be changed in place. The complement of the position of the piece to be moved is found, preparatory to an NC instruction which sets that one particular position to 0. The original

Fig. 11–17   Making a forward right move

```
*          SEGMENT TØ MAKE FØRWARD RIGHT MØVE,
*          GENERATE NEW BØARD PØSITION IN AREA ADDRESSED BY REG. 2
*          PIECE TØ BE MØVED RECØRDED IN REG. 9
           LR      8,9               CØPY MØVE
           X       8,=F'-1'          CØMPLEMENT
           ST      8,TEMP
           MVC     0(32,2),0(1)      MØVE CØMPLETE BØARD CØNFIG.
           NC      0(4,2),TEMP       REMØVE PIECE FRØM ØLD BFA PØSITIØN
           LR      6,9
           LA      7,0
           SRDL    6,5               MØVE BIT TØ SQUARE FØR'D. RIGHT
           STM     6,7,TEMP+4
           ØC      0(5,2),TEMP+4     PUT PIECE IN BFA.
           N       9,8(2)            IS PIECE MØVED A KING?
           BZ      ØUT                 IF NØT, FINISHED
           NC      8(4,2),TEMP       IF SØ, REMØVE FRØM ØLD BBA
           ØC      8(5,2),TEMP+4       INSERT IN NEW PØSITIØN ØF BBA
ØUT
```

bit is next moved five bit positions to the right to represent moving the piece forward to the right. The piece is stored in the configuration in its new position with an ØC instruction. Note that the ØC is performed on five bytes, since any of the five might contain the new position. A test is necessary to ascertain whether the piece moved is a king; the test is an AND function of the piece with the black backward active (BBA) word, which yields 0 if the piece is not a king. If the piece is a king, it is expunged from its old square and entered into the new square of BBA in the same manner it was moved in BFA.

The student is urged to simulate execution of the segment as we did for Fig. 11–14.

Generating jumps

As one more segment of a checker-playing program we exhibit in Fig. 11–18 a segment that generates all possible jumps for black forward to the left. The strategy is first to generate the eligible squares that might be jumped into, in the same way that the segment in Fig. 11–14 found blank squares. Then we find positions in which a red piece has a blank square forward and to the left; this is done by an AND function whose operands are the red pieces and the blank squares shifted 4. Finally, the red pieces followed by blank squares are matched against black pieces, after the red pieces are shifted 4. Note that the fictitious squares preclude the possibility of generating a jump around the left edge of the board to the right edge.

Making an actual jump involves the same kind of manipulation that was shown in the segment in Fig. 11-17, but a little more of it, since the red piece that is jumped must be removed from the board.

Fig. 11–18   Generate black's forward jumps to the left

```
*         SEGMENT TØ GENERATE BLACK'S FØRWARD JUMPS TØ
*         THE LEFT.   STØRE IN FØRDLFJP.
*         FIRST, GENERATE ELIGIBLE ØPEN SPACES.
          LM    4,5,0(1)      BFA
          SLDL  4,4
          LM    6,7,24(1)     RBA
          SLDL  6,4
          ØR    4,6           CØMBINE
          Ø     4,MM4
          X     4,=F'-1'      ØPEN SQUARES REPRESENTED BY 1'S
*         FIND RED PIECES IN FRØNT ØF ØPEN SPACE
          N     4,24(1)
*         MATCH WITH BLACK PIECES
          SLL   4,4
          N     4,0(1)
          ST    4,FØRDLFJP
          :
MM4       DS    0F
          DC    BL4'10000000010000000010000000010000'
```

6. MAIN IDEAS

a. Logical arithmetic instructions AL, ALR, SL, and SLR allow arithmetic operations to be carried out on full-word quantities as unsigned integers; the condition code records a result of zero or nonzero, carry or no carry. Logical full-word compare instructions CL and CLR set condition codes showing whether the first operand is equal to, less than, or greater than the second operand, each considered as a full-word unsigned integer.

b. Shift instructions provide left and right, single- and double-register, logical and arithmetic shift capabilities. Logical shift instructions consider quantities to be bit strings, moving the entire contents of one or two registers and filling in with zeros at one end; they do not set a condition code. Arithmetic shift instructions move all bits but the sign bit; on a left shift zeros are filled in at the right, and overflows may result, but on a right shift copies of the sign bit are filled. The condition code is set, and an overflow exception may result.

c. Logical functions AND and OR have many uses, including interpretations in symbolic logic and Boolean algebra. Instructions in the IBM System/360 implement the AND, EXCLUSIVE OR, and INCLUSIVE OR, each in instruction types RR, RX, SI, and SS. These instructions are exceedingly useful in bit manipulation problems, and can selectively set any configuration of bits to 0's or to 1's, change them, or leave them alone. They are especially powerful in combination with the shift instructions.

PROBLEMS FOR REVIEW AND IMAGINATION

1. The process followed in execution of SL or SLR is addition of the 1's-complement of the second operand and of a low-order 1 to the first operand. Show that this process does, in fact, the logical subtraction of the second operand. Show also that a zero result is not possible without a carry (even when 0 is subtracted from 0!) and that therefore a condition code of 0 can never result from SL or SLR.

2. Write an extension to the program segment shown in Fig. 11–1 which will solve the problem of overflow, that is, store an indicator somewhere if and only if the sum c is incorrect because of overflow.

3. Write a program segment to simulate a "logical multiply" instruction, that is, one that finds the product of two operands considered as unsigned 32-bit numbers. The arithmetic multiply may be used, but adjustments must be made. Considering each logical operand as

$$\text{signed operand} + 2^{32}*(\text{high-order bit of operand})$$

will help in making clear what adjustments are needed.

4. Write a program segment to form the 4-word product of two 2-word signed integers. This entails some of the difficulties of problem 3.

5. The first operand in a division instruction must be placed in a register pair. A one-word operand is usually loaded into the odd-numbered register, with the sign bit extended to the preceding register. Show how the SRDA instruction helps make this easy.

6. In some computers a left shift is a circular shift; that is, bits lost from the left end of a register are inserted on the right end. This kind of shift is especially appropriate if negative numbers are represented in 1's complement form (subtracted from 1111 . . . 1 instead of from 10000 . . . 0). Why? Write an IBM System/360 or 370 assembler-language segment to perform a left circular shift of seven bits on the contents of register 5. It can be done in two or three instructions.

7. Write a program segment which will reverse the order of bits in the word at FØRWARD, placing the result at BACKWARD. That is, place the bit from bit position 0 of FØRWARD in bit position 31 of BACKWARD, the bit from position 1 of FØRWARD in position 30 of BACKWARD, . . . , the bit from position 31 of FØRWARD in position 0 of BACKWARD. A four-instruction loop, plus a few instructions outside the loop, can do the task.

8. Write program segments to simulate the arithmetic shift instructions by others. You can try two approaches, using either multiply and divide instructions or using logical shift instructions. If you are exceedingly brave, try to simulate the setting of the condition code too.

9. In Section 2, fields IND, P, and Q were packed into a word using left logical shifts. Can the packing be done using only right shifts? If so, how and under what conditions? If not, why not, and under what different conditions would right shifts be more useful in packing data into words?

10. Show how data fields that were once packed into a word can be unpacked and returned to separate registers.

11. Exhibit improvements that can be made in segments of previous chapters, or in segments you have previously written, through use of arithmetic shift instructions.

12. Write a program segment analogous to that in Fig. 11–9, which will construct a string of 32 printable characters 0 and 1, representing the binary number in register 5. This is a simpler problem than hexadecimal conversion, but employs the same principles.

13. The program segment shown in Fig. 11–8 for counting the 1-bits in a word can be written using an NR instruction instead of a shift instruction. If the word to be tested is in register 3, the count can be generated in register 5 by

```
        LA    5,0
P       LTR   6,3
        BZ    ØUT
        SL    3,=F'1'      (cont. on next page)
```

```
NR    3,6
LA    5,1(5)
B     P
```

Simulate execution of the segment to see how it works. How many repetitions of the body of the loop are required?

14. Write a sequence of instructions that sets bits 8–11 of the contents of register 4 to 1100, complements the bits in positions 16–21, and leaves the others unchanged.

15. The contents of registers 4 and 5 can be interchanged, *without* the use of a temporary storage location, by

```
XR    4,5
XR    5,4
XR    4,5
```

Show how this segment does the job.

16. Is it true that any two of the logical functions AND, INCLUSIVE OR, EXCLUSIVE OR, or NOT can be simulated by combinations of the other two? Try to do it. If it can be done, it would be sufficient to provide for only two of the functions in a computer instruction repertoire; we would assume that direct provision of more than two is for convenience and programming ease.

17. Show the difference between a NOT function on the bits of a word in register 6 and the operation of

```
LCR    6,6
```

18. Think of a bit manipulation function which is not implemented directly on the IBM System/360 or 370. What would be the uses of your function, and how can it be simulated on the IBM System/360 or 370?

19. The logical functions and their IBM System/360 and 370 implementation can be useful in set arithmetic. Suppose the 32 bit positions of a word represent 32 points or disjoint subsets of a space. The contents of any word can represent a set of the space: if a bit is 1, it indicates that the point or subset corresponding to that bit position is in the set, a 0 bit indicates that the corresponding point or subset is not in the set. If two words X and Y represent sets P and Q, respectively, then X AND Y represents the intersection $P \cap Q$. Similarly, X OR Y represents the set union $P \cup Q$. Continue and expand the interpretation: what represents the complement of a set? What does the EXCLUSIVE OR represent? What other set operations should be defined, and how can they be implemented?

20. Using the storage scheme described in Section 5, write a program segment to generate all the possible backward moves to the right for black kings. Also generate the possible jumps backward and to the right, and make one if you can.

21. It is convenient to store a board position in four double words, in order to be able to use Load and Load Multiple instructions. However, 14 of the 32 bytes used are empty. Show how one could store each 36-bit string in five bytes, keep the whole board position in 20 bytes, and then expand the position into a 32-byte area for actual manipulation. The savings in main storage space are very likely worth the extra instructions. How might one store a board position in the minimum space of 18 bytes and expand the configuration to double words for convenient analysis?

REFERENCES

IBM System/360 Principles of Operation, GA22-6821, or *IBM System/370 Principles of Operation*, GA22-7000, IBM Corporation. References on logical and shift instructions.

Preparata, Franco, and Raymond Yeh, *Introduction to Discrete Structures* (Reading, Mass.: Addison-Wesley, 1973). Boolean algebra and applications.

Samuel, A. L., "Some Studies in Machine Learning Using the Game of Checkers," *IBM Journal of Research and Development* **3** (1959), pp. 210–229. Samuel's original paper.

Samuel, A. L., "Programming Computers to Play Games," in *Advances in Computers*, Vol. 1, edited by Franz Alt (New York: Academic Press, 1960), pp. 165–192. A more accessible survey including analysis of the checker-playing experiments.

Chapter 12

Input and Output, Through the Operating System

In earlier chapters the functions of input and output were treated very lightly. We said that these functions were performed by the supervisor on request from the user's program, but did not examine the nature of the requests, let alone the variety of forms of requests available. In our examples we either concentrated entirely on processing within the computer, completely without reference to input or output, or hid the input and output in subroutines. It is now time to take up the subject of input and output, and explain just exactly how one makes requests of the operating system. In this chapter then, we discuss the various options available and the principles guiding selection among them, in various situations. Our discussion will include a foray into job control language, where various options and parameters are also specified.

The reader must be warned that the material here is a small representative subset of all the facilities and options available. It is quite specific, and usable in several systems, especially the IBM System/360 Operating System (abbreviated OS/360) and the OS/VS Virtual Storage Operating Systems for System/370 (including versions OS/VS1 and OS/VS2). The details are specific to these systems, and do not necessarily apply to other operating systems. As new versions of even these systems are released, some of the material here may become obsolete. Furthermore, each installation chooses parameters and options when it generates the operating system it will use, and many installations further modify or add to the systems provided by the IBM Corporation. We attempt to describe only the most standard features and methods of use, so that the explanations will have as wide and long applicability as possible. It is the author's belief that the material in this chapter will indeed be almost completely trustworthy.

1. BASIC STRUCTURE OF INPUT AND OUTPUT PROCESSING

During execution of a user's program, input and output actions are done by the supervisor, on request from the user's program. The requests may be of several sorts, and each has a variety of forms, parameters, and implications, as we shall see. Some of the requests are as follows:

a) Open a data set, which means prepare it for processing: make sure the device is available and ready, read or write the data set label, and generally set up or complete the communication patterns needed for further processing.

b) Retrieve a record from the data set and make it available to the user's program.

c) Wait until a particular event, such as retrieval of a record, is completed; this request is made when the user's program cannot proceed further until the event is completed, and the supervisor suspends operation of that program until control can be returned with the event completed.

d) Check on *correct* completion, without errors, of an event, which implies waiting for completion as well as examining possible error return codes.

e) Output a record (or block) onto a data set.

f) Position the reading or writing heads of the input or output device (magnetic tape or a direct access device) so that they are ready to read or write a certain record or block of a data set.

g) Control the device on which a data set resides, in some way that is particular to the device, such as backspacing on a magnetic tape.

h) Close a data set: write a trailer label on an output data set, and generally break the communication patterns established for use of the data set.

What is a data set?

It would be helpful if we could define data set at this point, in terms of concepts already established. We are unable to do this. A data set must be defined operationally in the discussions that follow, as a set of data that we and the operating system treat in some sense as a whole. The data set is made up of records and blocks, which we will define shortly. A data set is both a conceptual entity and a physical one; the operating system helps to adjust the physical to our conceptions.

For example, a reel of magnetic tape may contain several short data sets if we choose, and the operating system will help us to retrieve data from the one we choose at any moment. On the other hand, a long data set may occupy several reels of magnetic tape, and the operating system makes the transition from one to the other during processing. By writing and keeping track of records containing housekeeping information, the operating system is able to overcome some of the physical limitations, such as reels of magnetic tape of particular lengths, and thus allow a data set to conform to our concept rather than to some physical necessity.

Let us introduce here some conceptual examples of data sets and explore some possible physical representations of them. We shall explore the processing of each of these data sets in the course of the remainder of this chapter.

The first data set is meant to be a data set used as input in a program. It contains results obtained from questionnaires, and can reasonably be thought of as a deck of punched cards. Questionnaire results are most likely punched into cards, so the data set may still *be* a deck of punched cards. There may be more than 80 characters of information for one subject, and so more than one card per subject. There may be almost any number of subjects, though most likely somewhere between 50 and 5000. The data set would be used as input by programs making tabulations of results or various statistical analyses. The user may submit the data set on cards the first time he wants to use it, but he may want the data set written on perhaps a magnetic tape so that further uses will not require reading cards and will therefore be more efficient. A program to make tabulations, for example, should be able to process the data set from *either* cards or magnetic tape or even a direct-access device, and we will see that the operating systems for the IBM System/360 and 370 easily allow this kind of flexibility.

The second data set to consider is purely an output data set, perhaps the tabulations developed by a program working on the first data set. The data set will certainly appear on the printer, and may be quite long. The user will most likely want to control the page format and cause a skip to the top of a new page here and a double or triple space there. For the sake of efficiency in use of the printer, the data set will probably be first written on a magnetic tape or direct access device, then later printed if several copies must be produced or if the printing can be done on a cheaper computer.

The third example data set is a file of reference data. It may be a table of physical characteristics of a number of chemicals, of meanings and grammatical properties of English words, or of costs and ordering characteristics of a number of airplane parts. But whatever the application, we have in mind an ordered file of data, any record of which may be required at any point in a user's program. We may call this a "random-access" application, because so far as the operating system knows, the demands for the next record are random, and decidedly not in the same order as the file itself. However, the file is for reference use only; it is never changed.

The fourth example of a data set is a file of information, perhaps inventory information, which is to be updated by the user's program. Quantities on hand are to be modified as a result of the day's or week's transactions, so this data set has both input and output aspects. It is an ordered file, most likely ordered on something like part number, and if the data set of reports of transactions is sorted into the same order, our data set can be processed sequentially. The data set may be kept on one or more magnetic tapes, or on a direct-access device, especially if a sophisticated online information system wants access to the inventory information. But that is beyond the scope of our current discussions.

Therefore, in summary, a data set is defined by what we can do with it; we try to define our data sets as naturally as possible for each application, and the operating system helps us to treat the conceptual unit as a programming unit.

The data control block

The physical connections necessary between the various parts of the computer system are reasonably evident, and more detail about channels and the commands given to accomplish physical input and output will be given in Chapter 17.

The programming connections embodied in a chain of communication between data set, job control statements, the supervisor, and the user's program are far from obvious, and must be sketched at this point.

The operating system maintains a *data control block* for each data set in use by a user's program. The data control block is kept in the user's own main storage area, and the user has opportunities to modify parameters and addresses in the data control block during execution of his program. However, this is not really common or desirable; most of the time the user is content to set parameters through the assembler and the operating system, and let the supervisor maintain the data control block. The user must include in his program a DCB macro-instruction, including several parameters for the data control block. The DCB macro-instruction (see Section 6.5 for an introduction of the macro concept) is a pseudo-operation which defines the skeleton of the data control block. It is expanded by the assembler into a sequence of constants, addresses, etc., but it contains no executable instructions itself. Therefore it has the status of, and is usually placed with, constant and symbol definitions in the user's program. The user gives each data control block a name (which the assembler of course translates into an address) through his DCB macro-instruction, and uses this name when making requests to the operating system for action regarding the data control block and the data set to which it corresponds.

The supervisor completes the data control block with information from several sources. One source is the DD (Data Definition) statement included in the job control statements for the job. Every data set needs a DD statement, which may contain a number of items of information about the data set. The main advantage to having some data-set definitions and parameters specified in a DCB macro-instruction and others in a DD statement is flexibility; certain parameters can be fixed (in the DCB macro-instruction) for all executions of a given program while others (in the DD statement) can vary from one execution of the program to the next. Items like the name of a data set, the device on which a data set resides, or the amount of space to be reserved on a direct access device, *should* be variable between executions.

A *ddname* must be included as one of the parameters of the DCB macro-instruction. The same ddname must appear on the DD statement, which is to correspond to and supplement the particular DCB macro-instruction. The operating system uses the ddname to make the correspondence and to take information from the DD statement to help complete the data control block.

The third source used in completing the data control block is the label from the data set itself, if the data set already exists before execution of the program begins. Such information as record length and format can be included in the label, which every data set on a direct access device or magnetic tape should have, and this information will be used in completing the data control block if the information has not been provided by the DCB macro-instruction or the DD statement.

The operating system must be told how to find the right data set to go with a particular data control block and DD statement. The operating system keeps a *catalogue* of the data sets under its control. A user may have any direct-access data set or magnetic-tape data set catalogued, and the operating system will remember where it is (it cannot tell, of course, whether a particular reel of magnetic tape is in Pasadena or Madrid, but it knows the serial number of the tape, and if it is not mounted on a tape unit it can ask the operator to mount it). So if a data set is catalogued, the user may give the data-set name (dsname) in his DD statement, and the operating system will find it by using the information in the catalogue. If the data set is not catalogued, the user directs the operating system to it by designating an input or output unit, such as a card reader or magnetic tape drive. In the case of magnetic tape, it will also be necessary, perhaps, to give the serial number of the tape to ensure that the correct one is used.

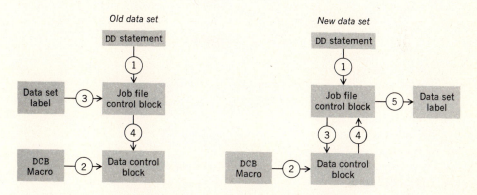

Fig. 12–1   Construction of the data control block.

The sequence of operations followed in setting up the data control block is roughly as follows and is summarized in Fig. 12–1. While the job scheduler is in control, at the beginning of a job or between job steps, the job control statements are read, and a *job file control block* is set up with the information from each DD statement. Each job file control block is identified by a ddname and contains at least a unit specification or a dsname. Second, while the program is loaded into main storage for execution, the expansion of the DCB macro-instruction made by the assembler becomes the skeleton of the data control block. The data control block is identified by an address (which in the assembler-language program was the *dcbname*), and it contains at least a ddname. Third, the user's program, during execution, "opens" the data set and causes completion of the data control block. The program requests the opening of the data control block by giving the supervisor the address of the data control block (dcbname). The supervisor finds the job file control block whose ddname matches that in the to-be-completed data control block. If the data set already exists, it is located through use of the dsname or unit specifications, and any uncompleted entries in the job file control block are

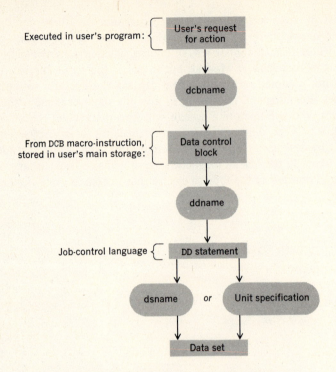

Executed in user's program:

dcbname

From DCB macro-instruction,
stored in user's main storage:

ddname

Job-control language

dsname *or* Unit specification

User's request for action

Data control block

DD statement

Data set

Fig. 12–2 The chain of data set identification.

filled in with information from the data set itself. Finally any uncompleted items in the data control block are filled in from the job file control block. For new data sets, the job file control block is completed by information from the data control block and in most cases a label is written for the new data set. The chain of identification that is followed is shown in Fig. 12–2.

2. ORGANIZATION OF A DATA SET

Blocking

First we make a distinction between *logical records*, which we shall hereafter call just plain *records*, and *physical records*, which will henceforth be called *blocks*. A logical record is the quantity of data (input or output) that the user wishes to process as a unit, the quantity that makes sense to the *logic* of the program. He usually issues his requests to the supervisor in terms of logical records, and in the processing sections of his program he need not concern himself with anything else. A block, on the other hand, is the quantity of data which is physically read or written by the computing system. The block consists of one or more records, which are grouped into a block for more efficient input and output processing.

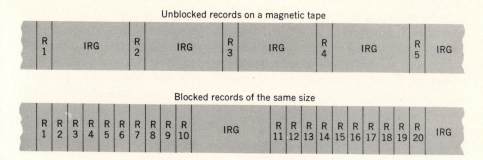

Fig. 12-3 Blocked and unblocked records.

While the user requests records from the supervisor, the supervisor reads a block, then doles out the logical records from the block one at a time.

The economy of blocking records is best understood from a discussion of data sets on magnetic tape. On magnetic tape a block is the quantity of information physically read or written in one operation, i.e., the data (we called it a record in Chapter 1) between inter-record gaps. If we consider logical records to be, for example, 80 characters long, a record occupies 0.1 in., at 800 bpi density. If each record is a block, it is followed by a half-inch (approximately) inter-record gap, and a series of a hundred logical records will occupy 60 in. of tape. On the other hand, if the tape is blocked with 10 logical records to a block, each block (1.0 in.) is followed by a half-inch inter-record gap, and a hundred logical records occupy only 15 in. of tape. Thus the blocking cuts the length of tape necessary by a factor of four. The comparison is shown graphically in Fig. 12-3. The elapsed time required to read the tape is cut by at least a factor of four, and most likely much more, since usually the tape comes to a halt at the center of each inter-record gap and thus its average speed in passing inter-record gaps is less than half of its reading or writing speed.

For devices other than magnetic tape, the blocking advantages are less pronounced, but the convenience of the concept is still very much present. On direct access devices such as magnetic disks, blocking can save time by permitting a larger segment to be read continuously before waiting for the disk to rotate to the appropriate spot for beginning the next record. As to a data set on punched cards, a block is a card and that is that.

Sequential, indexed sequential, and partitioned data sets

There are a number of different ways in which a data set can be organized, and we shall explore some of them now. These organizations correspond directly to concepts implemented under OS/360 and OS/VS, and indirectly to options available with other computing systems.

The first and simplest type to discuss is the *sequential* organization. Under a sequential organization each record follows the preceding one, and the records must be processed in that order. It may sometimes be possible to back up one record, or to go back to the beginning of the data set, but not to jump around otherwise. This type of organization is that necessarily followed physically on a magnetic tape: the actions possible are to read the next record, to backspace a record, to rewind, and no others. A data set being read by a card reader is the same except there is no going back at all. A data set being printed must also be sequential, with the addition of a few options as to line spacing. A data set on a direct-access device may be treated sequentially, and *can* even be created so that the beginning of the next record is known only after the previous one is read, so that the data set *must* be read sequentially.

Another type of organization is called *indexed sequential*. Associated with each record is a *key*, which is part of the record, and the records are arranged so that the keys are in ascending order. For effective use, the data set is kept on a direct access device, and a set of indexes is kept, showing the locations of blocks of the data set whose last records are associated with various keys. Then when access to a particular record is desired, its key is looked up in the index, and sequential retrieval of records begins with the block containing the desired record. Thus the file is sequential, but the indexes facilitate jumping into the middle at a number of different points. Maintenance of such a data set becomes a little difficult when records (which are not even all the same size) are added and deleted at various points. Maintenance procedures are built in, however, in some of the access routines.

A third organization type is called *partitioned*. A *partitioned* data set is divided into several *members*, each of which can be referred to as a sequential data set in its own right. A *name* is associated with each member, but the names of members, unlike the keys of records in an indexed sequential data set, are not ordered. A *directory* allows the operating system to find any member of the data set; this obviously requires that the data set be kept on a direct access device. Once a member is selected, it is processed like an ordinary sequential data set, although some extra handles are provided for use by the sophisticated user. Furthermore, a jump to another member is possible at any time.

The data set of questionnaire responses and the data set of program output, which were introduced in the previous section, would both be examples of data sets organized sequentially. The third example, the table of reference information, should be organized as an indexed sequential data set, so that the indexes kept by the operating system will facilitate rapid direct access to any item in the table. The fourth example, the file of inventory data, is again a sequential data set; since the processing we envision can treat the data set sequentially, there is no advantage, and considerable overhead, to organizing it as either an indexed sequential or partitioned data set.

All three of these organizations—sequential, indexed sequential, and partitioned—are recognized and handled by OS/360 and OS/VS. The *access methods*, sets of routines for processing the data sets, are identified with one or more of these types (or a few others, such as *direct*, which leaves almost everything to the user, and VSAM, which does even more for the user and enables more device independence). We shall select the simplest one, the sequential organization, for investigation in greater detail. Many of the points we discuss will be relevant to indexed sequential and partitioned data sets, but the details will be with particular reference to the sequential data sets recognized by OS/360 and OS/VS.

Record and block formats

Records and blocks may be of almost any size. We have seen that small blocks are uneconomic; there are also practical limits to the maximum length of a block. Since an entire block must be read into main storage at once, areas called *buffers* must be provided to hold entire blocks. Thus long blocks cut down on the main storage available for other purposes. Second, but less important, no records from a block can be made available to the user until the entire block is read, so a very long block delays the beginning of a user's processing. Third, an input/output hardware error will cost more time in correction procedures if blocks are long, and if the error cannot be corrected, the data loss is larger. A balance must be reached; the balance depends mostly on how restricted main storage will be *in all programs and on all occasions* in which the data set is to be used. In practice, reasonable lengths of blocks are from 400 to 4000 characters.

It may not be convenient for all (logical) records to be the same length. Certain records may need to contain more information than others. For example, in a dictionary some words have more meanings and a greater variety of syntactic uses than others. Access methods under OS/360 and OS/VS allow for data sets with fixed-length records and for data sets with variable-length records.

If records are of fixed length, all the blocks will be of the same length (except perhaps the last which may be shorter). If the supervisor is informed, either by the DCB macro, the DD statement, or the data set label, of the length of a record and of a block, the block need contain only the records themselves, without any other control information.

On the other hand, if the length of a record is variable, the length must be written just prior to the record.

For data sets destined for printing on the line printer, we control vertical spacing by appending a spacing control character at the beginning of each record. The common codes and their actions:

blank	normal single spacing
0	double space to the next line
–	triple space to the next line
+	suppress spacing before printing the next line
1	skip to the top of the next page before printing the next line

The spacing control (also called *carriage control*) character is not itself printed, but is used merely to give spacing control commands to the printer. However, if we are using a spacing control character, we must include it when counting record length and block size.

Variable-length records may be blocked or unblocked; if they are blocked, the length of a block is variable too, and that length must be written at the beginning of a block. The supervisor will handle the blocking and furnish the block and record descriptor words, and the programmer need only work with logical records. Requirements, formats, and procedures are more fully explained in *OS Data Management Services Guide*, GC26-3746, *OS Data Management Macro Instructions*, GC26-3794, and *OS/VS Data Management Services Guide*, GC26-3783. Provision is made for blocks which the supervisor considers to have "undefined" format, but for these blocks the programmer must do his own blocking and unblocking.

3. BUFFERING AND EXIT OPTIONS

In Section 2 we investigated various options for the organization of a data set: blocking of fixed- and variable-length records, in sequential, indexed sequential, and partitioned data sets. Now we examine some of the more important techniques and options used during the processing of a data set.

Buffering

The supervisor's input and output routines read blocks into and write blocks from areas called buffers. The areas are called buffers because they are intermediate between the user's own areas and the input and output devices themselves, protecting, in a way, each from the other. The idea is that the supervisor can be processing input and output through the buffers while the user's program is working in its own areas which are not affected by the simultaneous reading and writing. This simultaneity would not be possible without buffers.

Usually, the supervisor has more than one buffer assigned to each data set. For sequential data sets, this affords still more economies by enabling simultaneity of operations more of the time. For example, when an input data set is opened, two buffers may be assigned to it, and immediately the supervisor starts reading a block into the first one. As soon as the first block is read, the user's program may be given the first record from the first block. But immediately the supervisor also starts reading the second block into the second buffer. Thus one buffer is being filled, character by character, from the data set, while the other is being emptied, record by record, by the user's program. When all records of the first block have been taken by the user's program and the second block is read, the buffers interchange roles, and the third block is read into the first buffer while records are doled out to the user's program from the second buffer. Figure 12–4 illustrates the simultaneous uses of the two buffers and their interchange of roles. Assuming three records to a block, for simplicity, we first see the status at the time the user's program requests the first record (part a). The first block is in buffer 1, waiting to be given to the user's program, and the second block is being read into buffer 2. Figure 12–4(b) shows the action when the fourth record is being given to the user's program; the third block is already being read into buffer 1, whose first contents—records 1, 2, and 3—are no longer needed there.

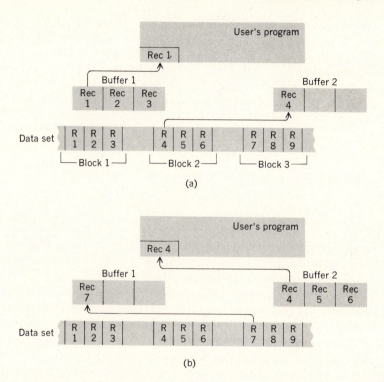

Fig. 12-4 Buffering action: (a) during request for first record, and (b) during request for fourth record.

During output the process is more or less reversed. As the user delivers each output record to the supervisor with a request to write it, the supervisor puts the record in the first output buffer. When the first buffer is filled, physical output of the block is begun, and while it proceeds, the user's program can deliver other records to the second buffer. When the second buffer is full and output of the first buffer is completed, the roles of the buffers are interchanged: the second block is written from the second buffer while more records are delivered to the first buffer.

There are many possibilities for variation in the implementation of this elementary but important concept of buffering. The options provided, such as the number of buffers associated with each data set and the method of managing buffers, can give the user a very flexible system.

Buffers associated with a data set are organized into a *buffer pool*. Each buffer in the pool is as long as the longest block in the data set; the buffers are normally provided automatically by the supervisor, though it is possible for a user to build his own pool. Two buffers are usually provided, but in some circumstances it is desirable to request more buffers either in the DCB macro-instruction or in the DD statement.

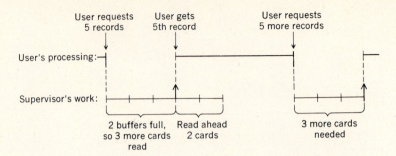

Fig. 12–5 Concurrency of operations: limited by insufficient buffers.

Consider our questionnaire response data set, as it exists on cards. If five cards hold an individual's responses, the requests for five records will be issued almost simultaneously. If we first suppose that the time the user's program needs to process an individual's responses is exactly equal to the time required to read five cards, the processing, given two buffers, would proceed as shown in Fig. 12–5. When the user's program wants five records before his analysis of the individual's responses begins, and only two are available, he must wait while the other three are physically read. On the other hand, while the user processes the data, the supervisor fills the two buffers and then waits for them to be emptied before it can read farther ahead. If, however, five buffers are provided, the flow of processing is as shown in Fig. 12–6. The provision of five buffers enables both the user's program and the supervisor to continue their work without waiting, and cuts the total processing time by $37\frac{1}{2}$ percent. However, if the time required for internal processing is only, say, 40 percent of the time required for input, then two buffers are again sufficient to keep the input going continuously, as we see in Fig. 12–7.

The general guide, then, is to provide enough buffers to hold the information requested in a spurt, unless the process is input or output bound, in which case enough buffers should be provided to make the input or output continuous.

Access methods under OS/360 and OS/VS are generally provided in two forms; there are "basic" access methods, in which a great deal is left to the user, and "queued" access methods, in which many more things, especially buffering, are done automatically for the user. Under the *Queued Sequential Access Method (QSAM)*, for example, reading ahead and filling buffers is done automatically, but under the

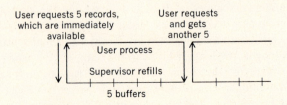

Fig. 12–6 Full concurrency provided by buffers.

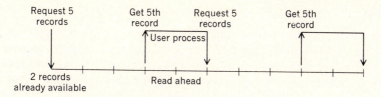

Fig. 12-7 Concurrency during an input-bound process.

Basic Sequential Access Method (BSAM) such functions must be performed by the user's program, using macro-instructions that allow him much more control, but which require more careful work. We shall restrict our attention now to facilities available under QSAM; these are the most often used, and most easily used by beginners. After the user has become reasonably conversant with the concepts and facilities embodied in QSAM and with the channel structure and commands, which we explore in Chapter 17, he will be in a good position to learn about BSAM and other access methods from the appropriate IBM manuals when he needs them.

Control of buffering under QSAM is done by the supervisor, but there are several options the user may choose. First, there is a decision between *simple buffering* and *exchange buffering*. Under simple buffering each buffer is associated with only one data set. Under exchange buffering, on the other hand, a record may be read into a buffer while it is associated with one data set, and the supervisor gives the record to a user's program by exchanging the buffer for an area of the same size belonging to the user's program. The first buffer now belongs to the user's program, and can be exchanged again, this time becoming the property of an output data set. The advantage of exchange buffering is that a record which is read, used, and then written again need not be physically moved. It can stay where it is while only possession of the buffer containing it changes hands.

Move and substitute modes

There are several *modes*, which indicate how the record is given to (or from) the user's program. Under simple buffering, *move mode* is the most used; an input record, when requested, is physically moved by the supervisor from its input buffer to an area designated by the user's program. The buffer is then immediately available for further use by the input routines. With output under move mode, a record which is ready to be output is physically moved by the supervisor from the area in which the user's program prepared it to a buffer. If no buffer is available, i.e., if all are full of other records waiting to be output, execution of the user's program is suspended until an output buffer can accept the current record.

Under exchange buffering, we use a *substitute mode*. Upon an input or output request in substitute mode, a work area belonging to the user's program is substituted for a buffer segment. In processing an inventory file, for example, we read a record, perhaps update it with a new transaction, and write it in a new data set.

Exit options

The user has options as to what should be done in a few special situations. If an error is encountered during input or output processing, the system automatically follows procedures that attempt to correct the error. If the error proves uncorrectable, the supervisor will, upon orders from the user's program, either accept the record anyway, skip the erroneous record, terminate the job abnormally, or give control to a routine specified by the user.

Similarly, when the end of an input data set is encountered and a request for an input record is made after there is no more input, the supervisor will branch to a routine specified by the user. This allows the user to build a loop for normal processing of records, with exit from the loop provided automatically to a location of the user's choice upon end of the data set.

The options mentioned in this section for the processing of data sets are mostly exercised in the macro-instructions of the user's program and in the DD statement. In the next section we show how the options in macro-instructions are specified, and in Section 6 we shall examine in more detail the parameters of the DD statement.

4. USING QSAM MACROS IN A PROGRAM

Most of the ideas, options, and structures of input and output processing that we shall consider have already been introduced. It remains to describe exactly how they are used and specified, and to illustrate their uses with examples. In this section we attempt to do that with the use of QSAM macros, and in later sections we shall show their relationship to job control language.

Under the QSAM access method, requests to the supervisor for input and output actions are made through the use of macro-instructions. There are only a few, and all but the DCB macro are simple to use. Briefly the macros are:

ØPEN	prepare the data set and complete the data control block,
GET	get a logical record for the user's program,
PUT	present a logical record for output,
CLØSE	terminate processing of a data set, and
DCB	organize the data control block.

All except the DCB macro-instruction are translated into executable statements and thus need entries in the name field only if the programmer wishes to branch to one. The DCB macro-instruction sets up the skeleton of the data control block and is not executable. It *must* have a name (called the *dcbname*), and all other macro-instructions refer to a particular data set by giving the dcbname associated with the data set.

The input and output macros are expanded into calls on subroutines, the subroutines residing in the supervisor. Therefore a routine that does not call subroutines of its own must still save registers 13, 14, 15, 0, and 1, and must provide a register save area if it uses the input or output macros. Registers 14, 15, 0, and 1 will not, in general, have the same contents after one of the macros as before, since these registers are changed by the calling sequence built into the user's own routine.

ØPEN and CLØSE macros

The first macro-instruction to be executed, with respect to any data set, must be the ØPEN. The supervisor prepares the data set for processing: it completes the data control block and either analyzes the label of an input data set or writes the label of an output data set. The syntax is

Name	Operation	Operands
[symbol]	ØPEN	(dcbname[,(options)])

where dcbname may be given in any form allowable in an A-type constant.

Under QSAM, one or two options are specified for each data set opened. The first must be one of the words INPUT, ØUTPUT, RDBACK (to prepare a magnetic tape to be read backwards), or UPDAT (to prepare a direct access data set for being read and written in place). The default option is INPUT, so the first option need not be explicitly stated for an input data set. The second option controls positioning of the data set, but if we want to start reading or writing the data set at the beginning, we need not specify this parameter. If only the first option is specified in the macro-instruction, the option need not be enclosed in parentheses, although the entire operand list must be. For example,

```
        ØPEN    (CARDIN,INPUT)
```

opens an input data set whose dcbname is CARDIN, and

```
        ØPEN    (INVFILØ,ØUTPUT)
```

opens an output data set whose dcbname is INVFILØ. Several data sets can be opened with one ØPEN:

```
        ØPEN    (CARDIN,INPUT,INVFILØ,ØUTPUT)
```
or
```
        ØPEN    (CARDIN,,INVFILØ,ØUTPUT)
```

are equivalent to the sequence of two ØPENs. When there is only one operand for a macro-instruction, it need not be put in parentheses:

```
        ØPEN    CARDIN
```

will correctly open the input (by default) data set whose dcbname is CARDIN.

The CLØSE macro-instruction is the converse of the ØPEN. It causes records remaining in output buffers and a data-set trailer label to be written, repositions the device, and, in general, disconnects the data set from the program. The syntax is

Name	Operation	Operands
[symbol]	CLØSE	(dcbname[,option])

Again, dcbname may be given in any form that could be used in an A-type constant. One option may be specified REREAD, LEAVE, or DISP. This option controls the positioning of the data set after it is closed: REREAD positions it for rereading, LEAVE positions it at the end, and DISP passes the buck to the DISP parameter of the DD statement. It is possible, with a magnetic tape or direct access data set, to process a data set, close it with REREAD, then open it again and reprocess it from the beginning. Under QSAM this is the only way to perform a rewind operation on a magnetic tape.

The CLØSE macro-instruction can sometimes be omitted; if data sets remain open when the program is terminated, they are automatically closed by the operating system. Still, the best practice is to close data sets explicitly.

GET and PUT macros

The GET macro-instruction retrieves for the user's program a record from an input data set. If the data set is exhausted, control is returned to the location given in the EØDAD parameter of the DCB (see below), and if there was a persistent error in the reading, return of control depends on the ERØPT parameter of the DCB (also see below); otherwise control is returned to the instruction immediately following the GET macro-instruction as soon as a record is available. The syntax of the GET macro-instruction is

Name	Operation	Operands
[symbol]	GET	dcbname[,area address]

The mode (move or substitute) of the GET is determined by a parameter in the DCB macro-instruction for all GETs referring to a data set. If the move mode is specified, the area address must be included in the GET statement; the record is placed by the supervisor in the area beginning at the given address. If the substitute mode is specified, the address of the record returned is placed by the supervisor in register 1. In substitute mode the area-address parameter must be included, but it is the address of the area given to the supervisor as a substitute for the area containing the current record. For example, in the move mode

        GET   CARDIN,INAREA

will retrieve a record from the data set associated with CARDIN; the supervisor will store the record starting at INAREA. In the substitute mode

        GET   INVFILI,(3)

will retrieve a record from the data set associated with INVFILI; the address of the new record will be in register 1. The second parameter (3) indicates that the address of the area to be substituted for the buffer containing the new record is in register 3. This form is common in macro-instructions; where an address is required but the address to be given is in a register and cannot be given symbolically, the register address in parentheses can be used. It is particularly appropriate here; the address of the area to be substituted is most likely the address of the most recent record *received* in exchange, and therefore not an address known symbolically to the programmer.

The PUT macro-instruction is quite similar to the GET. It presents a record to the supervisor, with orders to output the record when convenient. The syntax is

Name	Operation	Operands
[symbol]	PUT	dcbname[,area address]

The operands have precisely the same meanings as the corresponding operands of the GET macro-instruction. In GET and PUT macros the dcbname and area address may be given in any form allowable in an RX-type instruction.

The DCB macro-instruction

The general form of the DCB macro-instruction is

Name	Operation	Operands
dcbname	DCB	operands, separated by commas

The DCB macro-instruction is nonexecutable, so it is placed with the constant and symbol definitions in one's program. The operands in a DCB macro-instruction are all *keyword parameters*, which means that each is specified as

keyword = option.

For example, one of the keywords is DSØRG; the operand specifying it may be written DSØRG=PS, where PS is the option taken. Keyword parameters can be written in a list in any order, and if one is omitted, no extra comma or other adjustment need be made. The data control block is built in the space reserved by the DCB macro-instruction, and much of the control information is supplied from the DCB operands, which we now take up, one at a time. Our list will not be exhaustive, but for the operands we discuss we must make clear whether the information is required or optional, and whether it can be supplied in the DD statement or data-set label instead of the DCB macro-instruction. The user should remember the order in which information is taken to complete the data control block. It is taken first from the DCB macro-instruction. If certain items are omitted from the DCB macro-instruction, they are filled in from the DD statement, if the DD statement includes the items. If any remain unfilled, they may be filled from the data-set label. If an item is specified in both DCB macro and the DD statement, the DCB parameter takes precedence. The DCB operands with which we are concerned are as follows:

DSØRG stands for *Data-Set ORGanization* and must be specified in the DCB. For sequential data sets one specifies DSØRG=PS or DSØRG=PSU, the PS standing for *Physical Sequential*. The U, meaning Unmovable, is included only if the data set contains location-dependent information that would prevent its being moved; this is unlikely for sequential data sets.

RECFM specifies the *ForM* of data *RECords*: fixed or variable length, blocked or unblocked. This information is essential, but it may be given in the DD statement or in the data-set label instead of the DCB macro-instruction. If given in the DCB macro-instruction, it is given as

RECFM=V	Variable, unblocked;
RECFM=VB	Variable, Blocked;
RECFM=F	Fixed, unblocked; and
RECFM=FB	Fixed, Blocked.

To each of the codes V, VB, F, FB, we add the code A if we are using printer spacing control characters as explained in Section 2, thus making four additional allowable codes, VA, VBA, FA, and FBA. Other letters S, T, and M are sometimes included in defining record form, but we shall ignore them here.

BFTEK stands for *BuFfer TECHnique* (be careful not to spell it with a U). The options are simple buffering (coded S) and exchange buffering (coded E), as introduced in the preceding section. Buffering technique may be specified in the DD statement instead of the DCB macro-instruction, or it can be omitted from both, in which case simple buffering is assumed. So in the DCB macro-instruction we have

BFTEK=S   or   BFTEK=E

or neither.

MACRF, *MACRo Form*, is the fourth and last of the major parameters. In this parameter the user specifies which macros he is going to use with the data set and in which mode they are to be used. This parameter is required in the DCB macro-instruction. The letters used to code the information for this parameter are

G	GET macro will be used;
P	PUT macro will be used;
M	move mode; and
T	(watch this one) substitute mode.

As we have learned, GET or PUT can be used in either mode. The parameter can be coded

GM	GET used in Move mode
GT	GET used in Substitute mode

PM   PUT used in Move mode
PT   PUT used in Substitute mode

If the same data set is opened for both input and output, we specify which modes of both GET and PUT are to be used; the possibilities therefore are

(GM,PM)   (GT,PM)
(GM,PT)   (GT,PT)

BLKSIZE is the *BLocK-SIZE* parameter, which is specified as the length of the largest block to be processed in the data set. For fixed-length-record data sets, the block size must be an integral multiple of the record length; for variable-length-record data sets, BLKSIZE is the length of the largest block that may have to be processed. For a data set being created, BLKSIZE must be specified in either the DCB macro-instruction or the DD statement. For already existing data sets, the data-set label is another possible source. Absolute maximum block size is 32,760.

LRECL is the *Logical RECord Length.* This parameter is required and can be provided from the same sources as BLKSIZE. There must be a relationship between BLKSIZE and LRECL:

a) For fixed-length unblocked data sets, BLKSIZE = LRECL.

b) For variable-length unblocked data sets, BLKSIZE = LRECL + 4. This is in recognition of the block descriptor word which the operating system furnishes at the beginning of a variable-length record.

c) For fixed-length records blocked, BLKSIZE must be a multiple of LRECL.

d) If a printer spacing control character is included, it must be included as the first character of every record, and it must be counted along with other characters in calculating LRECL; other above rules then apply.

For example, if fixed-length 80-character records are blocked into 800-byte blocks, the DCB statement would include

RECFM=FB,BLKSIZE=800,LRECL=80

Unblocked records, each of 80 characters, would be specified as

RECFM=F,BLKSIZE=80,LRECL=80

Variable-length records to be printed would normally have a maximum of 132 characters to be printed since there are 132 print positions on the most standard printers. Adding the spacing control character results in LRECL=133. If the records are to be blocked, the DCB could contain

RECFM=VBA,BLKSIZE=1100,LRECL=133

BUFNØ is the *Number of BUFfers* assigned. This operand is optional: it may be specified in the DCB macro-instruction or in the DD statement, or it may be omitted, in which case two buffers are supplied.

DDNAME is the name which must be included as the ddname in the corresponding DD statement. Any name up to eight characters long, composed of letters and digits and beginning with a letter, is acceptable, but the user soon learns that using certain standard names saves trouble. For example, SYSIN is usually used for the standard input data set, SYSPRINT for the output to be printed, and SYSPUNCH for any output to be punched into cards. The user may discover other more-or-less standard names used in his installation, but he may still use his own names if he wishes. The DDNAME operand is mandatory in the DCB macro-instruction.

DEVD stands for *DEVice Description*, and it allows the user to specify the type of device to be used for the data set. This operand is optional. There are subparameters which allow him to specify certain options within the device class, such as the density used on a magnetic tape, character codes used in paper tape, etc. To preserve maximum flexibility, this kind of specification should be left to the DD statement if possible. We shall not list the possible parameters for this operand here, but refer the potential user to the manuals *OS Data Management Macro Instructions*, GC26-3794, or *OS/VS Data Management Macro Instructions*, GC26-3793.

EØDAD stands for *End-Of-Data-ADdress*, and is an optional operand. The user specifies by any relocatable expression the address of the segment of his program that is to be executed when the end of an input data set is encountered. The supervisor transfers control to this address when a record is requested by a GET statement after the data set is exhausted. If EØDAD is not specified, a GET statement appearing after exhaustion of the data set causes abnormal termination of the program.

ERØPT, *ERror OPTion*, specifies the action to be taken upon an uncorrectable input or output error if the SYNAD routine gives up or if none has been provided. Any one of the following options may be chosen:

ACC	accept the record anyway,
SKP	skip the record and proceed to the next, or
ABE	abnormally terminate the program.

Fig. 12–8 DCB operands

Operand	Required in DCB	Optional sources of information	May be entirely omitted
DSØRG		DD statement, data-set label	
RECFM		DD statement, data-set label	
BFTEK		DD statement	x
MACRF	x		
BLKSIZE		DD statement, data-set label	
LRECL		DD statement, data-set label	
BUFNØ		DD statement	x
DDNAME	x		
DEVD		DD statement	x
EØDAD			x
ERØPT			x

On output, however, SKP cannot be chosen, and ACC can be chosen only for printer output. If ERØPT is not specified in the DCB macro-instruction, a default option of ABE is assumed.

The above DCB parameters include the important ones. We summarize the methods of specifying their information in Fig. 12–8. This table may be used as a checklist by the user to ensure that he does not forget any of the parameters. The reader should remember that the list, if exhausting, is not exhaustive even for QSAM; anyone who intends to become a sophisticated input/output programmer still has many hours of manual-reading ahead of him.

Examples

We close this section by showing how a program may actually use the QSAM macros. First, consider a simple program that reads cards and transfers the records to magnetic tape or a direct access data set. There are only two data sets, one input and one output. In Fig. 12–9 we show the complete program for this job. The processing loop consists of only three instructions: GET and PUT, in move mode, and branch back. The exit from the loop is provided by the EØDAD parameter of the CARD DCB. Opening and closing sequences are standard, and the entire program is almost too easy after the long discussions in this chapter.

The first DCB, for the input card data set, includes almost all of the necessary parameters, leaving almost nothing to the corresponding DD statement. After all, if one is convinced that cards are being read, there is not much remaining variation possible. Default options are accepted for ERØPT, BUFNØ, and BFTEK. The second DCB, for the output data set, specifies the data set as blocked, but leaves block size to the DD statement.

Actually, the program as written can be improved in a number of ways. This is a classic case where exchange buffering can increase efficiency. Using substitute

Fig. 12-9   A card-to-tape-or-direct-access program

```
CARDCØNV  START   0
          SAVE    (14,12)
          BALR    12,0
          USING   *,12
          ST      13,SAV+4
          LA      13,SAV
          ØPEN    (CARD,INPUT,ØUT,ØUTPUT)
LØØP      GET     CARD,AREA
          PUT     ØUT,AREA
          B       LØØP
FINISH    CLØSE   (CARD,,ØUT)
          L       13,SAV+4
          RETURN  (14,12)
SAV       DS      18F
AREA      DS      CL80
CARD      DCB     DSØRG=PS,RECFM=F,MACRF=GM,BLKSIZE=80,               X
                  LRECL=80,DDNAME=SYSIN,EØDAD=FINISH
ØUT       DCB     DSØRG=PS,RECFM=FB,MACRF=PM,LRECL=80,                X
                  DDNAME=DATACØNV
          END     CARDCØNV
```

mode with both data sets, one would insert the instruction

```
            LA    2,AREA
```

before the loop. The loop itself would be changed to

```
        LØØP    GET    CARD,(2)
                LR     3,1
                PUT    ØUT,(3)
                LR     2,1
                B      LØØP
```

Of course, a few parameters of the DCBs would be changed, and BFTEK=E would be added to both. Action of the buffering would be as follows (assuming that there are only two areas for output):

	Belong to CARD	Belong to user	Belong to ØUT
After the open	In1, In2	AREA	Out1, Out2
After 1st GET	AREA, In2	In1	Out1, Out2
After 1st PUT	AREA, In2	Out1	In1, Out2
After 2nd GET	AREA, Out1	In2	In1, Out2
After 2nd PUT	AREA, Out1	Out2	In1, In2
After 3rd GET	Out2, Out1	AREA	In1, In2
After 3rd PUT	Out2, Out1	In1	AREA, In2
etc.			

After each GET, the address of the buffer segment containing the record is left in register 1; it is then moved to register 3 to be given to the output processors in exchange for another area.

Another improvement that can be made in the existing program is the loosening of the input restrictions. The DCB parameters could easily state that the input is blocked, and if BLKSIZE is left for the DD statement to specify, the input data set could be on practically any input device, and the program could thus serve as a more general data-set move program.

Next, consider a questionnaire analysis program. Since this is a simple but somewhat general program, there will be three data sets: the data, control cards specifying in detail the analysis desired, and printed output. The second set should certainly be input from cards, but the first could be on cards, disk, or magnetic tape. The DCB's for the three data sets may be as follows:

```
DATA        DCB    DSØRG=PS,RECFM=FB,MACRF=GM,                        X
                   DDNAME=INDATA,EØDAD=FIN
CØNTRØLC DCB       DSØRG=PS,RECFM=F,MACRF=GM,                         X
                   BLKSIZE=80,LRECL=80,DDNAME=SYSIN,EØDAD=D
ØUT         DCB    DSØRG=PS,RECFM=FBA,MACRF=PM,LRECL=133,             X
                   DDNAME=SYSPRINT
```

In the DATA   DCB, both LRECL and BLKSIZE are left unspecified; they can be supplied by the data-set label. The parameter BUFNØ may be given in the DD statement if the default option of 2 is not acceptable. In the ØUT   DCB, LRECL is specified to be 133 (to include a carriage-control character and 132 print positions) but BLKSIZE is left to be fixed in the DD statement.

The structure of the processing would be something like the following:

1. After standard beginnings, ØPEN the CØNTRØLC data set.
2. Read control cards and set up the analysis areas and procedures accordingly. The data-reading is accomplished by statements like

    GET   CØNTRØLC,CØNT4

3. After all control cards are read, the segment at D is given control; it concludes the set-up phase, closes CØNTRØLC, and ØPENs the DATA:

    D   CLØSE CØNTRØLC
               ØPEN DATA

4. Data records are read and analyzed, one at a time, through the instruction

    GET   DATA,DATAREA

5. The reading and analyzing continues until there are no more records, at which time the operating system gives control to the segment starting at FIN. Here DATA is closed and the output data set opened, and the final analysis performed and results printed. At FIN, then, we have

    FIN   CLØSE DATA
             ØPEN (ØUT,ØUTPUT)

and during output we have statements like

PUT   ØUT,RESULT

Finally, the ØUT data set is closed and the program terminated.

There are a number of things that can be done differently. All data sets could be opened at the beginning of the program and left open until the end; we choose not to tie up the devices longer than necessary. In some operating environments this permits gains in efficiency. Secondly, it may be that main storage space will not permit generation of all the desired tables with one pass through the data; further passes are needed. If the data are assumed to reside on a magnetic tape or on a direct-access data set, this is possible; at FIN we perform

FIN   CLØSE   (DATA,REREAD)

and reopen DATA again when ready to make another pass.

The job control, especially the DD statements, for these two example programs will be introduced in the next several sections.

5. SURVEY OF JOB CONTROL LANGUAGE

In Section 6.6 we gave a lick and a promise to job control language in order to prepare the student to submit jobs of the simplest kind. We now expand on that treatment and treat the syntax and use of job control statements in more detail. The treatment will still neither be exhaustive nor extremely sophisticated. The emphasis is on manipulation of data sets. Comprehensive information can be found in the manual *IBM System/360 Operating System Job Control Language Reference*, GC28-6539, or *OS/VS Job Control Language Reference Manual*, GC28-0618.

Structure of job control

The largest unit a user is concerned with is a job. The user submits a job to the computer as a request for execution of one or more programs. The execution of an individual program is a *job step*, and within the job there can be a certain amount of interdependence between steps. Between jobs there is none, except that, of course, different jobs may use (at different times) the same data sets. A user may call for execution in a step of either a single program or a sequence of programs defined by a catalogued procedure. The catalogued procedures are introduced in order to enable users to request in a very simple way any of a number of standard sequences of programs, operating on a more-or-less standard series of data sets. A catalogued procedure is, in turn, composed of steps, each step being the execution of a single program; procedures do not call on other procedures.

The user submits, along with his programs and data sets, a series of job control statements that define his requests. His job control statements for a job always begin with a JØB statement. Following this statement are one or more EXEC (for EXECute) statements, each defining a step, each calling for execution of a program or a catalogued procedure. Following each EXEC statement are the DD (Data Definition) statements necessary to the step. The standard DD statements supplied by a catalogued procedure can be replaced or supplemented by the user to fit his own requirements of the moment.

The format of job control cards, containing the job control statements, will be defined next. Each of the three kinds of job-control statements begins with two slashes (//) in columns 1 and 2 of the card. Most statements need names, and the names begin in column 3. A name is composed of from one to eight letters and digits, but begins with a letter. After the name and at least one blank comes the *verb* field; the allowed verbs are JØB, EXEC, and DD. After the verb and at least one blank are operands, which are separated from each other by commas but no blanks. Finally, following at least one blank after the operands may appear comments. We may therefore summarize the syntax requirements as

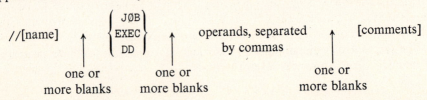

A job control statement can be continued onto a second and subsequent cards. Columns 1 to 71 are available for slashes, names, verbs, operands, and comments; operands may be interrupted after a parameter or subparameter and its succeeding comma (*don't* forget that comma!) at or before column 71. A character in column 72 is optional. The next card must have // in columns 1 and 2 (and *woe* if you forget those slashes!); operands must resume with any column from 4 to 16, and they can continue to column 71 and be followed by more continuation cards similarly if necessary.

There is one more job control statement, the *delimiter statement.* It has /* in columns 1 and 2, with only comments thereafter. The delimiter statement is used to signal the end of a data set in the main job stream.

Syntax of the JØB statement

A JØB statement must have a name, which is called a *jobname.* The user should try to make his name different from others in the batch, to avoid possibility of confusion in the operations staff, but it is not worth checking other jobs to make sure of not duplicating their names. Operands requirements are somewhat dictated by the particular installation, but the general structure can be laid out.

The first operand, in parentheses, is accounting information, and what that should include is really up to the individual installation. The second operand is the programmer name. This can be coded with, say, a period or hyphen between first or last names, as GEØRGE.STRUBLE or GEØRGE–STRUBLE, or it may be enclosed in apostrophes, in which blanks are permitted: 'GEØRGE STRUBLE'. The forms of both the accounting information and the programmer name may be prescribed by the installation.

The other operands are all keyword parameters, and are all optional. One is MSGLEVEL; an operand of MSGLEVEL=1 directs the operating system to print in the system output the job control statements used by the job. MSGLEVEL=0 directs that printing of the job control be suppressed. Each installation chooses which case is the default option in its system.

A parameter commonly required to help the job scheduler in a system which does multiprogramming is the CLASS parameter. It is coded CLASS= *a letter*; classes are assigned to types of jobs with similar attributes to help the scheduler balance the load on the system or respond appropriately to priorities. Each installation develops its own definition of job classes.

The last operand of the JØB statement we shall discuss is the CØND parameter, which allows the user to give conditions for terminating his job. Each program, when terminated, returns a value called the *return code* to the job scheduler. The return codes can be used, as they are by the assembler, linkage editor, FORTRAN compilers, etc., to indicate the success of execution: a low number may mean no errors and a high number may mean grave errors which render the result useless. The return code can be compared with values given in the CØND parameter to determine whether the remainder of the job should be canceled. The syntax is

$$CØND=((code,operator), \ldots , (code,operator))$$

with up to eight (*code,operator*) pairs. The value *code* is compared against the return code given by each program; *operator* can be any of

GT greater than,
GE greater than or equal to,
EQ equal to,
LT less than,
LE less than or equal to,
NE not equal to.

If a comparison

code   operator   return code

makes a true statement, the job is terminated. For example,

CØND=((12,LE),(7,EQ))

means that the job is to be terminated after any step which returns a return code such that 12 is less than or equal to the return code or 7 equals the return code.

Sample JØB statements would be

```
//GTRY    JØB    (321414),GEØRGE.STRUBLE,MSGLEVEL=1,CLASS=B
//MWILKR   JØB    (400261),'A. LINCØLN',CØND=((12,LE),(7,EQ))
```

Syntax of the EXEC statement

The name of an EXEC statement, called the *stepname*, is optional, but it must be used if the step or a data set in the step is referred to from another step.

The important and only required operand in the EXEC statement is the one designating the program or procedure to be executed. A program is kept as a data set; its execution is requested by data-set name. The data set may be catalogued and always known to the job scheduler, or it may be known temporarily as the result of a previous step in the same job. These two cases are recognized in the two optional forms:

$$\left\{ \begin{matrix} \text{PGM=program name} \\ \text{PGM=*.stepname.ddname} \end{matrix} \right\},$$

where * stands for "this job" and is further qualified by the name of the step in which the data set was defined and the name of the DD statement within that step. The third possible case is the request for execution of a catalogued procedure:

$$\left\{ \begin{matrix} \text{PRØC=procedure name} \\ \text{procedure name} \end{matrix} \right\},$$

where PRØC= is optional.

Other operands are CØND and PARM. The CØND parameter is like that described under the JØB statement, but it enables the user to specify conditions for bypassing each step individually. The syntax of the CØND parameter in the EXEC statement is

CØND=((*code,operator,stepname*), . . . ,(*code,operator,stepname*)), where up to eight triples, enclosed in parentheses, specify conditions for bypassing the current step. *Code* and *operator* have the same meanings given above, but the name of a particular step must be supplied for each, and the return code from that step is the one tested. For example,

```
//STEP3    EXEC    PGM=*.STEP2.DD2,CØND=((12,LE,STEP2),(7,EQ,STEP1))
```

asks for execution of the program in the data set defined under the name DD2 in STEP2, unless either 12 is less than or equal to the return code issued by STEP2 or 7 is equal to the return code issued by STEP1.

Up to 40 characters of control information may be passed to a program from the PARM operand of an EXEC statement. The information is enclosed in apostrophes, for example,

```
                    PARM='LIST,NØDECK'
```

Control information can be passed to a step of a procedure when calling for the procedure by naming the step:

```
    //    EXEC    ASMFCLG,PARM.ASM='LIST,NØDECK'
```

passes the control information to the program named in the ASM step of the ASMFCLG procedure.

Syntax of the DD statement

There are more rules for the syntax of the DD statement than for the JØB or EXEC statements, because there are more different options and parameters to be specified. OS/360 and OS/VS provide a very flexible and powerful facility for allowing various data sets to be used with any given program. We shall not exhaustively describe all options, but shall consider several which are felt to be the most important.

Almost every DD statement has a name, which we call the *ddname*. When a data set is used in a step of a catalogued procedure, the user must qualify the ddname by the name of the procedure step: procstep.ddname. For example, ASM.SYSIN specifies a ddname of SYSIN for a data set to be used in the ASM step of a catalogued procedure.

When a data set is entered in the main job stream with the job control statements, the single operand * on the defining DD statement will inform the job scheduler that the data set immediately follows the DD statement. The delimiter card (/*) must then follow the data set. For example,

```
            //ASM.SYSIN    DD    *
            cards containing the data set
            /*
```

is the complete definition for a data set whose ddname is SYSIN for use in the ASM step of a catalogued procedure.

Another simple variety of statement is the one assigning an output data set to be printed. The simple operand SYSØUT=A defines the data set to have a printer as its ultimate destination; the operating system, for the sake of efficiency, may write the data set on an intermediate device first and print it later, but this should not bother the user. In more sophisticated systems or for data sets with special requirements (special forms, exceptional length, etc.) more operands may be required in addition to SYSØUT=A; the user must learn such things in his own installation. For example,

```
//GØ.RESULT    DD    SYSØUT=A
```

can direct toward the printer the data set whose ddname is RESULT in the GØ step of a catalogued procedure.

If the data set to be defined is not one of these simple kinds, a minor host of operands may be needed in the DD statement. We attempt next a brief outline of them, and follow that with a more detailed description of each. In the next section we shall examine a number of complete DD statements used in a variety of situations.

The location of a data set must be specified; it can be named with a *dsname* in a DSNAME operand if it is already known to the operating system, or a UNIT can specify a specific device or device class to be used. For magnetic tapes or magnetic disk packs etc., which are demountable, a VØLUME specification identifies a particular reel, disk pack, or whatever to be used. In any case a DISP operand will usually be needed to tell the job scheduler whether the data set is new or already exists, and what to do with it after the current job step or procedure step. If the data set is to be created on a direct-access device, the job scheduler needs direction as to the SPACE to be allocated. Finally, a DCB operand may specify parameters, such as block size, to be included in the data control block for the data set.

The DISP operand has three subparameters. The first gives the previous status of the data set, and the others the disposition to be made of the data set at the end of the step. Possible entries for the first subparameter are ØLD, NEW, and MØD. ØLD and NEW speak for themselves; the data set either already exists (ØLD) or else it is to be newly created (NEW). The entry MØD is used for an existing sequential data set which is to have new information tacked on at the end. When opened, the data set is positioned at the end of the existing information, ready for writing.

The MØD subparameter introduces a very dangerous mode of operation. When an existing data set is modified, either on magnetic tape or on a direct access device, there is always the possibility that if the job step is abnormally terminated or writes the wrong information (these happen more often than we care to admit), the data set is left in a state from which it is difficult to recover even the previous status. It is far better practice to make a new data set by copying the information from the old and then adding on the new; this preserves the original data set in case something goes wrong. It is always good practice anyway to keep back-up copies of data sets, so that if one is accidentally destroyed or lost through some mishap, it can be reconstructed from a recent copy or version.

There are five possible dispositions of the data set after the step is completed: DELETE, KEEP, PASS, CATLG, and UNCATLG. We must first discuss further the system catalogue. In this catalogue the operating system keeps a list of data sets, by dsname and exact location, i.e., the serial number of magnetic tape reel, magnetic disk pack, etc. and the location on a disk pack. The operating system tries to ensure that the data sets listed in the catalogue are protected from accidental destruction, and it locates the data sets automatically for use in a job.

A data set, new or old, may be catalogued after successful completion of a step if CATLG is specified. A previously catalogued data set can be removed from the catalogue, but its space still not be made available for other use, if UNCATLG is specified. KEEP is specified for a data set, new or old, which is to be kept but not catalogued. A disposition of PASS directs that the data set be kept temporarily—either until the end of the job or until it is used in a subsequent step, whichever is sooner. Another disposition may be specified in a subsequent step. If no further disposition is specified in any subsequent step, the data set is deleted at the end of the job. Finally, a disposition of DELETE directs that the data set immediately be deleted, and its space be made available for other data sets.

The second subparameter directs the disposition to be made of the data set if the job step is completed successfully, the third if the step ends abnormally. If the first subparameter is left unspecified, NEW is assumed; if the second is omitted, the default is its disposition before the beginning of the step: DELETE for new data sets, KEEP for old, but DELETE for PASSed data sets. If the third subparameter is omitted, the second is taken to cover both normal and abnormal termination.

As examples, we may have an old data set which is to be read and to keep its original status after the step, whatever the outcome:

$$DISP=(\emptyset LD,KEEP)$$

On the other hand, we may be able to delete a data set at the end of the current step if it was successful, but otherwise keep it for a rerun:

$$DISP=(OLD,DELETE,KEEP)$$

A temporary data set perhaps has no further use if the step runs satisfactorily, but must be kept to aid in the diagnosis of trouble otherwise:

$$DISP=(NEW,DELETE,CATLG)$$

Conversely, a new data set is created for future use, but if the step was not successful, it must be rerun and this copy is useless:

$$DISP=(NEW,CATLG,DELETE)$$

Because direct access space required for the catalogue is usually at a premium and since the number of magnetic tapes being saved seems to grow without bound, many installations prefer that data sets on magnetic tape not be catalogued. They can be protected in other ways and identified by serial number. Data sets on magnetic tape are usually given dsnames, however.

A data set to be entered in the catalogue, or retrieved by reference to the catalogue, must have a dsname. The name is specified in the DD statement as

DSNAME=dsname, or if the data set desired is a member of a partitioned data set, DSNAME=dsname (member name). We can shorten DSNAME to DSN if we wish. If a temporary data set is to be used in a subsequent step of the same job, however, it need not be given a dsname when first created, and DD statements in subsequent steps may refer to it by the DD statement creating it: DSN=*.stepname.ddname. However, when the defining DD statement was used in a step of a catalogued procedure, both the step calling the procedure and the step within the procedure must be referred to:

$$\text{DSN=*.stepname.procstepname.ddname}$$

For example, DSNAME=*.STEP2.SYSLIN is a valid reference to the data set with ddname SYSLIN, used in STEP2, but if STEP2 were a call on a catalogued procedure which had a step LKED, then DSNAME=*.STEP2.LKED.GØDATA refers to a data set GØDATA defined in that step.

The UNIT parameter is required unless

1. the data set is retrieved by reference to its dsname and no volume (see below) information is given, or
2. the data set is passed from a previous step and no volume or unit information is given in the preceding definition, or
3. the location of the data set is defined, currently or previously, by VØLUME=REF (see below).

The UNIT may be indicated as a particular unit or class of units. There are three kinds of unit specification:

a) UNIT=address, where address is the channel address (channel addresses will be discusssed in Chapter 17) of a particular input or output device. The addresses are three-digit hexadecimal numbers specific to the individual installation. A card reader may have address 00A and a tape unit 191, for example. The address is specified only whan a *particular* tape unit or card reader, etc. is desired; otherwise the other types of UNIT specification are preferable.

b) UNIT=model, where model stands for a model number of input or output units; UNIT=2314, for example, requests that the data set be created by a model 2314 disk storage drive, but any 2314 drive in the system is acceptable. A user will know, or must learn, the model numbers of devices he is likely to use, so we do not attempt a list here.

c) UNIT=group, where group is an alphabetic designation of a class of units, for example, SYSDA for *all* direct-access devices, SYSSQ for all direct-access devices and magnetic tape units, which can handle sequential files, TAPE9 for all nine-channel tape units, etc. The classes and names are set up by each installation, so the user must learn them locally.

The specification of a unit group or class is preferable to the others, since it allows the job scheduler the widest latitude in employing devices for maximum efficiency.

When a data set is not catalogued, it can be requested by

UNIT=class,VØL=SER=serial number

A volume is an integral unit of peripheral storage capacity, such as a magnetic tape reel or a disk pack. A labeled magnetic tape has a serial number as part of its label, and a disk pack or any other demountable storage unit also has a serial number. Uncatalogued data sets on such volumes are usually requested by volume serial number. The keyword can be written VØLUME or VØL.

When a temporary (or nontemporary) data set is being created, and the user wishes it to occupy the same volume as another already-existing data set, he can request that by specifying VØL=REF=dsname, where dsname is the catalogued data-set name or one of the forms discussed under the DSNAME parameter: *.stepname.ddname or *.stepname.procstepname.ddname.

When a data set is to be created and a possible location for it is a direct access device, an allocation of space must be requested. The space can be requested in terms of average block size or, more device-dependent, tracks or cylinders. A quantity of the units chosen is requested by SPACE=(unit,quantity); for example, SPACE=(800,50) requests 50 blocks each of length 800, SPACE=(TRK,12) requests 12 tracks, and SPACE=(CYL,4) requests four cylinders. To request tracks or cylinders, the user should have some understanding of the structure and capacities of devices. For example, on disk packs for model 2314 disk storage units, a track holds 7249 bytes, and a cylinder consists of the 20 tracks that read-write heads are positioned to at any given moment. On disk packs for model 3330 disk storage units, a track holds 13,030 bytes and a cylinder consists of 19 tracks. If one requests space in terms of a block size, this is regarded as an "average" block size, and the user is not restricted to blocks of that length.

A user can avoid having to request *exactly* the space his data set will need. The quantity of units requested may be only an initial quantity and an *increment* specified—the number of units to be assigned when the already allocated space is exhausted. This kind of request is phrased as SPACE=(unit,(quantity,increment)). For example, SPACE=(800,(50,10)) requests an initial allocation of space for 50 blocks of 800 characters each. If that space is used up during the execution of the program, an increment of space for ten 800-character blocks is allocated. If *that* is used up, an additional increment of ten 800-character blocks is allocated. If necessary, this process continues until either 15 increments have been allocated or the space available on the volume is exhausted. Wonderful though this facility is, there is significant overhead, in both time and space, required for the additional increments, which are called *extents*, so the user is well advised to estimate his needs as well as possible, but not to make his increments too small. On the other hand, we should release the space allocated but unused after creation of the data set is completed. The third subparameter of SPACE directs the operating system to release the unused space; for example,

SPACE=(800,(50,10),RLSE)

The last of the DD operands to be presented here is the DCB operand. It is written DCB=(parameter list), where the parameter list is a list of keywords and corresponding values, coded exactly as they would be in a DCB macro-instruction in assembler language. All parameters not supplied by the corresponding DCB macro-instruction, by the data-set label, or by default, must be supplied in the DCB operand of the DD statement. Such an operand might be

$$DCB=(BLKSIZE=800,LRECL=160,RECFM=FB)$$

In summary, the DD statement can include as operands

*	data set follows directly,
SYSØUT=A	direct toward printer,

or any combination of

DISP=(status,disposition)	previous and future status,
DSNAME=dsname	name is used in catalogue references,
UNIT=ident	ident = address, model, or group,
or $\begin{cases} VØL=SER=ser.\ no. \\ VØL=REF=dsname \end{cases}$	identify specific volume,
SPACE=(unit,(quan.,incr.),RLSE)	required for direct access data sets,
DCB=(parameters)	parameters as in DCB macro-instruction.

This is not a complete list of possible operands, or a complete list of the options within each operand, but it presents the user with enough machinery to use until he needs more.

6. EXAMPLES OF SPECIFIC DATA-SET OPERATIONS

In the preceding section we introduced operands of DD statements and explained in a general way when and how the individual parameters should be used. Now we shall see how the operands and parameters are put together in specific situations.

Creating and using a data set on magnetic tape

First, let us suppose that a data set is to be created and kept on magnetic tape for use in later jobs. Operands DISP, UNIT, and DSNAME must be specified. Optional operands include DCB and VØLUME. Supposing that the program creating the data set does it under a ddname of TAPØUT, we see that a possible DD statement is

```
//TAPØUT    DD   DISP=(NEW,KEEP),UNIT=TAPE9,DSN=TAP349
```

A disposition of KEEP is given to reserve the tape but not to catalog it. Any nine-channel tape drive is admitted as acceptable for creating the tape, and the data set is given the unimaginative name of TAP349.

After the job is run and the tape is created, the user is informed of its serial number, which may be 101378. To use the tape in a later program, with a ddname of INTAP2, the user may write a DD statement

```
//INTAP2    DD  DISP=ØLD,UNIT=TAPE9,DSNAME=TAP349,VØLUME=SER=101378
```

The tape will be kept after this use too. I do not recommend a disposition of (ØLD,DELETE) or even (OLD,DELETE,KEEP); wait to delete your tape until you are sure your program ran correctly and you are indeed through with it. Deletion can easily be done then by the operations staff. DCB operands could, of course, be added to either or both DD statements.

Creating data sets on direct access volumes

To create a data set to be used only in one job step is very simple; only UNIT and SPACE parameters need be given. The data set can be written, read, reread, and changed within a program, as required, by a program that needs more storage space than is available in main storage. Supposing that the data set is used under a ddname TEMPSTØR in the GØ step of a catalogued procedure, and that it requires space for approximately 250 blocks of 400 characters each, we see that the DD statement could be

```
//GØ.TEMPSTØR    DD  UNIT=SYSDA,SPACE=(400,(250,25))
```

No DISP parameter is necessary, as (NEW,DELETE) is the default value supplied.

If a newly created data set is to be saved for use by later jobs, DISP and DSNAME parameters must be added. Besides, if the data set is to be kept, one ought to pay a little attention to where it is kept, so a VØLUME specification may be appropriate. Usually, however, the policies of the installation, plus the operating system's classification of private and public volumes, keep the user out of trouble if he neglects a VØLUME specification. However, suppose that we would like our new data set put on the same disk pack as the output (with ddname of DBREC) of our previous STEP1. A DD statement could be

```
//SKBLØC   DD  UNIT=2314,SPACE=(TRK,(25,5)),DISP=(,CATLG),
//             DSN=SKBLØCK3,VØL=REF=*.STEP1.DBREC
```

To use this particular data set in a later job is much easier; we can let the job scheduler find the data set through the catalogue, and space is already allocated. So the required DD statement is simply

```
//NØTHER    DD  DSNAME=SKBLØCK3,DISP=ØLD
```

Passing a data set

Suppose that a data set, created during one step of a job, is to be kept only for use during one subsequent step of the same job and then abandoned. This is the situation for PASSing a data set. The data set may be created either on magnetic tape or on a direct access volume. Let us assume we have a direct access volume and a DD statement in a step named STEP1 of

```
//DNEXT    DD   DISP=(,PASS),UNIT=2314,SPACE=(CYL,(4,1))
```

As in other DISP operands, we omit NEW, which is assumed by default. A dsname is not necessary, nor is a VØLUME designation.

Suppose now that STEP2 of the job does not refer to this data set, but STEP3 does, under a ddname of INTERMED. The DD statement in STEP3 could be

```
//INTERMED   DD   DSNAME=*.STEP1.DNEXT,DISP=(ØLD,DELETE)
```

Once the data set is identified as existing from the previous step, all the information about it is retrieved from the DD statement which guided the creation of the data set.

Complete job control for a simple step

Now let us examine the job control for a complete but simple job step. We shall illustrate with the card-to-tape convert program of Fig. 12–9. An EXEC statement and two DD statements are required, one each for the DCBs

```
CARD      DCB    DSØRG=PS,RECFM=F,MACRF=GM,BLKSIZE=80,            X
                 LRECL=80,DDNAME=SYSIN,EØDAD=FINISH
ØUT       DCB    DSØRG=PS,RECFM=FB,MACRF=PM,LRECL=80,             X
                 DDNAME=DATACØNV
```

The second DCB left BLKSIZE to be specified in the DD statement, but other DCB parameters are complete. Let us suppose that the first data set is actually on cards, and that the second is to be written on a magnetic tape. Assuming that the program CARDCØNV is in a system library in load module format under the name CARDCØNV (the name would not *necessarily* be the same as the name on the START statement), we find that the complete job control for the step is

```
//CØNVSTEP  EXEC   PGM=CARDCØNV
//DATACØNV  DD     UNIT=TAPE9,DISP=(NEW,KEEP,DELETE),DSN=QUEST215,
//                 DCB=(BLKSIZE=960)
//SYSIN     DD     *
```

Cards of first data set

```
/*
```

The definition of a data set in the main job stream is usually the last definition for the job step. This may be necessary so that other definitions can be made before the card data set is read!

Job control for a questionnaire analysis program

As a further example, we present the job control statements for a questionnaire analysis program which was outlined at the end of Section 4. This time, suppose that the program has been assembled and link-edited in the current job, and that it exists in a temporary data set whose ddname is SYSLMØD, which was created during a step named LKED. The data set of questionnaire data is the tape created in the above example, which we now assume to be on the reel with serial number

102139. Though LRECL and BLKSIZE are not specified in the DCB macro-instruction
for the data set, the data-set label can supply them. We may direct the output
to the printer, but because BLKSIZE was not specified in the DCB macro-instruction,
it must be supplied in the DD statement. The DCBs, themselves, from the previous
section are

```
CØNTRØLC  DCB   DSØRG=PS,RECFM=F,MACRF=GM,                             X
                BLKSIZE=80,LRECL=80,DDNAME=SYSIN,EØDAD=D
DATA      DCB   DSØRG=PS,RECFM=FB,MACRF=GM,                           X
                DDNAME=INDATA,EØDAD=FIN
ØUT       DCB   DSØRG=PS,RECFM=FB,MACRF=PM,LRECL=133,                 X
                DDNAME=SYSPRINT
```

The job control for the step is

```
//STEPGØ    EXEC   PGM=*.LKED.SYSLMØD,CØND=(5,LT,LKED)
//INDATA    DD     DISP=ØLD,UNIT=TAPE9,DSNAME=QUEST215,
//                 VØLUME=SER=102139
//SYSPRINT  DD     SYSØUT=A,DCB=(BLKSIZE=133)
//SYSIN     DD     *
```

Control cards

```
/*
```

Overriding and adding DD statements to catalogued procedures

Each step within a catalogued procedure has a name called the procstepname.
All modifications to data-set definitions for each step must be identified by the
procstepname, and must come before modifications for the next step. Furthermore,
modifications overriding DD statements in the procedure must appear in the same
order as the corresponding statements in the procedure itself, and before additional
definitions for the step. For example, if a procedure step consists of the statements

```
//GØ         EXEC   PGM=*.LKED.SYSLMØD,CØND=((5,LT,FØRT),(5,LT,LKED))
//FT03F001   DD     SYSØUT=A,DCB=(RECFM=VA,BLKSIZE=137)
//FT02F001   DD     UNIT=SYSCP,DCB=(LRECL=80,RECFM=F,BLKSIZE=80)
//FT01F001   DD     DDNAME=SYSIN
```

we may wish in executing this step, to redefine FT02F001 to write a tape instead
of punch cards, and add definitions for data sets SYSUDUMP and FT09F001,
as well as including a data set, to be used as FT01F001, in the main job stream.
The redefinition of FT02F001 must be first, and the inclusion of the data set in the
job stream itself must be last. This data set is included under the name SYSIN;
the definition of FT01F001 essentially *deferred* the definition of FT01F001 until a
later statement; this avoids the conflicting requirements that redefinition of
FT01F001 must come before definition of additional data sets, and that it come

last because it defines a data set in the main job stream. Job control statements to accomplish the modifications and additions are

```
//GØ.FT02F001 DD   UNIT=TAPE9,DISP=(,KEEP),DSNAME=SPECTR21
//GØ.SYSUDUMP DD   SYSØUT=A
//GØ.FT09F001 DD   DISP=ØLD,UNIT=TAPE9,DSNAME=ØBSERV47,
//                 VØLUME=SER=102483
//GØ.SYSIN   DD  *
```

Card data set

```
/*
```

A catalogued procedure for assemble, link-edit, and execute

The reader is by now in a position to understand the catalogued procedure ASMFCLG, which was introduced in Chapter 6. Each installation, in cataloguing its own procedures, makes slight variations to adjust to local conditions, so the procedure we exhibit in Fig. 12–10 will not be identical in all parameters to the one at any particular installation. It is very close to the procedure suggested by

Fig. 12–10   The ASMFCG procedure

```
Notes
  1  //ASM       EXEC  PGM=IFØX00,PARM=ØBJ
  2  //SYSLIB    DD    DSN=SYS1.MACLIB,DISP=ØLD
  3  //SYSUT1    DD    UNIT=SYSSQ,SPACE=(1700,(600,100))
     //SYSUT2    DD    UNIT=SYSSQ,SPACE=(1700,(300,50))
     //SYSUT3    DD    UNIT=SYSSQ,SPACE=(1700,(300,50))
     //SYSPRINT  DD    SYSØUT=A,DCB=(BLKSIZE=1089)
  4  //SYSPUNCH  DD    SYSØUT=B
  5  //SYSGØ     DD    DSN=&&ØBJSET,UNIT=SYSSQ,SPACE=(80,(200,50)),
  6  //                DISP=(MØD,PASS)
  7  //GØ        EXEC  PGM=LØADER,PARM='MAP,PRINT,NØCALL,LET',
  8  //                CØND=(8,LT,ASM)
  9  //SYSLIN    DD    DSN=&&ØBJSET,DISP=(ØLD,DELETE)
 10  //          DD    DDNAME=ØBJECT
     //SYSLØUT   DD    SYSØUT=A
```

Notes

1. IFØX00 is the name of the data set in the system library which contains the assembler.
2. SYS1.MACLIB holds the macros currently defined within the system.
3. SYSSQ (SYStem SeQuential) specifies a class including magnetic tape *and* direct-access devices.
4. In most systems SYSØUT=B directs data toward the card punch.
5. &&ØBJSET is a temporary name, used here for the object program produced by the assembler.
6. DISP=(MØD,PASS) defaults to (NEW,PASS) if the data set cannot be found. MØD is useful if several assemblies or compilations all contribute to the same executable module.
7. PGM=LØADER invokes a program which will link together all the modules necessary to run the assembled program, load them into main storage, and execute the loaded program. The PARM parameters invoke options in the LØADER.
8. The step is executed unless the return code from the ASM step is greater than or equal to 8. A return code of 8 or higher indicates serious assembly errors that result in a non-executable object program.
9. The temporary data set &&ØBJSET created by the assembly is the input to the LØADER.
10. A DD statement without an entry in the name field concatenates the defined data set. In this case, it permits an object deck (or object module anywhere) to be supplied at execution time, and accepted by the loader on an equal basis with the program at &&ØBJSET.

IBM, however (in the manual *IBM System/360 Operating System Assembler F Programmer's Guide*, GC26-3756), so it should be close to any a user may encounter. There are operands that we have not discussed, and they are noted and discussed specifically. The procedure is comprised of two steps. The first assembles a program (input SYSIN, printed listing SYSPRINT, punched object deck SYSPUNCH, data set for immediate link, load, and execute SYSGØ). The second step calls the loader, which links and loads all the object modules presented to it. The assembly of step one produced object modules lodged at &&OBJSET, and others can be supplied under the ddname of ØBJECT. The loader links the modules as it loads them into main storage, ready for execution. Finally it gives control to the assembled and linked program. *All* data set definitions required during execution of the user's program are left to the user; none are provided by the catalogued procedure.

A possible complete job, including the ASMFCG procedure but including reference to a routine in the data set USERLIB and an object deck of another subroutine, is shown in Fig. 12–11. This example is drawn from the questionnaire analysis example discussed previously, and the GØ step data sets are identical to those discussed earlier in that connection.

Fig. 12–11   A complete job, using ASMFCG

```
//QUESTNAR     JØB    (204121),MARCØ.PØLØ,MSGLEVEL=1
//             EXEC   ASMFCG
//ASM.SYSIN    DD     *
```
Program to be assembled
```
/*
//GØ.ØBJECT    DD     DSNAME=USERLIB,DISP=ØLD
//             DD     *
```
Object deck of subroutine
```
/*
//GØ.SYSPRINT  DD     SYSØUT=A,DCB=(BLKSIZE=133)
//GØ.INDATA    DD     DISP=ØLD,UNIT=TAPE9,DSNAME=QUEST215,
//                    VØLUME=SER=102139
//GØ.SYSIN     DD     *
```
Data cards, perhaps control cards for the program
```
/*
```

An inventory update program

Let us now explore an entire problem or at least all input and output pertaining to it. Suppose that we have a reel of tape, call it an inventory master, containing inventory data for a warehouseful of items. Each item has a part number, and the information on the tape is recorded in ascending order by part number. In the record for each item there is, of course, the number of pieces currently on hand, as well as other information such as perhaps number on order and bin location. Periodically, perhaps once or twice a day, perhaps once or twice a week, the inventory file must be brought up to date. Each transaction, such as an order placed, order received, quantity shipped out, change of bin location, is punched into a card, with the part number. The transactions are sorted into part number order (see the next section), and written onto a magnetic tape which we may call the transaction tape. Now the two tapes must be compared and merged into a new inventory master. At the same time a printed listing of exceptional conditions, such as negative quantity on hand, will be printed for human attention, since errors *will* creep in and they must be found and corrected. It is this program that we shall explore.

Suppose that a record on the inventory master or the transaction tape, including the information on one item, is 60 characters, and that the part number is the first eight of the 60 characters. The records may be blocked, perhaps with 1200-character blocks on all tapes. We may use exchange buffering with substitute mode for reading and writing the inventory master records, but we might as well use simple buffering and move mode for reading transaction records. Therefore the DCB macro-instructions can be written

```
ØLDMAST   DCB    DSØRG=PS,RECFM=FB,BFTEK=E,MACRF=GT,BLKSIZE=1200,      X
                 LRECL=60,DDNAME=INVMASØL,EØDAD=FINØLD,BUFNØ=4
NEWMAST   DCB    DSØRG=PS,RECFM=FB,BFTEK=E,MACRF=PT,BLKSIZE=1200,      X
                 LRECL=60,DDNAME=INVMASNW,BUFNØ=4
TRANSACT  DCB    DSØRG=PS,RECFM=FB,BFTEK=S,MACRF=GM,BLKSIZE=1200,      X
                 LRECL=60,DDNAME=SØRTRANS,EØDAD=FINTRAN,BUFNØ=4
EXCEPT    DCB    DSØRG=PS,RECFM=FA,MACRF=PM,BLKSIZE=133,LRECL=133,     X
                 DDNAME=SYSPRINT,BUFNØ=20
```

The inventory update program will be a standard program in the installation, so it will be kept in a library, perhaps under the name INVUPDAT. Supposing that the old inventory master has dsname INVMAS38 and is on tape reel number 202135, and that the sorted transaction tape has dsname TRANS39 and is on tape reel 201604, we see that the complete job control for the job would be

```
//INVUP39   JØB    2136,E.SCRØØGE
//          EXEC   PGM=INVUPDAT
//INVMASØL  DD     DISP=ØLD,UNIT=TAPE9,DSNAME=INVMAS38,
//                 VØLUME=SER=202135
//INVMASNW  DD     DISP=(,KEEP),UNIT=TAPE9,DSNAME=INVMAS39
//SØRTRANS  DD     DISP=ØLD,UNIT=TAPE9,DSNAME=TRANS39,
//                 VØLUME=SER=201604
//SYSPRINT  DD     SYSØUT=A
```

Neither old tape is deleted after use. Old inventory masters and transaction tapes should be kept for about four tapes back, so that if any mishap should destroy the most recent tape or even two tapes, the information could be recreated merely by running the update program a few more times. After a tape is more than five updates out of date, it can be returned to reusable status by the operations staff.

It remains of interest to explore the logic and the input-output manipulations of the program itself. The logic is essentially that of a *merge*: records from the two files are compared, and the one with the lower key is written. If the keys match, they are combined and at least one new record is read. There may be several transactions relating to one item in the inventory, so when an inventory record is updated by a transaction, it is held while another transaction record is read. If a dummy inventory record with key (part number) higher than any real key ends the inventory master tape, we are guaranteed that the transaction file will be exhausted first. Except when a new item is added to the inventory, every transaction should match an inventory master record. The new item case causes problems and requires a whole processing section of its own. We must hope that the new master information *precedes* any further transactions dealing with the new item. A flowchart for the processing, somewhat simplified and naive, is as shown in Fig. 12–12.

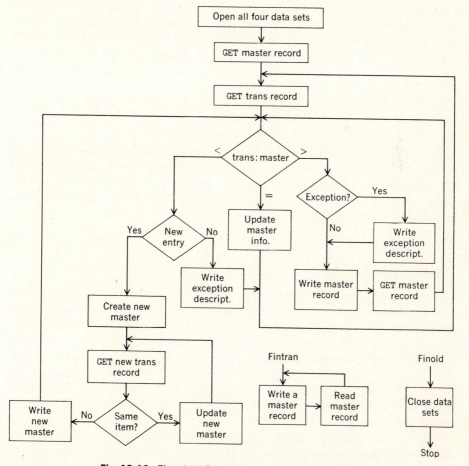

Fig. 12–12 Flowchart for the inventory update program.

Now let us examine a few of the instructions. At the beginning, just after the standard beginning instructions, the data sets are open by

```
ØPEN   (ØLDMAST,INPUT,TRANSACT,INPUT)
ØPEN   (NEWMAST,ØUTPUT,EXCEPT,ØUTPUT)
```

The statements for reading the first records are

```
         LA    2,BUFAREA    AREA SUPPLIED FØR EXCHANGE
         GET   ØLDMAST,(2)  ADDRESS ØF RECØRD IN REG. 1
         LR    4,1            MØVE ADDR. TØ REG. 4
READTR   GET   TRANSACT,TRANSAR
```

These instructions could be followed immediately by

```
CØMPR    CLC   TRANSAR(8),0(4)
```

which compares the first eight characters of the transaction with the first eight characters of the inventory master record. Branches can then lead to various sections of the program. Register 4 will always contain the address of the current inventory master record, and it can be used for addressing the record. Writing a master record and reading a new one are accomplished in substitute mode by

```
         PUT   NEWMAST,(4)
         LR    2,1
         GET   ØLDMAST,(2)
         LR    4,1
```

The address of the record to be written is given to the output routines from register 4, and the address of a substitute area is given in exchange in register 1. The address of this area is immediately moved to register 2 and the area is given to the input processor in return for another inventory master record, whose address is immediately moved to register 4, completing the cycle.

7. SORTING BY MERGING

Sorting methods can be divided into two classes. One class is called *serial*, because each file of items is treated only in a sequential manner. The other class uses items in nonsequential orders, effecting rearrangements or testing keys in various places. Since a method of this class is usually used in the internal storage of a computer, this class is called *internal*. Internal sorts can be most efficient if a fast direct-access storage of sufficient capacity for the entire file is available, but if the file is too large, serial sorts are required. We describe a serial sort in this section, partly to illustrate an important technique and partly to illustrate further input and output methods.

Our procedure accepts an input file on a sequential device, and assumes that we can write as well as read records there. In any one pass, however, we read or write but not both. The sorted file is finally generated on a second device capable of both reading and writing, and two scratch data sets are used internal to the process. Each record is identified with a key, and for brevity we speak of writing the key, when we mean of course writing a record identified with the key. We assume that the actual keys are composed of characters in the EBCDIC format, and order the file so that the keys, considered as unsigned integers, will be in ascending order. A quick glance at a table of EBCDIC representations will assure the reader that alphabetical order is thus preserved, with digits following the alphabet and other special characters sprinkled throughout.

We may speak of a *string* of records, meaning a sequence whose keys are in ascending order. In fact, we mean by "a string" a maximal sequence in ascending order, so that no larger sequence from the file, including the given string, is still a string. Obviously, the entire point of the sort is to merge the whole file into one string, and our procedure does that, in stages. If the entire file is divided into two data sets, a string from one can be merged with a string from the other to form a single string: 04,13,27 and 10,11,16,32 can be merged to form a string 04,10,11, 13,16,27,32. The mechanism is simple: two items, the first from each string, are compared, the one with smaller key is written, and so long as eligible items remain in both strings, another is read to replace in consideration the one just written. When one string is exhausted, the remainder of the other is written.

If there are n strings, approximately $n/2$ in each of two data sets, they can be merged to form $n/2$ strings, and if two output data sets are available, the output can be alternated so that each output data set contains only $n/4$ strings. Furthermore, the data sets are ready for another merge, using the previous output as input and the previous input data sets for output. Each merge pass of this kind is called a *phase*. The file containing n strings can be completely sorted in $[\log_2 n] + 1$ merge phases, where $[\log_2 n]$ represents the largest integer less than the logarithm to the base 2 of n. For example, a file of 300 strings can be sorted in nine phases and a file of 7000 strings in 13 phases. The process is illustrated in Fig. 12–13. The brackets show the strings but have no physical representation in the data sets.

Fig. 12–13　Sort illustration

Data set 1:　01, 27, 82, 34, 33, 69, 11, 87, 92
Data set 2:　19, 12, 74, 53, 58, 84, 95

　　　merge into

Data set 3:　01, 19, 27, 82, 33, 53, 58, 69, 84, 95
Data set 4:　12, 34, 74, 11, 87, 92

　　　merge into

Data set 1:　01, 12, 19, 27, 34, 74, 82
Data set 2:　11, 33, 53, 58, 69, 84, 87, 92, 95

　　　merge into

Data set 3:　01, 11, 12, 19, 27, 33, 34, 53, 58, 69, 74, 82, 84, 87, 92, 95
Data set 4:　——

Figure 12–14 shows a flowchart of the logic of the process. The flowchart is not specific to System/360 or 370, though we follow it shortly with an IBM OS assembler language program. The keys K_0, K_1, and K_2 are central to the process. Keys K_1 and K_2 are keys (associated with records) from the current input data sets f_1 and f_2, respectively. The key just written is K_0, and output continues into the same string so long as either K_1 or K_2 or both are greater than K_0. The section of flowchart headed by SL is thus the heart of the process. When either a new K_1 or K_2 is found to be less than K_0, that key begins a new string; but first the remainder of the current string from the other data set (f_2 or f_1) must be copied to finish the current merged string; that happens in the segment starting at ES.

There are two special values given to keys: 0 and 1. Assuming that real keys are EBCDIC characters, real keys cannot possibly be 0 or 1. The key 1 is used at the beginning of generation of an output string, to make any valid key eligible. A key of 0 is assigned to K_1 or K_2 only if there are no more records in the corresponding data set; this forces continuation of the process solely from the non-empty data set. In particular, at the very beginning when all records are on the original data set f_1, $K_2 = 0$ enables the regular procedure to split the strings from f_1 onto f_3 and f_4.

The process can be generalized from the two-way merge illustrated to an m-way merge, with m input and m output data sets; merging would be from m input data sets simultaneously, and output strings would be cycled among the m output data sets. A complete sort would take $[\log_m n] + 1$ phases.

A program for the sort procedure of Fig. 12–14 is shown in Fig. 12–15. The program follows the flowchart slavishly, except for: (1) method of alternation of direction of data flow, and the influence this method has on all input and output statements, and (2) the method of copying data set 1 to data set 3 if necessary at the end of the process. Therefore we confine our comments mostly to these features of the program.

We need two kinds of alternation of data set references; one is to interchange the pair of DCBs D1 and D2 with D3 and D4, each pair taking its turn as input and then as output. Second, we alternate writing strings between the two data sets which are designated output at the moment. This means that a PUT may be directed at any of four data sets, under control of program logic. It is possible to juggle DCB addresses among registers, and indicate the dcbname to PUT by leaving the DCB address in register 1 (we have not introduced that option before; it is only one of many the serious input/output programmer must learn by studying manuals), but we choose to illustrate instead the technique of using a *transfer vector* to control program choices. Each macro-instruction is treated as an elementary kind of sub-routine, and we use two vectors of branch instructions, one to access each set of macro-instructions. We keep the address of the appropriate transfer vector in register 10, and use that address and a displacement to branch to the correct place

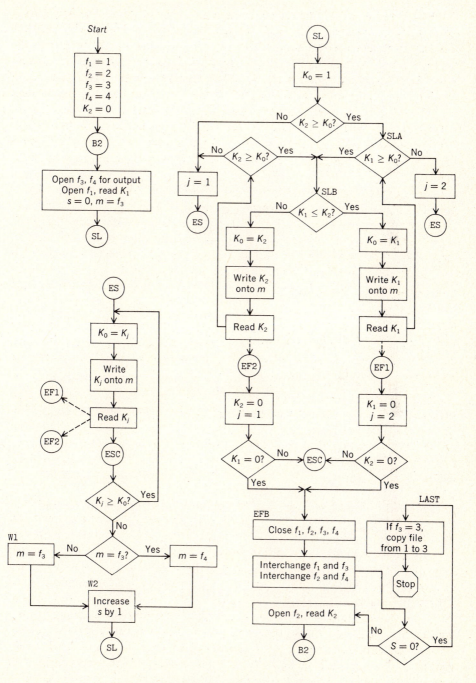

Fig. 12–14 Flowchart of a serial sort.

Fig. 12–15   Program for serial two-way sort

```
*       PRØGRAM USING TWØ-WAY SERIAL SØRT TECHNIQUE
*       INITIAL FILE IS ØN DATA SET D1
*       FINAL SØRTED FILE IS ØN DATA SET D3
*       DATA SETS D1, D2, D3, AND D4 ARE USED TEMPØRARILY.
*       RECØRDS ARE ASSUMED TØ BE NØT MØRE THAN 200 BYTES LØNG,
*       WITH EBCDIC KEYS IN FIRST 6 BYTES.
SERSØRT  START  0
         SAVE   (14,12)
         BALR   12,0
         USING  *,12
         ST     13,SAV+4
         LA     13,SAV
         LA     10,INØUTY    ADDRESS ØF LIST ØF ADDRESSES WHICH
*                            TREAT D1, D2 AS INPUT, D3, D4 AS ØUTPUT
         MVC    K2(6),ZRØ    MAKE D2 UNAVAILABLE FØR FIRST PASS
*       START A NEW PASS
B2       BAL    11,0(10)     ØPEN FILES F1, F3, F4
         BAL    11,8(10)     READ K1
         LA     8,0          REG. 8 CØNTAINS S
         MVC    24(4,10),16(10)     SET M=F3. WRITE ØN F3
*       START A NEW STRING FØR ØUTPUT
SL       MVC    KO(6),ØNE
         CLC    K2(6),KO
         BL     SETJ1        IF K2 LESS THAN KO, BRANCH TØ PRØCESS
*                            F1 ØNLY
SLA      CLC    K1(6),KO
         BL     SETJ2        IF K1 LESS THAN KO, BRANCH TØ PRØCESS
*                            F2 ØNLY
SLB      CLC    K1(6),K2
         BNL    SLC
         MVC    KO(6),K1     IF K1 LØW, SET KO=K1
         LA     2,K1             WRITE K1
         BAL    11,24(10)        ØNTØ CURRENT ØUTPUT STRING
         BAL    11,8(10)         READ ANØTHER K1
         B      SLA
SLC      MVC    KO(6),K2     IF K2 LØW, SIMILAR ØPERATIØNS ØN K2
         LA     2,K2
         BAL    11,24(10)
         BAL    11,12(10)
         CLC    K2(6),KO     MAKE SURE K2 NØT LESS THAN KO
         BNL    SLB
SETJ1    MVC    28(4,10),8(10)     SET INPUT TØ CØNTINUE K1 STRING
         LA     2,K1
         B      ES
SETJ2    MVC    28(4,10),12(10)    SET INPUT TØ CØNTINUE K2 STRING
         LA     2,K2
*       FINISH CURRENT ØUTPUT STRING FRØM ØNE DATA SET
ES       MVC    KO(6),0(2)   KO=K(J)
         BAL    11,24(10)    WRITE K(J)
         BAL    11,28(10)    READ K(J)
ESC      CLC    0(6,2),KO    CØMPARE K(J) WITH KO
         BNL    ES
*       AN ØUTPUT STRING IS CØMPLETE. WRITE NEXT ØN ØTHER
*       DATA SET, STARTING NEW STRING
         CLC    24(4,10),16(10)
         BNE    W1
         MVC    24(4,10),20(10)
         B      W2
W1       MVC    24(4,10),16(10)
W2       LA     8,1(8)
         B      SL
*       END ØF FILE PRØCESSING.
```

(continued)

Fig. 12-15 (continued)

```
EF1        MVC    K1(6),ZRØ    END ØF DATA SET F1
           MVC    28(4,10),12(10)    PREPARE TØ PRØCESS REST ØF F2
           LA     2,K2
           CLC    K2(6),ZRØ    (IF ANY REMAINS)
           BNE    ESC
           B      EFB          AND IF NØT, GØ TØ EFB
EF2        MVC    K2(6),ZRØ    END ØF DATA SET F2
           MVC    28(4,10),8(10)     SIMILARLY
           LA     2,K1
           CLC    K1(6),ZRØ
           BNE    ESC
*     BØTH INPUT DATA SETS EMPTY.  IF FILE NØT IN ØRDER
*     YET, REVERSE SENSE ØF ALL DATA SETS, MERGE AGAIN
EFB        CLØSE  (D1,REREAD,D2,REREAD,D3,REREAD,D4,REREAD)
           C      10,=A(INØUTY)     IF REG. 10 CØNTAINS
           BE     Z1           ADDRESS INØUTY, LØAD INØUTZ
           LA     10,INØUTY    ØTHERWISE, LØAD INØUTY
           B      Z2
Z1         LA     10,INØUTZ
Z2         LTR    8,8
           BE     LAST
           BAL    11,4(10)     ØPEN AND READ FRØM F2
           BAL    11,12(10)
           B      B2
*     IF FULLY SØRTED FILE IS ØN ØRIGINAL DATA SET, SØRT ØNCE MØRE
LAST       C      10,=A(INØUTY)          TØ MØVE IT TØ FINAL DATA SET
           BE     FIN
           MVC    K2(6),ZRØ    NØTE F2 AS INITIALLY EMPTY
           B      B2
FIN        L      13,SAV+4
           RETURN (14,12)
*     MISCELLANEØUS AREAS AND CØNSTANTS
SAV        DS     18F
ZRØ        DC     FL6'0'
ØNE        DC     FL6'1'
K0         DS     CL6
K1         DS     CL200
K2         DS     CL200
*     INPUT AND ØUTPUT STATEMENTS
D1         DCB    DSØRG=PS,RECFM=FB,MACRF=(GM,PM),DDNAME=INFILE,          X
                  EØDAD=EF1
D2         DCB    DSØRG=PS,RECFM=FB,MACRF=(GM,PM),DDNAME=TEMP1,           X
                  EØDAD=EF2
D3         DCB    DSØRG=PS,RECFM=FB,MACRF=(GM,PM),DDNAME=ØUTFILE,         X
                  EØDAD=EF1
D4         DCB    DSØRG=PS,RECFM=FB,MACRF=(GM,PM),DDNAME=TEMP2,           X
                  EØDAD=EF2
*     STATEMENTS TREATING D1, D2 AS INPUT, D3, D4 AS ØUTPUT
ØPENY1     ØPEN   (D1,INPUT)
           ØPEN   (D3,ØUTPUT,D4,ØUTPUT)
           BR     11
ØPENY2     ØPEN   (D2,INPUT)
           BR     11
READY1     GET    D1,K1
           BR     11
READY2     GET    D2,K2
           BR     11
PUTY1      PUT    D3,(2)
           BR     11
PUTY2      PUT    D4,(2)
           BR     11
```

Fig. 12–15 (continued)

```
*     LIST ØF STATEMENTS TØ BRANCH TØ. ADDRESS ØF LIST TØ REG. 10
*
INØUTY   B      ØPENY1     0(10) TØ ØPEN D1, D3, D4
         B      ØPENY2     4(10) TØ ØPEN D2
         B      READY1     8(10) TØ READ D1
         B      READY2     12(10) TØ READ D2
         B      PUTY1      16(10) TØ WRITE D3
         B      PUTY2      20(10) TØ WRITE D4
         DS     CL4        ADDRESS TØ WRITE D3 ØR D4 (M)
         DS     CL4        ADDRESS TØ READ D1 ØR D2 (J)
*     STATEMENTS TREATING D3, D4 AS INPUT, D1, D2 AS ØUTPUT
ØPENZ1   ØPEN   (D3,INPUT,D1,ØUTPUT,D2,ØUTPUT)
         BR     11
ØPENZ2   ØPEN   (D4,INPUT)
         BR     11
READZ1   GET    D3,K1
         BR     11
READZ2   GET    D4,K2
         BR     11
PUTZ1    PUT    D1,(2)
         BR     11
PUTZ2    PUT    D2,(2)
         BR     11
*     LIST ØF STATEMENTS TØ BRANCH TØ. CØRRESPØND TØ PREV. LIST
INØUTZ   B      ØPENZ1
         B      ØPENZ2
         B      READZ1
         B      READZ2
         B      PUTZ1
         B      PUTZ2
         DS     CL8
         END    SERSØRT
```

within the correct transfer vector. For example, suppose that we are treating D1 and D2 as input, and D3 and D4 as output. Then register 10 contains the address INØUTY of one of the transfer vectors. When we wish to read from D1, with the same instruction that will later read from D3, we execute the instruction

$$\text{BAL} \quad 11,8(10)$$

which stores a return address (address of the next instruction) in register 11, and branches into the transfer vector to the instruction

$$\text{B} \quad \text{READY1}$$

which branches to the desired instruction

$$\text{GET} \quad \text{D1,K1}$$

After the GET is taken care of, the instruction

$$\text{BR} \quad 11$$

returns control to the instruction following BAL   1,8(10). Later, when register 10

Fig. 12-16   Job control for a sort

```
//SØRTDATA  JØB   100023,PAUL.BUNYAN,MSGLEVEL=1
//          EXEC  PGM=SERISØRT
//INFILE    DD    DSNAME=RAWDATA,DISP=(ØLD,DELETE),VØLUME=SER=102397,
//                UNIT=TAPE9,DCB=(BLKSIZE=1200,LRECL=60)
//ØUTFILE   DD    DSNAME=SØRT39C,DISP=(NEW,CATLG),UNIT=SYSDA,
//                DCB=(BLKSIZE=900,LRECL=60),SPACE=(900,(800,100))
//TEMP1     DD    UNIT=SYSSQ,DCB=(BLKSIZE=900,LRECL=60),
//                SPACE=(900,(800,100))
//TEMP2     DD    UNIT=SYSSQ,DCB=(BLKSIZE=900,LRECL=60),
//                SPACE=(900,(800,100))
```

contains the address INØUTZ, the same kind of structure will cause

$$\text{GET} \quad \text{D3,K1}$$

to be executed.

For output, the situation is still more complicated, since we wish to output strings alternately to D1 and D2 or to D3 and D4. We accomplish this by alternating the contents of the seventh word in the appropriate transfer vector between

$$\text{B} \quad \text{PUTY1} \quad \text{and} \quad \text{B} \quad \text{PUTY2}$$

or

$$\text{B} \quad \text{PUTZ1} \quad \text{and} \quad \text{B} \quad \text{PUTZ2}$$

if in the other transfer vector. Analogous instructions take care of reading from file f_j.

The final copy loop, putting the file on data set 3, if it is not already there, is accomplished as an ordinary merge phase. Data set 4 is marked empty and not opened, but the regular procedure does everything else correctly, just as it would if one asked in the first place for a sort of an already sorted file.

The job control for a possible execution of this program under the name SERISØRT, is shown in Fig. 12-16. It shows a sort of a tape containing records of 60 characters and blocks of 1200 characters onto a direct access data set catalogued under the name SØRT39C. The two temporary data sets are assigned to the class SYSSQ, which could be either tape units or direct access devices.

8. MAIN IDEAS

a. A user's program requests input and output service from the *supervisor* through macro-instructions written in assembler language. The supervisor honors the requests when possible, protecting data sets from depredations by other programs, finding desired data sets in collaboration with the job scheduler, and taking advantage of all concurrency possible in handling input and output.

b. The supervisor builds a *data control block* for each data set in use. The skeleton is provided by the programmer's DCB macro-instruction, which specifies, among other parameters, a ddname. A DD statement in job control language, identified with that ddname, helps complete the data control block and gives the job scheduler information to help locate or create the data set. If the data set already exists, its label may also help complete the data control block.

c. Data sets can be organized as sequential, indexed sequential, or partitioned, and the IBM System/360 Operating System has access methods to handle each of these organizations.

d. *Logical records* are records desired by the logic of the user's program, but logical records can be *blocked* into larger units for efficient processing. The operating system can deal simultaneously with the user in logical records and with the data set itself in blocks. Logical records in a data set may be of fixed or variable length.

e. An operating system manages concurrency of operations partly by having more than one *buffer* for each data set. The supervisor, in reading a data set, can pull ahead of the program's use of records, storing records in buffers so that future requests can be met immediately. Options for the management of buffers include simple and exchange buffering.

f. Under QSAM (Queued Sequential Access Method) the macro-instructions requesting input and output actions are:

ØPEN	complete the data control block, prepare for action;
GET	retrieve a logical record;
PUT	output a logical record;
CLØSE	terminate processing.

Each refers to a data control block through the name of a DCB macro-instruction. GET and PUT operate in move and substitute mode, which extend the options for management of buffer segments.

g. The DCB macro-instruction contains specifications of many options available to the user, including data-set organization, record form, block size, logical record size, number of buffers allocated, macro forms used, and an address to branch to when a request for a record follows the end of the data set. The operands are summarized in Fig. 12–8.

h. A user specifies in *job control statements* directions about what programs to use, locations of data sets, and other information about data sets that is particular to each run. A user submits a *job*, headed by a JØB statement, to the computer requesting execution in each *job step* with an EXEC statement of a program or a catalogued procedure. Data sets are defined by DD statements for use in each step.

i. Important parameters in JØB statements are accounting information, programmer name, CLASS, MSGLEVEL, and CØND. Important in EXEC statements are program or procedure name, CØND and PARM. A checklist of DD parameters needed for the most common tasks is shown in Fig. 12–17.

Fig. 12-17   Summary of DD parameters by task

Task	Always required	May be necessary
Creating a temporary data set:		
Unit record	UNIT	DCB
Output stream	SYSØUT	DCB,UNIT,SPACE
Tape	UNIT	DCB,VØL
Direct access	UNIT,SPACE	DCB,VØL
Creating a nontemporary data set:		
Tape	UNIT,DISP,DSN	DCB,VØL
Direct access	UNIT,DISP,DSN,SPACE	DCB,VØL
Retrieving a data set:		
Cataloged	DISP,DSN	DCB,UNIT
Noncataloged tape	DISP,DSN,UNIT,VØL	DCB
Noncataloged direct access	DISP,DSN,UNIT,VØL	DCB
Passed data set	DISP,DSN	DCB,UNIT,VØL

j. A *catalogued procedure* allows the user to request simply a standard sequence of programs and associated data sets. However, he may modify and add data-set definitions.

k. Serial sorts are done by merging strings of records whose keys are already in order. When strings can be merged back and forth between two pairs of devices, the sort can be quite efficient.

PROBLEMS FOR REVIEW AND IMAGINATION

1. Think of examples of data sets, preferably from problems in fields related to your own experience, and write DD statements to describe them.

2. A program library is a partitioned data set consisting of members (programs), each of which is a sequential data set. Think of other possible examples of partitioned data sets.

3. Think of data-set organizations you think might be useful that do not fit any of the patterns of organization of sequential, indexed sequential, or partitioned data sets.

4. We have showed blocking, in which the logical record is smaller than the block. The opposite case, where one logical record spans several blocks, is called *spanned records*. Try to imagine what kind of software facilities would be appropriate for handling spanned records, then look up the actual options in the IBM manuals.

5. In addition to move and substitute mode, a *locate* mode is also provided. When input is done under locate mode, the address of the buffer area containing a record is placed by the supervisor in register 1; the program can use the record in place, and the time required to move the record to the user's own area is saved. When the next GET is executed, the supervisor automatically takes back the buffer area in which the previous record was given to the programmer. Output under locate mode requires the user to generate his output record in the buffer area given him (in register 1) by the previous PUT macro-instruction. Think of instances where locate-mode input, output, or both would be advantageous.

6. The order of filling items in a data control block could have been the reverse of the practice implemented in OS/360 and OS/VS. Namely, items from the data set label would have first priority, items not specified there would be taken from the DD statement, and items not specified in either would be filled in from the DCB macro-instruction. This would have the advantage that the DCB macro-instruction could contain a full description of all parameters, which would be controlling unless overridden; any parameter could be overridden by specifications from the other sources. Think of other advantages, and disadvantages of this proposed scheme.

7. In some computing systems no such thing as an EØDAD is provided; if a request for a record is made after the data set is exhausted, the program is terminated. Review the strategems necessary in place of the EØDAD option, and evaluate the relative merits of EØDAD and the other strategems.

8. What would you expect to happen if your program declared register 15 as your implied base register, and also used the input and output macros?

9. Construct for yourself the READATA and PRINT subroutines suggested for use in earlier chapters. Pay special attention to the need to ØPEN a data set the first time a call is made on a subroutine but not thereafter. What about closing the data sets?

10. In what sense, and under what conditions, can a decision about simple or exchange buffering be meaningfully left for the DD statement?

11. In the program CARDCØNV in Fig. 12–9, no provision is made for anything except abnormal termination of the program in the event of an input or output error. Think of circumstances in which some other action would be preferable; what information would you need from the system in order to put your ideas into effect? Design an implementation of your ideas, making assumptions where necessary.

12. The CØND parameter in the EXEC statement gives sharper control of continued executions than the CØND parameter in the JØB statement. Is the provision for a CØND parameter in the JØB statement superfluous, or what are its uses?

13. A data set put on tape at one System/360 or 370 installation can be used at another with the same job control, as if it had been written at the same installation. A data set written on a direct access volume at one installation, however, is certainly not catalogued at another and so must be addressed differently from catalogued direct access data sets. However, each direct access volume has a serial number and a *volume table of contents*, and if directed to the correct volume, the operating system can find any named data set on it. This makes the job control similar to that of a tape data set; write a DD statement for an

uncatalogued data set named FØREIGN on a direct access volume whose serial number is WØRKO3.

14. Trace the creation, passing, and deletion of the various data sets used by ASMFCG. What advantages does PASSing a data set have over cataloguing and then deleting it?

15. Learn about the catalogued procedures available at your installation.

16. The card-to-tape convert program of Fig. 12–9, the sort program of Fig. 12–15, and the inventory update program sketched in Section 6 are not completely compatible in their input and output assumptions, or at least not with the job control presented. Can the problems be taken care of by different job control? Of those that cannot, which would you fix by generalization of the existing programs, and how?

17. The sort program of Fig. 12–15 can benefit from the use of exchange buffering and substitute mode. Make this change to the program for use with all four data sets.

18. If the data sets used by the sort program in Fig. 12–15 are on direct access volumes, the CLØSE (*dcbname*,REREAD), ØPEN sequence takes practically no time. If the data sets are on tape units, this sequence involves a rewind which is time-consuming. Some tape units are capable of reading (but not writing) backwards. This gives us the opportunity to eliminate rewind time. Data sets are written forward, then *read backward;* the backward read can begin immediately, and the other tape drives, having just *been* read backwards, are at the load points and ready to start writing immediately. Note that the *file* is read forward, then backward, alternately. Consider the changes in comparisons and branches that would have to be made, and do what you can toward changing the program to accommodate the backward read.

19. Examine or design internal sort procedures, and then consider hybrid methods. Hybrid methods can be especially valuable during the early phases of a sort; an internal sort can immediately develop strings of significant length, which can afterwards be merged in a serial sort.

20. A Key-Word-In-Context (KWIC) index of, say book titles, indexes each title by every nontrivial word in the title. The entire title is shown in each entry if it is short enough, but the title is shifted so that the key words, which are ordered, form a column. Thus the title *Indians in North America* would be listed three times, once each under "Indians," "North," and "America." The word "in" is a trivial word and nothing is listed under it. A segment of the index might be

```
ENGLAND AFTER THE NORMAN CONQUEST
        INDIANS IN NORTH AMERICA
                     NORTH FROM ALASKA
  JUMPING OVER THE NORTH POLE
```

When a title is shifted over either edge of the column for alignment, it is brought around the other edge, but with a slash to show the boundary, as in

```
AND THE NATIVES OF NORTHERN RHODESIA        /CECIL RHODES
```

Outline, and program as much as seems interesting, the generation of a KWIC index. Pay special attention to data sets and their treatment. The usual procedure is to read items (title plus location information), then to generate all the lines that should appear for that title in the index. Each word must be compared to the "trivial word" list, to determine whether it should generate a line. Then the data set of all lines is sorted by a serial method.

21. Suppose that transcripts of students at a university are to be kept in a data set which is accessible to a computer, probably a magnetic tape. Design an efficient representation or layout of the data set. Then consider the problem of updating the transcripts with a term's grades. Design procedures, DCB macro-instructions, DD statements, and as much program as you like for taking a large mass of unsorted grade reports and updating the transcripts with them.

22. In many situations in which a file is updated, several reports are desired as a by-product. During transcript updating, for example, every student must get a report of his term's work, the dean's office wants a file of everybody's term grades, preferably broken down by sex, the financial aids office wants the grades of every student who has a scholarship or loan, somebody wants the honor roll, somebody else the list of students with grades low enough to flunk out, and so forth. A computer does not have enough printers to print all these lists simultaneously. Should the lists be put on direct access data sets for later printing, one by one, or should the entire file be processed once for each list to be produced? Are there other alternatives? What considerations would guide your decisions on what approach to take?

REFERENCES

IBM OS Linkage Editor and Loader, GC28-6538, IBM Corporation. Descriptions and use instructions for the linkage editor and the loader.

IBM System/360 Operating System Introduction, GC28-6534, IBM Corporation. Overview of operating system services.

IBM System/360 Operating System: Job Control Language Reference, GC28-6704, or *OS/VS JCL Reference*, GC28-0618, IBM Corporation. Complete rules for job control statements and parameters.

IBM System/360 Operating System: Job Control Language, User's Guide, GC28-6703, or *OS/VS JCL Services*, GC28-0617, IBM Corporation. Survey of facilities and options provided through job control language.

Knuth, Donald E., *The Art of Computer Programming, Vol. 1: Fundamental Algorithms*, *2nd ed.* (Reading Mass.: Addison-Wesley, 1974). A good description of input and output techniques, especially buffering.

Knuth, Donald E., *The Art of Computer Programming, Vol. 3: Sorting and Searching* (Reading, Mass.: Addison-Wesley, 1973). A discussion in depth of external sorting and merging techniques.

Martin, William A., "Sorting," *Computing Surveys* **3**, 4 (December 1971), pp. 147–174. A tutorial survey of sorting techniques.

Mealy, G. H., B. I. Witt, and W. A. Clark, "The functional structure of OS/360," *IBM Systems Journal* **5** (1966), pp. 2–51. A study of the then current philosophy and structure.

OS Data Management Macro Instructions, GC26-3794, or *OS/VS Data Management Macro Instructions*, GC26-3793, IBM Corporation. Detailed descriptions of the macros and their parameters.

OS Data Management Services Guide, GC26-3746, or *OS/VS Data Management Services Guide*, GC26-3783, IBM Corporation. More detailed description of services and options.

Chapter 13

Floating-Point Arithmetic

In Chapter 1 the concept of floating-point representation of numbers was introduced, and the floating-point registers and arithmetic capabilities were mentioned.
Since that time, the arithmetic used has been binary integer arithmetic. Binary
integer arithmetic is most useful for address computation and modification, for
counting events (like repetitions of a loop) and for miscellaneous computations
involving fairly small integers. Execution of binary integer arithmetic instructions is fast.

For computations in which numbers of widely varying magnitudes may arise,
integer arithmetic does not suffice; fractions and numbers larger than 2^{32} must
be recorded. In some instances it is possible to keep a portion of a number,
remembering that this portion, represented as an integer, is really some scale
factor—a power of 2 or 10—times the true value of the number represented.
Programming must then take account of the scale factors. This becomes quite
burdensome. The floating-point representation is a major blessing: In accord
with the principle that the computer is to do as much of our clerical work as
possible, the floating-point representation allows the computer to keep a scale
factor, which we call a *characteristic*, with the number, and automatically take
account of scale factors in all arithmetic operations, attaching the correct scale
factor to the result.

This chapter explains floating-point representation in System/360 and 370
in more detail than in Chapter 1, and discusses the floating-point arithmetic
instructions. Examples show conversions between integer and floating-point
representations, and the analysis of a regression problem.

1. REPRESENTATIONS OF FLOATING-POINT NUMBERS

Floating-point quantities in the IBM System/360 may occupy either 32 or 64
bits, and are called *short* and *long*, respectively, or sometimes *single-* or *double-
precision*. In either case, the first bit in position 0 represents the sign of the number:
0 for positive numbers, 1 for negative numbers. The bits in positions 1–7 are the
characteristic; we shall return to an explanation of the characteristic shortly.

The remaining bits of the floating-point number, either in positions 8–31 in the case of a short floating-point number or in positions 8–63 in the case of a long floating-point number, contain what is called the *fraction,* or sometimes the *mantissa.* The fraction is always recorded as a positive number; negative floating-point numbers are *not* represented in complement form. The (binary) point of the fraction is understood to be just before bit position 8. That is to say, a digit 1 in bit position 8 represents 2^{-1}, a digit 1 in bit position 9 represents 2^{-2}, etc.

A floating-point number is represented by its fraction times a power of 16, with its sign attached to the result. The exponent indicating the power of 16 by which the fraction is multiplied is coded in the characteristic. The characteristic, in bit positions 1–7 of the representation, can hold numbers ranging from 0 to (decimal) 127. The characteristic is coded in what is called *excess-64* notation, meaning that the characteristic is 64 greater than the exponent. Thus a characteristic of 66 represents an exponent of $66 - 64 = 2$, and the magnitude of the floating-point number is the fraction $\times 16^2$. Similarly, a characteristic of 61 represents an exponent of $61 - 64 = -3$, and the magnitude of the floating-point number with a characteristic of 61 is the fraction $\times 16^{-3}$. The excess-64 notation is used so that a wide range of magnitudes, roughly from 16^{-64} to 16^{63}, can be represented.

The quantity 64 (or hexadecimal 40) is also sometimes called a *bias quantity.* Another way of considering the characteristic is to say that the exponent is coded in 2's complement notation, except that a 0 in bit position 1, the sign position of the characteristic, represents a *minus* sign and a 1 represents a plus sign.

Some examples of System/360 and 370 floating-point numbers should help to clarify the representation. First are several examples of short floating-point numbers, shown in binary. The pattern

$$0 \quad 1000000 \quad 10000000 \quad 00000000 \quad 00000000$$

sign   charac-   fraction
        teristic

includes a characteristic of 64 (2^6 or hexadecimal 40) and therefore an exponent of 0. The fraction is (binary) $.1000 \ldots$, or 2^{-1}, or decimal 0.50. Therefore, since the sign bit of 0 denotes a positive number, the number represented is $+.5 \times 16^0 = 0.50$. The pattern

$$1 \quad 1000001 \quad 01010100 \quad 00000000 \quad 00000000$$

includes a characteristic of 65 and thereby codes an exponent of 1. The fraction is $.010101 = 2^{-2} + 2^{-4} + 2^{-6}$. The sign bit of 1 denotes a negative number, so the quantity represented by this pattern is $-(2^{-2} + 2^{-4} + 2^{-6}) \times 16^1 = -(2^2 + 2^0 + 2^{-2}) = -(4 + 1 + 0.25) = -5.25$. The pattern

$$0 \quad 0111111 \quad 11001100 \quad 11001100 \quad 11001100$$

includes a characteristic of 63 (hexadecimal 3F) and thereby codes an exponent of -1. Therefore the magnitude of the number is the fraction times 16^{-1}. As the reader can verify, the fraction is the first 24 bits of the binary representation of 0.8, which cannot be represented exactly by a finite binary expansion. The number represented by the pattern is thus an approximation to $+16^{-1} \times 0.8 = 0.05$.

Systems 360 and 370 can be called hexadecimal machines, and it is helpful to think of floating-point representation in this light. Since the exponent is a power of 16, adding one to the exponent multiplies the quantity represented by 16. Thus in some sense the numbers represented in floating-point by the patterns (in hexadecimal)

$$4162E0A0 \quad \text{and} \quad 42062E0A$$

are the same.

Let us now examine some long floating-point representations, and do it in hexadecimal to avoid writing 64 binary bits. The pattern

$$436D1000 \quad 00000000$$

includes a sign of 0, or plus, since the first hexadecimal digit is less than 8. The characteristic is hexadecimal 43 or decimal 67, so the exponent is $+3$. The fraction is (.)6D100000000000, so the entire quantity represented is (still in hexadecimal) 6D1.00000000000. The reader can verify that this number is the decimal number 1745. The pattern

$$BE34A20B \quad 68F1998C$$

represents a negative number since the first hexadecimal digit is greater than 8. The characteristic is 3E, or decimal 62, and codes an exponent of $62 - 64 = -2$. The fraction is (.)34A20B68F1998C, so the quantity represented by the full pattern is, in hexadecimal, $-.0034A20B68F1998C$.

Users of IBM System/360 Model 85 or System/370 computers also have access to *extended-precision* floating-point, in which each number is represented in 128 bits. Other installations may make extended-precision floating-point available by macros and interrupt routines. Extended-precision floating-point is presented in Section 9, but will be ignored until then.

Normalization

The representation of a nonzero floating-point number is said to be *normalized* if the first (high-order) hexadecimal digit of its fraction is not zero. It is almost always to our advantage to keep and generate numbers in normalized form, since this gives us the most digits of precision in our numbers (the digits we keep may not all be correct, but we generally make less error by keeping inexact digits than by throwing them away). The number 4162E0A0 is normalized, since the first hexadecimal digit of its fraction, 6, is nonzero. The equivalent number 42062E0A is not normalized.

Normalized nonzero floating-point numbers in System/360 and 370 can represent quantities whose magnitudes are

$$16^{-65} \quad \text{to} \quad (1 - 16^{-6}) \cdot 16^{63} \qquad \text{in short form}$$

and

$$16^{-65} \quad \text{to} \quad (1 - 16^{-14}) \cdot 16^{63} \qquad \text{in long form.}$$

Magnitudes of nonnormalized floating-point numbers can range down to 16^{-70} in short form and to 16^{-78} in the long form. The reader should verify these assertions by writing representations of the smallest and largest numbers possible and finding the corresponding magnitudes.

In most other computers, floating-point binary representations include an exponent which is a power of 2. That is, adding 1 to the exponent multiplies the quantity represented by 2. In these computers, normalization means that the highest-order binary bit of the (nonzero) fraction is nonzero. Since the exponent in System/360 and 370 is a power of 16, it is not possible to represent every number in such a way that the high-order bit of its fraction is nonzero. Normalized representations of some numbers (1.0, for example) have three leading zeros in the fraction.

When a number has a zero fraction, zero characteristic, and plus sign, it is called a *true zero*. When a zero fraction results from most floating-point operations, a true zero is forced. In any case, when the fraction in the result is zero, the sign of the result will be set positive.

The reader is urged to refer to Section 6.2 at this point to refresh his memory of the definition of floating-point constants, types E and D, in assembler language.

2. FLOATING-POINT REGISTERS; LOAD AND STORE INSTRUCTIONS

There are four floating-point registers in System/360 and 370, as was mentioned in Chapter 1. The registers are each 64 bits long, and thus are capable of holding and working with either short or long floating-point numbers. The addresses of the four registers are 0, 2, 4, and 6.

We now begin a description of the floating-point instructions. Since all floating-point arithmetic is done in registers, all the instructions are of RR or RX type. But since floating-point numbers are stored in main storage as bit patterns just like any other information, any instructions can operate on floating-point numbers. The MVC instruction, for example, can move floating-point numbers from one place to another within main storage.

In all floating-point instructions to be introduced in this chapter, the registers specified are floating-point registers. This must be understood as part of the specification of the instructions.

Addresses of main storage operands (S2) are formed as in other RX-type instructions; the *general registers* contain X2 and B2, which are used in the address computations. The main storage address S2 of any short-precision RX-type instruction must be divisible by 4, placing the operand on a full-word boundary. The main storage address S2 of any long-precision RX-type instruction must be divisible by 8, placing the operand on a double-word boundary.

First we introduce the floating-point load instructions. There is a group of four instructions which load a floating-point register but do not set a condition code. Two load a short floating-point number (32 bits) and two load a long floating-point number; two load from main storage and two from floating-point registers. The instructions are as follows, if we denote a floating-point register as *FPR1* when used as first operand and as *FPR2* when used as second operand.

Instruction	Type	Action
LER	RR	$FPR1 \leftarrow c(FPR2)$
LE	RX	$FPR1 \leftarrow c(S2)$
LDR	RR	$FPR1_{0-63} \leftarrow c(FPR2)_{0-63}$
LD	RX	$FPR1_{0-63} \leftarrow c(S2)_{0-63}$

The LER and LDR instructions load a (floating-point) register from a (floating-point) register, and the LE and LD instructions load a register from main storage. The LER and LE instructions load a short floating-point number into the high-order 32 bits of the 64-bit floating-point register, *leaving the low-order 32 bits unchanged*. The LDR and LD instructions load all 64 bits of the register.

There are helpful consistencies in the naming of floating-point instructions. All the RR-type instructions have mnemonic assembler-language ,names ending in R, but none of the RX-type instructions do. The short-precision instructions contain the letter E, and the corresponding long-precision instructions the letter D. Besides, the function of the instruction is suggested in the name: L for Load, ST for STore, A for Add, M for Multiply, etc.

If main storage locations and registers have initial contents (hexadecimal)

Location	BETA:	41100000 00000000	(on double-word boundary)
	GSQ:	3F3429E2 9B76C870	(on double-word boundary)
	GSQ+8:	C5113D6A BD473F88	
General register	3:	00000008	
Floating-point			
register	0:	42326EE4 00000000	
	2:	D0F63984 7B38C420	
	4:	BC98624B 8849CF01	
	6:	40CCCCCC 44444440	

before each of the following instructions, the instructions will have the effects indicated:

Instruction		Register	New contents	
LE	4,BETA	4	41100000	8849CF01
LD	6,BETA	6	41100000	00000000
LER	0,2	0	D0F63984	00000000
LDR	6,2	6	D0F63984	7B38C420
LD	2,GSQ(3)	2	C5113D6A	BD473F88
LE	4,GSQ+4	0	9B76C870	8849CF01

Note that the first, third, and sixth of these instructions leave unchanged the low-order halves of their first operand registers. The sixth instruction, LE   4,GSQ+4, is legal since GSQ+4 defines a full-word boundary; LD   4,GSQ+4 would *not* be legal since the LD instruction requires a double-word boundary.

The next group of load instructions are all of RR type, and set a condition code. There are short-precision and long-precision forms, and they correspond to the integer instructions LTR, LCR, LPR, and LNR. They can be described as

Instruction	Type	Action	Condition code
LTER	RR	$FPR1 \leftarrow c(FPR2)$	Yes
LTDR	RR	$FPR1_{0-63} \leftarrow c(FPR2)_{0-63}$	Yes
LCER	RR	$FPR1 \leftarrow -c(FPR2)$	Yes
LCDR	RR	$FPR1_{0-63} \leftarrow -c(FPR2)_{0-63}$	Yes
LPER	RR	$FPR1 \leftarrow \|c(FPR2)\|$	Yes
LPDR	RR	$FPR1_{0-63} \leftarrow \|c(FPR2)_{0-63}\|$	Yes
LNER	RR	$FPR1 \leftarrow -\|c(FPR2)\|$	Yes
LNDR	RR	$FPR1_{0-63} \leftarrow -\|c(FPR2)_{0-63}\|$	Yes

The LTER and LTDR do exactly the same operations as the LER and LDR instructions, respectively, except that LTER and LTDR set the condition code. The other six instructions, LCER, LCDR, LPER, LPDR, LNER, and LNDR, all load a floating-point register from a (same or different) floating-point register, but perform various operations on the sign of the result. Since the numbers are represented in sign-and-absolute-value form, changing the sign of a number results in complementing only the bit in position 0 of the result register. The LCER and LCDR instructions change the sign of the number; the LPER and LPDR instructions set the sign bit to 0 (making the number positive) regardless of its previous value; the LNER and LNDR instructions set the sign bit to 1, making the number negative regardless of its previous value. A true zero can be changed into a negative zero by the LCER, LCDR, LNER, or LNDR instructions; the sign bit is changed or set to 1 regardless of the value of the number.

After the instruction has loaded a register with its new contents, the sign and fraction of the number are tested, and the condition code is set accordingly. The same condition code, in PSW bits 34 and 35, is used for floating-point instructions as for any other. The settings of the condition code are also similar to the settings resulting from other instructions:

CC = 0   if the fraction is zero,
CC = 1   if the result is less than zero (fraction nonzero, sign = 1),
CC = 2   if the result is greater than zero (fraction nonzero, sign = 0),
CC = 3   is not used.

No overflow is possible in this set of instructions, since the fraction is never changed. In the short-precision instructions, the low-order 32 bits of the floating-point result register are neither changed nor tested.

If the floating-point registers have initial contents

Floating-point register 0:   42326E24   00000000
2:    D0F63984   7B38C420
4:    BC98624B   8849CF01
6:    00000000   00000000

before *each* of the following instructions or instruction pairs, the results will be as shown:

Instruction		Register	New contents		Cond. code
a) LTER	0,2	0	D0F63984	00000000	1
b) LTDR	4,6	4	00000000	00000000	0
c) LCER	0,4	0	3C98624B	00000000	2
d) LCDR	2,0	2	C2326E24	00000000	1
e) LPER	4,6	4	00000000	8849CF01	0
f) LER	4,6				
LPDR	4,4	4	00000000	8849CF01	2
g) LNER	4,6	4	80000000	8849CF01	0
h) LNDR	4,2	4	D0F63984	7B38C420	1
i) LNDR	4,0	4	C2326E24	00000000	1
j) LPDR	4,2	4	50F63984	7B38C420	2
k) LCER	2,6	2	80000000	7B38C420	0
l) LCDR	4,4	4	3C98624B	8849CF01	2

Note the settings of the condition code in the various cases: the single-precision instructions load *and test* only the high-order portions of their registers; tests can yield zeros when the sign is negative.

Finally, we introduce the two store instructions. They are of RX type, for storing either short- or long-precision floating-point numbers from the floating-point registers into main storage. The instructions are

Instruction	Type	Action	
STE	RX	$S2$	$\leftarrow c(FPR1)$
STD	RX	$S2_{0-63}$	$\leftarrow c(FPR1)_{0-63}$

The STE instruction requires a main storage address on a full-word boundary; the STD instruction requires a double-word boundary. Neither instruction affects the condition code. The first operand remains unchanged by either instruction. If floating-point register 2 contains D0F63984   7B38C420,

$$STE \quad 2, GAMMA$$

will cause D0F63984 to be stored at GAMMA, and the instruction

$$STD \quad 2, ALPHA$$

will cause D0F63984   7B38C420 to be stored at ALPHA, assuming that there is correct boundary alignment for GAMMA and ALPHA.

3. FLOATING-POINT ADD, SUBTRACT, AND COMPARE INSTRUCTIONS

In this section we discuss the normalized add and subtract instructions and the compare instructions; unnormalized addition and subtraction are left until Section 5. Normalized add, subtract, and compare instructions of RR and RX types permit the second operand to be either in a floating-point register or in main storage. Short-precision and long-precision forms are provided. We first give a gross description of the process.

If we understand that $+$ and $-$ denote floating-point operations, the instructions can be described as shown in Fig. 13–1.

The operations of addition and subtraction take account of sign, characteristic, and fraction in producing the result. The short-precision addition and sub-

Fig. 13-1 Action of floating-point add, subtract, and compare instructions

Instruction	Type	Action	Cond. code set
AER	RR	$FPR1 \leftarrow c(FPR1) + c(FPR2)$	Yes
AE	RX	$FPR1 \leftarrow c(FPR1) + c(S2)$	Yes
ADR	RR	$FPR1_{0-63} \leftarrow c(FPR1)_{0-63} + c(FPR2)_{0-63}$	Yes
AD	RX	$FPR1_{0-63} \leftarrow c(FPR1)_{0-63} + c(S2)_{0-63}$	Yes
SER	RR	$FPR1 \leftarrow c(FPR1) - c(FPR2)$	Yes
SE	RX	$FPR1 \leftarrow c(FPR1) - c(S2)$	Yes
SDR	RR	$FPR1_{0-63} \leftarrow c(FPR1)_{0-63} - c(FPR2)_{0-63}$	Yes
SD	RX	$FPR1_{0-63} \leftarrow c(FPR1)_{0-63} - c(S2)_{0-63}$	Yes
CER	RR	——	Yes
CE	RX	——	Yes
CDR	RR	——	Yes
CD	RX	——	Yes

traction operations, AER, AE, SER, and SE, change only the high-order 32 bits of the first operand register; the low-order 32 bits remain unchanged. Condition codes are set by the addition and subtraction operations as follows:

if the result fraction is zero, the condition code is set to 0;
if the result is less than zero, the condition code is set to 1;
if the result is greater than zero, the condition code is set to 2;
condition code 3 is not used.

The whole purpose of a compare instruction is to set a condition code. The result of the comparison is as if the two operands were subtracted; thus the condition codes set by the compare instructions are:

if the first operand equals the second operand, the condition code is set to 0;
if the first operand is less than the second operand, the condition code is set to 1;
if the first operand is greater than the second operand, the condition code is set to 2.

Some examples will illustrate the behavior of the instructions. If contents of registers and storage locations are (hexadecimal)

Floating point register	0:	41100000	00000000
	2:	BCCCCCCC	CCCCCCCC
	4:	C41362E5	23A97230
	6:	3E450000	4594FDC1
Main storage location	GRAD:	C41362E5	1347B8E0
	BSQ:	41484000	
	GBD:	441362E5	00000000
	GRAB:	BEC00000	00000123

before *each* of the following instructions, results will be as follows:

Instruction		Register	New Contents		Cond. Code
a) AE	0,BSQ	0	41584000	00000000	2
b) SE	0,BSQ	0	C1384000	00000000	1
c) ADR	0,6	0	41100450	0004594F	2
d) AE	4,GBD	4	00000000	23A97230	0
e) AD	4,GBD	4	BE23A972	30000000	1
f) SD	6,GRAB	6	3F105000	04594FEE	2
g) AER	2,6	2	3E443333	CCCCCCCC	2
h) SER	2,6	2	BE45CCCC	CCCCCCCC	1
i) SER	6,2	6	3E45CCCC	4594FDC1	2
j) SDR	6,2	6	3E45CCCD	1261CA8D	2
k) CER	0,6				2
l) CE	4,GBD				1
m) CE	4,GRAD				0
n) CD	4,GRAD				1
o) CDR	2,4				2

The reader is urged to verify, from the definition of the floating-point representation and the gross description of the instructions, the essential correctness of these results. If the reader is puzzled by the last digit or so of the result, the description we shall give next of the procedure followed by the floating-point instructions should clear up most questions.

In more detail then, floating-point addition and subtraction are performed as follows. First the second operand is moved to a special nonaddressable working register; this improves access to the operand in subsequent steps of the process and allows the original operand to be left unchanged. Actually, both operands are moved to special registers, but this need not concern us. We shall ignore these special registers in all further discussion; we mentioned them only to show that the second operand is not changed in its original location. Next there is a comparison of characteristics; the fraction of the number with the smaller characteristic is shifted right a number of hexadecimal characters equal to the difference. We may call this an *alignment* step. Thus if the first operand has a characteristic of 42 and the second operand a characteristic of 45, the fraction of the first operand is shifted right three hexadecimal positions or twelve bits.

Next, addition or subtraction of the fractions takes place, depending in the usual way on the signs of the operands and whether an add or subtract instruction was ordered. The sum or difference is formed in the first operand register, and the larger characteristic of the two characteristics is inserted. The correct sign of the result is inserted.

Either of two special actions may be necessary to complete the second step. If the fraction is zero and the fourth bit of the program mask (more about that later) is 0, a zero characteristic and sign are inserted, leaving a true zero. The condition code is also set to zero. The second case is one in which addition of the two fractions produced a carry out of the high-order hexadecimal digit (or high-order bit, which amounts to the same thing). In this case, all digits of the fraction are shifted right one hexadecimal position or four bit positions, truncating the number *without* rounding, and a hexadecimal 1 is inserted as the highest-order hexadecimal digit of the fraction. The characteristic is increased by 1 to record the shift, and this can cause an exponent overflow.

Thus, in the addition of the numbers 41C12345 and 41523456, the sum of the fractions is

$$
\begin{array}{r}
\text{C12345} \\
\text{523456} \\
\hline
\text{113579B}
\end{array}
$$

where the first 1 of the sum represents a carry. The result cannot hold all these digits, so the result given is 42113579. The digit B is lost, and the preceding digit, 9, is *not* rounded up to A.

The third step, called *normalization*, consists of a loop of the following actions given that the fraction is nonzero. The high-order hexadecimal digit is examined; if it is nonzero, normalization is finished. If it is zero, all digits of the fraction are shifted *left* one hexadecimal position, and the characteristic is correspondingly *decreased* by 1. The process of examining digits, shifting the fraction left, and decreasing the characteristic is continued until the high-order hexadecimal digit of the fraction becomes nonzero. The condition code is set according to the sign of the result.

In the addition of 41C12345 and C1C10123 we see that the signs are different, so the fractions are subtracted. The result of the subtraction is

$$
\begin{array}{r}
C12345 \\
- \ C10123 \\
\hline
002222
\end{array}
$$

to which the characteristic 41 is attached. The normalization process requires two shifts, and the final result is 3F222200.

In every short- or long-precision floating-point arithmetic operation, each operand is furnished with a *guard digit*. The guard digit is essentially a hexadecimal digit just after the regular (6 or 14) digits of the fraction. The guard digit for each operand is zero at the beginning of an operation, but during the alignment step, digits shifted right go through the guard-digit position. Therefore the last digit shifted out of the normal part of the register is saved as a guard digit. The guard digits participate in addition, subtraction, and comparison, and during the normalization step the guard digit may reappear into the regular part of the result register. Thus addition of 4210778A and C1112217 is done as follows, with the guard digit shown in brackets:

Alignment:	4210778A	[0]
	C1011221	[7]
Addition yields:	420F6568	[9]
Normalization:	41F65689	[0]

and the final result is 41F65689. The guard digit provides one more hexadecimal digit of accuracy than would be kept otherwise.

Action of the compare instructions can be thought of as being exactly like the action of the corresponding subtract instructions.

It remains only to point out the behavior of the instructions when presented with unnormalized operands. The steps are exactly as have been described above, which has certain consequences. During the alignment step, the number with the smaller characteristic is shifted right, even though it might be possible to align the numbers by shifting the other left (which would be called prenormalization). Therefore the numbers 44000100 and 41100000 are equal and will be recorded as equal by a compare instruction, but so will the numbers 44000100 and 411000FF. The alignment step yields

44000100 [0]
44000100 [0] FF → lost,

which obviously leaves the numbers equal. Note that the guard digit would prevent 44000100 and 41100100 from being called equal.

Complete normalization is carried out after addition or subtraction, regardless of whether one or both operands were unnormalized.

4. FLOATING-POINT MULTIPLY AND DIVIDE

Multiplication and division instructions are provided for floating-point numbers, four of each, which include all combinations of RR- and RX-type, single- and double-precision. There are also two Halve instructions. We may represent the instructions in tabular form as follows, but the table must be understood to be only an outline or point of departure for the necessary discussion of the features of the instructions.

Instruction	Type	Action	Cond. Code Set
MER	RR	$FPR1_{0-63} \leftarrow c(FPR1) \qquad \times c(FPR2)$	No
ME	RX	$FPR1_{0-63} \leftarrow c(FPR1) \qquad \times c(S2)$	No
MDR	RR	$FPR1_{0-63} \leftarrow c(FPR1)_{0-63} \times c(FPR2)_{0-63}$	No
MD	RX	$FPR1_{0-63} \leftarrow c(FPR1)_{0-63} \times c(S2)_{0-63}$	No
DER	RR	$FPR1 \qquad \leftarrow c(FPR1) \qquad / \quad c(FPR2)$	No
DE	RX	$FPR1 \qquad \leftarrow c(FPR1) \qquad / \quad c(S2)$	No
DDR	RR	$FPR1_{0-63} \leftarrow c(FPR1)_{0-63} \; / \; c(FPR2)_{0-63}$	No
DD	RX	$FPR1_{0-63} \leftarrow c(FPR1)_{0-63} \; / \; c(S2)_{0-63}$	No
HER	RR	$FPR1 \qquad \leftarrow c(FPR2)/2$	No
HDR	RR	$FPR1_{0-63} \leftarrow c(FPR2)_{0-63}/2$	No

Prior to multiplication, both operands are normalized; this step is called *prenormalization*. The multiplication step itself involves a characteristic addition (and subtraction of the bias quantity 64 or hexadecimal 40 from the sum) and a fraction multiplication. Only 24 bits of fraction from each operand take part in short-precision multiplication, but the full floating-point register is used for the product. The fraction product is 48 bits long, so the low-order eight bits of the full register will always be zero. In a double-precision multiply instruction, all 56 fraction bits of each operand take part. The product is truncated to 60 bits (including a guard digit). In either a short-precision or long-precision multiplication, post-normalization finishes the operation. The highest-order digit of the intermediate product may be zero (but not more than the highest-order digit unless the entire fraction is zero; why?), so one normalizing shift of four bits (including, in long-precision multiplication, shift of the guard digit into the four low-order bit positions of the register) and a corresponding reduction of the characteristic by 1 may be necessary. The ordinary rule of signs governs the result; in other words, an EXCLUSIVE OR is performed on the sign bits of the operands to yield the sign of the product. However, if all bits of the fraction of the result are zeros, a true zero is forced.

We illustrate this with a few examples. If floating-point register 0 contains 41200000 00000000 and CHI contains 42335421 23001632, execution of ME   0,CHI will take place in the following steps:

Prenormalization:	none necessary
Multiplication:	200000 × 335421 = 066A8420000000
Characteristic:	41 + 42 − 40 = 43
Sign:	0 (EXCLUSIVE OR) 0 = 0
Yielding a result:	43066A84 20000000
Postnormalization:	4266A842 00000000

With the same initial contents, execution of MD   0,CHI will be:

Prenormalization:	none
Multiplication:	200000 00000000 × 335421 23001632 =
	066A84 246002C6 40000000 000000

Characteristic and sign as above, yielding

43066A84 246002C6 [4]

Postnormalization:	4266A842 46002C64

Note the contribution of the guard digit. If floating-point register 4 contains AE000900 12345678, execution of MER   4,0 proceeds as follows:

Prenormalization:	register 4 (or special register)
	becomes AB900000 12345678
Multiplication:	900000 × 200000 = 120000 00000000
Characteristic:	2B + 41 − 40 = 2C
Sign:	1 (EXCLUSIVE OR) 0 = 1
Yielding:	AC120000 00000000.

No postnormalization is necessary.

In the divide operations the first operand is divided by the second operand; the quotient replaces the first operand, and no remainder is preserved. In short-precision only the 24 bits of each short floating-point number participate, and the low-order half of the first operand register remains unchanged. The process of division involves first prenormalization of both operands, then division of the fractions and subtraction of the characteristics (and addition of the bias quantity to the difference; why?) and adjustment of the sign of the quotient. Postnormalization is never necessary, but a right shift of one hexadecimal digit may be necessary, as we shall see.

Suppose floating-point register 0 contains 41400000 00000000, and SIX contains 41600000 00000000. Then execution of DE   0,SIX will be as follows:

	No prenormalization is necessary
Division:	400000/600000 = AAAAAA
Characteristic:	41 − 41 + 40 = 40
Sign:	0 (EXCLUSIVE OR) 0 = 0

yielding a result of 40AAAAAA, an approximation to 2/3. Next, suppose that floating-point register 6 contains C4300000 00000000. Execution of DDR 0,6 is as follows:

No prenormalization is needed
Division: 400000 00000000/300000 00000000
Yields: 1555555 55555555, where the 1, as normally developed, is in a carry position.
Characteristic: 41 − 44 + 40 = 3D
Sign: 0 (EXCLUSIVE OR) 1 = 1
Yielding an intermediate result of
BD(1)555555 55555555.

A right shift to make room for the leading digit of quotient yields a final result of BE155555 55555555.

There are also "Halve" operations, HER and HDR, which divide a short or long, respectively, second operand by 2 and place the result in the first operand register. The result is always identical to that upon a regular division by 2.

5. UNNORMALIZED ADD AND SUBTRACT OPERATIONS

System/360 and 370, like many other computers, have a set of instructions which perform addition and subtraction in exactly the same way as the ordinary add and subtract instructions except that no normalization step takes place after the intermediate sum is developed. A carry from the high-order digit in the addition causes a right shift, but if the fraction contains any leading zeros, they remain.

The instructions are as follows, where the lack of normalization is understood:

Instruction	Type	Action				Cond. code set
AUR	RR	$FPR1$	$\leftarrow c(FPR1)$		$+ c(FPR2)$	Yes
AU	RX	$FPR1$	$\leftarrow c(FPR1)$		$+ c(S2)$	Yes
AWR	RR	$FPR1_{0-63}$	$\leftarrow c(FPR1)_{0-63}$	$+ c(FPR2)_{0-63}$		Yes
AW	RX	$FPR1_{0-63}$	$\leftarrow c(FPR1)_{0-63}$	$+ c(S2)_{0-63}$		Yes
SUR	RR	$FPR1$	$\leftarrow c(FPR1)$		$- c(FPR2)$	Yes
SU	RX	$FPR1$	$\leftarrow c(FPR1)$		$- c(S2)$	Yes
SWR	RR	$FPR1_{0-63}$	$\leftarrow c(FPR1)_{0-63}$	$- c(FPR2)_{0-63}$		Yes
SW	RX	$FPR1_{0-63}$	$\leftarrow c(FPR1)_{0-63}$	$- c(S2)_{0-63}$		Yes

The mnemonic operation codes are designed to help the user remember the right instruction; U is inserted in place of E to stand for Unnormalized, and W is inserted as a convenient pun (DOUBLE-U) standing for Double-precision Unnormalized.

For example, if floating-point register 0 contains 44100022   3456789A and HP contains C3FFC834, the instruction AU   0,HP will proceed:

Alignment:	second operand fraction becomes 0FFC83 [4]
Addition:	100022 [0]
	− 0FFC83 [4]
	00039E [C]

The insertion of sign and characteristic 44 leaves the result in floating-point register 0: 4400039E   3456789A, and the condition code is set to 2. All operations standard to floating-point addition have taken place except normalization. Note that the guard digit never has a chance to enter the result of an unnormalized operation.

Uses for the regular addition, subtraction, multiplication, and division instructions are reasonably evident. Uses for unnormalized numbers and unnormalized operations are more obscure, so some uses should be mentioned here.

One use for unnormalized numbers is the intentional truncation of numbers. For example, suppose that we have a short floating-point number TSUB in main storage, and we want its integer part. Its integer part can be put at TSUBINT by

```
LE     0,UNFLZ        UNFLZ=X'47000000'
AE     0,TSUB
STE    0,TSUBINT
```

The constant X'47000000' (we assume the correct boundary) is an unnormalized zero; if TSUB is, for example, 44345F9E, action of the addition instruction is

Alignment:	the fraction of TSUB is shifted right 47 − 44 = 3:
	000345 [F]
Addition:	000000 [0] + 000345 [F] = 000345 [F]
Normalization:	44345F00.

The fraction digits representing negative powers of 16 (we call this the *fractional part*) are lost during the alignment step. If TSUB had been a negative number, the action of the fraction would be exactly the same; we say that rounding *toward zero* takes place. The reader can verify that the sequence of three instructions above will not affect a number which is too large to have digits representing negative powers of 16, and that it will completely annihilate any number whose magnitude is less than 1. Characteristics other than 47 with a zero fraction will have similar results, truncating numbers at different places. We may say that zeros with non-zero characteristics are "bigger" than a true zero.

Unnormalized numbers and arithmetic are useful in conversions between floating-point representation and printable characters, as we will see in Section 7.

Experiments have been made, and schemes developed for using unnormalized numbers and arithmetic to help keep track of the significance of the digits in floating-point computations. The idea is that significant digits are lost most quickly when an addition or subtraction results in leading zeros. Therefore if the leading zeros are kept instead of removed by normalization we have an estimate of the number of significant digits of our result. Because of the radix 16 used by System/360 and 370 floating-point representation, this measure is rather too coarse to be useful, and the complete normalization done by multiplication and division instructions makes it very difficult to keep the leading zeros one has developed in a series of computations. Therefore other techniques of keeping track of significance are to be preferred to use of unnormalized numbers in the IBM System/360 and 370.

6. EXCEPTIONS AND INTERRUPTS

There are a variety of exceptions that may arise from the attempted execution of floating-point instructions. We have postponed discussion of them until this section where we can give a unified treatment.

First, if the floating-point feature is not installed on the particular model, an *operation* exception is taken, with resulting interrupt, on attempted execution of any floating-point instruction, including the load and store instructions. Second, access exceptions can be caused by reference to main storage for operands, according to the usual rules. A *specification* exception, the most common during the debugging of programs, is taken and results in interrupt if a floating-point register address, *FPR1* or *FPR2* in our instruction descriptions, is other than 0, 2, 4 or 6. A specification exception can also occur if an RX-type single-precision instruction specifies a second operand address *S2* not on a full-word boundary, or an RX-type double-precision instruction specifies a second operand address *S2* not on a double-word boundary. These exceptions were all explained in Chapter 9, and it should be sufficient here to remark that they apply.

There are also four types of exceptions that are peculiar to floating-point instructions. First is the *exponent overflow*. An exponent overflow results whenever, by following the procedures described for each instruction, the final characteristic of the result would exceed 127 (hexadecimal 7F) and the fraction is nonzero. The overflow can occur as the result of a carry out of the high-order fraction position during normalized or unnormalized addition or subtraction and the following characteristic adjustment after a right shift, or during the characteristic computations in multiplication or division. An exponent overflow exception will always cause interrupt. The operation is completed first, however, and the result is correct except that the characteristic is 128 smaller than the correct characteristic.

An *exponent underflow* exception occurs when the final characteristic of the result of a floating-point instruction would be less than 0. The underflow could occur as a result of normalization during normalized addition or subtraction, and either during computation of the intermediate characteristic during multiplication or during the postnormalization. An underflow during prenormalization does *not* cause an exponent underflow exception. An exponent underflow may result from division, but if the underflow is rectified by a right shift to give the final quotient, no exponent underflow results. No underflows are possible in unnormalized addition or subtraction.

Action on an exponent underflow depends on bit 3 of the program mask. If this bit is 0, the result of the operation is forced to a true zero, that is, sign, characteristic, and fraction all become zero, and interrupt does not take place. If the bit is 1, the operation is completed, with a result whose characteristic is 128 larger than the correct characteristic, and an interrupt takes place.

In addition or subtraction instructions, normalized or unnormalized, when the fraction of the result is zero, a *significance* exception occurs. The point is that all significant digits of the result have been lost, and it is possible that further computations will be meaningless. Interruption because of a significance exception is controlled by bit 4 of the program mask. If the bit is 0, a true zero is forced, the condition code is set to 0 and no interrupt takes place. If the bit is 1 when a significance exception occurs, the characteristic is left as it is, the condition code is set to 0, and an interrupt takes place.

The last of the special floating-point exceptions is the *floating-point divide* exception. This exception occurs when a floating-point division is attempted by a divisor whose fraction is zero. The condition is discovered during attempted prenormalization of the divisor, and the dividend is left unchanged while the operation is suppressed and interrupt takes place.

The exceptions and the instructions that may cause them are summarized in the unified instruction list in Fig. 13–9.

7. CONVERSIONS

For conversions between printable characters and binary integers, the IBM System/360 and 370 have the simple helpful instructions PACK, CVB, CVD, and UNPK, which were introduced in Chapter 6. For converting to floating-point, there are no correspondingly easy instructions. One reason is that the conversion requirements, involving a wide range of values of floating-point numbers and several different external forms desired, are too varied to be serviced by any simple instruction. Let us therefore examine some sample segments that perform some conversions between floating-point and other forms.

First, in Fig. 13–2 is a segment that converts a binary integer in register 3 into a short normalized floating-point number stored at NØRMINT. Let us follow execution of this segment on a particular number. Suppose register 3 contains hexadecimal FC8034A3. Since floating-point numbers are not stored in 2's-complement form but in sign-and-absolute value form, the first thing to do is find the absolute value of the number. The absolute value, 037FCB5D, is put in register 5. An unnormalized zero is loaded into register 4; the characteristic is 4E, so the number whose floating-point representation is now in registers (general, not floating-point) 4 and 5 has its actual hexadecimal point at the far right of register 5. The number 4E000000037FCB5D is actually already a floating-point representation of the integer 37FCB5D. The instruction N   3,MASKSGN annihilates all 1-bits in

Fig. 13–2 Conversion of an integer to floating-point

```
*              THIS SEGMENT CØNVERTS AN INTEGER IN REG. 3
*              TØ SHØRT NØRMALIZED FLØATING PØINT FØRM,
*              STØRING THE RESULT AT NØRMINT.
               LPR   5,3            TAKE ABSØLUTE VALUE
               L     4,UNZRØ        CREATE UNNØRM. FLØATED NUMBER
               N     3,MASKSGN      ISØLATE SIGN
               ØR    4,3            ATTACH SIGN
               STM   4,5,UNNØ       UNNØRMALIZED SIGNED NUMBER
               LD    0,UNNØ
               AD    0,=D'0'        NØRMALIZE
               STE   0,NØRMINT
               ...
               DS    0F
UNZRØ          DC    X'4E000000'    UNNØRMALIZED ZERØ
MASKSGN        DC    X'80000000'    ANNIHILATES ALL BUT SIGN
UNNØ           DS    1D
NØRMINT        DS    1F
```

register 3 except the sign bit; in our example the sign bit is 1, so the result is 80000000. The next instruction attaches the sign to our floating-point number (XR would do just as well as ØR), making it CE000000 037FCB5D. This number is stored at UNNØ, then loaded into floating-point register 0. A zero is added; this is the easiest way to normalize the number, which then is C737FCB5 D0000000. The last instruction stores the upper half of the result. In this case, one significant hexadecimal digit is lost in the truncation to short floating-point form; in the worst case, two may be lost. They can be retained, of course, by storing the double-precision instead of single-precision result.

As a second example, suppose that the number in the preceding example was merely the integer part of a number whose EBCDIC form also included seven decimal fraction digits. We now convert these digits to floating-point form and attach the result to the preceding one.

This segment, Fig. 13–3, assumes that no minus sign is coded in the digits of DECFRAC, but that the sign is to be taken as the sign of the integer. This simplifies

Fig. 13–3 Conversion of a fraction to floating-point

```
*              THIS SEGMENT, FØLLØWING DIRECTLY THE SEGMENT 13–2
*              CØNVERTS 7 DIGITS ØF FRACTIØN FRØM EBCDIC FØRM
*              AT DECFRAC INTØ FLØATING–PØINT FØRM, ATTACHING
*              THE NUMBER TØ THE PRECEDING RESULT.
               PACK  DBL(8),DECFRAC(7)
               CVB   7,DBL          ASSUME NØ MINUS SIGN ØN DECFRAC
               L     6,UNZRØ
               ØR    6,3            ATTACH SAME SIGN AS TØ INTEGER
               STM   6,7,UNNØ
               LD    2,UNNØ
               DD    2,=D'1.0E7'    MAKE INTØ FRACTIØN, NØRMALIZE
               ADR   0,2            CØMBINE INTEGER AND FRACTIØN
               STD   0,RESULT
               ...
DBL            DS    1D
RESULT         DS    1D
```

the segment somewhat. The process of "floating" the fraction is the same as that for floating the integer. The division by 10^7 not only reduces the digits to fraction status but prenormalizes and leaves a normalized result.

As a last example we show an example of the converse process of converting a floating-point number to an integer. Suppose that we have a short-precision floating-point number FLT, whose integer part, if it will fit, is to be stored as an integer at INTGR.

Fig. 13–4 Conversion from floating-point to integer

```
*            THIS SEGMENT CØNVERTS A SHØRT NØRMALIZED FLØATING—PØINT
*            NUMBER AT FLT TØ A BINARY INTEGER AT INTGR.
*            IF THE NUMBER IS TØØ LARGE, BRANCH TØ TØØBIG.
             LD      0,=D'0'     CLEAR LØWER HALF ØF REGISTER
             LE      0,FLT
             LPER    2,0         IF ABS. VALUE IS NØT LESS
             CE      2,TWØ31           THAN 2**31, NUMBER IS TØØ LARGE.
             BNL     TØØBIG
             AW      0,TWØ32     UNNØRMALIZE, CØMPLEMENT IF NEGATIVE
             STD     DINT          STØRE RESULT
             MVC     INTGR(4),DINT+4
             ...
DINT    DS   1D
TWØ32   DC   X'4E00000100000000'
TWØ31   DC   X'48800000'
```

In this example, Fig. 13–4, all adjustments are made in floating-point registers. First, note that in order to make the short floating-point word into a double-precision one, we must clear the lower half of the register. If the absolute value of the number is greater than 2^{31}, the number is too large to be represented as an integer in one general register, so a branch to TØØBIG is provided. Let us suppose that the number in FLT is C553F049 as we follow the remainder of the segment. The instruction AW 0,TWØ32 accomplishes several things. First, the alignment phase unnormalizes the number so that the actual (hexadecimal) point is just to the right of the register. All digits representing a fraction less than 1 are eliminated, and the absolute value of the desired integer is in the lower half of the register. In our example, the register contains CE000000 00053F04. Integer representation requires that negative numbers be represented in 2's-complement form, so this low-order portion must be complemented if the number is negative. This is accomplished very cleverly by the instruction AW 0,TWØ32. If the result is negative as in our case, the addition is of

$$4E000001 \quad 00000000$$

and

$$CE000000 \quad 00053F04,$$

which is in effect a subtraction yielding 4E000000 FFFAD0FC, whose low-order 32 bits are the desired complement. If, on the other hand, the original number

were positive, say 4E000000   00053F04, the result would be 4E000001   00053F04.
In either case, the lower half is in correct 2's complement form. Finally, the whole
number is stored (there is no way to store only the lower half of a floating-point
register) and the desired portion moved to INTGR.

8. AN EXAMPLE: A REGRESSION CALCULATION

One of the common problems in the analysis of data is the fitting of a line or curve
to a set of observations, which can be called *regression*. In its simplest form, which
we carry through here, this involves a set of observations—pairs of values—and
the fitting of a straight line to the observations. Usually, a perfect fit is unobtain-
able; the data simply do not lie on a straight line. We need a measure of the
deviation from a perfect fit, and a way of drawing the line that will minimize
that measure.

We choose then to denote one variable as "independent" and the other as
"dependent," which is natural in most cases: we choose a temperature independently and observe the pressure in a physical system. The pressure can properly
be termed dependent on the temperature we choose. Or we may survey a group
of people, denoting age as one variable and yearly medical bill as another; we may
at least adopt the hypothesis that yearly medical bill is dependent on (among other
things) age. For the mathematical statement of the procedures we will denote x as
the independent variable and y as the dependent variable. If we have n observations, each observation can be represented as the pair x_i, y_i, and the equation for
the line we seek will be $y = a + bx$.

We choose as our measure of goodness of fit the sum of squares of deviations
of predicted values $a + bx_i$ from actual values y_i of the dependent variable:

$$E = \sum_{i=1}^{n} [y_i - (a + bx_i)]^2 \qquad (13\text{--}1)$$

When we choose a and b so as to minimize this measure E, we are doing what is
called fitting by *least squares*. One reason for choosing this particular measure is
that it weights heavily any large deviations $y_i - (a + bx_i)$, so that minimization
of E is an attempt to eliminate large deviations. Another reason is that the measure
E has a number of very nice mathematical properties, and a large body of theory
has grown around least-squares curve-fitting.

One of the nice properties of E is that the coefficients a and b of the regression
line are easily shown, by taking partial derivatives of E with respect to a and b,
to be the solutions of the equations

$$an + b \sum_1^n x_i = \sum_1^n y_i,$$
$$a \sum_1^n x_i + b \sum_1^n x_i^2 = \sum_1^n x_i y_i. \qquad (13\text{--}2)$$

This pair of equations, requiring only computation of the sums

$$\sum_1^n x_i, \qquad \sum_1^n y_i, \qquad \sum_1^n x_i^2 \qquad \text{and} \qquad \sum_1^n x_i y_i,$$

is easily solved. Another of the nice properties of E is that after a and b have been computed according to Eqs. 13–2, E itself can be computed as

$$E = \sum_1^n y_i^2 - a \sum_1^n y_i - b \sum_1^n x_i y_i, \qquad (13\text{–}3)$$

which requires only the additional computation of $\sum_1^n y_i^2$.

Computation, then, can be divided into three parts. First is the computation of the necessary sums

$$\sum_1^n x_i, \qquad \sum_1^n y_i, \qquad \sum_1^n x_i^2, \qquad \sum_1^n x_i y_i, \qquad \text{and} \qquad \sum_1^n y_i^2.$$

Second is the solution of Eqs. 13–2 for the coefficients a and b, and third is the computation of E, which can be done according to Eq. 13–3.

Let us now exhibit a program segment computing the necessary sums. We assume that the observations are all in main storage, and that the number n of observations is given in register 5. We assume further that each observation is in a record, and that the address of the beginning of one record is a quantity p greater than the address of the beginning of the previous record, and that p is in register 4. Finally, we suppose that the address of the beginning of the first record is in register 3, and that x_i and y_i, both in short floating-point form, are at the beginning of each record.

We must do some address calculation and looping control as well as the floating-point calculations. We control looping with a BCT instruction, decrementing register 7, and let register 6 always contain the address of the beginning of the current record, namely, the address of the current x_i. We keep $\sum_1^n x_i$ and $\sum_1^n y_i$ in floating-point registers 4 and 6, but keep the other sums in main storage. All computations are in short precision. Figure 13–5 shows the segment, which is reasonably straightforward. At the very end, n is stored as a floating-point number because it is needed in that form in the next segment. It is stored unnormalized, and because of prenormalization in multiplication and division, it can be used that way.

We now turn to the solution of the set of two equations in a and b. There are many schemes for solving a set of simultaneous linear equations, and we choose here an *elimination* scheme due to Gauss. This scheme is quite efficient and lends itself well to computer use; many other schemes are based on this one. We can describe the elimination procedure as follows. We start with two equations with more or less arbitrary coefficients that we denote by c's, which are subscripted for

Fig. 13-5 Calculation of sums

```
*                    INITIALIZATIØN
          LE     4,=F'0'            SUM X = 0
          LER    6,4                SUM Y = 0
          STE    4,SUMX2                  = 0
          STE    4,SUMXY                  = 0
          STE    4,SUMY2                  = 0
          LR     7,5                N
          LR     6,3                ADDRESS ØF CURRENT RECØRD
*                    BØDY ØF LØØP     CØMPUTE SUMS
BØDY      LE     0,0(6)             X
          AER    4,0                SUM X
          MER    0,0                X SQUARED
          AE     0,SUMX2
          STE    0,SUMX2            SUM X SQUARED
          LE     0,4(6)             Y
          AER    6,0                SUM Y
          ME     0,0(6)             X Y
          AE     0,SUMXY
          STE    0,SUMXY            SUM X Y
          LE     0,4(6)
          MER    0,0                Y SQUARED
          AE     0,SUMY2
          STE    0,SUMY2            SUM Y SQUARED
*                    INCREMENT AND LØØP CONTRØL
          AR     6,4                UPDATE ADDRESS ØF CURRENT RECØRD
          BCT    7,BØDY
*                    STØRE RESULTS AFTER LØØP
          STE    4,SUMX
          STE    6,SUMY
          LR     7,5
          A      5,UNZ              UNZ = X'46000000'
          ST     5,FLN              STØRE N IN UNNØRM. FLØATING—PØINT
          . . .
```

row and column of the array we can construct of the coefficients:

$$c_{11}a + c_{12}b = c_{13},$$
$$c_{21}a + c_{22}b = c_{23}.$$

First we divide the first equation by c_{11}, changing it to

$$a + c'_{12}b = c'_{13},$$

where $c'_{12} = c_{12}/c_{11}$, $c'_{13} = c_{13}/c_{11}$.   Next we eliminate a from the second equation by subtracting c_{21} times the new first equation from the second, leaving

$$c'_{22}b = c'_{23},$$

where $c'_{22} = c_{22} - c_{21} \cdot c'_{12}$, $c'_{23} = c_{23} - c_{21} \cdot c'_{13}$.   Now b is simply c'_{23}/c'_{22}, and with this value of b we can compute a from the new first equation. This procedure must be modified if c_{11} or c'_{22} turn out to be zero, and it can be extended to any number of equations in the same number of unknowns. With many equations the coefficients are kept in what is considered a two-dimensional array, as

Fig. 13–6   Computation of regression coefficients

```
  *             CØMPUTATIØN ØF REGRESSIØN CØEFFICIENTS.
        DE    4,FLN        SUMX/N = C12 PRIME
        DE    6,FLN        SUMY/N = C13 PRIME
        LE    0,SUMX2
        LE    2,SUMX
        MER   2,4
        SER   0,2          C22 PRIME = C22 - (C12 PRIME)*C21
        STE   0,C22
        LE    0,SUMXY
        LE    2,SUMX
        MER   2,6
        SER   0,2          C23 PRIME = C23 - (C13 PRIME)*C31
        DE    0,C22        B = (C23 PRIME)/(C22 PRIME)
        STE   0,B
        MER   4,0          (C12 PRIME)*B
        SER   6,4          A = (C13 PRIME) - (C12 PRIME)*B
        STE   6,A
```

suggested by our subscripts, and the address calculation for an efficient program is a good exercise.

We show a segment in Fig. 13–6 which is specific to Eqs. 13–2 and is designed to follow Fig. 13–5 directly.

As the third phase of our calculation we compute E, the measure of goodness of fit. Figure 13–7 accomplishes the computation according to Eq. 13–3.

When this sequence of segments is executed with a data set comprised of the ten observations (values given in decimal),

Observation	x	y
1	−21.23	65.72
2	−11.80	37.45
3	−6.12	20.34
4	−1.68	7.07
5	0.01	1.99
6	0.42	0.73
7	1.00	−1.01
8	2.56	−5.72
9	4.99	−12.93
10	18.00	−52.00

results include (here we give decimal and hexadecimal values)

	Decimal	Hexadecimal
a	2.007661	2.01F61
b	−3.000979	−3.00403
E	−0.003906250	−0.010000

The fit seems successful, since E is quite small. However, E is defined to be a sum of squares, so it should *not* be negative! The mathematics of deriving Eq. 13–3 is

Fig. 13-7   Computation of E according to Eq. 13-3

```
*               CØMPUTATIØN ØF ERRØR E
        LE      0,SUMY
        ME      0,A
        LE      2,SUMXY
        ME      2,B
        AER     2,0
        LE      4,SUMY2
        SER     4,2
        STE     4,E
```

correct, and there are no bugs in the program, so we are forced to think about accuracy and rounding errors. The fact that so few hexadecimal digits of E are nonzero is no accident; it is because the numbers that were subtracted to give E are large and of nearly equal magnitude:

$$\sum_{1}^{10} y_i^2 = 2386.\text{B9} \quad \text{(hexadecimal)};$$

$$a\sum_{1}^{10} y_i + b\sum_{1}^{10} x_i y_i = 2386.\text{BA} \quad \text{(hexadecimal)}.$$

Since each of these numbers can be expected to include some effect of rounding errors, their last hexadecimal digits are not to be trusted. Since their first five hexadecimal digits agree, their difference has *no* significant digits, and the computed estimate of E is pure rounding error! This scheme for computing E then, while involving very little computational labor, yields at most one hexadecimal digit of accuracy. Of course, we could do some or all of the computations in double precision, but the same kind of calamity would still happen in larger problems. The point is that the scheme of Eq. 13-3 is computationally poor from the standpoint of accuracy. The alternative is to compute E directly from its defining equation, 13-1; the segment in Fig. 13-8 does this. The segment is intended to replace that in Fig. 13-7; the four instructions of Fig. 13-5 computing SUMY2 can also be deleted, since SUMY2 is used only in Fig. 13-7.

Fig. 13-8   Computation of E according to Eq. 13-1

```
*               INITIALIZATIØN FØR CØMPUTATIØN ØF SUM ØF SQUARED DEVIATIØNS
        LR      7,5             N
        LR      6,3             ADDRESS ØF CURRENT RECØRD
        LE      2,=F'0'         SUM SQ. DEV.
*               LØØP FØR CØMPUTING AND ADDING A SQUARED DEV.
ELØØP   LE      4,0(6)          X
        ME      4,B
        AE      4,A             A + B*X
        SE      4,4(6)          A + B*X - Y = -DEV.
        MER     4,4             SQUARE DEV.
        AER     2,4             ADD TØ SUM
*               INCREMENT AND CØNTRØL LØØPING
        AR      6,4
        BCT     7,ELØØP
*               STØRE E
        STE     2,E
```

Computation of E by Fig. 13–8 yields 0.006762601 decimal or .01BB31A hexadecimal, of which roughly three digits are accurate. Approximately three significant digits remain in each deviation and in the square of each deviation, and during the summing process these digits are not lost.

Least-squares regression can be generalized to problems of finding coefficients in an equation involving several independent variables: $y = a_0 + a_1x_1 + a_2x_2 + \cdots + a_kx_k$, where the $x_1, \ldots, x_k$ are values of independent variables in one observation. It can also be generalized to problems involving more complicated functions than linear ones, such as $y = a_0 + a_1x + a_2x^2 + \cdots + a_mx^m$. The computational schemes are roughly the same. The work involved increases linearly in phase 1, generation of sums, with the number of coefficients to be determined, and increases as the cube of the number of coefficients in phase 2, solution of the simultaneous linear equations. The biggest increase in work, however, comes when there are too many observations to be kept in main storage, so that the records must be read and the information taken from them, not only in phase 1, but in phase 3, the computation of E according to Eq. 13–1.

9. EXTENDED-PRECISION INSTRUCTIONS

An extended-precision number is formed by two double-precision numbers. The first double-precision number contains the most significant 56 fraction bits; the second double-precision number contains another 56 fraction bits, in positions 8–63. Bits 0–7, the sign and characteristic bits of the second double-precision number are ignored in extended-precision calculation. There are seven instructions supplied in the extended-precision feature, which is included in some IBM 360 and 370 models. Included in the seven instructions are two round instructions, an add, a subtract, and three multiply instructions.

Extended-precision arithmetic is performed in the floating-point registers. An address of 0 can specify the pair of floating-point registers 0 and 2 which can hold an extended-precision operand or result; similarly 4 can specify the floating-point register pair 4 and 6. There are no special extended load and store instructions; extended-precision numbers must be loaded and stored by the LD, LDR and STD instructions, each moving half of an extended-precision number.

The instruction Load and Round Double (LRDR) is of RR type; it rounds an extended-precision number (second operand) to a double-precision number which is placed in the first operand register. Similarly, Load and Round (LRER) rounds a double-precision number to single-precision form. The LRER instruction therefore has nothing to do with extended-precision numbers, and is included in the extended-precision feature because it was introduced at the same time as the extended-precision instructions, several years after the implementation of the ordinary floating-point instruction set.

The RR-type instructions AXR, SXR, and MXR, respectively, add, subtract, and multiply two extended-precision operands, and leave an extended-precision result.

The operations are completely analogous to the single- and double-precision operations with respect to guard digit, normalization, condition code, and exceptions.

The instructions MXDR and MXD each multiply two double-precision operands, leaving an extended-precision product. MXDR is of RR type, and MXD of RX type.

Any double-precision number can be loaded as an extended-precision number merely by appending a second double-precision number, with zero fraction and any characteristic, in the second register of the pair. Thus

```
        LD    4,A
        LD    6,D'0'
```

loads an extended-precision number in the register pair 4,6; the extended-precision number has the same value as the double-precision number at A.

There is no extended-precision divide instruction implemented in hardware, but a macro named DXR is provided. Its accessibility to a program also depends on provision of an appropriate SPIE macro; the user must consult systems programmers at his installation for detailed arrangements. Similar arrangements can be made for simulation through macros of the other extended-precision instructions in installations where the extended-precision feature is not implemented in hardware.

As an example of the use of extended-precision arithmetic, we will show how the quotient of two extended-precision numbers can be formed without using a divide instruction.

The Newton-Raphson iterative process solves approximately an equation $f(x) = 0$ by computing successively

$$x_1 = x_0 - \frac{f(x_0)}{f'(x_0)}, \qquad x_2 = x_1 - \frac{f(x_1)}{f'(x_1)}, \dots .$$

Under certain conditions the sequence $x_0, x_1, x_2, \dots$ converges nicely to the solution of the equation. If we take $f(x) = (1/x) - b$, the solution of $(1/x) - b = 0$ is obviously the inverse of b. The iteration

$$x_{i+1} = x_i - \frac{f(x_i)}{f'(x_i)}$$

becomes

$$x_{i+1} = x_i(2 - bx_i),$$

which has two happy properties:

1) each iteration more or less doubles the number of accurate digits of the approximations;
2) the inverse of b is obtained without division.

We can easily generate a good first approximation of $1/b$ using double-precision arithmetic, and just one iteration beyond that generates $1/b$ correct to about 27 hexadecimal digits. Multiplying this inverse by a, we get a good approximation to an extended-precision a/b.

Fig. 13–9   Division of extended-precision numbers

```
LD    0,=D'1.'
DD    0,B                DØUBLE PRECISIØN 1./B=X
STD   0,X
LD    4,B                EXT. B
LD    6,B+8
LD    2,=D'0.'           EXTEND X BY ZERØS
MXR   4,0                FØRM     B*X
LD    0,=D'2.'
SXR   0,4                          2. −B*X
LD    4,X
LD    6,=D'0.'
MXR   0,4                          X*(2.−B*X)
LD    4,A                          =EXT. PREC. 1./B
LD    6,A+8
MXR   0,4                FØRM A*(1./B)
STD   0,X
STD   2,X+8             STØRE A/B AT X
```

Fig. 13–10   Actions of extended-precision instructions

Instruction	Type	Action	Cond. code set	Exceptions
LRER	RR	$FPR1 \leftarrow$ rounded $c(FPR2)_{0-63}$	No	S,E
LRDR	RR	$FPR1_{0-63} \leftarrow$ rounded $c(FPR2)_{0-127}$	No	S,E
AXR	RR	$FPR1_{0-127} \leftarrow c(FPR1)_{0-127} + c(FPR2)_{0-127}$	Yes	S,U,E,LS
SXR	RR	$FPR1_{0-127} \leftarrow c(FPR1)_{0-127} - c(FPR2)_{0-127}$	Yes	S,U,E,LS
MXR	RR	$FPR1_{0-127} \leftarrow c(FPR1)_{0-127} \times c(FPR2)_{0-127}$	No	S,U,E
MXDR	RR	$FPR1_{0-127} \leftarrow c(FPR1)_{0-63} \times c(FPR2)_{0-63}$	No	S,U,E
MXD	RX	$FPR1_{0-127} \leftarrow c(FPR1)_{0-63} \times c(S2)_{0-63}$	No	A,S,U,E

Suppose then that A and B are extended-precision numbers in main storage. The segment shown in Fig. 13–9 generates at X the quotient A/B correct to about 27 hexadecimal digits.

In summary, the instructions in the extended-precision feature are represented as shown in Fig. 13–10.

10. MAIN IDEAS

a. Floating-point numbers, in 32- and 64-bit lengths, represent quantities of widely varying magnitudes. The representation uses a characteristic—indicating an exponent of 16—and a fraction. Nonzero numbers are normalized if the first hexadecimal digit of the fraction is nonzero. Normalization enables the preservation of a maximum number of significant digits in a series of computations.

b. Floating-point registers, each 64 bits long, are numbered 0, 2, 4, and 6. Floating-point instructions are of RR and RX types; all the register operands of these are in floating-point registers, but general registers are used in the usual way to specify addresses of main storage operands.

c. Floating-point instructions perform load, store, add, subtract, compare, multiply, and divide operations. Add and subtract instructions are available in both normalizing and unnormalizing forms; multiply and divide instructions always normalize. See Fig. 13–11 for summary.

Fig. 13–11   Summary of floating-point instructions [4]

Instruction	Type	Action	Cond.[2] code	Exceptions[3]
LER	RR	$FPR1 \leftarrow c(FPR2)$	—	S
LE	RX	$FPR1 \leftarrow c(S2)$	—	A,S
LDR	RR	$FPR1_{0-63} \leftarrow c(FPR2)_{0-63}$	—	S
LD	RX	$FPR1_{0-63} \leftarrow c(S2)_{0-63}$	—	A,S
LTER	RR	$FPR1 \leftarrow c(FPR2)$	(a)	S
LTDR	RR	$FPR1_{0-63} \leftarrow c(FPR2)_{0-63}$	(a)	S
LCER	RR	$FPR1 \leftarrow -c(FPR2)$	(a)	S
LCDR	RR	$FPR1_{0-63} \leftarrow -c(FPR2)_{0-63}$	(a)	S
LPER	RR	$FPR1 \leftarrow \lvert c(FPR2)\rvert$	(a)	S
LPDR	RR	$FPR1_{0-63} \leftarrow \lvert c(FPR2)_{0-63}\rvert$	(a)	S
LNER	RR	$FPR1 \leftarrow -\lvert c(FPR2)\rvert$	(a)	S
LNDR	RR	$FPR1_{0-63} \leftarrow -\lvert c(FPR2)_{0-63}\rvert$	(a)	S
STE	RX	$S2 \leftarrow c(FPR1)$	—	A,S
STD	RX	$S2_{0-63} \leftarrow c(FPR1)_{0-63}$	—	A,S
AER	RR	$FPR1 \leftarrow c(FPR1) + c(FPR2)$	(a)	S,U,E,LS
AE	RX	$FPR1 \leftarrow c(FPR1) + c(S2)$	(a)	A,S,U,E,LS
ADR	RR	$FPR1_{0-63} \leftarrow c(FPR1)_{0-63} + c(FPR2)_{0-63}$	(a)	S,U,E,LS
AD	RX	$FPR1_{0-63} \leftarrow c(FPR1)_{0-63} + c(S2)_{0-63}$	(a)	A,S,U,E,LS
SER	RR	$FPR1 \leftarrow c(FPR1) - c(FPR2)$	(a)	S,U,E,LS
SE	RX	$FPR1 \leftarrow c(FPR1) - c(S2)$	(a)	A,S,U,E,LS
SDR	RR	$FPR1_{0-63} \leftarrow c(FPR1)_{0-63} - c(FPR2)_{0-63}$	(a)	S,U,E,LS
SD	RX	$FPR1_{0-63} \leftarrow c(FPR1)_{0-63} - c(S2)_{0-63}$	(a)	A,S,U,E,LS
CER	RR	—	(b)	S
CE	RX	—	(b)	A,S
CDR	RR	—	(b)	S
CD	RX	—	(b)	A,S
AUR[1]	RR	$FPR1 \leftarrow c(FPR1) + c(FPR2)$	(a)	S, E,LS
AU[1]	RX	$FPR1 \leftarrow c(FPR1) + c(S2)$	(a)	A,S, E,LS
AWR[1]	RR	$FPR1_{0-63} \leftarrow c(FPR1)_{0-63} + c(FPR2)_{0-63}$	(a)	S, E,LS
AW[1]	RX	$FPR1_{0-63} \leftarrow c(FPR1)_{0-63} + c(S2)_{0-63}$	(a)	A,S, E,LS
SUR[1]	RR	$FPR1 \leftarrow c(FPR1) - c(FPR2)$	(a)	S, E,LS
SU[1]	RX	$FPR1 \leftarrow c(FPR1) - c(S2)$	(a)	A,S, E,LS
SWR[1]	RR	$FPR1_{0-63} \leftarrow c(FPR1)_{0-63} - c(FPR2)_{0-63}$	(a)	S, E,LS
SW[1]	RX	$FPR1_{0-63} \leftarrow c(FPR1)_{0-63} - c(S2)_{0-63}$	(a)	A,S, E,LS
MER	RR	$FPR1_{0-63} \leftarrow c(FPR1) \times c(FPR2)$	—	S,U,E
ME	RX	$FPR1_{0-63} \leftarrow c(FPR1) \times c(S2)$	—	A,S,U,E
MDR	RR	$FPR1_{0-63} \leftarrow c(FPR1)_{0-63} \times c(FPR2)_{0-63}$	—	S,U,E
MD	RX	$FPR1_{0-63} \leftarrow c(FPR1)_{0-63} \times c(S2)_{0-63}$	—	A,S,U,E
DER	RR	$FPR1 \leftarrow c(FPR1) / c(FPR2)$	—	S,U,E,FK
DE	RX	$FPR1 \leftarrow c(FPR1) / c(S2)$	—	A,S,U,E,FK
DDR	RR	$FPR1_{0-63} \leftarrow c(FPR1)_{0-63} / c(FPR2)_{0-63}$	—	S,U,E,FK
DD	RX	$FPR1_{0-63} \leftarrow c(FPR1)_{0-63} / c(S2)_{0-63}$	—	A,S,U,E,FK
HER	RR	$FPR1 \leftarrow c(FPR2) / 2$	—	S,U
HDR	RR	$FPR1_{0-63} \leftarrow c(FPR2)_{0-63} / 2$	—	S,U

Notes

1. Addition and subtraction in these operations are unnormalized.
2. Condition codes are set to:

   a) 0 if result fraction $= 0$
      1 if result less than 0
      2 if result greater than 0

   b) 0 if $Op_1 = Op_2$
      1 if Op_1 less than Op_2
      2 if Op_1 greater than Op_2

3. Exception codes: A: Access
   S: Specification
   U: Exponent underflow
   E: Exponent overflow
   LS: Significance
   FK: Floating divide by zero
4. See Fig. 13–10 for extended-precision instructions.

d. Action of addition or subtraction involves the comparison of characteristics and a right shift in the alignment step, then addition or subtraction, then normalization. Multiplication and division operations include a prenormalization step.

e. In addition to exceptions for specification, operation, and access, special exceptions for exponent overflow, exponent underflow, significance, and floating-point zero divide may occur. All except exponent underflow and significance always cause interrupt; interrupts on exponent underflow and significance are controlled by program mask bits 3 and 4.

f. Regression, the fitting of a linear equation to a set of data minimizing the squares of the deviations, is accomplished by accumulating sums and sums of squares and cross products, and then solving a set of linear equations.

QUESTIONS FOR REVIEW AND IMAGINATION

1. Write short floating-point representations for the decimal numbers

3.0	12.0	−0.75
−3.0	24.0	−0.1875
6.0	4212.0	0.1
		0.3

2. What decimal numbers are represented by the following floating-point numbers?

42360000	3F200000
C12F0000	BF240000
C310A680	5E000000

3. Show the normalized equivalents of the following:

41010000	05000002
FF000001	5400068E
CE003CE0	800F0000

4. In most binary computers, the characteristic is used as a power of 2. To get the same range of magnitudes that System/360 and 370 do, these computers need three more bits for their characteristics than are required by the System/360 and 370. System/360 and 370 thus gain three bits for significant digits; however, they lose some again because of the necessity of up to three leading zero bits in normalized numbers. Making the reasonable assumption that numbers with 0, 1, 2, and 3 leading zeros occur equally often, what is the net gain or loss in significant bits carried by the IBM System/360 and 370, compared to a binary 32-bit-word computer whose characteristics are powers of 2? What other advantages and disadvantages can you think of for the power-of-16 system?

5. Assuming that the contents of floating-point registers and storage locations are:

Floating-point register	0:	42345200	00000000
	2:	C01E0000	EC86904A
	4:	BE003456	00000000
	6:	3D2136E1	02D46A71
Main storage locations:	TT:	42439A72	
	UU:	00000000	
	VV:	46000000	
	WW:	FE200000	
	XX:	00200000	
	YY:	D8400000	
	ZZ:	BC345678	

prior to execution of *each* of the following instructions or segments, give results of each, including condition code and any exceptions generated.

a) LPER	0,2	i) ADR	4,=D'2'	q) ME	4,XX
b) LCDR	2,6	j) LE	2,YY	r) SE	4,UU
c) LNER	2,4	SDR	0,2	s) ME	4,UU
d) CE	4,ZZ	k) AU	4,ZZ	t) DE	4,UU
e) LE	0,ZZ	l) ME	2,YY	u) DE	4,XX
CDR	0,4	m) ME	4,YY	v) DE	4,WW
f) AE	0,TT	n) ME	0,WW	w) SE	4,ZZ
g) SE	0,VV	o) ME	2,WW	x) SU	4,ZZ
h) ADR	0,6	p) ME	2,XX	y) LD	4,=D'-8.0'
				MDR	6,4

6. The LCR instruction can produce an overflow; the LCER instruction cannot. Why?

7. If two numbers are compared by the C instruction and also by the CE instruction, will the results of the comparisons be the same? If the numbers are both positive, will the results be the same? If the numbers are both positive and, as floating-point numbers, normalized, will the results be the same? If the numbers are both negative and normalized, will the results be the same? If one number is positive and one negative, will the results be the same?

8. In what cases does the guard digit affect the result of a floating-point compare instruction?

9. When floating-point numbers are computed with rounding errors, a test for whether one number is equal to another should take account of the rounding errors and ask only whether they are *approximately* equal. For example, one may ask whether they agree to within some preassigned tolerance. Show several ways in which such a test can be programmed.

10. In what cases does the guard digit affect the result of an unnormalized add or subtract instruction?

11. What principles would guide you in deciding, for a particular program or program segment, whether to allow interrupt on exponent underflow, and if so, what action should be taken by the interrupt processor? What actions might be taken, and under what circumstances, on an exponent overflow exception?

12. Put together and supplement the program segments of Figs. 13–2 and 13–3 so that a number in character form stored at main storage locations INPUT to INPUT+14 as

INPUT:	sign:	$+$ or $-$
INPUT+1 to INPUT+6:		integer
INPUT+7:		decimal point
INPUT+8 to INPUT+14:		fraction

is converted to floating-point form. Correct the segment to allow for a negative number whose integer part is zero.

13. What action might be taken in the segment beginning at TØØBIG referred to in Fig. 13–4? Try to write such a segment that will generate a double-word integer containing the correct value.

14. Write a program segment that will convert the *fractional* part of a floating-point number to character form. You may assume that your segment is given a number whose magnitude is less than 1.

15. Derive the equations necessary to generate a least-squares regression function of the form $y = ax + bx^2$.

16. Derive the equations necessary to generate a least-squares regression function of the form $y = a_0 + a_1x_1 + a_2x_2$, where each observation consists of a measurement each of variables y, x_1, and x_2. Extend the Gauss solution of linear equations to a set of three equations in three unknowns, and write a program segment to follow this procedure.

17. Suppose we have n linear equations in n unknowns, $x_1, \ldots, x_n$:

$$a_{11}x_1 + a_{12}x_2 + \cdots + a_{1n}x_n = c_1,$$
$$a_{21}x_1 + a_{22}x_2 + \cdots + a_{2n}x_n = c_2,$$
$$\cdots$$
$$a_{n1}x_1 + a_{n2}x_2 + \cdots + a_{nn}x_n = c_n.$$

The coefficients are stored consecutively as short floating-point numbers beginning at location CØEF in the order $a_{11}, a_{12}, \ldots, a_{1n}, c_1, a_{21}, a_{22}, \ldots,$ $a_{2n}, c_2, \ldots, a_{n1}, a_{n2}, \ldots, a_{nn}, c_n$, which is called storing the coefficient array row-wise. Use the Gauss procedure to solve this set of equations, leaving the results $x_1, \ldots, x_n$ in consecutive locations starting at X. Assume during your first attempt that none of the diagonal coefficients are 0.

18. One of the time-honored procedures for finding the square root of a positive number A is the Newton-Raphson iterative scheme

$$x_{i+1} = x_i + \frac{1}{2}\left(\frac{A}{x_i} - x_i\right),$$

which from an initial estimate x_0 computes successive approximations $x_1, x_2, \ldots$ that converge to the square root of A. If the initial approximation is chosen as $x_0 = \frac{1}{2}(1 + A)$, which is greater than the square root of A, all the approximations are (theoretically, in the absence of round-off error) greater than the square root of A. Therefore a good criterion for stopping the iteration in a computer is that $x_{i+1} \geq x$. Program a segment that will use this procedure to compute a square root. Then, maintaining $x_0 > \sqrt{A}$, improve the procedure by computing an initial approximation x_0 whose exponent (characteristic $-$ 64) is approximately half that of A.

19. A reasonably efficient procedure for finding the natural antilog e^x of a number x is to use the Taylor series

$$e^x = 1 + x + \frac{x^2}{2!} + \frac{x^3}{3!} + \frac{x^4}{4!} + \cdots,$$

where $n!$ (read n factorial, where n is a positive integer) is the product of the integers from 1 to n. Computation can proceed by computing partial sums, adding on terms one at a time until the sum does not change any longer. Each term can be derived from the preceding one by

$$t_0 = 1, \quad t_i = \frac{xt_{i-1}}{i}, \quad i = 1, 2, \ldots$$

Program a segment that will compute e^x by this procedure for a given x. Then analyze the number of significant digits produced by the computation, considering both positive and negative values of x.

REFERENCES

Efroymson, M. A., "Multiple regression analysis," in *Mathematical Methods for Digital Computers*, edited by Ralston and Wilf (New York: Wiley, 1960). Development and description of an algorithm for regression. The volume, and volume 2, contain algorithms for solution of other mathematical problems as well.

IBM System/360 Principles of Operation, GA22-6821, or *IBM System/370 Principles of Operation*, GA22-7000. For reference on the floating-point instructions.

IBM OS/360 Operating System Supervisor Services and Macro-Instructions, GC28-6646, IBM Corporation.   Reference on calling extended-precision floating-point simulator routines.

Knuth, Donald E., *The Art of Computer Programming, Vol. 2: Seminumerical Algorithms* (Reading, Mass.: Addison-Wesley, 1969).   Chapter 4 includes a study of the properties of floating-point arithmetic.

Kuki, H., and J. Ascoly, "FORTRAN extended-precision library," *IBM Systems Journal* **10**, 1 (1971), pp. 39–61. An analysis of problems and techniques using extended-precision arithmetic.

Moore, Ramon, *Interval Analysis* (Englewood Cliffs, N.J.: Prentice-Hall, 1966).   An approach to automatic analysis of rounding error.

Wilkinson, J. H., *Rounding Errors in Algebraic Processes* (London: H.M. Stationery Office, 1963).   A good introductory discussion of rounding errors.

Chapter 14

Decimal Arithmetic

The IBM System/360 has three modes of arithmetic; it can perform arithmetic operations on integers represented in binary or in decimal, and on floating-point (binary) numbers. The decimal arithmetic seems at first superfluous, but as implemented in System/360 and 370 it offers a number of conveniences. First, the packed decimal representation, which allows fields of greatly varying sizes, is a very efficient one for storage of numbers. Also, we have noted how convenient are the conversions from character representations to binary integer and back, with packed decimal forms as intermediate.

But aside from the mere representation of numbers, the decimal arithmetic has advantages in a number of situations. First, if numbers to be treated exactly grow rather large, requiring more than 32 bits for an exact binary representation, yet are of foreseeably bounded size, decimal representation offers a precision greater than binary integer arithmetic and greater convenience, especially in conversions, than double-precision floating-point. Many accounting problems are of this type: numbers ranging into the millions of dollars must nevertheless remain exact to the penny.

There are other situations in which numbers must be computed and rounded to the nearest penny, and for which no other rounding rules will do. In these situations binary integer arithmetic could be used, but decimal arithmetic is more convenient and straight-forward.

There are still other situations in which either binary integer or decimal integer arithmetic would be satisfactory but the fact that decimal arithmetic is storage-to-storage makes it more convenient than arithmetic in registers. One storage-to-storage addition can consume less space (but usually more time) than a load, add, store sequence.

We describe here in more detail than previously the packed decimal representation, the definition of decimal constants and symbols in assembler language, and the packed decimal instruction repertoire. Examples and a description of the exceptions possible close the chapter.

1. PACKED DECIMAL REPRESENTATIONS: INTERNAL AND ASSEMBLER LANGUAGE

In the packed decimal form of a number, two decimal digits are packed into each byte, with the exception that the lower-order half of the low-order byte contains a sign code. The length of a number may be from 1 to 16 bytes, and therefore 1 to 31 decimal digits:

Digit	Digit		Digit	Digit	Digit	Sign

Each digit or sign is coded in four bits. The digits 0–9 are each coded into their natural binary representations 0000 to 1001; 1010 to 1111 are not permitted as digits. On the other hand, 1010 to 1111 are recognized as signs—1010, 1100, 1110, and 1111 as plus, and 1011 and 1101 as minus; 0000 to 1001 are invalid as signs. Thus

0001 1001	0110 1100

is recognized as $+196$,

1000 0000	0111 1101

is recognized as -807, but

0110 1100	1010 0001

has invalid representations of both digits and signs. Note that a negative zero is perfectly possible.

It is easier to show and understand packed representations if they are stated in hexadecimal. The valid digits are 0–9, the valid signs are A–F, with A, C, E, and F defined as $+$, B and D as $-$. So the two-byte field 196C represents $+196$, 807D represents -807, and 6CA1 has both signs and digits in inappropriate places.

The IBM System/360 generates signs in either of two codes, the EBCDIC or ASCII, under control of bit 12 of the program status word: If the bit is 1, A is generated for $+$, B for $-$. This feature is not currently supported in software, and EBCDIC codes only are generated. The IBM System/370 uses bit 12 of the program status word for other purposes, so it does not include the ASCII code generation as an option at all.

In Chapter 6 packed decimal constants in assembler language were introduced, but we review them here. An operand of a DC statement defining a packed decimal constant is of the form P'decimal number' or PLn'decimal number'. The decimal number is a string of decimal digits, an optional decimal point, and an optional sign. The sign, if present, precedes the digits. The decimal point has no effect on the constant assembled and is allowed merely to help readability of the program. Thus P'3.25', P'+.325', P'325', and P'32.5' all define the same packed decimal constant, whose hexadecimal value is 325C. Signs C and D, the EBCDIC forms, are generated.

No boundary alignment is performed for packed decimal constants. If no length modifier is included, the number of digits given determines the length of the constant: 1 digit, 1 byte; 2 or 3 digits, 2 bytes; 4 or 5 digits, 3 bytes, etc., with an extra zero supplied as a high-order digit in the packed representation when necessary. When a length modifier (in bytes) is specified, the constant is further padded with high-order zeros or else loses high-order digits, depending on the specified length. Several constants can be defined in one DC operand, either by listing or by use of a duplication factor. Packed decimal constants can be specified in literals. The following generate the constants shown.

```
JONES   DC   PL4'-2.19'           0000219D
FZER    DC   6PL7'0'              six consecutive repetitions
                                  of 0000000000000C
TARIFF  DC   P'2.01,1.20,9.75'    201C120C975C
BG      DC   PL2'3296'            296C; note loss of digit
RT9     DC   P'-.21,.1474'        021D01474C
```

Decimal constants may also be defined in literals:

```
        MVC     RATE(2),=P'.26'
```

The DS statement used with a P-type operand will have the same syntax and define the same amount of space as the DC statement. In the absence of a specified value or length modifier, one byte will be reserved. Thus

```
GP3    DS   P          has length of one byte,
NXT1   DS   PL3        has length of three bytes, and
LAST   DS   P'4795'    has length of three bytes.
```

2. GENERAL STRUCTURE OF THE DECIMAL INSTRUCTION SET

All decimal arithmetic takes place in main storage, so all of the instructions are of SS type. The fields are of variable length, and the lengths of operands are not required to be equal, so the length field in each decimal instruction is split into $L1$, the length of the first operand (in bytes, not digits), and $L2$, the length of the second operand. The result always replaces the first operand, so the first operand field must be large enough to hold the result.

In assembler language, operands may be addressed as

$$D1(L1,B1)$$
$$D2(L2,B2)$$

where $D1$, $D2$, $L1$, $L2$, $B1$, and $B2$ are absolute expressions, or as

$$E1(L1)$$
$$E2(L2)$$

where *E1* and *E2* are relocatable expressions, or as

$$E1$$
$$E2$$

where the lengths *L1* and *L2* may be supplied by the assembler. If *E1* or *E2* is a single relocatable symbol, the assembler would supply the length attribute of the symbol; If *E1* or *E2* is a more complicated relocatable expression, the assembler would supply the length attribute of the first symbol appearing in the expression. For example, if RECD is defined by

```
RECD    DC    P'-296'
```

an operand RECD in a decimal-arithmetic instruction is equivalent to RECD(2) since the symbol has a length attribute of 2.

As elsewhere, we speak of lengths *L1* and *L2* as actual lengths of the fields, as they would be specified in assembler language. The reader will remember that in machine-language instructions the length codes are each 1 less than actual operand lengths.

Arithmetic instructions are provided for addition, subtraction, multiplication, and division of packed decimal numbers. These instructions are supported by others for comparing numbers and moving numbers and parts of numbers. The add, subtract, compare instructions, and an instruction equivalent to a load, set condition codes; the values of the condition code have the same meanings as in other arithmetic modes. We shall now investigate the instructions in detail.

3. ADD, SUBTRACT, AND COMPARE INSTRUCTIONS

The add, subtract, and compare instructions have assembler language mnemonics of

AP	Add Packed
SP	Subtract Packed
CP	Compare Packed.

The add and subtract instructions place the sum and difference, respectively, of their two operands in the first operand field. For example, if locations and contents are

ACC	01362C
RECD	296D
PAYB	181C
BALANCE	21347C

prior to execution of each of the following instructions, the results of the instructions will be as indicated:

```
AP    ACC(3),RECD(2)        ACC:   01066C
AP    BALANCE(3),PAYB(2)    BALANCE:  21528C
```

```
SP    BALANCE(3),PAYB(2)        BALANCE:   21166C
SP    ACC(3),BALANCE(3)         ACC:   19985D
SP    RECD(2),PAYB(2)           RECD:    477D
AP    RECD(2),ACC(3)            Overflow
```

An overflow occurs if the result field cannot hold the result. In our last example, the second operand field was larger than the first, and an overflow resulted. If 842C is added to 258C, the result is also an overflow, since a three-byte field would be required to hold the sum. The second operand field may be larger than the first, however, if the result fits in the first operand field. For example, addition of 024C (first operand) and 0000703C (second operand) results in a correct sum of 727C in the first operand field with no overflow; similarly 136D (first operand) added to 01075C (second operand) yields a result of 939C, which fits nicely into the first operand field. In summary, an overflow occurs if for any reason the first operand field is too short to contain all the nonzero digits of the result.

The condition code is set by both AP and SP operations to

0   if the result is zero,
1   if the result is less than zero,
2   if the result is greater than zero, and
3   if an overflow occurs.

The sign of a zero is always set to + by the AP and SP instructions, except that when the zero is the residue of an overflow, the sign of the true result remains.

The compare instruction, CP, acts just as the subtract instruction except that it

1) changes *no* bytes of main storage, and therefore
2) cannot result in an overflow.

All digits of both fields are checked, and the shorter field is considered to be extended with high-order zeros if necessary. A negative zero is considered equal to a positive zero. Therefore the condition code, the sole result of the operation, is set to

0 if the two operands are equal,
1 if the first operand is less than the second operand, and
2 if the first operand is greater than the second operand.

4. MOVING A PACKED DECIMAL NUMBER

Moving a packed decimal number, as it is, from one main storage location to another is quite easy, but when one wishes to extend or reduce the field, especially on the right, the situation is not so simple. There are some instructions that help us, and we introduce them in order.

The MVC instruction can obviously be used to move a packed decimal field just as it can move any string of bytes. The length of the field can remain fixed, or if only the last part of the field is moved, the field is effectively shortened, with several digits wholly abandoned.

The instruction ZAP (Zero and Add Packed) moves a number from the second operand location to the first operand location, filling high-order zeros in the first operand field if it is longer than the second operand field. The ZAP instruction is equivalent in function to a Load instruction, but since lengths of first and second operands are specified separately, the instruction can expand or contract fields. The ZAP instruction also sets a condition code, exactly as though it had first placed a zero in the first operand location and then *added* the second operand to it, as with an AP instruction. Thus the condition code reports whether the number is zero, less than zero, or greater than zero, or whether an overflow occurred. For example, if

RECD	contains	296D,
BALANCE	contains	21347C,
ZP	contains	00000C,

and

SLS	contains	00021C,

the following ZAP instructions will have the results indicated:

ZAP	RES(2),RECD(2)	RES:	296D	CC = 1
ZAP	RES(5),BALANCE(3)	RES:	000021347C	CC = 2
ZAP	RES(2),ZP(3)	RES:	000C	CC = 0
ZAP	RES(2),SLS(3)	RES:	021C	CC = 2
ZAP	RES(2),BALANCE(3)	RES:	347C (overflow)	CC = 3

We see that moving a number and possibly changing its length by adding or subtracting zeros on the left is simple. Next we consider the problem of adding or eliminating digits on the right, an operation equivalent to a shift. This is accomplished fairly easily by multiplication or division by an appropriate power of 10, using the instructions we introduce in the next section. However, there are other ways, and we describe some of them.

Shifts of an even number of digits are conceptually simpler than shifts of an odd number of digits, since they involve only movement of the sign (and possibly the whole field), not a re-division of digits between bytes. To help us, there is an instruction MVN (MoVe Numeric), which is of SS type with single length, that moves the low-order four bits (!) of each byte of the second operand to corresponding positions in the first operand. Thus if GG contains 123456 and HH contains 789ABC, the instruction

MVN   GG(3),HH

will move the half-bytes 8, A, C to corresponding positions in GG, which is thus changed to 183A5C. This instruction is especially useful for moving the *sign* of a packed decimal number. A four-byte packed decimal field at QUANT can be short-

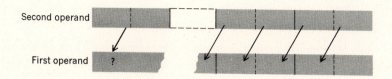

Fig. 14-1 The MVØ instruction.

ened to three bytes, with the loss of the least-significant two digits, by

        MVN   QUANT+2(1),QUANT+3

If QUANT contained 0027491C, this instruction would change it to 00274C1C.

To *add* two digits, presumably zero, to a packed decimal number, one can follow a sequence such as the following, which adds two zeros at the right of a four-byte field at SLT:

        MVI   SLT+4,X'00'   ZERØS IN EXTRA BYTE
        MVN   SLT+4(1),SLT+3   SIGN TØ NEW PØSITIØN
        NI   SLT+3,X'F0'   REPLACE SIGN IN ØLD PØSITIØN WITH O

The same operation could be done by

        MVI   SLT+4,X'0F'
        NC   SLT+4(1),SLT+3
        NI   SLT+3,X'F0'

For shifting a number by *one* digit, we have at our disposal an ingenious instruction: MVØ (MoVe with Offset), which is an SS instruction with two length subfields. It moves the second operand, starting at the rightmost half-byte, to the first operand location, *starting at the high-order half of the rightmost byte*, as shown in Fig. 14-1. No checking for valid decimal digits or signs is performed. Zeros are filled in the high-order positions of the first operand if the second operand is shorter than the first operand; otherwise high-order digits of the second operand are ignored. For example, if QUANT contains 36247D and NEWF contains 6093241C,

        MVØ   NEWF(4),QUANT(2)

will change NEWF to 0003624C. Note that the low-order byte of QUANT was lost in the move, and that high-order zeros were supplied. Note also that the sign of the result is left over from the first operand. Therefore it is usually necessary *first* to move the byte containing the correct sign to the new field, *then* to move the digits with the MVØ instruction:

```
MVC    NEWF+3(1),QUANT+2
MVØ    NEWF(4),QUANT(2)
```

To move while shifting *left* an odd number of places (inserting zeros on the right), three instructions are necessary, perhaps in a pattern like the following, which has results shown:

```
MVC    NEWF+4(1),QUANT+2        6093241C7D

MVØ    NEWF(5),QUANT(4)         036247D??D

NC     NEWF+3(2),=X'000F'       036247000D
```

In summary, we may suggest:

Move, adding zeros on left:	ZAP			
Move, deleting digits from left:	ZAP	or	MVC	
Move, keeping same digits:	ZAP	or	MVC	
Move, adding even number of zeros on right:	MVI	MVN	NI	or MP
Move, deleting even number of digits from right:	MVC	MVN		or DP
Move, adding odd number of zeros on right:	MVC	MVØ	NC	or MP
Move, deleting odd number of digits from right:	MVC	MVØ		or DP

or minor variations of these patterns.

Users of the IBM System/370 have access to another instruction which makes movement of data easier than we have shown it. The instruction is Shift and Round Packed (SRP); it has three operands. Operand 1, with a 4-bit length field, identifies the field to be manipulated. Operand 2 gives the shift count. The *B2* and *D2* are added as usual, and the last six bits are considered a signed integer. If positive (bit 26 is 0), bits 27–31 indicate the amount of left shift. If negative (bit 26 is 1), the 2's-complement of bits 27–31 indicates the amount of shift to the right. Therefore a right shift of x positions is specified by a second operand of 64-x. In any case, shifting is by decimal digits, or half-bytes. Zeros are supplied for digit positions vacated by the shift.

Fig. 14–2   Examples of SRP.

	Instruction	Result in GROSS
SRP	GROSS(5),2,0	043026500C
SRP	GROSS(5),0(11),5	043026500C
SRP	GROSS(5),1(11),0	430265000C
SRP	GROSS(5),62,0	000004302C
SRP	GROSS(5),62,5	000004303C
SRP	GROSS(5),58,5	000000000C
SRP	GROSS(5),58(11),5	000000043C

The third operand, *I3*, which occupies the *L2* field in the usual SS format, specifies the rounding factor used in right shifts. The rounding factor is added, as a decimal digit, to the last digit shifted out of the field, and the carry, if any, is added to the right-most digit kept; this addition is carried out disregarding the sign of the operand. The usual values to be coded in *I3* would be 0, in case no rounding is desired, and 5, which produces normal rounding.

Suppose field GRØSS is a five-byte field containing (hex) 000430265C, and register 11 contains 00000002. The following instructions will have results indicated in Fig. 14-2. Note that either the contents of register *B2* or the displacement *D2* or a combination of both can specify the shift count; in practice, most shift counts will be specified as decimal integers.

The shift factor must be a valid decimal digit; if not, a data exception results. A decimal overflow exception results if significant digits are shifted left out of the field.

The condition code is set, even if a shift of zero positions is called for:

CC = 0   if the result is 0 (and a zero result is always made positive),
CC = 1   if the result is less than 0,
CC = 2   if the result is greater than 0,
CC = 3   if an overflow occurs.

A sequence of ZAP and SRP will accomplish any move of a decimal field, lengthening or shortening the field and positioning the number anywhere in the new field. For example,

```
ZAP     GRØSS(5),BAL(4)
SRP     GRØSS(5),63,5
```

will take a BAL field 0430265C, place it in a five-byte field GRØSS, shift it right one position and round: 000043027C.

5. MULTIPLY AND DIVIDE INSTRUCTIONS

The packed decimal multiply and divide instructions have some slightly odd features that mostly result from the limitation of the results to the first operand location. The *Multiply Packed* (MP) instruction multiplies the numbers in the first and second operands, and places the result in the first operand field. The size of the second operand is limited: it may not be more than eight bytes (15 digits + sign), nor may it be larger than the first operand field, even if high-order zeros in the second operand would actually permit the product to fit. Since the length of the significant portion of a product is the sum of the lengths of the significant portions of the operands, the first operand field must contain high-order zeros equal to the length of the significant portion of the second operand. The restriction actually imposed is more stringent: the first operand is required to have high-order zeros equal to the field length, including all digits and signs, of the second operand. This guarantees at least one high-order zero in every product.

Suppose that we have the following contents of storage locations:

UNIT1	00600C
UNIT2	030D
RATE1	0000411C
RATE2	00002C
RATE3	00052D
TEN	010C
FDC	0000791C

With these contents existing in storage prior to execution of each of the following instructions, the results will be as indicated:

MP	RATE2(3),UNIT2(2)	RATE2:00060D
MP	RATE3(3),UNIT2(2)	Invalid: only three high-order zeros
MP	RATE1(4),UNIT1(3)	Invalid
MP	RATE1(4),UNIT1+1(2)	RATE1:0246600C
MP	FDC(4),TEN(2)	FDC:0007910C

The ZAP instruction can be used to extend the first operand field with high-order zeros before a multiplication.

The first operand of the *Divide Packed* instruction (DP) is the dividend and the second operand is the divisor. The *quotient and remainder* replace the dividend in main storage. The quotient occupies the high-order portion of the first operand field, and the remainder occupies the low-order portion. The remainder will always have the same length as the divisor and, even when zero, the same sign as the dividend. Therefore the length of the quotient is $L1 - L2$. The sign of the quotient is determined algebraically from the signs of the dividend and divisor, even if the quotient is zero. The length of the divisor is restricted to be less than the length of the dividend, and in no case greater than eight bytes. If the quotient cannot be held in the space allotted to it, the result is a decimal divide exception, but we shall see more about exceptions in the next section.

For example, suppose that TØTAL contains 0034075C, and that QT contains 200C. The instruction

$$DP \quad TØTAL(4),QT(2)$$

will leave 170C075C in place of TØTAL. The quotient is 170C, which is addressed at TØTAL; its length is $4 - 2 = 2$. The remainder is 075C, which is addressed at TØTAL+2.

For further examples, suppose that we have the following contents of fields:

TØT1	0034075C
TØT2	000064010D
TØT3	00000000316C
UNIT1	200C

UNIT2   005D
UNIT3   00320C
TEN   010C

With these contents in storage prior to execution of *each* of the following instructions, the results will be as indicated, with quotient and remainder bracketed:

DP	TØT2(5),UNIT2(2)	TØT2: 12802C, 000D
DP	TØT2+1(4),UNIT2+1(1)	TØT2: 00 12802C, 0D
DP	TØT2+1(4),UNIT2(2)	Invalid
DP	TØT2(5),UNIT2+1(1)	TØT2: 0012802C, 0D
DP	TØT1(4),UNIT2+1(1)	TØT1: 06815D, 0C
DP	TØT2(5),UNIT1(2)	TØT2: 00320D, 010D
DP	TØT3(6),UNIT3(3)	TØT3: 00000C, 00316C
DP	TØT3+3(3),UNIT3(3)	Invalid: no space for quotient
DP	TØT2(5),TEN(2)	TØT2: 06401D, 000D

Note the treatment of signs and the lengths of the various results.

In general, one may say that the number of leading zeros required in the first operand must be two plus the number of leading zeros in the second operand, though if the leading nonzero digit of the dividend is less than the leading nonzero digit of the divisor it may in effect be counted as a leading zero. The reader is urged to test this rule in various examples.

The condition code is not affected by the DP instruction.

6. EXCEPTIONS

Decimal arithmetic instructions are liable to some of the same exceptions as are other instructions: *addressing*, *protection*, and to an *operation* exception if the decimal feature is not installed (this does not affect MVØ and MVN, which are part of the standard instruction repertoire).

Word boundaries are not a problem, but the *specification* exception is used with a new meaning: when in a MP or DP instruction the length of the second operand is greater than 8, a specification exception with interrupt occurs. In these cases the operation is suppressed, so contents of storage are unchanged.

If the quotient in a DP instruction would be too large for the available space, or if the divisor is zero, a *decimal divide* exception occurs, the divide operation is suppressed, and an interrupt is taken.

A *data* exception can arise in any of the instructions AP, SP, ZAP, CP, MP, and DP (and also the CVB instruction introduced in Chapter 6). Each of these instructions checks every half-byte it processes for a proper sign or digit code. If a digit code 0–9 appears in a sign position or a sign code A–F in a position that should contain a digit, the result is a data exception. The data exception is also taken if the first operand of a multiply decimal instruction has too few high-order zeros. A third cause of a data exception is improper overlap of first and second operand fields; in each of these instructions it is permissible to have the rightmost bytes of the operands coincide (you can add a number to itself, for example), but any other overlap of fields is prohibited. A data exception occurs during the execution of an instruction, and the operation is suspended at that point; the contents of the result field is unpredictable and should not be used further.

One last exception is *decimal overflow*. This exception occurs when the result of an AP, SP, or ZAP instruction cannot be held in the available field. The result is truncated on the left but lower-order digits and sign are exactly as they would be in a longer field which was sufficient to hold the result. For example, addition of 360C (first operand) and 02713C (second operand) places 073C in the first operand field; this is the low-order portion of the correct sum.

On decimal overflow the condition code is set to 3. Interrupt depends on bit 2 of the program mask: if this bit is 0, no interruption occurs, but interrupt does take place if this bit is 1.

7. EXAMPLES

In this section we illustrate the use of the decimal arithmetic instructions, and also some of the standard manipulations performed on packed decimal numbers.

First, let us suppose we have a field of length 7 named EXTEN, in which there are assumed to be five decimal places (and therefore eight digits before the assumed decimal point). Suppose that we wish to *round* the number in this field to the nearest cent (or hundredth), placing the result with its two decimal digits at a six-byte field CHARGE. The usual rounding method is the addition of 5 to the first place to be lost (this step is often called *half-adjust*), then truncation. If we know the number in EXTEN is positive, the half-adjust is a simple matter:

```
AP      EXTEN(7),=P'.500'
```

This would change 0000004732962C, for example, to 0000004733462C, and if the 462 is then stripped away, the result will be the rounded quantity desired. If we are not sure of the sign of EXTEN, we must generate a half-adjust quantity of the same sign, and add that:

```
MVN   HAJ+1(1),EXTEN+6       HAJ CØNTAINS 500C
AP    EXTEN(7),HAJ(2)
```

The reader should test the adequacy of this sequence. The field can then be truncated and moved to CHARGE by

```
MVC   CHARGE+5(1),EXTEN+6
MVØ   CHARGE(6),EXTEN(5)
```

Of course, in the IBM System/370, we can use the SRP instruction instead:

```
SRP   EXTEN(7),61,5
ZAP   CHARGE(6),EXTEN(7)
```

Second, if we wish to set or change the sign of a packed decimal number whose sign is represented by A, B, C or D (not E or F), we can do the job easily with logical operations. If the sign of a number is at, say FIELD+6, we can

> set the sign to +:   NI   FIELD+6,B'11111110'
> set the sign to −:   ØI   FIELD+6,B'00000001'
> reverse the sign: XI   FIELD+6,B'00000001'

If the sign may be E or F (a PACK instruction on an unsigned field would leave a sign code of F), as well as A, B, C or D, the situation is more complicated. We can set the sign at FIELD+6 to minus, for example, by

> MVN   FIELD+6(1),=P'−1'

To reverse the sign, we must first test it:

```
          MVN    G(1),FIELD+6              G CONTAINS 00
          CLI    G,X'0E'
          BL     RSP
          MVN    FIELD+6(1),=P'−1'
          B      AFTER
RSP       XI     FIELD+6,B'00000001'
AFTER     ...
```

Third, let us consider a billing problem. Suppose there is a list of items and that the count of items in the list is (a binary integer) in register 3. Each item consists of a four-byte packed decimal quantity (an integer) followed by a five-byte packed decimal unit price, with four decimal places. These fields occupy the first nine bytes of a 20-byte record for each item; the items start at location ITEM and follow each other immediately. Our problem is to compute quantity times unit price for each item, then round the total to two decimal places (cents) and store the result in the tenth through fifteenth bytes of the record. Finally, we want to keep a running sum of the totals, and to keep the grand total in an eight-byte field GRANDTØT.

Address modification is required in this example. If we keep the address of the current record in register 4, we can address quantity as 0(length,4), unit price as 4(length,4) and total as 9(length,4). In a loop, register 4 can be increased by 20 and loop control can be accomplished by a BCT on register 3.

The computation for an individual item will be

```
ZAP    PRØD(9),4(5,4)           UNIT PRICE TØ PRØD AREA
MP     PRØD(9),0(4,4)           MULTIPLY BY QUANTITY
MVN    HAJ+1(1),PRØD+8          HAJ CØNTAINS 050C
AP     PRØD(9),HAJ              HALF ADJUST
MVC    9(6,4),PRØD+2            MØVE 6 BYTES ØF PRØD
MVN    14(1,4),PRØD+8           MØVE SIGN
AP     GRANDTØT(8),9(6,4)
```

Fig. 14–3 Quantity times unit price loop

```
          ZAP   GRANDTØT(8),=P'0'
          LA    4,ITEM
*         NØ. ØF ITEMS ALREADY IN REG. 3
DECL      ZAP   PRØD(9),4(5,4)          UNIT PRICE TØ PRØD AREA
          MP    PRØD(9),0(4,4)          MULTIPLY BY QUANTITY
          MVN   HAJ+1(1),PRØD+8         HAJ CØNTAINS 050C
          AP    PRØD(9),HAJ             HALF ADJUST
          MVC   9(6,4),PRØD+2           MØVE 6 BYTES ØF PRØD
          MVN   14(1,4),PRØD+8          MØVE SIGN
          AP    GRANDTØT(8),9(6,4)
*         INCREMENT AND LØØP CØNTRØL
          LA    4,20(4)                 PASS TØ NEXT ITEM
          BCT   3,DECL
```

The MVC   9(6,4),PRØD+2 instruction moves the upper six bytes of PRØD to its designated field, leaving behind one digit and the sign. The next instruction, MVN   14(1,4),PRØD+6 moves the sign to the sign position of the six-byte result field, destroying a second digit in the process. Since this second digit is the one that 5 was added to in the half-adjust process, the total effect is that of rounding of the product. Note that the multiplication required a product area of nine bytes, but it is quite reasonable to dispense with the upper two bytes of the product. (Why?) The entire loop is shown in Fig. 14–3.

As a final example, we consider a questionnaire analysis. Suppose that cards containing responses to questionnaires contain in columns 21 through 40 single-digit answers to questions. The responses we are interested in are the digits 0–9; other characters may code uninteresting responses such as "no answer," "question does not apply," etc. For each of the twenty questions, we want the *average* (*mean*) of the responses made in the 0–9 range and the *mode*, which is the response of greatest frequency.

For each of the 20 questions we maintain a 30-byte area containing

10 two-byte counters, one each for the responses 0–9, in that order;
a two-byte counter of digits 0–9;
a two-byte counter of other responses;
a three-byte sum of the responses;
three bytes to contain mode and the two-byte average (two decimal places).

We keep each counter and sum as a packed decimal field.

The logic of the segment can be represented by the flowchart in Fig. 14–4 and is fairly self-evident. Let us then examine the implementation strategy of the segment, which is shown in Fig. 14–5. As we move through the inner loop, we keep in register 4 the address of the beginning of the area of counters and sums pertaining to the current question, and in register 3 the address of the current card column. We use registers 6 and 7 for loop control, i.e., testing the contents of register 3 for exit from the loop. We shall use the response itself, 0–9, to help us compute the address of the field in which it is to be counted. For this purpose the digit must be converted to binary and multiplied by 2 (with a SLA instruction), and

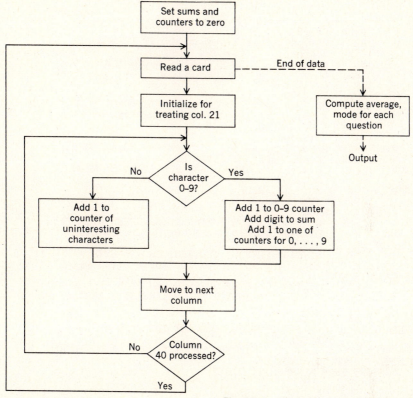

Fig. 14–4   The logic of questionnaire analysis.

Fig. 14–5   Program segment for questionnaire analysis

```
*     READ CARDS AND CØMPUTE AVERAGE AND MØDE ØF
*     DIGITS 0–9 IN CØLUMNS 21–40.
*     FIRST, SET SUM AND CØUNTER AREAS TØ ZERØS
INITØUTR  LA    8,20
          LA    9,CØUNT
INITØR    MVC   0(30,9),ZRØAR
          LA    9,30(9)
          BCT   8,INITØR
*     BEGIN ØUTER LØØP, READING CARD INTØ 'CARD' AREA
ØUTRLØØP  GET   IN,CARD
          LA    3,CARD+20   INITIALIZE FØR INNER LØØP,
          LA    6,1            WHICH CØNSIDERS EACH CARD CØL.
          LA    7,CARD+39
          LA    4,CØUNT
*     EXAMINE A CARD COLUMN
INNRLØØP  CLI   0(3),C'0'
          BL    UNINT       IF CHAR. IS LESS THAN 0
          CLI   0(3),C'9'        ØR GREATER THAN 9
          BH    UNINT       BRANCH TØ UNINT
          AP    20(2,4),=P'1'   CØUNT AN INTERESTING RESPØNSE
```

(continued)

Fig. 14–5   (continued)

```
           PACK   DBL(8),0(1,3)       PACK THE DIGIT,
           AP     24(3,4),DBL+7(1)    THEN ADD IT TØ SUM
           CVB    5,DBL               CØMPUTE ADDRESS ØF
           SLA    5,1                  APPRØPRIATE CØUNTER,
           AR     5,4                  THEN ADD 1
           AP     0(2,5),=P'1'        TØ IT
           B      INLPCTRL
UNINT      AP     22(2,4),=P'1'       CØUNT AN UNINTERESTING RESPØNSE
INLPCTRL   LA     4,30(4)             CØMPLETE INNER AND ØUTER LØØPS
           BXLE   3,6,INNRLØØP
           B      ØUTRLØØP
*      WHEN CARDS EXHAUSTED, AUTØMATIC TRANSFER TØ AVCØMP,
*      WHERE AVERAGE AND MØDE ARE CØMPUTED
AVCØMP     LA     8,20                INITIALIZE FØR AVERAGE, MØDE
           LA     9,CØUNT              CØMPUTATIØNS
AVLØØP     CP     20(2,9),=P'0'       IF NØ ENTRIES, BYPASS
           BNH    AVLPCTRL
*      CØMPUTE AVERAGE
           ZAP    DIVD(3),24(3,9) GENERATE DIVIDEND WITH TWØ
           MVC    DIVD+3(1),26(9)      EXTRA PLACES ØN RIGHT TØ PREPARE
           NC     DIVD+2(2),=X'F00F'  FØR TWØ DEC. PLACES IN QUØTIENT
           DP     DIVD(4),20(2,9) QUØTIENT IS TWØ-BYTE FIELD AT DIVD
           MVC    28(2,9),DIVD    AV. TØ LAST 2 BYTES ØF AREA
*      CØMPUTE MØDE
           LA     4,2(9)          STEP THRØUGH CØUNTERS ØF 1'S - 9'S
           LR     5,9             INDICATØR ØF LARGEST:  ZERØ AT FIRST
           LA     6,2
           LA     7,18(9)
MØDELP     CP     0(2,4),0(2,5)   CØMPARE TWØ CØUNTERS
           BL     MØDELPCT
           LR     5,4             IF NEW LARGEST, PUT ADDR. IN REG. 5
MØDELPCT   BXLE   4,6,MØDELP
*      CØNVERT FRØM ADDRESS TØ DIGIT
           SR     5,9
           SRA    5,1
           CVD    5,DBL
           MVC    27(1,9),DBL+7   STØRE MØDE AS PACKED DIGIT
*      LØØP CØNTRØL FØR AVLØØP
AVLPCTRL   LA     9,30(9)
           BCT    8,AVLØØP
*      READY FØR ØUTPUT
*      ...
*      CØNSTANTS AND SYMBØLS REQUIRED BY SEGMENT
DBL        DS     1D              DØUBLE WØRD FØR CØNVERSIØNS
DIVD       DS     PL4
CARD       DS     CL80
CØUNT      DS     20CL30          AREA TØ HØLD CØUNTERS
ZRØAR      DC     12PL2'0'        AREA ØF CØNSTANTS TØ INITIALIZE
           DC     PL3'0'              CØUNTER AREA
           DC     PL1'0'
           DC     PL2'0'
```

the result added to the address of the counter for the digit 0. The outer loop involves nothing particularly new, except the setup of the areas of sums and counters, which illustrates the definition of packed decimal storage and constants.

In the closing portion of the segment, beginning at AVCØMP, we have an example first of a division. In order to obtain two decimal places in the quotient, we extend the dividend two places on the right, thus creating two decimal places in the dividend. The reader should verify for himself that the instructions do, in fact, produce an average and that they cannot result in overflow. The computation of the mode is of course merely a search for the largest of the 10 counters. The addresses of next counter to be compared and largest counter found so far are kept in registers 4 and 5, respectively. After all 10 counters are examined, the address of the counter is converted to a packed decimal number in the reverse of the process that earlier generated the address of a counter.

This example could have been done in binary arithmetic, but decimal arithmetic is convenient and reasonably efficient in the use of storage. In particular, an instruction like AP   20(2,4),=P'1' can take the place of the three instructions, Load, Add, and Store. We lose some convenience, however, by not being able to index our fields.

8. MAIN IDEAS

a. The packed decimal representation allows expression of numbers of from 1 to 31 digits; the digits are packed two per byte, with the sign occupying the lowest-order half-byte.

b. The packed decimal instructions are all of SS type, with separate length specifications for the two operands. All packed decimal arithmetic is performed in main storage, and it can sometimes be quite convenient.

c. The instructions introduced for manipulation are summarized in Fig. 14–6.

Fig. 14–6 Instructions for manipulation of packed decimal fields

Name	Type	Action	Cond.[4] Code	Exceptions[5]
AP	SS[2]	$S1 \leftarrow c(S1) + c(S2)$	(a)	A, D,DF
SP	SS[2]	$S1 \leftarrow c(S1) - c(S2)$	(a)	A, D,DF
ZAP	SS[2]	$S1 \leftarrow c(S2)$	(a)	A, D,DF
CP	SS[2]		(b)	A, D
MP	SS[2]	$S1 \leftarrow c(S1) \times c(S2)$		A,S,D
DP	SS[2]	$S1 \leftarrow$ [quotient, remainder of $c(S1)/c(S2)$][6]		A,S,D,DK
MVN	SS[1]	$S1 \leftarrow [c(S1), c(S2)]$[7]		A
MVØ	SS[2]	$S1 \leftarrow [c(S1), c(S2)]$[8]		A
SRP	SS[3]	$S1 \leftarrow c(S1)$[9]	(a)	OP,A, D,DF

Notes

1. SS with single length specification describing both operand fields.
2. SS with separate length specification for each operand.
3. SS with *L1* specifying length of operand field, *S2* is shift count, *I3* is rounding factor. Operands written *S1(L1),S2,I3*.
4. Condition codes are set to

    a) 0 if result = 0   b) 0 if $Op_1 = Op_2$
         1 if result < 0   1 if $Op_1 < Op_2$
         2 if result > 0   2 if $Op_1 > Op_2$
         3 if overflow

5. Exception codes:

    OP: Operation (if System/360)   D: Data
      A: Access   DF: Decimal overflow
      S: Specification   DK: Decimal divide

6. Quotient occupies bytes 0 to *L1-L2*-1; remainder occupies bytes *L1-L2* to *L1-1*.
7. Only the low-order four bits of each byte of $c(S2)$ are moved; high-order four bits of each byte of $c(S1)$ remain.
8. Only the low-order four bits of $c(S1)$ remain.
9. Field shifted left by *S2* or right by 64-*S2*; right shifts rounded by *I3*.

QUESTIONS FOR REVIEW AND IMAGINATION

1. Given that the contents of main storage locations are as follows *prior to the execution of each* instruction, show the result of each instruction:

Main storage locations	Contents	Instructions	
GBS	21346C	ZAP	FERMAG+1(3),NLQC(2)
WHP	00120D	AP	GBS(3),NLQC(2)
NLQC	900C	SP	GBS(3),MPHY(4)
MPHY	0000024D	CP	NLQC(2),MPHY(4)
FERMAG	223344556C	SP	NLQC(2),WHP(3)
DRGN	000032500D	AP	NLQC(2),GBS(2)
		MP	MPHY(4),NLQC(2)
		MP	WHP(3),MPHY+2(2)
		MP	WHP(3),MPHY+3(1)
		DP	DRGN(5),NLQC(2)
		DP	DRGN(5),WHP(3)
		DP	DRGN(5),WHP+1(2)
		MVØ	DRGN(4),FERMAG(3)
		MVN	DRGN(4),FERMAG

2. Write as many different reasonably efficient segments as you can for moving a field by adding or deleting digits on the right. Be sure to include some segments which use multiplication and division.

3. There is an instruction similar to MVN which is named MVZ (MoVe Zones). It moves the *high-order* four bits of each byte from the second operand to the first operand field. The names of the MVN and MVZ instructions are derived from their possible use in moving numeric and zone parts of *zoned decimal* numbers. Can you think of any uses for the MVZ instruction in manipulating packed decimal numbers?

4. In the example segments we have seen, the MVØ instruction is used in combination with other instructions. What move or shift operations can be performed with one MVØ instruction by itself? Could you redesign the instruction so that fewer move and shift operations would have to be accomplished by several-instruction sequences? Would your design make other operations even more difficult?

5. From your knowledge that multiplication is performed by repeated shifting and addition and that division is performed by repeated subtraction, figure out the logical mechanism by which the MP and DP instructions are performed. It helps to postulate a working register of up to eight bytes which holds the second operand during either operation, and which conceptually is aligned in turn "under" various portions of the first operand. Make sure your mechanism explains all the rules by which the instructions operate.

6. Write a program segment to perform in packed decimal arithmetic a calculation of an employee's take-home pay. Suppose that available fields are

GRØSS   4 bytes   gross earnings for the month in dollars and cents
EXEMPT   2 bytes   number of exemptions, an integer
FICA   4 bytes   earnings for the year to date that have been subject to F.I.C.A. withholding in dollars and cents
DEDUCT   3 bytes   deductions for the month

Compute federal withholding, FED, as

$$14\% \quad \text{of} \quad (\text{GRØSS}-(\text{EXEMPT}*\$50.00))$$

Compute F.I.C.A. tax in a field FICATAX as

$$4.4\% \quad \text{of} \quad \text{GRØSS}$$

but only until a total of $6600.00 for the year has been taxed. Update the field FICA by the amount taxed. Then compute take-home pay as

$$\text{GRØSS}-\text{FED}-\text{FICATAX}-\text{DEDUCT}$$

Taxes withheld should be rounded *down*, that is, truncated; it hardly costs anything and makes somebody feel good.

7. Manufacture a small amount of sample data and simulate execution of the parts of the program segment in Fig. 14–4 in order to understand them better. Reprogram the entire segment using binary integer instead of packed-decimal arithmetic. Compare the two segments as to space required, number of instructions to be executed, limitations to be placed on the data, and straightforwardness of programming (a useful concept this, since it is inversely proportional to debugging time.)

8. Add to the program segment of Fig. 14–5 an additional section computing the *median* of the responses in any card column. Roughly speaking, the median is the middle number of the sorted set of data. More precisely, it is a number such that no more than half of the data are larger than the number and no more than half are smaller. This computation is more difficult than the computation of the mean or the mode; if the median, by our definition, should be fractional, take the next larger integer.

9. Write a program that will produce a mortgage amortization table. Input a card containing principal of the mortgage, nominal annual interest rate (e.g., .0500 for 5%), and the monthly payment. The printed table should consist of a line for each month of the life of the mortgage. Each line should contain

1) the time period: 1, 2, 3, . . . ;
2) the principal outstanding at the beginning of the month;
3) the interest for the month, computed as principal at the beginning of the

month times annual interest rate divided by 12, rounded to the nearest cent; and

4) the portion of monthly payment applied to the reduction of the principal, computed as the difference between the monthly payment and the interest.

The principal outstanding at the beginning of the next month is obtained by the appropriate subtraction. In the last period the payment required may be less than a full regular payment; it should be printed and labeled.

Printing the table with decimal points and without a sign appearing as part of the last digit of each number can be a major bother in this program. In the next chapter we shall see how the EDIT instruction eases this burden.

10. The program segment of Fig. 14–3 and the segment of Fig. 14–5 (especially the part that computes average) can be written more simply by using the SRP instruction. Make the changes.

11. Retry problem 21 of Chapter 11, specifically the expansion of the 18-byte area, making use of the MVØ instruction.

REFERENCES

IBM System/360 Principles of Operation, GA22-6821, IBM Corporation. Description of the decimal arithmetic instructions.

IBM System/370 Principles of Operation, GA22-7000, IBM Corporation. As above, but including the SRP instruction.

Chapter 15

Translate, Edit, and Execute Instructions

In this chapter we study some powerful special-purpose instructions that are representative of the sophistication found in instruction repertoires of modern computers. Just as early experience in numerical computation showed that keeping track of number magnitudes was a very common problem, leading to development of floating-point arithmetic instructions, more recent experience in nonnumeric problems has shown that certain problems are widespread and led to development of instructions that handle the problems well.

One of the instructions is a code translation instruction, and a second is a search instruction. Two others are designed for editing numbers into a nice form for printing; they are tailored to the problem, and fairly simple to use, but are among the most complex instructions in the IBM System/360 and 370 instruction repertoire. The fifth instruction has two functions: it permits execution of a single instruction outside the usual sequence of instructions, and it provides convenient modification of the length codes etc. that are specified in the second byte of an instruction.

1. TRANSLATE INSTRUCTIONS

In this section we discuss two similar instructions: TRanslate (TR) and TRanslate and Test (TRT). Each is an SS-type instruction, with a single length specification which refers to the first operand only. First we take up the TR instruction.

The purpose of the TR instruction is to translate the codes in the bytes of the first operand into other codes. The second operand is a table of codes defining the translation. Each byte b of the first operand acts as an index to the table; the sum of the second operand address and this index addresses the byte which replaces the first operand byte: the byte b is thus replaced by $c(S2+b)$. For example, if the second operand address is 00F604, an argument byte C6 is replaced by the byte at location 00F604+C6 = 00F6CA.

We may regard the table in the second operand as a table of function values of one byte each, and the first operand as a string of arguments to the function. The TR instruction replaces each argument by its function value. The table used in the second operand is ordered by the possible argument values and is therefore normally 256 bytes long. The length of the first operand is specified in the instruction and may be from 1 to 256 bytes.

As an example, let us suppose that our problem is to translate in an 80-byte card image the characters ( )+=' as punched on an IBM model 026 card punch into the proper EBCDIC codes for these characters, leaving all other characters unchanged. The codes are as follows:

Punched on IBM 026	Existing code	Desired code
)	4C	5D
+	50	4E
(	6C	4D
=	7B	7E
'	7C	7D

Therefore bytes in the source string whose hexadecimal values are 4C, 50, 6C, 7B, and 7C are to be translated into 5D, 4E, 4D, 7E, and 7D, respectively. A 256-byte table must be set up, perhaps starting at a location TRTAB1, to be the second operand of a TR instruction; the table will contain bytes 00, 01, 02, 03, . . . , FF, but 4C will be replaced by 5D, 50 by 4E, 6C by 4D, 7B by 7E, and 7C by 7D. If the card image is at location CARD, the codes will be translated as desired by the instruction

$$\text{TR} \qquad \text{CARD(80),TRTAB1}$$

The first character of CARD may be a blank, which is hexadecimal 40. The number 40 is added to TRTAB1, and the function byte at TRTAB1+40, which of course happens to be 40, replaces the 40 at CARD. Other bytes are translated similarly into copies of themselves, but when a 50, for example, is encountered, it is replaced by the function byte at TRTAB1+50, which is 4E. All data are valid, and the translation proceeds until all 80 bytes are translated. The second operand and the condition code are unchanged. If a segment of the string at CARD before the TR instruction is

40	C1	6C	C9	50	F2	4C	7B	6C	D2	60
blank	A	(	I	+	2	)	=	(	K	–

then the same portion of the string after the TR instruction will be

40	C1	4D	C9	4E	F2	5D	7E	4D	D2	60

A second type of standard chore is also handled very nicely by the TR instruction. This is the rearrangement problem, in which a string of bytes is to be moved from one area in main storage to another, but is to be rearranged in the process.

The rearrangement is accomplished by letting the string to be moved serve as the table in the second operand of a TR instruction, while the first operand is a series of pointers into the table. For example, suppose a 20-byte string is stored at SØURCE, preceded by one blank at SØURCE–1. If we desire to have at RESULT

3 blanks,
4th–8th bytes of the string at SØURCE,
1 blank,
18th–20th bytes from SØURCE,
2 blanks,
9th–12th bytes from SØURCE,

we first store at RESULT the following pattern, where the division into lines is only for visual correspondence with the specification above:

```
00 00 00
04 05 06 07 08
00
12 13 14
00 00
09 0A 0B 0C
```

The move with rearrangement is accomplished by

```
TR    RESULT(18),SØURCE-1
```

Wherever it appears in the pattern at RESULT, the argument byte 00 is translated into the function byte at (SØURCE–1)+00, which is the blank. The byte 04 is translated into the function byte at (SØURCE–1)+04, which is the fourth byte of the string at SØURCE. The translation process fetches and stores whatever characters we wish, and also makes repetitions and deletions of the second operand string as we wish. Note that the original string in the second operand is left intact by the TR instruction, but the pattern is destroyed. To rearrange more than one source string according to the same pattern, one would define the pattern as a constant, perhaps named PATT, then do the rearrangement by

```
MVC    RESULT(18),PATT
TR     RESULT(18),SØURCE
```

The TRanslate and Test (TRT) instruction uses an argument string as first operand and refers to a table of function bytes in exactly the same way that the TR instruction does. However, the argument string is not changed; the TRT instruction is a *search* for the first argument byte whose corresponding function byte is nonzero. The address of the argument byte found is placed in bit positions 8–31 of register 1, without alteration of bits 0–7, and the corresponding nonzero function byte is inserted into bit positions 24–31 of register 2, without alteration of bits

0–23. The operation terminates either when a nonzero function byte is found or when the end of the argument string is reached, and the condition code is set:

CC=0:   all referenced function bytes are zero;

CC=1:   a nonzero function byte is found before the argument string is exhausted;

CC=2:   the last argument byte corresponds to a nonzero function byte.

Thus the condition code is set to 0 or 2 if the entire first operand is examined, and to 1 if the search produces a nonzero function byte without examining the entire string. If no nonzero function byte is found, registers 1 and 2 are not altered.

The TRT instruction can, for example, find the length of the word or symbol beginning in a given location and extending to the first blank. Suppose that an 80-character string begins at STMT. A 256-byte table at SRCHBLNK consists entirely of zeros except for the byte at SRCHBLNK+64 (64=X'40'=C' '). The instruction sequence

```
LA     1,STMT+80
TRT    STMT(80),SRCHBLNK
S      1,=A(STMT)
```

will leave in register 1 the length of the character string up to the first blank, or 80 if there was no blank (in this case the TRT instruction does not alter register 1, so the address STMT+80 remains). If the first character of the string is a blank, the length will quite reasonably be reported as zero.

In combination with the EXecute instruction, the TRT instruction can be used to find addresses and lengths of all words delimited by blanks or other punctuation, as we shall see in Section 3.

The TR and TRT instructions are liable only to protection and addressing exceptions.

2. EDITING

One of the most common tasks in the use of a computer is generating the output in a readable format. The CVD and UNPK instructions help enormously and are reasonably sufficient for output of scientific computations. However, in many cases more gracious formats are desired, with

1. leading zeros eliminated,
2. punctuation inserted,
3. forcing of zeros after the decimal point,
4. designation of negative numbers by a CR suffix or by a sign just before the first significant digit,
5. a dollar sign preceding the first significant digit.

The EDit (ED) instruction and the EDit and MarK (EDMK) instruction were designed to provide these features. The two instructions are quite similar, but quite complex, so first we introduce the features of the EDit instruction, one by one, with examples.

The general structure of the ED instruction is somewhat like the TRanslate instruction, but it is also a generalization of the UNPK instruction. ED is an SS-type instruction with a single length; the length refers only to the first operand, called the *pattern*. Bytes of the second operand, which must be in packed decimal form and are called the *source*, are used as needed. Bytes of the pattern may be any of four kinds, with the definitions:

Code	Name
20	Digit selector
21	Significance starter
22	Field separator
All others	Message characters

The first byte of the pattern, however, is called the *fill character;* it is usually a blank, and during editing, it replaces other bytes before significance is established. A *significance indicator* is kept during execution of the instruction; this indicator keeps track of whether zeros or message characters are to be considered leading zeros, whether punctuation is to be replaced by the fill character, or whether significant zeros and punctuation are to be printed. The significance indicator is *off* at the beginning of the instruction.

In the simplest case, in which the pattern consists only of the fill character followed by digit selectors, the action of the ED instruction is as follows. The pattern is examined from left to right. For each digit selector encountered, a digit is fetched from the source. If the digit is nonzero, it is unpacked into a zoned decimal byte by the attachment of a zone (usually 1111) to replace the digit selector byte; it also turns *on* the significance indicator. If the digit fetched is zero and the significance indicator is off, the digit selector in the pattern is replaced by the fill character. If the digit fetched is zero and the significance indicator is on, the zero is expanded into a zoned digit to replace the digit selector. We can summarize these three cases by the following table:

Conditions on meeting digit selector		Result char.	Sig. indicator set
Nonzero digit	Sig. indicator on or off	Zoned dig.	On
Zero	Sig. indicator on	Zoned dig.	On
Zero	Sig. indicator off	Fill char.	Off

For example, if the pattern at RESLTA is 40202020 and the packed decimal number at PD is 020C (decimal 20), the instruction

$$ED \qquad RESLTA(4),PD$$

will yield the result 4040F2F0 at RESLTA, which is the character representation of bb20, where b stands for blank. In execution of the instruction, the fill character is 40 (blank). The first digit selector byte in the pattern causes the first zero to be fetched from PD; the significance indicator is off so the fill character is stored. The second digit selector causes the 2 to be fetched and inserted in the pattern; it also causes the significance indicator to be turned on. Since the significance indicator is on when the second zero is fetched, the zero is inserted in the pattern. The action taken on the sign will be described below.

Message characters included in the pattern do not cause fetching of a digit from the source string. They are subject to the influence of the significance indicator, however: if the indicator is off, the message character is replaced by the fill character. This feature is designed to enable the insertion of commas and decimal points at the right time. For example, if RESLTB contains

40	20	6B	20	20	20	6B	20	20	20	4B	20	20
b	ds	,	ds	ds	ds	,	ds	ds	ds	.	ds	ds

and the packed decimal number at PDB is

00	23	07	90	6C

the instruction

$$ED \quad RESLTB(13), PDB$$

will transform the pattern into

40	40	40	40	F2	F3	6B	F0	F7	F9	4B	F0	F6
b	b	b	b	2	3	,	0	7	9	.	0	6

The first comma is replaced by the fill character, since the significance indicator is not yet on; the second comma and the decimal point follow the digit 2, which turned on the indicator, so they remain unchanged in the pattern.

We would often like to force the decimal point and following zeros, for example, to print even if no previous digit is nonzero. This is done by the significance starter character. This character acts like a digit selector in fetching a digit, but even if the digit is zero, the significance indicator is turned on (to affect the *following* digits, not the current one). Therefore, whereas the pattern RESLTB above would produce the printed string bbbbbbbbbbbb6 if the source were 000000006C, the pattern RESLTC of

40	20	6B	20	20	20	6B	20	20	21	4B	20	20
b	ds	,	ds	ds	ds	,	ds	ds	sig. st.	.	ds	ds

and a source PDC of

00	00	00	00	6C

under the instruction

ED   RESLTC(13),PDC

would produce

40	40	40	40	40	40	40	40	40	40	4B	F0	F6
b	b	b	b	b	b	b	b	b	b	.	0	6

Each time a digit is fetched from the high-order four bits of a source byte, the low-order four bits are searched for a sign code. If a minus sign is present, the next digit to be fetched (if any) will be from the next byte. If a *plus* sign is present, not only will the next digit to be fetched be taken from the next byte, but also the *significance indicator will be turned off!* Thus the significance indicator plays a dual role. At the end of the instruction it becomes a sign indicator, on for minus and off for plus. Its function in controlling message characters is still important, as we see by the following example in which negative numbers are indicated by characters CR following the number. Let RESLTD be the pattern

40	20	20	21	4B	20	20	40	C3	D9
b	ds	ds	sig. st.	.	ds	ds	b	C	R

and PDD be

01	34	8D

Then the instruction

ED   RESLTD(10),PDD

will yield

40	40	F1	F3	4B	F4	F8	40	C3	D9
b	b	1	3	.	4	8	b	C	R

but if PDD is

04	97	2C

the same instruction and pattern will yield

40	40	F4	F9	4B	F7	F2	40	40	40
b	b	4	9	.	7	2	b	b	b

where the CR symbols in the pattern are replaced by the fill character because the plus sign at PDD+2 turned off the significance indicator.

The field separator symbol in a pattern is replaced by the fill character, but it turns the significance indicator off. This allows several numbers (fields) to be edited by one ED instruction.

The ED instruction sets a condition code:

CC=0:   last source field is all zeros;
CC=1:   last source field is less than zero;
CC=2:   last source field is greater than zero.

The EDit and MarK (EDMK) instruction is identical to the EDit instruction except that it also places in bits 8–31 of register 1 (leaving bits 0–7 unchanged) the address of a result character which is a zoned source digit fetched when the significance indicator was off—in other words, the address of the first significant digit of the result. We can use this address in placing a dollar sign or minus sign in front of the first significant digit. If the significance indicator is turned on by the significance starter byte, however, no address is loaded into register 1 by the EDMK instruction, so an appropriate address should be loaded *before* the EDMK instruction.

For example, suppose that the pattern RESLTE is

40	20	20	21	4B	20	20	40	C3	D9
b	ds	ds	sig st.	.	ds	ds	b	C	R

and the field PDE contains

01	34	8D

The instruction sequence

```
        LA     1,RESLTE+4
        EDMK   RESLTE(10),PDE
        BCTR   1,0
        MVI    0(1),C'$'
```

produces

40	5B	F1	F3	4B	F4	F8	40	C3	D9
b	$	1	3	.	4	8	b	C	R

as follows:

1. The address of the decimal point is placed in reg. 1, so that if significance is forced, the decimal point will be considered the "most significant digit."

2. The pattern is edited into bb13.48bCR, and the address RESLTE+2, the address of the digit 1, is placed in register 1.

3. BCTR 1,0 subtracts 1 from the contents of register 1.

4. The dollar sign is moved to RESLTE+1, just before the most significant digit.

If the source had been 00076C, the printable result would be bbb$.76bbb.

The ED and EDMK instructions are liable to several exceptions:

Operation: if the decimal feature is not installed,
Protection: store or fetch violation,
Addressing: attempt to use nonexistent storage locations,
Data: sign code (A–F) in high-order half of source byte.

Fig. 15-1   Action of ED and EDMK instructions

	Conditions				Results		
Pattern character	Significance indicator	Source digit	Low-order half of source byte		Result character	New state of significance indicator	Address placed in reg. 1(3)
Digit selector	Off	0	(1)		Fill char.	Off	No
Digit selector	Off	1–9	Not plus		Source dig.	On	Yes
Digit selector	Off	1–9	Plus		Source dig.	Off	Yes
Digit selector	On	0–9	Not plus		Source dig.	On	No
Digit selector	On	0–9	Plus		Source dig.	Off	No
Message char.	Off	(2)	(2)		Fill char.	Off	No
Message char.	On	(2)	(2)		Message char.	On	No
Signif. starter	Off	0	Not plus		Fill char.	On	No
Signif. starter	Off	0	Plus		Fill char.	Off	No
Signif. starter	Off	1–9	Not plus		Source dig.	On	Yes
Signif. starter	Off	1–9	Plus		Source dig.	Off	Yes
Signif. starter	On	0–9	Not plus		Source dig.	On	No
Signif. starter	On	0–9	Plus		Source dig.	Off	No
Field separator	(1)	(2)	(2)		Fill char.	Off	No

Notes

1) Irrelevant to the result.
2) Source digit not examined.
3) EDMK instruction only.

We conclude by presenting in Fig. 15-1 a summary of the rules for forming result characters and for turning on and off the significance indicator.

3. THE EXECUTE INSTRUCTION

The EXecute (EX) instruction is an RX-type instruction that directs the execution of an instruction called the *subject* instruction, which is addressed by the second operand. The EX instruction is unlike a branch instruction in that (unless the subject instruction is a branch) the next instruction to be executed is the one following the EXecute; the subject instruction is in effect a one-instruction subroutine. Furthermore, the subject instruction is modified before execution (though not altered at its main storage location): bits 8–15 of the instruction are ORed with bits 24–31 of register $R1$ to form the second byte of the instruction actually executed. Bits 8–15 of the instruction are the length codes in some instructions, register addresses in others, immediate operand bytes in others; the EXecute instruction is the best way we have of varying these specifications.

For example, suppose that we want to move a string of characters from B to A, but the length (actually, we need 1 less than the true length) has been computed and is in, say, register 9. We may include the definition

```
        VARMVC   MVC    A(0),B
```

in an area of constant and symbol definitions, and include the instruction

```
        EX     9,VARMVC
```

whenever we want the MVC instruction, with length supplied by register 9, executed.

The instruction to be executed after the MVC instruction will be the one following the EX instruction.

Any instruction other than another EX instruction may be a subject instruction for EXecute; an attempt to EXecute another EXecute causes an *Execute exception* and interrupt. Other exceptions possible are access, and specification, which occurs if the second operand address, the address of the subject instruction, is odd. Of course, any subject instruction is subject to the usual rules for its type.

If the subject instruction is a branch and the branch is taken, control does not return to the instruction after the EXecute but follows the branch.

Let us illustrate the use of TRT and EX instructions together in finding addresses and lengths of "words" of text. We say that words are composed of *text symbols*, including letters, digits, and perhaps a few special characters, delimited by *punctuation symbols*, which include blanks and most of the special characters. We define two tables for TRT instructions: one, named TEXTSYM, has zeros corresponding to punctuation symbols and nonzero function bytes corresponding to text symbols; using it as the second operand of a TRT instruction enables search for the first text symbol in a string. The other table, named PUNCTSYM, enables search for the first punctuation symbol; it has zeros corresponding to text symbols, and nonzero function bytes corresponding to punctuation symbols. The two are used alternately in a segment that records the addresses and lengths of words in the 80-character string beginning at TEXT. Let us suppose the existence of a blank at TEXT+80, just after the string; it simplifies exit from the loop. The length and address of each word are stored together in that order in a four-byte area; these areas begin at location WØRDADDR.

A segment for the problem is shown in Fig. 15–2. Register 5 always contains the address of the byte to start the next search from, and register 4 the length of

Fig. 15–2   Finding lengths and addresses of words of text

```
*     THIS SEGMENT SEARCHES THE 81 CHARACTERS AT TEXT
*     FOR SUBSTRINGS ØF TEXT SYMBØLS, AND STØRES LENGTHS
*     AND ADDRESSES STARTING AT WØRDADDR.
SEGMT   LA   8,WØRDADDR
        LA   4,80         LENGTH-1 ØF REMAINING STRING
        LA   5,TEXT       ADDRESS ØF STRING REMAINING
LØØP    EX   4,SRCHTEXT   SEARCH STRING FØR TEXT SYMBØL
        BZ   ØUT          IF NØNE, EXIT
        ST   1,0(8)       STØRE ADDRESS ØF SUBSTRING
        AR   4,5          FIND LENGTH ØF REMAINING STRING
        SR   4,1
        LR   5,1          PØSITIØN NEXT SEARCH AT FIRST BYTE ØF SUBSTRING
        EX   4,SRCHPUNC   SEARCH FØR NEXT PUNCTUATIØN SYMBØL
        SR   1,5          FIND LENGTH ØF SUBSTRING, STØRE
        STC  1,0(8)         ØNE BYTE IN WØRD WITH ADDRESS
        SR   4,1          LENGTH ØF REMAINING STRING
        AR   5,1          PØSITIØN NEXT SEARCH
        LA   8,4(8)       UPDATE PØINTER TØ ADDRESS AREA
        B    LØØP
ØUT     ...
*     CØNSTANTS AND SYMBØLS INCLUDE THE FØLLØWING
SRCHTEXT TRT   0(0,5),TEXTSYM
SRCHPUNC TRT   0(0,5),PUNCTSYM
```

the portion of string remaining to be searched. It is this use of register 4 to vary the length of the string to be searched that necessitates use of the EX instructions. Register 4 is ORed with the length code in each of the TRT instructions, and since the length codes in main storage are zero, the contents of register 4 *becomes* the effective length code. If the string at TEXT began, for example, with bbNØW IS THE TIME, the first TRT would insert in register 1 the address of the N. This address is stored as the address of the first substring (word) and also becomes the starting point for the next search. The next TRT finds the blank between NØW and IS, and the length of the word NØW, which it stores. The next time through the loop, the address and length of IS are found and stored; the process continues until the search yields no more text symbols.

Since MVCL and CLCL are interruptible instructions, special care must be taken if they are to be subject instructions of EXecute. First, neither *R1*, *X2*, or *B2* used in the EXecute instruction should be among those modified by the MVCL or CLCL instruction. Second, the area containing the EXecute instruction itself should not lie within the first (destination) operand area of MVCL. The reason for these restrictions is that if the MVCL or CLCL is interrupted, the EXecute instruction and the registers it uses must remain intact for re-interpretation upon resumption of the program.

4. MAIN IDEAS

a. The TR instruction enables translation of a string from one set of eight-bit codes into another.

b. The TRT instruction enables a search of a string for the first byte containing one of any desired set of codes.

c. The ED and EDMK instructions enable the unpacking of decimal numbers into fields with leading zero suppression, commas, decimal points, and other characters, and sign control and floating currency symbol placement.

d. The EX instruction permits the execution out of sequence of one instruction, whose second byte is modified by the contents of a register. This allows for convenient modification of lengths, masks, and register specifications.

e. These five instructions illustrate the tailoring of highly specialized instructions to the convenient performance of common but complex tasks.

QUESTIONS FOR REVIEW AND IMAGINATION

1. Suppose that each byte of a 16-byte string at SPREAD contains a number whose first four bits are zeros. Write a TR instruction and necessary function table to translate the hexadecimal digit in the low-order half of each byte into a character representation of the digits 0–9 or A–F.

2. Given a 32-bit word at Y, write a sequence of three TR instructions (and about three other instructions), and design tables to go with them, that will produce an eight-character string of printable characters representing the hexadecimal digits at Y. *Hint:* The first TR can translate the high-order hexadecimal digit of each byte; for example, all codes 00 to 0F would be translated into F0. The second TR can similarly translate the low-order digits, and the third TR can merge the two 4-character strings.

3. Write a TRT instruction (and table) that will determine whether the six-byte character string at U contains only the digits 0–9.

4. In addition to searching a field for the first blank, as was illustrated in Section 2, a TRT instruction can test the character string for illegal symbols; if different function byte codes are used for illegal symbols than for the blank, a test of register 2 after the TRT instruction will indicate what was actually found. Illustrate by designing an instruction sequence and function table that will test an assembler language statement for characters that are illegal in the name field.

5. A mailing address is stored in a 160-byte region, with a slash (/) marking the end of each line (the text is carefully edited, so this is the only way the slash occurs). Use the TRT instruction to move each line of the address to the beginning of a fixed area for printing, so that the address will be printed in its usual block format. The EX instruction helps too.

6. Write an EDit instruction and pattern which will produce a six-byte field from a two-byte packed decimal number. The numbers are to be printed with two digits before and one after the decimal point and a minus sign, if any, following the last digit; if the number is less than 1.0, one leading zero is to be printed. Examples are

$$67.9$$
$$3.4-$$
$$0.4$$

7. Write a sequence of instructions to edit a field and insert a dollar sign before the first nonblank character, but use ED and then TRT instead of EDMK.

8. Write a sequence of instructions, including EDMK, that will edit a number into some pattern you choose, but indicate a negative number by a minus sign just before the first nonblank character.

9. In order to maintain sign control in an ED or EDMK instruction, one must have significance starters and digit selectors in the pattern equal to the number of digits in the packed decimal number being edited. This means that the number of digits allowed must always be odd. Is this a burdensome restriction? If not, why not? If so, why, and what can we do about it?

REFERENCE

IBM System/360 Principles of Operation, GA22-6821, or *IBM System/370 Principles of Operation*, GA22-7000, IBM Corporation. Complete description of the instructions.

Chapter 16

Macro Definition and Conditional Assembly

In Chapter 6 we introduced the SAVE and RETURN macros, and in Chapter 12 the input and output macros. In IBM OS or OS/VS assembler language, the programmer also has the opportunity to define and use macros of his own design. Such macros can be included in a program to be assembled, or they can be kept in a macro library where the assembler can find them when they are needed.

Along with the macro definition capability, the assembler language programmer has access to variables that can be set, changed, and tested *during assembly*, and which can direct the assembler to jump around and even loop through the same statements in the assembler language program. This powerful facility, called *conditional assembly*, is most useful in macros, but it is available for use outside macros too.

A programmer who does a good deal of programming finds that there are certain instruction sequences which, with variations, are repeated often. The basic patterns of these sequences can be defined as macros, and the minor variations can be accomplished by use of parameters to the macros and by the conditional assembly feature. Macros can be simple or complex, but casual programmers will not bother to define any macros at all; only a reasonably sophisticated programmer can make use of the macro definition feature with profit.

Therefore we avoid here a comprehensive discussion of the macro definition and conditional assembly features of the assembler. We introduce the main points in enough detail so that the student can follow examples and write and use a few simple macros of his own. Thus he will be aware of the capabilities and ready to learn more about them when the proper occasion arises; he will also be equipped to learn from the Assembler Language manuals the additional facts he needs. In addition I recommend study of the system macros such as RETURN, CALL, GET in the system macro library for clues as to how things are done in the macro-definition language.

1. OUTLINE OF FACILITIES

The heart of the facilities for macro definition and conditional assembly is the provision for *variable symbols*, variables which are given values during assembly of the program. One important kind of variable symbol is the *symbolic parameter*, a dummy symbol used in the definition of a macro. During expansion of a macro-instruction at its proper place in the assembler-language program, actual parameters specified in the macro-instruction are substituted for the symbolic parameters in the macro definition; this provides flexibility in the use of macros.

A second class of variable symbol is the SET *symbol*. There are SET symbols with *arithmetic* (integer) values, others with *character* values, and still others with logical values, which are 0 or 1 (the manual calls them *binary*, so henceforth we shall too). In each of these types there can be *local* SET symbols, which are specific to each macro expansion and *global* SET symbols, whose values can be set in one macro and used in another, or be set and used outside macros entirely. Any of the SET symbols can be set, changed, and tested, and therefore used in various ways to control assembly.

In addition to the symbolic parameters and SET symbols, the programmer has certain *attributes* at his disposal. The attributes *type* and *length* of symbolic parameters can be used by the macro to adjust to specific types and lengths of the actual parameters used in a macro-instruction. The attribute *number* refers to a parameter list, and enables the macro to determine how many parameters are actually supplied in a macro-instruction. With this knowledge the macro can adjust to variation in the number of parameters.

Finally, in order to make effective use of attributes and SET symbols, the assembler instructions AIF and AGØ enable modification of the *order* of inclusion of statements in the source program. *Sequence symbols* can be attached to statements; AGØ (unconditional) and AIF (conditional) are branch instructions that direct the assembler to consider next the statement with a certain sequence symbol rather than the physically next one in the source program or macro definition. Assembler loops are even possible (and quite helpful) through the use of these branching instructions.

In the next sections we describe each of these facilities in more detail.

2. DEFINITION AND USE OF A MACRO

The specific form of any macro definition must include, in order,

    a) a header statement,
    b) a prototype,
    c) model statements, and finally
    d) a trailer statement.

The header and trailer statements are very simple: The header has no name and no operands, and the operation MACRØ. The trailer may have a name, which can be any sequence symbol (sequence symbols will be defined in Section 4), the operation MEND (for Macro END), and no operands. Neither header nor trailer may have a comments field.

The prototype follows the header statement. In the operation field is the name of the macro being defined. The name may be any symbol except the mnemonic operation code of any machine or assembler instruction or the name of another macro in the same program. A symbolic parameter may be placed in the name field, and a sequence of symbolic parameters, separated by commas, in the operands field.

A *symbolic parameter* is written as an ampersand (&) followed by one to seven letters and digits, of which the first must be a letter. Thus &N, &GZA, &ZABCDEF, and &Z123456 are valid symbolic parameters.

Valid forms of macro prototypes are therefore

```
        ADD    &A,&B,&C,&D
&NAME   MØVE   &TØ,&FRØM,&LENGTH
&N      ABØRT
        FILL
```

Model statements follow the prototype statement. Model statements can be rather normal machine or assembler instructions, and they follow more or less the same rules. The name field may be blank, or it may contain a sequence symbol or a variable symbol. The operation field may contain any machine or assembler instruction abbreviation (with a few exceptions such as END), the name of another macro, or a variable symbol.

The operands field may be formed as an operands field for any instruction, and it may include ordinary symbols and variable symbols. Apostrophes must be paired; characters inside a pair of apostrophes form a quoted string, and only within quoted strings are blanks permitted in the operands field. To represent a single apostrophe within a quoted string one must write two apostrophes. Exceptions to apostrophe pairing rules are made for attributes, which are discussed in Section 3. The ampersand has special meaning as the first character of a variable symbol; any other use of an ampersand requires two of them. A comments field may be written after the operands field.

To use a macro, a programmer writes a macro-instruction. The macro-instruction, as we saw in Chapters 6 and 12, has the name of the macro in the operation field, an optional symbol in the name field, and usually some parameters in the operands field. Comments may be included after the operands field. Operands entries must conform to the rules covering the use of apostrophes, ampersands, and blanks as noted above. In addition, equal signs are permitted only as the first character of an operand or in a quoted string or paired parentheses. Parentheses must be paired; that is, there must be an equal number of right and left parentheses, and they must be divisible into pairs in which the left parenthesis precedes the right parenthesis (parentheses in quoted strings are, of course, not subject to the pairing rule).

Expansion of macro-instructions precedes assignment of any addresses by the assembler. The macro-instruction is replaced by an appropriate (depending on parameters and execution of conditional assembly statements) sequence of model statements of the macro named. The symbolic parameters in the model statements are replaced by corresponding parameters from the macro-instruction; SET symbols are replaced by their current values, and sequence symbols are removed. The result is a sequence of ordinary machine and assembler instructions.

For example, consider the following macro definition.

```
            MACRØ                       Header
    &START  LAUNCH  &REG,&SAVAREA       Prototype
    &START  STM     14,12,12(13)    ⎫
            BALR    &REG,0          ⎪
            USING   *,&REG          ⎬   Model
            ST      13,&SAVAREA+4   ⎪   statements
            LR      2,13            ⎪
            LA      13,&SAVAREA     ⎭   Trailer
            ST      13,8(2)
            MEND
```

If the second statement in a program, after macro definitions and a START statement, is the macro-instruction

```
    BEGIN   LAUNCH    12,SAV
```

the macro-instruction is replaced by the model statements. The symbolic parameter &START is replaced by the corresponding parameter BEGIN, &REG by 12 and &SAVAREA by SAV, and the result is

```
    BEGIN   STM     14,12,12(13)
            BALR    12,0
            USING   *,12
            ST      13,SAV+4
            LR      2,13
            LA      13,SAV
            ST      13,8(2)
```

Symbols and variable symbols can be concatenated to form single symbols. If the second of two symbols to be concatenated is a variable symbol, its name is merely appended to the first symbol, as in SYMBØL&VAR. If something beginning with a letter, digit, left parenthesis or period is to follow another symbol, a period is placed between them, as in &VAR.SYMBØL. Values of variable symbols are concatenated with the other things (and the period removed) during expansion of the

Fig. 16–1 An addition macro

```
            MACRØ
    &N      ADD     &TYPE,&A,&B,&C
    &N      ST&TYPE 2,SAVE
            L&TYPE  2,&A
            A&TYPE  2,&B
            ST&TYPE 2,&C
            L&TYPE  2,SAVE
            MEND
```

macro. The example shown in Fig. 16–1 illustrates a concatenation. The concatenation of &TYPE to the operation codes in each of the model instructions allows the same macro to be used for integer addition, or for single- or double-precision floating-point addition. For example, the macro-instruction

```
LPAC       ADD     E,T,DELTA,TPRIME
```

will be replaced by the expansion

```
LPAC       STE     2,SAVE
           LE      2,T
           AE      2,DELTA
           STE     2,TPRIME
           LE      2,SAVE
```

Note that not only must T, DELTA, and TPRIME be defined as symbols in the main program, but SAVE must also.

If a parameter is omitted in a macro-instruction, a blank character value is assigned. Appropriate commas ensure that macro-instruction parameters correspond to the desired symbolic parameters. For example, with the macro ADD defined as in Fig. 16–1, the macro-instruction

```
ADD     ,CT,=F'1',CT
```

is replaced by the expansion

```
ST      2,SAVE
L       2,CT
A       2,=F'1'
ST      2,CT
L       2,SAVE
```

Parameters corresponding to both &N and &TYPE are omitted, and therefore &N and &TYPE are replaced by blanks.

Fig. 16–2   Use of a sublist

```
           MACRØ
&S         ADD        &TYPE,&A,&C
&S         ST&TYPE    2,SAVE
           L&TYPE     2,&A(1)
           A&TYPE     2,&A(2)           Macro
           A&TYPE     2,&A(3)           definition
           ST&TYPE    2,&C
           L&TYPE     2,SAVE
           MEND
LPAC       ADD        E,(Y,CØRR1,CØRR2),YP     Macro-instruction
LPAC       STE        2,SAVE
           LE         2,Y
           AE         2,CØRR1
           AE         2,CØRR2           Expansion
           STE        2,YP
           LE         2,SAVE
```

Operands in a macro-instruction can be supplied in a *sublist*, which is enclosed in parentheses. Individual parameters in a sublist can be used individually in the macro definition; the name of the entire symbolic parameter is followed by a position index in parentheses: &A(2) refers to the second operand supplied in the sublist corresponding to the symbolic parameter &A. Figure 16–2 shows an example of the use of a sublist in the macro definition and macro-instruction. The real value of having a sublist, however, appears when we can use conditional assembly features to accommodate sublists of varying length, as we shall see in Section 4.

3. SET SYMBOLS AND ATTRIBUTES

This section introduces the properties of SET symbols and attributes, and shows how SET symbols are defined and changed. This is preliminary to Section 4, where SET symbols and attributes are used to control conditional assembly.

A SET symbol is a type of variable symbol; its name is written the same as the name of a symbolic parameter: an ampersand followed by one to seven letters and digits, the first of which must be a letter. The distinction between symbolic parameters and various types of SET symbols is made by the manner of introduction: symbolic parameters by listing in a prototype statement, SET symbols by explicit declaration.

There are local and global SET symbols. *Local* SET symbols are particular to the macro in which they are used, and moreover to the particular expansion of a particular macro-instruction. The use or value of a local SET symbol named &VARSYM in one expansion of a particular macro-instruction has no bearing on the use or value of &VARSYM in another expansion of the same macro or on the use or value of a variable symbol named &VARSYM in any other macro. *Global* SET symbols, on the other hand, are common to the entire assembly, and a value of the global SET symbol &GLØBAL in one macro is available to be used by another macro.

There are three types of both local and global SET symbols: arithmetic (SETA), binary (SETB), and character (SETC). A local or global SETA symbol has an arithmetic value of from -2^{31} to $2^{31} - 1$. Such a symbol must be declared in a macro in which it is used by

> LCLA   symbol name

or

> GBLA   symbol name,

which declares the symbol to be a local or global SETA symbol. The name portion of a LCLA or GBLA statement (or LCLB, LCLC, GBLB, or GBLC, for that matter) is left blank. The declaration LCLA or GBLA in a macro must come just after the prototype and before any model statements; in a main program LCLA or GBLA declarations come after all macro definitions and before all regular statements. In either a main program or a macro definition, all global SET symbol declarations precede all local SET symbol declarations.

The value of a SETA symbol is initially 0. It may be changed by the SETA statement, which has the form

Name	Operation	Operands
Name of SETA symbol	SETA	An expression

The expression defining the new value may include self-defining terms (see Chapter 6), SETA symbols, attributes L (Length) and N (Number), and symbolic parameters whose values are self-defining terms, connected by arithmetic operators +,−,*, and /. Ordinary symbols, or symbolic parameters whose values are ordinary symbols, are not permitted, since their values are not yet defined when the macro is expanded. Thus

                   &VARS   SETA   &CT+3

is a valid statement if &CT is another SETA symbol, but

                   &VARS   SETA   LØØPA

is not.

A SETA symbol may be used in an arithmetic expression in any statement. It may also be used where characters are called for, as in the name of an operand; in this case the absolute value of the symbol is converted to an unsigned decimal integer, with leading zeros removed (the value 0 is converted to a single 0). Thus, if &VARS is a SETA symbol whose value is 7, and &A is a symbolic parameter to which a sublist corresponds, the model statement

              A   3,&A(&VARS)

will be expanded to an add instruction whose second operand is the seventh member of the sublist. On the other hand, if &B is a symbolic parameter whose value is AREG, then

              A   3,&B&VARS

will be expanded to

              A   3,AREG7

We bypass the SETB symbols, leaving them for investigation by the potential user after he has mastered SETA and SETC symbols.

The statements

         LCLC   name of SETC symbol

and

         GBLC   name of SETC symbol

declare SETC symbols in the same manner that LCLA and GBLA declare SETA symbols. A SETC symbol has a value which may be up to eight characters long. The initial value is *no* characters. A SETC symbol may be assigned a new value by the statement

Name	Operation	Operand
Name of SETC symbol	SETC	Character expression

A character expression may consist of a type attribute alone or a concatenation of one or more quoted strings; each quoted string can include a variable symbol and other characters. For example, if &BCD has the value GPDX, the character expression '&BCD.(2)' has the value GPDX(2). The statement

    &CHAR   SETC   'RST&BCD'

assigns the value RSTGPDX to the SETC symbol &CHAR.

SETC symbols may be used in name, operation, and operand fields of statements. If used in an arithmetic expression, a SETC symbol must have a value which is from one to eight decimal digits.

There are six attributes of a symbol or symbolic parameter: type, length, scaling, integer, count, and number. We shall describe type, length, and number but ignore scaling, integer, and count.

The *type* attribute is generally used in a macro to determine the type of value given to a symbolic parameter. The type of a symbolic parameter &S is written T'&S; exceptions to rules about paired apostrophes are made to accommodate this notation for attributes. The value of a type attribute is a single character; some of the more important are

A   A-type address constant or symbol;
C   character constant or symbol;
D   long floating-point constant or symbol, implied length;
E   short floating-point constant or symbol, implied length;
F   full-word fixed-point constant or symbol with implied length;
X   hexadecimal constant;
I   machine instruction;
M   macro-instruction;
N   self-defining term;
Ø   omitted operand; and
P   packed decimal constant or symbol.

For example, if the value of &S given in a macro-instruction is LØØP, where LØØP is defined by the statement

    LØØP   L   4,GWS

then the value of T'&S is I.

The *length* attribute of a symbolic parameter &S is written L'&S. Its value is an arithmetic quantity which gives the length associated with the symbol, either through explicit definition in a length modifier of a constant or symbol, or through the implied length associated with constants or symbols of that type (see Fig. 6–4). The length attribute can be used in any arithmetic expression, including definition of a SET symbol.

The *number* attribute of a symbolic parameter &S is written N'&S. Its value is the number of operands in the sublist corresponding to &S. Actually, the value is one greater than the number of commas, so leading omitted operands are counted. If the operand is not a sublist, the value of the number attribute is 1, except that if the operand is omitted entirely, the number attribute is 0. For example, number attributes of the following operands are

(ACT,DELTA,CØRR)	3
(ACT,,CØRR)	3
ACT	1
none	0

We shall see in the next section how the number attribute allows us to form a conditional assembly loop to treat sublist elements in turn.

4. CONDITIONAL ASSEMBLY

The assembler can be made to branch and loop among assembler language statements in much the same way that the computer branches and loops among machine-language instructions. The necessary elements are present: conditional and unconditional branch instructions and labels on statements to branch to. The labels are called *sequence symbols;* a sequence symbol is written as a period followed by from one to seven letters and digits of which the first is a letter. Some valid sequence symbols are .A and .Z23C4PQ. Sequence symbols may be attached (starting in column 1) to a machine or assembler instruction with some obvious exceptions like MACRØ and prototype statements.

The unconditional branch instruction is very simple:

Name	Operation	Operand
Sequence symbol or blank	AGØ	Sequence symbol

It causes the assembler to assemble succeeding statements beginning at the one with the designated sequence symbol.

The conditional branch is written as

Name	Operation	Operand
Sequence symbol or blank	AIF	A logical expression enclosed in parentheses, followed immediately by a sequence symbol

The logical expression is composed of one or more relations connected by the logical connectors AND, ØR, AND NØT, and ØR NØT. A relation consists of two arithmetic expressions or two character expressions connected by a relational operator:

EQ	equal to,
NE	not equal to,
LT	less than,
LE	less than or equal,
GT	greater than, and
GE	greater than or equal.

A relation has the value true (1) or false (0), and these values are combined by the logical connectors in the obvious way. If the value of the entire expression is true, the assembler branches to the statement named in the AIF statement; if the expression is false, the next instruction in sequence is taken.

The logical connectors and relational operators are immediately preceded and followed by at least one blank. The following are valid logical expressions:

```
&NØ GE N'&A      where &NØ has an arithmetic value,
&CT LT &NØ
&ØFF+255 LT &LEN
T'&REG NE 'Ø'
T'&INC EQ 'N' ØR &NØ EQ 0
```

One more statement is necessary. AIF and AGØ statements may not branch to statements named by regular or variable symbols; when such a branch is desired, the branch can be made to an ANØP statement, which is labeled with a sequence symbol and just precedes the desired statement. For example, an unconditional

Fig. 16-3   Conditional assembly in an ADD macro

```
        MACRØ
&S      ADD       &TYPE,&A,&C
        LCLA      &NØ
&NØ     SETA      1
&S      ST&TYPE   2,SAVE
        L&TYPE    2,&A(1)                  Macro
.B      AIF       (&NØ GE N'&A).E          definition
&NØ     SETA      &NØ+1
        A&TYPE    2,&A(&NØ)
        AGØ       .B
.E      ST&TYPE   2,&C
        L&TYPE    2,SAVE
        MEND

PH      ADD       D,(G,G+8,DECR,CØRR),G+16   Macro-instruction

PH      STD       2,SAVE
        LD        2,G
        AD        2,G+8
        AD        2,DECR                   Expansion
        AD        2,CØRR
        STD       2,G+16
        LD        2,SAVE
```

branch to

&N   DC 4F'0'

is accomplished by

     AGØ .STN

where the statement labeled .STN is

    .STN ANØP

and is placed just before the DC statement.

Figure 16–3 shows a macro using the number attribute, a SETA symbol, and conditional assembly to generate a sequence which will add a variable number of words. The SETA symbol &NØ is used as a counter of the number of operands in the sublist which have been used in Load or Add instructions, and the number attribute N'&A is used to cause exit from the assembler loop at the proper time. Note that sequence symbols are scrubbed from the expansion of the sample macro-instruction.

As a final example, consider Fig. 16–4. The macro defined is a further improvement in the macro of Fig. 16–3; it allows the programmer who has a register available to specify it as a last operand in his macro-instruction, thereby avoiding the expansion of instructions which save and restore the contents of register 2. Two SETC symbols are used; one holds the register number and is either the fourth operand if specified or 2 if the fourth parameter is omitted. The SETC symbol &N

Fig. 16–4   Use of type attribute and SETC symbol

	MACRØ		
&S	ADD	&TYPE,&A,&C,&REG	
	LCLC	&N	
	LCLC	&R	
	LCLA	&NØ	
&NØ	SETA	1	
&R	SETC	'&REG'	
&N	SETC	'&S'	
	AIF	(T'&REG NE '0').G1	
&R	SETC	'2'	
&N	ST&TYPE	&R,SAVE	
&N	SETC	' '	Macro definition
.G1	ANØP		
&N	L&TYPE	&R,&A(1)	
.B	AIF	(&NØ GE N'&A).E	
&NØ	SETA	&NØ+1	
	A&TYPE	&R,&A(&NØ)	
	AGØ	.B	
.E	ST&TYPE	&R,&C	
	AIF	(T'&REG NE '0').G2	
	L&TYPE	&R,SAVE	
.G2	MEND		
PH	ADD	D,(G,G+8,DECR,CØRR),G+16,6	Macro-instruction
PH	LD	6,G	
	AD	6,G+8	
	AD	6,DECR	Expansion
	AD	6,CØRR	
	STD	6,G+16	

holds the name field parameter of the macro-instruction. The name is to be attached to the ST instruction if it is present; if it is not present, the name is attached to the L instruction, but it must *not* be given to the L instruction if the ST instruction is included in the expansion. This is why a SETC symbol, which can be changed to a blank value, is used. The proper option is determined by an AIF statement testing (twice) the type of &REG to see whether it is '∅' (for Omitted) or not. This macro would expand the macro-instruction of Fig. 16–3 into exactly the same code as the macro of Fig. 16–3. The expansions of the two macros are different only if a fourth operand, corresponding to &REG, is specified. Note the use of the AN∅P statement labeled .G1 to accommodate a branch essentially to the statement

```
&N        L&TYPE    &R,&A(1)
```

5. OTHER FACILITIES

A number of facilities other than those described above are available and useful. Several of them deserve at least mention here.

The MN∅TE statement prints a message in the listing of the program. The macro definition may include checks for macro-instruction operand validity and print error messages when validity criteria are not met.

A system variable &SYSNDX has as its value a four-digit number which starts at 0000 and is incremented by 1 for every macro expansion. When a macro needs a symbol in the name field, two macro-instructions calling the macro may result in duplicate symbol definitions. However, if the symbol is concatenated with &SYSNDX, the combination will be a unique symbol in each expansion. For example, a name L∅∅P&SYSNDX will be expanded as L∅∅P0007 if it is in the macro called by the seventh macro-instruction, but if the same macro is called by the thirteenth macro-instruction, the name in the expansion will be L∅∅P0013.

Character strings, either introduced explicitly or as values of variable symbols, can be broken up and any substring used. This facility can allow a macro to examine each character of a macro-instruction operand, for example.

Finally, macro-instruction parameters can be specified as key-word as well as positional parameters. Key-word parameters are already familiar, both in job-control language and in input and output macro-instructions; the programmer can be assured that he may use them in his own macros too.

6. SUMMARY; MAIN IDEAS

It is instructive to compare a macro to a subroutine. A subroutine, sometimes called a *closed subroutine*, is a section of standard code to which the program branches when the functions of that section are desired. A macro expansion can be called an *open subroutine;* it is inserted bodily at each point where it is to be used. However, the macro definition has much of the appearance of a closed subroutine, and the macro-instruction is quite similar to a subroutine call, with parameters and a transfer of control (in the assembler) to and from the macro. As noted earlier, the discussion of macros in this chapter is far from complete. I have endeavored to introduce a sufficient subset of the features and rules so that the student can write and use macros and get an honest idea of their role. I hope that the rules as introduced are sufficient to keep the student out of trouble and yet not enough to completely overwhelm him with detail. The assembler language manual is obviously necessary to any serious user of macros.

In conclusion, we list the main ideas of the chapter:

a. A macro is defined by a sequence of a *header* statement, a *prototype, model* statements, and a *trailer* statement. The model statements, with suitable substitutions defined by the correspondence of macro-instruction operands and symbolic parameters listed in the prototype, and by conditional assembly, replace a macro-instruction as the *expansion* of the macro.

b. Variable symbols, written with an ampersand (&) as first character, include symbolic parameters and local and global SETA (arithmetic), SETB (binary), and SETC (character) symbols. SET symbols are declared by GBLA, GBLB, GBLC, LCLA, LCLB, and LCLC statements, and their values are changed by SETA, SETB, and SETC statements.

c. Attributes T' (type), L' (length), N' (number), and others permit the assembler to determine the nature of symbolic parameters and to adjust the expansion accordingly.

d. Conditional assembly is actually a mechanism for transfer of control by the assembler out of the sequence of statements in the source program or macro. Unconditional branch (AGØ) and conditional branch (AIF) statements transfer control to statements labeled with sequence symbols.

QUESTIONS FOR REVIEW AND IMAGINATION

1. Make a chart showing the objects (regular symbols, character strings, symbolic parameters, SETA symbols, SETC symbols, attributes, etc.) that are allowed in various places, such as operands of SETA and SETC statements, logical, arithmetic, and character expressions, macro-instruction operands, model statement operands; and list the operators that are allowed as connectors between the objects.

2. Learn more about partitioned data sets; then set up job control necessary to (1) create a private macro library and put a few macros in it, and (2) use these macros from the library in a program.

3. How can a macro distinguish between a simple macro-instruction operand, such as SUM, and a sublist containing one item, such as (SUM)? The solution is not trivial. Under what circumstances might the distinction be important?

4. The macro of Fig. 16–1 can be used to add full-word fixed-point numbers or single- or double-precision floating-point quantities. Why can it not add halfword integers with a macro-instruction whose first operand is H?   By using conditional assembly, can you remedy the flaw?

5. What would happen if a macro-instruction using the macro of Fig. 16–1 omitted the second operand?

6. Why are ordinary symbols not permitted in the defining expression of a SETA statement?

7. Type and length attributes may be written of ordinary symbols as well as of symbolic parameters.   When might this be useful?

8. Write a macro without SETC symbols which generates the same expansion from a macro-instruction that the macro of Fig. 16–4 does.

9. Write a simple macro that will generate a compare-and-branch sequence, and show sample macro-instructions that might use it.

10. Write a macro for a subroutine call.   With an appropriate DS or DC statement, generate an area in which to keep subroutine parameter addresses, and see that the addresses are placed there.

11. Write a macro that defines a 256-byte area and places in it the binary integers 0 to 255, one per byte.

12. Write a macro that will move a packed decimal number to a new location, adding zeros and deleting digits on the left and right as directed by the macro-instruction.   This should be a good review of the instructions and techniques introduced in Chapter 14.

13. Write a macro that will move a string of characters, from 1 to, say, 4096 bytes long, from one location to another, not using the MVCL instruction.   Have the expansion contain straight-line coding, i.e., no loops.

14. Modify the macro of problem 13 so that a series of strings, which are defined by location and length (perhaps you can permit the length to be omitted sometimes, and get the length by using a length attribute), are moved so as to follow one another in a new location.

15. Write a macro that will add a series of fixed-point quantities which are a specified distance (perhaps &INC) apart, for example, at &A, &A+&INC, &A+2*&INC, etc.   The number of quantities to be added is, of course, another parameter. Generate a straight-line expansion.

16. Write another macro for the same job as that in problem 15, but which generates a loop to do the addition.   It is interesting to note that to generate straight-line code, we must create an assembler loop, but to generate a loop in the expansion, the assembler does not need to go through a loop.

17. Combine the macros of problems 15 and 16 so that if, say, 10 or fewer numbers are to be added, a straight-line expansion is generated (as in problem 15), otherwise a loop is generated, as in problem 16.

18. The extended-precision floating-point instructions do arithmetic, but there are no explicit instructions for loading, comparing, storing, etc. extended-precision numbers. By analogy with the regular floating-point instruction repertoire, design a set of macros which will supplement the extended-precision instructions and round out the repertoire.

REFERENCES

Freeman, D. N., "Macro language design for SYSTEM/360," *IBM Systems Journal* **5** (1966), pp. 62–77.

Kent, William, "Assembler-Language Macroprogramming," *Computing Surveys* **1**, 4 (December 1969), pp. 183–196. A tutorial exposition of the System/360 macro definition and conditional assembly facilities.

OS Assembler Language, GC28-6514, or *OS/VS and DOS/VS Assembler Language*, GC33-4010. Reference description of the macro definition and conditional assembly facilities.

Wegner, Peter, *Programming Languages, Information Structures, and Machine Organization* (New York: McGraw-Hill, 1968). General and theoretical discussion of the structure and use of a macro definition facility.

Chapter 17

System Control Functions

Throughout the earlier chapters of this volume, references have been made to machine functions that are performed by the supervisor, or by machine elements controlled only through the supervisor. We have mentioned the program status word, control registers, the protection system, dynamic address translation and virtual storage management, the interrupt system, and performance of input and output, with almost no hint of how such things are used. This chapter introduces the capabilities of the IBM System/360 and System/370 which are usually reserved for use by the supervisor.

The features of the System/360 and 370 computer considered in this chapter can be divided into several groups. First is the dynamic address translation facility, which implements virtual storage in some models of the IBM System/370. Second are functions controlled through the program status word and control registers. These functions include the storage protection system and control over which interrupts are permitted and which are not. There are special instructions which manipulate the fields of the program status word and control registers.

As an important part of manipulation of the program status word, we will study the interrupt system: the nature and mechanism of interrupt, the various types, and some of the considerations involved in using the interrupt system.

The most complex of the topics considered in this chapter is the input and output system. The input and output instructions are simple enough, but the input and output channels are themselves programmed, and we shall study channel programming. States of the channels, subchannels, and devices must be explained, as well as the workings of the input and output interrupts and the means of providing information to the central processing unit on the status of the input and output processes.

No attempt has been made to be complete and definitive in this chapter. Our goal is to introduce the features used by the supervisor, so that a programmer will have a better understanding of what the supervisor does and how, and thus will be more effective in his use of supervisor services. Use of the interrupt system and of direct input and output commands is sometimes necessary for a programmer, and the supervisor includes provision for accommodating such use; this chapter can serve as an introduction to the facilities that are available to him when he needs them. Finally, since all sophisticated computers of the current generation have complex facilities that parallel those of the IBM System/360 and 370, study of the 360's and 370's interrupt and input/output systems can serve as an introduction to the kind of structure used by other computer systems as well.

The reader who wishes to concentrate on IBM System/360 features can skip Sections 1 and 3, and the treatment in other sections makes clear which features are included in System/370 models only.

1. DYNAMIC ADDRESS TRANSLATION AND VIRTUAL STORAGE

In earlier chapters we have presumed that each address refers to a particular and fixed location in main storage, though there were occasional hints that it was not necessarily so. Some IBM System/370 models implement virtual storage, which dynamically allocates real storage blocks to the virtual storage of several programs, as required.

Why virtual storage?

There are several reasons for implementing virtual storage. In a multiprogramming environment, programs and service routines are continually called in, executed, and finished. They come in all sizes, and seldom is the next one needed the same size as the one which just finished. Therefore storage assignments become fragmented, and it becomes difficult to find a contiguous block of storage, even though enough storage, in pieces, is available. Storage would be managed better if each program's required space could be broken into several areas of fixed size, not necessarily contiguously assigned. Each programmer can arrange this to some extent, but it would be better to have the operating system take over storage management, since the programmer cannot foresee what size blocks will be available. Second, programs include sections used for initialization and for treating various exceptional conditions and allowance for data storage space often in excess of that required during a particular run. In any small interval of time, only a subset of the program's entire program and data areas are in active use. This subset is called the *working set*; only the working set need be actually resident in main storage at any time, but the system must be able to bring in other pieces easily and automatically when they are needed. A quantity of main storage can serve many more programs if it need hold only their working sets than if it must hold their entire defined storage areas. Third, and by extension, a computer can execute a program whose total storage requirements exceed the actual main storage available.

These considerations lead to an implementation design with the following characteristics:

a) division of main storage into blocks (we will call them *pages*), each assignable to a program independently of other blocks;
b) a hardware-implemented means of translating logical addresses which the program thinks it is using into real addresses in the pages assigned.

Virtual storage   Main (real) storage

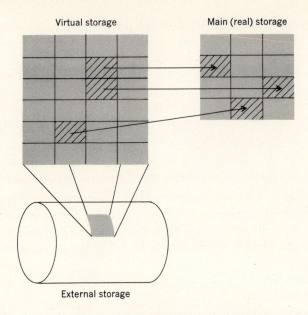

External storage

Fig. 17–1   Mapping virtual and real storage.

Figure 17–1 shows a representation of virtual and real storage and the mapping. The program assumes an area of contiguous pages, and the pages are actually kept in external storage, as shown. A few of the pages, the working set, reside in main storage in any blocks that may be available at the moment. An automatic translation is made so that addresses in virtual storage access the appropriate real storage and, when necessary, call for bringing a needed page from external storage to main storage for the use of the program.

The dynamic address translation feature

Since addresses in IBM System/360 and 370 are each 24 bits, they define an *address space* of 16,777,216 (16,384K) bytes. Theoretically, any program could use any addresses within that address space, but that is considerably more than most programmers need. The range of addresses actually used by a program may be called its *virtual storage* space, and it may be assigned by relocation exactly as shown in earlier chapters. For management, the virtual storage is divided into a hierarchy of *segments* and *pages*. A *segment* is 64K bytes, and each segment is divided into 16 *pages* of 4K bytes each (in OS/VS1, a segment is divided into 32 pages to 2K bytes each, but our explanation will continue with the larger pages). The 24-bit address therefore is subdivided into fields as shown in Fig. 17–2. We must emphasize that the addition of base, index, and displacements are followed exactly as described heretofore, and the resulting address is a virtual address since

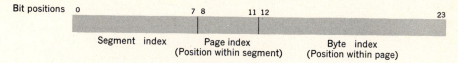

Bit positions   0   7 8   11 12   23

Segment index   Page index   Byte index
(Position within segment)   (Position within page)

Fig. 17–2   Fields of an address.

the program acts entirely in its virtual storage; it is the resulting virtual address which is interpreted in segment index, page index, and byte index.

Real storage is assigned in chunks of 4K bytes called *page frames*. We must distinguish between pages, which are the content of virtual storage, and page frames, which are physical portions of main storage assigned dynamically to hold pages. The assignment makes necessary a translation so that for every virtual storage address (which means to access some content) our program is directed to the page frame where that content is to be found.

Segment and page tables

The segment index and page index are arranged so that translation from virtual into real addresses can follow a two-step process, referencing, in turn, a *segment table* and a *page table*. First, the *segment table origin register* (STOR) gives the beginning address of the current segment table. For a given virtual address, the segment index determines the proper entry in the segment table. The most important part of the entry is the address of the relevant page table. The page index determines the proper entry in the selected page table. The entry in the page table gives the upper twelve bits of the page frame address; the address is completed by concatenation with the byte index.

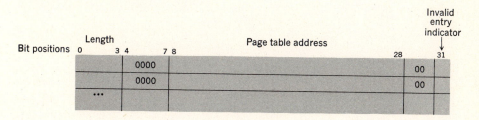

Fig. 17–3   Format of a segment table.

The format of a segment table is shown in Fig. 17–3. The length of a page table is given in bits 0–3, and the first 21 bits of the address of the page table are given in bits 8 to 28. The lower three bits of the page table address are supplied as zeros, which means that a page table always begins on a double-word boundary. Bit 31 indicates whether there is a currently valid page table for the segment or not; if not, address translation must be suspended and the supervisor given control until the page table is made valid.

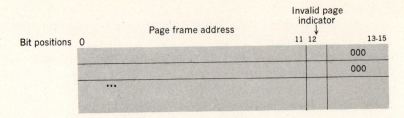

Fig. 17–4 Format of a page table.

The format of a page table is shown in Fig. 17–4. Bit 12 indicates whether the desired page is currently in real storage (valid) or not (invalid). If it is not, translation must be suspended until the needed page is brought into main storage and the page table gives its correct page frame address. When translation can be carried out, bits 0–11 of the page-table entry hold the first twelve bits (page frame address) of the desired location in real storage.

The translation process

An example of use of the tables in the translation of an actual (virtual) address is shown in Fig. 17–5. The address generated by base, index, and displacement is 013A8C. Since each segment table entry is four bytes long, the segment index must

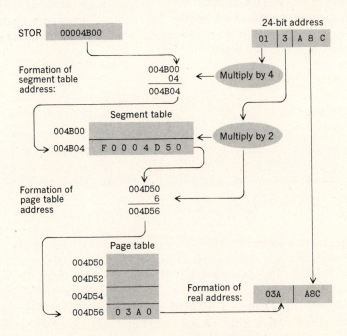

Fig. 17–5 Example of address translation.

be multiplied by 4; the result is added to the contents of STOR to give the proper address in the segment table. Similarly, since each page table entry is two bytes long, the page index is multiplied by 2 and the result added to the address found in the segment table. The result, 004D56, indicates the address in the page table where we find the address of the real page frame containing the desired page. The combination of the page frame address and the byte index yields 03AA8C, the real address of the desired operand.

If the above translation process had to be carried out for every reference to operands or instructions in main storage, execution of programs would be slowed significantly. A *translation look-aside buffer* (TLB) is provided to hold the page frame addresses of the most recently used pages. The translation process is carried out in parallel through the TLB and the segment and page tables; in most cases the TLB will contain the desired entry, and operands can be addressed immediately while the translation process through segment and page tables is aborted. The TLB is an example of an *associative* or *content-addressable* memory. See Foster (reference at the end of the chapter) for a discussion of content-addressable memory techniques.

Storage management

Next we outline some other steps and considerations in the management of a virtual storage system. Most important is the dynamic change in assignment of page frames and the process of storing and retrieving contents of pages which are not currently in real page frames.

The supervisor must know what pages are in which page frames at any time. A *page frame table*, managed entirely through software (the supervisor) must contain

> page frame address,
> ID of the program to which the frame is assigned,
> segment and page index,
> status.

When a new page must be brought into main storage, the supervisor must find an available page frame and bring the proper page from external storage into the selected frame. This implies an *external page table*, with content like the page frame table, but instead of the page frame address it must contain the address in the external storage medium (drum or disk) used for the purpose.

Swapping

The working sets of active programs change, and more pages must be brought into main storage. Eventually, all page frames will contain pages for various programs. The next time a page is needed, one of the pages in main storage must be replaced. We call the replacement of one page in a page frame by another *swapping*. Which page will be swapped out? We adopt a strategy that a page *least recently used* is most likely not to be needed again, at least for quite a while. To tell which page is least recently used, we add a *reference bit* to (essentially) the page frame table; every time the page in the frame is used by a program the bit is set to 1. If all reference bits are set to 0 every so often, those remaining at 0 when we must test have been used less recently than those whose reference bits have been set to 1.

We must now examine what the swapping entails. We must be sure we keep the most recent version of each page, so if the page to be swapped out of main storage has been changed since it was last brought from external storage, the changed version must be moved back to external storage. How will we know? We need a *change bit* in (essentially) the page frame table, to be set to 1 every time the contents of the page are changed. We must test the change bit when we need to swap out the page. We will learn in the next section that the reference and change bits are actually kept in special hardware locations where they are easy to set with no loss of time.

Since this is a brief description, we close this section with an outline of the steps followed in swapping in a new page.

1. By finding the *invalid* bit set to 1 in a page table, the hardware recognizes that a page must be brought from external storage. An interrupt passes control to the supervisor.
2. The supervisor scans the page frame table, searching for an available page frame. If one is available, it goes to step 9.
3. Otherwise, the supervisor examines the *reference bits* to pick a page that will be swapped out. A page whose reference bit is currently 0 will be chosen.
4. The invalid bit is set *on* in the page table for the page to be removed.
5. The page frame is marked *reserved* for swapping.
6. If the page to be swapped out has its change bit *off* (0), the supervisor goes to step 9.
7. Otherwise, it initiates transmission of the page from main storage to external storage.
8. Another program is activated until the transmission is completed.
9. After completion, transmission of the desired page is initiated from external storage into the assigned page frame.
10. Another program is activated until the transmission is completed.
11. The page table is updated to show the location of the new page.
12. The page frame table is updated to show use of the frame.
13. The program is reactivated, and will now be able to proceed with the instruction which was halted by the unavailability of the page just brought in.

This brief introduction to storage management can be supplemented by reference to the IBM student text *Introduction to Virtual Storage in System/370*, GR20-4260. The reference manuals *IBM System/370 Principles of Operation*, GA22-7000, and *OS/VS Supervisor Services and Macro-Instructions*, GC27-6979, provide more definitive information on the hardware and software respectively.

2. THE PROGRAM STATUS WORD IN BC MODE

There are two forms of the program status word (PSW). The first is *BC mode*; this
is the only form available in System/360 and the form we study in this section. The
second form, *EC mode*, is treated in Section 3. Various fields of the PSW have been
introduced in previous chapters, and we survey the PSW more comprehensively
here.

The PSW is 64 bits long, and it resides in a special part of the central processing unit, not in a part of addressable main core storage. Its format is shown
in Fig. 17–6. The condition code (bits 34–35) has been used extensively and needs
no further discussion. The instruction address is the main storage address of the
next instruction to be executed. It is usually increased by 2, 4, or 6, the length
of the current instruction, in passing from one instruction to the next; execution
of a branch is accomplished by loading the branch address into this portion of
the PSW.

The AMWP code reflects current status of the computer. In System/360, the
A position (bit 12) specifies whether sign and zone codes generated by decimal
arithmetic instructions are in the ASCII-8 code (when bit 12 is set to 1) or in the
EBCDIC code (when bit 12 is set to 0). Actually, current software does not support
the ASCII-8 setting. In System/370, bit 12 distinguishes between BC mode (bit 12
is 0) and EC mode (bit 12 is 1) of the PSW. The W bit (position 14) is 1 when the
central processing unit is in the *wait state*, and 0 when the CPU is in the running
state. In the wait state no instructions are processed, but an interrupt is allowed;
the interrupt can return the machine to the running state. The wait state differs
from the *stop state* in that the stop state does not permit interruption, but is left
(and entered) only by manual action. The P bit (position 15) denotes whether
the CPU is in the *problem state* (when the bit is 1) or the *supervisor state* (when the
bit is 0). Certain instructions, such as PSW manipulation and input and output
manipulations, are executable only in the supervisor state; thus the status of the
machine is protected against unwarranted change by a user.

Bits 32 and 33 of the PSW contain the Instruction Length Code (ILC), which
is normally 1, 2, or 3, showing the number of half-words occupied by the current
instruction. Since the instruction address is normally the address of the *next*
instruction to be executed, the ILC is necessary in finding the *last* instruction for
diagnostic purposes in case of interrupt.

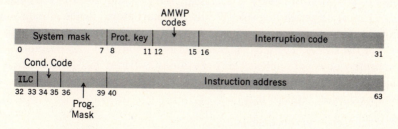

Fig 17–6   The format of the program status word in BC mode.

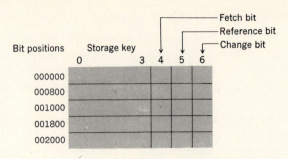

Fig. 17–7   Storage keys.

The storage protection system was introduced in Chapter 9. A four-bit storage key is associated with each block of 2048 bytes. A fifth bit, called the *fetch bit*, controls whether attempts to fetch information from the block are monitored as well as attempts to store information into the block; if the fetch bit is 1, fetch attempts are monitored, but if the fetch bit is 0 or if fetch protection is not implemented, fetch attempts are always permitted. The monitoring consists of comparison of the *protection key*, bits 8–11 of the PSW, with the storage key. If the two keys match or if the protection key is 0, access is permitted. A nonpermitted access attempt causes an interruption.

The reference bit and change bit, introduced in the previous section as an aid in the management of virtual storage, are in fact attached to the storage key, as shown in Fig. 17–7. This is a handy place to append the functions of reference and change bits, since the storage keys are accessed for every reference and change anyway. These bits are of course included in the hardware only in virtual storage systems.

There are two instructions that enable the supervisor to manage the protection system. They are ISK, Insert Storage Key, which loads a storage key into a register for inspection, and SSK, Set Storage Key, which sets a storage key from the contents of a register. Both are RR-type instructions. In both, *R2* indicates which block of storage the instruction pertains to. The block is identified by bits 8–20 of the register; for example, if the register contains 0000B800, the storage key for the storage block 00B800 to 00BFFF is accessed. Bits 0–7 and 21–27 are ignored, but bits 28–31 must be zero. Register *R1* bits 24–30 are stored as the storage key by the SSK instruction; other bits are ignored. In BC mode, the ISK instruction inserts bits 0–4 of the storage key into bit positions 24–28 (bits 0–3 into positions 24–27 if fetch protection is not implemented). Positions 29–31 (or 28–31) are set to 0, but positions 0–23 are unchanged.

As an example, suppose that

Register 8 contains 00000030
Register 9 contains 0000B800

Fig. 17–8   PSW bits masking interrupts in BC mode

PSW bit	Interrupt condition
0	Message from channel 0
1	Message from channel 1
2	Message from channel 2
3	Message from channel 3
4	Message from channel 4
5	Message from channel 5
6	Message from channels 6 and higher
7	Timer, interrupt key, external signal
13	Machine-check
36	Fixed-point overflow
37	Decimal overflow
38	Exponent underflow
39	Significance

The instruction SSK 8,9 will cause bit patterns 0011000 (or 00110 or 0011, depending on model) to be set as the storage key for the block of storage 00B800 to 00BFFF. Fetch access to the block will be permitted to any instruction, but store access only if PSW bits 8–11 are 0011 or 0000.

The ISK and SSK instructions are carried out without respect to segment and page tables, and accesses to the keys are not subject to the protection system itself. Both SSK and ISK are privileged, so they may be executed only in the supervisor state.

The other fields of the PSW have to do with interrupts, which will be discussed in more detail in Section 5. However, we describe here the PSW bits in positions 0–7, 13, and 36–39. These are all *mask* bits, controlling (*masking*) whether certain conditions cause interrupt or not. The conditions are as shown in Fig. 17–8; a 1-bit permits interrupt on the condition, a 0-bit suppresses it. Bits 0–7 are called the *system mask*, bits 36–39 the *program mask*. Interrupts caused by action in channels will be discussed in more detail in Sections 5 and 9; the conditions whose interrupts are controlled by the program mask have been discussed in Chapters 9, 13, and 14. External and machine-check interrupt conditions will be described in Section 5. The system mask should be under control of the supervisor, but the program mask is under control of the programmer, as we shall see in the next section. Finally, bits 16–31 of the PSW contain an *interrupt code*, which is stored in the event of interrupt, to identify the cause of interrupt.

3. EC MODE AND CONTROL REGISTERS

The IBM System/370 implements a number of features not included in the System/360. Several of these require information fields of the kind that could logically be part of the PSW. To extend the capabilities, a set of *control registers* is provided, some fields formerly in the PSW are moved and expanded into control registers while other fields are established in the PSW. The new format of the PSW is called EC (Extended Control) mode, while BC (Basic Control) mode is retained for compatibility when needed.

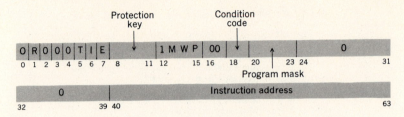

Fig. 17–9   The format of the program status word in EC mode.

The format of the PSW in EC mode is shown in Fig. 17–9. Bit 12 is 1 to indicate that the format is EC mode. The protection key, MWP codes, and instruction address are unchanged in function or location. The condition code and program mask occupy bit positions 18–23 instead of 34–39, but their function is unchanged.

Input/output interrupt masks for individual channels are moved to control register 2, and bit 6 of the PSW indicates whether *all* input/output interrupts are to be blocked (bit 6 = 0) or whether control register 2 will mask interrupts on the individual channels (bit 6 = 1). The same treatment is given to external interrupts, which are divided into subclasses, each masked by a bit in control register 0. Bit 7 of the PSW can block all interrupts of the class (in System/370, this is true in BC mode as well).

Bit 5 of the PSW in EC mode specifies dynamic address translation. When the bit is 1, addresses are translated as described in Section 1; when the bit is 0, no translation takes place.

Bit 2 of the PSW controls program event recording, which was mentioned in Chapter 9 and will be treated in a little more detail below. Other bit positions are unused, but, of course, new features yet to be announced at this writing may find a new use for them!

There are up to 15 control registers. As of this writing, the functions controlled are shown in Fig. 17–10. We will treat some of the features and functions here and in later sections; the reader will have to supplement this brief introduction with reference to the *IBM System/370 Principles of Operation* manual, GA22-7000, and other manuals which set forth the software facilities built upon the hardware features.

In Section 1 we mentioned that there were choices of segment and page size in the virtual storage system; bits 8–12 of control register 0 specify the sizes. Control register 1 is also associated with the virtual storage system; bits 0–7 specify the length of the segment table, in terms of 4-byte entries. If only the first few segments of address space are assigned, only the first few lines of the segment table need be filled in, and the length specified prevents code beyond the actual entries to cause spurious address translations. Bits 8–31 are the Segment Table Origin Register, whose function we showed in Section 1.

Control registers 9–11 are associated with program event recording. Program events such as a successful branch, fetching an instruction from a designated area

Fig. 17–10   Control register fields

CR	Bits	Name of field	Associated with	Init.
0	0	Block-multiplexing control	Block-multiplexing	0
	1	SSM suppression control	SSM instruction	0
	2	TOD clock sync control	Multiprocessing	0
	8–9	Page size control		0
	10	Unassigned (must be zero)	Dynamic addr. transl.	0
	11–12	Segment size control		0
	16	Malfunction alert mask		0
	17	Emergency signal mask		0
	18	External call mask	Multiprocessing	0
	19	TOD clock sync check mask		0
	20	Clock comparator mask	Clock comparator	0
	21	CPU timer mask	CPU timer	0
	24	Interval timer mask	Interval timer	1
	25	Interrupt key mask	Interrupt key	1
	26	External signal mask	External signal	1
1	0–7	Segment table length		0
	8–25	Segment table address	Dynamic addr. transl.	0
2	0–31	Channel masks	Channels	1
8	16–31	Monitor masks	Monitoring	0
9	0	Successful branching event mask		0
	1	Instruction fetching event mask		0
	2	Storage alteration event mask	Program-event recording	0
	3	GR alteration event mask		0
	16–31	PER general register masks		0
10	8–31	PER starting address	Program-event recording	0
11	8–31	PER ending address	Program-event recording	0
14	0	Check-stop control		1
	1	Synch. MCEL control	Machine-check handling	1
	2	I/O extended logout control	I/O extended logout	0
	4	Recovery report mask		0
	5	Degradation report mask		0
	6	Ext. damage report mask		1
	7	Warning mask	Machine-check handling	0
	8	Asynch. MCEL control		0
	9	Asynch. fixed log control		0
15	8–28	MCEL address	Machine-check handling	512

of main storage, storing an operand in the designated area, and alteration of specified general registers can cause interrupts and passage of control to a routine which will record the event, if the interrupts are not masked off. The monitored area of main storage is designated by addresses in control registers 10 and 11. Bits 0–7 of control register 9 mask those events that may cause interrupt. Bits 16–31 designate which general registers are monitored for change. Having a record of events of the sort indicated can provide a selective trace of program actions which can be very useful in debugging programs.

4. INSTRUCTIONS PERTAINING TO PSW AND ADVANCED FEATURES

There are instructions that change all or part of the PSW and that also load and store control registers. We consider these instructions in this section, along with some special instructions that are used in managing a virtual storage system. Note that in System/370 models, the functions controlled by these instructions, are not the same in EC mode as those controlled in BC mode.

First is the SI-type instruction Load PSW (LPSW). It has only one operand, a double word addressed by *D1* and *B1*. Bit positions 8–15, the *I2* portion of the instruction, are ignored. The double word from main storage addressed by *D1* and *B1* is loaded into the PSW, replacing the current PSW. Thus LPSW is a branch instruction, but it can also change all other status indications contained in the PSW. It is a privileged instruction, executable only from the supervisor state.

A second SI-type instruction is Set System Mask (SSM). Again, the *I2* portion is ignored; the system mask, bit positions 0–7 of the PSW, is loaded from the byte in main storage addressed by *D1* and *B1*. Other parts of the PSW are unaffected. The SSM instruction is also privileged, so it must be executed from the supervisor state.

The program mask is accessible to the programmer in problem state, and it is the only part of the interrupt system that can be controlled by the user that is not in supervisor state. The programmer can load a new program mask and condition code by the Set Program Mask (SPM) instruction, which is a nonprivileged instruction of RR type. The bits from positions 2 and 3 of register *R1* are loaded into the condition code portion of the PSW, and the bits from positions 4–7 of register *R1* are loaded into the program mask portion. The *R2* field of SPM is ignored. These functional fields are set regardless of whether the current program status word is in BC or EC mode.

The programmer gains access to the program mask by executing a BAL or BALR instruction. The register *R1* is loaded with ILC, CC, the program mask, and the address of the next instruction, in that order. These fields are exactly bits 32–63 of the PSW in BC mode, but the same content is loaded regardless of current mode of the PSW. For example, if a programmer wishes at some stage in his program to enable interrupt on decimal overflow, the following instructions would do the job:

```
          BALR   9,0
          Ø      9,ENDECØV
          SPM    9
          ⋮
ENDECØV   DC     X'04000000'
```

A final nonprivileged RR-type instruction is SuperVisor Call (SVC). Its format is actually different from that of other RR-type instructions; bits 8–15 are a byte of "immediate" data and not references to registers. The action of the SVC instruction is to force an interrupt of SVC type (more about the type in the next section) and to store the second byte of the instruction in the last eight bits of the interrupt code in the old PSW. The SVC is used by a programmer to request actions from the supervisor. The second byte of the instruction carries a message to the supervisor indicating what action is requested; for example,

SVC   19

may request the opening of a data set (certain other parameters to the request are assumed to be in registers), and

SVC   13

may request abnormal termination of the job step.

In addition to the instructions described above, System/370 models implement several others. To allow greater control over the system mask (PSW bits 0–7) there are two SI-type instructions: STore then aNd System Mask (STNSM) and STore then Or System Mask (STØSM). Each first stores the current system mask at the first operand location. Then the *and* or *or* function, respectively, is carried out with the system mask and the *I2* field of the instruction; the result is the new system mask. This allows any particular bit in the system mask to be set to 0 (by STNSM) or 1 (by STØSM), storing the previous system mask for later restoration. The instruction is privileged, and installed only as part of the dynamic address translation feature.

Three other privileged instructions deal specifically with dynamic address translation. Load Real Address (LRA) is an RX-type instruction. The (virtual) address generated as the second operand (base, index, displacement) is translated into a real address, if possible, using the current segment and page tables; the resulting real address is loaded into register *R1*. The condition code is set to 0 if translation is successful; other condition code settings report various mishaps (e.g., encountering an *invalid* bit in one of the tables). The supervisor must every now and then generate a real address equivalent to a given virtual address; we shall see examples when we study input and output.

The instruction Purge Translation Lookaside Buffer (PTLB) must be executed whenever a page or segment table changes; otherwise the old entry would still be used through the Translation Lookaside Buffer. When the instruction is executed, the entire buffer is cleared; it will be reloaded automatically by the hardware, an entry at a time, as new pages are referenced. The instruction is of S type, with no operands.

The Reset Reference Bit (RRB) instruction is also of S type. It resets to 0 the reference bit associated with the block of storage designated by bits 8–20 of the operand address. The operand address itself is not subject to address translation. It is convenient to be able to reset the single reference bit without bothering any other portions of the storage key.

Two instructions provide for loading and storing control registers. They are Load ConTroL (LCTL) and STore ConTroL (STCTL). Both are of RS type, and load and store control registers as LM and STM load and store general registers. Two differences must be noted, however: LCTL and STCTL are privileged, and we are not promised what will be stored if we attempt to store a control register not implemented on the computer. No other manipulation (arithmetic, logical instructions, shifts, etc.) can be done with control registers, so it is necessary to store their contents, perform any desired change, then reload the control registers.

One final instruction is introduced here because it was not convenient to do it elsewhere. The IBM System/360 has one internal clock which can be used in timings and can be accessed through macros. The System/370 has several additional clocks with various functions. The *time-of-day clock*, which we introduce specifically, is a double-word binary integer whose value behaves as if 1 is added to position 51 every microsecond. Depending on model, a larger number may be added less often, but it is a fairly high-resolution clock. A user program operating in problem state can receive the value in this clock by executing the S-type instruction STCK. The

Fig. 17–11   System control instructions

Instruction	Format					Action	Exceptions
SSK	08	R1	R2			Key for storage block addressed by $c(R2)_{8-20} \leftarrow c(R1)_{24-30}$	M,A,S
ISK	09	R1	R2			$R1_{24-30} \leftarrow$ Key for storage block addressed by $c(R2)_{8-20}$	M,A,S
LPSW	82	/////	B1	D1		$PSW_{0-63} \leftarrow c(S1)_{0-63}$	M,A,S
SSM	80	/////	B1	D1		$PSW_{0-7} \leftarrow c(S1)_{0-7}$	M,A
SPM	04	R1	////			$[CC, \text{Prog. Mask}] \leftarrow c(R1)_{2-7}$	
SVC	0A	I				$PSW_{24-31} \leftarrow I; \text{Interrupt}$	
STNSM	AC	I2	B1	D1		$S1 \leftarrow PSW_{0-7};$ $PSW_{0-7} \leftarrow PSW_{0-7} \wedge I2$	M,A
STØSM	AD	I2	B1	D1		$S1 \leftarrow PSW_{0-7};$ $PSW_{0-7} \leftarrow PSW_{0-7} \vee I2$	M,A
LRA	B1	R2	X2	B2	D2	$R2 \leftarrow$ translated $S2$	M,A
PTLB	B20D	/////////////				$TLB \leftarrow 0$	M
RRB	B213	B2	D2			Stor. Key $(S2_{0-12})_5 \leftarrow 0$	M,A
LCTL	B7	CR1	CR3	B2	D2	$CR1, \ldots, CR3 \leftarrow c(S2), \ldots$	M,A,S
STCTL	B6	CR1	CR3	B2	D2	$S2, \ldots \leftarrow c(CR1), \ldots, c(CR3)$	M,A,S
STCK	B205	B2	D2			$S2_{0-63} \leftarrow$ time-of-day clock	A

Fig. 17–12   Instructions affecting system control features

Field	BC-mode Location	EC-mode Location	Instructions affecting the field
Storage key	special area		ISK,SSK,RRB
System mask	PSW_{0-7}	PSW_{0-7}	LPSW,SSM,STNSM,STØSM
Prot. key	PSW_{8-11}	PSW_{8-11}	LPSW
ASCII mode	PSW_{12} (360 only)		LPSW
Control mode	PSW_{12} (370 only)	PSW_{12}	LPSW
MWP	PSW_{13-15}	PSW_{13-15}	LPSW
Interrupt code	PSW_{16-31}	main stor. locs.	an interruption
ILC	PSW_{32-33}	main stor. locs.	———
Cond. code	PSW_{34-35}	PSW_{18-19}	SPM, LPSW, any instruction which sets condition code
Prog. mask	PSW_{36-39}	PSW_{20-23}	SPM,LPSW
Inst. address	PSW_{40-63}	PSW_{40-63}	LPSW, any branch instruction
Control register			LCTL,STCTL
Time-of-day clock			STCK

double-word value is stored at the second-operand location. The value is arranged so that the *first word* of the clock (bit 31) is incremented every 1.048576 seconds, so often measurement of time intervals can be done accurately enough by computing the difference between two values of the first word of the clock. The condition code is set by STCK, to

0   if the clock is set,
1   if not set (but still running, so available for interval calculation),
2   error state,
3   not operational.

The instructions introduced in this chapter are summarized in Fig. 17–11. The formats are shown explicitly, since the instructions differ from other instructions of their respective types. Figure 17–12 shows by control field the instructions which deal with each control function.

There are a number of system control instructions not mentioned at all. They deal with yet more specialized control functions, and little purpose would be served by descriptions here. The reader may feel we have tried to cover too much already!

5. INTERRUPT HANDLING

The mechanism of interrupt is very simple. The current program status word, with appropriate instruction length code and interrupt code indicating the condition causing interrupt, is stored at a fixed location in main storage. A new program status word is loaded into the PSW (we now distinguish between PSW, the physical register, and a program status word, which is the information currently or formerly held in the PSW) from another fixed location. Processing then resumes, according to directions and status given in the new program status word.

There are six classes of interrupts, and each class has its own set of fixed addresses for old and new program status words. The types and fixed addresses

Fig. 17–13   Classes of interrupts and program status word addresses

Interrupt class	Old program status word stored at:	New program status word loaded from:
Restart	000008	000000
External	000018	000058
Supervisor call	000020	000060
Program	000028	000068
Machine check	000030	000070
Input/output	000038	000078

are shown in Fig. 17–13. A *restart* interrupt (System/370 only) is caused by depression of the *restart* key at the operator's console. An *external* interrupt is caused by a signal from any of several clocks or timers, the interrupt key on the console, or external lines (perhaps attached to other computers—not to be confused with channels). The *supervisor call* interrupt is caused by execution of the SVC instruction. A *machine check* interrupt is caused by detection of a machine malfunction in the CPU; it can be masked off by PSW bit 13, but should be masked off only during processing of a machine check interrupt. An *input/output* interrupt is caused by conditions in the input/output system, as will be discussed further in Sections 6 through 9.

A *program* interrupt is caused by some condition, usually an invalid instruction or data for the instruction, arising from execution of the user's program. Fifteen program conditions were discussed in previous chapters; four of them can be masked by the program mask.

Three program conditions are associated with dynamic address translation. One is caused by a *segment fault*, in which the *invalid* bit for a needed entry in the segment table is found to be 1. A second is caused by a *page fault*, in which the *invalid* bit for a needed entry in the page table is found to be 1. Either of these is a signal that a needed page is not in main storage, and a swapping action must be taken, after which control is returned to the program. The third condition is a *translation specification* condition, caused by improper codes in control register 1 or in the segment and page tables.

Another program interrupt, called "special operation," occurs when attempted SSM execution is masked off by bit 1 of control register 0. Another is caused by a *program event*, to enable recording as defined in Section 3. One last program interrupt is caused by a *monitor call* instruction; the monitoring system is beyond the scope of the treatment of this chapter. A summary of interruption codes and actions is provided in Fig. 17–14.

Several interrupt conditions can arise simultaneously. When they do, interrupts occur in order of priority as follows:

Machine check
Supervisor call
Program
External
Input/output
Restart

Fig. 17–14   **Interrupt action**

Source	Inter-ruption Code	PSW Mask bits		Mask bits in Control Register		Execution of instruction identified by old PSW
		BC	EC	Reg.:	Bits	
Machine check		13	13	14:	4–7	completed if possible
Supervisor call	*12*					completed
External		7	7	0:	20–21, 24–26	unaffected
Input/Output:						
Channels 0–5		0–5	6	2:	0–5	unaffected
Channels 6 & on		6	6	2:	6 and on	unaffected
Restart						unaffected
Program:						
Operation	1					suppressed
Privileged op.	2					suppressed
Execute	3					suppressed
Protection	4					suppressed or terminated
Addressing	5					suppressed or terminated
Specification	6					suppressed
Data	7					suppressed or terminated
Fixed-pt. overflow	8	36	20			completed
Fixed-pt. divide	9					suppressed or completed
Decimal overflow	A	37	21			completed
Decimal divide	B					suppressed
Exponent overflow	C					completed
Exponent underflow	D	38	22			completed
Significance	E	39	23			completed
Floating-point divide	F					suppressed
Segment trans.	10					nullified
Page translation	11					nullified
Translation spec.	12					suppressed
Special operation	13			0:	1	suppressed
Monitor event	40			8:	16–31	completed
Program event	80			9:	0–31	completed

If conditions of, say, fixed-point overflow and input/output interrupt arise simultaneously, the fixed-point overflow interrupt is taken first. However, immediately afterwards the input/output interrupt is taken, so it is really *processed before* the fixed-point overflow interrupt.

The program status word stored at each of the locations 000000, 000058, 000060, 000068, 000070, and 000078 is obviously associated with the portion of the supervisor which is to handle the corresponding type of interrupt. Each of these program status words will contain a 0-bit in position 15 to put the CPU in the supervisor state. It will contain, in positions 40–63, the address of the routine which handles the particular type of interrupt. Finally, it will contain bits to mask out further interrupts of the type it is treating. For example, the program status word at location 000058 contains the address of the routine which handles external interrupts; it also contains a 1-bit in position 7 so that no further external interrupts may occur. The prohibition is necessary at least until the information in the old program status word from the current interrupt is safely stored; otherwise, a new interrupt would put another program status word in location 000018, destroying the previous information. This is why masking provisions are necessary for external, input/output, and machine check interrupt conditions; presumably, if the interrupt handling routines are written correctly, they will not *cause* program check or supervisor call interrupts, so masking provisions for these are not necessary.

If the programmer wants to handle interrupts of certain types resulting from his program, he can provide in a SPIE (Specify Program Interruption Exit) macro-instruction the address of his interrupt-handling routine and the interrupt conditions under which he wants it to operate. When one of these interrupts occurs, the supervisor will put register contents and program status word information, including the interrupt code, in a special region and give control (in the problem, not the supervisor state) to the programmer's own routine.

6. THE BASIC STRUCTURE OF INPUT AND OUTPUT PROCESSING

The structure of the input and output (we use the abbreviation I/O) system of System/360 and 370 is rather complex, designed for flexibility and the maximum decentralization of control possible consistent with standardized treatment wherever possible. There are four main I/O instructions executed by the CPU, and they are quite simple: Start I/O, Halt I/O, Test I/O, and Test Channel. The actual activity takes place in the channels, control units, and I/O devices under direction of programs executed by the channels. Channel programs consist of *commands;* a channel program is initiated by a Start I/O instruction, but is then executed independently of the CPU. The format of channel programs is standard for all devices, but a channel command may include a device-oriented code which will be translated by an I/O control unit into an *order* to a device.

A given System/360 or 370 computer may have one or more channels. A *selector channel* operates in the *burst mode*, in which the channel is dedicated completely to the device using it at the moment, and no other device may use the channel until the channel program is completed or terminated. Selector channels are generally used for servicing high-speed devices. A *multiplexor channel*, called byte-multi-plexor in System/370, may have several subchannels, each one capable of executing a channel program concurrently with others. Devices attached to a multiplexor channel are usually slow-speed. A multiplexor channel has elements that can be used for only one operation at a time, but in the *multiplex mode*, operations are broken into short intervals so they can be serviced in turn. A multiplexor channel can also operate in the burst mode.

The System/370 can also have a *block multiplexor* channel. The block multiplexor channel has subchannels and permits multiplexing of several channel programs, but actual data transfer is carried out only in burst mode for one subchannel at a time.

Commands are kept in main storage, each in a double word. Information being transferred by the channel moves into or out of main storage; the use of main storage for both instructions in the CPU and for I/O operations causes the program in the CPU to slow slightly, but otherwise the CPU and the channels run independently. Communication is maintained, however; the CPU can halt an I/O operation with the Halt I/O instruction, and the channel can cause an interrupt of the CPU. At appropriate times information on the status of a channel is stored in a channel status word (CSW), which is accessible to the program in the CPU.

In the next three sections we examine the I/O structure in somewhat more detail.

7. INPUT AND OUTPUT INSTRUCTIONS AND STATES OF THE SYSTEM

All I/O instructions are of S type. In System/360, the listed I/O instructions are called SI-type instructions. There is no conflict; all the System/370 instructions have 0's in bits 8–15 of the operation code; the System/360 instructions do not use the $I2$ field (bits 8–15) of the instruction. The instructions are also written the same in assembler language; for example,

SIØ   190

is proper form for either System/360 or System/370. The sum of the displacement $D2$ and the contents of the register $B2$ is formed as usual, but it does not refer to a main storage location. The low-order half of the sum specifies a channel and a device on the channel as shown in Fig. 17–15.

Ignored	Channel address	Device address
0 15 16	23 24	31

Fig. 17–15   Addressing a channel and device.

The channel and device addresses have nothing to do with addresses of main storage locations but are used to identify particular channels and devices attached to channels. For example,

9C000190

is the hexadecimal code for a Start I/O instruction, addressing channel 1 and device 90 on the channel—$B2$ is 0, so no register is used.

The four I/O instructions are as shown in Fig. 17–16. All four instructions set a condition code, as we discuss below. All are privileged. But before we

Fig. 17–16   Input/output instructions

Instruction	Type	Action	Cond. code[1]	Exceptions[2]
SIØ	S	Start an I/O operation	Yes	M
HIØ	S	Halt an I/O operation	Yes	M
TIØ	S	Set cond. code, perhaps store Channel Status Word	Yes	M
TCH	S	Test a channel	Yes	M

Notes

1) Condition code settings partially explained in text.
2) M: Privileged operation.

describe in any detail the actions of the individual instructions, we must describe states of the I/O system.

Each of the channels, subchannels, and control units and devices (let us consider the control unit and device to be merged into one unit) may be in one of the four states: *available*, *working*, *interrupt pending*, or *not operational*. A channel is in the *working* state if it is operating in the burst mode; a subchannel or device is in the working state if it is performing an operation. Devices, control units, subchannels, and channels are *not operational* mainly if not provided in the system, or if power is turned off. If a condition which can cause interrupt is present, the channel, subchannel, or device is said to be in the *interrupt-pending* state. If a channel, subchannel, or device is in either the working, not operational, or interrupt-pending state, it is said to be *not available;* the *available* state is the absence of the not-available state. Many combinations of states are possible, but fortunately only a few are detectable or significant; for example, if the channel is not operational, states of subchannels and devices on the channel are irrelevant. Furthermore, channel and subchannel effectively coincide in a selector channel. The condition codes set by the I/O instructions depend on these states. We can now study the instructions, one by one.

The Start I/O (SIØ) instruction starts an input or output operation: read, read backward, write, sense, or control, if the designated channel, subchannel, and device are available. A *channel address word* (CAW) at fixed location 000048 gives to the channel the address of the channel program to be executed, and the protection key to be used by the channel in its main storage accesses. The information in the CAW is promptly stored in the channel itself, so location 000048 can be used for other things. The SIØ instruction takes very little time; the operation is initiated, if possible, and left to the channel. The condition code is set to reflect the result of the initiation attempt, as follows:

CC=0:   Operation is initiated and undergoing execution by the channel.
CC=1:   Some kind of exceptional condition exists, such as interrupt pending; information is stored in a channel status word.
CC=2:   Channel or subchannel is busy (in the working state).
CC=3:   Channel, subchannel, or device is not operational.

If the condition code is 1, 2, or 3, the operation is not initiated.

The Halt I/O (HIØ) instruction terminates the operation in a device, subchannel, or channel; data transmission stops immediately, but the mechanical operation of the device usually continues until the end of the block of data. The condition code reports the result of the HIØ instruction:

CC=0:   The subchannel was in an interrupt-pending state; no action taken.
CC=1:   A CSW is stored, giving details of the termination, which may or may not have been completed.
CC=2:   A burst-mode operation is terminated.
CC=3:   Channel, subchannel, or device is not operational.

The HIØ instruction is not often used; normally, an operation is allowed to run to completion. However, if the user's program is being terminated, if the channel is desperately needed for another operation, or if it is found that the current operation is somehow erroneous, the HIØ instruction is necessary.

The Test I/O (TIØ) instruction tests the status of a designated channel, subchannel, and device. Status information is recorded in the condition code and sometimes in the CSW. An interrupt-pending condition is cleared. The condition code is set:

CC=0:   Subchannel and device are available.
CC=1:   The device is busy, or the device or subchannel has an interrupt pending; the CSW gives the details.
CC=2:   Channel or subchannel is busy.
CC=3:   Channel, subchannel, or device is not operational.

An I/O-handling piece of the supervisor may well be carried out with I/O interrupts masked off. Before returning control to an interrupted program, it may test all operating devices to see if one has an interrupt-pending condition; the discovery of one enables the interrupt condition to be serviced without actually causing interrupt.

The Test Channel (TCH) instruction is very simple. The channel only is tested; subchannels and devices are not. The condition code is set:

CC=0:   The channel is available.
CC=1:   The channel has an interrupt-pending condition.
CC=2:   The channel is operating in a burst mode.
CC=3:   The channel is not operational.

Since operations in the multiplex mode are not sensed, the channel is left available for still further multiplex-mode operations.

8. CHANNEL PROGRAMMING

If all goes well, the SIØ instruction initiates execution of a channel program to carry out an operation or sequence of operations using a particular channel, subchannel, and device. The channel then proceeds until the operation or sequence of operations is complete, a HIØ instruction is given, or an exceptional condition, signaled by interrupt, makes completion impossible. We now study how operations are specified to the channel and how the channel executes its commands.

The sequence of operations to be performed by a channel program is defined by one or more *channel command words* (CCW's). The address of the first CCW in the channel program is given to the channel in the Channel Address Word

Prot. Key	0000		Command address
0 3	4 7	8	31

Fig. 17–17 Format of a Channel Address Word (CAW).

(CAW) at location 000048. The format of the CAW is as shown in Fig. 17–17. Bits 0–3 of the CAW contain a protection key which is compared to the storage key of any main storage location referenced, just as the protection key in the PSW is compared during instruction execution. The channel command words are double words which have the format shown in Fig. 17–18. The command code specifies the type of operation to be performed: Sense, Transfer in channel, Read backward, Write, Read, or Control. These types are described in more detail below. The data address is the address of the first byte to be used in information transfer (except when indirect data addressing is specified, as will be explained below); the count is the number of bytes to be transferred under control of the CCW. The flags in positions 32 to 37 carry further information about how the channel program is to proceed.

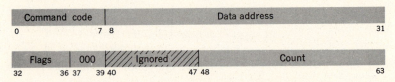

Fig. 17–18   Format of a Channel Command Word (CCW).

Two of the flags in the CCW control *chaining*. When the processing defined by one CCW is completed and the CCW indicates chaining, another CCW is fetched by the channel from main storage following the given CCW, and the channel program continues. If a CCW does not indicate chaining (and is not a transfer in channel command), it is the last CCW of the channel program. There are two types of chaining: *data chaining* and *command chaining*. Under data chaining, one operation—read, for example—is carried out using several main storage areas not necessarily contiguous. For instance, if a block contains three logical records of 80 bytes each, the block can be read in one operation while the three logical records are placed in three buffer areas. Command chaining allows several operations, for example, the reading of several blocks in one channel program. Data chaining can take place within command chaining.

Sequences of CCW's in a channel program need not be contiguous in main storage. The *transfer-in-channel* command is an unconditional branch in a channel program, giving the location of a further sequence of CCW's. Thus a loop may be formed in a channel program!

When a block is being read or written, the count in the current CCW is decremented by 1 for each byte read or written. If the block is not completed when the count reaches zero, and data chaining is indicated, the next CCW is used for a continuation of the operation. If the count reaches zero before the block is completed and data chaining is *not* indicated, or if the block is completed before the count reaches zero, an incorrect length is indicated. The indication can be suppressed by the SLI (Suppress Length Indication) flag, but otherwise it causes the end of the channel program and generates an interrupt condition.

Another useful flag is the Program Controlled Interruption (PCI) flag, which generates an interrupt condition but allows the channel program to continue. The interrupt can be used by the supervisor to determine the current progress of the channel program. An interrupt could be generated after every block read, for example, so the user's program could start using the block while the channel program went on to read another block.

A *control* command causes the information sent to the device through the subchannel to be interpreted as control information instead of as data to be written. Control commands become *orders* to devices, causing rewinding of a magnetic tape, positioning of read-write heads to a particular cylinder of a magnetic disk pack, skipping the paper in a printer to a new page, etc.

Although read and write commands are the most important commands, they are obvious. Only a few devices, such as some magnetic tape units, can read information backwards, but a separate command is necessary for *read backward*.

A *sense* command asks for detailed information on the status of the device and any unusual conditions detected in the last operation. The information is placed in main storage as though it came from a read operation, and it is often more extensive than information given in the CSW.

As an example, suppose that we want to read two blocks from a direct-access device, and that each block consists of two logical records which are to be read into noncontiguous buffer areas. The supervisor issues an SIØ instruction after storing the address of our first CCW and an appropriate protection key (probably 0) in location 000048 as a CAW. The SIØ instruction designates the channel, let us suppose a selector channel, and the device address; then the channel takes over. The CCW's required could be the following:

1. A *control* command to position the beginning of the read; a few bytes at a main storage location which contain the address of the desired area on the direct-access storage device are sent to the device as control information; the command chaining flag is on.

2. A *read* command, containing the address of the first buffer area and length of the logical record; the data chaining flag is on.

3. The command code is ignored, but the read operation continues, reading into the second buffer area; the command chaining flag is on.

4. Another *control* command, positioning the reading heads to read the second block; the command chaining flag is on, and so is the PCI flag; the PCI flag signals the supervisor that the first block has been read, but it does not affect execution of the channel program.

5. Another *read* command, including the data-chaining flag, and giving the address and length of the third buffer area.

6. The command code is ignored, but the address and length of the fourth buffer area enable continuation of the read operation; *no* flags are on, so the channel program ends here.

When the channel program is terminated, either by an HIØ instruction, by detection of an error in the transmission or the channel program, or by normal completion, an interrupt condition is generated; it causes an interrupt unless interrupts for the channel are masked off.

We have not yet considered the implications of virtual storage management on input and output in System/370. There are two major implications we explore:

1. Input and output are initiated and left to proceed while the CPU serves other tasks. Until the data transmission is completed, the main storage allocated for input/output areas must *not* be swapped out or made available for other uses; the reader can readily imagine the chaos that would result otherwise.

2. Main storage addressing for data transmission is *not* subject to dynamic address translation. This means that data addresses in channel programs must be real, not virtual addresses. It also means that a buffer that looks like one continuous block of main storage to the program may be, through paging, a set of several noncontiguous areas! While the reader gets over his initial shock at this complication, let us point out why this design is necessary. First, data transmission is rapid and must not be hindered by address translation. Second, several input/output operations often proceed simultaneously, while several user programs and sections of the supervisor use the CPU in turn. One set of segment and page tables would be terribly strained trying to accommodate all users.

The remedy for point 1 is for the supervisor to "lock" the input/output areas into main storage, and mark the page frames (in the page frame table) as not available for swapping.

For the second problem, the *indirect data addressing* feature, available only in System/370, is helpful. If the IDA flag in the CCW is on, the data address portion of the CCW is interpreted as the address of a list of addresses of areas to be used in the actual information transmission. The count field of the CCW is still controlling; transmission begins with the address given in the first word of the IDA chain, and continues to the end of the 2048-byte block containing the first address (or until the count field is satisfied). If the count is not satisfied, transmission continues, starting at the second address in the chain (which will point to the beginning of a 2048-byte block), and it continues to the end of that block unless the count is satisfied first. Additional addresses in the chain are used similarly until the count is satisfied.

What then must the supervisor do when requested to execute a channel program in a virtual system? The channel program will be expressed in virtual addresses; the supervisor makes a copy which will be the one executed. The copy must then be modified. Each data address must be converted to a real address (this is where the LRA instruction comes in handy). The real address and count must be examined to see whether the data area crosses a page boundary. If so, the supervisor generates an IDA chain, puts its address in the CCW, and turns on the IDA flag.

The appropriate page frames must be locked into main storage by changing their status in the page frame table. Then the supervisor may initiate execution of the channel program.

9. INTERRUPTS AND THE CHANNEL STATUS WORD

The channel status word (CSW) occupies a double word at fixed main storage location 000040; information is stored there regarding the status of an I/O device or conditions under which a channel program is terminated. The information is provided upon I/O interrupt or when a SIØ, HIØ, or TIØ requires more information than can be given in the condition code. The general form of the CSW is as shown in Fig. 17–19. The channel, subchannel, or device whose status is given is indicated in the stored program status word in case of interrupt; for a CSW resulting from SIØ, HIØ, or TIØ the channel, subchannel, and device are those addressed by the SIØ, HIØ, or TIØ. The protection key which was sent to the channel through the CAW is included in the CSW, as well as the address of a CCW, usually the one beyond that producing the current condition. The residual count, that is, the number of bytes not yet processed under the current CCW, is given in bits 48–63; bits 32–47 indicate certain conditions, some of which are: busy, control-unit end, device end, channel end, unit check, unit exception, program-controlled interruption, incorrect length, program check, protection check, channel data check, and chaining check. The reader can gather from this list the general nature of the information conveyed even without detailed explanation of each of these conditions.

Detection of an error in any phase of an I/O operation will cause the channel program to be terminated and an interrupt generated. A parity error in the data read or written, which is reflected in a channel data check, does not cause interrupt until completion of the current I/O operation. Other errors actually caused by invalidities in the channel program are detected as a new CCW is being interpreted, and execution of the command is suppressed.

The example channel program described in Section 8 could be interrupted at any of several points. A channel data check in the execution of the second CCW does not terminate the channel program until after the read operation is completed, that is, at the end of the third CCW. However, an error in specification of the third CCW itself, called a program check, would terminate the program in the middle of the read operation. An exceptional condition in the device, such as

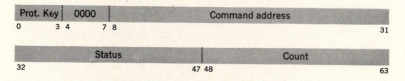

Fig. 17–19 Format of a Channel Status Word (CSW).

equipment error or not-ready status, generates a unit-check and signals the program that more information can be obtained through execution of a sense command.

10. REENTRANT AND RECURSIVE SUBROUTINES

A subroutine is called *reentrant* if it is written so that more than one execution can be in progress or suspended at once, yet all executions can ultimately be completed correctly. In a computer system that permits more than one program to run independently at more or less the same time, commonly used subroutines should be reentrant, so that only one copy of the subroutine need be kept in main storage. Routine A may call the reentrant subroutine C, and while execution of subroutine C is in progress, an interrupt may occur and routine B may be given control. Routine B may call subroutine C before the initial execution for routine A is completed; depending on possible further interrupts, either execution of subroutine C may be completed first, but if C is written properly, its execution for either routine will have no effect on the other.

The requirements put on a subroutine to make it reentrant are simple. The storage (including registers and indicators) used by any subroutine can be divided conceptually into two parts: the first is the *fixed* part, including instructions and constants—whatever remains fixed or immutable during the execution of the subroutine. The second part is the *variable part;* it includes anything that may vary during execution of the subroutine. A reentrant subroutine must distinguish

Fig. 17–20   Non-reentrant and reentrant subroutines

```
(a) Non-reentrant
SBRC     SAVE    (14,12)
         BALR    12,0
         USING   *,12
         LM      2,3,0(1)    ADDR. ØF TWØ PARAMETERS
         . . .
         X       5,NQ
         ST      5,G(6)      STØRE INTØ ØWN AREA
         . . .
         RETURN (14,12)
G        DS      9F
NQ       DC      F'-1'
         END
(b) Reentrant
SBRC     SAVE    (14,12)
         BALR    12,0
         USING   *,12
         LM      2,4,0(1)    ADDR. ØF TWØ PARAMS.
*    AND ADDR. ØF 9-WØRD WØRK AREA
         . . .
         X       5,NQ
         ST      5,0(6,4)    STØRE INTØ WØRK AREA SUPPLIED
         . . .
         RETURN (14,12)
NQ       DC      F'-1'
         END
```

carefully between these two parts. The fixed part can be used in common, but provisions must be made so that for the variable part, storage is provided that is particular to each call. If a subroutine is to be reentered after interrupt suspends another execution, information kept in registers and in the PSW is automatically kept in storage particular to each call by the interrupt processors. Main storage used must be treated differently. One of the parameters to the call can be the address of a block of main storage to be used for the variable part of the sub-routine. The address of this block would be kept in a register and used for addressing locations in the block.

Figure 17–20 sketches two versions of a subroutine. The first, shown in part (a) of the figure is *not* reentrant. It stores information in the work area G; if the subroutine is interrupted and reentered, it will store new information in area G, and proper resumption of the first execution is not possible because the needed information in G has been destroyed. The second version, shown in part (b) is reentrant. Each user is required to supply the address of a nine-word work area; if one execution is interrupted, the subroutine can be reentered, with another call including the address of a *different* work area. Neither execution interferes with the work area of the other, and both can be completed properly. Note that the constant NQ can be kept in the subroutine's own area, because it is used but not destroyed.

We have described one reason for making subroutines reentrant: in multi-programming systems one avoids duplication in main storage of the fixed part of common routines, and thus saves storage space. A second purpose, with different requirements, is implementation of *recursive processes*. A recursive procedure calls on itself; this does not necessarily lead to circular definitions but allows what we may call "spiral" definitions, which go around and around but descend, hopefully to some end which serves as a base for the spiral.

As a simple example of a function defined recursively, the factorial function can be expressed

$$n! = \begin{cases} 1, & \text{if } n = 0, \\ n \times (n-1)!, & \text{if } n \text{ is a positive integer.} \end{cases}$$

The function is defined in terms of itself, but is perfectly well defined. The value of 3!, for example, is

$$3! = 3 \times 2! = 3 \times (2 \times 1!) = 3 \times (2 \times (1 \times 0!))$$
$$= 3 \times (2 \times (1 \times 1)) = 6.$$

Let us consider a less trivial recursive procedure. A strategy for reaching a certain goal—like solving a puzzle or proving a theorem—is to define the goal, work backwards to define a subgoal, then a subgoal of that subgoal, and so on until given initial conditions are reached. One may have to backtrack in this process, abandoning subgoals that apparently cannot be reached and searching for an alternative subgoal. Thus the procedure to generate a subgoal may have to call on itself. After the execution defined by that call is completed, the original must be resumed.

A related procedure is finding a good move to make in a game of, say, chess. One wants to look ahead several moves. To do this, we generate a list of possible moves, and create from these some hypothetical next board positions. Then we generate a list of possible moves for our opponent and construct further board positions. To be feasible, the process must ultimately evaluate board positions for their desirability by means other than examining further moves, and how far one goes and how one makes the evaluations are rather difficult and sensitive questions. But the process up to those evaluations is a recursive one: from one board position one generates moves; to evaluate the different moves one constructs board positions, further moves, and evaluates *those* moves, *using the same subroutines.*

The programming requirements for a recursive subroutine are more stringent than on a merely reentrant one. From the subroutine, the call to the subroutine must be such that a new block of storage is made available for the variable part of the subroutine. Yet *that* execution may have to make available, with the same calling sequence, a *still* different block. Registers are no longer safe, and to keep variable information in the PSW from before a call until after it is almost impossible. We need what we call a *push-down stack.* The idea behind a push-down stack can be illustrated by a pile of plates. We can put down a plate, then a second plate on top of it. If we take a plate off the stack, it will be the second one. We can put more plates on the stack, and always the last plate put on is the first to be taken off. When that is taken, the plate set down before that is accessible. The push-down stack can also be characterized as a queue organized in a Last-In First-Out (LIFO) basis.

Subroutines must keep arguments, any working storage, and the return address in the push-down stack. Let us consider a subroutine which computes the factorial function. It must keep the argument, a space for the argument to feed to another execution of itself, and a return address. Let us follow the use of the stack as the subroutine, named FACT, is called with argument 3 and return address 003988.

1. Since the argument is not zero, the subroutine stores in the stack the argument n, $n - 1$, and the return address.

3	2	003988

2. Call FACT, with argument 2 and return address (within FACT) of 004A76.

3. FACT stores information in the stack, which reads:

2	1	004A76
3	2	003988

4. Call FACT, with argument 1 and return address 004A76.

5. Store information in the stack:

1	0	004A76
2	1	004A76
3	2	003988

6. Call FACT, with argument 0 and return address 004A76.

7. With argument 0, FACT returns to 004A76, with result 1.

8. In the resumption of FACT, the result 0! is multiplied by 1, to yield the result 1. Before return, a line of the stack is "popped up," so upon return to 004A76, the stack shows

2	1	004A76
3	2	003988

9. The resumption of FACT multiplies its argument (2) by the result 1! = 1 to yield a new result 2. Return is made to the return address after popping the stack to

3	2	003988

10. The resumption of FACT multiplies its argument (3) by the result 2! = 2 to yield a new result 6. Return is made to 003988 after popping the stack.

11. The calling program resumes with the result 3! = 6.

Implementation of this concept requires a separate subroutine which manages the stack and doles out a new block when asked. The stack can be organized in a variety of ways. One form is a simple block of sequential subblocks; the management would consist entirely of keeping a pointer to the current subblock. The pointer moves down when a new subblock is needed, and moves up when the stack is popped and a subblock is no longer needed. If the program uses linked lists, the push-down stack may well be kept as a linked list. This has several advantages, including more flexible use of storage. In some languages in which recursion is provided for explicitly, a number of push-down stacks used essentially as registers are created. These can be pushed down, used, and popped up individually as required; this is helpful when an application requires several recursive subroutines (*A* calls *B* which calls *C* which calls *B* which calls *C*, etc.) with different temporary storage requirements.

11. MAIN IDEAS

a. Virtual storage systems assign page frames of main storage as needed to hold pages for a program, allowing more efficient use of main storage. The mapping of virtual to real storage requires dynamic address translation hardware, and segment table, page tables, page frame tables, and external page tables.

b. The program status word contains information about the state of the CPU and the program currently in execution, and about the categories of interrupts allowed. System/370 employs two different modes or forms of the program status word, and also keeps related information in control registers.

c. During execution of a program, instructions changing contents of main storage are monitored by the protection system, if it is installed on the model. The protection key in the PSW must either be zero or match the storage key associated with the referenced storage block, or a protection interrupt occurs.

d. Some instructions, called privileged instructions, can be executed only when the computer is in the supervisor state. Among them are the protection-system instructions ISK and SSK described in Section 2, the PSW-manipulating instructions LPSW and SSM described in Section 4, and the I/O instructions SIØ, HIØ, TIØ, and TCH described in Section 7.

e. An interrupt causes the contents of the PSW to be stored at a fixed location in main storage, and causes another program status word, corresponding to an interrupt-handling routine, to be loaded from another fixed location. A pair of such locations is provided for each of the interrupt classes: external, supervisor call, program check, machine check, restart, and input/output.

f. Input and output operations are carried out through channels from the CPU to control units and devices. Each selector channel has one subchannel and operates in the burst mode. A multiplexor channel may have several subchannels, all operating in the multiplex mode concurrently, thus handling several slow-speed devices. The block multiplexor channel in System/370 allows several subchannels to execute programs concurrently, but only one at a time may transmit data, in burst mode.

g. An I/O instruction is initiated by the SIØ instruction, which sends to the channel a channel address word (CAW). Thereafter the channel executes a channel program consisting of channel command words (CCW's) in main storage which specify the operations read, read backward, write, control, sense, and transfer in channel, as well as the address and length of the main storage area to be used. Several CCW's may define several areas of main storage to be used in an I/O operation through data chaining; and through command chaining, several operations may be executed under control of one channel program. Since channels do not use dynamic address translation, the supervisor must map virtual addresses into real explicitly for channel programs, and often break virtual blocks into real discontiguous subblocks.

h. In addition to SIØ, the instructions HIØ, TIØ, and TCH manipulate and get information from the channels. Each one sets a condition code which depends on whether the addressed channel, subchannel, and device are available, working, have interrupts pending, or are not operational; if necessary, more information is supplied in a channel status word (CSW).

i. An I/O interrupt can be generated as specified in a command or upon normal or abnormal termination of an I/O operation. The interrupt is always accompanied by further information about its cause in the CSW.

QUESTIONS FOR REVIEW AND IMAGINATION

1. Given the special meaning of a protection key of 0, what areas of main storage might have a storage key of 0?

2. Write sequences including SPM instructions which set the program mask to allow various combinations of the maskable program-check interrupts.

3. The LPSW instruction loads a new program status word; how can one store the current contents of the PSW for examination? Design an instruction sequence, including an interrupt-handling routine if necessary, that will change bit 13 of the current PSW to 1, not changing anything else except, of course, the instruction address.

4. An interrupt-handling routine should mask out interrupts of the type it is handling, but one can see problems of an interrupt of type x, followed by an interrupt of type y, followed by another interrupt of type x which wipes out information on the first x-type interrupt. The priority hierarchy given in Section 5 should therefore be consulted in determining which interrupt-handling routines should allow which other interrupts. Design such a scheme; would you make special provision for machine-check interrupts?

5. In a multiprogramming system, there are subroutines which should be common to several jobs but which cannot be reentrant. One example is a storage allocation subroutine. When two routines each want a block of storage, we must arrange that one gets the first available block and the other gets the second available block. Some mechanism must be set up so that before the storage allocation subroutine (or at least a certain critical section of it) is entered, the mechanism makes sure that the subroutine is not currently in use. Some indicator must therefore be set upon entrance to the subroutine and reset upon exit, but *tested before entrance*. Show that if testing and setting of the indicator are done by separate instructions, an interrupt *between* testing and setting would permit a second routine to enter the subroutine concurrently with the first.

There is an instruction Test and Set (TS) which helps us in this problem. This instruction is of SI type with one operand which is one byte in main storage. Test and Set first tests the leftmost bit of the first operand byte. The condition code is set to

0 if the leftmost bit is 0,
1 if the leftmost bit is 1.

Then, regardless of the outcome of the test, it sets the byte to (binary) 11111111. Show how an indicator byte can be tested and set by the TS instruction to try to gain entry to and reserve the subroutine. Should the TS instruction be used inside or outside the subroutine? What configuration of the indicator byte represents that the subroutine is in use? What configuration represents that the subroutine is available? How is the indicator reset, and when?

6. Revise some subroutine defined in previous chapters in order to make it reentrant.

7. Write a simple routine to manage a push-down stack as a simple block with pointers. The lengths of all cells in the stack are equal, but write the routine so this length is easily varied.

8. Write a recursive subroutine which computes a factorial. Use the push-down stack management routine constructed in problem 7.

9. Write, or at least sketch, a routine which manages a push-down stack as a linked list.

10. There is an instruction Test under Mask (TM), of SI type, which tests bits of a one-byte first operand and sets a condition code. The second operand, the $I2$ portion of the instruction, controls which bits of the first operand are tested. Only first operand bits in positions where second operand bits are 1 are tested, and the condition code is set to

0 if all tested bits are 0's or if all the mask (second operand) is zero,
1 if the tested bits are mixed 0's and 1's,
3 if all tested bits are 1's.

For example, if the byte at IND8 contains 11100001, the instruction

```
TM    IND8,B'11000000'
```

will cause only the first two bits of IND8 to be tested, and since they are 1's, the condition code will be set to 3. Similarly,

```
TM    IND8,B'00001110'
```

will set a condition code of 0, and

```
TM    IND8,B'11110000'
```

will set a condition code of 1. Show how several one-bit indicators can be packed into a byte, and tested singly or in various combinations using the TM instruction.

11. Think of as many different situations as possible that require different status indications in the page frame table, and outline some of the routines that would be required in managing page frame table, segment and page tables.

12. Design a program segment which will examine CCWs, translate virtual addresses to real addresses, and construct an indirect data addressing chain.

13. Design a program segment which will temporarily set a bit of the system mask to 0 (or 1), then later restore the system mask to its previous state.

14. Design a program segment that will set reference bits for all page frames to 0.

15. Design a program segment that will add 2 to the number in bit positions 0–7 of control register 1.

16. Outline the routine that would handle a page fault interrupt and the swapping actions that must be taken. Either make assumptions about details we have left unspecified or look up the actual conditions in appropriate manuals.

REFERENCES

Auslander, M. A., and J. F. Jaffe, "Functional structure of IBM virtual storage operating systems. Part I: Influences of dynamic address translation on operating system technology," *IBM Systems Journal* **12**, 4 (1973), pp. 368–381.

Brown, D. T., R. L. Eibsen, and C. A. Thom, "Channel and direct access device architecture," *IBM Systems Journal* **11**, 3 (1972), pp. 186–199. The design of block multiplexor channel and other System/370 input/output features.

Denning, Peter J., "Virtual Memory," *Computing Surveys*, **2**, 3 (September 1970), pp. 153–189. A tutorial exposition of virtual storage techniques (not restricted to System/370).

Foster, Caxton C., *Computer Architecture* (New York: Van Nostrand Reinhold, 1970). A discussion of content-addressable memory and its uses, among other architectural features.

IBM System/360 Principles of Operation, GA22-6821, IBM Corporation. A full description of the machine's facilities.

IBM System/370 Principles of Operation, GA22-7000, IBM Corporation. Likewise for System/370.

Introduction to Virtual Storage in System/370, GR20-4260, IBM Corporation. A student text on virtual storage.

Morrison, J. E., "User program performance in virtual storage systems," *IBM Systems Journal*, **12**, 3 (1973), pp. 216–237.

Padegs, A., "The structure of SYSTEM/360: Part IV—Channel design considerations," *IBM Systems Journal* 3 (1964), pp. 165–180. An explanation of the rationale of the input-output structure of System/360.

Scherr, A. L., "Functional structure of IBM virtual storage operating systems. Part II: OS/VS2-2 concepts and philosophies," *IBM Systems Journal*, **12**, 4 (1973), pp. 382–400.

APPENDIXES

Linking Assembler Language
and Fortran Routines

There are a number of situations in which it is very desirable to use assembler language routines to do part of a job, and use some higher-level language for other parts. It makes sense to use higher-level languages such as Fortran, COBOL, or PL/I for parts of procedures for which they are well suited, and supplement with assembler language routines for those parts of procedures for which the higher-level languages are awkward or inefficient. Since it is not difficult to link OS or OS/VS assembler language routines with those of other languages, the programmer can have a powerful and flexible bag of tools to use on his problems.

For purposes of this text, there can be another reason. It takes a while to learn enough to do a complete program in assembler language, and good pedagogy calls for earlier opportunities to do laboratory exercises. Subroutines such as READATA and PRINT, supplied as per examples of Chapters 3 to 6, can help. A teacher can supply a shell of a program, and ask the student to provide certain restricted manipulations. Another alternative is to combine elementary assembler language routines with routines in higher-level languages, especially to do conversions, input, and output. For example, given the main program shown in Fig. A–1, the beginning assembler language programmer can write a small routine which will accept two binary integers as parameters, do some arithmetic, and return two binary integer results. The linkage can be reversed, with an assembler language main program which calls Fortran subroutines to do input and output.

We present here requirements of linkage with Fortran; linkage with COBOL is similar. So is linkage with PL/I routines, though information about parameters is passed differently. The programmer interested in these languages is directed to the *Programmer's Guide* for the appropriate system. Indeed, the programmer interested in

Fig. A–1   A simple Fortran calling program

```
      READ (1,91) I,J
      CALL ASSEM (I,J,K,L)
      WRITE (3,92) I,J,K,L
91    FØRMAT (2I5)
92    FØRMAT ('1DATA',2I7,4X,'RESULTS',2I11)
      STØP
      END
```

427

doing sophisticated things with Fortran must still find in Appendix C of *IBM System/360 Operating System Fortran IV (G and H) Programmer's Guide*, GC28-6817, more information than can be presented here.

We distinguish two cases. The first is an assembler language routine, called by a Fortran routine but which does not call others in turn. The second is an assembler language routine calling a Fortran routine.

There is a sort of Fortran submonitor which in some ways controls execution of Fortran programs; it opens and closes data sets appropriately, and tries to provide some diagnostic information in case of failure. The submonitor requires information not usually included in subroutine linkages, but linkage generally conforms to the conventions described in Chapter 5.

We will first concentrate on the case of an assembler language routine which does not call any other routines, but is called by a Fortran routine. As in other linkages, register 13 contains the address of a register save area, whose format is the same as described in Chapter 5. Register 14 contains the return address. Register 1 contains the address of a parameter address block, conforming to normal conventions. However, a 1-bit should be placed in the high-order position of the last word of the parameter address block, as described in problem 16 of Chapter 6. If there are *no* parameters, register 1 should contain 0. Upon entry to the routine, register 15 contains the entry address. Just before return from the routine, register 15 should be loaded with a *return code*. Upon normal return, the return code should be 0; if the subroutine wishes to report a terminal error condition, it should load a return code of 16, and the Fortran submonitor will halt execution and print an error message. Other codes may be used, but they will not be discussed here. If the assembler routine is called as a FUNCTIØN, the result should be left in general register 0 or floating-point register 0, depending on whether the name of the FUNCTIØN establishes the result as INTEGER or REAL. If the routine is called as a SUBRØUTINE, results are left as values of parameters.

Two additional conventions must be followed. The length of the routine name, and the name itself, must follow the entry instruction of the routine. For example, the first statements for a routine named PINK would be as follows:

```
PINK      START     0
          B         10(15)
          DC        X'5'
          DC        CL5'PINK'
          STM       14,12,12(13)
```

The length of the name is given in one byte; the name itself follows. The name must be of odd length, but can be padded with a blank, as above. The second convention is that the routine should enter X'FF' in the first byte of the fourth word of the calling routine's register save area just before return to the calling program; this is a signal to the Fortran submonitor that the assembler routine has finished its processing.

Figure A–2 shows the actions necessary for a subroutine which calls no others. Parameters are accessed through register 1 and the parameter address block; if the routine is a FUNCTIØN subprogram with INTEGER name, its result must be placed in general register 0, and if a FUNCTIØN with REAL name, the result must be left in floating-point register 0.

If the assembler routine calls other routines, especially Fortran subprograms, usual conventions apply, complementary with those described above. Two more conventions

Fig. A–2   Linkage for lowest-level routine

```
name      START     0                    name is name of routine
          B         m+5(15)              m is length of name
          DC        X'm'
          DC        CLm'name'
          SAVE      (14,12)
          USING     name,15               or declare and set another
                                            base register
          ...
          LA        15,0                 return code = 0
          LM        2,12,28(13)
          MVI       12(13),X'FF'
          BR        14
```

must be noted. First, forward links between register save areas should be stored, as described in problem 1 of Chapter 5. Second, if the assembler language routine is the *main program*, it must call (once only) an initialization routine of the Fortran submonitor by executing

```
          L         15,=V(IBCØM#)
          BAL       14,64(15)
```

Fig. A–3   Linkage for higher-level routine

```
name          START     0                      name is name of routine
              B         m+5(15)                m is the length of name
              DC        X'm'
              DC        CLm'name'
*     SAVE ROUTINE
              SAVE      (14,12)
              BALR      12,0
              USING     *,12
              LR        2,13
              LA        13,SAVAREA
              ST        13,8(2)
              ST        2,SAVAREA+4
              ...
*     CALLING ANOTHER RØUTINE
              LA        1,PARAMAD
              L         15,=V(name of routine)
              BALR      14,15
              ...
*     RETURN FRØM THIS RØUTINE
*         ASSUME RESULTS ARE PRØPERLY PLACED
              LA        15,0                 return code=0
              L         13,SAVAREA+4
              LM        2,12,28(13)
              L         14,12(13)
              MVI       12(13),X'FF'
              BR        14
*     DEFINITIØNS
SAVAREA       DS        18F
PARAMAD       DC        AL4(param 1)
              DC        AL4(param 2)
              ...
              DC        X'80'                last parameter flag
              DC        AL3(last param)
              END
```

A summary of actions of an assembler language subroutine which calls a Fortran subprogram is shown in Fig. A–3.

We refrain from showing the Job Control Language necessary to compile Fortran routines, assemble Assembler Language routines, link, load and execute the resulting combination. Each installation will have its preferred set of procedures. The main idea is either to assemble and compile all routines into the same object data set for loading, or to assemble and compile into different data sets which are concatenated at load (or link-edit) time.

Notation for Action
Description of Instructions

1. Entities

R1	General register specified as first operand
R2	General register specified as second operand
R3	General register specified as third operand
FPR1	Floating-point register specified as first operand
FPR2	Floating-point register specified as second operand
Reg. 1	General register 1; implied operand in certain instructions
Reg. 2	General register 2; implied operand in certain instructions
S1	First operand (specified by *D1* and *B1*) in main storage
S2	Second operand (specified by *D2*, *B2*, and sometimes X*2*)
$c(R1)$	Contents of register *R1*
$c(R2)$, $c(R3)$, $c(FPR1)$, $c(FPR2)$, $c(S1)$, $c(S2)$ have similar meanings
M1	M1 portion of Branch instruction
M3	M3 portion of masked character instruction
I2	I2 portion of SI instruction
I3	I3 portion of SRP instruction
PSW	Program status word

2. Lengths of entities

a) Register and main storage operands are presumed to be 32 bits long unless otherwise noted.
M1 is always four bits and *I2* always eight bits.

b) Bit positions of a portion of an entity are designated by subscripts:
Entity $_{a-b}$ designates bit positions a to b of an Entity.
$c(\text{Entity})_{a-b}$ designates contents of bit positions a to b of an Entity.
Bit positions are always numbered from 0 at the left (high-order) end.

c) Lengths of operands are also indicated in notes.

d) [Entity 1, Entity 2] indicates the concatenation of Entity 1 and Entity 2.

3. Actions on entities

a) Operations + − * / AND OR Ex. OR and absolute value (| |) are shown.
Mode of the operation—signed binary integer, unsigned binary integer (logical),

floating point, decimal—is implied by the instruction name or notes. Mode of comparison is also implied in compare instructions.

b) Placement of a result is indicated by a left-pointing arrow:
   $R1 \leftarrow c(S2)$ designates placement of $c(S2)$ in register $R1$.

c) Branch is indicated by a right-pointing arrow:
   $\rightarrow S2$ designates a branch to the location $S2$.

IBM System / 360 Instructions

Mnemonic	Name	Type code	Num. op. code	Operands	Cond. code	Exceptions[19]	Action (see Appendix B)	Ref. chapter and sec.	Notes
A	Add	RX	5A	R1,D2(X2,B2)	(1)	A,S, IF	$R1 \leftarrow c(R1)+c(S2)$	4.3	
AR	Add Register	RR	1A	R1,R2	(1)	IF	$R1 \leftarrow c(R1)+c(R2)$	4.3	
AH	Add Half-word	RX	4A	R1,D2(X2,B2)	(1)	A,S, IF	$R1 \leftarrow c(R1)+c(S2)_{0-15}$	4.3	
AL	Add Logical	RX	5E	R1,D2(X2,B2)	(3)	A,S	$R1 \leftarrow c(R1)+c(S2)$	11.1	
ALR	Add Logical Register	RR	1E	R1,R2	(3)		$R1 \leftarrow c(R1)+c(R2)$	11.1	
AP	Add Decimal	SS	FA	D1(L1,B1),D2(L2,B2)	(1)	A, D, DF	$S1 \leftarrow c(S1)+c(S2)$	14.3	(20,26)
AD	Add Double	RX	6A	R1,D2(X2,B2)	(5)	A,S,U,E,LS	$FPR1 \leftarrow c(FPR1)+c(S2)$	13.3	(21,23)
ADR	Add Double Register	RR	2A	R1,R2	(5)	S,U,E,LS	$FPR1 \leftarrow c(FPR1)+c(FPR2)$	13.3	(21,23)
AE	Add Floating	RX	7A	R1,D2(X2,B2)	(5)	A,S,U,E,LS	$FPR1 \leftarrow c(FPR1)+c(S2)$	13.3	(21)
AER	Add Floating Register	RR	3A	R1,R2	(5)	S,U,E,LS	$FPR1 \leftarrow c(FPR1)+c(FPR2)$	13.3	(21)
AU	Add Unnormalized	RX	7E	R1,D2(X2,B2)	(5)	A,S, E,LS	$FPR1 \leftarrow c(FPR1)+c(S2)$	13.5	(21,24)
AUR	Add Unnormalized Register	RR	3E	R1,R2	(5)	S, E,LS	$FPR1 \leftarrow c(FPR1)+c(FPR2)$	13.5	(21,24)
AW	Add Double Unnormalized	RX	6E	R1,D2(X2,B2)	(5)	A,S, E,LS	$FPR1 \leftarrow c(FPR1)+c(S2)$	13.5	(21,23,24)
AWR	Add Double Unnormalized Register	RR	2E	R1,R2	(5)	S, E,LS	$FPR1 \leftarrow c(FPR1)+c(FPR2)$	13.5	(21,23,24)
AXR	Add eXtended	RR	36	R1,R2	(5)	S,U,E,LS	$FPR1_{0-127} \leftarrow c(FPR1)_{0-127}+c(FPR2)_{0-127}$	13.9	(39)
BAL	Branch And Link	RX	45	R1,D2(X2,B2)			$R1 \leftarrow c(PSW)_{32-63}; \rightarrow S2$	5.Prob.3	(35)

(continued)

IBM system/360 instructions (continued)

Mnemonic	Name	Num. op. Type code		Operands	Cond. code	Exceptions[19]	Action (see Appendix B)	Ref. chapter and sec.	Notes
BALR	Branch And Link Register	RR	05	R1,R2			$R1 \leftarrow c(PSW)_{32\text{-}63}; \rightarrow c(R2)$	5.2 7.4	(29,35)
BC	Branch on Condition	RX	47	M1,D2(X2,B2)			$\rightarrow S2$ if $(M1)_{cc}=1$	7.4	
BCR	Branch on Condition to Register	RR	07	M1,R2			$\rightarrow c(R2)$ if $(M1)_{cc}=1$	7.4	(29)
BCT	Branch on Count	RX	46	R1,D2(X2,B2)			$R1 \leftarrow c(R1)-1; \rightarrow S2$ if $c(R1) \neq 0$	8.6	
BCTR	Branch on Count to Register	RR	06	R1,R2			$R1 \leftarrow c(R1)-1; \rightarrow c(R2)$ if $c(R1) \neq 0$	8.6	(29)
BXH	Branch on Index High	RS	86	R1,R3,D2(B2)			$R1 \leftarrow c(R1)+c(R3);$ If $R3$ is even, $\rightarrow S2$ if $c(R1) > c(R3+1)$ If $R3$ is odd, $\rightarrow S2$ if $c(R1) > c(R3)$	8.5	
BXLE	Branch on Index Low or Equal	RS	87	R1,R3,D2(B2)			$R1 \leftarrow c(R1)+c(R3);$ If $R3$ is even, $\rightarrow S2$ if $c(R1) \leq c(R3+1)$ If $R3$ is odd, $\rightarrow S2$ if $c(R1) \leq c(R3)$	8.5	
C	Compare	RX	59	R1,D2(X2,B2)	(2)	A,S		7.3	
CR	Compare Register	RR	19	R1,R2	(2)			7.3	
CH	Compare Halfword	RX	49	R1,D2(X2,B2)	(2)	A,S		7.3	
CL	Compare Logical	RX	55	R1,D2(X2,B2)	(2)	A,S		11.1	
CLR	Compare Logical Register	RR	15	R1,R2	(2)			11.1	
CLC	Compare Logical Character	SS	D5	D1(L,B1),D2(B2)	(2)	A		10.2	(25)
CLI	Compare Logical Immediate	SI	95	D1(B1),I2	(2)	A		10.2	
CLM	Compare Logical under Mask	RS	BD	R1,M3,D2(B2)	(15)	A		10.6	(36,37)
CLCL	Compare Logical Characters Long	RR	0F	R1,R2	(2)	A,S		10.6	(36,38)
CP	Compare Decimal	SS	F9	D1(L1,B1),D2(L2,B2)	(2)	A, D		14.3	(20,26)
CD	Compare Double	RX	69	R1,D2(X2,B2)	(2)	A,S		13.3	(21,23)
CDR	Compare Double Register	RR	29	R1,R2	(2)	S		13.3	(21,23)

(continued)

Mnemonic	Instruction	Fmt	Op	Operands	(n)	Cond./Int.	Operation	§	Ref
CE	Compare Floating	RX	79	R1,D2(X2,B2)	(2)	A,S		13.3	(21)
CER	Compare Floating Register	RR	39	R1,R2	(2)	S		13.3	(21)
CVB	Convert to Binary	RX	4F	R1,D2(X2,B2)		A,S,D, IK	R1 (binary) ← c(S2)$_{0-63}$(packed dec.)	6.1	
CVD	Convert to Decimal	RX	4E	R1,D2(X2,B2)		A,S, IK	S2$_{0-63}$(packed dec.) ← c(R1)(binary)	6.1	
D	Divide	RX	5D	R1,D2(X2,B2)		A,S, IK	R1 ← Rem. of [c(R1),c(R1+1)]/c(S2); R1+1 ← Quot. of [c(R1),c(R1+1)]/c(S2)	4.5	
DR	Divide Register	RR	1D	R1,R2		S, IK	R1 ← Rem. of [c(R1),c(R1+1)]/c(R2); R1+1 ← Quot. of [c(R1),c(R1+1)]/c(R2)	4.5	
DP	Divide Decimal	SS	FD	D1(L1,B1),D2(L2,B2)		A,S,D, DK	S1 ← [quot. of c(S1)/c(S2), rem. of c(S1)/c(S2)]	14.5	
DD	Divide Double	RX	6D	R1,D2(X2,B2)		A,S,U,E,FK	FPR1 ← c(FPR1)/c(S2)	13.4	(20,26)
DDR	Divide Double Register	RR	2D	R1,R2		S,U,E,FK	FPR1 ← c(FPR1)/c(FPR2)	13.4	(21,23)
DE	Divide Floating	RX	7D	R1,D2(X2,B2)		A,S,U,E,FK	FPR1 ← c(FPR1)/c(S2)	13.4	(21,23)
DER	Divide Floating Register	RR	3D	R1,R2		S,U,E,FK	FPR1 ← c(FPR1)/c(FPR2)	13.4	(21)
ED	Edit	SS	DE	D1(L,B1),D2(B2)	(1)	A, D	S1 ← c(S2)	15.2	(20,30)
EDMK	Edit and Mark	SS	DF	D1(L,B1),D2(B2)	(1)	A, D	S1 ← c(S2); Reg.1$_{8-31}$ ← Addr. of 1st sig. digit	15.2	(20,30)
EX	Execute	RX	44	R1,D2(X2,B2)		A,S, EX	Execute instr. c(S2), mod. by c(R1)$_{24-31}$	15.3	(21)
HER	Halve	RR	34	R1,R2		S	FPR1 ← c(FPR2)/2	13.4	(21,23)
HDR	Halve Double	RR	24	R1,R2		S	FPR1 ← c(FPR2)/2	13.4	(21,23)
HIØ	Halt I/O	S	9E00	D2(B2)	(7)	M	Halt an I/O operation	17.7	
IC	Insert Character	RX	43	R1,D2(X2,B2)		A	R1$_{24-31}$ ← c(S2)$_{0-7}$	10.1	
ICM	Insert Characters under Mask	RS	BF	R1,M3,D2(B2)	(16)	A	R1 ← c(S2)	10.6	(36,37)
ISK	Insert Storage Key	RR	09	R1,R2		M,A,S	R1$_{24-30}$ ← Stor. key of c(R2)$_{8-20}$	17.2	(22)
L	Load	RX	58	R1,D2(X2,B2)		A,S	R1 ← c(S2)	4.2	
LH	Load Half-word	RX	48	R1,D2(X2,B2)		A,S	R1$_{16-31}$ ← c(S2)$_{0-15}$; R1$_{0-15}$ ← c(S2)$_0$	4.2	
LA	Load Address	RX	41	R1,D2(X2,B2)		A,S	R1$_{8-31}$ ← S2; R1$_{0-7}$ ← 0	4.7	
LM	Load Multiple	RS	98	R1,R3,D2(B2)		A,S	R1,...,R3 ← c(S2)...	4.6	
LCTL	Load ConTroL registers	RS	B7	R1,R3,D2(B2)		M,A,S	(Control Reg.)R1,...,R3 ← c(S2)	17.4	(27)
LR	Load Register	RR	18	R1,R2			R1 ← c(R2)	4.2	(27,36)
LCR	Load Complement Register	RR	13	R1,R2	(1)	IF	R1 ← −c(R2)	4.2	
LNR	Load Negative Register	RR	11	R1,R2	(5)		R1 ← −|c(R2)|	4.2	
LPR	Load Positive Register	RR	10	R1,R2	(1)	IF	R1 ← |c(R2)|	4.2	
LTR	Load and Test Register	RR	12	R1,R2	(5)		R1 ← c(R2)	7.2	

IBM system/360 instructions (continued)

Mnemonic	Name	Num. op. Type code	Operands	Cond. code	Exceptions[19]	Action (see Appendix B)	Ref. chapter and sec.	Notes
LD	Load Double	RX 68	R1,D2(X2,B2)		A,S	$FPR1 \leftarrow c(S2)$	13.2	(21,23)
LDR	Load Double Register	RR 28	R1,R2		S	$FPR1 \leftarrow c(FPR2)$	13.2	(21,23)
LE	Load Floating	RX 78	R1,D2(X2,B2)		A,S	$FPR1 \leftarrow c(S2)$	13.2	(21)
LER	Load Floating Register	RR 38	R1,R2		S	$FPR1 \leftarrow c(FPR2)$	13.2	(21)
LCDR	Load Complement Double Register	RR 23	R1,R2	(5)	S	$FPR1 \leftarrow -c(FPR2)$	13.2	(21,23)
LCER	Load Complement Floating Register	RR 33	R1,R2	(5)	S	$FPR1 \leftarrow -c(FPR2)$	13.2	(21)
LNDR	Load Negative Double Register	RR 21	R1,R2	(5)	S	$FPR1 \leftarrow -|c(FPR2)|$	13.2	(21,23)
LNER	Load Negative Floating Register	RR 31	R1,R2	(5)	S	$FPR1 \leftarrow -|c(FPR2)|$	13.2	(21)
LPDR	Load Positive Double Register	RR 20	R1,R2	(5)	S	$FPR1 \leftarrow |c(FPR2)|$	13.2	(21,23)
LPER	Load Positive Floating Register	RR 30	R1,R2	(5)	S	$FPR1 \leftarrow |c(FPR2)|$	13.2	(21)
LTDR	Load and Test Double Register	RR 22	R1,R2	(5)	S	$FPR1 \leftarrow c(FPR2)$	13.2	(21,23)
LTER	Load and Test Floating Register	RR 32	R1,R2	(5)	S	$FPR1 \leftarrow c(FPR2)$	13.2	(21)
LRA	Load Real Address	RX B1	R1,D2(X2,B2)	(13)	M,A	$R1 \leftarrow$ Address translated from $S2$	17.4	(40)
LRDR	Load and Round Double	RR 25	R1,R2		S,E	$FPR1_{0-63} \leftarrow c(FPR2)_{0-127}$ rounded	13.9	(39)
LRER	Load and Round	RR 35	R1,R2		S,E	$FPR1 \leftarrow c(FPR2)_{0-63}$ rounded	13.9	(39)
LPSW	Load Program Status Word	SI 82	D1(B1)			$PSW \leftarrow c(S1)_{0-63}$	17.4	
MC	Monitor Call	SI AF	D1(B1),I2	(6)	M,A,S	Interrupt if $c(\text{Control R8})_{16+I2_{0-3}} = 1;$ $148_{0-15} \leftarrow [0,I2]; 157_{0-23} \leftarrow S1$	17.5	(36)
M	Multiply	RX 5C	R1,D2(X2,B2)		A,S	$[R1,R1+1] \leftarrow c(R1+1)\times c(S2)$	4.4	
MH	Multiply Half-word	RX 4C	R1,D2(X2,B2)		A,S	$R1 \leftarrow (c(R1)\times c(S2)_{0-15})_{16-47}$	4.4	
MR	Multiply Register	RR 1C	R1,R2		S	$[R1,R1+1] \leftarrow c(R1+1)\times c(R2)$	4.4	
MP	Multiply Decimal	SS FC	D1(L1,B1),D2(L2,B2)		A,S,D	$S1 \leftarrow c(S1)\times c(S2)$	14.5	(20,26)
MD	Multiply Double	RX 6C	R1,D2(X2,B2)		A,S,U,E	$FPR1 \leftarrow c(FPR1)\times c(S2)$	13.4	(21,23)

Mnem.	Instruction	Type	Op	Operands	Notes	Flags	Operation	Sec.	Notes
MDR	Multiply Double Register	RR	2C	R1,R2		S,U,E	$FPR1 \leftarrow c(FPR1) \times c(FPR2)$	13.4	(21,23)
ME	Multiply Floating	RX	7C	R1,D2(X2,B2)		A,S,U,E	$FPR1 \leftarrow c(FPR1) \times c(S2)$	13.4	(21)
MER	Multiply Floating Register	RR	3C	R1,R2		S,U,E	$FPR1 \leftarrow c(FPR1) \times c(FPR2)$	13.4	(21)
MXR	Multiply eXtended Register	RR	26	R1,R2		S,U,E	$FPR1_{0-127} \leftarrow c(FPR1)_{0-127} \times c(FPR2)_{0-127}$	13.9	(39)
MXDR	Multiply eXtended from Double Registers	RR	27	R1,R2		S,U,E	$FPR1_{0-127} \leftarrow c(FPR1)_{0-63} \times c(FPR2)_{0-63}$	13.9	(39)
MXD	Multiply eXtended Double	RX	67	R1,D2(X2,B2)		A,S,U,E	$FPR1_{0-127} \leftarrow c(FPR1)_{0-127} \times c(S2)_{0-63}$	13.9	(39)
MVC	Move Character	SS	D2	D1(L,B1),D2(B2)		A	$S1 \leftarrow c(S2)$	4.2	(25)
MVCL	MoVe Characters Long	RR	0E	R1,R2	(17)	A,S	$c(R1) \leftarrow c(c(R2))$	10.6	(36,38)
MVI	Move Immediate	SI	92	D1(B1),I2		A	$S1_{0-7} \leftarrow I2$	4.2	
MVN	Move Numerics	SS	D1	D1(L,B1),D2(B2)		A	$S1 \leftarrow c(S2)$	14.4	(25,31)
MVØ	Move with Offset	SS	F1	D1(L1,B1),D2(L2,B2)		A	$S1 \leftarrow c(S2)$	14.4	(26,32)
MVZ	Move Zones	SS	D3	D1(L,B1),D2(B2)		A	$S1 \leftarrow c(S2)$	14.Prob.3	(25,33)
N	And	RX	54	R1,D2(X2,B2)	(4)	A,S	$R1 \leftarrow c(R1) \text{ AND } c(S2)$	11.4	
NC	And Character	SS	D4	D1(L,B1),D2(B2)	(4)	A	$S1 \leftarrow c(S1) \text{ AND } c(S2)$	11.4	(25)
NI	And Immediate	SI	94	D1(B1),I2	(4)	A	$S1_{0-7} \leftarrow c(S1)_{0-7} \text{ AND } I2$	11.4	
NR	And Register	RR	14	R1,R2	(4)		$R1 \leftarrow c(R1) \text{ AND } c(R2)$	11.4	
Ø	Or	RX	56	R1,D2(X2,B2)	(4)	A,S	$R1 \leftarrow c(R1) \text{ OR } c(S2)$	11.4	(25)
ØC	Or Character	SS	D6	D1(L,B1),D2(B2)	(4)	A	$S1 \leftarrow c(S1) \text{ OR } c(S2)$	11.4	
ØI	Or Immediate	SI	96	D1(B1),I2	(4)	A	$S1_{0-7} \leftarrow c(S1)_{0-7} \text{ OR } I2$	11.4	
ØR	Or Register	RR	16	R1,R2	(4)		$R1 \leftarrow c(R1) \text{ OR } c(R2)$	11.4	
PACK	Pack	SS	F2	D1(L1,B1),D2(L2,B2)	(4)	A	$S1 \text{ (packed dec.)} \leftarrow c(S2)\text{(zoned dec.)}$	6.1	(26)
PTLB	Purge Translation Lookaside Buffer	S	B20D	none		M	Clear translation lookaside buffer	17.4	(40)
RRB	Reset Reference Bit	S	B213	D2(B2)	(14)	M,A	Stor. key $(S2)_5 \leftarrow 0$	17.4	(40)
S	Subtract	RX	5B	R1,D2(X2,B2)	(1)	A,S, IF	$R1 \leftarrow c(R1) - c(S2)$	4.3	
SR	Subtract Register	RR	1B	R1,R2	(1)	A,S, IF	$R1 \leftarrow c(R1) - c(R2)$	4.3	
SH	Subtract Half-word	RX	4B	R1,D2(X2,B2)	(1)	A,S, IF	$R1 \leftarrow c(R1) - c(S2)_{0-15}$	4.3	
SL	Subtract Logical	RX	5F	R1,D2(X2,B2)	(3)	A,S	$R1 \leftarrow c(R1) - c(S2)$	11.1	
SLR	Subtract Logical Register	RR	1F	R1,R2	(3)		$R1 \leftarrow c(R1) - c(R2)$	11.1	
SP	Subtract Decimal	SS	FB	D1(L1,B1),D2(L2,B2)	(1)	A, D, DF	$S1 \leftarrow c(S1) - c(S2)$	14.3	(20,26)
SD	Subtract Double	RX	6B	R1,D2(X2,B2)	(5)	A,S,U,E,LS	$FPR1 \leftarrow c(FPR1) - c(S2)$	13.3	(21,23)
SDR	Subtract Double Register	RR	2B	R1,R2	(5)	S,U,E,LS	$FPR1 \leftarrow c(FPR1) - c(FPR2)$	13.3	(21,23)

(continued)

IBM system/360 instructions (continued)

Mnemonic	Name	Type	Num. op. code	Operands	Cond. code	Exceptions[19]	Action (see Appendix B)	Ref. chapter and sec.	Notes
SE	Subtract Floating	RX	7B	$R1,D2(X2,B2)$	(5)	A,S,U,E,LS	$FPR1 \leftarrow c(FPR1) - c(S2)$	13.3	(21)
SER	Subtract Floating Register	RR	3B	$R1,R2$	(5)	S,U,E,LS	$FPR1 \leftarrow c(FPR1) - c(FPR2)$	13.3	(21)
SU	Subtract Unnormalized	RX	6F	$R1,D2(X2,B2)$	(5)	A,S, E,LS	$FPR1 \leftarrow c(FPR1) - c(S2)$	13.5	(21,24)
SUR	Subtract Unnormalized Register	RR	2F	$R1,R2$	(5)	S, E,LS	$FPR1 \leftarrow c(FPR1) - c(FPR2)$	13.5	(21,24)
SW	Subtract Double Unnormalized	RX	7F	$R1,D2(X2,B2)$	(5)	A,S, E,LS	$FPR1 \leftarrow c(FPR1) - c(S2)$	13.5	(21,23,24)
SWR	Subtract Double Unnormalized Register	RR	3F	$R1,R2$	(5)	S, E,LS	$FPR1 \leftarrow c(FPR1) - c(FPR2)$	13.5	(21,23,24)
SIØ	Start I/O	S	9C00 $D2(B2)$		(8) M		Start an I/O operation	17.7	
SLA	Shift Left Arithmetic	RS	8B	$R1,D2(B2)$	(1)	IF	Left shift bits 1–31, fill (with) 0's	11.2	(28)
SLL	Shift Left Logical	RS	89	$R1,D2(B2)$			Left shift bits 0–31, fill 0's	11.2	(28)
SLDA	Shift Left Double Arithmetic	RS	8F	$R1,D2(B2)$	(1)	IF	Left shift bits 1–63, fill 0's	11.2	(28)
SLDL	Shift Left Double Logical	RS	8D	$R1,D2(B2)$			Left shift bits 0–63, fill 0's	11.2	(28)
SRA	Shift Right Arithmetic	RS	8A	$R1,D2(B2)$	(5)		Right shift bits 1–31, fill $c(R1)_0$	11.2	(28)
SRL	Shift Right Logical	RS	88	$R1,D2(B2)$			Right shift bits 0–31, fill 0's	11.2	(28)
SRDA	Shift Right Double Arithmetic	RS	8E	$R1,D2(B2)$	(5)	S	Right shift bits 1–63, fill $c(R1)_0$	11.2	(28)
SRDL	Shift Right Double Logical	RS	8C	$R1,D2(B2)$		S	Right shift bits 0–63, fill 0's	11.2	(28)
SRP	Shift and Round Packed	SS	F0	$D1(L1,B1),D2(B2),I3$	(1)	A,D,DF	$c(S1)$ shifted $S2$ digits right or left, rounded by factor $I3$	14.4	(28,36)
SPM	Set Program Mask	RR	04	$R1$	(6)		$PSW_{34-39} \leftarrow c(R1)_{2-7}$	17.4	(22)
SSK	Set Storage Key	RR	08	$R1,R2$		M,A,S	Storage key of $c(R2)_{8-20} \leftarrow c(R1)_{24-30}$	17.2	
SSM	Set System Mask	SI	80	$D1(B1)$		M,A	$PSW_{0-7} \leftarrow c(S1)_{0-7}$	17.4	
STCK	STore ClocK	S	B205 $D2(B2)$		(18)	A	$S2_{0-63} \leftarrow c(\text{Clock})$	17.4	(36)
ST	Store	RX	50	$R1,D2(X2,B2)$		A,S	$S2 \leftarrow c(R1)$	4.2	
STH	Store Half-word	RX	40	$R1,D2(X2,B2)$		A,S	$S2_{0-15} \leftarrow c(R1)_{16-31}$	4.2	
STM	Store Multiple	RS	90	$R1,R3,D2(B2)$		A,S	$S2 \ldots \leftarrow c(R1),\ldots,c(R3)$	4.6	(27)

		Fmt	Op	Operands	Note	Type	Operation	Timing	Ref
STC	Store Character	RX	42	$R1,D2(X2,B2)$		A	$S2_{0-7} \leftarrow c(R1)_{24-31}$	10.1	
STCM	STore Characters under Mask	RS	BE	$R1,M3,D2(B2)$		A	$S2 \leftarrow c(R1)$	10.6	(36,37)
STCTL	STore ConTroL registers	RS	B6	$R1,R3,D2(B2)$		M,A,S	$S2 \leftarrow c(R1),...,c(R3)$(Control Registers)	17.4	(27,36)
STD	Store Double	RX	60	$R1,D2(X2,B2)$		A,S	$S2 \leftarrow c(FPR1)$	13.2	(21,23)
STE	Store Floating	RX	70	$R1,D2(X2,B2)$		A,S	$S2 \leftarrow c(FPR1)$	13.2	(21)
STNSM	STore then aNd System Mask	SI	AC	$D1(B1),I2$			$SI_{0-7} \leftarrow PSW_{0-7}; PSW_{0-7} \leftarrow PSW_{0-7}$ AND $I2$	17.4	(36)
STØSM	STore then Or System Mask	SI	AD	$D1(B1),I2$		M,A	$SI_{0-7} \leftarrow PSW_{0-7}; PSW_{0-7} \leftarrow PSW_{0-7}$ OR $I2$	17.4	(36)
SXR	Subtract EXtended	RR	37	$R1,R2$	(5)	S,U,E,LS	$FPR_{0-127} \leftarrow c(FPR1)_{0-127} - c(FPR2)_{0-127}$	13.9	(39)
SVC	Supervisor Call	RR	0A	I			Interrupt; PSW(old)$_{24-31} \leftarrow I$	17.4	
TCH	Test Channel	S	9F00	$D2(B2)$	(9)	M		17.7	
TIØ	Test I/O	S	9D00	$D2(B2)$	(8)	M		17.7	
TM	Test Under Mask	SI	91	$D1(B1),I2$	(11)	A	$SI \leftarrow c(S2)$	17.Prob.10	
TR	Translate	SS	DC	$D1(L,B1),D2(B2)$		A	Reg.$_{18-31} \leftarrow$ Address of Arg. byte;	15.1	(34)
TRT	Translate and Test	SS	DD	$D1(L,B1),D2(B2)$	(10)	A	Reg.2$_{24-31} \leftarrow$ Function byte		
TS	Test and Set	SI	93	$D1(B1)$	(12)	A	$SI \leftarrow FF$	15.1	
UNPK	Unpack	SS	F3	$D1(L1,B1),D2(L2,B2)$		A	SI(zoned dec.) $\leftarrow c(S2)$(packed dec.)	17.Prob.5	
X	Exclusive Or	RX	57	$R1,D2(X2,B2)$	(4)	A,S	$R1 \leftarrow c(R1)$ Ex. OR $c(S2)$	6.1	(26)
XC	Exclusive Or Character	SS	D7	$D1(L,B1),D2(B2)$	(4)	A	$SI \leftarrow c(SI)$ Ex. OR $c(S2)$	11.4	(25)
XI	Exclusive Or Immediate	SI	97	$D1(B1),I2$	(4)	A	$SI_{0-7} \leftarrow c(SI)_{0-7}$ Ex. OR $I2$	11.4	
XR	Exclusive Or Register	RR	17	$R1,R2$	(4)		$R1 \leftarrow c(R1)$ Ex. OR $c(R2)$	11.4	
ZAP	Zero and Add Positive	SS	F8	$D1(L1,B1),D2(L2,B2)$	(1)	A, D, DF	$SI \leftarrow c(S2)$	14.4	(20,26)

(continued)

Notes

Condition code settings:

	0	1	2	3
1)	Result = 0	Result < 0	Result > 0	Overflow
2)		$Op_1 = Op_2$	$Op_1 < Op_2$	$Op_1 > Op_2$	—
3)	Result = 0, No carry	Result $\neq 0$, No carry	Result = 0, Carry	Result $\neq 0$, Carry
4)	Result = 0	Result $\neq 0$		—

439

	0	1	2	3
5)	Result = 0	Result < 0	Result > 0	—
6)	(Condition code loaded by instruction)			
7)	Interrupt in subchannel	CSW stored	Burst Op. terminated	Not operational
8)	Available or Operation Proceeding	CSW stored	Channel or subch. busy	Not operational
9)	Available	Interrupt in channel	Operating in Burst mode	Not operational
10)	All function bytes are zero	Nonzero before 1st Op. exhausted	Last function byte nonzero	—
11)	$SI_i = 0$ for all i for which $I2_i = 1$	For i such that $I2_i = 0$, some $SI_i = 0$, some $SI_i = 1$	—	$SI_i = 1$ for all i for which $I2_i = 1$
12)	$SI_0 = 0$	$SI_0 = 1$		
13)	Translation available	Segment table entry invalid	Page-table entry invalid	Table length violation
14)	Ref bit = 0, change bit = 0	Ref bit = 0, change bit = 1	Ref bit = 1, Change bit = 0	Ref bit = 1, Change bit = 1
15)	Selected bytes equal, or mask = 0	Selected bytes of Op1 low	Selected bytes of Op1 high	—
16)	All inserted bits = 0, or mask = 0	First inserted bit = 1	First inserted bit = 0, but not all inserted bits = 0	—
17)	Lengths of operands equal	Op1 shorter	Op1 longer	Destructive overlap; no movement
18)	Clock in set state	Not-set state	Error state	Not-operational state
19)	Exceptions:			
	M Privileged operation	D Data	DF Decimal overflow	FK Floating-point divide
	A Access (Protection, Addressing, Translation)	U Exponent underflow	LS Significance	EX Execute
		E Exponent overflow	IK Fixed-point divide	
	S Specification	IF Fixed-point overflow	DK Decimal divide	

20) Instructions available only if decimal feature is installed; operands and results in packed decimal form.

21) Instructions available only if floating-point feature is installed; operands and results in floating point form, normalized unless otherwise indicated by note (18).

22) Instructions available only if protection feature is installed.

23) Double-length floating-point instructions—each operand is 64 bits long.

24) Normalization not performed on result.

25) Length of each operand given by L.

26) Length of first operand given by L1; length of second operand given by L2.

27) Registers participate as follows, and bytes of main storage are correspondingly treated as shown:

If $RI < R3$, register $RI, RI+1, \ldots, R3$, $4\times(R3-RI)+4$ bytes.

If $RI = R3$, register RI,   4 bytes.

If $RI > R3$, register $RI, RI+1, \ldots, 15, 0, \ldots, R3$, $4\times(16+R3-RI)+4$ bytes.

28) Only the low-order six bits are used in defining the length of the shift.

29) No branch takes place if $R2 = 0$.

30) First operand is pattern, with length L; second operand is source, in packed decimal format, with length dictated by pattern.

31) Only the low-order four bits of each byte are moved.

32) Low-order four bits of rightmost byte of $S1$ are unchanged; move proceeds from right to left, thus offset by four bits.

33) Only the high-order four bits of each byte are moved.

34) Each byte of the first operand designates which byte from the second operand replaces it: $S1_{0-7} \leftarrow c(S2 + c(S1))_{0-7}$.

35) In System/370 in EC mode, RI is loaded with $[c(PSW)_{16-23}, c(PSW)_{40-63}]$.

36) System/370 only.

37) Op_1 = Concatenation of bytes $RI_{8i \text{ to } 8i+7}$ for which $M3_i = 1$, $i = 0,1,2,3$; $Op_2 = c(S2)$, of length equal to length of Op_1.

38) Length of Op_1 specified by $c(R1 + 1)$; length of Op_2 specified by $c(R2 + 1)_{8-31}$; fill character taken from $c(R2 + 1)_{0-7}$.

39) Instructions available only if extended-precision floating-point feature is installed; $FPR1_{0-127}$ is understood as abbreviation for $[(FPR1)_{0-63}, (FPR1 + 2)_{0-63}]$; FPR2 similarly.

40) Instructions available only if dynamic address translation feature is installed.

8-bit code	Hexa-decimal	Decimal	Punched card code	BCD characters	EBCDIC characters
0100 0000	40	64	no punches	space	space
0100 1010	4A	74	12–8–2		¢
0100 1011	4B	75	12–8–3	.	.
0100 1100	4C	76	12–8–4	□)	<
0100 1101	4D	77	12–8–5	[	(
0100 1110	4E	78	12–8–6	<	+
0100 1111	4F	79	12–8–7		|
0101 0000	50	80	12	&+	&
0101 1010	5A	90	11–8–2		!
0101 1011	5B	91	11–8–3	$	$
0101 1100	5C	92	11–8–4	*	*
0101 1101	5D	93	11–8–5	]	)
0101 1110	5E	94	11–8–6	;	;
0101 1111	5F	95	11–8–7		¬
0110 0000	60	96	11	–	–
0110 0001	61	97	0–1	/	/
0110 1011	6B	107	0–8–3	,	,
0110 1100	6C	108	0–8–4	%(	%
0110 1101	6D	109	0–8–5		—
0110 1110	6E	110	0–8–6		>
0110 1111	6F	111	0–8–7		?
0111 1010	7A	122	8–2		:
0111 1011	7B	123	8–3	#=	#
0111 1100	7C	124	8–4	@'	@
0111 1101	7D	125	8–5	:	'
0111 1110	7E	126	8–6	>	=
0111 1111	7F	127	8–7		"
1100 0000	C0	192	12–0	?	

(continued)

Representation of characters (continued)

8-bit code		Hexa-decimal	Decimal	Punched card code	BCD characters	EBCDIC characters
1100	0001	C1	193	12–1	A	A
1100	0010	C2	194	12–2	B	B
1100	0011	C3	195	12–3	C	C
1100	0100	C4	196	12–4	D	D
1100	0101	C5	197	12–5	E	E
1100	0110	C6	198	12–6	F	F
1100	0111	C7	199	12–7	G	G
1100	1000	C8	200	12–8	H	H
1100	1001	C9	201	12–9	I	I
1101	0000	D0	208	11–0	!	
1101	0001	D1	209	11–1	J	J
1101	0010	D2	210	11–2	K	K
1101	0011	D3	211	11–3	L	L
1101	0100	D4	212	11–4	M	M
1101	0101	D5	213	11–5	N	N
1101	0110	D6	214	11–6	O	O
1101	0111	D7	215	11–7	P	P
1101	1000	D8	216	11–8	Q	Q
1101	1001	D9	217	11–9	R	R
1110	0010	E2	226	0–2	S	S
1110	0011	E3	227	0–3	T	T
1110	0100	E4	228	0–4	U	U
1110	0101	E5	229	0–5	V	V
1110	0110	E6	230	0–6	W	W
1110	0111	E7	231	0–7	X	X
1110	1000	E8	232	0–8	Y	Y
1110	1001	E9	233	0–9	Z	Z
1111	0000	F0	240	0	0	0
1111	0001	F1	241	1	1	1
1111	0010	F2	242	2	2	2
1111	0011	F3	243	3	3	3
1111	0100	F4	244	4	4	4
1111	0101	F5	245	5	5	5
1111	0110	F6	246	6	6	6
1111	0111	F7	247	7	7	7
1111	1000	F8	248	8	8	8
1111	1001	F9	249	9	9	9

Selected Problem Solutions

Chapter 1

5. Binary 10101 = Decimal 21
Binary 1110111 = Decimal 119

6. Hexadecimal A8 = Decimal 168
Hexadecimal 24D = Decimal 589

7. Hexadecimal 24D = Binary 1001001101
Binary 11011001110001 = Hexadecimal 3671

8. Decimal 18 = binary 10010
32-bit 2's complement: 11111111111111111111111111101110

9. Decimal 7:   00000000000000000000000000000111
+Decimal −18: 11111111111111111111111111101110
          11111111111111111111111111110101
which is the representation of decimal −11.

12. The break-even ratio is 1.0; if there are more decimal digits stored than characters, the eight-bit representations are more efficient than six-bit ones. Of course, this is only one component of the question of desirability of an eight-bit or six-bit scheme.

Chapter 2

2.

Base	Index	Displacement	Effective address
2	—	104	0025A6
3	—	000	005310
0	—	0CE	0000CE
1	3	101	00B624
2	0	233	0026D5
0	2	233	0026D5
0	0	FFF	000FFF
3	1	101	00B624

3. Effective address desired: 00958A

Base   −009336

Displacement needed: 254

5. All RR-type instructions whose result is in a register and SS-type whose results are in main storage (there are a few exceptions) are defined so that the first operand is the destination or result. SI-type instructions can also be defined so that the first operand is the destination, since one should never want the result to be put in the instruction itself.

Chapter 3

1. Valid symbols: A3, \$3, GIH2J3K4, #34\$Q

Invalid: (B9)   includes special characters ( )

         7X   does not begin with a letter

         GIH2J3K4L5   too long

         #@\$&   includes special character &

2. Valid absolute expressions:

$$G, \; X'123F', \; X'123F'+G, \; *-P, \; Q-(P-K)+B'10100',$$
$$C'4578'-G-X'F4F23E4A'$$

Valid relocatable expressions:

$$P, \; =X'123F', \; X'123F'+P, \; P+4*X'CE', \; *, \; *-7,$$
$$*+X'123F', \; *+G, \; R+G+H, \; P+Q+R-W-(*+4)$$

Invalid: =X'123F'+G   expression including a literal

         G-(P-K)   pairing violated: (P-K) is subtracted

3. Invalid instructions:

L	19,19(H)	No register 19
L	7,W(H,K)	W is relocatable, K is supplied as explicit base
L	W,4(4)	Relocatable W may not be register address
L	4(4),W	4(4) is invalid *R1* specification
LR	4,P	Relocatable P may not be *R2*
LM	K,W	Needs three operands
LM	3(4),Q	3(4) is invalid for *R1*, *R2*
LM	3,4,Q(5)	No indexing of RS instructions
MVI	R,Q	*I2* must be absolute
MVC	W(8),P(8)	P is valid second operand, P(8) invalid
MVC	W(8,9),*+8	Explicit base with relocatable W

4. Second operand address: 009A48

5. Assuming that =F'24' has not been encountered in a previous statement, the assembler must put the constant F'24' in the word at relocatable 0003CC; note that the next available location in the literal pool is now 0003D0. The second operand of the current instruction will be assembled with base A, index 0, displacement 0003CC−00000C=3C0.

6. L   409452

    LM   569822 $V-4 = 000828$

    AR   45

    A   6A9452   A is hexadecimal value of index G

    MVI   FF982A

    ST   4A9456

    MVC   07900C982B

7. Pairing rules ensure that any valid expression be either absolute or relocatable.

Chapter 4

1. LNR   2,7

    LCR   2,2

2. LA   5,0

    L   5, some location known to contain zero

4.

Instruction		Result	
LPR	7,2	Reg. 7	00000040
LNR	8,4	Reg. 8	CDEF0123
AR	1,2	Reg. 1	FFFFFFEE
AR	2,1	Reg. 2	FFFFFFEE
SR	1,2	Reg. 1	0000006E
SR	2,1	Reg. 2	FFFFFF92
A	1,K	Reg. 1	00000024
S	1,K	Reg. 1	00000038
SH	1,K	Reg. 1	0000002F
AH	3,Q+2	Reg. 3	4567FFFF
MVI	Q+5,17	Q+5	11 (hexadecimal), replacing 10
MVC	K+1(5),Q+2	K+1	76543210FE
STM	2,4,Q	Q	FFFFFFC0
		Q+4	456789AB
		Q+8	CDEF0123
LM	5,6,Q	Reg. 5	BA987654
		Reg. 6	3210FEDC
LH	7,Q+6	Reg. 7	FFFFFEDC
STH	3,K	K	89AB
LA	8,2(3,4)	Reg. 8	00568AD0
S	2,Q	Reg. 2	4567896C

5. Both LR 5,4 and LA 5,0(4) load contents of register 4 into register 5. However, the latter strips off the first 8 bits and replaces them with zeros. LA 5,4 loads the number 4 into register 5. L 5,4 and L 5,0(4) both load register 5 from main storage locations: the former from absolute locations 000004 to 000007; the latter from a full word whose address is in register 4.

6. Instruction		Result(Decimal)

Instruction		Result (Decimal)	
MR	8,9	Reg. 8	0
		Reg. 9	900
MR	6,9	Reg. 6	0
		Reg. 7	-360
M	8,U	Reg. 8	0
		Reg. 9	-480
MH	7,U+2	Reg. 7	192
DR	2,7	Reg. 2	1
		Reg. 3	4
DR	4,7	Reg. 4	0
		Reg. 5	-7
DR	4,9	Reg. 4	-24
		Reg. 5	2
D	2,Y	Reg. 2	4
		Reg. 3	-9

7.
```
L    5,K
M    4,=F'1'
D    4,Q
ST   5,Z       QUOTIENT
```

10. Dividend: hexadecimal 80000000
Divisor: hexadecimal   FFFFFFFF

11. E = K+3:
```
L    2,K      ⎫      ⎧ LA   2,3
A    2,=F'3'  ⎬ or   ⎨ A    2,K
ST   2,E      ⎭      ⎩ ST   2,E
```

E = (K+3)/Q
```
L    3,K
A    3,=F'3'
LA   2,0
D    2,Q
ST   3,E
```

E = (K+U)*R
```
L    3,K
AR   3,6
M    2,R
ST   3,E
```

E = (K–T+R*P)/(Y–5)
```
L    3,R
M    2,P
SH   3,T
A    3,K
L    4,Y
S    4,=F'5'
DR   2,4
ST   3,E
```

Chapter 5

2. The branch address is determined *before* the address of the next instruction is stored. Since in BALR 12,12 the *previous* contents of register 12 determines the branch address, the result will not, in general, be the same as that of BALR 12,0.

4. The key fact is that only one subroutine is active and using the save area at a time.

5. *Hint:* The difficult part is restoring registers, because some base address must be used for addressing the save area. Subroutine B is presumably using all registers for its own purposes. But what about contents of register 14?

7. No difficulties would be encountered at all. But a save area trace (see Chapter 9) would be impossible.

8. Suppose subroutine B is interrupted while the address of the save area of the calling routine (the one that called B) is in register 13. If the supervisor stored register contents in that same area, it would destroy register contents belonging to the calling routine. Therefore the supervisor must save registers in its own area.

10. Base C, Index 0, Displacement 00061C–000608 = 014

11. Reg. 4: 0000E844, as left by RDIGIT; irrelevant to RANDØM

12. RANDØM returns 400D2019 = decimal 1074602009
RDIGIT returns 00000005

14. The instruction

$$\text{LA} \qquad \text{15,RANDØM}$$

could be substituted for

$$\text{L} \qquad \text{15,RANDAD}$$

if RANDØM were assembled *after* RDIGIT (and within 4096 bytes after RDIGIT). Otherwise RANDØM could not be addressed in base + displacement form from RDIGIT.

17.
```
CUBE    STM   14,12,12(13)
        BALR  12,0
        USING *,12
        L     3,0(1)        ADDRESS OF PARAMETER
        L     5,0(3)        PARAMETER
        MR    4,5           SQUARE
        M     4,0(3)        CUBE
        LR    0,5           RESULT TO REG. 0
        LM    1,12,24(13)   RESTORE REGISTERS
        BR    14
```

20. The instruction LA 4,=A(TENNIS) loads register 4 with the address of a full word containing the address of TENNIS. Both LA 4,TENNIS and L 4,=A(TENNIS) load register 4 with the address of TENNIS. Finally, L 4,TENNIS loads register 4 with the contents of a full word *at* location TENNIS.

Chapter 6

1. PACK overflows if there are more than $2d$-1 digits (leading zeros do not count) in the source field, where d is the length in bytes of the destination field.

UNPK overflows if there are more than d' significant (after leading zeros) digits in the packed decimal field, where d' is the length of the destination field.

CVB overflows if the number to be converted has a magnitude of over 2^{31}, or 2,147,483,648.

CVD can never overflow.

3.
```
MVC   D(5),=XL5'0'    D IS ØN A DØUBLE WØRD
MVC   D+5(3),N
CVB   4,D
```

4. PACK   D(8),Q(1)   D: Hex. 000000000000007C
   CVB   4,D   Reg. 4: Hex. 00000007

5. CVD   7,D   D: 000000000000107C
   UNPK   U(3),D(8)   U: F1F0C7

   The instruction UNPK   U(3),D+5(3) would have the same effect.

7.   Statement   Bit pattern

DC	C'0'	11110000
DC	CL4'0'	11110000010000000100000001000000
DC	X'0'	00000000
DC	XL4'0'	00000000000000000000000000000000
DC	F'0'	00000000000000000000000000000000
DC	E'0'	00000000000000000000000000000000
DC	P'0'	00001100
DC	PL4'0'	00000000000000000000000000001100
DC	C'A'	11000001
DC	X'A'	00001010
DC	F'19'	00000000000000000000000000010011
DC	XL4'19'	00000000000000000000000000011001
DC	HL4'19'	00000000000000000000000000010011

9. 1) DC   F'-11,373,0'
   2) DC   10F'0'
   3) DS   0H
      DC   B'1100100100100100'
   4) DS   0D
      DC   C'EGC123*$'
   5) DC   3X'E4'
   6) DC   4CL120'RESULT ='

10. The difference in each case is in boundary alignment. If a length modifier is written, *no* alignment is done.

15. a) No good: the address of BBB is loaded into register 1 instead of the conventional address of the address.
    b) No good: exactly like the previous case.
    c) Good.
    d) Confusing, but okay.
    e) No good: the address of FF is loaded into register 1, which neither conforms to convention nor helps at all to make GG and HH accessible.
    f) Okay.
    g) Okay.
    h) Okay. The address of the third parameter is stored in the block.
    i) Okay, if the BAL statement is on a full-word boundary. This is known as an *in-line* parameter list. Note how the BAL instruction loads register 1 with the address of the parameter block and also jumps around the block. Problem 10 of Chapter 7 will show how to ensure proper alignment on a full-word boundary.

18. a)   ØRG   X'100'
    b) PØRG   EQU   256
    c) DEC300   DC   F'300'
    d) ØUTBUF   DC   A(ØUTSTR)

e) ØUTSTR   DS   CL132
f)   END

Chapter 7

3. Instruction   Condition code

SR	3,4	3
S	2,W	2
SH	2,W+2	2
A	4,Q	1
C	4,Q	1
CR	4,3	1
CR	3,4	2
C	3,Y	2
LTR	3,3	2

4. 1) $c(\text{Reg. } 9) \leq c(T)$ 2) $c(\text{Reg. } 9) < c(T)$
3) $c(\text{Reg. } 9) + c(T) < 0$, or overflow
4) Difference between $c(\text{Reg. } 9)$ and $c(T)$ not 30 or -30

5. LTR   5,5
BNL   CØNTIN
LCR   5,5
B   CØNTIN

7. *Hint:* What happens if the addition results in overflow?

8. *Hint:* Define some data item to be a "termination symbol," so that you can mark a cell as empty by putting the termination symbol in it.

10.   CNØP   0,4
         B   *+8
A   DS   1F
         L   3,A

Note that the CNØP statement must precede the branch instruction.

11. We will show two solutions. For the first, it is necessary to know the length of the instruction to be skipped. If the instruction is four bytes long,

> LTR   1,1
> BE   *+8
> four-byte instruction

If the instruction to be skipped is two or six bytes long, the branch destination must be *+6 or *+10, respectively. The second solution is not dependent on length of the instruction:

> LTR   1,1
> BE   JUMPARØU
> instruction to be skipped
> JUMPARØU   EQU   *

We can use an EQU statement like this whenever we want to attach a symbol to a location without putting it on the same card.

Chapter 8

3. a)

```
          LA    3,0
          LA    6,4
          LA    7,72
   LP     L     5,AA(3)
          S     5,AA+4(3)
          ST    5,BB(3)
          BXLE  3,6,LP
```

b)

```
          LA    3,0
   LP     L     5,AA(3)
          S     5,AA+4(3)
          ST    5,BB(3)
          LA    3,4(3)
          C     3,=F'72'
          BNH   LP
```

5. Blanks are stored from PRTAREA to PRTAREA+1999

6. The second operand of the ST instruction is always on a full word boundary; each time through the loop the S instruction subtracts 3 and the BCT instruction, 1. Copies of the contents of register 4 are stored at C+48, C+44, . . . , C+4.

7. When the segment is completed, the half-word at LP+2 contains the address BB+40 in base+displacement form. Therefore initialization is not complete. It can be remedied by including

$$\text{MVC} \qquad \text{LP+2(2),LPDUMMY+2}$$

just before the loop, where the "constant" LPDUMMY is defined with other constants by

$$\text{LPDUMMY} \quad \text{A} \qquad \text{6,BB}$$

Why and how?

8. 1)

```
          LA    6,FF+112
          LA    7,BB
          LA    8,4
          LA    9,BB+112
```

2)

```
          LA    8,0
          LA    9,112
          L     7,=F'-4'
```

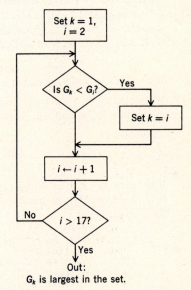

Set $k = 1$, $i = 2$

Is $G_k < G_i$? Yes

Set $k = i$

$i \leftarrow i + 1$

No $i > 17$?

Yes

Out:
G_k is largest in the set.

10.

```
          LA    4,GG     K
          LA    5,GG+4   I
          L     6,0(4)
          LA    8,4
          LA    9,GG+64
   LP     C     6,0(5)
          BNL   TEXIT
          LR    4,5
          L     6,0(4)
   TEXIT  BXLE  5,8,LP
   *      AT EXIT, REG. 4 CONTAINS ADDRESS OF LARGEST NUMBER
```

11. Adaptation of Fig. 8–16:

```
POLEVAL    SAVE    (14,12)
           BALR    12,0
           USING   *,12
           LM      2,4,0(1)
           L       7,0(2)      ADDRESS OF FIRST COEF
           L       11,0(3)     ORDER OF POLYNOMIAL
           L       3,0(4)      VALUE X
           L       5,0(7)      SUM = A SUB 0
           LA      9,0           I = 0
           LA      10,1        INCREMENT = 1
LOOP       BXH     9,10,OUT    ADJUSTMENT AND TEST FOR EXIT
           LA      7,4(7)      ADJUST ADDRESS
*    ***BODY OF LOOP***
           MR      4,3         SUM*X
           A       5,0(7)      NEW SUM = SUM*X+AI
           B       LOOP
OUT        LR      0,5         RESULT TO REG. 0
           RETURN  (1,12)
```

Chapter 10

1. Substitute for

```
    IC    4,AB
```

```
ST    4,TP
MVC   TP+3(1),AB
L     4,TP
```

Substitute for

```
STC   6,G
```

```
ST    6,TP
MVC   G(1),TP+3
```

5. We set up an area of, say, four bytes just beyond the 10-byte count area. The four bytes are divided into two cells. The first byte of each cell contains the digit that is being counted in the cell: 0 if 0's are being counted, etc. This byte is set initially to 15 (hexadecimal F) to show it is not in use. The second byte of the cell is the overflow counter, in which 1 is added for each 256 counted in the ordinary counter in the 10-byte area. This requires additional initialization of

```
MVC    10(4,10),=2X'0F00'
LA     7,0
```

The segment shown in Fig. 10–4 is left intact; the overflow area and program segment are used only when one of the 1-byte counters overflows. The segment is therefore

```
TILT1    LA    8,0             FIRST OVERFLOW CELL
         LA    6,0
UPA      IC    7,10(10,8)
         CR    5,7             IF OVERFLOW COUNTER ALREADY
         BE    UPB               ASSIGNED TO THIS DIGIT, COUNT
         C     7,=F'15'
         BNE   UPC             IF CELL IS EMPTY,
         STC   5,10(10,8)        ASSIGN IT
*        SEGMENT TO COUNT THE OVERFLOW
UPB      STC   6,0(10,5)       RESET ORIGINAL COUNTER TO ZERO
         IC    6,11(10,8)      ADD 1 TO OVERFLOW CELL
         LA    6,1(6)
         C     6,=F'255'
         BH    TILT2
         STC   6,11(10,8)
         B     CONTINUE        COUNTING FINISHED
```

```
*           BRANCH TO TILT2 IF OVERFLOW CELLS NOT SUFFICIENT
*           SEGMENT TO LOOK FOR ANOTHER CELL
UPC     C       8,=F'0'         IF MORE THAN 2 CELLS, USER MAY
        BH      TILT2                 CHANGE VALUE OF LITERAL
        LA      8,2(8)
        B       UPA
```

To put the counts, including those from the overflow cells, in full words, we can employ a segment such as the following, in which we assume that register 10 again contains the address of the small count area, and register 11 contains the address of a 10-word block that is to receive the counts.

```
        LA      6,0
        LA      7,0             INDEX FOR SMALL AREA
        LA      8,0             INDEX FOR FULL-WORD AREA
        LA      9,10            FOR LOOP CONTROL
*   LOOP TO TRANSFER ONE-BYTE COUNTS
TRANSLP IC      6,0(10,7)       INSERT A BYTE
        ST      6,0(11,8)       STORE A WORD
        LA      7,1(7)
        LA      8,4(8)
        BCT     9,TRANSLP
        LA      8,0             INDEX FOR OVERFLOW AREA
TRANSLPA IC     7,10(10,8)
        C       7,=F'15'        IF CELL EMPTY,
        BE      OUT                   FINISHED
        M       6,=F'4'         COMPUTE INDEX FOR STORING OVERFLOW
        IC      6,11(10,8)
        STC     6,2(11,7)       STORE BYTE OF OVERFLOW COUNTS
        C       8,=F'0'         IF MORE CELLS, LOOP BACK
        BH      OUT
        LA      8,2(8)
        B       TRANSLPA
```

13. If the first division is by 509, the second could overflow.

15.
```
        L       4,=CL4' '       LØAD BLANKS
        LA      5,HEAD          INITIALIZE ADDRESSES
        LA      6,DHEAD
        LA      8,4             LØØPING CØNTRØL
        LA      9,DHEAD+798
LP      ICM     4,B'1010',0(5)  LØAD 2 BYTES
        ST      4,0(6)          STØRE BYTES AND BLANKS
        LA      5,2(5)
        BXLE    6,8,LP
```

Chapter 11

2. This segment follows immediately the segment shown in Fig. 11–1:

```
        MVI     OVIND,X'0'      0 MEANS NO OVERFLOW
        L       4,A                   OVIND WILL BE CHANGED TO 1 LATER
        X       4,B                   IF OVERFLOW IS DETECTED
        LTR     4,4             IF OPERAND SIGNS ARE DIFFERENT,
        BM      OUT                   RESULT OF EX. OR APPEARS NEG.  NO OVER
```

```
        L      4,A          IF RESULT SIGN IS SAME AS THE
        X      4,C          OPERAND SIGNS, EX. OR GIVES
        LTR    4,4          NON-NEG. NUMBER, SHOWING NO OVERFLOW
        BNM    OUT
        MVI    OVIND,X'1'   SET OVIND TO SHOW OVERFLOW
OUT     ...
```

3. If the logical operand a is represented as $a = a_s + 2^{32}a_0$, where a_s is the same bit pattern considered as a signed number, and a_0 is the high-order bit, and similarly, $b = b_s + 2^{32}b_0$, then

$$ab = (a_s + 2^{32}a_0)(b_s + 2^{32}b_0) = a_sb_s + 2^{32}a_0b_s + 2^{32}b_0a_s + 2^{64}a_0b_0.$$

From this we can deduce that to the upper half of the ordinary arithmetic product a_sb_s we must add b if a appears negative and a if b appears negative. If the two numbers are in words at A and B, the logical product is stored at C by the segment:

```
        L      5,A
        M      4,B
        CLI    A,X'80'
        BL     P1
        AL     4,B
P1      CLI    B,X'80'
        BL     P2
        AL     4,A
P2      STM    4,5,C
```

6.
```
   SLR   4,4      CLEAR REG. 4           ⎫              ⎧ LR    4,5
   SLDL  4,7      SHIFT INTØ REG. 4      ⎬   or         ⎨
   ØR    5,4      BRING ARØUND INTØ REG. 5 ⎭           ⎩ SRDL  4,25
```

7. The logic of the reversal is shown in the following diagram, assuming that the original word is loaded into register 7. Original contents of other registers are irrelevant.

```
        L      7,FORWARD
        LA     8,32
LOOP    SLDL   6,1
        LR     4,6
        SRDL   4,1
        BCT    8,LOOP
        ST     5,BACKWARD
```

9.
```
   SRDL  6,15
   LR    6,5
   SRDL  6,15
   LR    6,4
   SRDL  6,2
   ST    7,W
```
This segment is shorter in time and space than that given in the text, but the difference is marginal. In most packing problems left and right shifts are equally efficient.

10. Unpacking is quite analogous to packing. To unpack the word at W, for example, returning IND, P, and Q to separate registers 4, 5 and 6, the following segment suffices

```
        L      4,W
        SRDL   4,15
        SRL    5,17
        LR     6,5         Q TO REG. 6
        SRDL   4,15        ISOLATE IND IN REG. 4
        SRL    5,17        P IN REG. 5
```

```
12.               LA      6,0
                  LA      8,1
                  LA      9,31
       LOOP2      LA      4,B'1111000'   1111000 ARE FIRST 7 BITS OF C'0' OR C'1'
                  SLDL    4,1            ADD 0 OR 1, TO MAKE C'0' OR C'1'
                  STC     4,CHAR(6)      STORE
                  BXLE    6,8,LOOP2
```

```
14.               Ø       4,MASK1
                  N       4,MASK2
                  X       4,MASK3

                  . . .
                  DS      0F
       MASK1      DC      X'00C00000'
       MASK2      DC      X'FFCFFFFF'
       MASK3      DC      X'0000FC00'
```

17. A NOT function changes all bits of the word; LCR   6,6 leaves unchanged the lowest-order 1-bit and all 0's below that.

21. a) Assuming that a 20-byte string at BD20 contains four groups of 36-bit strings each followed by four zeros, the following segment will transfer each 36-bit string to the beginning of a double word in an eight-word area BD32:

```
       MVC     BD32(32),=XL32'0'
       MVC     BD32(5),BD20
       MVC     BD32+8(5),BD20+5
       MVC     BD32+16(5),BD20+10
       MVC     BD32+24(5),BD20+15
```

b) If the 36-bit strings are packed into an 18-byte area BD18, and are not aligned on any particular boundary, the job is more complicated. The following segment will do the job, but the MVØ (MoVe with Offset) instruction to be introduced in Chapter 14 could help do the job easier.

```
       MVC     BD32(5),BD18
       NC      BD32+4(4),=X'F0000000'   CLEAR LOW-ORDER 28 BITS
       MVC     DBL+3(5),BD18+4
       LM      4,5,DBL                  DBL ON A WORD BOUNDARY
       SLDL    4,28
       STM     4,5,BD32+8
       MVC     BD32+16(5),BD18+9
       NC      BD32+20(4),=X'F0000000'
       MVC     DBL+3(5),BD18+13
       LM      4,5,DBL
       SLDL    4,28
       STM     4,5,BD32+24
```

In System/370, the pair of instructions

```
       MVC     DBL+3(5),BD18+4
       LM      4,5,DBL
```

can be replaced by

```
       IC      4,BD18+4
       ICM     5,X'F',BD18+5
```

The ICM instruction, in effect, loads register 5 but does not care about boundary alignment. A similar pair of instructions later in the segment can be similarly replaced.

Chapter 12

7. One possible strategem is to follow the data cards with a card which contains in some field a value which by the programmer's convention means end of data. A second possibility is to require that the data cards be counted and the count fed in on a card at the head of the data.

8. Register 15 would be changed by the execution of the macros, and from the point of return from the first macro-instruction addressing of main storage would be completely haywire.

13. `//YØURDD DD   DISP=ØLD,UNIT=2314,VØLUME=SER=WØRK03,DSNAME=FØREIGN`

Chapter 13

1.

Decimal	Hexadecimal floating point
3.0	41300000
−3.0	C1300000
6.0	41600000
12.0	41C00000
24.0	42180000
4212.0	44107400
−0.75	C0C00000
−0.1875	C0300000
0.1	4019999A
0.3	404CCCCD

2.

Floating point	Decimal
42360000	54.0
C12F0000	−2.9375
C310A680	−266.40625
3F200000	.0078125
BF240000	−.0087890625
5E000000	0.0

4. The hexadecimal system permits, on the average, 1.5 more significant bits to be kept in a floating-point word.

7. a) If two normalized, positive floating-point numbers are compared by a C or a CE instruction, the results are the same.

b) If two unequal, normalized, negative floating-point numbers are compared by a C or a CE instruction, the results are opposite: the one that appears larger to a CE instruction appears smaller to the C instruction.

c) If one number is positive and one negative, C and CE give the same results.

d) If two floating-point numbers, at least one of which is unnormalized, are compared by CE and C instructions, the situation is more complicated.

8. The guard digit affects a compare instruction only when one number is unnormalized, and after shifting, the numbers agree except for the guard digit.

9. Several possible segments for testing approximate equality of two floating-point numbers involve high risk of a significance exception; the following does not:

```
          LE     2,A          COMPARE A AND B
          CE     2,B              FOR AGREEMENT WITHIN TOL
          BE     APPEQ        BRANCH TO APPEQ IF EQUAL
          SE     2,B
          LPER   2,2
          SE     2,TOL
          BM     APPEQ             ALSO IF DIFF LESS THAN TOL
```

10. Never.

14. Suppose the fraction is stored in short floating-point form at FRAC and the character form, including sign, decimal point, and seven digits, is to be stored at CHAR.

```
          LE     2,FRAC
          MVC    CHAR(2),=C'+.'
          LTER   2,2
          BNM    P2
          LPER   2,2          IF NEGATIVE,
          MVI    CHAR,C'-'        CHANGE BUT RECORD SIGN
P2        AU     2,UNZRO      UNZRO=X'40000000'
*  UNNORMALIZE SO BINARY POINT IS JUST BEFORE BIT POSITION 8
          STE    2,DT         DT IS A DOUBLE WORD
          MVI    DT,0         CLEAR THE EXPONENT
          L      5,DT
          M      4,=F'10000000'
          SLDA   4,8          10000000 * NUMBER IN REG. 4
          CVD    4,DT         CONVERT INTEGER PART
          UNPK   CHAR+2(7),DT(8)
          OI     CHAR+8,X'F0'
```

18. a)
```
          LE     4,A
          LTER   2,4          IF A NOT POSITIVE, GIVE IT BACK
          BNP    DONE             THIS IS EASY, BUT IS IT GOOD?
          AE     4,=E'1.0'
          ME     4,=E'0.5'        FIRST APPROX
LP        LER    2,4          SAVE LAST APPROX.
          LE     4,A
          DER    4,2
          SER    4,2
          ME     4,=E'0.5'
          AER    4,2
          CER    4,2
          BL     LP
DONE      STE    2,X
```

b)
```
          LA     6,0
          L      7,A
          LTR    7,7
          BP     P1
          MVC    X(4),A
          B      DONE
P1        SLDL   6,8          EXPONENT INTO REG. 6
          LA     6,66(6)
          SRA    6,1          DIVIDE (EXP+64) BY 2, ADD 1
          SRDL   6,8          ATTACH NEW EXPONENT TO FRACTION
          ST     7,X          THIS IS FIRST APPROX.
```

Then continue with loop, more or less as previously. In the worst case, the first approximation is within a factor of 16 of the true square root. Can you show that? Can you do better?

Chapter 14

1.

	Instruction	Result		Condition code
ZAP	FERMAG+1(3),NLQC(2)	FERMAG+1:	00900C	2
AP	GBS(3),NLQC(2)	GBS:	22246C	2
SP	GBS(3),MPHY(4)	GBS:	21370C	2
CP	NLQC(2),MPHY(4)			2
SP	NLQC(2),WHP(3)	NLQC:	020C	3
AP	NLQC(2),GBS(2)	Data exception: 4 in sign position		
		of second operand		
MP	MPHY(4),NLQC(2)	MPHY:	0021600D	—
MP	WHP(3),MPHY+2(2)	Data exception: insufficient number of		
		high-order zeros in first operand		
MP	WHP(3),MPHY+3(1)	WHP:	00480C	—
DP	DRGN(5),NLQC(2)	DRGN:	00036D100D	—
DP	DRGN(5),WHP(3)	DRGN:	270C00100D	—
DP	DRGN(5),WHP+1(2)	DRGN:	00270C100D	—
MVØ	DRGN(4),FERMAG(3)	DRGN:	02233440	—
MVN	DRGN(4),FERMAG	DRGN:	02033455	—

6.

```
        ZAP   PROD(5),EXEMPT(2)
        MP    PROD(5),=P'50.00'        $50.00 EACH EXEMPTION
        ZAP   PROD2(6),GROSS(4)
        SP    PROD2(6),PROD(5)         NET INCOME BASE FOR WITHHOLDING
        BP    FEDTAX
        ZAP   FED(4),=P'0'             IF NET NOT POSITIVE, WITHHOLD 0.
        B     FICACOMP
FEDTAX  MP    PROD2(6),=P'.14'         WITHHOLD = 14% OF NET
        MVC   FED(4),PROD2+1
        MVN   FED+3(1),PROD2+5         TRUNCATE, STORE IN FED
FICACOMP ZAP  PROD2(6),GROSS(4)
        AP    FICA(4),GROSS(4)
        ZAP   PROD(4),=P'6600.00'      IF PREVIOUS FICA + GROSS ARE
        SP    PROD(4),FICA(4)          LESS THAN $6600, COMPUTE
        BNM   FICAPCT                  FICATAX AS PERCENTAGE OF GROSS
        AP    PROD2(6),PROD(4)         OTHERWISE, REDUCE AMOUNT TAXED
        MVC   FICA(4),=P'6600.00'      BY THE EXCESS
FICAPCT MP    PROD2(6),=P'.044'        FICATAX = 4.4% OF GROSS OR
        MVC   FICATAX+3(1),PROD2+5     REMAINDER
        MVO   FICATAX(4),PROD2(4)      TRUNCATE AND STORE
        ZAP   TAKEHOME(4),GROSS(4)     COMPUTE TAKE-HOME PAY
        SP    TAKEHOME(4),FED(4)
        SP    TAKEHOME(4),FICATAX(4)
        SP    TAKEHOME(4),DEDUCT(3)
```

8. The strategy is to add the counters of individual digits until the sum is more than half the total number of digits 0–9. The segment directly precedes AVLPCTRL, and puts the median in packed form in the 27th byte of the counter area.

```
*              COMPUTE MEDIAN, STORE IN BYTE 27 OF AREA
        LR     5,9
        ZAP    DIVD(3),20(2,9)    GENERATE HALF THE TOTAL COUNT
        DP     DIVD(3),=P'2'        AS A 2-BYTE QUOTIENT AT DIVD
        ZAP    DBL(2),=P'0'
MEDLOOP AP     DBL(2),0(2,5)
        CP     DBL(2),DIVD(2)     IF SUM GREATER, MEDIAN FOUND
        BP     MEDST
        LA     5,2(5)
        B      MEDLOOP            EXIT FROM LOOP IS ASSURED BY METHOD
MEDST   SR     5,9                PUT MEDIAN IN PACKED DECIMAL FORM
        SRA    5,1
        CVD    5,DBL
        MVC    26(1,9),DBL+7
```

When we want the median of a set of numbers which can take on a great many different values, it becomes impractical to count frequencies of each different value. One approach then is to sort the set and find the "middle" number of the sorted set. Can you do better?

Chapter 15

1. TR   SPREAD(16),=C'0123456789ABCDEF'

2. Besides the solution suggested by the hint with the problem, the following slick solution presented by Tim Hagen takes much less space in tables:

```
        L      2,Y
        L      4,=X'0F0F0F0F'
        LR     3,2
        SRL    3,4
        NR     3,4
        NR     4,2
        STM    3,4,WØRKB
        TR     WØRKB(8),=C'0123456789ABCDEF'
        MVC    WØRKA(8),=X'0004010502060307'
        TR     WØRKA(8),WØRKB       RESULT IN WØRKA
        ...
WØRKA   DS     2F
WØRKB   DS     2F
```

```
        TRT    U(6),TABLE09
3.      BC     8,ALLDIGIT    COND. CODE = 0 IF ALL DIGITS ZERO
        B      BADDIGIT
TABLE09 DC     240X'01'
        DC     10X'00'
        DC     6X'01'
```

5. The essence of the following segment is that a TRT instruction finds the next slash, and from that is computed the length of the current line to be moved by an MVC instruction. Modification of the length in the MVC instruction is accomplished by an EX instruction; another EX is used to modify the length in the TRT instruction. We assume five printable lines of 50 bytes each. Be critical of this segment: it (and others) can be improved.

```
          MVC   LINE(250),=CL250' '
          LA    4,160              161 CHARACTERS TO SCAN
          LA    7,LINE
          LA    5,ADDR             BEGINNING OF CURRENT STRING
LOOP      EX    4,ITRT             FIND A SLASH
          LA    6,1(1)             ADDR OF "/" + 1
          SR    6,5                LENGTH OF STRING INCLUDING "/"
          SR    4,6                NEW LENGTH FOR TRT
          BNH   OUT                EXIT IF LAST "/" REACHED
          C     7,=A(LINE+250)
          BNL   ER42               TOO MANY LINES
          SH    6,=H'2'            COMPUTE LENGTH FOR MVC
          EX    6,IMVC
          LA    5,1(1)
          LA    7,50(7)
          B     LOOP
OUT       ...
ITRT      TRT   0(0,5),SLTAB
IMVC      MVC   0(0,7),0(5)
SLTAB     DC    97X'00'
          DC    X'01'                    SLASH IS 98TH CHAR.
          DC    158X'00'
LINE      DS    CL250
ADDR      DS    CL160
          DC    C'/'
```

6. MVC   CHAR(6),=X'4021204B2060'
ED   CHAR(6),SØURCE

Pattern contains

Fill character:	40 (blank)	Decimal pt.:	4B
Sig. starter:	21	Digit selector:	20
Digit selector:	20	Minus sign:	60

7.

```
          MVC   FIELD(8),PATT
          ED    FIELD(8),SOURCE    SOURCE IS ONE WORD PACKED
          TRT   FIELD(8),BLTEST
          BZ    ALLZ
          S     1,=F'1'
          MVI   0(1),C'$'
ALLZ      ...
          ...
PATT      DC    XL8'4020202020202020'
BLTEST    DC    64X'01'
          DC    X'00'
          DC    191X'01'
```

Except for the fill character, the content and length of the pattern are irrelevant, and could be whatever is wanted to take care of other aspects of the problem.

Chapter 16

1. See Appendix G: Macro Language Summary, of the *IBM System/360 Operating System Assembler Language* manual, GC28-6514.

3. The use of a substring notation helps us to test for the difference between an operand and a sublist. We can test whether the first character is a left parenthesis:

```
          AIF   ('&A'(1,1) EQ '(').GØSUB
```

This is a start, but not a general solution. A parameter could, for example, be (1)+X. Some system macros adopt the convention that (5) signifies that the operand is to be found in register 5. However, these system macros require that ordinary operands *never* begin with (, so they can use a test like the one above.

5. Blanks would be used as the operand value, and a generated instruction

$$\text{L} \qquad \text{2,}$$

would not be acceptable to the assembler.

6. Values of ordinary symbols are not yet defined at the time SETA symbols are set and used. The complete macro expansion is done before definition of the first ordinary symbol.

9.
```
        MACRØ                                          ⎤
&NAME   CBR      &TYPE,&A,&B,&CØND,&BRAD               ⎥ Macro
&NAME   C&TYPE   &A,&B                                 ⎥
        B&CØND   &BRAD                                 ⎥
        MEND                                           ⎦

        CBR      D,2,PI,NL,REITER              ⎤ Macro-instruction
        CD       2,PI                          ⎥ Expansion
        BNL      REITER                         ⎦

        CBR      LC,STRING(18),BLANK,NE,TRAP   ⎤ Macro-instruction
        CLC      STRING(18),BLANK              ⎥ Expansion
        BNE      TRAP                           ⎦
```

10. Refer to description of an actual CALL macro in *IBM OS/360 Supervisor Services and Macro-Instructions*, GC28-6646, or *OS/VS Supervisor Services and Macro-Instructions*, GC27-6979, and to the listing of your local macro library for the complete macro definition.

11.
```
        MACRO
&NAME   BYTASCEN
        LCLA     &N
&NAME   DS       OC
&N      SETA     0
.P      DC       AL1(&N,&N+1,&N+2,&N+3,&N+4,&N+5,&N+6,&N+7)
&N      SETA     &N+8
        AIF      (&N LT 256).P
        MEND
```

Chapter 17

2. For example,
```
        BALR  3,0
        N     3,MPM      MPM=X'F5000000'
        SPM   3
```

set bits 36 and 38 of the PSW to 0's, thus preventing interrupt on fixed-point overflow and exponent underflow. Other mask bits are not affected.

3. The only way to store an entire program status word is to cause an interrupt. Suppose we decide the SVC   133 is to mean change bit 13 of the program status word

to 1. The SVC interrupt-handling routine must include something like

```
            ØRG    96
            CLI    39,133
            BE     P12T1
                   . . .
    P12T1   ØI     33,X'04'
            LPSW   32
```

Note that if P12T1 is within the first 4096 main storage locations, this requires *no* register contents, therefore none need be saved and restored. Of course, we users are not at liberty to write and insert code like this into the computer. However, we can define our own interrupt-handling routines; conventions are described in *IBM OS/360 Supervisor Services and Macro-Instructions*, GC28-6646, or *OS/VS Supervisor Services and Macro-Instructions*, GC27-6979.

12. Suppose a CCW is in main storage, its address is in register 4, and it has already been determined that the command calls for data transfer and that the indirect data addressing flag is off. We will construct a new CCW at location NCCW, and if an indirect data addressing chain is necessary, it can start at location ADCHAIN.

```
            MVC    NCCW(8),0(4)
            L      5,NCCW              VIRTUAL STARTING ADDR
            LRA    6,0(5)
            STCM   6,X'7',NCCW+1       STØRE REAL ADDRESS
            LA     7,0
            ICM    7,X'3',NCCW+6       BYTE COUNT
            LA     8,0(5)
            AR     8,7                 ENDING VIRTUAL ADDR
            N      5,=X'00FFF800'
            AH     5,=H'2048'          STARTING ADDR. NEXT
    *                                     BLØCK
            CR     5,8                 CHAIN NECESSARY?
            BNL    FIN

    *    INITIALIZE CHAIN
            ØI     NCCW+4,B'00000100'  IDA FLAG ØN
            MVC    ADCHAIN+1(3),NCCW+1 REAL ADDR TØ CHAIN
            MVC    NCCW+1(3),=AL3(ADCHAIN)
            LA     9,ADCHAIN+4
    *    LØØP TØ PUT SUCCESSIVE BLØCK ADDRESSES IN CHAIN
    LPAD    LRA    6,0(5)
            ST     6,0(9)              STØRE REAL ADDR IN
    *                                     CHAIN
            LA     9,4(9)              UPDATE CHAIN ADDR.
            LA     5,2048(5)           VIRTUAL ADDR. NEXT
    *                                     BLØCK
            CR     5,8                 MØRE CHAIN NEEDED?
            BL     LPAD
    FIN     EQU    *
```

14.   LA   9,0   ASSUME MAIN STØRAGE
                                                  SIZE
     BRR   RRB   0(9)   786432 BYTES
                LA   9,2048(9)
                C   9,=F'786432'
                BL   BRR

In practice, one would reset reference bits on a smaller subset of main storage, as some portions are not available for swapping pages.

15. STCTL   1,1,B
     LA   4,0
     IC   4,B
     LA   4,2(4)
     STC   4,B
     LCTL   1,1,B

INDEX